THE OXFORD HISTORY OF
THE CHRISTIAN CHURCH

Edited by
Henry and Owen Chadwick

EDITOR'S NOTE

The history of the Church in the British Isles, and in non-European countries including the Americas, is to be found elsewhere in the Oxford History of the Christian Church.

A History of the Popes
1830–1914

OWEN CHADWICK

CLARENDON PRESS · OXFORD

OXFORD
UNIVERSITY PRESS

Great Clarendon Street, Oxford OX2 6DP

Oxford University Press is a department of the University of Oxford.
It furthers the University's objective of excellence in research, scholarship,
and education by publishing worldwide in

Oxford New York

Athens Auckland Bangkok Bogotá Buenos Aires Calcutta
Cape Town Chennai Dar es Salaam Delhi Florence Hong Kong Istanbul
Karachi Kuala Lumpur Madrid Melbourne Mexico City Mumbai
Nairobi Paris São Paulo Singapore Taipei Tokyo Toronto Warsaw

with associated companies in Berlin Ibadan

Oxford is a registered trade mark of Oxford University Press
in the UK and in certain other countries

Published in the United States
by Oxford University Press Inc., New York

British Library Cataloguing in Publication Data

Data available

Library of Congress Cataloging in Publication Data
A history of the popes, 1830-1914 / Owen Chadwick.
(The Oxford history of the Christian Church)
Includes bibliographical references and index.
1. Papacy—History—1799-1870.   2. Roman question.
I. Title.   II. Series
BX1386.C48   262'. 13'09034—dc21   97-47470
ISBN 0-19-826922-6

3 5 7 9 10 8 6 4 2

Printed in Great Britain on acid-free paper by
Biddles Ltd., Guildford and King's Lynn

CONTENTS

ABBREVIATIONS

AAS	*Acta apostolicae sedis* (*ASS* until 1908)
AHP	*Archivum Historiae Pontificiae* (Rome, 1963–)
ASS	*Acta sanctae sedis* (*AAS* after 1908)
CC	*La Civiltà Cattolica* (Rome, 1850–70; Florence, 1872–87; Rome, 1888–)
CH	*Church History*, Scottdale (1932–)
CHR	*Catholic Historical Review*, Washington (1915–)
DACL	*Dictionnaire d'archéologie chrétienne et de liturgie*, ed. F. Cabrol and H. Leclercq (Paris, 1907–53)
DBEC	*Diccionario Biografico Español Contemporaneo* (Madrid, 1975)
DBF	*Dictionnaire de biographie française* (Paris, 1933–)
DBI	*Dizionario biografico degli italiani* (Rome, 1960–)
DC	*Documentation catholique* (Paris, 1919–)
DDC	*Dictionnaire de droit canonique*, ed. R. Naz (Paris, 1935–65)
DDI	*I Documenti diplomatici italiani* (Rome, 1960–)
DHEE	*Diccionario de Historia Eclesiastica de España* (Madrid, 1972–87)
DHGE	*Dictionnaire d'histoire et de géographie ecclésiastiques*, ed. A. Baudrillart *et al.* (Paris, 1912–), later R. Aubert
DIP	*Dizionario degli Istituti di Perfezione*, ed. G. Pelliccia and G. Rocca (1973–)
DS	*Dictionnaire de spiritualité ascétique et mystique*, ed. M. Viller (Paris, 1932–)
DTC	*Dictionnaire de théologie catholique*, ed. A. Vacant and E. Mangenot, later E. Amann (Paris, 1903–)
HJHC	*Handbook of Church History, History of the Church*, ed. H. Jedin and J. Dolan, Eng. trans., 3rd edn. (1965–81)
JCH	*Journal of Contemporary History* (1966–)
LTK	*Lexicon für Theologie und Kirche*, ed. J. Höfer and K. Rahner, 2nd edn. (Freiburg im Breisgau, 1957–)
MHP	Miscellanea Historiae Pontificiae
NCE	*New Catholic Encyclopedia* (Washington, 1966–87)

NDB	*Neue Deutsche Biographie* (Berlin, 1952–)
ODCC	*Oxford Dictionary of the Christian Church*, F. L. Cross and E. Livingstone (1974); 3rd edn. (1997)
OHCC	*Oxford History of the Christian Church* (1976–)
OstKSt	*Ostkirchliche Studien* (Würzburg, 1951–)
PP	Parliamentary Papers
RB	*Revue bénédictine* (Maredsous, 1884–)
RGG	*Die Religion in Geschichte und Gegenwart*, 3rd edn. (Tübingen, 1957–62)
RHE	*Revue d'histoire ecclésiastique* (Louvain, 1900–)
RSCI	*Rivista di storia della chiesa in Italia* (Rome, 1947–)
SCH	Studies in Church History
Schm.	J. Schmidlin, *Papstgeschichte der neuesten Zeit* (4 vols.; Munich, 1933–9)
TRE	*Theologische Realenzyklopädie* (Berlin, 1976–)
ZKT	*Zeitschrift für katholische Theologie*

I

GREGORY XVI

THE ELECTION OF 1831

The most famous pope of the Middle Ages to assert papal power against emperors and kings was Pope Gregory VII, Hildebrand. Ever since the high Middle Ages popes were conscious that in Gregory VII they made an emperor to kneel in the snow at Canossa, that in Innocent III they acted as the international authority of Europe, that in Boniface VIII they asserted the ultimate secular power of the pope as well as his ultimate spiritual authority. They were also aware that these tremendous claims were not often recognized and sometimes were repudiated with contempt or with force. Gregory VII died in exile, Boniface sickened and died after being kidnapped and rescued. In the Counter-Reformation, when Spanish and afterwards French power became strong in Italy, they grew hesitant of using such names lest they remind Europe of the contrast between the past glories of the Holy See and the weakness of its present occupant. No one had chosen the name Boniface since 1389, when the see was divided by the Great Schism. Gregory XIII was a famous name of the Counter-Reformation and shortly afterwards there were two more Gregorys; one ruled for less than a year, the other for two years, yet they were important. Towards the end of the seventeenth century and early in the eighteenth century there were three weighty popes who took the name Innocent. But in the eighteenth century they preferred to take gentler-sounding names, such as Clement (four of those), Pius, or Benedict. The coronation of Pius VI in 1775 started the age of the Piuses—during the next 183 years there were only fifty-four years in which the pope was not named Pius. And when they were not called Pius they avoided high-and-mighty sounding names—with one exception.

For books cited in footnotes, place of publication is London unless otherwise stated.

When the Camaldolese friar Cappellari was elected pope in the first weeks of 1831, he took the name Gregory XVI. He was the son of a lawyer, born at Belluno in the republic of Venice (and some thought it a disadvantage to him that he was not born a Roman), and was now aged 65. A Camaldolese from the age of 18, he was at first at Murano in the lagoon of Venice, went to Rome in 1795 and was abbot there from 1805; three years later he was expelled by the French but was able to return after the fall of Napoleon, and was cardinal from 1826.

The name Gregory was a claim. This was a cardinal who reacted against the French Revolution and all that it stood for. He seems to have had Gregory VII in his mind; but also, while a cardinal, he did a lot for the Congregation de Propaganda Fide, and the last Gregory had founded that Congregation. When the French Revolution kidnapped the Pope, he published a cry of resistance to the revolution, *The Triumph of the Holy See and the Church against the attacks of Innovators* (1799).

Just when the papacy looked moribund, and many said that Pius VI was the last pope in the history of Europe, and no one could see how the institution could survive even in Italy, he published this book, which rejoiced in the coming victory of the Church over its enemies. Not many people read it. He once said humorously how remarkable it was that after he became pope readers suddenly discovered the excellence of this book. Within three years of his election it was translated into four languages.

His was a mind of the eighteenth century. When he attacked the 'innovators', he had no idea of the novelties that he and his successors were fated to meet. His innovators were those whose day was swept away by the Revolution. He had not liked the way the world went in 1799, when a pope was dying in exile and prison. Thirty-two years later, when he was elected pope, Napoleon was a ghost of the past, and conservative princes ruled most of Europe. King Ferdinand of Spain was a devout Catholic, though one of the worst sovereigns of that country. Austria under Metternich was powerful, Catholic, and conservative, the kingdom of Naples had repressed a revolution with Austrian aid, Catholic Belgium had just freed itself from Protestant Holland. But he still disliked the way the world went. That was not surprising since his election was a hurried, vain, twelfth-hour effort to avert revolution in the Papal States.

In not liking the way the modern world was going Gregory XVI was characteristic of the popes, with one possible exception, for the next 127 years. This was a mark of the age with which we have to deal: the popes not only as encouragers of the modern world, or creators of its qualities, or guides to its moral aspirations—but the popes as against it.

Gregory XVI was ugly and coarse in appearance and did not look like a pope or even a sovereign, for he was short and broad and round, but he was the best-educated pope for nearly three-quarters of a century. His visitors found him interesting to talk with, as well as jolly. The three popes before him had delicate health, but he had abounding energy. He was a monk and did not stop the monk's way of life. He slept on a palliasse, and kept the Camaldolese rule; he rose at 4 a.m., was spare in diet, and unwavering in the old custom that popes ate their meals alone. For all its quality his mind was set hard. He had not the defect of the monk which cardinals feared, that of being poor in business. As he had been secretary of the Congregation of Propaganda, responsible for missions in tormented continents, he was used to administration. What he could not understand was Europe and its politics. He had never travelled outside Italy, nor anywhere except his homeland round Venice and Rome, and he spoke no languages but Italian and Latin (both of which he spoke fluently). He had never needed to concern himself with politics except (no small exception) with the troubles in Latin America and with missionary India and Armenia.

Gregory XVI was elected on 2 February 1831. The election was no act of enthusiasm or acclamation. It was always harder for a monk to be elected, because electors expected that a monk would not know enough about the world. The cardinals almost reached the point of electing Giustiniani who had been nuncio in Spain. But at the crisis of the Conclave (9 January 1831) the Spanish government vetoed the name of Giustiniani and the electors of Giustiniani's party turned to Cappellari as the next best of the same mind. The French government had recorded Cappellari as a possible among their list of cardinals not too Austrian in outlook. But the opponents of Giustiniani kept steady in their opposition for three more weeks.

One of the problems of an institution which represented a high ideal was a lack of reality. The cardinals were urged to elect someone with every conceivable virtue heaped together. Angelo Mai begged them to elect someone with the *faith* of St Peter, the *resolution* of the

centurion Cornelius, the *good fortune* of Pope Silvester, the *elegance* of
Pope Damasus, the *learning* of Pope Gelasius, the *piety* of Pope
Gregory, the *strength* of Pope Eugenius, the *friendliness to princes* of
Pope Hadrian, a *reconciler of the Churches* like Pope Eugenius, a *wise
counsellor* like Pope Julius, with *generosity* like Pope Leo, *Holy* like
Pope Pius, with *mental power* like Pope Sixtus, *erudition* like Pope
Benedict, and *munificence* like Pope Pius VI, with *courage and charita-
bleness* like Pope Pius VII, and *vigilance* like Pope Leo XII, and a *great
legislator* like Pope Pius VIII.[1] To find these nineteen virtues in one
person the cardinals had forty-five people to choose from, all of
whom were human beings.

A few of them could be crossed out at sight: one because he was a
fool, another because he was a nepotist, a third because his age put
him beyond it, a fourth because he was a friend of the deposed King
Charles X of France and the French government was sure to veto
him.

As the weeks passed in deadlock, skits and pamphlets, satires and
caricatures spread round the streets of Rome, and a harmless bomb
exploded inside the Conclave. A message was sent into the Conclave
from the city threatening to create a Roman republic unless they soon
elected. What finally drove them to elect was a message from the
Duke of Modena saying that the revolution was about to break out
in the northern Papal States. Then at last the party against Cappellari
gave way. There were still thirteen refusing to vote for him, but he
secured the necessary two-thirds, 32: 13.

REVOLUTION IN THE PAPAL STATES

Revolution broke out in Bologna, the provincial capital of the northern Papal States, three days later. From Bologna it spread instantly
through the papal provinces, into Umbria and the Marches and
throughout the northern territories beyond the Appennines known
as the Legations. The best of the papal seaports, Ancona, which was
also a fortress, fell to the revolutionaries.

This was not because the revolution particularly objected to Pope
Gregory, whom it did not know. Since the Middle Ages an interregnum in the papal office was a time when conspirators got to work

---

[1] Schm. i. 512.

because of the vacuum of power. The French Revolution of 1830 made it seem as though the season of revolution had once again come to Europe. The example of France usually infected Italy. The new French government made sympathetic noises towards its like-minded friends among the Italian States. It looked as though revolution there would have backing from France.

It seemed also as though Gregory would be the third pope, after Pius VI and Pius VII, to lose his Papal State to a revolutionary army. In the city of Rome trivial meetings of conspirators and displays of tricolour were easily suppressed. A revolutionary army marched south and neared Rome. The papal troops vanished or joined the rebels. The young Louis Napoleon Bonaparte, nephew of the emperor and then aged 22, joined its advance. He sent a letter to the Pope telling him that it was best to abandon his temporal power. The new government in Bologna issued a statement that they did not question the Pope's spiritual power, but Christ had declared that his kingdom was not of this world, and therefore the Papal State could find no warrant in the authority of the Lord of whom the Pope claimed to be the vicar:

Considering that public opinion in a thousand forcible forms demands that without delay we declare the smashing of the bond which has made us subjects of the Pope . . . Article 1. The temporal power of the Pope over this province [Bologna] has ended in fact and for ever by law. Article 2. A general assembly of the representatives of the people is summoned to choose the deputies who will form the new government . . .

The Pope's northern territories, the Legations, were governed corruptly, with an excess of debt, favouritism in promotion, an Inquisition that could act irresponsibly, lawcourts that judged without knowing the law, low stipends, and high customs duties—but not high taxes. This was not a revolt against tyranny but against large inefficiency. The rebel leaders had memories of Napoleon's kingdom of Italy, and they wanted a tricolour flag, but in origin this was not a plan for a dream-world of a united Italy but for a Papal State with a secular government. The leaders were not proletarians but middle-class gentry. When they found themselves a government they had no future without allies. They appealed to all the States of Italy to join them and make a united State, and invited everyone to a feast (planned for 2 March 1831) to celebrate.

In Rome the Pope's advisers debated plans by which he should flee to Genoa or Venice. The Austrian envoy Lützow warned him not to go, it could only help revolution. Gregory and his advisers tried every sort of concession—to free political prisoners, to lower the low taxes, to call up soldiers.

Just over three weeks after his election Gregory XVI appealed to the Austrian government to suppress the rebellion. He had not wished to do this. It was not good to be seen to depend on a foreign army. He hoped that the papal police and troops could contain the rebellion. But the papal governors and police surrendered without trouble and the former officer of the Emperor Napoleon, Sercognani, though with only 3,000 men, was not far from Rome and was greeted by friendly towns as he moved south.

The rebel leaders in Bologna assumed that the new French government would protect them from the Austrians. To their bitter surprise, the French did not intervene. It took an Austrian army just over a month to suppress the rebellion. This was not much of a revolution, the leaders were not fierce, their soldiers were keener on cockades and parades than on fighting, and they collapsed easily in face of a regular army. The only thing the French did was formally to protest to the Pope against his request for Austrian help, on the ground that it meant 'an end to the independence of the Holy See'.

These events made the pattern of the next forty years which conditioned the psychology, and the place in the European state system, of the papacy.

First, the pope could no longer be an absolute ruler of a ramshackle and unprosperous State without the aid of a bodyguard—that is, a foreign army—and an army that was more than a battalion or two of Swiss mercenaries. Since the arrival of Spanish power in Italy during the Counter-Reformation, popes had depended for their stability on powerful governments outside Italy; and that stability was always shattered when the powers fought each other for Italy, as in the War of the Spanish Succession or the Napoleonic wars. But the events of 1831 gave this predicament a new turn for the worse.

Formerly the pope could not defend his State from Austria without French help, or from France without Austrian help. Now he could not defend himself from his own subjects without Austrian or French help. He had inherited a mission as ruler. He was as legitimate a ruler as anyone in Europe. He was a more legitimate ruler than most if not all. His rebel critics liked to say that he acquired his government through an early medieval forgery, the Donation of Constantine. But if there were to be an examination into how the sovereigns of Europe acquired their sovereignty, the other rulers of 1831 needed to blush more than the pope. No one had more right to rule his territory.

This legitimate government was fortified by religion. It was believed to be a sacred mission. Benefactors—a Charlemagne, nobles, counts, kings, gave an inheritance to the Church. They gave it because they wanted to give something to God and to do good to society. The rule of the Papal State was a kingdom given directly by God to his Vicar for the good of the Church and of Christendom. It was a trust which popes could not imagine that they could agree to desert. They had a moral duty, they believed, to maintain what they had been given.

There was a Whig theory that 'legitimacy' to govern did not rest on birth (a form of legitimacy which could not apply to popes), nor on acceptance by the élite of the State (as with the Hanoverian line in Britain, or with King Louis Philippe in France of that moment), but on acceptance by the people. No one thought that 'the people' included women, or the poor, or (in the United States) the slaves. Louis Philippe's new title was not 'King of France' but 'King of the French by the grace of God and the will of the people'; here the phrase 'the will of the people' was a hoodwinking phrase to describe the result of a compromise between two sets of armed men who were on the brink of civil war. The pope's legitimacy was by this means, acceptance by the élite of the State; they chose a king by an electoral board of some fifty carefully picked electors. It was as effective a system for choosing a sovereign as any other in Europe at that moment. The British system had produced George IV, the French system Charles X, the Spanish system Ferdinand VII who was worst of all— unless Miguel of Portugal was still worse. Never was there such a set of monarchs in Western Europe. But papal election had the defect that hereditary systems were invented to cure. Monarchies by birth were devised to ensure that everyone knows who is sovereign and there is never an interregnum during which generals and politicians struggle for power, since experience showed that the worst form of constitution is one that allows the death of a ruler to lead inevitably to civil war. But Papal States were a monarchy in which no one knew what would happen at the election nor how long the interregnum would be. There was a vacuum of sovereignty. This time it lasted three months. That was too long.

Moreover, the secular monarch's child was educated to expect political responsibility, or, if the question was of choice by an élite, the electors were likely to pick someone with political experience. But the cardinal-electors might choose a monk who knew nothing whatever about politics. Political ability stood low in their list of qualities. What they wanted was a man of God who was sensible and respected by religious persons. In their eyes his task as head of a Church was of more weight than his task as the king of Central Italy.

Everyone agreed that a tyrant was not a legitimate ruler, however legitimate the inheritance he had received. He had misused his inheritance and could be overthrown. No sensible person suggested that the pope was a tyrant. Theoretically a pope was the most absolute of rulers who controlled Church as well as State with an unquestionable power. Nobody believed in this theory. It corresponded to nothing visible. The problem of the Papal State was not that it was despotic but that it was weak. Partly it was weak because it was the government of a clergyman who preferred to treat culprits with compassion, and tended to trust the human race even when they were corrupt; but mainly it was weak because it was very old-fashioned, indeed hidebound. It hardly liked to interfere with well-established practices of government even when they were out of keeping with the axioms of the modern world.

The second problem, therefore, of the legitimate inheritance was weakness. If the government, however sacred, was so far the opposite of a tyranny that it could not bring good government to the people who lived within its territories, then questions had to be asked about its legitimacy, as severely as if it had passed into a tyranny. If a government could not get an adequate administration of law and order into its territories, or ensure a reasonably speedy system in the courts of justice, in which its people had confidence, that made a case, not for overturning the government, but for drastic constitutional change in the way that government worked; and if the old-fashioned government was unwilling to accept constitutional change, and persisted in its archaisms and inefficiencies, that could lead to the overthrow of the government as surely as if it had been a tyranny, although it was the opposite.

In 1831 and the thirty-nine years following until the papal government was finally overthrown, it was (and still is) difficult to get a fair picture of how inefficient the papal government was. What is certain is that to all the States of Western Europe except Spain, Portugal, and Naples it appeared to be backward and out of keeping with the times. It was an absolute government (in theory) in an epoch when the world outside Russia pushed towards various forms of constitutional government. It was government by clergymen—for although the bulk of the administration in the Papal States was run by laymen, and Gregory XVI opened more posts to laymen, all the highest offices were reserved to the clergy—and it had got into the head of Western Europe that government by clergymen was not likely to be the most practical way of ruling modern humanity. They did not take into account the reality that some of these clergymen, such as Tommaso Bernetti, Gregory XVI's first Secretary of State, were laymen who took minor orders to qualify for the civil service and were clergymen only in name. And it was government for the sake of a particular religious denomination, at a time when Europe outside Russia and the Ottoman empire was in the course of accepting the doctrine (despite many limitations and exceptions in practice), that a State must be run for the benefit of all its citizens whatever their religion.

Bernetti, when young, had been taken by Napoleon's troops to France when they seized Pope Pius VII; he was imprisoned at Rheims and after the Restoration was the first police chief of the restored Papal State. He had spent years dealing with conspirators. He was able but solitary, worldly, and unclerical in spite of being a cardinal, and had no ideas but those of reaction, and no notion that what happened in religion (as distinct from politics) could affect the pope. He took the view that all liberal governments were sure to fall, that the new king of France Louis Philippe could last only a few months. In the north of the Papal State he created a nasty body of irregulars called the Centurions who behaved as though they had power to shoot anyone they suspected.[2]

THE FIVE POWERS AT ROME

Early that summer of 1831 representatives of five of the powers met in Rome and drafted a memorandum to the Pope demanding that he

---

[2] Bernetti was forced to resign in 1836. Three years later he was ordained priest. At the papal election of 1846 Metternich made sure that he would not be elected, but he would have had no chance anyway as he had made too many enemies. In 1848 he fled from Rome at the murder of Rossi and joined the Pope in exile, and helped to govern Rome in the Restoration of 1850; he died in 1852. See *DBI* and *DHGE* s.v. for his biography.

reform his government. These powers were Austria, Russia, France, Britain, and Prussia. An observer might ask what business Russia, Britain, or Prussia had to interfere with the government of Central Italy, and why the classical power of Italy, Spain, was not invited. It could reasonably be conceded that since Austrian soldiers were all over the Papal States the Austrians had a status to recommend reform; and whenever the Austrians had armies in Italy, it could be conceded that France had a political interest; apart from the circumstance that France and Austria could be said to be two Roman Catholic powers while the other three were Protestant or Eastern Orthodox.

The justification of this intervention was the international system set up after the Congress of Vienna in 1814–15. The victor powers, together with a defeated France, became a Concert of Europe to ensure peace and good order and avert the dangers of revolution. More than once they carried out this task by force. They overthrew liberal governments in Spain and southern Italy. But the most conservative of them, whether the Tsar or Metternich the Austrian Chancellor, saw that to avert revolution one must remedy the causes of revolution, which were bad forms of administration. Hence the plea that the great powers could press the Pope to reform his State. Two of the powers, France and Britain, had just acquired, or were about to acquire, more liberal forms of government likely to be unfriendly to 'absolute rule' even when it was a legend and a sham.

The five powers demanded that laymen be admitted to the higher posts in the papal administration; that the cities and provinces in the Papal States be permitted elected self-governing councils, municipal or provincial; and above them a cabinet or assembly of laymen and clergy who would be a form of government to advise the pope. Austria wanted to include a promise to preserve the Papal States from revolution. But this was impossible for the French and unwelcome to the British, since it could justify Austrian intervention in Italy.

The intervening powers did not practise what they preached. Britain still had pocket boroughs, the Tsar was a tyrant, Metternich wanted to be a tyrant, France in the aftermath of revolution was affected by areas of chaos; and they demanded reforms in a third of Italy which were not required of the rest of the country. They entered the long-lasting era of international conferences where efforts to do good were marred by hypocrisy.

Nothing happened except committee meetings and a fever of laws and decrees. Cardinal Bernetti met the demand for change by changing everything: courts, police, bank, army, monopolies, communes, waterworks, taxes, pensions, censures, honours, curricula, post-office, smuggling, cemeteries, coinage, and ceremonial. No courts nor administration nor the public could keep up with the new orders that were supposed to make things better but multiplied confusion and left the civil service still doing what it thought sensible. This obsessive drive to new decrees was an example of the doctrine: when powerful forces press for reform, be seen to change much and the intruders will go away.

Some good came out of it. Coins were better minted; Tivoli was not flooded by the River Anio; the too-powerful police improved public order; the banking system was a little less archaic. There was no possibility of the Papal States accepting a modern form of administration; because such would sacrifice certain things which the existing administrators found valuable—the forced celibacy of all the higher posts meant that they were less likely to be corrupt because they would have no families; they were accustomed to a very conservative way of doing things and went on in the same way because if anything was changed people would lose their posts and salaries and that would be unjust. This was the dilemma that must sooner or later (as is now obvious) end in the destruction of the Papal States. Europe would not for long bear them as they were. They had no power to reform themselves. Therefore sooner or later they would be overthrown. It took a surprisingly long time, nearly four decades, before the end.

To hold its influence in the peninsula Austria needed to keep Italy weak. It already ruled Venice and Lombardy, had a satellite State in Tuscany and influence in Naples. To keep the Pope in his State was the guarantee of Austrian power in Italy. The Papal States could not be ended unless both Austria and France suffered disaster. Thus far the Pope was safe politically.

In 1831 the Austrian army thought that it had restored the Pope, and withdrew. Cardinal Albani who was put in charge of Bologna appealed to them to come again as early as January 1832. France promptly occupied Ancona so then there were two foreign armies maintaining the Papal State. The French had no idea of helping the rebels against the Pope, their motive was to spite the Austrians at the Pope's expense.

Italy—or rather the Italian middle class, or some of its members—had not forgotten Napoleon and his kingdom of Italy. And the more

Italian their consciousness, the less they were willing to endure the presence of French or Austrian armies on 'their' territory. The presence of the French and the Austrians, especially the Austrians because they ruled directly the provinces of Lombardy and Venice, gave a sudden new stimulus to the idea of 'Italy for the Italians', which was hard to reconcile with a ruler of Central Italy who could not be maintained without the aid of foreign armies. Fortunately for Pope Gregory XVI, the idea of 'Italy for the Italians' was feeble; though, so far as it existed, it was stronger in the north than in the south. For the Austrians governed two Italian provinces of the north: Milan and Venice were Austrian capitals.

LAMENNAIS AND THE IDEA OF TOLERATION

The French were divided on the meaning of their 1830 Revolution. One party thought this a glorious revolution which overthrew the settlement imposed on vanquished France fifteen years after the Battle of Waterloo and restored the ideals of liberty, equality, and fraternity. The other party thought that there was no revolution, and all they had done was to get rid of a king who would not do and put in his place a close relation who would do.

When the revolution of 1830 broke the archbishop of Paris, Quelen, was a Breton count who had lost eleven close relatives to the guillotine and had visited the September prisoners in gaol shortly before they were massacred. Like most boys who grew up in the Revolution after 1789 he was ordained late but at the Restoration was picked to deliver the funeral oration for the executed Louis XVI and spoke a national act of penitence for what had happened. Thence he rose rapidly and was more publicly dedicated to the Bourbon family than any other clergyman in France. He was a Gallican from the old world, who could be thought haughty, but was devout, and honourable, and pleasant, and had courage.

Like others he was astonished by the disorderly crowds of July 1830. A band of armed men spotted him coming into the city and put swords to his chest. He went into hiding first in a hospital, then he was hunted out into a hospice run by nuns, then out of the hospice into a hole in the nunnery, before being rescued by the non-Catholic director of the nearby Botanic Garden. There he vanished for a fortnight. Meanwhile a crowd attacked his palace and demanded the

Archbishop, and said they would hang him with the tricolour they had just flown from the tower of Notre Dame. They sacked the palace, threw the books into the Seine, tore up the archives, and smashed all the rooms. They put about the rumour that the Archbishop had fired out of a window and killed a workman. They shouted that he was hiding 4,000 rifles and a lot of Jesuits in the cellars.

Five months later, though still in an unknown lodging, he was able to celebrate mass at Notre Dame. But three days after the mass, unknown to Quelen, legitimists turned a requiem at Saint-Germain into a little demonstration. The press reported it and next morning a crowd sacked the church, and when they had wrought all the damage they could they moved on the archbishop's palace and destroyed whatever was not destroyed already. During the next fortnight most of the churches in Paris suffered damage from demonstrators. Police came to arrest Quelen but could not find his hiding-place, for he was now in a Normandy château.

The government of the new King Louis Philippe approached Pope Gregory XVI to force Quelen to resign the see of Paris. The Pope was told that there were riots in the streets because Quelen was hostile to the new government. But the Paris nuncio, the future Secretary of State Lambruschini, told Rome that Quelen was guilty of nothing. The new French ambassador to the Vatican told his government that they might get Quelen out if Rome made him a cardinal in exchange for resignation. The Pope and his Curia thought this a bad suggestion. Meanwhile no one knew where Quelen was. He wrote letters to the ministry and they asked him to say where he was but he refused.

So the government removed the statues of Louis XIII and Louis XIV from each side of the altar at Notre Dame; ordered the demolition of the ruined archbishop's palace (a medieval building rebuilt by Cardinal de Noailles at the end of the seventeenth century and then made more eminent by Napoleon when he wanted to force the pope to live in Paris); removed the crucifixes from the lawcourts; turned all the Christian symbols out of the Panthéon, which Quelen himself had restored to Christian worship; refused to compensate Quelen for the loss of his private fortune in the damage; and refused to give money for the repair of Saint-Germain. On the dome of the Panthéon was a cross; this was taken down and replaced with Fame— but a gale threw her down, to the pleasure of the Catholics. She was replaced by the Genius of France, but people ridiculed her and she was taken down; so the government put statues on the façade and to Quelen's horror chose Voltaire and Rousseau.

Quelen was rigid. He refused to visit King Louis Philippe on occasions when by custom the archbishop should call on the sovereign. He tried not to call him 'king' in public documents. He did not think the monarchy of Louis Philippe could last (and he was right, though its fall took longer than he expected). He said that he would call on the King if they rebuilt his palace and reopened the church of Saint-Germain. He refused to move into the house they offered him instead of the palace. He accused the government of wanting him assassinated. He issued public notices to the effect that what the government did at the Panthéon was a profanation and that Voltaire and Rousseau were impious corrupters. The Pope, and even Lambruschini, told him that his rigidity was wrong and that it was his duty to call on the King. He was politely disobedient to the Pope. He said that no archbishop could be seen to bless the idea of the sovereignty of the people. He tried to stop the Pope from allowing Louis Philippe's heir to marry a Protestant German princess. The legitimists loved him.

Seven years after the 1830 Revolution the archbishop of Paris was at last reconciled with the King whom the revolution made. He agreed to baptize his grandson, and sang a Te Deum at Notre Dame, and the King came. They were still arguing over the archbishop's palace, but Saint-Germain was open for worship. Quelen died the next year.

These tense circumstances between the Church and the Revolution made the French priest Felicité de La Mennais powerful. He was then known as La Mennais and his disciples and doctrine as Mennaisian. In 1836 he asked to be called Lamennais; everyone followed his wishes, and that is how history spells him.

In Belgium and in France some Catholics saw that a parliamentary system, with freedom all round, would loose Catholics also from State restrictions, to be at liberty to advocate their faith as any other group could propagate its point of view. That is, they realized that freedom of the press was a friend and not an enemy. This required an act of faith: that truth did not need State protection to prevail but could be left to stand in its inherent strength, and that in the long run the mind of humanity would distinguish between what was true and what was false. How many people believed this as early as 1830 is debatable, but at that moment it fitted the party conflict in both Belgium and France. Probably many of those who professed it regarded it as a temporary expedient in a political predicament, and did not think of freedom of the press as a doctrine which Catholics should countenance as a matter of principle. For it seemed obvious that since the truth is a matter of life and death, both for the individual in the next world and for a healthy society in this world, a State must protect truth when it has the power to do so; and must discourage the teaching of other faiths, or of atheism.

Lamennais was a youth during the French Revolution and for eight years was without faith. After his conversion he was ordained priest, because of the times without any training. Later, when he was famous as a theologian, it was a complaint of his critics that he had no proper knowledge of the traditions of theology and that he had read too freely in Voltaire. He wrote with genius and a brilliant style, and soon was one of the two most famous French writers of that age, the other being Chateaubriand. From the first he assailed the Gallican tradition and Napoleon's State control of religion and when Napoleon came back from Elba he fled to England, which was when he decided to be ordained. He wrote an apology for Christianity, a big work in four volumes, *The Mind of Christianity*, later called *Essay on Indifference in the Matter of Religion*.[3] Its premiss is that reason common to humanity is more profound than individual reasonings, and it is through this natural rationality that religion is justified. His experience of Napoleon convinced him that the State has no right to interfere with the Church, and therefore that popes are free to act in any State without government taking the right to stop their bulls or veto their approval of the choice of bishops. Hence he came before the world as a strong papalist. His *Religion Considered in the Political and Social Order*[4] won him a trial and a fine in a French court.

In his earlier life he believed not at all in toleration, nor in freedom, nor in the rights of man, nor in democracy. But now he saw how dangerous it was for Catholicism, in the climate of developing liberalism, to be always on the side of the despots. From this recognition he proposed that the Church is not the enemy of freedom but its protector; that the doctrine of the rights of man is derived from Christian foundations. After the French Revolution of July 1830 he started a journal, *L'Avenir* (*The Future*), which first appeared that

[3] *Esprit du Christianisme* (1817–23); soon *Essai sur l'indifference en matière de religion.*
[4] *De la religion considerée dans l'ordre politique et civil* (1826).

October. The newspaper had as its motto the words, 'God and
Liberty'. It was to stand for all the freedoms; to prise the Catholic
Church apart from its defence of reactionary regimes; to reinspire
Catholic thought; and to demand that the Church support the claim
of oppressed Catholic peoples—in Poland, or Belgium, or Ireland, or
Holland—to equality in their States. It advocated the separation of
Church and State. Catholics were to place themselves at the head of
the radicals and utter the loudest cry for liberty the world had ever
heard.

Not many people bought this paper. But it had the widest influence. In France there was a generation gap: the older clergy and bishops found it dangerous nonsense, the younger clergy found it
inspiring. Wherever a Catholic country was either in revolution, as
in Belgium against Holland and Poland against the Tsar, or mutter-
ing angrily about its government, as in Southern Ireland against
Westminster and Rhineland Prussia against Berlin, it was inspiring.
When the July revolution broke out in Paris, Brussels seethed with
discontent against its Dutch and Protestant government and was well
peopled with refugees from absolutist regimes in France, Italy, or
Spain. When the revolution succeeded and made Belgium independent, it needed a constitution; and that was when Lamennais's ideas
were fertile.

The new Belgian constitution of 1831 embodied most of his principles. *L'Avenir* was more weighty in Belgium than in France. Just out
from under the weight of Protestant Holland, the new Belgium was
excited that the Church was free. *L'Avenir* was reprinted at Louvain
and sold more copies than in France. Catholic priests did not ask the
new State for privileges, only for liberty.

The new constitution of Belgium removed special privileges for
the Church in the State; though the State, which possessed the old
Church endowments confiscated in the French Revolution, still continued to pay the stipends of the clergy. In return the Church was
given a freedom that it then possessed in no other Catholic State. It
could at will open schools and run them with religious orders. The
State would have no say in the choice of bishops (this was an extraordinary thing for a Catholic State to abandon—it was a historic
axiom that a State could not dispense with a measure of control over
the choice of bishops—it remained an axiom with most of the States
of Europe till the Second World War). The Pope chose the bishops,
the bishops chose the priests. The State could not stop the publica-

tion of papal bulls. Censorship was abolished. The historic method of
a Concordat between the papacy and the State was abandoned. This
Belgian constitution became a model for the more liberal Catholics
of the nineteenth century. The one provision that the Church
regarded as offensive to its liberties was the law that ordered civil
marriage to precede marriage in Church. But Belgians accepted a law
of civil marriage, with which they were familiar from the rule of
Napoleon, more easily than any other body of Catholics in Europe.[5]
In the conditions of Europe and the papacy such a constitution of
Church and State required statesmen to work it with success.
Belgium was fortunate in its Archbishop of Malines, Sterckx, able
and moderate and in office for thirty-six years from the new constitution.

In France Lamennais had many enemies. France was still under the
Concordat of Napoleon, which gave bishops advantages. To conservatives Lamennais appeared to be a political priest preaching revolution and pretending that it was religion. He lost support, even from
the younger clergy, because he said that the clergy should cease to be
paid by the State and should instead depend upon a just endowment
(presumably provided by the State from the old endowments confiscated in the French Revolution) and from the gifts of their people.
Everyone could see that if this happened French priests were sure to
be poorer, and they were poor already. Bishops who had to finance
seminaries and good works were shocked at the idea of abolishing
the Concordat of Napoleon, by which their finances were (fairly)
safe. In an unsettled time after 1830 they were anxious not to disturb
the politics of Church and State when no one yet knew what would
happen in France. The bishops could discern signs of a religious
revival. The middle classes were tired of revolutions, and mobs, and
local risings, and wanted stability, and thought that religion could be
a help. Theorists of revolution frightened them—Proudhon's
doctrine that all property is robbery, Saint-Simon's socialism, and
soon Karl Marx. The middle class might not think much of the clergy
but found what they stood for not to be trivial. The bishops did not
wish to choke this sign of sympathy by letting a famous priest tell
France that religion was the cause of revolution and revolution was
its hope.

[5] They revived a see, Bruges, in 1834, to add to the five existing sees. Bruges was one of
the sees created by Philip II under Spanish rule but was abolished by Napoleon.

Lamennais was so convinced that his was the only way forward that he believed it possible to appeal to the Pope. He fancied that he received cold air from the Church authorities because the French bishops and the Curia in Rome kept the truth away from Pope Gregory. He needed only to go personally to the Pope, explain himself, and gain the approval which would win him backing for his work in France.

Lamennais believed that the Pope should bless democracy. But only a few months earlier this pope had summoned an Austrian army into the Papal State to stop democracy, or at least to stop armed men who claimed to be democrats. *L'Avenir* had not said pleasant things about the suppression of the rebellion in the Papal State.

Archbishop Quelen of Paris told him to his face that he was not a realist; that he had adopted the language used by demagogues and had praised revolution, and there was no chance that Rome could give him approval. Lamennais did not believe his archbishop, whose views, legitimist and Gallican, he knew to be outmoded.

On the journey to Rome he was accompanied by his young colleagues Lacordaire and Montalembert. Lacordaire, who had suggested the voyage, was a young priest beginning to be well-known; Montalembert was a young hereditary peer, and that gave the trio more weight. Of an ancient family, Montalembert's father was ennobled because of his resistance to the French Revolution. The son Charles was born in London, and after the Battle of Waterloo gained a European experience because his father served as French ambassador first in Württemberg and then Stockholm. He was unusual among French Catholics because he was much influenced by English conservative-liberals such as Burke. At the age of 20 he became a colleague of Lamennais on *L'Avenir*. But the weight he added was minimal compared with that of the principal person. Here was not merely a priest whose teaching was criticized going quietly to Rome to ask for advice. Here was a famous writer who blazoned his journey to the world. Europe watched as *this* priest, who raised the pope's power above that of all governments, went to Rome to persuade Gregory XVI that he ought to be a democrat; or, if that were not realistic (which Lamennais could see), to persuade him that a thinker who taught Catholicism to be the foundation of democracy said nothing contrary to faith or due order.

For a century and a half the documents that told what happened lay unpublished. Then Le Guillou persuaded Pope John XXIII to

allow his Dominican brother to copy the bulky dossier, and later persuaded Pope John Paul II to allow the two Le Guillou brothers to
publish the papers (1982).[6]

Before Lamennais reached Rome, powerful men told the Pope
that he was bad. The nuncio in Paris, Lambruschini, who had been a
friend of Lamennais, now gave a warning; and after Lambruschini left
Paris his substitute Antonio Garibaldi sent another warning. A
mounting number—though not a majority—of the French bishops,
led by the archbishop of Toulouse, made their opinion plain; they did
not at first include the two whom Lamennais knew best, his own
bishop, of Rennes, and his kind critic Archbishop Quelen of Paris.
Metternich, whose job was to keep Italy in order, whose troops held
down the Papal States at the Pope's request, who was the most powerful person in Rome though he was in Vienna, must have been horrified at the idea that the Pope might fail to condemn a dangerous
democrat. Possibly the Tsar, through his agent Gagarin in Rome,
pressed also. The Tsar was busy stamping on Polish revolutionaries
and for the Pope to declare that Lamennais was to be approved (and
so good Catholics could be revolutionaries) was as abhorrent to the
Tsar as to Metternich. Lamennais and Montalembert believed that
the Russian did all that he could, which was likely, because
Lamennais abused the Russian government and backed the revolution in Poland. But there is no firm evidence of such Russian pressure on Gregory XVI; and if it happened it must have weighed lightly
in comparison with the nagging of Metternich, without whom the
Pope was not safe in Rome.

The portrait of Lamennais sent to the Pope by the French nuncio
and the deputy was not ill-considered: here is a devoted and prayerful priest. He has a brilliant mind and is a famous writer but is not a
deep theologian and his judgement is not equal to his intelligence. He
is dedicated to the Pope and a high believer in his authority. He is
proud, and believes he has a mission to save the truth and the Church
of France. To justify revolution he appeals to St Thomas Aquinas, and
Suarez, and even the *Unam Sanctam* of Pope Boniface VIII. He is hostile to the bishops and they to him. He is dangerous. If he is condemned he and his numerous followers might go for a schism. If he

---

[6] Published as *La Condamnation de Lamennais*. Where the documents were in Italian or
Latin they are published in a French translation. The French Jesuit Paul Dudon was allowed
to see the dossier for his book *Lamennais et le St-Siège* (1911) but the result did not satisfy
historians.

is approved he will misuse the approbation. If Rome keeps silence he will treat it as tantamount to approval.

Before Lamennais arrived, the French ambassador in Rome received an assurance from Bernetti the Secretary of State that the Pope would give no approval to Lamennais. Gregory told the ambassador that he found the doctrines of Lamennais a threat to the peace of the Church and of France, and that he felt personally wounded by some of the articles in *L'Avenir*. He told the Austrian ambassador Lützow of his extreme grief at this expected arrival which he believed aimed to compromise him. More than once he informed Lützow that he was placed in a very difficult predicament.

Although the letters which poured into Rome were mostly negative there were others. The Theatine Father Ventura was a friend of Lamennais and was consulted. Ventura told Rome that Lamennais had done a great work: he had refuted the cries of the Church's enemies that it always stood on the side of tyranny, saved the Church in France from a far worse fate during this revolution, and broken the power of French Gallicanism. He ought not to have set out for Rome, but the intention was very pious. 'A great writer, an apologist of the first rank, who has dedicated 24 embattled years of his life to defend and spread truth, is accused of being a person of feeble faith, and comes of his own accord to the supreme Pastor and judge of doctrine to find out whether he may face condemnation—nothing could be more edifying.' If Rome receives courteously some of its worst enemies it ought not to receive with discourtesy one of its best defenders. He is the first writer of his generation; he is heroically disinterested; he is influencing all Europe, and has his hand on all the younger clergy not only in France but from Ireland to Prussia. 'I do not say that he will rebel. He is too faithful a Catholic. Still—in prudence it is a mistake to count too much on human virtue—and especially when it is French virtue.' (Ventura was a Sicilian.)[7]

Ventura was not alone. And the dossier proves what surprises: that Gregory XVI himself was one of those who had no wish to condemn, and presents a portrait of the Pope different from that which historians formerly assumed.

Lamennais and his two companions passed through Lyons, where they found the city in the power of the workers, who welcomed them as friends and whom Lamennais thought to be not 'the brig-

---

[7] Ventura's plea in *La Condamnation de Lamennais*, 105 ff.

ands' whom the French army suppressed a few weeks later. At Assisi they grieved that the great convent, once with many friars, was so declined that there were now but fifteen. In the Tiber valley Lamennais was upset at seeing a chain-gang of convicts under an escort of the pope's police. The trio arrived in Rome at the end of December 1831, sure that they were perfectly orthodox. Difficulties were constantly put in their way about seeing the Pope; most cardinals were cool to them. They were fêted by the Polish community, and from the Poles, who gave him a chalice, he learnt much of the Russian onslaught in Poland.

The three wrote frank letters to their friends in France. What they never knew was that Metternich's spies secured copies of their letters and that Metternich personally read them and forwarded what he wanted for the Pope's eyes.

Lamennais's portrait of the Pope (whom he had not yet met) was written in a letter to Gerbet of 28 January 1832.

He is a good monk. He knows nothing of the world. He has no idea what the Church is like. He is deeply pious and this fills him with a passive courage—he will suffer anything rather than hurt his conscience . . . He is surrounded by men of affairs, several of them laymen, to whom religion is not important; they are ambitious, greedy, cowardly, blind and stupid like the eunuchs of the late (Roman) Empire; that is how this country is governed. (*Correspondance générale*, ed. L. le Guillou (Paris, 1971–), v. 80–1.)

On 15 March 1832, after two and a half months of waiting, they won their audience with the Pope. It was very surprising. They waited an hour in anterooms. The French Cardinal Rohan (whom Ventura declared to be one of their prejudiced enemies and whom Lamennais regarded as a *bambino*, a person with no more weight in the world than a child) arrived and took them into a modest little room which was the Pope's study. They went through the ritual, knelt and kissed his feet. Then they stood and faced him, and he stayed standing to face them, wearing a plain white cassock and with one hand in his pocket. Montalembert was moved by the sensation that in front of him stood such power among the nations, 'the only authority in the world I want to obey'. They talked in a friendly way—the Pope simple, almost without dignity, and not formidable, with a healthy but not a spiritual demeanour, kind and welcoming. For a quarter of an hour they chatted of people they knew, and of Geneva, and of the piety of French Catholics, and of Michelangelo.

He offered them a pinch of snuff. Then he gave each of them a medallion of St Gregory, blessed the chaplets they presented, and said goodbye graciously. Not a word was exchanged on the mission for which they came to Rome.[8]

The way this interview went can mean only one of two things. Either the Pope was too shy, or too nervous, or too gentle, to *confront*—yet in history he has a formidable reputation—or he can have had no intention of condemning, for all are agreed that he was not capable of hypocrisy. If there was to be a condemnation of Lamennais, it could only be because Metternich forced it upon his client State, or because the engines of the Inquisition churned away and could not be stopped even by a pope. It is not astonishing that the three young men—one famous and two to become famous, one of whom was a peer—should not have started to ask him questions about their predicament, for the Curial officials had made it a condition when fixing the audience that they should not raise with the Pope the subject of their mission; what surprises is that the three should have accepted that condition.

Six days after the audience the secret service picked up a letter from Lamennais in which he described the tyranny of papal government in the Legations of North Italy: how the Pope's armies had murdered several nuns, and sacked a Benedictine monastery; how the despot who tyrannizes over Poland is all-powerful at the Vatican; how religion is decadent or worse and the Austrians are useless—and Lamennais and his sympathizers must fight on because one day a pope will come who will bring a rebirth to the Church.[9] All this was brought to the eyes of Gregory.

Lamennais hung on in Rome until 1 July 1832. In mid-June the Pope issued a brief condemning the revolution in Poland as a wrong act against a lawful sovereign (the tsar) and telling the bishops and clergy that they must take no part in fostering the revolutionary spirit. The repression of the Poles was brutal. Whether the then tsar was actually the lawful sovereign of Poland (though of course he had the power over Poland) was debatable. This encyclical hurt the Poles very much. Since *L'Avenir* had vehemently backed the Poles, denounced the tsar, and talked of the murder of Poland, Lamennais

---

[8] Montalembert's partly unpublished diary in *La Condamnation de Lamennais*, 141–2; E. Lecanuet, *Montalembert* (Paris, 1895–1912), i. 286–7.

[9] Lamennais to Charles de Coux, *Corr. gén.* v. 84 ff.; *La Condamnation de Lamennais*, 144; cf. *Corr. gén.* v. 83, to Coriolis.

was 'appalled' (said the secret Austrian informant) and at last accepted that nothing was to be gained from this pope and that the best he could hope for was silence. He half-exempted the Pope on the supposition that this anti-Polish brief was a payment forced out of him as a fee for the military protection of the Papal States.

It was odd that no one in Rome had even discussed his ideas with him. It was odd that if they meant to criticize him they had given him no chance to explain himself. At least he could presume that he was free to act further and could restart *L'Avenir* when he came back to Paris.

Nearly all the Pope's advisers were persuaded that it was impossible for Rome to say nothing. If he kept silence, he would be taken by a large part of the world not to disapprove of the doctrines of Lamennais. So the encyclical, when it came, avoided condemning Lamennais by name. Instead it condemned most of what he stood for as general principles.

Mirari vos (15 August 1832) condemned freedom of conscience for everyone—'a false doctrine, really a bit of madness'. It condemned the freedom of the press—'a hateful freedom, impossible to execrate enough'. It condemned the doctrine of a just revolution—or at least the encouragement by the Church of rebellion against a lawful sovereign (which were not the same thing, but felt to be at that moment the same thing). It condemned the doctrine that Church and State ought to be separated. No pope could be expected to preach the equality of all religions. This encyclical condemned the Napoleonic and Lamennaisian doctrine that the practitioners of all religions ought to have the same legal rights in the State. Most out of keeping with Catholic tradition on a historic view, the encyclical condemned the doctrine that the people are the source of power in the State. It did not preach the divine right of kings in so many words—but it was near it.

Moreover the encyclical spoke in strong terms—depressing terms—about the state of society. Such language became a habit with the Curia of the nineteenth century: 'Wickedness is exultant. Shameless science exults. Licentiousness exults. Truth is corrupted. Errors of every kind are spread without restraint. Wicked men abuse holy laws and rights and institutions and discipline. . . . They attack the divine authority of the Church . . . a terrible disaster for religion and morality . . . the destruction of public order . . .'[10] This tone of

---

[10] *Mirari vos*, in A. M. Bernasconi (ed.), *Acta Gregorii Papae XVI* (Rome, 1901), i. 170.

lament had roots in the curial tradition. But the new music of tragedy became characteristic of the Roman organization as it contemplated the ways in which Europe developed its politics, its civilization, and its opinions. It may have been the way to help a supportive party to form, but it was not the way to persuade the world.

One tradition in Catholic (and equally in Protestant) thought had always understood the doctrine of power in an authoritarian sense. Power comes from God, that is common doctrine. Therefore it always comes from above, not only in a spiritual sense but also in the meaning that we have a duty always to obey the lawful ruler. If this were true, the doctrine 'the voice of the people is the voice of God' is not a Christian doctrine. But a long tradition of Catholic (and Protestant, especially Calvinist) thought had allowed that the idea of the voice of the people being the voice of God had truth. The law of God is in part natural law, the principles of justice; and natural law is known because it is found in the general mind or conscience of humanity.

After the French Revolution the authoritarian looked more Christian than the popular interpretation. And the Pope had made his name, when a younger priest, as a resister of the Revolution.

The encyclical denounced those who appealed that the clergy be allowed to marry. It denounced the Italian secret societies that worked to overturn the lawful governments of the Italian States. It declared divorce to be unlawful, and the marriage bond permanent. It said that the Church's censorship of books was extremely useful.

The Protestant countries, and most Catholic countries once ruled by Napoleon—France, Belgium, the Rhineland, North Italy, but not Spain or southern Italy—now accepted that if a society were to be happy it must tolerate people who practised cults which were not the religion of the majority of the country. The wars of Napoleon intermingled Catholics with Protestants in many areas of Europe; very few States were now of one denomination only; intolerance of harmless dissenters was coming to be seen as immoral.

In the Pope's eyes the State has a moral duty, not only to be a weapon for defending the bastions, nor merely to be a hirer of policemen, nor is it a device for making the citizens richer, but it is called of God to help the people to behave according to the laws of God and man. Therefore it has a duty to restrain, not only the immoral, but persons who promote immorality. Since everyone is agreed (so he could then assume) that religious error leads to immorality because it pulls away from the truth that is the cause and safeguard of keeping God's law, the State must stop the promotion of religious error. To provide legally that speakers or writers shall be free to promote what is not true, or to utter words that declare racial prejudice, or paederasty, or pornography, or adultery, or murder not to be sins, cannot be what God demands of any State.

This was a conflict within the Church of the nineteenth century. It was a dispute between two moral judgements, with good Catholics on both sides. And the world went the way that was not Pope Gregory's.

The copy of the encyclical reached Lamennais in Munich where he spent nearly a month on his way home. Montalembert wrote from Munich to a friend: they had meant to go back to Paris to restart *L'Avenir* with new energy. But, he said, the encyclical has come and puts the Church in direct enmity with science and liberty and calls us and our system 'impudent, execrable and even stinking', and says liberty of conscience is madness and it is only the sequel of the brief 'dictated by the Russian prince Gagarin' against the Poles and it destroys the Catholic party in France. So we must give up trying to defend the Church in the way we thought, and we will hold ourselves in silence.

Lamennais himself thought that the encyclical could be disregarded; it mentioned neither him nor his work. He said that no one could take its contents seriously. He wrote to his friend the Countess of Senfft (20 August 1832), 'We need scarcely take the trouble to read it. Its ideas are like the swaddling bands that wrap up Egyptian mummies. It talks of a world that does not exist any more. Its sound is like those remote rumbles that are heard in the consecrated tombs of Memphis.'

The three published an act of submission to Rome. The words were chosen carefully. 'We cannot continue our work except by putting ourselves against the formally expressed will of him whom God has made the governor of the Church. . . . Respectfully submitting to his authority we give up the fight which we have loyally fought for two years and encourage our friends to submit likewise. Paris 10 September 1832.' Lamennais gave no public sign of anything but a resignation which his friends admired.

But the fight was not over. Neither the disciples nor the enemies of Lamennais were content. In Belgium and in Poland his doctrines were Catholic comfort and people said that it was only necessary to accept the pope's decrees when he taught religious doctrine and not necessary when he talked of political constitutions. Young French priests pointed out that Lamennais was not condemned. In several dioceses of France the debate still raged—if Lamennais was silent his disciples were not. And his opponents were discontented with Rome. Lamennais had retracted nothing. This was, in the old Jansenist phrase, 'a respectful silence'. He did not say that he no longer held the doctrines, he only said that he would not talk about what he did hold. The archbishop of Toulouse was militant against him. 'This submission', he told Rome, 'is captious and inadequate and Rome may not realize that.' He did not even think it a promise of respectful silence. He had secured the copy of a private letter from Lacordaire—even archbishops had their agents—which declared how they had chosen their words with care and avoided any hint of recantation and 'our opinions are still what they were'.[11] To this Rome answered quietly: patience; prudence; charity. Not until the end of February 1833 did the Congregation of Extraordinary Affairs, with the Pope in the chair, meet to consider what to do next. And it decided to do nothing—as yet; to avoid a formal condemnation, and to see if Lamennais kept the silence he had promised. In France Lamennais's private letters showed a mood of complete submission. This was not the mood of the French bishops, and their mood was changing what the Pope felt it right to do. Some of the bishops refused to ordain candidates who did not first make a declaration that they would not follow Lamennais or that they accepted the sense of the encyclical *Mirari vos*. Archbishop Quelen of Paris forced a public disciple of Lamennais to recant publicly. In briefs to Lamennais's chief enemy the archbishop of Toulouse, and then to his diocesan the bishop of Rennes, Gregory XVI evidently approved of the acts of the French bishops. Newspapers kept speculating on Lamennais's discontent and whether or not he was a rebel. It appeared that Lamennais's position was untenable unless he uttered a further recantation; silence about what he had taught was no longer enough, but he must say that he no longer believed what he had taught.

The dossier of letters exchanged proves that he was pressed too hard. Leading French bishops, as well as Metternich, were more convinced of the necessity than the cardinals in the Curia or the acting nuncio in Paris. But on 5 November 1833 Lamennais wrote the Pope

[11] d'Astros, archbishop of Toulouse, to Mgr. de Gregorio, 3 Nov. 1832; *La Condamnation de Lamennais*, 277.

another letter of submission on all matters of doctrine and of church administration and discipline declared in *Mirari vos*; and added a fifth paragraph which finally disturbed the Curia at Rome: 'In conscience I have a duty to affirm that while Christians have only to hear and obey in the realm of religion, they remain entirely free in their opinions and words and acts in the sphere that is purely temporal.'[12]

The Curia were disturbed not only by the failure to submit fully, but because Lamennais assumed that the world accepted this principle of a division between the spiritual sphere where Christians obeyed and the sphere of the world where they were free to think and say what they liked. They demanded more. And in a short letter of five lines in Latin (11 December 1833) Lamennais accepted absolute submission to the sense of *Mirari vos* as stated by the Pope. Archbishop Quelen thought that all was achieved and expressed his great joy. Two days later Lacordaire sent him a submission on the same lines.[13]

Something was sinister about the words in which the bishop of Rennes expressed his joy: 'Lamennais has committed suicide. His style and genius cannot avoid that. He is a spark put out. He is a lesson and a victim of his refusal to obey.' 'One knows his immense capacity for suffering', wrote a friend, 'It is surprising he goes on living. His friends say he won't live more than two years. They have killed him. Do you know of a worse murder than that of a Catholic genius armed to defend the faith? . . . What shall we do without him?'[14] One or two of the letters of his enemies express too much pleasure that he was brought to a nothing.

But the troubled soul was not dead. Three months later, on 30 April 1834, there appeared in Paris *Paroles d'un Croyant* (*Words of a Believer*). It had no author's name. It quickly sold many copies. When Archbishop Quelen of Paris contrasted it with his undertaking to write no more *on religious matters*, Lamennais replied that he wrote it a year before and that the book was not about religion but about politics. It was later clear that in earlier editions he left out paragraphs which said hostile things about Gregory XVI.

Written in prose, it is a meditative poem on the original sin of human society. Its burden was this: human beings were born free and equal in a Garden of Eden. But they fell, and so made themselves

---

[12] *La Condamnation de Lamennais*, 391.   [13] Ibid. 430–1.
[14] Rennes to the Pope, 14 Dec. 1833, ibid. 437–8; Maurice de Guérin to his sister, *Œuvres*, ed. H. Clouard (Paris, 1930), ii. 114 ff.

governments to keep sin in handcuffs, or sinners seized power to pretend that they kept order but really to enjoy themselves in comfort and idleness, and so the world is full of oppression and injustice; and only Christ can save us by bringing the true brotherhood of humanity; *it is upon the heart of Christ that the sick peoples revive, and that the oppressed peoples receive strength to free themselves*; and this is not achieved by laws, nearly all of which are bad, nor by governments which are tyrannical much of the time, and which ban workers from even trying to combine to get more just conditions, and which kill people who think differently from themselves—but by us the people; and we the people cry out to Thee, Lord, out of the depths of our misery, like a shipwrecked crew on a barren coast, or like a wounded bird hunted by a dog, or like Christ crying upon the cross, *why hast thou forsaken me?* We look up to thee in prayer that in time, little by little, we may rid ourselves of this poverty; but we know that we are exiles upon this earth and the exile is everywhere lonely—*cease to lament poor exile; all are banished like thee—our true Country is not here below—that which we take for it is but a resting-place for a night.* The poor are restless, and soon a tempest shall sweep over the nations; be ready, the time is at hand, and there shall be terror, and kings on their thrones shall cry in fear and will clutch their crowns which the gale is carrying away, and the powerful shall run naked out of their palaces for fear that the stones will fall upon them in the earthquake and will beg a morsel of bread from the passers-by. *It is the peoples that make the kings; and the kings are made for the peoples and not the peoples for the kings.* The book was full of parables and little stories. There was an old widow, in near-destitution because her man had died; and her young daughter wept at seeing her work so hard with her needle; and the mother said '*Our hope is not here, below . . . While I bore you in my womb, I prayed fervently to the Virgin Mary, and she came in my sleep and I dreamt that she held out to me, with a smile of heaven, a little child. And I took the child which she held out to me and when I held it in my arms, the Virgin-Mother placed upon its head a crown of white roses—and a few months later you were born . . .*'

It alarmed the printers. Sainte-Beuve, who in these years of his life was more than half a disciple of Lamennais, visited the press while they printed and found them excited and wondering whether what they did was legal. Republicans were radiant, and Poles, and some Belgians, and some French who were not so republican. The Marquis de Corioli wrote, 'It's Job, it's Isaiah, it's St John: it's more

still, it's you.'[15] Guizot said that by writing this book he had put himself among the bad men of the age.[16] It shocked the hierarchy. It
preached democracy; the tyranny of kings; the absurdity of hereditary lines of kings; the oppression of the peoples. Human beings, it
seemed to say, have no rulers except Christ, and no law to follow but
that of justice and human brotherhood, and cannot obey God without disobeying governments; which to sustain their tyranny have
enlisted the clergy by giving them money and honours and so priests
became the valets of kings instead of the servants of Christ.

The acting nuncio called it '*infamous . . . He is a man lost for ever*'.[17]

Metternich was reported to be in consternation. 'It is a book worth
more to our cause than a thousand bayonets', said a writer in the
French left-wing press *Le Populaire*. One hundred thousand copies
were soon sold, it was translated into several languages; the police of
certain countries tried to stop its sale.

The Pope ordered Cardinal Lambruschini to read it and report,
and the cardinal said that the book filled him with horror; the worse
because the style is so brilliant and poetic; 'as great or greater than that
of Paradise Lost'.

Archbishop Quelen thought that the right policy was to take no
notice and to treat the book as the idealistic vision of an unbalanced
mind which no one could take as literal. To condemn would mag-
nify it and would treat a poem as though it was prose. This was a wise
view. It was an apocalypse and apocalypses flee into heaven and hide
in mystery and so escape the censorship because no reader can pin
down what they mean in propositions. Cardinal Lambruschini did
not agree. There are propositions—for example that the king is made
by the people, or that punishment for heresy is wrong. Everyone will
read it. The literary will value it because it is literature. If Rome is
silent the silence will only help the influence of the book. We need
a formal brief, addressed to the French bishops, condemning the
book by name. This was bad advice from Cardinal Lambruschini
even though, or because, he had served as nuncio in Paris.

The Pope accepted the advice but changed the destination of the
encyclical to all bishops everywhere; and so on 25 June appeared
Singulari nos, which condemned the book 'little in size but vast in
perversity'. 'I am very pleased at the welcome which everyone has
given to *Mirari vos*.' But, he said, the evil has not quite ceased. There

---

[15] *Corr. gén.* ii. 280.   [16] F. P. G. Guizot, *Mémoires* (Paris, 1858–61), iii. 99–100.
[17] Antonio Garibaldi to Bernetti, 9 May 1834, *La Condamnation de Lamennais*, 466.

are little books full of imprudence, and there are dark machinations. I was so glad about the submission which Lamennais made on 11 December 1833. And now I am filled with horror even at the first glance at this book; and how it breaks the bonds of loyalty to princes and encourages sedition and disobedience to law.

This encyclical used an unusually heavy hammer for a short book. Popes ought not publicly to express the horror they felt 'at the first glance' (*ex primo oculorum obtutu*). Normally they did not use all their weight to condemn single publications. The Index of Prohibited Books would issue a ban, that no Catholic might read book X by author Y. To use an encyclical magnified the importance of the book that was published and ensured that it became a best-seller and stayed so all the century. This misuse of the method can only be explained by a sense of shock in Gregory XVI. But the encyclical did not excommunicate Lamennais. It prayed that he might return to a better mind.

Anyone else publishing this book would not have been censured in this way. The moment was important. The Papal State was in revolution and held down by Austrian troops. Metternich was potent and pressed for an outright condemnation of so dangerous a thinker who pretended that democracy was the Christian way. The French bishops fancied they achieved a *modus vivendi* with a government which after a revolution came out more moderate than they expected, and could hardly bear it if their most famous priest cried for disestablishment. But above all, it was the context. *Paroles d'un Croyant* might contain parable and mystery in its pages but it must be read in the light of the propositions earlier stated by the author and which had been publicly condemned in *Mirari vos* and then, apparently, recanted by the author. St Paul declared that power came from God, Lamennais said that power came from hell. The two minds were less apart than they seemed, for everyone agreed that government was a consequence of sin. But at that moment of time, and in that context, they seemed as far apart as possible.

Here was a famous priest, publicly disapproved and humiliated, and in such a way that bishops could not allow him to act as a priest unless something more happened. He had not been excommunicated. He could have gone on as a Catholic writer saying what he liked until fate struck him down with direct excommunication. But he had lost any desire to write as a Catholic. What he believed to be true Christianity the Pope said was not. It took about a year after

Singulari nos before Paris was aware that he no longer regarded himself as a Catholic. He wrote one more book on this part of his life— a historical description of the visit to Rome, *Affaires de Rome*. It is surprising in that it has no rancour. It is the only calm book he ever wrote. But he made it very clear that he was no longer a servant of the Pope; and he passed among the working leaders of the radical French left, who at first did not trust him. His close disciples submitted to the condemnation, without exception. The way this was done by Lacordaire and Montalembert pained him.

Though he turned to the extreme left, his friends went on. Lacordaire gave lectures at the College Stanislaus. The chapel was too small, people put ladders to the windows. Chateaubriand came, and Lamartine, and Victor Hugo. The clergy protested to Archbishop Quelen who made him stop the course. Before Advent Lacordaire asked if he could preach a course. Quelen said that he must first see the text and on this condition Lacordaire refused to preach. But early in 1835 to his astonishment Quelen invited him to be the Lent preacher in Notre Dame Cathedral if he would submit not the text but the general theme. Lacordaire preached to 6,000 people. Famous anticlericals appeared at these sermons. Was that a sign of religious revival, or was it also a sign of the interest which not very religious persons felt in a priest who was known to be of the left in politics and disapproved of by his archbishop? Probably it was more a sign of revival than of interest in rebellion, but both feelings were present among the people. Quelen attended the course and invited Lacordaire to do another the following year, 1836; which was attended with the same success.

BOURGEOIS FRANCE AND THE CHURCH

The liberal ideas were less anticlerical than they appeared to be when competing for power. They were of the middle class. Seven years after the Revolution of 1830 the French State was increasing the financial provision for the clergy, and in various areas of France where Catholicism was strong local officials encouraged the life of the Church. Government controlled the choice of bishops. But it did not try to appoint very liberal Catholics. It tried to keep out the clergy who would not accept its lawful authority, and clergy who might be democrats of any variety, or followers of Lamennais. A liberal bourgeois government tried to establish good relations with moderate leaders of a conservative Church; and on the whole successfully, to the benefit of both parties.

Here also was a reason for the development of the authority of the pope. In France the bishops had absolute power over their clergy, under Napoleon's Concordat. The clergy needed the pope. He must be their protector against the acts of State or bishops. The religious orders, always under attack in the press, and continually questioned whether they were legal in society, needed an international backing, if they could get it. The only way to get it was through the pope as the mouthpiece of Catholic opinion through Europe. During the age of Gregory XVI the lower French clergy became conscious of a need for the authority of Rome.

The State, seeing the need for more elementary schools, was aware of the service that religious orders might render, as also in nursing. It did not discourage the religious and occasionally encouraged them. A so-called Guizot law (1833) recognized that members of religious orders could be teachers in schools and provided that religion be taught in primary schools. There was an astonishing growth in the number of French Jesuits—seventy-four houses in 1840.

Jesuits were illegal in France, but at first no one tried to stop them. The anticlerical world had it in its head that the Jesuits were the pope's shock troops and the symbol of everything that was reactionary, which led to loud disputes between Jesuits and anticlericals during the middle years of the 1840s, the last years of Pope Gregory. This clamour was important in the growing cleavage of France into clerical and anticlerical. The historian Michelet, who had academic weight, gave a course on the history of the Jesuits which proved how historians use history for prejudiced ends.

Government was asked to apply the old law which made Jesuits illegal. The government behaved wisely, and asked its ambassador in Rome, Pellegrino Rossi, to persuade Gregory XVI that it was better to withdraw the Jesuits by his command than to suffer them dissolved by the State. That Gregory agreed to such a painful demand is one more sign that he could act more flexibly than was expected from his reputation.

The division was at its worst in education. Some members of the teaching profession were free-thinking or agonistic. Catholic newspapers were ferocious in their attacks upon the way in which teachers tried to make their children non-Christian. On one side a few

Church leaders still demanded that the Church must control the whole system of State education. On the other side, a profession grew up which escaped the influence of the Church and claimed its autonomy. Many teachers were devout Catholics; and one in twenty teachers was a priest. Still, the strife over how, or whether, to educate the children in religion led to a rift within French society.

Two possible ways lay ahead for a French Catholic educationalist wanting children educated in the faith. One way was to claim an exclusive right to control education, on the grounds that religion is the foundation of character in homes and families and the moral basis of society, that France is a Catholic country and therefore it is right that the Church control education and that religion be taught in all schools.

The other way was to appeal to liberal principles. If such principles are practised properly they mean freedom for people to educate their children in the way they want to, and therefore freedom for Catholics to educate their children in the Catholic faith. It means freedom for non-Catholics to educate their children in the way they want, but it is better to accept this for the sake of Catholic freedom. This second was the only policy which could bring results; as it had done already in Protestant Britain, and in Catholic Belgium, where with the encouragement of the Protestant King Leopold the Catholics used the constitutional freedoms to bring strong influence into the schools. A few French Catholics tried to follow this policy. Montalembert was their leader; his ally was a young priest of future eminence, who had nothing to do with Lamennais, the Abbé Dupanloup. But in the age of Gregory XVI, when many Catholics were still so frightened of liberal principles that the Pope was known to be against, it was the 'exclusive right' claim that was mostly tried. It did not work.

Under the regime of the French Restoration all secondary teaching was controlled by the University—appointments, syllabus, examiners. No one could get the qualification to go on to higher education without attending a school approved by the University; therefore the little seminaries which taught so many Catholics, and in which the teachers were controlled by the bishops, did not qualify to pursue higher degrees. All through the reign of Louis Philippe and the pontificate of Gregory XVI the two sides fought each other over education without any change in the law; the Catholics demanding freedom for denominational secondary schools, the professors saying that University control was the only safeguard of proper standards, and a few of them saying that University control was the only safeguard against narrow churchy education. The fight was lamentable; talk by one side of the University massacring souls and being a main sewer of vice, by the other side of children being indoctrinated with superstition. The sharp political division over education produced for the first time in modern France an embryo Catholic political party, led by Montalembert—with a call to vote for candidates who will work for freedom in education. It had success in attracting voters.

GERMANY AND MARRIAGE

The reconstruction of Germany by and after Napoleon, threw many Catholics into Protestant States. The kingdom of Württemberg, a stalwart Protestant State since the Reformation, now had many Catholics in the Swabian mountains. Bavaria, a stalwart State of the Counter-Reformation, had many Protestants. Prussia, one of the big Protestant States of the Reformation, and the chief weight of Protestant power in Germany, now had a large Catholic population, partly in the east, where there were many Poles, and even more in the Rhineland, where the disappearance of the old Catholic elector-States increased Prussian power and threw Catholics under Prussian government.

The Congress of Vienna had one article (no. 16) on religion in Germany. It affected the settlement of the Treaty of Westphalia in 1648, which was still based upon the success of the Reformation in establishing peace, that each State should have its own established religion (Catholic, Lutheran, or Reformed) and those who would not conform need not have civil rights. The age of German Enlightenment weakened this constitution as toleration grew. Then Napoleon everywhere introduced civil equality irrespective of religion. The Congress of Vienna formally accepted this constitution for the German Confederation, and established the gain of the revolutionary epoch.

To establish civil equality in law was not the same as establishing it in practice. In 1829 the British established civil equality for Roman Catholics and a century and a half later the problem of civil equality still caused bombs and murder in Northern Ireland. A large population, which associates its religion with its nationhood or liberties, does not surrender religious privilege to a minority which it thinks not merely wrong in religion, but disloyal to the State.

The pope must find it easier to defend Catholic rights under a Protestant government than under a Catholic government. If the Austrian emperor or the Spanish king interfered with the bishops or the pastoral system they behaved only as good Catholics expected, and they had so behaved for centuries. If the British government treated Irish Catholics similarly, or the Dutch government its Catholics, the pope could appeal to justice and the freedoms of the Church against interference from outside. And the local Catholics could also appeal to those ideas of tolerance and liberty which their Protestant rule now accepted as the ideal of their State.

If a society had a mixture of Catholics and Protestants, many more of them would marry each other.

On the validity of mixed and non-Catholic marriages the canon law of the Catholic Church was obsolete and unworkable. It rested on a decree (*Tametsi*) of the Council of Trent, which had remained in force since the sixteenth century. This declared that no marriage was valid unless celebrated by a Catholic priest. Since this draconian decree turned all Protestant or other non-Catholic marriages into adultery, it was interpreted, to save the situation, by the understanding that the decree only applied in countries where it was published; and it was not published in Protestant countries.

The theoretical question thereby raised about the status of Protestant marriages, which the Protestants did not mind even if they were aware of it, was less important than the consequence for a mixed marriage between a Catholic and a Protestant. The Catholic could not remain a Catholic, or would lose rights as a Catholic, if he or she married a Protestant in a Protestant church, unless the marriage was also celebrated in a Catholic church. Even more, canon law laid it down that a mixed marriage could only be approved if a pledge was given that the Catholic partner in the marriage should exercise the Catholic religion freely; and if both bride and bridegroom gave an undertaking that children of the marriage would be baptized as Catholics and educated in the Catholic religion.

During the eighteenth century German bishops and the popes treated these rules with flexibility. Prussia disliked this canon law and refused to apply it and had not faced any strong protest. The Prussian law code laid it down that in a mixed marriage the sons should be brought up in the religion of the father and the daughters in the religion of the mother. The Catholic clergy of that epoch followed this Prussian rule without questioning it. Then in 1803 the Prussian government issued a declaration that all legitimate children should be educated in the religion of their father. The Catholic clergy contin- ued to conform. The rule could still be said to be impartial between the two denominations.

Such contradictions between the law of the Church and its admin- istration could only survive while mixed marriages were few. With the mingling of denominations, the number grew. In 1825 the Prussian government applied the rule of 1803 to the Rhineland. That is, they applied a rule which fitted the old State of Prussia where the Protestant Church was established, to an area with long traditions of Catholic faith and practice and with no tradition of Protestant estab- lishment. The Prussian government welcomed mixed marriages because it welcomed schools mixed in religion, believing that they would prepare the young to live in a unified state.

The bishops of the Rhineland conformed to the law, but it was certainly a breach in individual freedom. Some Catholic priests refused to accept the decree. They were supported by some non- Catholic liberals, for Rhinelanders did not like the authoritarian behaviour of Berlin. The State demanded that the priests should not try to dissuade their parishioners from mixed marriages; that no pledges should be given beforehand; and that parish priests should on request marry the couple without receiving any pledges. With heavy pressure it persuaded its bishops more or less to accept the system. It could do nothing to make many parish priests do what it wanted, nei- ther could its censors stop the circulation of hostile pamphlets outside Prussian territory, even if they were suppressed within.

Committed to toleration by past history, by circumstances, by numbers of Catholics, by sane policy, and by the Congress of Vienna, the Prussians nevertheless accepted that theirs was a Protestant State, and if possible should become more Protestant. In education Catholics had their place. The ruling Prussians disliked them in the more influential parts of government. Though the majority of Rhinelanders were Catholic, the provincial government never had a Catholic as its president throughout the nineteenth century. Trier and Cologne, former Catholic prince-bishoprics and electoral states, had a Catholic president only for a few weeks during the 1848 Revolution. When a leading civil servant in the Ministry of Cultural Affairs was converted to Catholicism, King Frederick William III, who had a soldierly mind, ordered him not to continue in his post. One of his circle said of the King, 'He practised toleration—so far as that did not diminish the Protestant stamp of Prussia.'[18]

German Protestant States attributed power in religion to the sovereign. This was not a clear distinction from the Catholic States, which behaved in much the same way towards their churches. Catholic States saw such powers over the Church as matters of expediency, so that the State be not too weak. Protestant statesmen saw them as a moral principle—ground of religious freedom, prevention of little tyrannies by pastors or synods. The Prussian minister for Church Affairs, Altenstein, had more power over the Protestant Church of Prussia than any pastor or synod, more than any bishop or pope in the Catholic Church. Archetype of a deskbound bureaucrat, he combined stern conservatism in politics with radical philosophy in religion. He regarded Rhineland Catholicism as obscurantist and to be separated, whenever possible, from its links with Rome.

During the Napoleonic wars the archbishopric of Cologne was abolished because the French annexed much of its territory when they secularized the prince-bishopric. By agreement with Prussia the pope recreated the archbishopric in 1821. At once the archbishop became a potential leader of resistance to the Prussian government in the Rhineland.

In 1835 the Prussian government, which could veto the choice of archbishop, failed to prevent the election of Count Droste zu Vischering, because they knew that he was very conservative and against radicals in politics. Altenstein hoped to gain credit with Rome and the Rhineland by so Catholic a nomination. They asked Droste zu Vischering whether he would follow the moderation of the last papal brief (of Pius VIII) on the subject of mixed marriages. This had gone far; it allowed parents not to take a pledge, and recognized marriages by a Protestant pastor as valid, as long as the pastor warned the couple that the Catholic faith was necessary for the saving of their souls. Droste, asked whether he would follow this, said that he would interpret it with charity and peacefulness. Altenstein was content with this assurance.

From the point of view of government the choice was a mistake. In mentality Droste was an ox-like Becket, with a sense of mission to fight the government to the point of martyrdom. He was an

[18] F. Schnabel, *Deutsche Geschichte im 19. Jahrhundert*, rev. edn. (Freiburg im Breisgau, 1948–55), 115–16, 119.

unintelligent aristocrat who stayed in his study rather than go out into his diocese. He listened to no advice, avoided public ceremonies, and was half inclined to the life of a solitary.

He consciously chose mixed marriages as his battle-ground. He knew that Gregory XVI would back him in disobedience to the rules of the Prussian government. Several other German bishops had no desire for trouble, and it was reported to Rome by a papal envoy in Vienna that they were lukewarm prelates.[19] Prussian officials tried to persuade Droste zu Vischering to conform—in vain. A decree ordered that he perform no duties of his office—in vain. On 20 November 1837 police arrested the Archbishop and confined him in the fortress at Minden.

The French Revolution and Napoleon kidnapped two popes and left Europe relatively unmoved. That a Protestant government should throw an archbishop into gaol caused vast indignation. The State claimed that this was necessary because of the revolutionary acts of the Archbishop. Pope Gregory XVI made an allocution to the cardinals (10 December 1837),[20] that the Prussians trampled upon the liberties of the Church, that the office of bishop was treated with a total disrespect, and that the just rights of the pope were overthrown. The lawyers doubted whether the arrest was legal, and demanded to know the nature of the charge.

For the first time in the century, but by no means the last, the papacy was in public conflict with the Prussian government. The cause was chiefly the change of boundaries by the Napoleonic wars, which put so many Catholics under a Protestant regime. Both this pope and his archbishop of Cologne were products of a revolutionary era that made resistance to tyrannical authority into a virtue.

The papacy thus fulfilled for the first time a function that was to be its characteristic office during the nineteenth century—and the source of a vast increase in papal power within the Catholic Church. Local bishops hard pressed by governments—whether those governments were Catholic or Protestant—could appeal to Rome if they were prepared to resist, and could get the approval of the pope. Thereby their resistance to government could acquire a backing in international opinion, and by the growing influence of the press in various countries. It was a paradox. The more authoritarian the pope, the more he was able to help local churches and bishops against inter-

---

[19] Capaccini's report to Lambruschini, 17 July 1837, in Schm. i. 567.
[20] *Acta*, ed. Bernasconi, ii. 237 ff.

ference by their governments. It became the interest, and the conviction, of many Catholics in Germany, France, and Britain—even in Spain and Austria—that the power of the pope was indispensable to their freedoms. They must be able to plead the moral duty of obedience to a spiritual power coming from outside the frontiers of their State. Despite the liberal age in which they lived, and the liberal axioms from which they profited, an authoritarian pope like Gregory XVI was welcome to them in their quest for freedom.

At first many Catholics of Germany were far from wanting this conflict with the State into which Archbishop Droste zu Vischering set them. As minorities they preferred a quiet life and not too much publicity, and they were now in the headlines of the German press. From Munich the chief lay Catholic publicist of Germany, the romantic writer Görres, issued a booklet entitled *Athanasius*, which treated the conflict of Church and State in Germany as if, absurdly, Droste were another St Athanasius of the fourth century who, at the cost of prison and exile, had fought for what he saw as the foundations of the faith. But the booklet was not absurd. It rallied a wave of Catholic opinion behind resistance to the orders of Berlin. In the streets of Cologne were organized demonstrations against the cathedral chapter because they were willing to administer the diocese without the archbishop.

The conflict made the friendliness between Catholics and Protestants in Germany, where it existed, more difficult. It was a sign that relations between Churches became, contrary to expectation in a world of toleration, more acrimonious instead of more ecumenical.

At first Prussian Protestants were content. Altenstein believed that Prussia could never be happy until a battle was won against Rome, and laboured at his desk under the delusion that he went the right way to divide the German Church from Rome. The policy split Prussia into camps which plagued Germany for the next seventy-five years.

The partition of Poland put many Polish Catholics under Prussian rule. In the east, Catholic resistance was a part of Polish nationalism, and more deep-seated among the people. In 1838 the archbishop of Gnesen-Posen, Martin von Dunin, issued two pastoral letters ordering his clergy to conform to the rules of the Church, not the State, over mixed marriages. Pope Gregory was strong for Dunin. Prussian Protestants found it an anachronism that their politics could be troubled by a pope after an age in which the powers seemed to have put popes in order.

The Prussian lawcourt in Posen deposed Dunin from office and imprisoned him in a fortress. Gregory said the deposition was invalid. That made Dunin a hero among the educated Poles. But despite the difference in race, the eastern conflict aroused less passion. There was no Polish middle class. Polish noble ladies wore mourning; Polish peasants hardly knew. In the Rhineland Catholics were identified with middle-class liberals who cared for freedom and the rule of law.

It was not to the advantage of the Prussian government to go on imprisoning archbishops. A government order gave the clergy a much freer hand in what they did over mixed marriages. Droste zu Vischering was released, though not allowed to return to exercise his functions, and two years later was forced into resignation—a very conciliatory concession by a pope who had not the name of being a compromiser. Altenstein, still sure that he was right, resigned. Martin von Dunin was not released until August 1840, in return for the assurance that he would do all he could for peace between the denominations. He returned to his diocese as a national hero in a triumphant procession. The prince-bishop of Breslau, Count Sedlnitzky von Choltitz—who believed in conciliation with the government, accepted its rules, and in this was supported by his suffragan bishop and most of his cathedral chapter—was persuaded or forced by Pope Gregory XVI (and by the hostility of his people) to resign his see. In his old age, twenty-two years later, he became a Protestant.

King Frederick William IV, who became king of Prussia in 1840, wanted to treat Catholics with respect and to settle the dispute which divided his kingdom. He opened negotiations with Rome. Gregory XVI behaved diplomatically. But with the exception of the Prussian refusal to reinstate Droste zu Vischering, it was a total victory for the Church over the State. The Church got its way over mixed marriages; the government withdrew any claim to interfere in the rules of the Church, and agreed to free communication between Rome and the Catholic authorities in Prussia; schools with Polish children began to teach in the Polish language; a chair of Slav language and literature was founded at the university of Breslau; the oath of loyalty that new bishops had to take was altered to suit Catholic consciences. The Ministry of Church Affairs was divided into two sections, Catholic and Protestant, each with a head of that denomination. There was a new agreement about choice of bishops: the chapter sent a list of names and the Crown struck out what it would not accept.

A national rite consecrated the new harmonies. Cologne cathedral became a symbol of reconciliation. In 1842 the Protestant king laid the foundation stone of the restoration, in the presence of Metternich and many of the princes of Germany.[21] Some Catholics refused to take part in these ceremonies because the Protestant king was the central figure. When the cathedral was consecrated at long last in 1880, it was the time of the *Kulturkampf*, the big fight between Bismarck and the Catholic Church, and most Catholics stayed away as a demonstration of protest. The completion of the building was not so harmonious in its effect as was hoped by those of irenical mind.

Throughout Germany and Austria, in whatever States there were now mixed denominations, the Cologne affair caused difficulty. Under the impact of the Enlightenment and then of Napoleon, all the States moved towards tolerance, part of which included an insistence that their citizens could marry in church without first needing to make promises about the future religious education of the children. It was natural that a Protestant country such as Saxony or Württemberg should practise this, but Austria was equally tough in its legal practice; and in Hungary, where the population was mixed, many local administrations fined parish priests if they tried to exact conditions before marriage. In all these States the task of government was easier because they retained the Josephist system of State control of the Catholic Church in their territories, and chose bishops who would conform, and could ban communications with Rome or the publishing of Rome's messages.

The Prussian trouble affected Catholic opinion in all these States. Some bishops had a sense that it was their duty to imitate Droste of Cologne. No bishop outside Prussia had much success. But this trying series of conflicts proved to the various governments in Germany that they needed to be more careful of Rome, and of the claims of their Catholic prelates, than they had expected. The reason was their new Catholic population, who now had their own newspapers, and representatives in the local Parliaments who could be vociferous against ruthless State interference.

Germany had another unique difficulty. The Catholic professors of divinity were part of a much larger university system, most of which

---

[21] Original foundation stone laid in 1248; the plan was ambitious and the main part was not finished until 1560. Early in the 19th cent. it was determined to complete the plan. From 1821–42 restoration of the existing building took place, and it was finally completed in 1880. It was badly damaged in the Second World War and not fully reopened until 1956.

was Protestant. This Protestant system of teaching and research led Europe in its higher education. That meant that the Catholic professors must reach for the highest standards of scholarship and not be afraid of arguing with non-Catholic scholars; for the whole of the nineteenth century and even beyond, a majority of the Catholic minds most independent and critical of Rome were Germans or Austrians in universities. Rome excommunicated more German professors that century than any other class of Catholic—if we except umbrella excommunications, as of 'all those who robbed the Church of its territories'.

The professors became entangled in the marriage trouble. It came about because the Rhineland had a problem, in that its two old Catholic universities, Cologne and Trier, were destroyed by the French Revolution. When the Congress of Vienna gave the Rhineland to Prussia, the State founded a new university at Bonn but it was to be of mixed denomination with two separate theological faculties. The leader of the Catholic faculty was a brilliant teacher, Georg Hermes, who died in 1831 and left a faculty stamped with his ideas. Unlike the great school tradition that believed that the human reason could prove the existence and being of God and so could move on to show the reality of revelation, Hermes taught that theology must begin with the critical doubt and that the only initial certainty was the consciousness of reality in oneself; so that doubt is the source of faith; and no one may take as 'supernatural truth' what is contrary to the common rational judgement of humanity. The Roman inquisition of those days took little trouble to understand what was taught, did not ask the opinion of the German bishops, and was told to hurry up by Metternich. Hermes's books were posthumously condemned by a brief of 1835. Here was a second case, like that of Lamennais and *Singulari nos*, where the Pope intervened personally, and with an almost equal vagueness; and with the condemnation of books without that of their authors.

When the Prussian State gave way over mixed marriages, as part of the bargain it agreed not to defend the Bonn disciples of Hermes in their professorships. Their best mind, the historian Braun, ejected from his chair, turned like Lamennais to politics, in his case the Prussian Parliament. His colleague Achterfeldt, the professor of preaching, refused to accept the condemnation and was ejected. He resubmitted to Rome only at the age of 85.[22]

22 The Roman decree in *Acta*, ed. Bernasconi, ii. 85 ff.

THE TRIER ROBE

In 1844 the Rhineland celebrated a Catholic feast: that of the Seamless Robe of Christ. In the early Christian centuries it was supposed that this robe might exist somewhere in the East, perhaps in Jerusalem, perhaps in Georgia, perhaps in Constantinople. The Crusades made the idea familiar among the French; and soon after the First Crusade a legend-maker (or falsifier) of Trier claimed that Queen Helena had brought the robe to Trier. It remained in the altar of the east choir until its first exhibition to the people in 1512. But it was put away in the elector's castle for safety, and during the wars of the French Revolution was given refuge at Augsburg. It was returned with a little ceremony in 1810. But what happened in 1844 was extraordinary: it was exhibited to the public, and more than a million pilgrims came to Trier. Never before had it received this magnitude of devotion. The event was a sign of the new Catholic fervour and self-consciousness that the Cologne troubles helped to create. The record number of pilgrims to the holy robe was in the year 1933, the summer when the Nazis were first in power and Catholic life was tense.

This event hurt moderate Catholics of the old tradition of the Enlightenment. They thought it a reversion to superstition. A priest, Ronge, founded at Breslau a 'German-Catholic Church'—fifteen congregations at its first meeting, but two years later about 80,000 members. The speed of its spread was intelligible—the Prussian government was of the right, and wished to use the Catholic Church as an agent of good order and social discipline; and some supporters of Ronge came from Catholics of the political left who resented the way in which the Catholic revival seemed to be on the side of government. Ronge was most successful in the industrial areas. He was exiled as a political radical after the Revolution of 1848 and spent twelve years in England. His movement had little depth or devotional power. What was unusual was the place of women, for in the organization of congregations and synods women had an equal place with men. They concentrated on social welfare and organizations for charity and education. Bit by bit the people fell away, either into Protestantism or into free-thinking. For three years it was important, but in the longer run it was not a weighty protest within Catholicism. Europe at the time, for a moment, wondered whether this was the beginning of a new German Reformation.

THE SONDERBUND

A microcosm of the problem of the European Church lay in the Catholic Church of Switzerland. The Catholic cantons were part of a State with a militant Protestant majority. They felt beleaguered.

The canton governments, whether Catholic or Protestant, had won their liberties by resistance to the foreign bishops in whose spheres some of them lay, Constance or Besançon, Milan or Como. At first sight national Swiss dioceses would be better. But on reflection the presence of a bishop as head of their Church, whether he resided in their canton or in the next canton, would intimidate canton governments. He would be too big a piece on too small a chessboard. They usually preferred nuncios or temporary legates from Rome to permanent bishops.

The Protestant middle class of the northern cantons was determined that all Switzerland should have liberal laws. They were offended that Catholic cantons should lag behind the standards of what they regarded as modern civilization. As the Protestant cantons felt their strength, and resented the antiliberal atmosphere which came out of Rome, the constitution of the Swiss Confederation began to be misused.

In January 1834 at a conference at Baden near Zurich seven cantons headed by Lucerne and Berne and prompted from Saint-Gall agreed to ask the Pope for an archbishop for all Switzerland; while in return the State should control the publishing of documents of the pope or bishops, should oversee the seminaries, and should require that ordinands pass a state examination. The meeting also declared that mixed marriages were valid. These Baden decisions were at once rejected by Gregory XVI,[23] but Swiss Catholics were not agreed whether it was good to refuse them.

This caused the first of several crises which afflicted the canton of Berne during the century. It was the strongest of the Protestant cantons. But high in the Jura it had mountaineers who had never ceased

---

[23] *Commissum divinitus*, 17 May 1835; Bernasconi (ed.), *Acta*, ii. 33 ff. There was a historic diocese of Chur, first proven in the fourth century, but since the Reformation with not many Catholics; the old see of Basel was moved to Solothurn in 1828; the bishop of Lausanne, whose diocese now included Geneva, lived at Fribourg. Saint-Gall was created as a see, separate from Chur, in 1836. The Swiss sees were poorly endowed and their occupants had then little influence. The newest canton, Ticino, was wholly within the dioceses of Milan and Como, until in 1888 the see of Lugano was created.

to be Catholic, were French-speakers, and not for one moment felt that they ought to belong to the German-speaking Berne canton; and so their religious and racial/linguistic dissent was a unity. The Baden articles evoked a call to rebel, demands to separate from Berne, shouts of 'Die a Catholic!', and calls for union with France. When the canton sent soldiers into the mountains and restored order, France— Louis Philippe's France!—threatened to march in unless the Baden articles were withdrawn. Berne allowed the articles to be a dead letter. The teachers at the Jura seminary lost their posts and two of them died in exile. Yet it was a big Catholic victory, under the threat of a France which said that it was no longer a specially Catholic State.

In 1841 the canton of Aargau, which had almost equal numbers of Protestants and Catholics, dissolved all its eight religious houses (four of monks and four of nuns) and took the property. The excuse was that monks contributed to unrest and disorder when the canton (just) accepted a change of constitution. They were turned out of their homes with little consideration. The Swiss diet declared the act unconstitutional and ordered the reopening of all eight houses within six weeks. Only the four nunneries were revived.

As the radicals advanced, the Catholics acted with belligerence. The Catholic canton of Lucerne made the mistake of recalling the Jesuits to the canton to reform the schools. They gave them two dissolved Franciscan houses as seminaries to train priests. This was legal but provocative. The Jesuits at once began to conduct parish missions, which were crowded. Then they were given charge of all the higher education in the Lucerne canton. A war of paper ensued against 'the Jesuit government in Lucerne'.

The radicals and Protestants—these two groups were not always easy to distinguish—determined to alter the constitution so that government would be centralized, dominated by Protestants, and able to control the Catholic cantons. They started using bands of soldiery to trouble the Catholic cantons. The Catholic peasant leader Leu, who had brought in the Jesuits and founded a brotherhood (approved by Gregory XVI) for the defence of the faith, was shot in his bed by a peasant.

Seven Catholic cantons (Lucerne, Uri, Schwyz, Unterwalden, Fribourg, Zug, and Valais) found the Confederation powerless to help them because it was too divided. They therefore formed (December 1845) a separate Confederation, to be a league of defence, called the Sonderbund (League of Secession) by its enemies, a name that was taken over by the members. Their aim was freedom and independence,

if necessary at the cost of separation from the Swiss Confederation.
They planned to redraw the frontiers of the cantons in Catholic favour,
and to give the Catholics along the Jura their own canton and abolish
the Aargau canton. It was a secret agreement. The secret could not be
kept more than a few months. It was the immediate cause of civil war.

The armies of the Sonderbund were easily overthrown by the
army of the Protestant cantons (November 1847). This war had other
causes of division besides religion—industrial versus rural cantons,
different types of economy, different attitudes to the constitution
over the right of secession from the Confederation. It was not solely
a war of religion, for no war of religion is ever solely thus. The general of the Sonderbund army was a Protestant, the general of their
opponents was a Protestant devout enough to treat his defeated
Catholic enemies with courtesy and respect. Two Catholic cantons,
Ticino and Solothurn (Solothurn was a canton with a mostly
Catholic people but a liberal–Protestant government) fought against
the Sonderbund. Nevertheless religion was the chief cause; this war
has rightly been regarded as the last occasion in Europe where a religious war was fought between Protestants and Catholics.

Quick defeat in the war diminished Catholic power in the
Confederation but the victors preserved the religious autonomy of
the cantons, without which the Swiss Confederation could not have
survived. The new constitution contained the illiberal prohibition of
the Jesuit order. Various liberal measures were forced upon the
Catholic cantons.

The result was to make everything for which Pope Gregory XVI
stood more admired by Swiss Catholics. They ceased to want anything to do with liberal ideas. They retired into their communities
and erected walls against the general society of their country. Not
allowed to secede politically, they seceded psychologically; they
made more of a division between a Swiss Catholic and Swiss anything
else. And naturally they also looked to Rome, and wished to raise its
authority, to have the right to appeal to Rome, and to see the
supreme if not absolute authority of the pope in the church.

THE MISSIONS

Before he became pope, Gregory, as Cardinal Cappellari, was
the prefect of the Congregation de Propaganda Fide. That is, he

was the chief director of the missionary policy of the Catholic Church.

The Congregation of Propaganda suffered destruction from Napoleon with the loss of much of its money and all its archives. It got back some of both in the Restoration, but it was weak. Its communications with the overseas territories were broken and needed restoring. In Africa and the East good men and women went on with the work; even in China. The single useful aid from a government was the belief of the French State that to protect missionaries in the East was to promote its political influence. By the time Gregory XVI became pope, French priests were the leaders of Catholic missions. At Lyons (1822) was founded an association, L'Œuvre de la Propagation de la Foi. This collected money and was soon indispensable.

Many papal decrees which sounded mighty were moral aspirations. Rome was long opposed to the exploitation of Indians or blacks. But the slave trade grew fast. Profit demanded it. In North and South America, and in the Arab States, the economies needed labour in a climate where Europeans were incapable of hard physical toil, and where Africans had the physique which could supply the need. Central Africa was impoverished and had little to trade, and its chaos allowed plenty of scope for a few people with guns to mount raids. The Arabs in East Africa, the Portuguese in East and West Africa, and other adventurers of any nation, even the French in the island of Réunion, though they concealed the trade under a form of apprenticeship, bought Africans from their chiefs, and exported them to the Arab States or the Americas. To stop slave-running would require warships and better forms of trade.

The Pope condemned the slave trade in 1839. It made no difference. The Arabs never heard of it; the Portuguese, if they heard of it, took no notice; adventurers never bothered with popes. It had the appearance of an enactment but was in reality a moral plea. This was characteristic of a growing number of pronouncements through the nineteenth century as the popes felt that they must do what they could about some immorality or other.

The old organization of the Spanish and Portuguese empires remained; forty bishops in Spanish America, seven in Brazil. The structures were shaky because they had relied on the Spanish and Portuguese establishment which now was dead. Many of the higher clergy worked against revolution, but many younger clergy were in favour of it, so that among the ordinary people the parish priest was often popular. Despite the imposing framework of dioceses, these Churches had lost most of their leaders, and were cut off from the supply of new bishops out of Spain and Portugal. They lost the money which revolutionaries, or bandits, or governments took to win their wars against Spain or each other. This hit religious orders particularly hard; monks were cut off from their high command in Europe.

Like the Spanish, the new States thought it advantageous to dominate the Church. They claimed the controls that Spanish or Portuguese kings had exercised in the choice of bishops (or, often, of the vicars-capitular elected by cathedral chapters to stand in for the bishop because no bishop could be elected in the turmoil). Revolutionary States installed persons as administrators of dioceses or as superiors of monasteries without any right in canon law. The prudent recognized these hierarchs, but the stout-hearted refused them. Some of the prelates whom revolutionary governments installed were less than satisfactory, because of ambition, immorality, compromise with buccaneers, or merely because they were too ignorant to do the work to which they were appointed.

While the future Pope Gregory XVI was the cardinal-prefect of Propaganda he made Rome a benefit to these Latin-American Churches that battled with impossible politics. They needed a power to sanction changes in the old laws, and therefore a pope who would have confidence in the plenitude of papal authority to override existing laws in the Church, one who had such conviction about the supreme power of the Holy See that he would take no notice of the screams of the Spanish and Portuguese governments if their (now nominal) authority over Churches was diminished or abolished. They needed a realist; a man willing to treat de facto governments as real, or even lawful. In other areas Gregory XVI, because his doctrine of the papacy was so high, had not the reputation of a realist. In Latin America he saw that the day of Spanish and Portuguese empire was over and did what was necessary to recreate the Churches, at the risk of trouble in Europe from the Spanish and Portuguese governments. He had not been pope for a month before he appointed six bishops for Mexico, contrary to the legitimist principle that old canon law must be obeyed and that the Spanish government still had rights. He followed this by appointments to sees in Argentina and Chile. Before the end of his reign he had settled the worst schism in revolutionary

Latin America, which occurred in the State of San Salvador. Before he died he formally recognized the legitimacy of four (but only four) of the new States—Colombia (under the name New Granada), Mexico, Chile, and Ecuador.

Gregory offered the agonized Latin American Churches an exit from their immediate dilemmas. This was another way in which the pontificate of Gregory marked the rising tide of opinion towards papal absolutism in the Church.

He was helped because the revolutions passed into their second stage. They started by thinking the Church to be part of the establishment that needed to be overthrown. When they won the war and settled down—they never quite settled down—they realized that simple priests still affected opinion in the parishes and that it was wise to keep them reconciled to the regime. Their constitutions continued to make Catholicism the religion of the State.

Portuguese-speaking Brazil was less difficult for the Church than any of the States formerly Spanish. The continuity between the old regime and the new was nearly legitimate. There was no guerrilla revolution. The government of Brazil exercised the rights over the Church that Portugal had exercised. Everyone was used to it. But as the nineteenth century wore on, and the power of the papacy grew, Erastian control over Catholic Churches bred friction.

In South America, Belgium, Ireland, Holland, and the Rhineland, the power of Rome stood for an adjustment to liberal constitutions or revolutionary regimes. In Poland, Italy, Spain, and Portugal, as well as all the northern Protestant countries led by Britain and Prussia, it had the reputation of being reactionary and against everything for which liberals contended.

THE PAPAL STATES IN ITALY

As a secular sovereign in Italy, Gregory XVI could not govern his people efficiently, as the States now understood effective government. Yet, for historic reasons, because he was a trustee of what had been given to God, and because of his need for a spiritual independence which meant that he must be no other man's subject, the pope could not do without secular sovereignty. On the one side he must have it. On the other side to have it was bad for his reputation and a weakness to his international authority. This incompatibility was the chief problem of the papacy and the Church for the next hundred years.

Gregory XVI could not rule his territory without a foreign army. That could only be possible so long as Italians did not mind the presence of a foreign army, and so long as it was in the interest of a foreign power to provide an army.

Gregory was an educated person who worked hard. His two Secretaries of State, Bernetti till 1836 and then Lambruschini, though men of different types—the first a politician and the second more of an ecclesiastic—were dedicated to the politics of the old regime and distrusted every cry for reform. The Curia was a self-generating body. Like-minded men co-opted like-minded men. Once it had received a particular stamp, that stamp marked its behaviour whatever the variations in the opinions of popes. The revolutionary epoch under Napoleon left the Curia full of very conservative clergymen; for they were those who were most loyal in the opposition to the French Revolution and its armies. Bernetti was imprisoned by Napoleon, Lambruschini was nuncio in France during the 1830 Revolution, and so resisted the new government that it forced Gregory to recall him. Few members of the Curia were different in their experience. This cast of curial mind was the third problem of the papacy that first became apparent under the pontificate of Gregory XVI.

Although quick to encourage steamships, the Pope would not allow a railway to be built in his territory. This refusal had a justification. A railway would bring the cheap manufactured goods of north Europe to destroy the still rural markets of the Papal States. But though the refusal appealed to economics, a railway would also bring ideas. The Pope had more than a rational conviction about railways—he was afraid. A railway group tried to bribe him by a lavish toy, a model railway in beautifully worked silver, which they asked the secretary Moroni to give to the Pope—but Moroni would have nothing to do with the plan.[24]

This refusal of a railway was not so important as it afterwards sounded, for even in northern Italy the terrain made the building of railways slow and costly. But it had an effect on reputation. Northern Europe regarded the invention of the railway as the instrument of modern civilization. For the Pope to refuse a railway made him look

[24] F. Hayward, *La Dernier Siècle de la Rome pontificale* (Paris, 1927–8), ii. 209.

like a Luddite. The decision was at once reversed by Gregory's successor, who even travelled in a train.

ITALY FOR THE ITALIANS

Meanwhile in Italy the movement for 'Italy' became articulate, although it still had small influence. No one had ruled all Italy as a unity since the heirs of Charlemagne, perhaps not even since the Roman empire. The Italians were used to being Sicilian, or Neapolitan, or Roman, or Lombard, or Venetian, etc., and preferred it that way. They were like Irishmen who had no desire to be members of a United Kingdom of Great Britain. Some great writers, conscious of Italian literature as a unity, had spoken of Italy as one country. It meant little to the ordinary member of one of the Italian States. If ever Italy were one country, what would happen to its several sovereigns, of whom the pope was chief?

This indifference to a political Italy was affected by Napoleon, and then by the Congress of Vienna. Napoleon wanted to bring all Europe into his empire, and took in Italy, although not quite as a unit of administration—the king of Italy (Napoleon himself) who ruled in the north was a different person from his brother or his general Murat who ruled in the south. But Italians who served Napoleon, especially in the north, remembered the idea of the Italian nation. The Congress of Vienna gave Venice to Austria—which already ruled Lombardy. To have Venice and Milan as Austrian towns was not comfortable. Milan had been ruled by Spaniards or Austrians from time immemorial and no one minded till Napoleon. But the Venetian empire had been great in politics and greater in culture, and was a source of Italian influence in the Adriatic and the Eastern Mediterranean. Napoleon's destruction of Venetian power was one of the worst consequences of his imperial rule.

MAZZINI

Giuseppe Mazzini, while an expelled Genoese revolutionary in exile in Marseilles, started the periodical *Young Italy*. It did not last long, nor did it have many readers. It was flowery, rhetorical, and impracticable. However, it put forward an ideal in a way that touched feelings in Italy and turned radicals into Italian patriots or nationalists. Mazzini prophesied the future of Italy as a unified State which would rid itself of kings, dukes, and the Austrians, take into itself all the separated Italian States, and be a democratic republic. He sang this song—it was a sort of song—with a poetic prose that sounded as though the result would bring peace on earth and goodwill towards all. He thought that the world needed a new religion, with the old hierarchs vanished; a religion of fraternity, of God and the people, a faith of human brotherhood which, somewhere in his not always clear mind, he contrasted with Catholicism. He asked himself why revolution had failed, and decided that it was because it lacked religion. The revolution must have spiritual power. It must appeal to what was mystical and transcendent.

No one can mistake the similarity between these ideas and those of Lamennais after he rejected the Pope. Mazzini wrote a little *Life of Lamennais*. He revered the book *Paroles d'un Croyant*, and talked of a giant soul, of a powerful intellect rising between a world in ruins and a world newborn: 'He weeps like a child at a symphony of Beethoven; and will give his last franc to the poor; and tends flowers like a woman; and steps out of the path so as not to squash an ant— this is he whom they declared to be a man of blood and a preacher of anarchy.' He regarded Rome's pressure on Lamennais for more and more absolute submission as a moral torture. He was sure that Lamennais was right: revolution and religion are brothers, but the religion could not be Catholicism in its present shape.

It was certain that if the Italians were going to have religion at all it would be more or less Catholicism and not a new invented doxy. But Mazzini also appealed to more practical feelings—to justice, and to equality, and to the right of Italians not to live under foreign rule. In his vision there would be a Republic of Italy in which the pope, if he still survived, would be just one clergyman, though an important one, among others, and would lose his secular authority as the monarch of an important Italian State.

Mazzini was only intelligible—only influential—as a romantic in a romantic age. He was truly pious; but the religion that he professed was professed by no one else. He was excited, and exciting to read; he cared passionately for the ideals of humanity, and therefore stirs his readers at times—even now—but at other times leaves them cynical. He had no idea how to come anywhere near bringing his ideals into effect.

In the reality of power politics, the question was how the powers would use or be affected by such sentiments as they grew in Italy. The Austrians dominated Italian politics. If the past were a guide, sooner or later the French would try to replace the Austrians as the chief political force in Italy; such at least was the law and precedent of Italian history. And now Austria was an old-fashioned and conservative Catholic monarchy, France was a constitutional half-democratic and half-secular State. It was possible that the French left, or even the French moderates, could use the slogans of democracy, republicanism, and equality as a way of weakening Austrian strength in Italy and increasing the power of France. If the French used the ideas of Mazzini to weaken Austria's grip, the ideal of a united Italian republic might be no longer the dream of a few impractical journalists, but a real alternative for the future of Italy—in which the Papal State, as then constituted, could not have a place.

In 1838, after six years, the two occupying armies in the north were persuaded to withdraw and leave public order to the Pope's Swiss mercenaries, and the nasty volunteers enlisted by the Secretary of State. The result of withdrawal was not an outbreak of further rebellion against the Pope but a succession of little riots or attempted coups against his government.

THE NEO–GUELFS

Before Mazzini died, and in expectation of his death, a few Catholics put forward a compromise between Catholicism and Italian nationalism, which soon became known as the neo-Guelf movement. Was it possible that the key to Italian unification was not nationalism, which hardly existed, nor anti-Austrian feeling, which only unified persons threatened by Austrians, but the common religion of Italy? The chief neo-Guelf was Gioberti, a priest from Turin who was banished to France and Belgium for his sympathy with revolutionaries such as Mazzini. He was no revolutionary but a wordy moderate. He published (1843) a long-winded but curiously persuasive book, *On the Moral and Civil Primacy of the Italian People.* It rambled over the long history of Italy with its sporadic outbursts of liberal and republican ideals, linked with the best of European civilization and always with the Catholic religion. Catholicism was not the enemy of Italian nationalism but the key to its growth and success. The way forward was to ally the Church with the constitutional monarchies or duchies, unite the States of Italy into a single federation, and put the pope as the head of State, the constitutional leader of the Italian people, and the sovereign or president of a United States of Italy. Naturally this could not be done without Austrian withdrawal and without drastic changes in the mode of government of the Papal State and all the other States of Italy.

The papal government would have none of this. Italian nationalists could not imagine how the papacy of Gregory XVI would fulfil the function to which Gioberti called it. But the reputation of the book inspired those who wanted an Italy which should be united, liberal, and Catholic because it envisaged for the first time a liberal Italy that was not against, but led by, the pope; Gioberti and his friends drew portraits of a pope who should come: loving freedom, wanting the strength and united harmony of the Italian people, and ready to promote the reforms that would be necessary to that end. At that moment they were like the medieval dreams of a Joachim of Flora, an impossible vision. But they had political consequences. They prepared minds to work towards the goal of the vision. Gregory XVI could not last for ever.

These dreams were not shared by many of the devout Catholics of Italy. Most accepted the Pope's personal horror of the propaganda of the Bible societies, the Protestants, the secret societies, or freedom of the press. If devout Catholics in Italy wanted reform, they were likely to derive their ideas not from new liberalism out of France, but from the old-fashioned Jansenism of the Enlightenment, where State control was the chief instrument for reform of the Church and the guide of the Church's influence in society.

The most important person in all that world, so far as the future would see, was not Gioberti but Rosmini. He was a north-Italian priest from Rovereto in the Trentino, and therefore an Austrian subject. He came of a well-to-do family and could choose his own way. This took him up into the Alps to a hermitage at Domodossola. There he lived a very austere life—bad for his health—and dedicated himself to the study and the writing of philosophy. He founded what at first appeared to be a small religious order of a type which was then becoming common. Up in his hermitage his mind developed freely. He became a critic of the bishops, of the system of training clergy, of the ignorance of the priests, and of the dangers of a Latin liturgy that people could not understand. Out of touch with academics in the

university, he formed a romantic picture of the glories of the primitive Church and the age of the Fathers, and contrasted this rosy picture with the Church that he observed from his mountain. He
revered the Pope. He was neither a Jansenist reformer nor a disciple
of the French Revolution. But he began to think about freedom, and
the connection of freedom with modern civilization, and the vocation of a nation to be itself and to develop its own best qualities. With
all this he saw that the bishops, as he imagined them, were not in
tune. He supposed that the papacy would lead a reconciliation
between Catholicism and the best of modern civilization, for in his
view Catholicism lay at the heart of the best in civilization. It was
necessary therefore that the Catholic Church should be free from the
control of secular States. And the most important part of this wrest-
ing of freedom for the Church lay in gaining freedom for Italy from
the Austrians.

From his mountain he could see that the Church as then operat-
ing would not fulfil the vocation to which he summoned it, that of
creator and protector of human freedom. The programme was based
upon a renewal of the Church which he conceived to be spiritual. In
1832–3 he started to write a strange book, *The Five Wounds of the
Church*. He did not—could not—publish it yet. Written in a style of
charm, gentleness, and holiness, but very wordy, it was a savage
attack upon the condition of the clergy of his age. It held up the
virtues of primitive Christianity as the model for the age in its revival
of spirituality.

Much of the book is fanciful history. It contrasts the Church of
the present with a Church that never was, but which Rosmini supposed to have existed. The weight of the book lay in the
'wounds', to which he attributed decline or corruption. They were
the division between clergy and people, which rested upon the
inability of the people to understand the Latin liturgy, causing lay
worshippers to stand more like statues or pillars than living people
at prayer. There was inadequate education of the clergy, stemming
from the gulf between them and the bishops, which came about
because bishops were over-busy as men employed by the State,
which in turn arose from the right of sovereigns to choose bishops. So the Church must be freed from dependence on wealth and
feudal rights, from control by the State. It must be shown how the
gospel turns absolute rulers into constitutional monarchs. Bishops
must be freely elected by clergy and people and the free writ of

the Holy See (to which Rosmini submitted all) run through the Church.[25]

At one point in the book Rosmini blamed people for excess of prudence and for not having the courage to say these unpalatable things. On reflection he did not dare to publish his own book so long as Gregory XVI was on the throne. Under a new and much more promising pope, fifteen years later, he published it. And sixteen years after he wrote it he recanted its main positions, which were attacked by the Curia.

Rosmini now accepted that the Church had its proper discipline in the Latin liturgy; that it was not necessary for bishops to be elected by clergy and people; that he had only meant that in the choice of bishops it should be discovered whether they were likely to be acceptable to the people. He denied that he intended to preach the necessity for the separation of Church and State; although it was his opinion that the Church does better without privileges. These recantations were not in the mood of the young Rosmini on his mountain at Domodossola.

This was not quite in continuity with the reforming tradition of Jansenism in the eighteenth century. It was too papal. And underneath Rosmini's gentle style and spiritual mind it was too passionate. But the Jansenist influence can still be seen working away towards a marriage of Italian civilized aspirations with Catholic ideals. The novelist Alessandro Manzoni had a half-Jansenist background and a Jansenist sort of conversion. As his mind grew, he perceived the conscience of man in religion as the source of liberty and simultaneously as the guide which would prevent the cry of liberty turning to anarchy, mob-rule, or military dictatorship. It was nothing like Christian Socialism, or like Lamennais's democratic Catholic liberalism. Its centre was the individual; his freedom, his soul, his conscience, his piety—and the need for a free Church and so of a free society for the development of that free personality.

These liberal Catholics—they would have disliked the name as a description of their ideals—were not yet important. They were literary, and quiet, and studious. They affected the politics of Italy hardly

---

[25] The eminent Victorian Anglican H. P. Liddon made an English translation of *The Five Wounds* (1883). Much work on Rosmini has been published in recent years, both the philosophical works and the correspondence. There is an important study of the turning-point of his life, M. F. Mellano, *Anni decisivi nella vita di A. Rosmini 1848–54* (Rome, 1988), with new evidence from the papers of Tizzani.

at all. But they represented a yearning among intellectuals in Italy, who saw the needs of society, and longed to marry their quest of political reform with devout faith and with a loyalty to the see of Rome; where the present occupant, for all his learning, love of scholarship, and care of monuments and art, understood almost nothing of the things for which they were striving.

GREGORY XVI'S REPUTATION

A hundred years after the death of Gregory XVI, by the end of his life the most hated pope for two centuries, it was possible to publish two volumes which declared, in nearly all their pages, what a good pope he was.[26]

In North Italy, Spain, Portugal, and parts of France, Gregory was regarded as an outrage. In the missions, in parts of Latin America, among the French lower clergy, in the remoter cantons of the Swiss mountains, in the world of books and scholarship and archaeology, he was respected or revered. He was good at charities; he visited hospitals during the cholera epidemic, ordered that unemployment should end (not thinking about the effect of this order on the plight of the public finances), defended vaccination, and took Galileo off the index of prohibited books. He encouraged art, architecture, painting, and scholarship. He made cardinals of Angelo Mai, one of the greatest of classical scholars, and Giuseppe Mezzofanti, one of the greatest of oriental linguists, who was alleged to speak twelve languages and to understand fifty-eight. (In the next hundred years it became rare for a scholar to become a cardinal.) This pope cared about Etruscan vases, and better museums, and the much-neglected catacombs, and the restoration of the Coliseum. As the Vatican librarian, Mai discovered a scientific but damaging way to read palimpsest manuscripts, and found Cicero's *Republic* (which had been hunted in vain during the Renaissance), letters of Marcus Aurelius, together with an amazing number of other texts of the classics and the early Christian Fathers.

Gregory took an interest in the catacombs. Till then they were under the Custodian of Relics, and were neglected, and many of those that we know now were unknown then, and their value for

---

[26] A. Bartoli *et al.* (eds.), *Gregorio XVI: Miscellanea Commemorativa* (2 vols.; Rome, 1948).

history and archaeology was still hidden. Marchi, a Jesuit professor at
the Roman college, took a scholarly interest, and Gregory made him
'custodian of the Roman cemeteries'. Marchi attracted the young student De Rossi, and the pair became inseparable. The systematic study
of primitive Christian Rome began.[27] This made one of the chief
advances of the nineteenth century in the understanding of the earliest Christianity.

Another act of patronage, and the most extraordinary, was that of
Gregory's barber's apprentice and then his secretary, Gaetano
Moroni. He had beautiful handwriting and was used by Cappellari
even to copy confidential documents. After Gregory became pope,
Moroni was his favourite companion. He had an obsequious manner
and, using the Pope's favour, and subventions of money, he was
able to gain access to otherwise closed libraries. In 1840 he started
an encyclopedia of church history, *Dizionario di erudizione storia-
ecclesiastica*, which was planned in 30 volumes but rose to 109. It
became one of the tools of the modern age, full of unexpected items
of rare knowledge, especially concerning remote areas of the subject.
It was not critical, but had information not otherwise obtainable on
all sorts of corners of church history. Its compilation was an extraordinary feat for a person of Moroni's background and lack of opportunity for formal education. Never did a private favourite use his
chances to more profitable effect.[28]

The nearer Gregory came to death, the more change was expected
and the more unsettled were the northern Papal States. After the
Austrian and French armies withdrew there were five years of no
worse discomfort than that of Northern Ireland in the 1990s—nothing that could overthrow the State, but murders of policemen and
Swiss soldiers, shooting of individual terrorists, gatherings of refugees
abroad (Marseilles, Corfu, Malta, Corsica, Algiers) to threaten
descents on the coasts. The foreign armies had withdrawn but the
people saw the Swiss, who were now the mainstay of papal order, as
another form of foreign army. Observers believed that but for the
Swiss the State would not last more than a day or two.

---

[27] G. B. De Rossi's 3-vol. *La Roma sotteranea cristiana*, which is the foundation of all subsequent study, was not published till 1968–77, after the dedication of many years to the catacombs and to the sources which shed light upon them.

[28] Alessandro Gavazzi, in his Recollections of 1858 (which were not recollections mostly)
said that Moroni's power was due to the Pope's affection for his beautiful Venetian wife.
Gavazzi's evidence was the gossip of Rome plus words said to him by a coachman.

From the summer of 1843 this changed for the worse. Lone terrorists grew into guerrilla bands. On 15 August such a band ambushed a papal column, killing some and wounding many. Government reacted, made meetings of five or more illegal, and instituted a form of martial law with a commission sitting in Bologna. The murders went on, the court had six terrorists shot in a meadow outside Bologna. The middle class, who wanted order, believed that only a return of the Austrians could keep the peace. Most of the people were against the Austrians and the Pope's government. Radetzky, the Austrian commander in Lombardy, reinforced his corps along the border. In Rome they blamed Mazzini for stirring up murder by issuing violent pamphlets from London. But many others did the same and Rome only magnified Mazzini's importance by blaming him.

On 20 September 1845 one of the guerrilla bands, which collected first in Paris and then in Algiers, landed near Rimini to start the revolution, and seized the town in spite of its garrison. Radetzky thought this was the start of an attempted revolution in the whole peninsula and moved his battalions in preparation; Austrian warships cruised off the port. All ended in fiasco when the guerrillas failed to seize Ravenna, and Rimini was easily reoccupied by the Pope's men. The band fled into Tuscany, losing people in the running fight, and a couple of ships got away from Leghorn to Marseilles. But that November 1845 there was again a need for Austrian cruisers along the coast, and in March 1846 there were two Austrian battleships at Ancona where the garrison was in such a state of nerves that the officers dared not walk the streets.

To a later age the record of the stream of orders that was issued is not always pleasant to read. There was a decree of April 1842 on how a condemned prisoner is to be shot, who may attend, whether medals may be worn, and more of such detail.[29] It is probable that Gregory never saw it, but it came out under his name. To the twentieth century such a decree is distasteful. That is because the expectations on the office of the pope changed during the nineteenth century. At that moment the decree caused no stir and gave no handle to adversaries. It was part of the inescapable duty of a head of State.

Everyone abroad—British, French, Piedmontese, Germans, even some of the Austrians—were agreed that things could not go on as

---

[29] Bernasconi (ed.), *Acta*, iv. 606.

they were; that drastic change of some sort must happen, though few could imagine what.

Pope Gregory died on 1 June 1846. He was not lamented, even in Rome; he died as the most unpopular of popes. The world wanted him to go. It wanted change in Italy, change in the Papal State and its administration, change in the attitude to the liberal pleas. He left a people with a sense of breach between government and governed, with an idea that the sovereign was a remote monarch who did not wish his people to progress. The crowds of the city of Rome showed indifference to the death except for an anxiety whether they were in for trouble; and the cardinals in charge hastily doubled the pay of the soldiers. For liberals and many of the middle class he was the pope who summoned Austrian bayonets to his rescue. For everyone who cared about just government his name stank because of the police state in the Romagna. Objectively, he might be seen as an honourable old man who was not unique in failing to understand where the century was going. Unjustly or not, his notoriety was enough to cause gladness when he died, and a naïve longing for his successor.

This mood of expectation made possible the melodrama of the next three years. The people yearned that now there would be a different kind of pope. They were not disappointed.

2

A LIBERAL POPE, 1846–1848

THE CONCLAVE OF 1846

The Conclave of 1846 met for only two days—it was one of the shortest Conclaves ever. The short space of time that it took to elect was the beginning of a new era. Four scrutinies were taken, one held invalid, with a speed that was to become characteristic of papal elections. The cardinals could not forget that the stalemate of the last Conclave helped to cause revolution in the Papal State, and the mood of the State was again as menacing.

The usual satires were posted in Rome. A litany amused the people:

That thou wouldest be pleased to choose a Pope who is not a cardinal
That thou wouldest be pleased to allow railroads to be built
That thou wouldest be pleased to give amnesty to political prisoners
We beseech thee to hear us.[1]

The French wanted an 'Italian'—that is, a pope not tied to Austria—and allowed their cardinals to use the veto against any candidate too Austrian. But they did not say who that might be. They ought to have specified Lambruschini since he was the obvious candidate and they had refused to have him as nuncio in Paris because they so much disapproved of him. But they did not mention a veto against him. Metternich identified the interests of Catholicism with the preservation of order, that is, of the treaties made at the Congress of Vienna, and with the interests of the Austrian empire. He had a religious belief in the mission of the Habsburgs, while this new force of nationalism stalked through Europe—a delusion, he thought it— to stand for a non-racialist world of law and order. He saw the Catholic religion as a key political instrument in a non-nationalist Europe. He wanted a pope who saw how the safety of the papacy depended on Vienna.

[1] G. Martina, *Pio IX, 1846–50* (Rome, 1974), 84–5: the ground-breaking book on these years.

But Metternich always knew that conservatism was easier to defend if it was neither intransigent nor provocative. Like everyone else he saw that the northern Papal States could not go on as they were. He wanted a moderate pope, willing to allow suitable reform in the administration. The only cardinal whom he could not tolerate, as an extremist and chiefly responsible for the police state in the Romagna, and too 'French-minded', was Bernetti the former Secretary of State, whom he had practically forced Gregory XVI to dismiss. He entrusted Archbishop Gaysruck of Milan with a veto against Bernetti. But Gaysruck failed to arrive at the Conclave in time, and the veto was not necessary, the cardinals were not mad. In the election not one cardinal gave Bernetti a vote at any of the scrutinies.

The ordinary people of Rome wanted Cardinal Gizzi. He was an experienced diplomat who in the worst years after 1844 was governor of the Forlì Legation in the north, and despite that office retained the respect of the liberals. He suffered from gout, but was effective. The people of Rome were under an illusion about his 'liberalism'. Beneath the diplomat's cover he was a deep-dyed conservative. In an election like this it was not an advantage to a candidate to be the favoured son of the liberals outside. He received a steady pair of votes but never more. The poor had a wish for the Capuchin Micara, but that was not sensible, first because he was a friar and then because he was already ageing. Rumours afterwards spread that the Austrians intended to veto both the candidates Gizzi and Mastai-Ferretti because they were believed to be moderates. The rumours were false.

This was a very Italian election, in the sense that the Italian cardinals had rarely achieved such a dominance in numbers as when Pope Gregory XVI died. There were sixty-two cardinals altogether, and fifty-four were Italians. Only fifty, and none of the eight foreigners, appeared at the election, and no foreigner received a vote. (Cardinal Acton, the first and so far the only student at Magdalene College Cambridge to receive a vote in a papal election, has to be treated as a Neapolitan.) The Italian weight had this peculiarity, that the cardinals from the Papal States were especially powerful when compared with those from other Italian States. This was one of the explanations of the speed of election. At this moment the College of Cardinals was a college which as largely as possible represented the Curia.

In this unusual situation the curial candidate, he of the establishment, Lambruschini the Secretary of State, was the obvious choice. He was steady, strong, and politically experienced. At the first scrutiny he received the most votes, 15 (32 were needed to achieve two-thirds). But no one, except perhaps King Ferdinand of Naples, could want the world, or Rome, or the north of Italy, to think that the repressive regime of Gregory XVI would continue unchanged. The election of Lambruschini might provoke instant revolution. To look around for a credible choice, they must find an Italian, a cardinal of the Papal States—yet not, emphatically, one of the many cardinals of the Curia—and they must find a person respected for his qualities. Such they found in Mastai-Ferretti, the bishop of Imola. He would be very young for a new pope, only 54. He was liked in his diocese, no small feat for a northern bishop in the bad time of the last three years. He was conciliatory, friendly, without pomposity, cheerful, open, and very religious. He was also known to think that the police state in the north must change. He had never been identified with the central Church government in Rome. The drawback was that of the two experiences that prepared a pope for an over-complicated world, curial administration and international diplomacy, he had neither. They opted for a simple pastor who had presence, and charm, and piety.

At the first scrutiny, in this last Conclave to be held in the Quirinal Palace (15 June 1846), Lambruschini led with 15 and Mastai-Ferretti had 13; which from the start meant that if Lambruschini were to be defeated, Mastai had the best chance. It was not unanimous. He was elected on the fourth ballot with 36 votes, so that ten went to the end for Lambruschini and four others abstained.

When the smoke rose on the morning of 17 June 1846, the crowd caught the rumour that the successful candidate was Gizzi, and Gizzi's servants followed the old custom of sacking the new pope's private rooms. When Mastai was announced few had heard of him and the crowd was disappointed and cold. When he was crowned four days later spectators made the chill too plain. What France, Austria, and the world were grateful for was not the man, of whom they knew nothing, but the speed—the cardinals had saved them from weeks of stalemate that might have fermented revolution.

THE AMNESTY

A new pope was expected to begin his reign with acts of generosity— dowry for a thousand girls, free redemption of objects pawned by

debtors—and Pius IX was no exception. One traditional act was the
release of prisoners. In the wake of a heavy-handed police state, this
release would be a political act different in quality from normal
releases of the past. Never before had a new pope, expected to pronounce amnesty, found prisons full of several hundred political prisoners and others who could be proved to have murdered policemen
or Swiss guards. This was the first difficulty of the reign of Pius IX.
Everyone expected an amnesty for most, if not all, of the political
prisoners. Yet to release them all would be seen across Europe as the
act of a pope with a different policy from that of his predecessor, and
he would be hailed as a liberal. Lambruschini, who *was* the previous
regime, was totally against any amnesty whatever. The majority of
cardinals said that an amnesty could not be avoided, the allegiance of
the State could not be held without it.

It was not known how many prisoners there were and it could not
be discovered because the records were in such a muddle that the
police chief could not tell them. The cardinals decided that the Pope
should issue an amnesty from which ecclesiastics and state officials
were excluded but which applied to everyone else, whether in prison
or in exile, who made a declaration of loyalty. The text of the
amnesty was drafted by a young monsignor, Corboli Bussi, already
the most trusted curial officer of the new pope. About 400 people
were freed, and more than 200 came back from exile. A few hundred
exiles refused to declare loyalty.

These freed men were not like those who came out at earlier
amnesties; they were fêted like heroes, and given receptions, processions, and banquets. This little amnesty, so conventional, so modest
in intention, was a spark to light a train of powder that ran thinly at
first but then more widely and furiously until there was fire in Paris,
and Vienna, and Frankfurt, and Milan, and Budapest. All over
Europe people hailed the advent of a liberal pope and looked for
change not only in papal policy but in the papacy. They marvelled at
the idea of a liberal pope. Pius IX was expected to turn the Papal
State into a constitutional monarchy. He was expected to commend
the Catholics of Europe who longed to marry their Catholicism with
liberalism; to open the heart of the Church to a friendly relationship
with Protestant countries; and perhaps to put himself at the head of
the movement to create out of the separated States a national, free,
and federated Italy with himself as its president or constitutional
suzerain.

The Pope was embarrassingly popular when he moved about Rome. The people filled the streets with *evvivas* and demonstrations, the cafés with banquets and speeches, the windows with illuminations and placards, the Piazza del Popolo with a triumphal arch. They made processions to the Quirinal Palace and shouted till the Pope came out upon his balcony and blessed them. They surrounded his coach, took the horses from the shafts, and drew it themselves. As he drove down the Corso crowds knelt on each side. He was to be the last pope, up to the time of writing, upon whom flowers rained down from Roman balconies as he drove by. Nothing like it had been seen since Pope Pius VII returned after his exile under Napoleon. Giuseppe Pecci, bishop of Gubbio, told his people in a pastoral letter that this was the start of a new era of peace and happiness when all hearts would be reconciled. This sugar-plum of rhetoric was printed in the Roman newspapers, recited in public, and turned into verse.[2] When Pius IX saw it he was not displeased—which was his first sign of weakness. It was a demonstration of his faith that what was happening would turn out right.

All over the Papal State the enthusiasm produced crowd demonstration and threats to public order. Father Ventura di Raulica, a Theatine from Sicily, was the most famous speaker in Rome. He was a disciple of Lamennais, and at one time the general of the Theatine order but had resigned the responsibility to dedicate himself to preaching. He was not a neo-Guelf because he was against the fancy that the Pope should be sovereign of all Italy. But he believed in the marriage between the papacy and democracy. A generous man with a warm heart, and not a demagogue, he used his oratorical ability with the crowds, wrote a plan for a constitution with a general election and two houses of Parliament, and devised a scheme for railways. He was a strong supporter of Sicilian liberty against the Bourbon rule in Naples. The best-known of his utterances was his funeral panegyric at Sant'Andrea della Valle on the Irish 'liberator' Daniel O'Connell (28 June 1847); O'Connell came to Italy to ask the Pope for a word of comfort for the Irish and died on the way at Genoa, leaving his body to Ireland and his heart to Rome. Ventura's sermon was a hymn to the union between Catholicism and liberty. 'The Church will know how to resort to democracy, she will christen this savage lady, will make her Christian . . . and will seal her forehead

[2] Martina, *Pio IX (1846–50)*, 103.

with the sign of the cross . . . and will say, Reign; and . . . she will reign.'

In Rome the government treated these demonstrations and crowd scenes as natural outlets, but in the provincial cities the crowds and the people's orators showed signs of displacing constituted authority. A new, untried government was losing control of its provinces, as well as being in trouble over the desperate state of papal finances. The archbishop of Fermo spoke of 'a revolution in the name of Pius IX'.[3] The provincial authorities began to ask how it would end, and whether the Pope knew what was happening. Groups of conservatives in the north protested against a Jacobin pope, nuns were called to prayer against the evil of a liberal pope, and a forgery was circulated in Umbria purporting to show that Pius IX had enlisted in Mazzini's Young Italy. It was rumoured that the Pope would soon abolish the Jesuits, ban permanent vows for monks and nuns, and disband the Swiss Guard. In the pulpit at Imola a preacher shocked the congregation by attacking the Pope as though he were Antichrist.[4]

The dream of the pope as head of a federated Italy was propagated by the neo-Guelfs. The Pope gave it no countenance. The French ambassador Pellegrino Rossi attended a big service at the French church of Saint-Louis in Rome, 25 August 1846. The Pope came. Next day Rossi went to see him and afterwards reported to Paris on the interview. The Pope said, among other things, 'A Pope ought not to throw himself into utopias. Will you believe it, there are people who even talk of an Italian federation with the Pope at its head? As if that were possible! As if the Powers would let it happen! It's all a chimera.' Rossi had remarked that there were other things to do, which required time, such as putting the finances of the Papal State in order. The Pope talked of economizing on the Swiss Guard. 'The Swiss, they don't please, and they cost a lot. Could I get rid of them at once?' Rossi said, 'That too needs time. You must not deprive yourself of an army till you have organized what will take its place.'[5]

It will be noticed that at this moment of his long reign the Pope rejected the idea of heading a united Italy, not because no pope could ever risk such a thing for his office, as because it would be politically impossible in the then state of Europe.

    [3] Martina, *Pio IX (1846–50)*, 109.
    [4] C. Spellanzon, *Storia del Risorgimento e dell'unità d'Italia* (Milan, 1933–), iii. 16.
    [5] F. Guizot, *Mémoires pour servir à l'histoire de mon temps* (Paris, 1867), viii. 345.

Whatever the Pope said in private, liberal optimists continued, not without reason, to believe that a federated Italy was where a reformed, liberal, and national-minded pope must lead them. The progress towards these ends seemed to the liberal observers very marked. The Pope appointed Gizzi as Secretary of State on 8 August 1846. This was not his own idea, but was forced upon him by public opinion, which wrongly fancied that Gizzi was chief liberal among the cardinals. The new Secretary of State started plans for the railway that Gregory XVI had refused. The Pope sent greetings to a scholarly congress, from which his predecessor tried to exclude scholars from the Papal State.

In March 1847 Gizzi reformed censorship, to make it the freest in Western Europe apart from Britain. The rules were retained for religious publications, which could be stopped if heretical or offensive; but for political publications the area of liberty was widened—anyone could now discuss 'contemporary history' or the 'administration of the State', provided that the book or article did not lower the reputation of religion or the government—'directly or indirectly' the Pope added personally. Right of appeal against the verdict of the censors was also given.

At first the policy of the papal government, to reform what needed reforming, keep the executive strong, and let the crowds demonstrate till they were weary, seemed to be winning. The difficulty was to distinguish reform that showed strength from concessions that looked like weakness. In the prevailing conditions the executive weakened steadily. As early as the autumn of 1846 Metternich made the famous remark, to the Piedmontese ambassador in Vienna, that he had been prepared for everything but a liberal pope; and this they now had, therefore he could no longer predict what might happen. By July 1847 Metternich was convinced that tragedy lay ahead—'my pessimism is extreme'.[6] Cardinal Bernetti prophesied that coming events included first revolution, and then, by consequence, French and Austrian take-over—precisely his experience when he was in charge in 1832. Metternich said that this pope was like a novice sorcerer who conjured up spirits that he then could not control. 'He's caught in a net . . . and in the ordinary course of events he will be chased out of Rome.'[7]

---

[6] Metternich to Lützow, 18 July 1847, *Aus Metternich's Nachgelassenen Papieren*, ed. H. von Fürsten and Richard Metternich-Winneburg (Vienna, 1883), vii. 410.
[7] Ibid. 339 ff.

Moderates thought such views alarmist. Here was a moderate pope; a moderate movement that had every wish to keep Austrians out of any more of Italy; and a real chance of a Papal State with a constitutional form of government. Pius IX was not a liberal, he knew nothing about politics, and knew that he knew nothing; but he had faith in God, and anything that happened that was not sinful was likely to be in the providence of God. He did not get on with his Secretary of State Gizzi, and the most powerful among the cardinals was still Lambruschini who was not his kind of person and who was surrounded by other cardinals of Gregory XVI. But he had at his side a person picked with brilliant judgement: Corboli Bussi. Bussi had come into Gregory XVI's Curia and was found to have an exceptional mind. He was only 33 when Pius IX first met him, a delicate consumptive who was to have a very short life. They quickly formed a close friendship. They were both warm-hearted, religious, and cheerful. The elder did not know what to do in politics, so the younger proposed and drafted. He perfectly understood the basic difficulty, that democracy and papal authority did not agree. But he also saw, and persuaded his master to see, that many good people had ideals that ought not to be dismissed out of hand. Their idealism should be turned to benefit, and bad consequences remedied by good administration. But it was important to have an objective, and not to drift, giving way here and there as the pressure of the piazza mounted.[8]

It took them time to get going. The Pope's first encyclical, *Qui pluribus*, had no impact.[9] It was written by Cardinal Lambruschini, and sounded like the encyclicals of Gregory XVI—it is against Bible societies and communism, said priests must be better trained, and the times are deplorable, and people are preparing war against Catholicism, and 'we cannot imagine errors madder than the monsters of our age'. There was not a sparkle of light to be seen. It did not help the looming struggle in Rome; it did not help anyone. But it showed that this new pope, on matters of faith and the duty of the State to support the Church, stood with his predecessor.

One trial afflicted a papal regime attempting to move towards a form of government more acceptable to its people. It was deep in the minds of conventional liberals that Jesuits were sinister. This belief

---

[8] Baron A. Manno published a large part of his correspondence: *L'opinione religiosa e conservatrice in Italia dal 1830 al 1850, ricerecata nella corrispondenze e confidenze di Giovanni Corboli Bussi* (Turin, 1910).

[9] *Acta Pii IX* (Graz, 1971), I. i. 4–24, 9 Nov. 1846.

corresponded little to the truth about the members of the Society of Jesus since their revival. But they inherited a burden of reputation from the past of the Counter-Reformation, heavy because once a pope had abolished them. Crowds when demonstrating and orators when moving assemblies in the streets needed enemies for their rhetoric. Since the pope was now a friend they identified the enemy as the Jesuits, and it became unsafe for them to move about Rome.

Authentic liberalism demanded the protection of Jesuits as it demanded the protection of every other citizen. The Swiss Protestants breached the principle when their new constitution excluded Jesuits from the Swiss Confederation. The British government breached the principle when it banned Jesuits simultaneously with the concession of the vote to Catholics under Catholic emancipation. The French government breached the principle when it made its ambassador in Rome, Pellegrino Rossi, persuade the Pope to withdraw the Jesuits from France. But a papal government could not ban Jesuits. There was discussion, even among informed persons, whether it would be necessary for a liberal-minded pope to follow a predecessor of the previous century and abolish the Jesuit order. In reality any such act was not unthinkable, apart from its injustice. If the Jesuits could not be protected in the city of Rome then they must be advised to leave the city quietly until the streets were more settled. Pius IX did not mind much. The Jesuit general Roothaan was a very reserved Dutchman, and the open-hearted Pius could not get on with him. But he also had the reason of policy: the Jesuits whom he knew were stout enemies of reform in the State.

A second problem was the influence that Rome exerted elsewhere. A constitutional monarchy in Rome was so miraculous an innovation that it generated calls for reform all over Italy, and demonstrations when their rulers failed to grant the demands of the crowds. Tuscany and its grand duke were troubled during the summer of 1847, as were Turin and Genoa in the kingdom of Piedmont. In the kingdom of Naples there were risings at Reggio and Messina, though easily suppressed. In the autumn of 1847 Charles Albert the king of Piedmont and Sardinia granted a moderate reform of the constitution.

In April 1847, still conceding step by step to the pressure of lay politicians, Gizzi announced a plan for a rudimentary representative system, which soon won the name of the Consulta, to show that it was for consultation only. Each province was to send a list of three names from which the pope would choose one; and the function of

the resulting body would be to advise on finance and general administration. But before this plan could take effect, the modest possibilities of the Consulta were enhanced by two decisions. The first
concerned a civil guard.

It was a criticism of the old regime that it had to rely on foreign
mercenaries like Swiss guards and could not rely for its defence upon
its own people. Pius IX, popular as few popes before him—perhaps
as no pope before him—believed that he need no longer rely on foreign mercenaries but could trust the loyalty and affection of his people. In July 1847, against the advice of the Secretary of State Gizzi,
who thought it better to strengthen the regular police and not to
hand out weapons to a new and unreliable body, the Pope allowed
the formation of a civil guard—though only in the city of Rome.
Before Cardinal Gizzi published the decree, he quietly, and without
telling his master (!), asked the Austrian government what would be
its attitude to a request for military help. Two days later he published
the decree establishing the civil guard—and resigned. Metternich,
who had doubted Gizzi for being too open, was sad at his resignation: 'What has happened in the Papal State is revolution. It is disguised as reform . . . Cardinal Gizzi's successor will have a difficult
job. I pray that it is not an impossible job.'[10]

The new Secretary of State was Cardinal Ferretti, a relative of the
Pope. He had commanded part of Gregory XVI's army during the
revolution of 1831, was self-sacrificing in the cholera epidemic, and
made enemies for sternness in his northern diocese of Fermo. His
family record was not conservative, for a brother commanded a
brigade in Napoleon's retreat from Moscow and another brother was
a revolutionary of 1831. Perhaps because of this past record he
believed that the people could be trusted: 'Let us prove to Europe
that we are capable of protecting ourselves.' He began to allow back
political exiles though they had not affirmed their loyalty. The chief
of those who came back was Terenzio Mamiani, a prominent member of the rebel government in Bologna in 1831. It was a mark of the
pendulum change in papal policy that this unreconciled liberal should
soon find himself Prime Minister of the Papal State.

[10] Metternich to Lützow, 18 July 1847, *Nachg. Pap.* vii. 409.

THE POPE AS LEADER OF ITALY

The second change, after the civic guard, which affected the Consulta, was a failure of judgement by the Austrian commander in Lombardy, Marshal Radetzky, whom the Austrian army revered for his past history of courage and his part in beating Napoleon, and whom Metternich always backed. It was a failure of judgement caused by nervousness at what was happening to his south.

On the border in papal territory was Ferrara. By the Treaty of Vienna the Austrians had the right to man the 'piazza', whatever that meant; it was taken to mean the citadel. In the city, as authority was weak, theft and murder rose. In July 1847 the Austrians precipitated disaster by an illegal step. They moved troops into Ferrara town itself to ensure public order; under protest from the papal legate.

In 1831 Gregory XVI summoned Austrians to keep order. But all Italy, indeed all Europe including Austria, saw this new pope as part of the national movement of Italy that was against foreign occupation. Everyone believed that he must be against the Austrian occupation of Ferrara. They were correct in that belief. The affair of Ferrara raised him to new heights of popularity as defender of Italy against the foreigner. Far away in Rio de Janeiro, Garibaldi offered his sword to the Pope's representative. The Pope's reputation stood still higher when in December 1847 the Austrians yielded to the pressure and withdrew the troops to the citadel.

Ferrara weakened the fear of Metternich in Italy and excited the dislike of the Austrians. It made the Pope look more liberal and nationalistic, and the natural leader of military resistance to Austria. Metternich or Radetzky had made him the hero of Italy. To defend Italy was now to defend the Pope and the Church.

If it were not impossible to attribute cynicism to Mazzini one would suspect his next move of being cynical. He published an open letter to the Pope, beseeching him to place himself at the head of the national movement for a united Italy. He declared that he was no revolutionary, nor a communist, nor a man of blood. 'I adore God, and for me an idea that is equal to God: an Italy that is one, a cornerstone of moral unity, and of the progressive civilization of the European nations' . . . 'I believe deeply in religious principle, and in a divine order which we ought to seek to bring on earth . . . I believe you good. No one has more power than you today' . . . 'Thanks to your predecessor, and the old hierarchy, faith is dead. Catholicism is lost in despotism. Protestantism is lost in anarchy. No one believes, they only have superstitions.' Humanity cannot live without heaven. You can guide them to truth out of materialism. To do this, you must unite Italy and abhor being a king or politician. To unite Italy you have no need to *do*, only to *bless*. Let the pen go free. Throw the Austrians out of Italy . . . Bless the national flag—and leave the rest to us.[11]

The Pope had a warm nature and was a patriot. He shared the aspirations of those who wanted Italy to be free of Austrian rule. Thus a deception entered the public mind. The people identified liberal and constitutional government with the national hopes against Austria; both aims were necessary to freedom. The Pope wanted Italy to be free of foreigners, and to prosper, but saw that a fully constitutional government was not compatible with the temporal sovereignty of the pope. Therefore the people had a false expectation of him. They enthused over his 'liberalism'. When he called for God's blessing on Italy (10 February 1848) they imagined that he asked a blessing upon the liberal cause.

On 14 October 1847 the Consulta began to sit, after absurd pomp at the opening. Soon it was in heavy disagreement over whether its debates should be public. Those who wanted them public, knowing that the Pope was against it, held that the Consulta had a responsibility to the people as well as to the sovereign, for they saw themselves to be a sort of Parliament and not just a team of advisers; the argument between sovereign's rights and Consulta's rights went on for two months until it lost relevance. Whatever it advised had little effect upon what the administration did. By then it looked less like a mini-Parliament than like one more of those committees which the Curia appointed to make a complex situation yet more complex.

But the Consulta had one result that mattered. Until now all the Ministers of State were clerics. At the beginning of 1848 it was accepted that except for the Prime Minister (who was also Foreign Secretary) they could be lay. This was sensible. The moderates could never hold the radicals unless they were allowed responsibility. But still they had a chance—as did the Pope—of coming through without a revolution and with a rational type of constitution that did not hurt his supreme spiritual authority. That chance was smashed by what happened outside the Papal States.

[11] G. Mazzini, *Scritti Politici*, ed. T. Grandi and A. Comba (Turin, 1972), xxxi. 560 ff.

In January 1848 the people rose in revolt at Palermo and within a month forced a constitution upon King Ferdinand of Naples. In February a revolution in Paris overthrew King Louis Philippe. This revolution was infectious for it sounded as if revolutionaries everywhere might get the backing of a great power. Within a few weeks risings forced constitutions upon the rulers of the separated states of Western Germany. And all Italy was aflame when, on 13 March 1848, revolution in Vienna overthrew the symbol of European conservatism, the statesman responsible for maintaining Austrian power in Italy, the Chancellor Metternich. Every bell in Rome was rung at the news of Metternich's fall.

It was a wave of enthusiasm, even ecstasy, an ardour to sacrifice self for freedom and independence; an enthusiasm not only of the middle classes but of the poor. This enthusiasm focused in affection for and hope in the pope, its sovereign symbol; a pope as the longed-for saviour of Italy. Pius IX felt no danger. To him this was evidently God's will, who was casting down the mighty from their seats and raising the humble. He said in a proclamation that what had been happening was the work of God.

In March 1848, not under this new pressure from outside but continuing the limping movement towards a Papal State with a representative government which should nevertheless reserve the absolute rights of the pope in the matters which he regarded as essential to his freedom and independence, the Pope sanctioned a Parliament, with two chambers—the lower house elected, the upper house nominated by the pope. But there was a third chamber, namely the college of cardinals, with the right to veto bills and which would debate in private. The pope reserved to himself all ecclesiastical matters or 'mixed matters', that is part ecclesiastical and part not, e.g. education, marriage, censorship of books on religion, public morality. The 'confessional State' was maintained, except that the existing liberty of the Jews to worship was preserved, and shortly afterwards (17 April 1848) the chains at the gates of the ghetto were removed, and Jews could in theory live where they liked.

The statute, that is the new constitution with its Parliament, might have held. As it was, it held longer than in most States where it was conceded in that age. If it had held, there would have been a fascinating example of a Papal State where in secular affairs the pope was a constitutional monarch and where he was free to be absolute as an international spiritual authority. Those old disciples of Gregory XVI,

Cardinals Lambruschini and Bernetti, kept saying that the sure end of all this was revolution followed by occupation by the Austrian and French armies. It was far from certain that it was inevitable, though it was what happened.

When Milan and Venice and the cities of northern Italy revolted against the Austrians and fortified themselves against an Austrian reaction, would other Italian States help the rebels? Pius IX was infected with the public excitement. He probably thought that Marshal Radetzky's retreat from Milan was forced by the barricades in the streets, that the Austrians were more beaten than they were, and that under God's providence a new Italy was being born. 'The Pope', he said, 'cannot be silent, when his children's souls are moved by their aspirations. He prays for Italy. He is bound to love all Catholic Christendom, and does not love Italy more than other lands. But Italy is nearest to him.' On the day after the news of the Vienna revolution reached Rome, the crowd invaded the Austrian embassy at the Palazzo Venezia, and—alleging the agreement of the Pope— tore down the Austrian eagle, trampled upon it, and burnt it in the Piazza del Popolo. The Pope's government made no formal apology to Vienna.[12] The Austrian ambassador no longer felt safe in the city.

When all northern Italy, headed by the king of Sardinia-Piedmont, engaged in patriotic war against the foreigner, what would the Pope's army do? He had an army under General Durando defending his frontiers near Ferrara. These troops had asked for his blessing. He blessed their representatives, but told them not to cross the frontier. They were to be an army defending against aggression, not an aggressive force.

If the papal troops on the Austrian border were ordered not to help the Lombard rebels and the Piedmontese army, they would not have obeyed. Therefore at Rome, in the government, among the cardinals, and by the Pope, there was anxious debate about the morality of war.

Most of the clerics were strong for neutrality, for these reasons: Austria held Lombardy and the Veneto by an international treaty. Could it be said that the treaty of 1815 was unjust? It had held Europe at peace for more than thirty years. Against it was the plea of 'nationalism'. But what was this nationalism, had it any moral right, or was it the consecration of a racialism that would trouble Europe endlessly

---

[12] F. Engel-Janosi, *Österreich und der Vatikan* (Graz, 1960), i. 35, from the Viennese archives out of Rome.

if it were accepted? The Church was a symbol of peace among the peoples. Austria had done no harm to it; indeed they were a Catholic people, therefore it must be immoral to go to war. If Rome were to say that it was neutral, it would probably suffer a revolution. But the wish to avert revolution could not justify an immoral policy.

On the other hand a few clerics, including Corboli Bussi and Rosmini, were decisive for intervention. They argued that by general agreement the pope had the right to defend his subjects. There could be circumstances where defence would only be possible by crossing the other side's frontier. Austria had caused the troubles in which the Italian States found themselves. And it should be considered what would happen if Rome did not fight—a fervent nationalist movement in Italy would be fiercely anti-Catholic and cause grievous harm to religion. To fight was not only a possible course, it was a moral duty.

This pope was to be a military defender of his lands later during his pontificate and it did not feel strange, many Catholics revered it as noble and courageous. But in 1848 the pope's armies, for the sake of an Italian cause, were invading the lands that another power received by a treaty which the popes accepted. And the other power was Catholic and had a hold on the Church in its empire. Pius IX appeared to the Austrians to be, and almost was, a political ally of their enemies in a war. Threats against the Austrian Church soon began. The Redemptorists were thrown out of Vienna, then the Mechitarists; there were calls in Vienna for a separate non-Roman Catholic Church with its own patriarch.

The Pope was trained as a churchman and a pastor. By the force of history he found himself the king of a kingdom at a crisis in its long story. The situation was hardly workable. His cabinet ministers said that they could not get near him to get vital decisions out of him about the affairs of State, because he was closeted with an official from the Curia to discuss the disciplinary case of some monk or nun in America. The future Italian Prime Minister Minghetti, who was a member of the Consulta in 1847–8, put down in his memories of that time: 'The care of religious things absorbed the Pope's mind. He did not take pleasure when cabinet ministers came to see him. Some cardinals profited by this to sow fear into his mind. He shut himself up with the grand penitentiary, and then it was vain to hope for an audience.' Minghetti said in old age that Pius IX always remained for him a dear and reverent memory and blamed Cardinal Antonelli for the

disasters that were to happen; for the Pope, with his 'fervent faith
. . . the storms that tossed the ship of Peter were passing proofs of the
sins of humanity and would in time give place to serene years for the
Church'; but Antonelli had none of this faith—he was *scaltro*, sly or
smart, without a big idea in his head.[13] The Pope's embarrassment at
his predicament appeared in the evidence of the Netherlands ambassador Count Liedekerke to whom he talked at this time as though he
considered that, if the worst came to the worst, he could resign his
see and retire to a monastery.[14]

Not for the first time in history, but for the clearest time in modern history, the pope's office as Italian sovereign and national leader
was in opposition to his office as a spiritual and international leader.
If he declared war he would be in trouble with conservatives all over
Europe and the Church in Austria-Hungary would suffer. He would
probably have a schism in Austria and possibly in Bavaria. That damage could later be repaired when the situation changed. And if the
war of liberation were successful and the Austrians driven out of Italy
partly by the Pope, his future place in Italian hearts would be secure,
and he was likely to be the president of whatever Italian federation
came into existence. If he failed to declare war his government in
Rome was likely to be overthrown by violence, with consequences
for Italy and the Church which no one could predict. Both courses
were bad but war was the lesser evil. So his advisers, though not his
leading ecclesiastical advisers, believed.

If Pius IX failed to declare war he was like a sovereign, who had
just accepted that he was a constitutional sovereign, refusing to carry
out a policy on which all his ministers were agreed. He could see that
his ministers, moderate liberals almost to a man, were better in every
sense, from his point of view, than the radicals who would follow if
he refused to support the moderates. But he was not capable of
declaring war. His moral personality made the act impossible.

Afterwards it was said that Pius IX, for all his liberal decisions
between June 1846 and April 1848 (and even afterwards) was never a
true liberal pope but a weak man, basically reactionary, who was carried on the wave of events in the first years of his pontificate, and
asserted his true self in the moment when he realized that things were
out of hand. That is a just tenable theory, and afterwards was widely

[13] M. Minghetti, *Miei Ricordi* (Turin, 1889–90), i. 349–50, 380.
[14] F. C. A. Liedekerke-Beaufort, *Rapporti delle cose di Roma*, ed. A. M. Ghisalberti (Rome,
1949), 39; Engel-Janosi, *Österreich und der Vatikan*, i. 37.

held, even until today. But the evidence points the other way. Pius IX *then* was a genuine moderate; a lover of Italy; a man with a readiness to trust good men about him; and a willingness to pick advisers whom he knew to be liberal in their approach to problems. He was not an intellectual. He had small experience of the world. He was not fitted for secular monarchy whether it were absolute or constitutional. But he opened his heart to the best that he could see around him and tried to let the liberal cause, provided it went moderately and with circumspection, take its course. And then came the moment when events made the liberal course demand of him a decision for war that he knew he could not take. A defensive war was one thing—a war of liberation was a war of aggression. There was contradiction between the policy which his advisers told him was the only sane policy and the policy which his convictions told him was the only moral policy. The notion that he was always a concealed reactionary, always another Gregory XVI pretending to be a different sort of pope, is contradicted by the evidence.

THE REFUSAL TO GO TO WAR

On 29 April 1848 he made an allocution to the cardinals. He said: Some people speak about us as though we caused all this commotion. The Austrians spread rumours that the Pope sends agents to stir the people to rebellion against them. I have been told that some Germans talk of separating their church from Rome. I do not doubt that the Catholics and bishops are wholly against this. But it is right to refute the rumours. When there was revolution over Europe, I sent troops to guard the frontiers. But when some demanded that these troops join with other states to war against Austria, I must say solemnly, that I abhor the idea. I am the Vicar of Christ, the author of peace and lover of charity, and my office is to bestow an equal affection on all nations. I repudiate all the newspaper articles that want the pope to be president of a new republic of all the Italians. I warn the peoples of Italy to obey their princes. If they do not there will be more blood shed in civil war. I am determined to work for the kingdom of God and want peace and reconciliation. I lament the sordid attacks on religion now so common. We must pray God to defend his Church and bring us peace.[15]

[15] *Acta Pii IX*, I. i. 92 ff., summary.

To speak thus was to reject the advice of his cabinet. It resigned *en bloc* that evening. He was surprised by the reaction. His draft of the allocution said more than the public text; it spoke of his enthusiasm for the Italian cause and for an Italy that could face up to the other powers of Europe; said that he could not hold back his own subjects who were determined to fight; but neither could he accept a war to shed Christian blood; and he moved off into quietness and prayer for the true good of Italy, with talk of the religious mission of the see of Rome.

It is proved that a hand in the Curia redrafted the allocution to make it much stronger for neutrality and to omit both the enthusiasms for the Italian cause and the retirement of a troubled soul to prayer for the good of Italy. The redrafting made the allocution far more offensive to the cabinet and the people. The person most likely to have been the redrafter was Cardinal Antonelli.[16] If so, Antonelli played a double game: as drafter making the Pope say what he, Antonelli, as a minister with cabinet responsibility, must publicly disagree with.

It was at once put about that the Pope condemned Italy's struggle for freedom. The higher the enthusiasm before, the fiercer now the reaction. Street orators talked of the Pope's treason. A delegation asked him, not to declare war, but to hand over power to a lay cabinet which could declare war. Thus he would save his priesthood and his conscience. He allowed an envoy (Farini) to go to the king of Sardinia-Piedmont to ask that the papal troops in the north should come under his command and his protection, otherwise they could be shot by the enemy as irregulars.

For the government of his State, the Pope continued to seek out moderate liberals. No one could say that the refusal to declare war turned him into a reactionary. As a private man, as an Italian, he longed to take part in a patriotic war; and there was a lesser motivation: he had been the most popular of popes, had loved the plaudits of the crowd, and wanted to know that his people still loved him. But he could not declare war—it was a block in his moral being.

He tried three lay Prime Ministers in succession, but only the third had a chance. The choice was intelligent: Mamiani had been in exile for his liberalism and was the person whom the streets of Rome wanted—he had been a revolutionary. The programme of any lay

---

[16] See the discussion in Martina, *Pio IX (1846–50)*, 241 ff.

Prime Minister must be to persuade the Pope to separate his spiritual power, which could not go to war, from his temporal power, which had to go to war, and therefore to free himself from the secular responsibilities. Mamiani was bold enough to say this in the newly elected Parliament at Rome (he could hardly do other) and raised the issue of war in the Chamber. On 10 July 1848 the Pope publicly rebuked Mamiani, who resigned.

The war began to go badly and to evoke less enthusiasm. On 8–9 June 1848 Radetzky swung round on the papal troops under General Durando at Vicenza, drove them back, and reoccupied the town. Vicenza was a blow to the morale of the Pope's men. The Austrians reoccupied Ferrara—the government in Rome told the Pope that he must go to war, but he refused. On 18 July 1848 the news reached Rome that victorious Austrian forces had entered papal territory. Was the war now no longer a war of aggression but a defensive war that the Pope could join? Pius IX was sure that he was entitled to defend his people and said so. That eased his situation a little with public opinion. On 24–5 July Radetzky smashed the Piedmontese army at Custoza—the government in Rome told the Pope that he must go to war, but he refused—indeed it began to look like a demand to war on the losing side. At the end of July Radetzky reoccupied Milan, where the rising was the origin of the war, without a fight. On 7 August an Austrian force occupied Bologna—and the city rose in fury, the streets saw fearful anarchy, and the Austrians evacuated the town.

But public order in Rome was worsening as troops or wounded from the beaten papal army in the north appeared in the city. The sight of them raised the fury of the crowds.

For the first time Pius IX asked for a foreign army. He had a body-guard of 100 or more Swiss. On 14 August 1848 he asked the new French President, General Cavaignac, whether he could spare him up to 3,000 soldiers—to defend the integrity of his State (against Austrians?), to maintain the constitution, to defend the liberties of the Church. Cavaignac had lately suppressed the Paris revolutionaries in the terrible street fighting through Paris on 23–6 June, during which Archbishop Quelen's successor, Affre of Paris, was shot dead at a street barricade as he tried to persuade both sides to stop firing. Cavaignac had no desire to risk doing the same through the streets of Rome. He could see that to do what was asked by the Pope risked war between France and Austria. He did not say no, but no troops came. There are historians who believe that if the French army had arrived in September 1848 instead of ten months later, the constitutional Papal State could have survived, with big consequences for Italian history and for the history of the popes.

At one point the Pope considered bringing the priest Rosmini from Stresa on Lake Maggiore. Rosmini had engaged in the drafting of a constitution for the Papal State, and was very loyal, so he combined the principles of constitutional government with the supremacy of the pope. He wanted an Italian federation, with a congress that would meet in Rome under the presidency of the pope. Pius IX greeted him with the warmest of welcomes, and spoke of making him Secretary of State and a cardinal.

The extent of Rosmini's radicalism at this moment is shown by his decision to publish the reforming book which he wrote in retirement in 1832, *The Five Wounds of the Church*. That made him impossible as a moderate political leader and suspect to all the Pope's ecclesiastical advisers. The Curia knew that Rosmini believed that a war of liberation was moral and were nervous that he would push the Pope to war. From August 1848 for three months he was the most important ecclesiastic to be at the side of the Pope.

The new Prime Minister Fabbri had a past that was even more radical than Mamiani's; as a republican who had written songs to celebrate Napoleon's victories, a friend of Manzoni, the author of thirteen tragedies, and condemned in Rome to life imprisonment for conspiracy, which he served till the revolution against Gregory XVI released him. He gloried in the election of Pius IX as a liberal pope and was willing to serve as his lay leader. His government lasted just over a month and was the weakest of all the Pope's governments in the rising tide of disturbance. He was too old, drifted, and resigned because his government could not keep order in the streets of Rome. He prorogued Parliament till 15 November.[17]

PELLEGRINO ROSSI

The Pope summoned Pellegrino Rossi to be his Prime Minister, on 16 September 1848. This was the best possible selection. If any politician of the time could have saved the Papal State it was Rossi.

---

[17] For Fabbri, see the important article, *DBI* (1993), s.v., by G. Monsagrati.

His career was dramatic. A lawyer from North Italy, he joined the revolutionary kingdom of Murat at the end of the Napoleonic wars and had to flee into exile. He became an academic at Geneva and made distinguished contributions to the history of law. Then he became a professor of political economy in Paris and soon a French citizen, and made more contributions of distinction to the theory of political economy. In 1845 he was sent to Rome as the French ambassador to Gregory XVI. The French Revolution of 1848 ended his duties. Here was one of the leading minds of Europe to be found in Rome. He was an expert in the workings of constitutional monarchy, and if anyone could fashion an Italian federation with the pope at its head it was Rossi. In Geneva he had married a Protestant wife. Gregory XVI minded about the Protestant wife; Pius IX did not.

Pellegrino Rossi knew exactly where he was going, a man of resolution. His popular position was weaker than it looked because, although he had been a man of Murat, the radicals could say that since the heady days he corrupted himself by serving the French conservative government of Guizot. If they disliked him they could say that now he was hardly even an Italian, how could he feel their sense of patriotism? The clergy suspected him because he instantly set about taxing them to help balance the budget.

And, more dangerously, he became a menace to everyone who was afraid of power. He cleansed the police force of unreliable men, ordered an army battalion out of Rome, protected the Jews in the old ghetto who were at risk from the mob, brought in a strong force of police from outside Rome, ejected to Naples a couple of well-known revolutionaries, established order in the streets of Rome, and reintroduced censorship of publications as part of creating order. He paid pensions to the wounded and to the widows of casualties and brought some contentment into the army. He started negotiations for a league of Italian States under the presidency of the pope, which would counter the plans of the king of Sardinia-Piedmont to be at the head of just such a league. His forces restored order in Bologna and scoured the country for the ex-soldiers who had become armed bandits.

To the revolutionaries he looked like a bourgeois governor putting down the revolution—which was what he was. His strengthening of the police in Rome caused wild fear that he planned a *coup d'état*. Two or three days before Parliament reopened on 15 November a group decided to use the opening as the moment of Rossi's death. The evening before the opening one or two politicians persuaded four or five young men to show their courage and patriotism by doing the deed.

Rossi was warned of trouble, and the square near the Parliament building was policed. As he walked up the steps, amid angry shouts of demonstrators, he was stabbed in the neck. He was carried, barely alive, to the room of a cardinal, where he died. The assassin easily slipped away in the confusion. A mob went through the streets of Rome brandishing torches and flags and singing revolutionary songs. The next day some of them gathered under Rossi's window to shout abuse at his widow and family. Not a single voice was raised in parliament to protest. Garibaldi, then with his few irregulars in the Romagna, thought the murder a noble tyrannicide.

The Pope's quest for a constitution compatible with the papal office and with the freedom of Italy from the foreigner had died, by the knife of an assassin.

Almost everyone who had a chance of wielding authority, almost anyone who could have stood by the Pope, most of his loyal disciples, the noble guard who were supposed to protect him, and many members of the Curia, hid or ran from Rome, and left a rampant mob; they abandoned their sovereign in the Quirinal Palace, protected by 100 Swiss guards, and helped by only three prelates—Antonelli, Soglia, and Pentini—and by the ambassadors, who went to the Quirinal to see if they could be of use.

THE ROMAN REVOLUTION

The Pope tried to find someone who would form a government. Minghetti? An excellent moderate leader, but he knew he had no chance of persuading colleagues. Galletti? He was one of the popular radical leaders and demanded by the crowd, and on Minghetti's advice the Pope charged him with the duty. At that moment the crowd arrived in the square outside the Quirinal and shouted for the government and the policy they wanted—including war. Galletti said he must accept. Pius IX said he would accept nothing under threats. The square filled with armed men, civil guard and soldiers. They tried to set fire to a door of the Quirinal and shooting broke out between the Swiss and the soldiers outside. A secretary, Monsignor Palma, standing next to the Pope at the Quirinal window, was shot dead. Cannon were brought to blow out the door.

The ambassadors and Cardinal Pentini told the Pope he had to accept the crowd's demand. He did so, provided that Rosmini was made Prime Minister of the new cabinet.

Like Minghetti before him, Rosmini was sure that it could not work. He sent a question into the Quirinal: Is this a command? The Pope sent back the reply: he would be happy if Rosmini accepted, but he was not sure that it would work and he refused to make it a command. Rosmini declined the task—'If I accepted I would be head of an unconstitutional ministry imposed by force'—and went into hiding so that no one could press him. The Pope chose Muzzarelli, chairman of the Chamber, a monsignor but a layman and a radical. Muzzarelli was in favour of the rebels and approved of the murder of Pellegrino Rossi, and talked cynically about it in the Pope's presence.[18]

This business of finding someone willing to give orders to somebody made no difference to the rule of Rome by a mob. The next day, 17 November, the Pope was forced to dismiss his 100 Swiss guards from the palace and accept civil guards as his 'protectors'; they were also his gaolers.

At this juncture historians have raised the question: Was another course possible? Postulate that this pope was not a gentle, emotional pastor from North Italy, who hated blood, but a tough like Pope Julius II. Could he have stood up to them? Could he have issued a call to good men and true, the majority that wanted law and order, to come and restore discipline and its legal constitution to the State? If he had stood stalwart, could he have averted most of the bloodshed that was to flow with the coming of the French army? Pius IX has been blamed for this failure. But he was not a tough and a Julius II would not have averted bloodshed. Historians have also asked whether Rosmini was at fault—he had a chance, the one person acceptable to the crowd and dedicated to the Pope. That is a conundrum harder to answer.

THE FLIGHT OF THE POPE

The day after the dismissal of the Swiss guards, the Pope began to plan flight from Rome. Cardinal Antonelli was chief planner. The

[18] G. Pasolini, *Memorie*, ed. P. D. Pasolini (author's son), 4th edn. (2 vols.; Turin, 1915), i. 217.

ambassadors of France, Spain, and Bavaria were drawn in. The Frenchman undertook to spirit the Pope out of the Quirinal, the Bavarian undertook to get him across the border of the Papal States— to where? No one knew, perhaps the monastery of Monte Cassino— and the Spaniard undertook to provide a ship so that he could sail to . . . no one yet knew, perhaps Majorca? Whisk him across the border and the other decisions could be taken at leisure. The task of the Frenchman was the most tense, to extract a pope with a very well-known face from under the eyes of his guards.

Eight days later, shortly before 6 p.m. on 24 November 1848, the French ambassador d'Harcourt was received, apparently for an audience in the Pope's room. The Pope disguised himself in the cassock of an ordinary priest, dark glasses, and a brown woollen muffler, and went down by a back staircase while d'Harcourt carried on talking in a loud voice to make the guards think that the audience continued. At the back door an aide greeted the guards outside and climbed, with the Pope, into an ordinary city coach. They drove off in the wrong direction, then reversed their tracks and, outside the church of Sts Peter and Marcellinus, transferred to the coach of Spaur the Bavarian ambassador. At the gate of San Giovanni Spaur used his diplomatic passport made out in his own name and that of his doctor. At Ariccia as they journeyed southwards Spaur met his wife who waited with a heavier travelling coach. In the early morning they crossed the border into the kingdom of Naples and by mid-morning they drew up at the port of Gaeta where Cardinal Antonelli waited to greet them.

A stay at Gaeta was not intended. A Spanish ship would be ready to take him to the Balearic Islands, or a French ship to France, perhaps to a restored Avignon. They talked also of Malta, although its government was Protestant, and the little state of Monaco, and an abbey in French Switzerland, the historic house at Agaune. Antonelli thought of the old papal enclave within the kingdom of Naples, Benevento. It seemed better not to commit the Pope too evidently to one of the great powers. Hence the quest for island retreats or little states.

The king of Naples begged him to stay at Gaeta. The argument for staying as near Rome as possible was strong. The snag was that liberals everywhere hated King Ferdinand of Naples. If he stayed at Gaeta, the Pope must live under Bourbon protection. The name Bourbon did not sound well in constitutional Italy. And King Ferdinand, whose absolute power was shaken because to his north the Pope allowed a constitution, might be expected to have small enthusiasm for giving him a home. The argument for staying on Italian soil and within easy reach of Rome prevailed. The stay was not expected to be long.[19]

THE ROMAN REPUBLIC

The revolutionary government in Rome was on sufferance. They were a legal government, their Prime Minister, Muzzarelli legal, for their sovereign had accepted them and it made no difference that their sovereign had gone away. On 27 November from Gaeta the Pope issued a declaration that they were illegal because imposed by force. On 4 December he issued a note to the powers of Europe asking for their help in the restoration of the temporal power of the pope so necessary to his liberty.

If the Pope wished to keep his constitution and his liberal State—if he wished to avoid bloodshed—he must compromise with the rebels in Rome. So saw his moderate advisers in Gaeta, such as Rosmini, who wrote verbose memoranda to this effect. Rosmini lost influence steadily, until in May 1849 the Congregation of the Index met at Naples and condemned his works.

For the weight of opinion in Gaeta was to the contrary: the Pope himself, who had stood near the window when a secretary was shot dead at his side; Cardinal Antonelli, who because of his steadfastness in the danger grew ever more powerful; their host the king of Naples—all were sure now that the liberal experiment had failed and the only resource was to restore order and the power of the pope in Rome, if possible by concession of the Roman leaders, if not, by force.

The Romans needed the Pope's presence if they were to survive as a government. They sent three deputations to persuade him to return, and these were turned back at the frontiers of Naples. They even asked him for instructions. But underneath the debates about conciliation there was a naked contradiction: the Pope could not return unless he was assured by a government in Rome of the security of his person and his freedom to act, especially in things of

---

[19] For the flight from Rome, A. M. Ghisalberti, 'Intorno alla fuga di Pio IX', in *Archivio storico italiano* (1969), 109 ff.; Martina, *Pio IX (1846–50)*, 295 ff.

religion. No possible government in Rome could give this assurance without doubt whether it would hold.

So the Romans must do what they were there to do—create a constituent assembly, organize elections, and form a popular government—that is, replace the pope's secular monarchy with a democracy. In that democracy the pope's authority, if any, could be no more than nominal or ceremonial. Every move they made to this end—summon a constituent assembly, order elections—was illegal in the eyes of Gaeta and dug deeper the chasm between themselves and the Pope.

On 8 February 1849 the Constituent Assembly in Rome declared that the Pope no longer had temporal power. The draft constitution declared that the Pope was guaranteed independence in the exercise of his spiritual authority. It abolished any distinction of citizenship on the basis of religion, and Catholicism was no longer the state religion. There was to be universal (male) suffrage. The next day a majority voted themselves a republic and went to St Peter's to celebrate. The canons of St Peter's refused to take a service, but the organizers found a priest willing. The government was entrusted to a triumvirate. The triumvirs imposed heavy fines on the canons of St Peter's because they declined to sing a Te Deum in thanksgiving for the republic. Foreigners kept arriving to help—the Roman republic was ceasing to be led by Romans. On 5 March 1849 Mazzini arrived in Rome, full of mysticism and ideals and the lovely language of freedom, and was made one of the triumvirs. The reputation of Mazzini ensured that the Roman republic lost credit with many who might have been disposed to look upon it with favour. The troubles with the republic were two: most of Europe saw that it could not last, and it was bankrupt, with vast inflation.

Garibaldi arrived in April, in command of a formidable little force which the Austrians had driven out of Lombardy. Yet the republic was not very Jacobin. It passed a resolution to secularize all church property. It requisitioned the church bells to make cannon—but there were still enough bells to warn the city of attack. Garibaldi made his headquarters at the nunnery of San Silvestro and ejected the nuns, who prayed as they went, to Santa Pudenziana. The government arrested five bishops who had not run away. But there was no organized attempt to attack the clergy in Rome. They walked in the streets and sat at cafés in the open, but many went out dressed as laymen because they were liable to insult. When zealots hauled confessional boxes out of churches to burn them, the government stopped the destruction. When robberies occurred in churches, guards were stationed to protect them. Nuns and monks were legally allowed to leave their houses and orders.

At Gaeta they heard and believed that priests were being murdered in Rome. Mazzini did what he could to protect them, but there were a few deaths. A Dominican was killed as he walked in the road. A gang forced its way into the monastery of San Callisto in Trastevere and slaughtered ten monks. There was violence at Santa Croce. Vandals destroyed the coats of arms of Pope Alexander VI at the Castel Sant' Angelo. These were exceptions. Like the Pope some clergy fled from Rome; chief among them the Secretary of State Soglia, leaving that office free for Cardinal Antonelli to act as Pro-Secretary of State and so open the door to his astonishing career. The State took over the buildings of the Inquisition and some monasteries as houses for the poor. Garibaldi's band had a Barnabite[20] priest, Ugo Bassi, as chaplain; he had a reputation as one of the most powerful, and most political, preachers in Italy, and had been more often banned from the pulpit than any other preacher; he joined the papal army as a chaplain when it passed northward through Ancona to fight the Austrians, was wounded at the battle of Treviso, and after their later defeat came south to the republic at Rome. In the square at Anagni he preached to Garibaldi's men for two and a half hours and then was carried in triumph by the soldiers. But he was asked by Garibaldi to change his black cassock for the red shirt which was their uniform, because his men disliked the black; so he wore his black clerical hat and his Barnabite crucifix over a red shirt. Another Barnabite, Alessandro Gavazzi, a friend of Bassi, had something of the same career. Already a famous preacher, he marched with the pope's legion as a chaplain and was even blessed by Pius IX at a personal interview; at Padua and Bologna he had audiences which were like those of Peter the Hermit as he summoned to the first Crusade. After

[20] The Barnabites were founded at the church of St Barnabas in Milan about 1530, as an order engaged in pastoral work mainly in north Italy. The headquarters moved to Rome only in 1662. They grew more upper class, engaged more in education, and provided a lot of Italian bishops, and even some famous physicists. They always remained small in number: at their maximum in 1731 with 788 members. In the age of Joseph II and then of Napoleon they had a bad time (suppressed in 1810). They began to be restored from 1823. In 1875 they were 186 (cf. *DIP* s.v. Chierici regolari di San Paolo, col. 974); but these small numbers fail to represent the extent of their pastoral influence especially in upper- and middle-class Italy, and in some areas of the missions.

the retreat he joined the republicans—he kept his habit but wore a tricolour cross on his cloak—organized ambulances, and ministered in a hospital. Once he assisted at mass in St Peter's when the canons refused.

At the end of March 1849 the situation was changed by Piedmont. They crossed into Lombardy to try to retake Milan, still with papal troops under General Durando in their command. On 23 March Radetzky smashed them at the battle of Novara: Sardinia-Piedmont had to plead for peace, and its king, Charles Albert, abdicated. North Italy lay open to the Austrian army. So far as the Roman republic existed in the north, in Bologna and Ancona, it was defenceless. Austrian victory meant that it was suddenly the interest of France to send troops to Rome so that they could restore the Pope before the Austrians restored him.

French troops under General Oudinot landed at Civitavecchia, without resistance, on 23 April. In Gaeta the cardinals were less happy than might be expected, as they knew the new president of France, Louis Napoleon, to be a revolutionary adventurer whom they had every reason to distrust. They would have preferred rescue by Austrians.

Oudinot expected no resistance, and was astonished on 30 April to be knocked back before the walls of Rome. This difficulty was due not only to the battle-hardened irregulars, such as Garibaldi's band, it was a sign that some Romans wanted and believed in the republic. The French general had no desire to lose life in so un–French a campaign, and while the Austrians overran Bologna and Ancona, it took the French till 3 July to take Rome. The republic held out long after its plight was desperate, and the French soldiers were received with every sign of dislike as they marched through the city. Oudinot held a Te Deum in St Peter's but hardly anyone attended. The Pope was advised not to return till order was secure; the new rulers of the city were not sure of the attitude of the people. He did not return for nine months.

Historians have said that the Pope ought to have been more moderate while in Gaeta. On 20 April 1849, misled by what he heard, he issued an extreme allocution:

All justice, virtue, honour, religious principle has disappeared, and the horrible unnatural system of socialism and communism is propagated and dominates the faithful to the destruction of humanity . . . Rome has been turned into a forest of wild animals—and apostates and heretics and so-called communists and socialists and haters of the faith flock in and teach their diseased errors and pervert minds . . .   (*Acta Pii IX*, I. i. 174, 183–4.)

Historians have said that he ought not to have declared the activities of that government illegal, even though they were; that he should have refrained from an appeal to the powers which was an appeal to force. Rosmini was one who wanted him to act moderately and had to leave Gaeta hurriedly, almost to flee. Historians argued that by refusing to treat with Rome he thrust the republic ever more into the hands of the republicans and lost any chance that the moderates would regain authority in the State.

The truth that underlies this view is the discovery that the Pope's outlook had changed. In theory a pope could have thought to himself thus: 'I have tried constitutional government for my State. It has not worked. It ended in murder and revolution. Nevertheless, this fate of representative government was brought on by accidental circumstances, for instance, the behaviour of the Austrian army on the northern borders. It does not follow that representative government must end in murder and chaos. Therefore let us overthrow this illegal regime—that is a duty—but in overthrowing it let us offer moderate terms to the opposition which moderates can accept. This demand for representative government is not going away. Somehow we must find a compromise between papal authority and the political axioms of the age. Therefore let us offer moderate terms which will be accepted under the threat of force and then engage in discussion to find a way forward which will take us out of the impasse into which events have forced both sides.' Something like this attitude a Rosmini would have liked to see in the Pope.

But on the other side, it was said, this plea for representative government did not produce it. It created a Parliament—and, they said, Parliament is a pretence of representation, where people tell lies, abuse each other, turn elections into a game, encourage corruption in the public service, and so weaken a government that it cannot keep order in the streets. These were the opinions that surrounded Pius IX at Gaeta. The cardinals were nonentities apart from Antonelli, now a real Prime Minister, and Lambruschini still in opposition to everything the liberals stood for. But the Pope took no notice of any but Antonelli.

On 12 September 1849, now moved from Gaeta to the Bourbon palace at Portici in the kingdom of Naples, and not back to Rome, the Pope issued a proclamation that was moderate, with an amnesty, and proposals for reform in the government. The amnesty was not all-embracing, and did not forgive exempted officials and commanders. The purging of the republicans went on for nearly four years, so slow was the course of justice. During the eight months after Oudinot occupied Rome (the Pope still being in the kingdom of Naples) some 20,000 left Rome, nearly half of them expelled; that is, the purgation cost the city nearly one in eight of its inhabitants.[21] At least there was now order in the city, at a cost. But the roads outside were still plagued with ex-soldiers turned bandits.

The Pope returned solemnly to Rome on 12 April 1850. He was greeted by prepared ceremonies, respectful though not ecstatic applause from the spectators, and a Te Deum. It did not compare with the shouting that hailed his appearances three years before. The republican leaders and some moderates had gone. Mazzini was back in London, Garibaldi hidden in Tangier, Monsignor Muzzarelli took refuge in Corsica and ended his life, with mind darkened, near Turin. Mamiani (who had refused to work with the republic) went to Piedmont and became a professor of philosophy, Fabbri was back in Cesena in the Papal States but thought it wise to attend the Te Deum in the cathedral there for the Pope's return. Rosmini was in disgrace and back at Stresa. Father Ventura (who had recognized the legality of the republic but refused to be one of its officers) fled to France, and found his sermon on the dead revolutionaries of Vienna condemned by the Index because it held that a revolt for liberty is Christian; Ventura immediately submitted and had a friendly letter from the Pope. They were troubled in the French dioceses, asking where they could rightly allow him to minister, but he became an adviser in Christian political philosophy to the Emperor Louis Napoleon, and on his death-bed twelve years later received a blessing from Pius IX. Father Gavazzi left Italy, with the aid of a passport provided by the Americans, and became a militant anti-Catholic speaker among the Protestants of England, Scotland, and North America; he then founded an evangelical church and became pastor of the Italian Protestants in London. In 1860 he returned to be chaplain to Garibaldi and ten years after that founded a free Church in Italy and became its only professor of divinity.[22]

---

[21] Figures in Martina, *Pio IX (1846–50)*, 399–400.

[22] See the proceedings of a congress of 1988 on Ventura: G. Guccione (ed.), G. *Ventura e il pensiero d'ispirazione cristiana* (Florence, 1991). For Gavazzi, who died in 1889, see his

Father Ugo Bassi, still odd in black clerical hat with red shirt, went as Garibaldi's chaplain on the northward flight from Rome. Gaeta thought it astounding that Garibaldi could retreat from Rome with 4,000 men, but Oudinot still wanted little bloodshed and Garibaldi's men soon drifted away as they marched. Bassi's was the cruellest fate of the republic. He was caught by papal police near Commachio on the Adriatic, in the company of a Garibaldine captain who was a deserter from the Austrian army. The papal police handed him over to a Croat unit which was hunting Garibaldi, with the statement that he was armed when arrested. Better evidence shows that he was unarmed; that his war career was spent ministering to the wounded, sometimes at risk to his life; that he never contradicted his priest-hood—though he often said words better not said from a pulpit. But the red shirt, the report that he was armed, and the company of a deserter, meant that he was shot with the deserter. The cardinal and the papal authorities did not intervene with the Austrians but the report to Rome shows that they knew nothing of the decision. The Austrian commander cajoled nine priests at Bologna to sign a paper that the execution was just.

Instantly Bassi's grave became a goal of pilgrimage, and the papal government in Bologna moved the body by night to an unmarked place in the Carthusian cemetery.[23]

THE RESTORATION TO ROME

The Pope could not bear to reoccupy the Quirinal and henceforth lived inside the Vatican. He may have felt that the Vatican, on the edge of the city, was easier to protect in time of tumult than the Quirinal in the centre of popular Rome. Possibly he felt that the Quirinal was linked with his secular mission and the Vatican with his

Recollections of the Last Four Popes (1858), written, not impressively, in answer to Wiseman's book of the same title; Basil Hall, in *Studies in Church History*, 12 (Oxford, 1975), 303 ff., with literature; study by Luigi Santini, *Alessandro Gavazzi: Aspetti del problema religioso del Risorgimento italiano* (Modena, 1955).

[23] Bassi's body was moved again in 1859 to the family tomb. Genoa published his writings in 1864. Best now on Bassi is M. L. Trebiliani, *DBI*, with bibliography; the earliest biography, by L. Gualtieri (written in 1851 but not published—nor publishable—till 1861 at Bologna), is interesting because it is written by a young man of 20 who had fought to defend Venice and had known Bassi on the walls, and is consequently passionate; a book remarkable for both its atmosphere and its documents.

religious mission. He was under the protection of French troops; the north of his domains, all the Romagna, the Marches, and Umbria, was under the protection of Austrian troops. He was a pope whose secular power existed by virtue of two armies of non-Italians, like Gregory XVI in 1831.

The new fact was that the Pope was resigned to this situation. He might still take moderate measures. For example he allowed lay officials more and more power in the administration of the Papal State. But he lost any belief that papal authority could be reconciled with constitutional government. The State must be treated as exceptional in Europe because of its history and its vocation as the safeguard of the spiritual independence of the Vicar of Christ. Whether or not other governments were rightly absolute, this government must in the last resort be so because the pope's power as the Vicar of Christ could not be truly exercised unless he had the ultimate authority.

When it is said that henceforth he conceived of papal government as necessarily absolute, that does not mean that he conceived of it as a despotism. It was absolute in the old sense of papal practice; a weak government with a theoretical supreme power, limited in theory because its sovereign was more committed than anyone else to obey the laws of God, and in practice by those long-standing customs which hampered any executive action. A once liberal-minded pope became a resolute conservative. But the strength of his conservatism was not at first plain.

Some contemporaries, and some historians, attributed this change in the mind of Pope Pius IX to the influence of a single ecclesiastic. During the exile at Gaeta Giacomo Antonelli gained the trust of the Pope. He kept this trust for the next twenty-seven years.

He had a legal training and his ability was spotted in Gregory XVI's Curia. Gregory XVI put him in charge of the papal finances, which were in trouble, and he handled them capably. Moroni the barber-valet said that he was one of the few people at Gregory XVI's death-bed. When Pius IX succeeded, it was odd that so secular a person became the right-hand man of so unworldly a pope. His administrative gifts won him the cardinal's hat in 1847, for at that moment he had the reputation of moderation in policy towards the liberals; he was used in the development of the liberal constitution in which he seemed to share without reservation, and was pleased at the fall of Metternich. He handled well the delicate business of expelling the Jesuits from Rome. Pellegrino Rossi, whose judgement was sane and impartial, thought him the most considerable of the cardinals; and in his turn he advised the Pope to name Pellegrino Rossi as Prime Minister. Not long before Rossi's murder he was made Master of the Sacred Palace, and as such stood by the Pope after the attack upon the Quirinal and helped to plan the flight to Gaeta.

The murder, the attack, and the flight reversed Antonelli's attitude to politics. He now regarded Gregory XVI's first Secretary of State, Bernetti, whom even Metternich thought too reactionary, to be the master of politics whom they ought to be following. Since March 1848 he was Pro-Secretary of State and in 1850 became Secretary of State. At Gaeta he took the view that no compromise was any longer possible with the liberal idea and was the leader of the antiliberal point of view among the Pope's advisers.

Some therefore imagined that it was he who caused the Pope to change his mind. But the later Antonelli, at least, did not have this kind of influence over the Pope, who made up his own mind and sometimes took not much notice of his Secretary of State.

The change in the Pope's outlook was not due to a single adviser. If a sovereign has a distinguished Prime Minister stabbed to death on the steps of Parliament; or sees a chaplain murdered at his own window by a shot from a crowd outside; or has to flee disguised while the French ambassador pretends that he is still in conversation in his room—those are experiences which change a man's outlook more drastically than pressure from a not very spiritual secretary.

Yet the dominance of Antonelli over the Curia during the next twenty-six years, as a result of his courage, sense, and lack of compromise in the storm, was not a good result of the Roman republic. Of all the secular business, Cardinal Antonelli gathered the reins. He preferred second-rate men about him, whether to avoid rivals or because he preferred second-rate men. He was the last director of the unreformed papacy. He was a career ecclesiastic in the civil service of the Papal State, who all his life, and for all his eminence as an ecclesiastic, never went further than the order of subdeacon. He was a worldly clergyman born out of time; and was still in that character even though later in life he was at mass at 6 a.m. every morning and confessed once a week.

About anyone who was so powerful a Secretary of State for so long Rome would pass rumours and gossip of corruption and immorality. After his death a woman who claimed to be his illegitimate daughter sued his estate. The evidence did not prove that she was his daughter but did prove indiscretion in his behaviour. What could not be denied was the nepotism: three of his four brothers appeared in well-paid posts in the civil service, while the fourth ran the family estate. The eldest brother, Filippo, became the governor of the Bank of Rome, but was so incompetent (or worse) that three years later he was forced out. In wealth, property, palace, and collections of jewels and coins, Antonelli was the last of the Renaissance cardinals. He had not been ordained to be priestly, he was ordained because that opened a career. Unlike the best of Renaissance cardinals, he was not widely read. He trusted no one. He did not hold meetings or discussions, he decided whatever the Pope was not interested to decide.

But he had qualities. He was totally loyal to his master; he was discreet; he commanded the Pope's trust because he had helped to save him in the revolution. He was efficient at working at his desk. At interviews he combined charm and ability to please with a refusal to commit himself, and that was one quality that made a first-class diplomat. In conversation he had a reputation as a wit. His answers to letters from distant parts of the world asking for advice were usually sensible. He understood machinery and the practical, he had no idea of the force of public opinion and no interest in ideas or doctrines, he kept his eyes on detail and never lifted them to look at a wider perspective. He had no notion that it could make a difference to his work, his most practical work, if his master were to say, for example, that he would never reconcile himself with the modern world; because that was not a practical thing to say and could not affect (he thought) his desk.

As a pair of close colleagues they were curious. The Pope was warm, friendly, at times passionate, full of piety, loving the simple. Antonelli was courteous and pleasant to meet but he was too cold to like. He was half respected and half despised. The Pope might think, 'The ship of the Church is being driven onto the rocks by pirates; the helmsman can do nothing but pray; we are sure that at the twelfth hour God will help.' Cardinal Antonelli would think, 'The ship is being driven onto the rocks; the crew can do nothing but crash; so they will go down with honour, bands playing and flags flying, and still manning the ship expertly.' Of the two chief officers on the bridge, the captain had his eyes fixed on the stars, the mate held the wheel hard for the reef while he protected the captain from worry.

3

CATHOLIC POWER

The nine years from 1850 to 1859 were the last years of Catholic power in Europe. The Pope was restored to his States by France and Austria. France reacted against its revolution of 1848 by accepting a dictator, who was a dubious Catholic and an unreliable man, but whose power rested on the support which French Catholics gave him and who must encourage Catholicism. Austria reacted against its revolution of 1848 by a desire to help its Church as a safeguard against more revolution, whether in its Italian domains or among its Slavs and Hungarians. These two, France and Austria, were believed to be the two great powers of continental Europe. So long as they did not quarrel, the Pope's power was secure. That was a proviso, because for three centuries they had quarrelled from time to time about northern Italy. But for this decade, all was almost happy.

In addition, after the civil wars in Spain, there were a few years when Queen Isabella looked like, indeed was, a truly Catholic sovereign doing all she could to foster Catholicism in Spain. And in the kingdom of Naples, Ferdinand, least democratic of kings, and troublesome to the Pope because he preferred to run his own Church rather than let the Pope interfere, was another truly pious Catholic and, after playing the host at Gaeta, a close personal friend of the Pope. No other sovereign wrote letters to Pius IX on such terms of familiarity.

LOUIS NAPOLEON

The Paris Revolution of 1848 created a French republic, and a constituent assembly and legislature in which Lamennais sat on the extreme left. He had been a solitary among the intellectuals of the French republicans, but won their backing when he served a year in gaol for issuing a violent republican pamphlet.[1] During the year

---

[1] *Le Pays et le gouvernement* (1840); sentence, 26 Dec. 1840: a year in prison, and a 2,000 fr. fine.

before the Revolution the conservative Prime Minister Guizot received private information that the political groups that had made most progress during the last ten years were the 'communists' of Lamennais.[2] When the Revolution came in February 1848 Lamennais hailed it with ecstasy and hope, and imagined that injustice would vanish. After the Revolution he drafted a constitution for the republic of France. He founded a journal which was the most interesting newspaper of the republican press but it was stopped by the government after a few months. Lamennais tried to force them to prosecute him but in vain.

The new republic lasted less than three years. On 10 December 1848 Louis Napoleon was elected president of the French Republic. Part of his electioneering was the liberty of the pope. Lamennais retired into silent votes in opposition, and when Louis Napoleon by a coup turned his presidency into a dictatorship Lamennais left politics and spent his last three years translating Dante. France looked back upon him as sad and lonely. He had dedicated the first half of his life to the pope and was repudiated; and dedicated the second half of his life to the people and then the people accepted denial of his democratic ideals. When he was known to be dying various Catholics strove to win access to bring him back to the faith; the only one with a chance was his old friend Father Ventura. But he let none of them in and refused to have any religious sign at the funeral, and insisted on being buried in a pauper's grave without a mark.

The funeral did not go unobserved. The government was afraid of a scene, and ordered it early in the morning, and provided a sizeable body of soldiers to keep order. Despite the hour a great crowd appeared to escort him home. The cortège went by back streets but in vain, there were scuffles, and fighting, and truncheons wielded, and blood spilled. The troops let only eight persons into the cemetery.

The key to the Pope's comfort was Louis Napoleon: he kept the French garrison in Rome. These troops were necessary to the Pope's freedom of action. It was important that Louis Napoleon should not decide to take them away. Therefore it mattered what sort of a person he was, what his attitude was to Catholicism, and whether he stayed in power in France.

He had taken part in the revolution against Gregory XVI: he was not a devout Catholic. In the spring of 1853 he married—in religious

    [2] D. W. J. Johnson, *Guizot: Aspects of French History, 1787–1874* (London, 1963), 241, citing the national archives.

splendour at Notre Dame, with five cardinals taking part—the beautiful Spaniard Eugénie de Montijo, who had been educated by the nuns at the Sacré Cœur in Paris, was devout, and found religion a heartful consolation to her, especially in the tragedies that afflicted her family. In the exile in England to which at last they both went she founded an abbey at Farnborough for the repose of their souls, and it seemed natural, when she died, to clothe her body in a nun's habit for the funeral. Eugénie loved Louis Napoleon and was faithful to him; he loved her and was unfaithful to her, the curious effect of which was to increase her influence upon him in politics, so that she began to sit with him at meetings of the cabinet; not always to advantage because when she started to talk she had no consciousness of time. By contrast he was silent at meetings.

She steadily believed that her husband ought to help and defend the pope. In her old age her memory told her that her admiration for Pius IX was qualified, because she admired his successor more. 'Leo XIII has all the virtues of Pius IX and also everything that Pius IX did not have. I often used to say (later) "If only the Emperor had had Leo XIII to deal with and not Pius IX!" ';[3] the implication being that they were both good religious men but that Pius IX had not the political wisdom of his successor.

Napoleon III had small belief in the Papal State as a sensible way of governing Central Italy. He did not know much about the Church and was not very interested in it. He surrounded himself with undevout cabinet ministers. He did not like it if liberal Italians saw France as the backer of an illiberal regime in Italy. He was a dictator and dictators need to stay in power by drama. The name of Napoleon sang of romantic conquests in Italy. It was inevitable that a French emperor would think about the weak Italian States as a field for French influence. The memory of Napoleon suggested someone who restored worship to France but who kidnapped two popes. Therefore his opinions, and his record of unreliability, carried danger for the Pope.

What should be the Church's attitude to a *coup d'état*? This moral difficulty kept appearing during the nineteenth and twentieth centuries. The old Catholic right wing, that is Brittany and the Vendée, was steady against Louis Napoleon because it was loyal to the Bourbon king/pretender. But since the alternative to Louis

---

[3] M. Paléologue, *Les Entretiens de L'Impératrice Eugénie* (Paris, 1923), 41.

Napoleon was a government of the anti-Catholic left, most Catholics—whether they were of the ultramontane right like the journalist Veuillot, or of the moderate centre like Montalembert the former disciple of Lamennais—must decide for Louis Napoleon whether or not he was illegal. Several bishops urged their flocks to vote 'Yes' in the plebiscite which was to confirm the dictatorship. Cardinal Gousset said that it was the finger of God. Pius IX heard the news of the *coup d'état* with pleasure and his attitude was conveyed to the French church leaders. When the plebiscite was past, Pius IX summoned the officers of the Rome garrison and thanked the French army 'for saving France and Europe from the calamitous bloody plots of anarchists'.[4]

The memory of the French henceforth linked the clergy with the *coup d'état*. That had consequences twenty years later.

Louis Napoleon was kind to the Church; restored the Panthéon to worship; wanted Sunday kept quietly; was willing for a tighter control of alcohol and the wine bars; arranged that cardinals should have seats in the Senate; made it easier for nunneries to be founded; exempted ordinands from serving in the army; allotted money to raise the very poor pay of curates; decorated bishops; stiffened the censorship on anti-Catholic books and tracts; exiled opponents. In the *Univers* Veuillot wrote articles in praise of absolutism (limited by the laws of God) as the best form of government and looked back with admiration on the reign of Louis XIV. Father Ventura, unexpectedly, hailed the person representative of all the people by universal suffrage.

Not all Catholics liked what was done. Montalembert (after a few months of optimism), Lacordaire, Dupanloup, and Falloux did not (but Dupanloup and Falloux were, like the Bretons, loyal to the Bourbon line of kings). Archbishop Sibour of Paris was indignant and refused to thank Napoleon for restoring the Panthéon to worship, because it would look like accepting the regime. He uttered a formal protest against the error of linking the Church with one political party. While Pius IX was at Gaeta he wrote the Pope a long frank letter.[5] He said that what had happened—the flight to Gaeta, the

---

[4] J. Maurain, *La Politique ecclésiastique du Second Empire de 1852 à 1869* (Paris, 1930), 13, from *Journal de Rome* and the *Moniteur*.

[5] Dated 24 Mar. 1849, summarized in Martina, *Pio IX (1851–66)* (Rome, 1986), 256. Sibour had translated the *Summa* of St Thomas Aquinas and had a part in the editing of *L'Avenir*. From 1836 he was bishop of Digne with a reputation for pastoral care; he loved St Augustine of Hippo and helped to translate his relics from Pavia back to Bone in Algeria, by

declaration of the Roman republic—had cancelled all the good that was done during the moderate years after the Pope's accession. There was again the feeling of hostility to the Church and clergy. Gaeta identified the Pope with the politics of reaction. Sibour asked for the revival of the earlier policy of moderation and respect for Italian nationality. The Pope replied but took no notice of the plea. And when there was a Te Deum in Notre Dame to say thanks for the dictatorship of Louis Napoleon, it was Sibour who celebrated the rite. Montalembert refused an invitation to be a senator.

Baillès, the bishop of Luçon, the diocese in which was the Vendée, refused to sing Te Deum in celebration of the new emperor when other cathedrals were asked to do so, and declined, despite pressure from the government, his archbishop, and even the Pope, to put the name of Napoleon into the state prayers. Since the Vendée was the heart of the Bourbon loyalties of old France, his people backed their bishop with enthusiasm and made it very hard to get rid of him. For three years the trouble went on, threats from prefects, vain prosecutions of clergy, appeals to Rome against the bishop. His priests suffered and then doubted the cause. In April 1855 Napoleon escaped an attempt to murder him and Te Deums were ordered, but the bishop of Luçon refused. He declined to order public prayers for the Empress Eugénie's pregnancy. Finally the French government told the Pope roughly that if he did not remove this bishop they would act by force. The Pope ordered him to Rome. He refused to go. The Pope commanded him to resign. He refused. So at last the Pope appointed an administrator for the diocese, and forced Baillès out. The French government had driven the Pope to a doubtful action, to be repeated nearly a century later in the plight of Cardinal Mindszenty of Hungary, getting rid of a bishop who was a good man and an excellent pastor. The result was remarkable. Instead of disgrace, Baillès was summoned to Rome and given responsible posts in the Curia.[6]

Sovereigns who lack constitutional authority need ritual blessing to persuade the people that all is well. Napoleon I had forced Pope Pius VII to preside at his coronation in Notre Dame. Pius VII consented because he thought that so he could obtain better conditions

the ruins of Hippo. In the troubles of 1848, after Quelen's successor Archbishop Affre was killed on the street barricade, he became archbishop of Paris, nominated by the temporary President General Cavaignac.

[6] For Baillès, see Maurain, *La Politique ecclésiastique*, 86 ff.

for the Church in post–revolutionary France and Italy; and because if he refused he might provoke reprisals.

The question reappeared. Should Napoleon III be crowned in Notre Dame? He had the idea that, like his uncle, he should persuade the Pope to come to Paris to anoint him emperor and confer a sacred approval of his empire. The Pope was not too indisposed to this idea. If he consented to the ritual blessing, however distasteful, could he do what mattered, gain more freedoms for the work of the Church in France? The Concordat by which the Church was restored after the years of terror had been supplemented by the so-called Organic Articles of 1802, which Napoleon I imposed to limit the freedoms of the pope; for example by controlling communications between pope and French clergy, making the decisions of synods liable to approval by the State, and compelling seminaries for training priests to teach the Gallican Articles which declared that General Councils are superior to popes.

But the support for a new coronation was tepid. The only enthusiasts were Bonapartists in France. The French legitimists, who looked back to the historic line of kings, the Bourbons, were shocked at the idea. The Austrian emperor was thought to be an objector. Gaston de Ségur in Rome invented a plan for a double coronation, in one journey the Pope should go to Paris for Napoleon—'marvellous effect in France, the death-blow to Gallicanism . . . once at Paris the Emperor would consent to everything that you want'—and then onward to Vienna to crown Francis Joseph—in Germany it would 'be a decisive stroke against the Protestants'. Cardinal Antonelli set up a committee to advise on what concessions by the Emperor were enough to pay for a coronation, and, if the Pope decided to refuse, how it could be done with least offence to the French.[7] It was not

---

[7] G. Martina, *AHP* 10 (1972), 212 ff.; Maurain, *La Politique ecclésiastique*, 46 ff.; Ségur, *Ségur*, Eng. trans. (London, 1884), 62 ff. Gaston de Ségur, born in Paris to a count (1820), studied to be a painter and was attaché to the French ambassador to the Pope; gave up his career and was ordained (1849); served in Rome (1852–6) but soon became totally blind; learnt the liturgy by heart and for 25 years exercised a blind apostolate in Paris—to prisoners, the young, artists, and at retreats, and spent hours a day as a confessor; he was a friend of the leading ultramontanes, and a close friend of Gounod who wrote some religious music under his inspiration. His book on the Pope, published in 1860, was in its 78th edition by 1899. His book on the holy communion, published in 1860, had its 143rd edition in 1906. One of his books, on piety and the interior life, was to his horror and shame banned by the Holy Office in its Italian translation and he instantly withdrew the French original and revised it. He started by being a dedicated advocate of Napoleon III but could never forgive him for what he did to Italy and in the last years of life was a royalist.

easy to refuse, because de Ségur advised it, and this monsignor had influence with the Pope, the Empress, and the more papal-minded of French churchmen. Empress Eugénie seemed to want it. De Ségur said that the effects of the coronation would reach further than France, to strengthen monarchy in Europe and so the stability of the nations. Pius IX decided that he would be prepared to do it, seeing it as a chance to dispense with the Organic Articles and perhaps ensure that marriage in church became the legal form of marriage for France. He thought it a marvellous vision that he travel across Europe crowning heads of State. But something told him that it would not do. Napoleon did not push hard, and his lawyers were fierce against tampering with the marriage law or sacrificing the control over the Church; and the plan faded away without the need for a rude and public 'No'.

If Louis Napoleon wanted to menace the Pope, he could threaten to withdraw his army from Rome and leave him to the mercy of Garibaldi and his guerrillas. Everyone, including the Pope, knew that he could not afford to do any such thing. It would destroy his power-base in France. The Emperor had to keep the Pope safe in Rome, not for the Pope's sake but for his own. The Pope could afford to take no notice of the wishes of the Emperor upon whom he depended physically.

In 1854 Napoleon III was fortunate that his two political needs, to be friendly to Catholics and to do things that were dramatic, coincided with a chance of martial glory.

In the fourteenth century the Franciscans had won the right to be the guardians of the holy places of Palestine under their Arab rulers; and from 1620 the French government was given the right of political protection for this Western oversight of the holy places. But many of the Christians in those lands were Orthodox. With growing Russian power, the pressure of Orthodox clergy to gain rights in the churches at Jerusalem and Bethlehem grew vehement, and the Franciscans were pushed out of customs which they regarded as theirs by immemorial usage.

They appealed to France with its duty of protection. Napoleon III, posing as the authentic Catholic ruler, protested in Constantinople and demanded that the customary rights be restored. The Turkish government had no desire for a quarrel and freely referred the dispute to a commission of inquiry. But no one that mattered wanted a settlement. Tsar Nicholas felt a religious duty to the Orthodox in

Jerusalem but he wanted a war because he thought that non-Christians ought to be turned out of Europe, which would entail a Russian protectorate in the Balkans. Napoleon III wanted a war because dictators need wars and because it was good to be seen as the protector of Catholics. And once the threat of war existed, Britain must help France, which meant helping Turkey against Russia, because it would not tolerate heavy Russian power in the Eastern Mediterranean. Hence the Crimean war, in which half a million men died to no purpose; except that the war did what it was expected to do, to raise the prestige of Napoleon III among the French people, confirm that he was the protector of Catholics, and prevent an excess of Russian power in the Balkans; and also what was not expected, that is, to produce far higher standards of nursing.

The Pope said nothing, either to encourage France to protect Catholics in the Levant, or to ask anyone not to go to war. He needed to say nothing because he must not risk worse persecution of the Poles inside the Russian empire. He told the Tsar that he commended the Catholics of Russia to his care and prayed for peace. The Tsar had the idea of using this friendship to persuade Austria, the nearest neutral power, that it was better to fight on the side of Christians and not to bolster a Muslim State. The sultan of Turkey countered this by making noises about an imminent toleration for all religions in the Ottoman empire. When the war was ended, the Pope asked the sovereigns of France and Austria to do what they could to protect Catholics in the East; and his language expected that their political 'protection' would diminish Islam and Eastern Orthodoxy and foster the Catholic faith. He begged Napoleon not to allow the Catholic representatives at the Peace Conference to slide into indifference to religion, which is 'so common in our days'.[8]

The climax of the alliance between Pope and Emperor came in 1856. Eugénie wished the Pope to stand godfather to her child. Pius IX agreed and sent Cardinal Patrizi to be his proxy at the baptism in Notre Dame. All the bishops of France were invited and nearly all attended; only one was known to refuse because he did not think Louis Napoleon legitimate.

In France itself, under these conditions, with an Emperor friendly to Catholics, the Church prospered. The number of monks and nuns

---

[8] Pius IX to Napoleon III, 8 Feb. 1856; in P. Pirri, *Pio IX e Vittorio Emanuele II dal loro carteggio privato*, MHP 17 (Rome, 1951), ii, pt. 2, 5 ff.; and cf. Angelo Martini, 'La Santa Sede e la questione d'Oriente', in *CC* (1958) 1: 587 ff., 2: 149 ff., 4: 169 ff., 494 ff.

increased rapidly. Nuns, in 1851, numbered approximately 34,000; ten years later nearer 89,000; monks, in 1851, only 3,000; ten years later more than 17,600.[9]

For the time being the French people accepted peace, of necessity, in the long quarrel over religious education. In 1850, the Minister of Education was a liberal Catholic viscount, perhaps a grandson by an illegitimate route of the executed King Louis XVI. Falloux was a natural diplomat who, it was said, could have stepped out of the age of Louis XIV. The Falloux law of March 1850 was an intelligent compromise. The State was maintained as the controller of all education. Churchmen were joined to the governing body, 'the University'. Any group could open secondary schools under the condition that the head teacher had a degree; the bishops could nominate assistant teachers who need not have a degree; but the examiners were appointed by the State. It had to be fought through Parliament: Victor Hugo made a speech against Church power in education, in which he mentioned Galileo, Torquemada, and the Inquisition. The law was resented by the radicals who wanted to take religion out of schools and who disliked monks and nuns. It was almost as fiercely resented by those Catholics, including several leading bishops, who regarded the compromise with the State as a treachery and could hardly think Falloux a loyal Catholic. But the moderates, the barely Catholic Thiers, and those such as Montalembert and Dupanloup, were strong enough to carry it (March 1850; voting 399:237). For the time it helped the Catholic revival in France.

Government raised the grants to the Church (not more than was just, since it still held all the old Church endowments confiscated by the Revolution). The French middle class were frightened by what happened in the 1848 Revolution and joined a revival of religious practice. Because there were far greater numbers of monks and nuns, and because there was more money everywhere in the Church, many more schools were run by religious, and many more middle-class children received a Catholic education in Catholic schools. Towards the end of the time of Louis Napoleon the number of children being educated by the Church approached the number educated in the public schools.

The growing number of religious meant that the French Church during those decades was to the missionary movement of the

---

[9] *HJHC* viii. 95.

Catholic Church what the American Church was during several decades of the twentieth century. By reason of its resources in money and its number of possible vocations, it was able to supply much the most numerous body of priests and nuns working in the mission fields.

In the midst of this revival of faith France grew more divided about religion. It has been proved by modern enquiry that the division was not by class nor by income nor by profession but by area or district; that is, the division of France was a curiously physical division. In the west, for example, they went to worship at mass, sent their sons into the priesthood, and produced vocations to the religious orders. In Paris the radical tradition of the French Revolution was strong. Hardly anyone went to church in some areas of the city. The absence of religious practice was accompanied, no doubt because of the long folk-memory of revolution, by an anticlericalism that was usually contemptuous, sometimes bitter, and at times ran to violence against demonstrations of religion in public. Surprisingly, Provence was a country district not unlike Paris, and was far from being the only such. It is possible that in some of these areas the deep-seated divisions of France over religion ran back far into history, even to the wars of religion of the sixteenth century. We find similar geographical differences in Spain, between the north and the south; but there it is easier to explain.

If these anticlerical areas were industrial, which several of them were, the division became a class division. The working man might not say that he was not a Christian, but he had no use whatever for the Church. He—but less so his wife—was alienated, and no amount of evangelism, missions, or public processions, could do anything to shake his conviction that the Church was not for him; and for some, that the Church was bad for society and on the side of capitalists.

In addition, this flourishing French Church was associated with a dictator. The one thing certain about dictators is that they do not last for ever. When a dictator is overthrown, anyone or any institution associated with his favour then suffers.

Still, what was clear in the 1850s and even 1860s was religious revival. The weaknesses of it, and the danger of the underlying bitterness, were not so clearly seen. This ardent though temporary revival, in that part of Europe where most were Catholics or nominal Catholics, was as strong a backing for an ultramontane pope as the presence of the protecting French troops in Rome.

THE AUSTRIAN CONCORDAT

Meanwhile in Austria Rome achieved one of its successes of the century.

The rule of Schwarzenberg was as absolute as, or more so, than the rule of Metternich—with one exception. Since the eighteenth century the Austrian government maintained strict control over its Church—the philosophy of State known as Josephism. But as in France, revolution caused statesmen to think that to avoid a repetition the Church must be encouraged; and the obvious way to make the Church more alive might be to give it more freedom.

The empire was far from being universally Catholic. Hungary had a lot of Protestants, and the Romanians were mostly Orthodox, with some hundreds of thousands of Protestants who were German by race and language. Still, Catholicism was the main religion of the empire—Austrians, especially Tyrolese; Croats, Slovenes, and Slovaks; many Hungarians; the North Italians; and some Czechs. Traditionally Catholicism was the established religion. The government therefore had the idea of using religion, as an alternative to race and language, in a unifying cement of the State. This motive made for friendly legal treatment of the Catholic Church.

On their side the Austrians needed the pope. They were troubled that they ruled northern Italy by force, and not with the affection of the people. Since crusading days against the Turks, they had won the vocation of being the protector of the Church. They saw that the Catholic Church was the one moral force in Italy that stood on the side of peace and against revolutionary war.

The Austrian Church was once one of the Churches in Europe to be led by aristocrats. The French Revolution changed that. Like the rest of Catholic Europe it began to be a Church led by the middle class.

Salzburg was a prince-bishopric secularized in 1803, and for years its beautiful palace was left in ruins. In 1823 it obtained an archbishop who was the first bourgeois after centuries of noblemen. Twelve years later the chapter elected an Austrian prince to succeed him: Schwarzenberg, only 26 when he became archbishop, and the brother of the future president of the reaction after the 1848 Revolution. He was a good archbishop. He gained for the college at Salzburg, as its professor of church history, the priest who became

identified with the revival of the Austrian Church during the middle
of the nineteenth century, Joseph Rauscher. In 1853 Rauscher
became prince-archbishop of Vienna. He was trusted by both
Church and State. He dedicated himself to freeing the Austrian
Church from the trammels of State control. By the respect his qualities won, he created the conditions for a Concordat between Rome
and the empire.[10]

The Concordat was signed in 1855. It meant the end of the historic control of the Catholic Church by the State. The pope was
given freedom to communicate with the Church in the empire and
his authority was formally recognized. Church pronouncements
needed no State licence. The emperor kept the right to put forward
the names of new bishops for approval by Rome, and also the names
of most of the canons of cathedrals, but the bishops freely chose the
incumbents and controlled the seminaries in which they were
trained, and had the free right to establish new monasteries (hence the
Austrian ban on the Jesuits ended). Religious teaching in State schools
must be in accordance with the Catholic faith. No one might teach
theology or canon law in the universities who was not approved by
the bishop. Church courts were given the right to supervise marriage
and should do it according to Catholic law. The State agreed to cen-
sor books that were against the Church. The Vienna government was
determined that it should apply to the whole empire. The Hungarian
primate Cardinal Scitovsky, worked to prevent it from applying to
Hungary, but in vain.

The key without which the Concordat could not have happened
was the new marriage law. This was the law most offensive to liberal
and Protestant Europe.

Here the Church of the second Catholic power of Europe, as in
France, gained new privileges and influence upon its government and
the legislation of the country. The Concordat helped the Church in
Lombardy and the Veneto—where it lasted only a few years. The
Pope was very pleased with it. The young Emperor Francis Joseph
had not a deep religious heart, but was conscious of the Habsburg
tradition that Austria was the protector of the Catholic Church. He

[10] Joseph Othmar Rauscher, 1797–1875; priest 1823, academic career, professor of church
history at Salzburg 1825 and published a 2-volume history of the Christian Church, head of
oriental academy at Vienna 1832, tutor to future emperor Francis Joseph 1844; prince-
bishop of Seckau 1849, the year after the Revolution; prince-archbishop of Vienna 1853,
cardinal 1855.

fulfilled the formal religious duties of his station faithfully and into extreme old age walked in the procession on Corpus Christi. Young though he was he already had influence in meetings of the cabinet. He thought that in return for the freedoms which he had given, the State could justly expect the clergy to help the government in building the society which it thought right. He believed that he was helping to make the law of Austria accord with the law of God. Some of his advisers also thought that by thus standing out as a great Catholic power Austria would gain the backing of the South German and Rhineland Catholics in disputes with the growing might of Prussia. They also hoped that they would weaken the influence of Louis Napoleon in Italy.

As in France this new privileged position of the Catholic Church caused fury among the liberals of the country. One of them described it as going to Canossa. Another said that it was made by women, children, parsons, and the Tyrolese who had united to make a new kingdom of God.[11] It shocked Protestant Germany. From London *The Times* expected the Austrian Concordat to be the ruin of the Austrian empire.

Its opponents in the empire were (1) all the non-Catholics, who expected trouble in mixed marriages and in schools; (2) most of the German-speaking middle class; (3) many civil servants, accustomed to the axioms of the Josephist tradition, who thought it wrong to lose control of Church leaders; (4) the Hungarian bishops; (5) the Lombard bishops; (6) many of the lower clergy who were afraid of bishops getting such power over them. But most non-German-speakers among the people were much in favour of the Concordat.

What happened carried the same danger which threatened France. The league between throne and altar linked the Church with an aristocratic State and made it one of the mainstays (in theory) of the unity of the empire. The emperor ruled a kingdom in which Hungarians and Italians resented Austrian government. He fancied that the State could only be healthy if Austria and Hungary ceased to be two distinct societies, and believed that only the pope had the power to achieve this in a common Church.

In North Italy there was alienation now between governors and governed, so that Italians boycotted cafés, theatres, and clubs that the Austrians frequented. Mazzini had disappeared to London, but the

[11] A. Wandruszka and P. Urbanitsch (eds.), *Die Habsburgermonarchie 1848–1918*, iv. *Die Confessionen* (Vienna, 1985), 30, 34.

Rome triumvirate had made his name inspiring and in Lombardy and Venice there were secret Mazzini societies. In Mantua the chairman of the group was a priest, professor of philosophy at the seminary, Don Enrico Tazzoli, their secretary Castellazzo an undergraduate at Pavia who had fought for Garibaldi in Rome. Some of them were absurd: one had a plan to kidnap the Austrian emperor when he visited Venice, and in his gaol the kidnapped emperor would buy his release by ceding Lombardy or would be blown up by the conspirators. But Tazzoli was not wild; not at all like Garibaldi's former crank-chaplains such as Gavazzi. He was a quiet, upright, and thinking clergyman. He distributed Mazzini's paper money (the wildest of Mazzini's schemes) and kept conscientious accounts. Because he knew that the accounts would betray the names of conspirators if found by the police, he encoded them, using *Pater Noster* as the key to the code.

In December 1851 the police traced one of Mazzini's notes to the house of a priest, Don Ferdinand Bosio. They tortured him and after three weeks he directed them to Tazzoli. It took them four months to break the code; there is still an argument whether they broke it by torturing the secretary Castellazzo or because the code-breakers in Vienna guessed that a priest might use the key *Pater Noster*, or whether they were competent code-breakers. In prison Tazzoli tried to take the blame for everyone. When attacked for misusing his priesthood he said that a priest must be of the mind of the people whom he served, and that their ideal of liberty was right and he was right to share it. The archbishop of Milan and the patriarch of Venice intervened on his behalf; Bishop Corti of Mantua appealed to the Pope to intervene, but what came out of Rome had no force, for Pius IX blamed what the guilty had done. The appeals were to no purpose, the government was rigid, it forced the bishop of Mantua to unfrock Tazzoli by the threat that if he refused they would execute other priests. Tazzoli was executed by hanging on 7 December 1852 outside the gate of Mantua fortress, and died serenely. The business of unfrocking him agonized Bishop Corti and he tried to resign his see but was not allowed to and the affair caused a loss of confidence between him and the Pope.[12]

---

[12] Two other priests were executed, five more had penalties commuted, and four of these at least were almost at once allowed to resume pastoral work, on the government's condition that they changed parishes. Bishop Corti tried to resign again six years later and was again refused; cf. F. Engel-Janosi, *Österreich und der Vatikan* (Graz, 1960), i. 75, and Martina,

THE POPE AND CATHOLIC POWER

The Church, whether in Italy, France, or Austria, built power in the 1850s; it also built resentment. Sooner or later the resentment would force the reversal of the power-building, in France with catastrophic consequences because of a divided society with class and religious tensions rooted in the past, in Austria with controversy far less bitter because it was a country with no successful radical revolutions in its own past, but still making for a strife which would affect the politics of the State for decades to come.

Pope Pius IX then was a pope who had rejected the liberal ideal; who could feel the rising tide of pro-Roman sentiment and devotion all over the Church; who was safe from the Italians because of French and Austrian soldiers, and who saw the Catholic powers of Europe becoming still more favourable to Catholicism and friendly to the Church, and giving more of that freedom which Rome had always wanted and which the Catholic governments of the eighteenth century refused to concede; and who saw Protestant powers like Britain and Holland powerless to stop very public Catholic advance.

This was a time when Rome felt again the sense of religious revival. The revolution was past, the Vicar of Christ had returned to his throne, Europe, except in Piedmont, Switzerland, and Baden, had returned or was returning to its senses. The papacy could sense the people rallying to its cause. From Hungary, especially from the Banat, came stories of the conversion of whole villages.[13] Those who looked to France could hardly find a Gallican priest, whatever the state of the bishops. Those who looked to Germany could hardly find a Febronian priest or a Josephist priest (or so at the time it seemed).

Irish emigration took many Irishmen to the United States. By 1850 the Catholic population of the United States was near double what it had been ten years before. Ten years after that the number of American Catholics was near five times what it had been in 1840, and

---

Pio IX (1851–66), 87–8, who includes letters between the Pope and Bishop Corti; Spellanzon, *Storia del Risorgimento dell'unità d'Italia* (Milan, 1933–), viii. 88 ff. The later career of Castellazzo was extraordinary: he fought as one of Garibaldi's Thousand and was one of his agents outside Rome before the battle of Mentana; he fought with his legion in France; and became an eminent Freemason. But when he was elected to the Italian Parliament, the blot—if it were a real blot, which was never settled—that he betrayed Father Tazzoli and others to the police wrecked his later career.

[13] Banat, *CC* (1856), 1: 242.

ten years later again it was about seven and a half times what it had
been in 1840, and had become a Church of four and a half million
souls, or 11 per cent of the population. Of course this increase was
not all Irish. Germans were very numerous after 1848, and there were
Spanish, and towards the end of the period the multitudinous Italian
emigration began. But the Irish were the most numerous in these
middle years. They gave the Church in America an Irish leadership
and an Irish atmosphere. For a long time it was almost impossible to
become an archbishop without being of Irish descent. To be a leader
in America it was necessary to speak English, which the other immigrants spoke less easily. Moreover they were always short of priests
and needed to import them from Europe, and Ireland was the best
source. In addition a seminary was founded at Louvain (1857) to train
Europeans who would agree to work in the United States. Two years
after that the Pope founded a college in Rome to give American
priests a better training. The Irish imparted to American Catholicism
an urbanized and working-class character. And since in Ireland
Catholicism was associated with Irish nationality, and the pope was a
counterweight to the queen of England, American Catholicism also
wanted strong links with Rome.

The free constitution of the United States served the Catholic
Church well. The Pope went on founding dioceses without objection from anyone that mattered. This freedom was important. The
organization of the ministry was a difficult and at times desperate
problem as the groups of immigrants came flooding in, often unable
to speak the language and usually too poor to contribute to the maintenance of a church or its priests. In relation to their numbers, they
had small influence on American public life or society during those
decades.

A like strengthening happened in Canada. There the French
Canadians were nearly half the people, at one time more than half,
but even when, as most of the time, a minority, a very numerous
minority. They had the attitude of a minority. They had the instinct
that they needed to preserve their French language and a way of life
against a dominant Anglo-Saxon language and culture. To effect this
they turned to the Church. Catholicism became the cement which
was to hold together French-Canadian nationality and civilization.
The bishops and priests grew powerful. They could control elections,
or make a big difference to them. Because of this nationalism in a
provincial form, it was a very conservative type of Catholicism.

Veuillot, most extreme Roman publicist in all the Church, had more influence in French Canada than in France.

Of emigrants from Great Britain the Irish were most on the move. Australia, opening up after 1830, attracted Irishmen and by about 1860 Catholics were about a quarter of the population. Catholicism was entangled with their nationality, and they were loyal in their allegiance to the see of Rome. But they were still so distant by length of voyage that they made no difference to the policy of the Church in Europe. And the British government was powerful enough to ensure that the Catholic leadership in Australia was kept within a charmed circle of English immigrant priests. They did not have a cardinal till 1885 and by then he was an Irishman.

It was a new consciousness of a world-wide authority. That for the last time in history the pope was surrounded by pious Catholic crowned heads, some of them with real power, was weighty in the psychology of the 1850s. The emperor of the French might not be a satisfactory Catholic but had a devout queen who was truly pious. The emperor of Austria might not be very religious but was certainly a practising Catholic and valued the Catholic faith in his empire— and still ruled Lombardy and Venice. The king of the Two Sicilies was a very devout Catholic and had absolute rule in his territories. Miracles happened at the tomb in St Clare at Naples of his queen, Maria Cristina. She was born in Sardinia as the youngest daughter of King Victor Emmanuel I. After her father's abdication of the throne she considered becoming a nun but was persuaded by her family to marry the young King Ferdinand of Naples, though Metternich did not like Ferdinand to marry into so liberal a family. She died at the birth of the heir to the throne Francis II (Bomba) who ever afterwards revered her. It was a very religious court. There were rumours in Italy that the marriage was unhappy and even that the king beat her brutally; but the rumours came from Italian liberals who hated her illiberal husband. Mazzini was glad at her death. Her letters show a happy person. She was beautiful and cared about the people and though she was shy they cheered her as she went by. Her days in Naples were never without masses, usually more than one, she used the rosary often, and whenever her husband went to a cabinet meeting she spent time on her knees. When the miracles started to happen, official investigators were cautious, but came to accept them when reliable witnesses, including physicians, gave their evidence; and devout persons wondered whether in so irreverent an age this was a sign from heaven to honour the mother and the wife and the daughter of a king; and it was special, because she was of the House of Savoy and by origin a Piedmontese. Fortunately for herself she died too early to be a symbol of reaction. The process to get her declared blessed was started at Rome in 1859 but did not get far and that was wise because by then her name stood for an ideal on the right wing of politics. Two years later a guerrilla band campaigning for the Bourbons in southern Italy fought under a flag with Mary of the Immaculate Conception on one side—a banner which they said was blessed by Pius IX—and on the other side a portrait of Maria Cristina kneeling before the Madonna with her feet upon the white cross of the Piedmontese.[14]

Queen Isabella of Spain had morals which were to be deplored but was a very devout Catholic and at times in the 1850s had real power in her country, at least over religion if not over politics. King Maximilian II of Bavaria was more satisfactory than his predecessor and if he was not so papalist a Catholic as Rome would have liked, at least he put up with a clerical ministry.

The strength of the authority of Pope Pius IX in the Catholic Church lay not in crowned heads, nor in the need of clergy under pressure from governments to appeal to Rome for help, nor in better communications, nor even, in the world-wide sense in Catholicism, that the Pope was in danger of persecution by the modern world. Though not a poet such as Frederick Faber or a man of literary mysticism such as Gaston de Ségur, Pius IX shared the people's affection for a warmth of devotion, for the cults of the Blessed Virgin and the Sacred Heart, and the coming forms of eucharistic devotion. He was a religious man and a pastor by instinct, not at all a politician. The development of the Churches in Europe during the next three decades elicited all the priestly side of him, so that his personal influence upon the Catholic Church became greater than any of his predecessors since the office of pope began.

This was partly because of the exceptional length of time during which he occupied the see of St Peter. But it was also due to his unusual personality. He was outgoing and unpompous. Everyone who met him, except on the rare occasions when he was angry, agreed on his charm and friendliness. He had an emotional weak-

---

[14] In 1937 she was declared to be of heroic virtue. Harold Acton, *The Last Bourbons of Naples 1825–1861* (1961), 59 ff., 82 ff.; *CC* (1853), 2: 452; B. Croce, *Uomini e cose della vecchia Italia*, 2nd edn. (1943), ii. 263 ff. is remarkable among Croce's essays about the past.

ness—possibly connected with a history of epileptic fits during his childhood—that from time to time caused him to flare up. He was not very well educated, not well informed, and not at all perceptive about complex situations. It was a disadvantage to the Church, at a time when all civilized society was in motion, and when the human intelligence confronted problems of a complexity not seen since the age of the Renaissance and Reformation, that the Church should have a pope with so small an intellectual range and so narrow a field of experience. But in harness with a nature that was otherworldly, he had at times an earthy common sense which saw with clarity the only thing that really mattered in a situation. He easily made friends. Nothing about him was remote, or shut away.

On 12 April 1855 Pope Pius IX went outside Rome to visit the students of Sant'Agnese. As the young men queued to kiss his toe, the floor collapsed and all but a scrambling few fell nearly twenty feet on top of each other, amid a choking cloud of dust and broken timber and paving. The Pope's throne fell on top of him and protected him from other falling fragments. A Canadian student found himself clutching the cross round the Pope's neck and asked him for absolution. The Pope's clothes were torn but he was imperturbable and after a short rest in the garden went to sing a Te Deum in the church and then to visit the injured in their beds. All over Catholic Europe there was talk of the *miracle* of Sant'Agnese.

He was the first pope who could reach out to the common man and woman, who at last began to be able to visit Rome. The railways were very slow in building, but they were built. Long before the end of his reign he received in audience trainloads of pilgrims. The railway made an enormous difference to the international influence of the papacy. The Catholic world knew this pope as no pope was known before. Then, in the 1860s, came the national newspapers with their foreign correspondents. This pope was news. He might be damaging news to the Church, in the eyes of Protestants, and even in the eyes of some Catholics. But the proverb 'All publicity is good publicity', was applicable to Pius IX. He was the first pope in the history of the papacy to be, in the modern sense of the word, news. And it so happened that this was a warm personality who in the end rose to the opportunities which modern media provided.

This made him more conscious of the international role of the papacy. All the reasons that existed under Gregory XVI for the rising centralization of the Church in the papacy, all the needs of French priests or German bishops, of Swiss or Irish Catholics, and of so many others to look to a larger authority in the Church at Rome, were not only present under this pontificate but rose to be a creative force in the structure of the Church. The Pope was conscious of what was happening, and took opportunity to foster the international authority of the see. In a more political pope the critic might suspect this as a defence against the threat to the papacy from the Italian republicans—an appeal to France, Germany, and Austria to defend the papacy from the menace. But Pius IX—it was part of his strength— was not that kind of pope.

Somewhere in Rome was a feeling that the Holy See could take on all the world; or, to put it more religiously, do whatever was right for the Church and not mind what the world thought. Diplomacy was out. Prudence was hardly seen as a cardinal virtue except in the textbooks of moral theology. Attitudes like caution looked weak.

This new-found confidence was visible in three spheres: church order, doctrine, and resistance to general opinion.

Church Order

The English Bishops

On 29 September 1850 a papal brief established a hierarchy of bishops for England: twelve dioceses and an archdiocese in Westminster. England had at that moment eight vicars-apostolic doing the work of the bishops. Vicars-apostolic were under the immediate direction of the Congregation of Propaganda in Rome. But they coped—or failed to cope—with a vast Irish immigration, speeded up by potato famine in Ireland. They were under desperate pressure, as a mass of poor Catholics flooded into English cities. They wanted quicker decisions, and not to have to refer everything to Rome. They wrongly imagined that properly constituted bishops would help them to run their affairs as they saw right. They asked Rome for bishops.

Fifty years before, Rome would not have tried to do such a thing without previous discussion with the government of Britain. The question was informally mentioned to the British government, which seemed not to mind, but no formal agreement was attempted or reached. By 1850 Rome took the view that the decision was purely for the Church and that a government, especially a Protestant government, had no status. The papal brief announced it, a little provocatively. Then Cardinal Wiseman issued a pastoral letter to the

English Catholics in which the language was of the most provocative; as though this was a campaign for the reconquest of England to the Catholic faith, instead of a desperate attempt to cope with starving Irish immigrants.

The result was the greatest storm of No Popery in England since 1778. It is always an argument whether anti-Catholic rioting does good or harm to the Catholic Church. In this case there were gains and losses. On one side the British government legislated against Catholic bishops' titles (so that they could be fined if they took the title of an Anglican see), but the legislation was trivial and con-temptible; and it was clear that the Pope had been right, and in the half-democracy of Britain the affairs of the Church were affairs only of the Church. On the other side it encouraged the feeling, with a measure of future peril in it, that the Church was hard against the world, and vice versa. In Britain it strengthened the more extreme, less conventionally English, less Gallican, or more Roman-minded, members of the Church. But this would have happened anyway. For with the stream of immigrants the Church in England became less English and more Irish in its mood. Irish churchmen were not likely to want to take notice of the British government or of conventional English Catholic society.

The mood in Rome was affected by these events. A country Protestant since the Reformation received a large number of Catholic immigrants. That must make a difference to the relations between the pope and England.

Almost more difference was made to the mood in Rome by the calamities of the Oxford Movement. Setting out in 1833 to draw the soul of the Church of England to its Catholic inheritance, the Tractarian leaders began to suffer the loss of some of their young men to the Roman Catholic Church. By 1843 it was clear that their leader John Henry Newman suffered from frustration or doubt about his mission. When in October 1845 he became a Roman Catholic the effect upon the hopes of Rome was marked; and this explained the overconfident language of Wiseman's pastoral letter of 1850. Famous Englishmen were received into the Church at Rome—especially Robert Wilberforce the son of the slave emancipator (1854). An Anglican bishop from the United States, Ives of North Carolina, was received in Rome on Christmas Day 1852 and persuaded his wife to come too; Rome could soon expect Pusey and with him all the Anglican high churchmen. The blazing heat of the No Popery agitation combined with the legal entanglements of the Anglican establishment to prompt another wave of conversions to Rome among the leaders of the Oxford Movement. Of these Henry Edward Manning was the most important, and Manning had all the fervour of the convert.

In the eyes of Rome at that moment, England, unsteadily but markedly, was moving back towards the Catholic faith; and, as part of that move, to a closer relationship between Catholic Church life in England and the authority of the see of Rome. Newman could preach one of his most famous sermons under the title 'The Second Spring'.

The Dutch Bishops

There was a long argument whether the Church could do the same in Holland and create Catholic dioceses in a country where Protestantism was so established. The chief advisers of the Pope thought it a mistake because it would be a provocation. Pius IX made up his own mind. The constitution of Holland gave government no right to interfere. In a touch of prudence he weakened the draft, probably given him by Cardinal Lambruschini whose style the text bears. It talked about the 'fury of Calvinists' and was absurdly provocative. But the Pope retained plenty of provocation: the 'Calvinist heresy', the 'atrocious storm' against the Catholics in the Dutch Reformation, the 'monstrous pest' of the Jansenist schism in the eighteenth century.

As in England, a 'No Popery' storm blew through Holland. The government formally protested to Rome against the tone of a document which hurt the honour of the country, but that was all that happened.

The Cardinals

Another sign of the confidence in Church structure was the making of cardinals. People always judged a pope in part by the kind of men whom he promoted to the cardinal's hat.

The Pope used them little in the government of the Papal State. Because of Cardinal Antonelli and the way the Pope preferred to work, one historic function of the cardinals was diminished. It declined over two decades before it was forcibly abolished by enemy action.

By reason of the length of his reign Pius IX made more cardinals than any previous pope: 122 in all. When he died he left in the

College sixty-four cardinals whom he had made. Among the 122 were seventy-one Italians and fifty-one non-Italians. That was a much larger proportion of non-Italians than was normal. Several of these foreign cardinals were famous and controversial names in their countries for their struggle for Church rights against their government: for example Archbishop Geissel of Cologne, prominent in the settlement of the strife over mixed marriages in Germany; Diepenbrock the prince-bishop of Breslau, who was strong for conservative order during the German revolutions of 1848; Wiseman the archbishop of Westminster, at that time (1850) the most unpopular clergyman among the English people; Mathieu of Besançon who was strong in the French Senate for the temporal power of the pope; Gousset of Rheims who was among the most strenuous ultramontane bishops in France; Ledochowski from Gnesen in Polish-speaking Prussia, the leader of Polish resistance to Bismarck's assault on the Catholic Church; Manning the archbishop of Westminster, also in his time the most unpopular clergyman in England.

As in former times, there was need of even-handedness between the nations, in order not to provoke jealousies among Catholic powers. The promotion of ten non-Italian cardinals in 1850 was distributed thus: four Italians, two Germans and one Austrian, three Frenchmen, three Spaniards, and one Englishman (Portugal, which was usually loud in its complaints if it failed to get into such a list, happened to be in political difficulty with the Holy See—the patriarch of Lisbon became a cardinal in 1858). He continued the old custom of rewarding the nuncios in the main Catholic capitals with the rank of cardinal when they were superseded. But since many of the cardinals at home had little enough to do this was an honorary push upstairs. And some of his promotions reached out towards the more distant areas of Church life—Michael Lewykyj who was the uniat archbishop of Lemberg/Lvov and the first Ukrainian ever to be a cardinal; Cullen, the first archbishop of Dublin, indeed the first Irish diocesan bishop, to be a cardinal; McCloskey the first archbishop of New York to be a cardinal; Antici Mattei, the patriarch of the very small Catholic community in Constantinople, when the Eastern Question hung heavily over the political tensions of Europe.

Gregory XVI left at his death fifty-four Italians and eight non-Italians to elect his successor. Pius IX left at his death thirty-nine Italians and twenty-five non-Italians to elect his successor. Formerly at papal elections the cardinals had to listen to the international Church because governments brought an intense pressure to bear through their ambassadors and their cardinals. Now government pressure was weaker. The international Church was better represented by the non-Italian cardinals inside the Conclave, who might take a lot of notice of their own government—or might not take any notice at all.

Not that the Pope listened much to the cardinals, foreign or not, in the conduct of affairs, even foreign affairs. On some complicated matters he was more likely to ask a monsignor in his neighbourhood, someone among the chamberlains with whom he was familiar; George Talbot, for example, on English affairs—and Talbot was far from a sane or well-informed guide; Mgr. de Ségur came to Rome as the French auditor to the Rota court, won the Pope's friendship, and remained his informant and adviser on French affairs after he returned to France. Xavier de Mérode was another adviser on French, Belgian, or Swiss affairs; Mérode was not so second-rate as Talbot, but no one could call him a sound adviser.

The international face of the Church was not reflected by much of an international face in the Curia. Because the monsignors were so important in this regime, and because most of them were not of first-rate calibre, they preferred to stick in the old ways which they understood, and to repeat the old formulas which had long precedent but hardly fitted modern circumstances. Yet they grew more and more powerful as more of the world looked to Rome for decisions. As the Holy See rose to more weight and importance in the world than at any time since the Reformation, little men in old-fashioned cassocks and with closed minds were too often the vehicles of this authority which grew so fast. The system was fixed; the Church was too kind to get rid of clergymen. Reach a humble position on the ladder of the ecclesiastical service and by stages the man was fairly sure to arrive near the top and attain a level above the ceiling of his abilities.

Another priest who won importance because of friendship with the Pope was a Barnabite, Luigi Bilio. The relationship began when he was asked to comment on a liberal Catholic document. He commented in such an illiberal sense that the Pope was very pleased and asked to see him. As they were both outgoing personalities a friendship developed; and Bilio was soon on the path from being an obscure Barnabite to a place where he was within distance of becoming the next pope.

The Church was governed with the aid more of monsignors than of cardinals. Cardinal Antonelli dominated the Papal State, Cardinal

Barnabò was the secretary of Propaganda and controlled the missions like an empire, Cardinal Reisach[15] directed the policy towards Germany. Cardinal Patrizi had weight as an adviser less because he was a cardinal than because he was a close friend of the Pope. These cardinals were exceptions.

But the sign of this sense of Catholic revival was not the non-use of the cardinals to run the Church, but the choice of a range of persons among the nations to receive the honour and thereby make the office more important among non-Italians.

Doctrine

Another sign of the confidence of Pius IX was the definition of the doctrine of the Immaculate Conception of the Virgin Mary. The people wanted this doctrine; no one should think it forced upon the simple people by hierarchs. At Cartagena in Spain an anticlerical enthusiast who spoke against it publicly was almost torn in pieces by a mob.

It was agreed that the Virgin was pure. Could she be so if she were part of the inheritance of original sin? The old Byzantines were the first to deny that she could be born with original sin. These ideas came from the East into Italy and then further west. By the twelfth century the Immaculate Conception became an argument between two schools of opinion, each with weighty representatives. Its opponents, led by the Dominicans, said that there was no evidence for it, and secondly that the human race without exception is redeemed through Christ. But the opinion continued to grow and be fostered by the people's devotion. During all the earlier nineteenth century the cult of the Immaculate Conception developed in popular devotion, especially in France and Spain, to a lesser extent in Italy, and still less in Germany and Britain. Bishops, friars, monks, and nuns kept asking Rome for leave to celebrate the Immaculate Conception, in so many words, in their services; and Rome steadily granted permission. Pope Gregory XVI encouraged the doctrine because he was known to be a devotee. In 1831 a French Sister of Charity, Catherine

---

[15] Karl August Graf von Reisach, 1800–69, bishop of Eichstätt from 1836. He won the confidence of Gregory XVI in the troubles over the see of Cologne. In 1846 he became archbishop of Munich but was almost instantly in trouble with Kings Ludwig I and Maximilian II of Bavaria who determined to get him out. In 1855 he therefore became one of the cardinals in the Curia at Rome.

Labouré, who was a nurse at a hospital in Paris, had a vision of Mary with an inscription 'conceived without sin', and believed that she received an order that a medal with this inscription be struck, and a promise that all who wore this medal should receive great graces by the intercession of the mother of God. Archbishop Quelen of Paris enquired, and allowed the medal. During the course of the nineteenth century millions of people must have worn copies of this medal.

Near the end of the reign of Gregory XVI Rome felt that almost the whole Catholic world wanted the Immaculate Conception to be made an article of faith which all Catholics must believe. The Secretary of State Cardinal Lambruschini even stepped from behind the anonymity of a public servant and published a book claiming that such a definition was much to be desired, and citing the miraculous medal. Pope Gregory was cautious. That year he told the bishop of La Rochelle, 'Nothing could be happier for me than solemnly to define . . . But I am held back by high considerations of prudence in the present circumstances . . .'. He was afraid of making the see of Rome hated among the nations.[16] Yet he was sure that this was the faith of the Church and would be seen to be so, and he was willing (he said in the language of a historic and controversial vow) to shed for it his last drop of blood. In May 1845 the American bishops at the Council of Baltimore declared Mary Immaculate the patroness of the United States.

When Pius IX was elected pope the debate already raged. He found himself in the middle of a far-flung popular movement demanding definition by Rome. The leading theologian of the Roman schools, Giovanni Perrone, published a thesis to show that the doctrine could be defined.[17] The Pope's troubles increased the fervour of his feelings. For it was at Candlemas 1849, when in the midst of his exile at Gaeta, and before the French army began to land at Civitavecchia to rescue papal Rome, that he issued to the bishops of the world a request that they should tell him how much desire there was among their peoples that the belief in the Immaculate Conception of the Blessed Virgin should be raised into a dogma of the Catholic Church. When the Pope asked the bishops what their people thought, he consulted them because he was aware of a widespread movement through the Church that it would be right to

[16] *DTC* vii. 1193.

[17] The long title explained it: *De immaculato B.V. Mariae conceptu an dogmatico decreto definiri possit disquisitio theologica* (Rome, 1847).

settle the argument and make it a dogma. It was not his private idea
that he would impose upon a reluctant Church. How deeply popular devotion had run is shown by Bernadette Soubirous of Lourdes;
for the little girl heard in her vision the beautiful lady say to her the
strange words, 'I am the Immaculate Conception'.

Most of the bishops wanted the Pope to act. Some bishops
doubted whether it was right to define. Archbishop Sibour of Paris
thought it was true but asked why the Church should define anything
when all is quiet and there is no raging controversy troubling minds.

Pius IX, man of a people's devotion, did not ask himself either of
the questions that the intellectuals among his bishops asked; whether
it was necessary to add to the number of doctrines that people must
believe for salvation and for obedience to the Church, or whether it
would be better to leave it as an opinion, even if a recommended and
pious opinion; and secondly, whether a pope had the power in the
Church to convert a widely held opinion into a dogma. The Pope
did not believe that he was an innovator. He was satisfied that this
faith was Catholic because it was held for centuries by many. He was
declaring what the Church always believed and what the faithful
ought to believe. He was sure that in his office as supreme teacher of
the Church he was protected by God from error. Therefore he took
it for granted that he did not need any consent by the organs of the
Church at large to what he proposed to do.

On 8 December 1854 he defined the doctrine of the Immaculate
Conception of the Blessed Virgin Mary.

To the honour of the Holy and Undivided Trinity, and to the grace and
dignity of the Virgin Mother of God, to the exaltation of the Catholic faith
and the advance of the Christian religion, by the authority of our Lord Jesus
Christ and of the blessed apostles Peter and Paul, *and by our own authority*,
we declare, pronounce and define . . .

And the bull went on still more formidably. For if anyone should dare
to believe now that Mary was not pure from the taint of original sin,
or dare to believe that this is not revealed by God, 'they are to know
that they have wrecked the faith and separated themselves from the
unity of the Church'.

No previous Pope in eighteen centuries had made a definition of
doctrine quite like this.[18]

[18] Perhaps *Unigenitus* (1713) may be held to come near it in intention. Many Catholics
never believed what Pope Clement in *Unigenitus* said they ought to believe, and even more
Catholics did not know what the encyclical contained. Not so in 1854 with Pius IX.

The bull caused gratitude in the Catholic Church, contempt or sadness among Protestants, and difficulty or anxiety to those Roman Catholics who believed neither the doctrine that the Blessed Virgin was unique in being free from original sin nor the doctrine that the pope had a power to define this without consulting the Church at large in a formal way. But at first this difficulty was small. These sceptical Catholics went their way with their minds still free. Archbishop Sibour of Paris, who doubted the wisdom of the definition, was present at the ceremonies in Rome and then ordered the doctrine to be proclaimed in his parishes. He suspended from saying mass a French priest who was outspoken in his attack upon the doctrine. Priests in Austria and Spain were disciplined for the same reasons. A French priest who served in various parishes and worked in London under Cardinal Wiseman and was now the *curé* of a French parish, preached against the doctrine when it was defined. Archbishop Sibour suspended him. He bought a long knife, and, as Sibour walked in solemn procession in the porch of a church, blessing the people, ran forward and stabbed his archbishop to death (1857). The see of Paris suffered in the forty years after 1830: first an archbishop who was threatened with murder and lost his palace to a sacking mob; then an archbishop killed on a revolutionary barricade trying to stop the bullets; now an archbishop murdered by a mentally disturbed priest; then at last an archbishop who died in his bed; and after him an archbishop whose death was the worst of all because the killers were not in the least insane, unless to take revenge on innocent persons is near insanity.

But neither outspokenness nor suspension were frequent. For it could not be said that the profession of the doctrine, or the refusal of profession, made a difference to pastoral care or the leading arguments in Europe. If sceptics were troubled by a phrase in the liturgy, they could accept it, as a Protestant like Jeremy Taylor could accept it, to mean that the Blessed Virgin was a very pure lady, which no Catholic wished to deny. Perhaps its historical importance lay in the bringing it home to Pius IX and the Curia that they had a right and a duty, acceptable to the Church, or much of it, to articulate the faith more precisely.

It would have helped a little in Protestant and anticlerical Europe if the title of the bull had been different. It gave rise to jokes in Piedmontese bars, and to Spanish ditties. The theatre at Vigevano in Piedmont celebrated the first anniversary of the bull with a comedy ridiculing the doctrine. But the people hated such crudity; most of them refused to go and the play was taken off after two days. The attitude of the Catholic Church as a whole was gratitude, even heart-felt gratitude. Queen Isabella of Spain sent a precious tiara as a sign of her pleasure. In Naples the bull was put into army orders. At Vienna the court went in procession to the statue of the Virgin erected in 1647.

From the Middle Ages the kingdom of Naples, as a sign of liege loyalty to the pope, had the duty to send to Rome each year the *chinea* (horse), an annual grant carried on a white horse to St Peter's. Just before the French Revolution Naples said it was an anachronism and stopped sending it; but each year Rome protested against the omission of a historic right, one of those ritual protests that had no importance to either side. During his stay at Gaeta Pius IX was moved by seeing the deep devotion of the people of the kingdom of Naples to the Immaculate Conception, and this experience helped him to make up his mind to the definition. Together with his friendship with King Ferdinand this made for the final solution of the *chinea*. In return for the end of the protest the king of Naples paid 10,000 *scudi* and with this money the Pope erected the ancient column in the Piazza di Spagna and put on the top a gilt statue of the Immaculate Virgin. Pope and king kept the agreement secret—neither wished their people to know that they surrendered old rights lest public surrender give ideas to other States.

The bull did nothing to weaken the Pope's influence in the Church—on the contrary—except among the few: German professors of divinity or history, ex-Anglican converts in England, clever French clergymen, Italians of the old Jansenist tradition. This way of piety was not being carved out for the Church by the Pope as by some explorer or engineer. His strength was that he represented, not just as a public figure but in his personal and private attitudes, the movement of a people's devotion.

What the bull did, in its political consequence, was to add another piece of portrait to the European image of the Pope and consequently of Catholicism; of a faith deeply pious, otherworldly even to excess, with a true religious sentiment, and with its corporate mind moving away from the general direction in which European culture moved; almost as though the faith was heading into an enclosure of piety.

Disregard of Opinion

The Church believed that it had the right of asylum; it said that courts of justice were not always able to protect an accused person from being murdered, or ill-treated in a police station, or sentenced by corrupt judges; if the accused fled to an altar then he or she could not be torn away from it by police, but there must be time for the bishop's pastoral care to operate. Protestant States abolished this in the Reformation, most Catholic States did so in the eighteenth century, and Piedmont had just abolished it. In the Papal State it still existed and was defended as a Christian part of seeing that justice is done. The opinion of Europe was that it was now a way of endangering justice by giving criminals a chance that they ought not to be allowed.

For example: in March 1856 a thief fled to the church of San Giacomo on the Corso in Rome and sat in a chair by the altar. Two policemen in mufti waited and watched. The scene gathered an interested crowd of spectators. But when dark fell the monks who ministered in that church spirited him away.[19]

POLITICAL REPUTATION

Against this sense of revival and Catholic power had to be set that both the revival and the power made more enemies, or made existing enemies more vocal. The Church flourished in France but its critics in France grew fiercer because it flourished. The Church secured a most favourable Concordat in Austria and thereby was more unpopular with many of the middle class. The Pope instituted hierarchies in England and Holland and in each country endured storms of 'No Popery'.

Enemies could see an Achilles heel: the Papal States, the government of Central Italy. They fastened on the old-fashioned nature of the regime restored in 1849–50. Was it right to have Central Italy governed by a ruler who could only remain in power with the help of two foreign armies?

During the 1850s the administration of the Papal State, in finance and provincial and municipal government, was slowly improved.

[19] F. Gregorovius, *Roman Journal*, Eng. trans. (1911), 26.

Pius IX had the strength that he cared not at all whether he was popular. But he had not solved the problem of the Papal State, or the temporal power of the pope, or his secular monarchy, or what was coming to be called the Roman Question. All these lay about him still to plague his pontificate and condition all his years as pope. The citizens of the Romagna towns, the prosperous part of the State, had shown that they wanted representative government and the Pope had no means of holding them under his rule if the Austrian soldiers were taken away, for a police state like that of Bernetti was now unthinkable. If the French soldiers were withdrawn it was not likely that he would be able to hold Rome.

He conceded little to the upper and middle classes who wanted more say in the State. In the northern provinces it was not only the middle classes. He went on a visit round the State; and as he left Bologna in his carriage he waved his hand to bless all the people, but there were no people to bless: they had stayed away, there was only the Austrian guard of honour silently presenting arms, and to an Italian observer it looked cold and empty. This observer thought of the tour as a pope's sad goodbye to a people who had been his subjects for a thousand years. His reception was not frigid in all the towns, and the Pope noted the cheers, the friendly greetings, and the triumphal arches.

It was the British who avenged what had happened over Dr Wiseman and the hierarchy. At Paris in 1856, at the making of the treaty after the Crimean war, the British Foreign Secretary, Lord Clarendon, made a speech which was nothing to do with the making of the treaty, but which resounded through Western Europe. Clarendon was a good Protestant and a liberal man who had experience of Catholicism. He had served the British in Spain during the Spanish civil war in the 1830s (which had not led him to think well of the extreme Catholic right in Spain) and governed Ireland during the famine and its aftermath of troubles, which had not led him to think well of the Irish bishops, although he wanted a liberal policy in Ireland. At Paris he had the difficulty that though Piedmontese soldiers fought, or at least appeared, on the Allied side in the Crimean war, the powers allotted her nothing in the peace treaty. Therefore he gave Piedmont a speech which pressed for the end of foreign occupation (by French and Austrians) in Italy and declared that the government of the Papal State was a scandal to Europe and that it must be reformed. All the press of Europe resounded with this cry.

It was like a little war of paper between Britain and the Pope. The Pope had sent bishops ostentatiously to Protestant England and issued a bull in provocative language. British politicians said his government was the worst in Europe. His Italian defenders then said that the English government was the most barbarous in Europe, with its labyrinth of a legal system, its baby-shows, its floggings in the army, its justice only for the rich, its seizure of bits of Arabia and Borneo, its overcrowded and squalid prisons, its seven million Irish groaning under English oppression, its holding down of an empire by hired mercenaries, its queen as head of a church, its slums of Westminster and its prostitutes in the West End of London—the incredible hypocrisy of Britain which dares to attack the pope's government; they asked, what of the mote and the beam?

The pope's government was under attack, said the defenders, because it was clerical. It was countered, did men lose their sense of justice, or their competence, or their financial acumen, when they received holy orders? 'Priests are indeed men, but laymen are not angels.' The pope was accused of relying on foreign troops, but every other state in Europe hired mercenaries. And there was this differ-ence: the pope was international, to him no Catholic was a foreigner. Swiss guards or French zouaves were also his sons. And why this attack upon the pope's army when it was the only army in the world that would not go to war? Some people said it was shameful to have a monarch who sang mass, but it meant also to have a sovereign who commanded two or three million men and women outside his own State, who every morning examined his conscience on the welfare of his subjects, and who consistently pursued peace.

Naturally the attack spilt over to the Church of England, the bish-ops of which were always referred to in Rome as pseudo-bishops; and from the Church of England to all the heirs of the Reformation—rationalism, socialism, revolution—as the children of Protestantism. At that time a Franciscan proved in a lecture at Rome that Protestantism was destructive of all faith, all morality, and all author-ity—and was applauded. Those were not ecumenical years, when the British Foreign Secretary Lord Clarendon said that the papal govern-ment was a disgrace to Europe.[20]

A more objective test may be found in the reports, between June 1855 and June 1857, of Lyons the British representative in Rome. He

[20] e.g. *CC* (1856), 2: 639–56; (1855), 11: 361–6; (1859), 1: 28.

began by being very critical of the papal regime. He remained critical, but the nature of his disfavour slowly changed with more knowledge. He started by thinking the papal government a bad government because it was clerical, illiberal, and dependent on foreign troops. He thought that these defects caused the budget deficits, the smuggling, the too frequent murders in the Romagna. Because the top posts were clerical, he thought that able young laymen would not go into the administration, and hence the weakness of the civil service. Immediately after the Congress of Paris Lord Clarendon sent Lyons to tell Cardinal Antonelli that Britain wanted the foreign troops out of the Papal States and the pope to have a national guard; and that Britain wanted the government of the Legations to be lay and autonomous. To Lyons Cardinal Antonelli was delightful in conversation, good-humoured, and courteous. He said that they also wanted foreign troops out of the Papal States as soon as possible, but that the speeches at the Congress of Paris made this more difficult to achieve. As to clerical government, he said that there were only eighteen clergymen in the administration outside Rome; as to the national guard, he said that the last time the pope instituted a national guard it ended in the murder of the Prime Minister and the flight of the pope; he said that to ask for autonomy in the Legations was the same as asking the pope to abdicate his throne.

Slowly Lyons realized that the working of the government (as distinct from the nature of the government, which he could not forgive) was not bad; that the number of political prisoners was few; that the behaviour in the Legations of the Austrian garrison was disliked in Rome; that the Pope was religious and dutiful, however unpopular with the bourgeois; that the roads were safer except in the Romagna; that prisons were being reformed, tariffs reduced, railways slowly built, and agriculture in progress. 'There is certainly nothing like the life and activity which liberal institutions have called forth in Piedmont, but the country is by no means at a standstill, nor in decay. On the contrary there are many signs of progress visible to an attentive observer.' Still, nothing could alter the insecurity of the papal government, and the hatred felt for it by 'Italians'; it was their credo that Austria must be pushed out of Italy, and because the pope was integral to Austrian power in Italy, his state must be destroyed.[21]

---

[21] PP (1860), lxviii. 381 ff., esp. 436; Antonelli's reply to him, 386. The number of eighteen clergymen only in the papal government outside Rome needs explanation. The 1848 return shows 243 clergymen in the civil service. This did not include professors at the

So far a civilized Protestant observer. His French Catholic colleague Rayneval drew a more favourable portrait of the papal government. He had political motives for his generosity. He said to Lyons, 'We do not choose to have a revolution in the Papal States. The question with us is mainly a religious question. We must have a pope, and we must have him at Rome, and he must be tranquil and secure there.' Therefore French troops must stay in Rome until this aim was achieved. Rayneval also confessed that the pope's government was unpopular. He allowed that the liberal constitution of Piedmont exercised a fascination on many educated Italians. But he took a cynical view of the nature of Italians. They complain about government; reform the administration of the pope's state and they will still complain. Topple the pope's state and they will complain just as acidly about its successor.[22] And Rayneval had a still friendlier view of the papal administration. He specially admired the 'clemency' with which it treated the revolutionaries of 1848–9, and the just and costly way in which their financiers honoured the paper money issued by the revolutionary government. He envied the average citizen of the Papal States that he paid half the taxes that a Frenchman paid. 'The expression "the abuses of papal government"', Rayneval told the French government, 'is now consecrated, and is above criticism or objection. It is held as gospel. What are the abuses? I have never yet been able to discover.' And yet he admitted the political problem to be insoluble.

The Jewish ghetto was a historic piece of the city of Rome, along the east bank of the River Tiber. It dated officially from 1556, when it was instituted by the fiercest pope of the Counter-Reformation, Paul IV. Under the system all Jews must live within a part of the city behind a wall, with gates across which chains were placed at night. The ghetto had two objects—to protect Christians from too close an association with persons of a different religion, and to protect the Jews from mobs or hooligans. The ghetto was welcome to some Jews

university, but included 134 chaplains to the forces. It also included certain 'prelates' (such as the Minister of the Interior in 1856) who dressed as clergymen but were not in holy orders. Thus there were about 100 clergy in the civil service, of whom eighteen were outside Rome, nearly all governors of provinces. The figures do not include the clergy employed in the curial offices, e.g. twelve in the Inquisition, forty at Propaganda in the administration of the overseas missions, and even four still at the almost obsolete Congregation of Immunity.

[22] Rayneval's report to Walewski, 14 May 1856; Eng. trans. in J. F. Maguire, *Rome and its Ruler*, 3nd edn. (1859), 473, cf. app. xiv; and PP (1860), lxviii. 414.

because it protected the small community from the drain which must follow from assimilation to the majority and enabled special religious customs to be observed without interference. During the hours of day they could come out to hawk their goods, usually cheap textiles and embroidery. Most were very poor. Inside the ghetto they were crowded because the space was too narrow for the people, some 4,000, and therefore the houses were built higher and the streets narrower so that the rooms had poor air and little light. When the Tiber flooded, which was not seldom, the river ran through the ground floor of their houses. They had four small synagogues, which were the only non-Catholic places of worship allowed within the city, each synagogue with its school and a choir where the music was admired. Christians could freely attend synagogue worship and priests could be seen there. They spoke Italian to each other, not Hebrew nor Yiddish, and they had Italian rather than Jewish names. The ghetto was self-governing, in that they elected three Jewish officers to be magistrates and to tax them for the sick and poor and to pay a heavy quota to the State; but their court of final appeal was the Cardinal Vicar of Rome. Sermons were provided on Saturdays to convert them to Christianity and they had to pay the fees of the preachers but only a token few needed to attend. They also had to pay the wages of the guards at the gates and a subscription to the house of such few converts as asked for Christian baptism. They were not all happy inside their walls for they were sharply divided over observances.

For three or four decades of the nineteenth century this was not a black mark to the papal government because so many other cities still had ghettoes—Vienna, Prague, Venice—and further East, in Russia and Poland, their treatment could be rougher. Pope Gregory XVI was kind to them in 1837 when, seeing how poverty and high taxes plunged the community into bankruptcy, he rubbed out all their debts, and helped them with medical aid during the cholera epidemic of that year. The year before he died the Rota court ruled that a Jew had the same right as a Christian to be exempt from arrest by the police while at a religious service—'The Jews are not to be treated as heathen. They pray to the same God as Christians.'[23]

The liberal regime of Pius IX felt to them like a miracle. He ordered that the insults against them, normal in the annual comedies

[23] A. Berliner, *Geschichte der Juden in Rom* (Frankfurt am Main, 1893), ii. 144.

of the Carnival, should cease. He abolished the sermons to convert them. On 26 March 1848 Father Ambrossoli preached in St Mary's in Trastevere a sermon of such power against the intolerance of the ghetto walls that the congregation talked of going out to pull down the gates. Less than a month later, on the night of 17 April, without warning to the occupants of the ghetto, the gates were destroyed by the police, and the astonished Jews sang hymns of praise. They could live where they liked. Most of them could not afford to live any-where but in their old ghetto. The Roman republic put three Jews on their municipal council.

When the reaction came, the ghetto was restored; it was at first worse, because Jews were rumoured to have robbed churches during the anarchy. The French army moved into the ghetto and for three days hunted after stolen goods, vainly. Afterwards, though the old laws were still supposed to be in force, and the sermons to convert were revived, the chains were not maintained, they were still free in practice to live where they liked, the insults at the Carnival were not renewed; and the community began to be helped by rich northern Jews, especially Rothschild who was also aiding the Pope's treasury.

But in 1858 an accident swung the attention of Europe to the predicament of Jews in the Papal State. In the house of a Jewish fam-ily at Bologna, named Mortara, a Christian nurse saw that the baby was dying. She was told by a good lady outside that it would be kind to christen him and that in the imminence of death she, the maid, could be the minister of baptism. She baptized him without telling the parents. Fortunately the baby did not die. When the baptism came to light, six years later, government ruled that the child, being a Christian, could not grow up in a Jewish household. To abstract him from his parents' home, a Dominican made what was described as 'a little use of the secular arm'. The child was taken to Rome and educated as a pious Catholic. He grew up to be a faithful priest and did not die till 1940.

The French ambassador appealed to the Pope, who said that it was repugnant to his conscience to allow a Christian to be brought up in the Jewish religion and that the parents caused their misfortune when they hired a Christian as nursemaid. He said, with evident sincerity, that nothing could be more precious to him than an individual soul and above all the soul of a child. He did not accept that the other side cared about the child. He thought that they only wanted the child as a bludgeon to bang the Pope. But even that devout papalist the

Empress Eugénie believed the Pope to be wrong. Napoleon III had it printed that he did not approve. Piedmont said that it would do all it could to get the child back to its parents, but in the end could do nothing.[24]

Not all governments then looked as modern as modernity supposes. At that very date the British were only just admitting Jews to Parliament. In the next years the Russian government forced hundreds of thousands of Roman Catholics to become Orthodox. But a State where justice still ran according to the precepts of the canon law of the Middle Ages did not look comfortable in the Europe of the mid-nineteenth century. The Pope's enemies made sure that the world knew what kind of a government he headed in Central Italy. Even today it is hard to read with equanimity the curial defences of what was done: a State stealing a little boy from his mother, persecution of the Jews—the rights of the family, and the rights of humanity.

The papal government was old-fashioned because oligarchy had come to be seen so; and it looked even more old-fashioned than it was. Most States had a censorship; the Papal States called their censorship by the name of Inquisition, which sounded like a thumbscrew sort of censorship. Europe looked upon the Papal States as it would have looked upon Britain if its high court were called the Star Chamber.

This Achilles' heel, the weak point of so apparently flourishing an institution, was seized upon, at last fatally for the Pope, when in 1852 there came to power in the kingdom of Piedmont the most dangerous enemy that he ever knew: Cavour.

[24] G. L. M. Zannini, 'Nuovi documenti sul "Caso Mortara"' in *RSCI* 13 (1959), 239 ff.; D. I. Kertzer, *The Kidnapping of Edgardo Mortara* (1997).

4

THE MAKING OF ITALY

The revolutions of 1848–9 and the reaction afterwards left Piedmont as the only State in Italy with a constitutional government. Italian nationalists still wanted to drive the Austrians out of Italy and to that end unite the Italian peninsula as an Italian State. The Pope had shown that he would take no part in this. He refused to war against Austrians, and he did not want to be the head of State in an Italian federation or make himself responsible for acts or policy of which, as head of the Church, he must disapprove. Therefore Piedmont now collected the aspirations of nationalists and liberals in Italy. And as such it won the sympathies of liberals and Protestants all over Europe.

The attack upon the old rights of the Catholic Church in Piedmont, from 1850 onwards, was a parliamentary necessity. The government must prove that it was a liberal and constitutional government or it could not survive without a coup.

In Piedmont the Church was privileged. By European standards it started as a backward State in church law. Church courts dealt with marriage and with crimes committed by clerics. A death sentence on a cleric went to a special court of bishops chosen by king and pope. This privilege was known by the historic but vague term 'forum', used to mean the exemption of clerics from ordinary secular courts.

Of all Italian States most influenced by France because many of its people spoke French, Piedmont wanted to be a modern State in which all citizens were subject to the same law, and that law must be determined by the State and not accepted from outside, e.g. in canon law. The constitution of 1848 had among its articles that all citizens are equal before the law. The forum contradicted this article. Parliament debated abolishing it. They negotiated with Rome. Cardinal Antonelli defended the forum thus: the State is helped if the clergy have prestige, and the forum is a condition of that prestige; the bishops' authority over their clergy rests upon it. Pius IX did not mind abolition much if this were part of a general settlement of Church and State in Piedmont. If Piedmont had conceded to him the free choice of bishops, he would have compromised. But everyone suspected this attack upon the forum to be the start of a course followed in other countries, leading to civil marriage, divorce, and dissolution of monasteries.

In 1850 Piedmont debated bills from a lawyer, Siccardi, that abolished the right of sanctuary and the forum, and put the clergy under the ordinary lawcourts. Siccardi was a moderate and a practising Catholic but his name afterwards came to symbolize attack upon the Church.

Government argued that the bill only made clear what was stated in the constitution, that all citizens are equal before the law. Against them speakers argued that because the constitution also declared that this is a State of the Catholic religion, the forum could not be abolished without the agreement of Rome; and further, that its legality rested upon a Concordat, a treaty between two powers which could not be ended by only one of the two. Government speakers replied that the constitution declared Piedmont to be a state of the Catholic religion and that legal arrangements about the clergy are nothing to do with religion; and as for the Concordat they argued that the treaties are only in force so long as the circumstances are unchanged.

During the hot debate on Siccardi, Cavour made a speech of such power that it turned him from an obscure back-bencher into a possible Prime Minister.

A second Siccardi bill reduced the number of holy days, which must be kept compulsorily, to every Sunday and seven feasts in the year. From the left it was argued that this was absurd, why should the State order anyone to do things on certain days? Siccardi replied that days of rest were needed and that we must not hurt the conscience of the nation. But the opposition was strong and the bill withdrawn; and Pius IX, three years later, agreed a reduction of compulsory feasts to Sundays and ten other days.

To posterity the passing of the Siccardi law looks easy and uncontroversial. The government had not expected the storm which now blew and was embarrassed. The pope withdrew his nuncio from Turin. But this was trivial compared with the behaviour of the archbishop of Turin. Fransoni, archbishop for the last nineteen years, was rigid and difficult. He issued a circular that clergy were not to obey summonses to a secular court; or, if they must, to obey only with a public protest that the court had no jurisdiction: these instructions to stand until Rome decided. The government seized his circular, asked him vainly to resign, arrested him and, when he refused to plead, the court sentenced him to a month in prison and a fine of 500 lire. His followers raised a subscription to help him; whereupon the public raised a subscription for a monument to the Siccardi law, which still stands massively in the Savoia piazza with the inscription, 'All are equal before the law'.

But this was not the worst. By ill fortune, that August the Minister of Agriculture Santa Rosa, a close friend of Cavour, lay dying. As a member of the cabinet he shared responsibility for the Siccardi law. He asked for a priest, the Servite friar Pittavino, member of an order which had the care of the sick as part of its vocation.[1] The friar said that he had a ruling from Archbishop Fransoni not to give absolution unless the dying man made a retraction of all acts hostile to the Church. Round the death-bed was played out an astounding scene, with Santa Rosa, his grieving wife, and another clergyman pleading with the Servite. Santa Rosa refused to give the assurance demanded and died on 5 August. The scene had an emotional effect upon Cavour.

Crowds besieged the Servite friary and church. The national guard had to defend them. The government ejected the Servites from Turin, for the sake of public order, and accused Archbishop Fransoni. He said that this was the responsibility of the friar. They arrested Fransoni. It was awkward; for he had committed no illegality, it was within an archbishop's right to accept or reject a soul for communion. Since public opinion would not tolerate a guiltless archbishop, they used an ancient obsolete statute from the old despotism, pretended that they had papers proving him to be a conspirator with the Austrians, and exiled him from the country. He tried to run his diocese from Lyons.

At bottom the trouble was caused by the archbishop. But his exile was unjust; and it made a running sore between Church and State in

---

[1] The Servites were founded in 1240 at Florence and had a special devotion to the Virgin of the Seven Sorrows. For the history see *DIP* s.v. Servi di Maria. The Enlightenment and then the French Revolution reduced them to very few. In 1848 there were sixty-four houses, all in Italy or the Austrian empire; the coming suppressions in Piedmont and then in united Italy brought them down to their lowest point, about 1885, with fifty-three houses and 359 friars.

Piedmont for several years and must not be forgotten in the background to the conflict that developed.[2]

There were more trivial breaches of the Concordat. In 1741, in return for gaining a feudal right, the Piedmontese government undertook to send to Rome every year a gold chalice, worth 2,000 silver *scudi* of Roman money. Except for the years of French revolution this was regularly sent—till 1851; and then, as a penalty for the Pope's attitude to the Siccardi laws, the Parliament at Turin struck it out of their accounts.

There was now, as nowhere else in Italy outside Austrian-ruled Lombardy and Venice, a middle class with a culture that felt superior to the old conservatisms associated with the Catholic Church. They believed true culture to be lay and liberal, and that the movements of history and society were on their side.

CAVOUR AND RELIGION

Cavour became Prime Minister of Piedmont in 1852 and held the office almost continuously for the next nine years until his death. He had a Swiss Protestant mother who converted to Catholicism and was pious. His father was a formal Catholic, conservative in feeling, but he had served under the Napoleonic regime, which was a sign of liberal attitudes. These elements affected Cavour's make-up. He truly professed a Catholicism, though it was vague; he cared for the Church as a historic institution; he admired Rousseau; even more he admired the British and their institutions. He had faith in the progress of society—and part of progress meant restraining the Church. He talked of the need for reform of the Catholic Church but never said what that implied. He made his first confession before he was 7 but as an adult he is not recorded as going to mass, except once at a time when in danger of death. At 18 he had some sort of crisis of faith when he saw church authorities fiercely trying to prevent the arrest of a friar who had committed murder. Altogether his mind was very lay. But he was no extremist. For all the anti-Church acts of Piedmont under his government, and their long consequences for Roman Catholicism, he was like a Josephist of the previous century:

[2] They also exiled Archbishop Nurra of Cagliari in Sardinia, but here the act was legal: he refused to co-operate with a government commission enquiring into the ecclesiastical revenues on the island.

his policy was to restrict monasteries rather than destroy them all; to let the Church have its due place in the State; to make sure that the State retained sufficient power to prevent the Church from being an obstacle to state policy. Before he was Prime Minister he once (23 August 1850) used the expression 'a free church in a free State', which became his most famous saying. It needs comment.

Cavour admired the separation of Church and State laid down by the constitution of the United States. But that was not what he wished for Italy. He associated the pope with Austrian power, and had no desire for a concordat with the Vatican. His idea of a free Church did not include freedom for anyone who wanted to become a monk; he was prejudiced against Jesuits and wanted them expelled from Piedmont. To him contemplatives were idlers, and he wanted friars abolished because they lived by begging. In his view society was damaged if holiness were associated with idleness. He assumed a direct connection between Protestant destruction of monasteries and the prosperity of modern Protestant States.

But Cavour's idea of the 'free Church' did include a measure of independence. He observed how the French government's control of bishops made their clergy more Roman, and he did not want that for Italy. The State must retain ultimate control over the Church but ought to treat it with moderation so that it would regard the State as friend and not enemy. His idea of freedom for the Church did not include the idea that priests should be free to interfere in politics—he could not bear the idea of political priests.

Cavour was very sure that he was in the right. He often used phrases such as 'enlightened persons', 'enlightened government', as though no sensible person could disagree about the nature of enlightened policy. He was rather complacent about his virtues.

He underestimated the pope's person and office. He did not scorn the clericals in Piedmont because he feared what they could do. Whether because of his once-Protestant mother, his French experience, or his lay habit of mind, he felt small need to take any notice of the pope, even though the churches of Piedmont were full of devout worshippers. He would have helped Italy if he had had more respect for forces that were intangible.

In 1855 his government brought in a bill—Rattazzi's bill—to suppress many monasteries. The purpose was to save the State grant, nearly a million lire, which was given to keep the parish system working and to increase the pay of the curates. But in Cavour's mind the gain was not only financial; too many monks were bad for a State, a modern State should have few of them.

The mood was such that churches were full of people praying against the bill. In Parliament opponents argued that the State could not take away people's property, and certainly could not take the property of the Church without asking Rome. The bill was unjust because it stopped citizens dedicating themselves to a way of life which they chose and which was not antisocial. It violated the free right of association which was part of their liberties. It was replied by government speakers that monasteries were corporations which the State recognized and from which the State was free to withdraw recognition. Nothing in the bill stopped men and women from living together in communities.

As Prime Minister Cavour was pressed from the left. Why did the bill leave any monasteries? Brofferio said,

There are 490 convents in the State. Will the minister propose to abolish them all? I vote for him with exultation. Will he propose to abolish half? I vote resignedly to abolish 245. Will he ask to abolish 100? I vote for 100. Will he ask to suppress ten? I vote for ten. For one convent? I vote for one. For one friar? I vote to abolish one friar [loud laughter in the House].

The left proposed an amendment to abolish all monks and nuns. Cavour said that if this were carried the government would withdraw the bill.[3]

Brofferio's numbers were wrong. There were 604 houses of which 372 were nunneries, and a total of 8,563 monks and nuns. Of these, 334 houses were suppressed—that is, 5,506 persons of whom 4,308 were monks. That left 274 houses, and a monastic population of 4,050, substantially less than half the monastic population before the law.[4] The figures show that this dissolution bore comparison rather with the 'enlightened' dissolutions of the eighteenth century than with those of the Spanish, Portuguese, or French Revolutions. The

[3] Brofferio was a very able representative of the new Piedmontese world; was a deputy in Parliament for eighteen years from 1848; edited the radical paper *Messaggiere*; and wrote political poems. He had been a Freemason in Paris, was anticlerical, wrote histories of his time which were journalistic but full of information, had a legal wife and children in Turin and a mistress on Lake Maggiore. He was determinedly against a free Church in a free State, believing the State must control the Church to stop it damaging society; strongly against any compromise with the pope; and strongly against Piedmont joining in the Crimean war: cf. *DBI*; and E. Bottasso (ed.), *Angelo Brofferio: Mostra bibliografica nel centenario della morte* (Turin, 1966).

[4] W. R. Thayer, *The Life and Times of Cavour* (2 vols.; Boston, 1911), i. 343–4.

plan allowed for monasteries or nunneries considered useful—those that cared for the sick, ran schools, or trained preachers.

In Cavour's mind the main importance of the legislation, apart from financial gain, was the image of the State—to be modern and secular instead of a State behind the times, and therefore to collect the sympathy of modern Europe. For when the Piedmontese bishops, with Bishop Calabiana of Casale as their mouthpiece, offered to hand over an income equal to endowments the State would obtain from the monasteries, if only the 'sacrilegious' law were withdrawn, Piedmont regarded this proposal as an insult by the bishops, which it was not. The bishops had made it a condition that the offer be part of a negotiation for a new concordat with the Pope. Calabiana never again attended the Senate when this plan failed.

King Victor Emmanuel was disturbed at the breach between his country and the pope. The King tried to insist that the offer of Bishop Calabiana be accepted. Cavour resigned, after one of his great speeches; no one else could form a government, there were anti-clerical demonstrations in the streets; the King had to summon him back. He conceded only that monks and nuns could continue in their own houses if they liked or in others prescribed by the government.

During 1855 agents visited the monasteries and nunneries to make inventories. In Ovada the people gathered to resist and had to be stopped from force by the Capuchins. Some masons and locksmiths refused to be hired to break into religious houses; a few local officials resigned. But on the whole there was little trouble. The Pope excommunicated all who proposed or approved the Rattazzi law (*Cum Saepe*, 26 July 1855), but his Penitentiary allowed clergy to receive pensions from the fund and so pleased Cavour.[5] Monks were ordered by Rome not to resist the taking over of their houses, but to come out under protest. Rome allowed Catholics to buy the monastic property at auction, 'provided they intend one day to restore it to the Church'.

Such a law, though in utilitarian terms sensible, and enforced peacefully with the local respect for individuals, created a new class of landowners and smaller capitalists who backed the State; it produced hardship for the poor who had relied on monastic charity; damage, as always in such dissolutions, to works of art and libraries; and suffering to men of principle because the act was condemned by

[5] *Acta Pii IX* (Graz, 1971), ii. 436 ff.

the Pope and by the exiled archbishop of Turin. Don Menzio, the parish priest of Verres, when taking a christening, found that a godfather was the officer who dissolved the local convent. He refused to baptize the baby unless a different godfather was found. The father of the child took him to court. Menzio was imprisoned and, after a long legal struggle, was acquitted. But the antagonists made the parish impossible for him, and forced him out into destitution and a premature death.[6]

The money from the dissolved houses went into the Cassa Ecclesiastica to sell property, pay the pensions, and raise the stipends of parish priests; any surplus went to the State. The plan failed to go as well as the estimates: three years later the Cassa was in heavy deficit, had to borrow money from the State, and had still not raised the stipend of a single impoverished priest.[7]

THE ELECTION OF 1857 AND ITS CONSEQUENCES

One of Cavour's less worthy acts affected the future history of Italy and of the Catholic Church. In November 1857 he held a general election. To his surprise and vexation he lost his large majority and became the head of a minority government—if left and right voted together, which was almost impossible. What was worse was the number of seats, 65, that went to the Catholic right. Cavour himself reckoned the result thus: his party, 116; strong clerical, 58; right wing but not clerical, 14; extreme left but voting with government, 8: 'I hope the blow will not be mortal'. The Catholics calculated their group at 80.

A week later Cavour began a policy with long consequences. He saw how bishops and parish priests drove their flocks to vote against his candidate. He decided that clerical influence was a form of corruption. Therefore elected candidates might justly be unseated for corruption. He had a vague idea of confessors bullying timorous consciences in their confessional-boxes, and imagined pulpit and altar to be a kind of political tribune—which the pulpit sometimes was. At Birago thirty-eight priests were alleged to act as canvassers, and to tell the people that they must vote for the Catholic candidate under pain of excommunication. At Strambino the priests were alleged to depict

[6] *CC* (1856), 1: 105; 4: 349.   [7] *CC* (1858), 12: 513.

the opponent of the Marquis Birago as a heretic and schismatic with a hellish policy.

Cavour first obtained a ruling that any canon was ineligible as a member of Parliament because the law excluded persons with cure of souls (though four canons sat in the last Parliament). Then he started enquiries into corruption in constituencies, and unseated thirteen candidates, plus five canons; two of the thirteen being of his own party. These enquiries were hardly impartial. One of the thirteen who was elected and afterwards unseated was the priest Margotti, who was the editor of the Catholic newspaper *Armonia*. They accused him of 'irregularities' with illiterate electors. Another unseated candidate was the owner of *Armonia*, the Marquis Birago.

The full title of the newspaper was *L'Armonia della Civiltà alla Religione*, 'Harmony between Culture and Religion'. It was founded by Giacomo Margotti at Turin in the revolutionary times of 1848, and financed by a rich and intelligent lay Catholic deputy of the political right, the Marquis Birago di Vische. He managed the paper personally, despite anonymous letters, threats of assassination, the burning down of four of his farms, and the murder of his land-agent. Margotti himself survived an attempted assassination in the street on his way home from the office, and several violent demonstrations at the building. It was alleged in 1858 that the newspaper paid 10,000 fr. a year in fines.[8]

This treatment of the Catholic party by Cavour was in the long view bad for both Italy and the papacy. Cavour thought it vital not to have in Parliament a powerful body of members who would support the pope and therefore Austria. But the method by which he achieved their weakening confirmed Catholic suspicion that democracy is bound to be a corrupt form of government; and that it is useless, perhaps even immoral, for honest Catholics to have anything to do with voting and polling-booths when the result is certain not to represent public opinion. 'The right to elect', said one right-wing deputy in Parliament, 'has vanished.'[9]

It was Margotti who invented a phrase destined to be a motto of political force in the Italy of the future: 'Nè eletti nè elettori' ('neither electors nor elected'). In other words, Catholics must neither vote in an election, lest they seem to approve it as a way of achiev-

[8] Cf. *CC* (1858), 9: 489; 12: 110.

[9] *CC* (1858), 9: 615. For Catholic analysis of the election of 1857, and the 'proof' that democracy is a tyrannical form of government, see Ponziglione, *Le Mene elettorali* ('The Electoral Plots') (Turin, 1858), reviewed *CC* (1858), 11: 216–21.

ing representative government, nor must they agree to be candidates when, if they are elected, they will end in a Parliament that poses as representative but is not, and which will almost certainly undertake legislation with which no Catholic conscience can agree.

Cavour's programme was successful in the international field. In the minds of Protestants the contrast grew between the archaic system of government by the pope in Central Italy, and the modern system of efficient government by the Piedmontese.

THE PLAN TO UNITE NORTH ITALY

There were now two Italian plans for the future of Italy. They both needed Piedmont to lead. The one, radical and backed by wiser allies of Mazzini, wanted to unite all Italy under the king of Sardinia-Piedmont; this would not do for Mazzini because kings were bad. The other was the idea of Cavour, to remove the Austrians from Milan and Venice, and the pope from the Legations, his northern territories where the people were discontented; and create a kingdom across the north, the more prosperous and richer part of Italy, leaving the pope with much less of a State, and the kingdom of Naples and Sicily untouched.

This second was the practicable plan. Neither plan could begin without the backing of the French emperor and his army. The emperor was committed to keeping the pope in Rome, therefore the republicans' plan would not work; but he was not committed to keeping the Austrians in Milan or Bologna. To push the Austrians out of Italy with the aid of Piedmont might attract him as a step in that age-long rivalry between the French and the Germans, so often in history fought out on the plains of North Italy. And it attracted him before Cavour even spoke to him. We know from the papers that, irresolute as he was, swaying hither and thither in mind, he was ambitious and power-hungry and aware that he needed success to be secure in his dictatorship, he could see the chance that lay open to French power: get the Austrians out of Italy by an alliance with Italian nationalism and so Napoleonic France would be 'the deliverer and civilizer of the peoples'.[10] The vague plan was not to unite Italy. His army must keep the pope safe in Rome.

[10] Napoleon III to Walewski, 20 Dec. 1858; R. Romeo, *Cavour e il suo tempo*, 2nd edn. (Bari, 1971–84), iii. 433–4.

Cavour perceived this. He saw it clearly enough to risk his own future on the bet that this was what the Emperor would do. In July 1858 the Emperor took the waters at Plombières in the Vosges and suggested secretly that Cavour might meet him there. Cavour camouflaged his journey with a passport bearing a false name. Travelling round Plombières together in a carriage, they agreed in one day. They would aim at the making of a kingdom of Upper Italy in which the king of Piedmont should rule Lombardy and Venice. There would be a kingdom of Central Italy with Tuscany and the pope's Marches and Umbria. The kingdom of Naples should remain as it was. The four resulting Italian kingdoms (North Italy, Central Italy, the remaining Papal State, and Naples with Sicily) should be a confederation with the pope as honorary President.

But there were conditions. Austria must be seen to be the aggressor if a French army in Italy were to gain the respect of Europe. And France must be paid: Piedmont must cede the large part of its lands that lay across the Alps, Savoy and Nice. Savoy was the origin of the kingdom of Piedmont, its kings were the house of Savoy—but it spoke French. Nice was different, its people spoke Italian, it was Nizza. Cavour protested about Nice.

This agreement was in the interests of everyone except the Austrians, the pope, the dukes of Modena and Parma in North Italy, most of the inhabitants of Nice, a few of the inhabitants of Savoy, and all the young men who would die on the coming battlefields of North Italy where the battle of Solferino was to be the bloodiest massacre of the century. It would turn Piedmont into the strongest power in Italy. It was kept very secret: could a pope be safe if an antipapal power were to be so weighty in the peninsula?

To make Austria look the aggressor was not easy. Piedmont and Cavour made warlike noises and hoped anxiously that the wavering Napoleon III would back them. The Emperor jerked so up and down as to drive Cavour to distraction, sleepless nights, and the contemplation of coming death and the burning of his papers. Piedmontese noises were such, invitation to volunteers (including deserters from the Austrian army) to join a coming war of liberation in Lombardy were so intolerable to the Austrians that Cavour hoped they could rely on the passions of the Emperor Francis Joseph to cause Austria to act rashly.

He was not wrong. The young Francis Joseph was persuaded that Napoleon was the menace of Europe; he must be got rid of, the

Bourbons restored, and Alsace-Lorraine given to Prussia. But the fact was, Piedmont was arming. Austria demanded that it disarm and dismiss the volunteers within three days, or there would be war. The Pope's two military defenders were at each other's throats.

So in the spring of 1859 the expected war broke out between Piedmont and France on one side and Austria on the other. All the Pope's northern provinces of the Romagna revolted against his authority and put themselves under the king of Sardinia-Piedmont. In Tuscany, Modena, Parma, and the Legations, popular movements demanded to join the campaign against Austria, and their rulers—one grand duke, two dukes, and a cardinal—fled. In a few papal towns further south, such as Fano and Sinigaglia, crowds tore down the papal arms, but vanished at the approach of papal troops. An attempted coup in Perugia was repressed by Swiss mercenaries of the pope, who sacked the town; the repression of a people's revolt by mercenaries did not raise the reputation of the Pope across liberal Europe, which talked of a massacre sanctioned by the Pope (ten Swiss and twenty-seven citizens lost their lives). The Piedmontese army could easily have retaken Perugia but it was under the orders of Napoleon III that the Pope's dominions were not to be entered. They finally won Napoleon's leave to send troops into the Legations. Cavour justified this advance to the Pope as necessary to prevent social revolution.

The war was ended by what was known as the armistice of Villafranca (11 July 1859). Napoleon III would not go further because he was afraid of the rising hostility across the Rhine. Venice stayed under Austrian rule—which horrified Italian nationalists and put Cavour into a rage, and made him resign, though he was indispensable and had to be called back in the spring of 1860. The idea of the Italian federation vanished. By March 1860, in return for the annexation of Nice and Savoy, France accepted that the kingdom of Sardinia now ruled Lombardy, Tuscany, Parma, Modena, and the papal Legations. The loss of Nice horrified Italian nationalists because it was so Italian, and made Garibaldi furious because he was born there. In the church in Nice where he was baptized they still display proudly the certificate of his christening. The clergy and people of Savoy cheerfully accepted union with France, though they were reluctant about civil marriage and the State's right (rarely exercised) to ban the bishops' choice of pastors. The Savoy clergy sang with spirit the Te Deums for the new union. The clergy of Nice, on the contrary, felt with the people of Nice. Their seminary was full of enemies of France. But as their pay was increased, they accepted what happened.

A powerful kingdom of Italy had come into existence on the Pope's northern border and in occupation of his only prosperous lands. On 26 March 1860 the Pope in a solemn bull excommunicated the usurpers of the lands of the Church.

Some popes would have tried to compromise. They would have sought the way of diplomacy. Pius IX had no weapons in this fight. The protector who alone kept him safe in Rome, the French emperor, was on the Italian side. The Spanish had no power; the king of Naples had an army less reliable than the pope's; the Austrians had just been beaten out of Lombardy; the British being Protestant preferred Piedmont to the Pope; the Prussians could hardly help him. He was defenceless.

There was secret talk of a Catholic league to save the Pope; for the army of Naples to advance northward against the Piedmontese; for the Spanish to act, no one knew how; for the Austrians to rejoin the men from Naples. No one practical believed in this scheming.

In these conditions, the Pope remained without compromise. He would never recognize the Piedmontese annexation of the northern Papal State. His attitude was that nothing earthly could happen to change this situation. But this was the cause of God and with Him all things were possible.

Possibly the history of the Piedmontese quarrel with the Catholic Church in Piedmont-Sardinia during the 1850s made any form of compromise impossible. It might involve recognizing conduct over the Church in the land of Piedmont, for example over Church property or monasteries, which the Pope still regarded as outrageous.

It has been argued that the policy of no compromise was a disaster for the Church, not only as the holder of property but as a spiritual society. The argument is that it made the Pope appear to be against the whole of Europe. But it is not probable that anyone, however statesmanlike, could have remedied the situation which was now coming to pass. And it focused the minds of the best Catholics—especially in France, England, and Italy—on an affair of political right and of property. For at least two decades the attentions of fine men and women were dedicated to loyalty to the pope because his State was overturned. This has been argued to be a distraction from their proper cares.

Nevertheless, the stance of no compromise had a wonderful effect in Catholic Europe and America. It drew the hearts of Catholics towards Rome. It elicited their protective instincts, and evoked their emotional sense of loyalty. If these feelings could do little or nothing to protect the Pope in his defencelessness, they could and did feed a wave of world-wide allegiance to the office, and the person who then occupied the office. We have seen how so many aspects of Church life made for centralization in Rome and the elevation of the papacy to power in the Church. This wave of emotion was almost the final influence necessary to bring modern popes to a greater authority in the world-wide Church than any of their predecessors were able to exercise.

In Anglo-Saxon and medieval Britain there was a voluntary tax called Peter's pence. It began as a collection round the houses but later the bishops paid out a single sum. Henry VIII abolished it. But now it was revived in Catholic countries as a way by which the faithful could send money to the Pope in his dire need. It began from below, as an idea of the congregations. After a time bishops took it over and issued letters of exhortation; and finally the Pope did the same. Some 40 per cent of the money was sent from France. It only helped a little to pay for the soldiers and expenses of the State but it was another way by which European laymen and laywomen outside as well as inside Italy felt that they could help the Holy Father personally.

In its new situation, the Papal State did not look viable. The Romagna which it lost contained its industry and many of the best of the middle class. To have a strong Italian power just across the northern border made it vulnerable. If the French agreed, the Piedmontese could take it over in a moment. There was already a magnetism working on other areas of the Papal State, such as the Marches and Umbria. Forecasters and pamphleteers talked as though sooner or later—and probably sooner—the Pope must be confined to the city of Rome and a stretch of country round; and only secure there because of a French garrison. The French would never go back on the acquisition of North Italy by Piedmont, for they had gained Nice and Savoy for France.

Yet Louis Napoleon, on whose power the Pope depended, had lost some of his authority in France. He had depended on the Catholic vote; and now his policy had overthrown the pope's dominions. It was anticlerical Frenchmen for the most part who backed the war against Austria in Italy. A few liberal-minded French Catholics, such as the learned Maret, and even Montalembert and Lacordaire, thought that Austrian power in Italy was bad for civilization and it was good to end it. But they were not many. Nearly all the French bishops were against the Emperor's war. The Empress Eugénie was against it on religious grounds. Numbers of priests preached sermons against it: the government wanted them prosecuted for misuse of the pulpit for political ends, but local magistrates saw that this would do more harm than good. The people, indifferent to begin with, were caught up in the fervour of patriotic war, especially after the victories, and resented it when their priests could not share their enthusiasm. Government ordered the priests to sing Te Deums, and though they were less difficult than the North Italian priests they showed little pleasure in the hymn.

Now came the suggestion of a Vatican City State, as the future would think of it. The argument ran thus: modern States must have liberty of conscience, therefore the pope, committed to a single denomination, is not fit to be head of a modern State. He is disqualified by reason of his spiritual function, yet he ought not to be the subject of any other sovereign, and international opinion would not tolerate it. His independence as a spiritual leader demands independence in politics. He needs a State; but it ought to be the smallest State consistent with its being viable. The city of Rome itself, certainly—the historic see and historic capital. But nothing else is important, except in so far as it provides food or endowment to the city.

This idea became widespread, and it looked as though the French Emperor was converted to it, for the most-read pamphlet advocating a scheme of this sort, *The Pope and the Congress* (Paris, 1859), was by his close friend, the Vicomte La Guéronnière. All the Curia thought this pamphlet wicked; Veuillot said it was the kiss of Judas.[11] But after what happened in 1859, even after what happened in 1848, it had the logic of history on its side. An Italian translation was at once published in Milan. Cavour thought it as important a service by Napoleon to Italy as the battle of Solferino.

Intelligent French friends of the Pope still argued for the maintenance of his State. It was covered by the international law of Europe. His northern provinces were seized from him by a lawless invasion.

---

[11] *Univers*, 24 Dec. 1859; J. Maurain, *La Politique ecclésiastique de Second Empire de 1852 à 1869* (Paris, 1930), 359.

People said that the form of government was out of date; but a constitution that elected a king for his life and ensured that he could not be elected unless he was a good man morally, might be held to be a better constitution than any other. And if at the same time this system held high in Europe the moral and spiritual past which was inherent to its better civilization, the needs of Christian Europe coincided with the dictates of justice and international law. Few people listened to such arguments.

The absolute refusal of Pius IX to compromise meant that he and the Emperor were now in as severe a tension as that longer dispute between himself and the Piedmontese. The bull of excommunication of 26 March 1860, which hit all those who encouraged the rebellion of the Pope's States, could be held to hit Napoleon, though it did not mention his name and could not be published in France. The French Church was indirectly the pope's political protector and now it no longer had confidence in the Emperor, neither did it receive his confidence. The old religious division of France, lately held to silence by police action, reappeared. In the French Senate Dupin made a rollicking speech—this claim of the Pope that he has taken an oath not to lose any territory—it is not meant to cover that readjustment of frontiers which happens to every State from time to time. It was designed to stop popes of old from giving away lands to their bastards and nephews. More than one bishop protested against this speech, but it was the speech and not the protest that was given publicity.[12]

When in February 1860 Piedmont asked the Pope to hand over the Marches and Umbria as well as the Romagna, the Paris nuncio Sacconi, an unspiritual member of the Curia, talked violently. The French Ambassador in Rome told how he threw oil into the flames by stirring up the Pope with malevolent remarks, telling him scandalous stories about the Emperor, and running down the French clergy—even Archbishop Morlot of Paris. It was said on good evidence that Sacconi talked of his duty to cause civil war in France and smash the Emperor's regime.[13]

[12] Maurain, *La Politique ecclésiastique*, 402; Merimée to Panizzi, P. Merimée, *Lettres à M. Panizzi, 1850–70*, 3rd edn. (Paris, 1881), 31 Mar., 1 Apr. 1860.

[13] Gramont (then French ambassador at Rome) to Thouvenel, 18 Feb. 1860 in Louis Thouvenel, *Le Secret de l'Empereur* (Paris, 1889), i. 38 ff.; and Merimée to Panizzi, 25 Mar. 1860, *Lettres*.

GARIBALDI IN THE SOUTH

It looked as though an attack on Rome would happen soon. All sorts
of people talked in public as well as in secret, about invading the
Papal States immediately; Mazzini, Garibaldi, even the king of
Piedmont himself, Victor Emmanuel. But it risked disaster, in a fight
against the French garrison of Rome; and once the Emperor committed an army, no one knew whether the whole recent union in
North Italy might be at risk.

During April 1860, the Sicilians, stirred by events in the north,
broke into rebellion. It was being suppressed, without much difficulty,
when Garibaldi landed in the western end of the island with his
'Thousand'. He recreated the revolt, and by 7 September 1860 he was
in Naples. He was not without a Franciscan as his chaplain: Father
Pantaleo ran away from his cloister at the Angeli di Salemi, met him as
he landed in Sicily, and offered his services, and persisted despite a cold
shoulder from the troops. As they advanced on Palermo they went to
church at Alcamo, and Garibaldi knelt and was blessed by Pantaleo,
crucifix in hand, and declared to be a warrior sent by God; the monks
of Alcamo celebrated a mass for the dead and called on God to bless
the liberators. Pantaleo wore the crucifix on his breast—but breeches
instead of a cassock; a friar's girdle—but a sword slung below. He was
an ecstatic popular preacher, and hoped to make all the Catholics of
Italy into followers of Garibaldi. When they took Naples they went to
a service in the cathedral, and Father Pantaleo sang Te Deum amid the
frightened canons, and preached a sermon in which Garibaldi, who sat
below the pulpit, was compared to Christ incarnate.

In Naples Garibaldi was sure that he could advance first on Rome
and then Venice, and unite all Italy. Cavour could not bear to think
of what might happen if Garibaldi's guerrillas advanced on Rome and
met a disciplined French garrison, and what might then be the fate of
the insecure northern kingdom of Italy. To stop the invasion of
Rome by Garibaldi it was necessary for Cavour to tell the Parliament
in Turin that his government intended to make Rome the capital of
Italy and that it would join Venice to Italy by the growth of Italian
power and the force of European opinion. But it was also necessary
to send the Piedmontese army to invade the Papal States—that is, the
Marches and Umbria—and so to make sure that southern Italy
belonged to the united Italian kingdom.

Lamoricière's career was the most extraordinary among those of all the defenders of Pius IX. He was a soldier and a republican; a Breton, but from a family of soldiers who had served the French Revolution. He accepted the influence of Saint-Simon towards socialism, and at Paris studied under the anti-Christian Comte. He did not resign from the army at the Revolution of 1830 and fought in Algeria with distinction. The painting of him standing in the breach at the capture of the city of Constantine was celebrated throughout France and he came back a hero. In Algiers he learnt Arabic and trained the Arabs and Berbers in a force with the Berber name of Zouaves; he believed in the French mission to 'civilize' Algeria. He entered Parliament and at the Revolution of 1848 was made the captain of the national guard to keep order in the Paris riots; he was twice wounded in street fighting. He believed in universal suffrage and it was said of him that when he spoke in Parliament it sounded as though he was calling his troops to a charge. He was the War Minister when France decided to save the Pope from the Roman revolution, but his motive was not to put down the revolution but to get there first, before Austria. He was moved by the murder of Pellegrino Rossi, whom he looked upon as a Frenchman.

Lamoricière was opposed to Louis Napoleon and fiercely against his dictatorship. The Emperor therefore got rid of him by sending him off to be French ambassador to Russia, but he quickly resigned, and in 1851 was arrested and imprisoned in the fortress of Ham before being allowed to go into exile in Brussels.

He had married a pious Catholic. In the fortress of Ham, he began to study the Bible, and was held by the devotional books of the Oratorian Gratry, and experienced what he felt to be true conversion.

Here was one of the two or three most famous soldiers in Europe, at a loose end, and known to be a new and ardent Catholic. He was sounded out from Rome, whether he could come to command an army to defend the Pope against his enemies. His advisers told him that he had no future but defeat, whatever volunteers were raised had no chance of standing up to a trained Piedmontese army. He accepted that this was true; but he replied that Rome was secure with its French garrison, that the Emperor had guaranteed the Papal States from the Piedmontese, and that the work lay in keeping out Garibaldi and the guerrilla bands, which he and his volunteers could do.

Under a false name Lamoricière went to Rome through Austria. No French citizen could legally enlist as a foreign mercenary without leave, for which Lamoricière refused to ask. For the Pope to name him as general was intended to be a blow to the Emperor. The French ambassador in Rome, Gramont, won him the French assent to make legal the *fait accompli*. Lamoricière at once issued a proclamation: 'The revolution now menaces Europe as once Islam used to menace it. Today as in old days the cause of the Pope is the cause of the civilization and liberty of the world.' He did not like what he found in the papal armoury if the object was to fight a war. In France they heard the story that he made a pun to Pius IX which was more than a jest, 'Get rid of canons and get more canons.'[14] He spent lavishly on credit and so caused worry to Cardinal Antonelli about bankruptcy.

The papal zouaves, mostly recruited from France and Belgium, made the Pope slightly less dependent on the French army. By September there were some 500 French zouaves, some of whom were ordinands; very few had asked for the legal leave necessary from their State, many were hostile to the Emperor and talked about him contemptuously in camp. No one had any confidence, army or no army, that the Pope could do without French protection.

Cardinal Antonelli, who really governed the Papal State, was totally opposed to this enlisting of an amateur force that could not defend the Pope against a serious attack. Pius IX believed it right and allowed Monsignor Mérode as War Minister to organize the defence. Lamoricière found the organization inefficient. He fortified the port of Ancona as a possible refuge for the Pope.

The Piedmontese could not afford not to move. All southern Italy was liable to be governed by ragged forces, the leaders of which were republican. To the new North Italian kingdom they seemed to be on the same side—but were more of a danger than the Pope. On 19 September 1860 the Piedmontese army crossed the north-east frontier, with the aim not to advance on Rome but to make sure of North Italian power in the South. They easily defeated Lamoricière's outnumbered force at Castelfidardo near the shrine of Loreto. He forced his way through to the fort at Ancona but surrendered sadly ten days later. The Piedmontese never came into contact with the regular French troops in Rome.

---

[14] Merimée to Panizzi, *Lettres*, i. 89.

There was talk of the Pope leaving Rome as the invaders approached—it was said that he might go to Spain, or Trieste, or Bavaria—but it was bluff by conservative diplomats, Pius IX had no such intention. The Empress Eugénie at Paris was in tears that her husband had allowed this to happen to the Pope;[15] and he had not intended it to happen, but now there was nothing that he could do to stop it.

French bishops celebrated memorial services for the twenty-five Frenchmen who were killed at Castelfidardo but not many of the people bothered to attend. Lamoricière returned to a hero's welcome in France.

Cavour was in an impossible situation for a statesman. On the one hand he had to say to Parliament, 'We must have Rome.' That encouraged the guerrilla bands, of which there were many because of recent history, to attack Rome; and the most famous guerrilla commander was now upon an Italian pedestal and revered. On the other hand, though he must say that Italy needed Rome, he must also use Piedmontese soldiers to stop anyone attacking Rome, lest everything so far gained be destroyed.

The Pope, protected by his French soldiers, was not reduced to the city of Rome alone. But he was left with a very small State—the city of Rome and Lazio which surrounded it. A united Italy existed, though without Venice and its surroundings, Rome and its surroundings, the Trentino, Trieste, Nice, bits of Savoy, Corsica, and the Italian towns on the Dalmatian coast which were relics of the Venetian empire.

No one with eyes could suppose that Italy could stay like that. The ideas of men such as La Guéronnière did not address the crucial difficulty. If there was to be a unified Italian State, it had to include Rome. That was not the same as saying, for instance, that it must include Nice; the name of Rome was magical in the history of Italians. Once it had ruled the world. A movement for the unity of Italy could not stop short at Rome, Rome had to be the goal. It alone was the final achievement by which the movement was seen to have won. To say, 'The Pope must not be a sovereign of more than a minimum but that minimum must include Rome', was still to confront all Italy, and all Europe, with a conflict. There was talk now that the Pope ought not to have a State at all: he should trust the Italians.

[15] Bixio to Cavour, 24 Oct. 1860, in *Il Carteggio Cavour–Nigra* (Bologna, 1929), iv. 264.

There were already those who suggested that since Rome must be Italian, and since the Pope must be independent, it would be enough—it would even be best for the Pope—if he only had the Vatican Palace to rule, together with the Leonine City, that piece of Rome, not large, between St Peter's and the River Tiber. Since this was almost the solution that eventually, and after many tears, was adopted, such prophets must be credited with unusual perception. But there was no chance of this solution at that moment. Any such plan would have required confidence by the Pope in an Italian government. Pius IX had no confidence whatever in Cavour and the Piedmontese. He took the view of his Secretary of State Cardinal Antonelli, who said, 'We never make pacts with burglars.'[16] And history gave the members of the Curia reason to doubt whether a pope whose kingdom was the Vatican Palace would rule a State which could have more than a ceremonial independence of the Italian State.

Rome was necessary to the pope because that was his see city and the sanctuary of the Catholic Church, and because a pope could be no one's subject. Rome was necessary to the Italians because in the ancient world the Romans made Europe what it was and made Italy; Italy could never be Italy if Rome were not part of Italy. This contradiction meant a fight between Italy and the pope that lasted sixty-nine years and conditioned the development of the papal office in the modern world.

Cavour tried negotiation; he found various liberal-minded clergymen who believed that the pope would be better off spiritually if he had no duty to be secular ruler; chief among them was Carlo Passaglia.[17] But there was nothing to negotiate about because the Pope would never surrender Rome nor even his claims to Bologna; and also because the French emperor was committed to keeping him sovereign of Rome and he knew it. And Cavour did not really want

[16] N. Bianchi, *Storia documentata della Diplomazia Europea in Italia 1814–1861* (Turin, 1872), viii. 448; *noi non patteggieremo mai cogli spogliatori.*

[17] It was April 1861, not long before Cavour's death, when Antonelli's more pious brother Gustavo used Passaglia, the leading Jesuit (ex-Jesuit from 1859) theologian of the doctrine of Immaculate Conception, for a further half-attempt at compromise. Passaglia was a Jesuit at the two Rome universities in succession (the Gregorian and the Sapienza), was learned in the Fathers, and published three vols. of theological commentaries and the two-vol. *De Ecclesia*; when he had to leave Rome and the Jesuits he became professor at Turin. He was suspended from the priesthood and for a short time was a member of the Italian Parliament. He reconciled himself with the Church near his death. Cf. *LTK, DTC.* Newman's letters are interesting about him as a teacher.

the concessions that he would need to make in a compromise: he had to offer what he described as 'the great principle', a free Church in a free State—but it would have pained him if the offer were taken up. The new Italian State was too insecure not to control the Church. Besides, he knew that he was safe, that the offer could not be accepted. In Lombardy, Tuscany, and Naples, the Josephist tradition survived: for the good of the State as well as the good of the Church, the State must keep reins on the Church. Such opinions disliked the phrase, 'A free Church in a free State'. They confessed their scepticism about it in Parliament. 'It is only a pun or epigram,' Ferrari told the Italian Chamber, 'it cannot mean that we intend to make concessions to the spiritual power, in return for the concession of the temporal power. Liberals could never allow it. It would be a step backwards. It would be a renunciation of the conquests we have already made.'[18]

THE DEATH OF CAVOUR

On the very dawn of the national feast of Italian unity Cavour was struck with a fever and died (June 1861). The priest of his parish had been exiled nine years before, mainly for declaring that civil marriage was merely a way of producing bastards. The man then put in charge of the parish, the Franciscan Father Giacomo di Poirino, was one of those priests, now plentiful in Turin, who approved of the new Italy and was not well regarded by the bishops. But he was simple, and friendly, and much liked.

When Archbishop Fransoni had refused religious burial to Santa Rosa, the Minister of Agriculture, Cavour had arrived at the deathbed just after the death, and used violent language about what had happened. He was determined that nothing like this should happen when he died. He put himself in touch with Father Giacomo and a few years later, at a time of cholera, asked for his help. In 1856 he used Father Giacomo as an emissary to carry a letter from him to the Pope seeking some sort of compromise. He described him to a friend as

---

[18] Atti, no. 922. 3581, *apud CC* (1863), 5: 20–1. Giuseppe Ferrari was a philosopher who believed in the general necessity of revolutions. He wanted a non-religious State but still a State that would keep a tight control of Churches. He wanted a democratic republic but disapproved of Mazzini as much as he disapproved of Cavour or the Pope: a loner but with weight; a professor at Milan.

'this devoted monk'.[19] It appears that there came to be a sort of agreement between them, that Giacomo should minister to him on his death-bed. 'I'm a Catholic,' he said to a friend Ruggero in 1856, 'I want to die in my religion, and I want my death not to be the cause of scandal.'[20]

During Cavour's final days a mob threatened priests of the Church if they refused to minister the last rites—for in effect he was excommunicated. While thousands stood silent outside in the street, Father Giacomo, who was aware of the risk that he ran, made no difficulty about the viaticum and extreme unction. He did his ministerial duty with piety and won the hearts of Cavour's family.

But had Cavour recanted? If he received the sacrament, he must have recanted. If he had not recanted and received the sacrament, Father Giacomo committed scandal? The debate sounded throughout Italy. Roughs prepared to attack the offices of the Catholic newspaper *Armonia* if it criticized Cavour in its obituary. But Margotti believed that Cavour must have recanted, and printed nothing but praise for the dead man. Liberal Italy found it important that the Church should bless the maker of Italy at his end without a recantation. Papal Italy found it important that the Church should not bless him at the end without a recantation. In the midst of the newspaper rhetoric and a wave of indignation against him, Father Giacomo stayed silent.

Four weeks later Pope Pius IX summoned him to Rome, to find out what happened. Giacomo was nervous of going, a little friar before the Pope, but the Piedmontese Foreign Secretary Ricasoli gave him a formal safe-conduct. In Rome he stayed at the house of his order at Aracoeli and was summoned to the Vatican on 27 July 1861. Father Giacomo replied simply and properly that he could not tell: 'What was said, was said under the seal of confession, your Holiness would not care to ask me about it.' He would only say that he did his duty as a priest. The Pope remarked, 'Some newspapers have said it was only a comedy, a performance, a bit of staging.' Father Giacomo replied, 'Newspapers can say what they like. But I can affirm to your Holiness that the Count of Cavour died a good Christian and I would be happy if any of my parishioners made such a good and exemplary end.' 'You have some rum parishioners,' the Pope said.

[19] *Questo zelante religioso*: Cavour to Cardinal Gaude, 20 Aug. 1856, *Epistolario* (Florence, 1992–), XIII. ii. 697–8.
[20] M. Mazziotti, *Le Comte de Cavour et son Confesseur* (Paris, 1919), p. xv.

The liberal press heard of efforts to break the seal of confession and there was a campaign on behalf of Giacomo. He was very troubled in Rome, but kept on saying that he could tell no more. His general deprived him of the charge of the Turin parish and suspended him from ministering the sacraments. All 1862 the quarrel in the newspapers went on. Cavour had wanted a quiet death but had not achieved it. Carlo Passaglia, the ablest theologian in Italy, printed a tremendous defence of Father Giacomo.[21]

Father Giacomo was given two rooms next to his old convent and had his monk's pension and something more from the government. He lived humbly and obscurely. Twenty years later a new archbishop of Turin asked a new pope that Giacomo be given back the right to hear confessions, and this was granted. He burnt all his private papers and when he died in poverty the newspapers did not notice.

To this little friar, of whom no one heard again, the future Italy owed a bigger debt than was ever realized. The chasm between the new-made Italy and old Catholic Italy would have grown far deeper if the hero of the Risorgimento was seen to die excommunicated, cast out by the Church. Various legends were circulated to help diminish the chasm—as that in dying Cavour said, 'I desire the good people of Turin to know that I die like a Christian', and that almost his last words were, 'A free Church in a free State.'[22]

Father Giacomo was not alone. A state funeral was needed at Santa Croce in Turin. The archbishop of Turin was in exile, and a state funeral needed a bishop to preside. One was found—Renaldi of Pinerolo—who celebrated the requiem in a church hung with black as for royalty, and at the portals an inscription that prayer was made for Cavour, 'a man sacred to Italy'.[23]

THE SEARCH FOR 'LIBERAL PRIESTS'

In Piedmont the government could easily find 'liberal priests', who liked the idea of a united Italy and saw nothing incompatible between loyalty to the pope and their Italian patriotism. In Lombardy most of

---

[21] *Mediatore*, May 1862, 586 ff.; repr. by Mazziotti, *Comte de Cavour*, 93 ff.
[22] *CC* (1861), 11: 65–78, 109–14, 613–14; *DBI*, s.v. Cavour; *CC* (1863), 7: 235; Thayer, *Cavour*, ii. 489–90; Romeo, *Cavour*, iii. 935 ff.
[23] *CC* (1861), 11: 359.

the people preferred being part of Italy to being part of Austria, and therefore Milan was second only to Turin or Genoa in the encouragement of liberal priests. In the old Legations of the pope Bologna had not been comfortable with him, and there could be found clergy who welcomed a united Italy. In Florence 'liberal clergy' were not rare. But the further south the less frequently could such clergy be found. The people of the two Sicilies were not fond of Piedmontese conquest. A civil war raged in the mountains of southern and central Italy. And most of the priests were on the side of the rebels, or (as it was called) 'the reaction'; though of course they could not declare themselves and often tried to prevent the foolish local uprisings which led to terrible executions.

The government of Turin fixed the first Sunday in June 1861 as a feast to celebrate a united Italy. Determined to avoid earlier troubles over singing the Te Deum, the government ruled that no priest who did not wish to sing should be compelled. But government could not control local feeling. Plenty of priests in Lombardy cheerfully sang Te Deum. In Milan Archbishop Ballerini could not act for eight long years because the people thought him 'Austrian'; the chapter elected Caccia Dominioni to act as bishop. He ordered that Te Deum should not be sung. A crowd hunted the vicar-capitular through his cathedral. He left Milan and tried to govern the diocese from the seminary at Monza. He founded the paper *Osservatore Cattolica* which later in the century was to be the chief ultramontane journal of North Italy. In the spring of 1861 no one in Milan could safely go out of his house without wearing in his hat the inscription, 'Down with the Pope-King! We want Rome!'

By the time Caccia Dominioni died in 1866 the Milan clergy were much more papist. Pope and Italian government then appointed a proper bishop, translating Calabiana, who was respected by both sides and at last achieved reconciliation. The trials of Milan cathedral were a type of the troubles that afflicted other cities in the north.

Some in Turin had the idea of creating a national Church of Italy without the pope; Bishop Renaldi of Pinerolo was regarded with hope by the Piedmontese; Bishop Caputo of Ariano in the kingdom of Naples was on the side of Italy. Turin formed the plan that Caputo should become its archbishop and then consecrate other bishops. Caputo wanted the clergy to hail Victor Emmanuel as a new Judas Maccabaeus, who won an eternal name for freeing his people. The money for Caputo's proposed Church would be found from the confiscated monasteries and nunneries; but the plan never passed beyond vague talk, the endowments of the monasteries were in deficit even for paying the monks' small pensions. Bishop Caputo suddenly died and with him died the plan of a National Church. He would not have made a good archbishop.

It is hard to know the number of 'liberal' priests in Italy. Several hundred priests signed a petition to the Pope to give Rome to Italy, but some signatures were extorted or fictitious. The best evidence comes from Lombardy where there were about 9,000 clergy and under 100 declared 'liberal' clergy. But out of the twenty-five parish rectors of Milan, ten said they stood on the side of united Italy. Whatever the merits of the 'liberal' clergy they were of ruined reputation because they were linked with the government of Turin which persecuted the Church.[24] The top moment of the clergy's willingness to sacrifice the temporal power was in 1862. Carlo Passaglia, transferred from the Roman chair from which he was ejected to a chair of moral philosophy at Turin (where he remained for twenty-six years) launched an appeal to the Pope to sacrifice the Papal State for the good of the Church, and obtained 8,943 signatures, representing one in every ten priests in Italy.[25] But such numbers, or anything like them, were never achieved again. The harder the Pope was pressed by the Italian State, and the tougher the behaviour of the State towards the clergy, the more loyally the clergy rallied to the Pope. The situation led to odd predicaments.

Luigi Prota was a Dominican of Naples. He was stalwart for the 'liberal' clergy, indeed became president of the Society for the Emancipation of the Clergy, which aimed at abolishing papal power in Italy. The Dominicans expelled him from their order, but he went on living in their house under the protection of the State, and continued to wear the Dominican habit. Later he became bishop of the National Church of Italy—though he had hardly any flock.

Truly the rift between the Pope's Italy and the King's Italy made life hard for the Church and for the people, and created war between the Risorgimento and official Catholicism. There was the instance of Archbishop Limberti of Florence, who consented to sing Te Deum for the coming of the kingdom of Italy. He was willing to receive King Victor Emmanuel with honour at the cathedral when he laid

---

[24] Cf. *DBI* s.v. Caputo; *CC* (1862), 1: 617; (1863), 5: 641–56; (1864), 9: 227–9.
[25] G. Martina, *Pio IX (1851–66)* (Rome, 1986), 134.

the foundation stone for the façade. But (in theory, for actually the Pope remained friendly towards the King) Victor Emmanuel was excommunicated. A fierce letter reached Archbishop Limberti who asked pardon. Then there was Abbot Pappalettere of Monte Cassino: impressive as an abbot of a great house should be and, unlike most abbots, scholarly, who kept his historic archive in perfect order. He had a reputation won by suffering months of imprisonment under the Roman Revolution of 1849. He had studied German philosophy and helped the Vatican with advice about the German professors. Now he was reduced to twenty monks, and was inside the new kingdom of Italy; he longed to preserve the most historic monastery in Europe from destruction or dissolution and he sang a Te Deum and invited King Victor Emmanuel to pay a visit to the abbey. Pius IX not only drove him out of the office of abbot but ordered him not to go back to the community.[26]

Cavour left the legacy, a free Church in a free State, as an ideal of life and hardly anyone knew that he did not believe in it: 'Let the pope give up Rome, we will guarantee his freedom to rule the Church.' Quickly the saying became a jest in Catholic Italy. Hardly an archbishop was not in prison or exile, most monks and nuns were either driven out or under threat of expulsion, many priests were troubled by police; government supervised, or tried to, the syllabuses of seminaries. 'What "a free Church in a free State" means,' said one Catholic, 'is a slave Church in a despotism.'[27]

To this mockery the Piedmontese had a reply: These troubles are the passing conflicts of a big change in society and politics. The Pope has refused to accept modern Italy—therefore his men will not say Te Deums for the making of Italy, and will not pray for the King; they talk of the Pope as still sovereign, refuse absolution to loyal Italians in the confessional, and may even refuse them the viaticum on their death-beds; they sympathize with the 'brigands' hidden in the Apennines, and by their behaviour, if not their words, encourage disloyalty to the new national government. Therefore we penalize and control. But let the Pope resign Rome. Let him accept a united Italy with a generous heart. Let his men be grateful for the coming of a free and united Italy. Then we will guarantee him

---

[26] Martina, *Pio IX (1851–66)*, 132. He was abbot from 1858. His fateful letter to the king, which was not meant to be public, was written in April 1862. Cf. F. Gregorovius, *Roman Journal* (1911), 68 ff.

[27] *CC* (1861), 12: 739.

(already they began to talk of guarantees) liberty to rule the Church as he likes.

In the Pope's mind his oath of office weighed. He had taken an oath not to sacrifice any of the rights of the Holy See. He was a legitimate sovereign and international law must prevail. He had a faith in the future, unlike that of most people it was a faith that the future would restore the immediate past. He was never reconciled to the invention of newspapers with wide circulations, and was never aware that they were one of the instruments that simultaneously lowered his reputation and magnified his international authority. He never lost the belief that liberty of the press is bad for society and especially for the morals of the people. He did not feel alone against the world: he could sense the simple people of ordinary Catholic congregations from various countries rallying in sympathy.

On 9 June 1862 bishops from different parts of the world were in Rome to make saints out of twenty-six Japanese martyrs. 'We recognize that the secular sovereignty of the Holy See is a necessity for its work and is instituted by God . . . In the present state of the world this secular sovereignty is needed by all of us for legality and that the Church's authority and care for souls should be free.'[28] Fifty out of eighty-five French bishops attended the celebration. The ship that carried most of them sailed from Marseilles as a reverent crowd sang hymns at the dock, and a smaller group with many Italians demonstrated with cries of 'Down with the Pope-King, down with parsons, long live the Emperor!'[29]

In that same year of 1862 Garibaldi raised his next little band to raid southern Italy. Lamoricière in France heard of it and offered his sword to the Pope, but Pius IX refused the offer. In the church at Marsala in Sicily Father Pantaleo invited the condottiere and all his comrades to renew their oath, or 'Rome or Death', raising their hands towards the altar. At Caltanisetta he climbed into the bishop's throne of the cathedral (the pulpit was locked) and to a crowded congregation denounced the absent bishop, whereat the cathedral emptied, not silently. At Aspromonte in Calabria the mismanaged raid collapsed before a small force of Italian regulars. Father Pantaleo was captured as he escaped towards Naples but was released at the armistice a few days later. Next year he left the Franciscan order. He

---

[28] *Collectio Lacensis*, vi. 883; Martina, *Pio IX (1851–66)*, 124.
[29] Maurain, *La Politique ecclésiastique*, 608 n. 3.

fought as one of Garibaldi's band in the war of 1866 against Austria and in the defeat of Mentana the next year. He followed Garibaldi to France to fight against the Prussians; and after the war he married at Lyons. He returned to Italy and died in poverty, not reconciled with the Church, at the age of only 57.

5

THE NEED FOR A COUNCIL

NAPOLEON III AND THE CHURCH OF THE 1860S

All through the 1850s the French government and the French Church were united in Catholic policy. All through the 1860s the French government and the French Church were at loggerheads with each other, partly because the Emperor let down the Pope in 1859–60, and even more because the realization of what the Emperor was like enabled the old oppositions to reappear. Under the dictatorship no one could freely publish or express opinions. That restriction could affect Church tracts, pastoral letters, and even sermons. But it was recognized that the Church had special liberties, the freedom to speak and to associate, which no one else had without the leave of government. Therefore the Church was now the chief vehicle of opposition to the dictatorship. Napoleon began to allow more freedom to the anticlericals.

One case was indirectly to affect the Pope. Ernest Renan was an ordinand at Saint-Sulpice and then renounced Catholicism and studied Oriental sources and worked as an archaeologist in Palestine. This gave him insight into daily life in Palestine and the chance to become the best Hebraist in France. The Hebrew professorship at the Collège de France was vacant and the government did not dare to allow it to be filled because they knew that the college would recommend Renan. The vacancy went on more than four years. At last they asked for candidates, the college asked for Renan, and the government approved. At his inaugural lecture (21 February 1862) there were hisses and boos drowned by applause so thunderous that for twenty minutes he could not speak, and the students afterwards escorted him home in triumph. There was an appeal to the government which after three days suspended the course—'he has taught in such a way as to hurt Christian doctrine and this might lead to trouble better avoided'.

A year later Renan was allowed to publish his *Life of Jesus*, a book shattering to traditional Catholic beliefs about the Bible. In a popular way it summarized the results of Protestant, and his own, biblical scholarship. It was well based in the countryside of Palestine, and written beautifully—though it made Jesus elegant. It had an enormous success in France and in all Protestant Europe. Within two months it appeared on the Index of Prohibited Books. In the French Senate speakers argued that the book ought to be banned—and got nowhere. The public prosecutor considered whether Renan could be prosecuted and believed that any attempt would fail. Finally the government suppressed the chair of Hebrew at the Collège de France. But the Emperor Napoleon respected Renan. For the first time in a Catholic country, still with Catholic control of printing, the great intellectual problem of the Christian modern age was presented, the challenge to treat the foundation documents of the faith like any other ancient documents, with the same methods of enquiry. This was hardly to affect Pius IX; but it affected his successor in his later years and was an agony for his successor but one.

In his new mood towards an uncompromising Rome, Napoleon wanted to push less papalist bishops into French sees. This was difficult because although he had the right of nomination the Pope had the right to disagree. In 1860 he proposed for the see of Vannes Maret, a fine scholar who was the dean of the faculty of theology at the Sorbonne and the leading representative of the old Gallican school in France; he believed that the pope was not infallible, and that the General Council was his superior; that he ought to have a State, but that it need not be so large. The nuncio Sacconi, who was not the most admirable of clergymen, campaigned against the choice of Maret. It was said that he was deaf—and he was a little deaf; it was said that he sometimes dressed as a layman—and it was true that this had happened when he was ill with trouble in the bladder; it was said that he was a man of books and not likely to be a good pastor of a diocese. All these were excuses, what mattered was that he was a Gallican. Everyone agreed that he was a very good man, and intelligent. The French ministers said that the Pope had no right to refuse to have a man against whom no real objection could be laid. The Pope won. He told the Emperor that he could not agree to a bishop whom his conscience told him he ought not to allow. And Maret had no wish to be a cause of trouble. He suggested that he might be made not a real bishop but a titular bishop, *in partibus*. Both sides agreed and he became the bishop of Sura.

There were other such cases. Much the most important was that of Darboy. He had the sharpest, quickest mind of all the French bishops of the century. He had ministered to the wounded during the street civil war of 1848 and was not far from his friend Archbishop Affre when he was shot at the barricade. Then he collaborated with Archbishop Sibour of Paris in the fight against the ultramontanes. In 1859 he became bishop of Nancy with no protest from Rome (which may not have known how Gallican were his opinions). When the Emperor launched his Italian campaign he became famous for his support. In 1863 he was translated to be archbishop of Paris. The nuncio protested, Rome hesitated, but this was a translation. Until his murder as a hostage by the Communard revolutionaries eight years later, Darboy was the most potent French critic of an uncompromising Rome. He appointed to preach in Notre Dame the Carmelite Father Hyacinthe Loyson, who was a fine orator but believed the French Revolution had done good. The Pope and Darboy wrote each other severe letters. Darboy's letters always remained courteous but during the time of Pius IX no other bishop wrote tougher letters to the Pope: 'You have made a vague accusation against my young people' . . . 'your blame of my vicar-general is unjust'. He reminded him that a pope interfering in a diocese must by the law of the Church be exceptional—in ordinary circumstances the bishop is in charge. 'I have not deserved your reproaches.' 'Such accusations are puerile and not worthy of either of us.' Darboy removed the right of the blind Monsignor de Ségur, the Pope's chief French adviser, and an acrid critic of Darboy to the Pope, to preach or hear confessions in his diocese on the grounds that de Ségur's criticisms of him were calumny. Since de Ségur's godly life consisted in hearing confessions and directing souls, he submitted to Darboy and withdrew his complaints against him. Darboy was in more trouble at Rome because as a senator he defended the Organic Articles which gave the State its control of the Church, and then because he celebrated the funeral of a high-ranking French Freemason.[1] Then the Curia was in big trouble with Darboy because, with the set purpose of diminishing his reputation with his clergy, they leaked to the press a severe letter of rebuke from the Pope, which was three years old and contained errors of fact. Darboy called this an outrage and worse than an outrage. The conflict between emperor and pope had caused one of the chief sees of all the Church to be held by an intelligent Gallican who

---

[1] See the letters between Darboy, the Pope, and Antonelli printed in *Revue d'histoire et de littérature religieuses*, 12 (1907), 240 ff. The Freemason was General Magnan.

was willing to say to Rome whatever he thought right without thought for the consequences to his own reputation. Pius IX, despite pressure from the Emperor, absolutely refused to make Darboy a cardinal, though the see and the person were of such eminence that the refusal was almost an insult to France.

The Pope's refusals were not always ill-founded. In his new hostility to the Pope, Napoleon tried to get bishops appointed not because, as in Darboy's case, they would be excellent bishops, but because they were against the Pope. The chief such case was Gérin. He was a parish priest at Grenoble who was warmly recommended by the prefect: his politics were excellent and his morals irreproachable, he was not at all clerical and disliked monks and he thought that the only solution for the pope's temporal power was to do what Napoleon wanted. The politicians all wanted him, the bishops thought him an ambitious political priest and not one would back him. Napoleon nominated him for the see of Agen. The Pope refused him with no explanation, though one of the Pope's men did say that he had not the qualities recommended by St Paul for a bishop. The see of Agen stayed vacant for four years.

The case of Gérin was very different from that of Darboy. At Paris the Pope refused an excellent man solely because he was a Gallican. At Agen he refused a man because he was selected on political grounds. Yet it was not certainly right. Gérin was of Grenoble, an able speaker and preacher. He was active in social welfare and won great influence among the working class of Grenoble; Napoleon III decorated him for his work. But Gérin recognized Napoleon to have done good in helping to make Italy. The nuncio told him, 'You are sold to the Emperor.' In the spiritual arena, he did not believe in the visions of the children at La Salette, which was near Grenoble, and said so plainly. The reasons against his appointment were not very good but were enough to make Pius IX refuse to accept his name, and the vacancy at Agen went on too long.

When the Emperor fell and German troops straddled France, the emergency government at Bordeaux (January 1871) nominated another for the see of Agen, Rome accepted and so did Gérin. He died wealthy fifteen years later and left his money to the poor, sick, and children of Grenoble.[2]

_____

[2] Cf. J. Maurain, *La Politique ecclésiastique* (Paris, 1930), and *DBF* s.v.

THE SEPTEMBER CONVENTION

Napoleon wanted to get his garrison out of Rome. But he could not afford to do that unless the Piedmontese would guarantee not to take Rome if the French troops left. This was difficult to achieve because Cavour had said that Italy must have Rome, and for the Italian government to guarantee that it would not enter Rome was asking it to declare something which must weaken it with its constituents, and might cause it to fall.

In 1864, by what was known as the September Convention, the French emperor agreed with the king of Italy. The French would withdraw their soldiers from Rome. The Italian government undertook not to occupy Rome thereafter. They promised to defend the pope's Rome if others attacked it. They undertook to transfer their capital from Turin to Florence as a sign of good faith. Neither side asked the opinion of the Pope about this agreement. Matters vital to his safety were now settled by monarchs over his head and without telling him.

Pius IX did not believe that the Italians would observe the Convention, and he was right. It was impossible for an Italian government to observe this agreement if it had a chance of taking Rome, or it would cease to be an Italian government. One of the French ministers told the Italian negotiators, 'Naturally the result of all this will be that you will get to Rome; but it is important that between our evacuation and your occupation there should be a sufficient interval of time, and some excuse in events, so that France is not obviously responsible for the Pope's loss of Rome.'[3] The Pope did not believe that the French withdrawal from Rome, completed in December 1866, would last long.

The Piedmontese might honour their troth for a time, but there was no reason why their guerrillas should obey. In autumn 1867 Garibaldi invaded the Papal States with his band. And instantly the French army was back in Rome, and at the battle of Mentana Garibaldi was beaten off.

The Emperor had begun to live dangerously. There were republican demonstrations in the streets of Paris against what happened at Mentana. The French clergy were very pleased with the battle. In the

---

[3] Nigra to Minghetti, 21 Apr. 1864, Maurain, *La Politique ecclésiastique*, 704–5.

Senate Cardinal Bonnechose demanded that after Mentana the French army must reconstitute all the old Papal State. The Senate was about to treat this with contempt when the honour of the bishop-senators was saved by Darboy in a moderate speech to the effect that the Emperor had done all that was needed in the crisis of the moment. The famous speech was Rouher's 'Never!': the French will *never* allow Rome to be taken by the Italians. Asked whether by 'Rome' he meant Lazio as well, he said that he did.

This 'Never!' was the moment when Italy realized that France, to which they owed their unity, was now their enemy. The feeling, often articulate, that France could upset the hard-gained unity of the nation, and might use the Pope in breaking it up, was to last until the outbreak of the First World War and cause the Italian alliance with Germany and Austria.

Despite such a 'Never!' the Pope had begun to live more danger-ously than the Emperor. Any accident of politics could take away the French and then he would be at the mercy of guerrilla bands or the Italian army. His personal attitude remained uncompromising: he was God's servant; he stood for the morality of Europe, and of the Italian people; he could do nothing to preserve his own safety. He was not above politics because he stood at the heart of one of Europe's chief political problems, but he behaved as if that had nothing to do with him.

The papal zouaves were very distinctive by their uniform, with bright colours and something Turkish in its rakishness. After the defeat at Castelfidardo young men continued to enlist in them to defend the Pope; mostly French or Belgian, and many of the French were Bretons; later some French Canadians, and Irishmen, and 300 or more Hungarians. Eventually they numbered just over 5,000. Their new general was a German, Kanzler, a good soldier and an honourable man. Like all such bodies of soldiers they varied; some were mercenaries who had come for pay or excitement, a few deserted after they found what was asked of them or discovered the odds against them, and some joined because they fondly imagined that no one would dream of warring against the pope and they would be paid but not need to fight. The number with the spirit of a cru-sade was higher than in most troops; and their devotion was fed by the expectation that if they had to fight in the pope's cause they would be outnumbered. At their best they hated it when their ene-mies called them 'the pope's mercenaries'. They disturbed Roman monasteries by being quartered in their buildings but political wisdom preferred to keep them out of Rome and usually they were camped near the frontier where the only action till 1867 was rounding up very elusive brigands in the mountains.

One of the zouaves was a French aristocrat who joined aged 19 and wrote diary-letters to his family and later made them into an anonymous book, under his first name Philippe, to describe his experiences. His emotions were strong. They were a mixture of personal admiration for the person of Pius IX, adherence as a sacred duty to the cause, and excitement that he took part in the historic rituals. The bombs exploding in the city, or antipapal posters put up on walls, or anonymous threats delivered to zouaves served only to increase his dedication. When at Easter 1864 a bomb went off under a wing of Bernini's colonnade and blew out many of the Vatican windows, his only thought was that Garibaldi and Mazzini were pygmies and the Church had stood up to monsters like Nero. He did not like it that if a zouave went into a café in Rome the other customers walked out. He did not like tourists and their intrusions, the English the worst, pushing insolently for the best seats, but some of the French almost as bad; but he confessed that the visitors enriched the Romans and he was amused by the fashionable hats which suddenly appeared on their heads.

When in December 1866 the French garrison withdrew under the September Convention, the defence was not left only to the zouaves because 1,000 French volunteers arrived as 'the legion of Antibes'. In October 1867 the zouaves were proud of their part in the battle of Mentana and the victory raised both their morale and recruitment. It was the first battle at which nurses (nuns) made field-stations in the midst of the fight.

Pius IX kept visiting the wounded in the hospital, and wrote personal letters to the families of the killed, and created a victory medal; a cross with tiara and keys in the centre and the words *Fidei et virtuti*, 'to faith and courage'; and on the back St Peter's upside-down cross with the words *Resurget fulgentior!*, 'he shall rise more gloriously'. Philippe the zouave still had a total conviction that he was in the noblest of causes but after Mentana was sure that Rome must soon fall to the Italians who would outnumber the defence. This certainty rested on his French perception that the Emperor Napoleon, the only person who could keep Rome safe, was marching towards his ruin.

He recorded the Pope's defence of his right to keep an army. Enemies asked what a minister of religion did with killing machines. Pius IX received Kanzler and the officers and said how they had come from all parts of the world to serve a noble cause; that critics denied his right to have an army; but on the Mount of Olives, when the Garibaldini came into the garden of Gethsemane, they fell to the ground before Jesus, who said how if his Father wanted he would send legions of angels; and how he said before the Sanhedrin that he was a king. 'And I have only the title of king, so I need a little army to defend a throne that is little in size and vast in its influence and the truth that comes from it . . . So be proud to serve and God give you courage—not for war, we hope there will be no war—but for the pitfalls that you will face . . . God bless you and your families and all who help this defence of the pope's throne.'[4]

Nevertheless, Pius IX was not so serene as he looked, for his language as head of the Church grew more extreme. We cannot prove the psychological connection between the growth in extreme expression and the dangers of his political life, but it is hardly possible to think that there was not an intimate connection. The pressure of Italian force affected the spiritual history of the Catholic Church.

THE SYLLABUS OF ERRORS

In Turin, and in London, they said that the Pope was behind the times, not in keeping with modern civilization. But why should he reconcile himself with modern civilization? Was that so marvellous a state of society, with its tearing up of treaties, its robberies, murders, and slums? In an allocution of 18 March 1861 the Pope said that he stood for eternal principles of truth and justice, and if modern civilization corrupted them, so much the worse for modern civilization. Civilization he would stand for, popes were its bearers to the barbarians. But modern civilization had elements that were vicious and with which no pope could reconcile himself.[5]

Europe took little notice of this allocution. But the habit of mind contained the seed of peril for the papacy. Its defenders started to think out the position: the Church brought civility to the barbarians; until the eighteenth century everyone believed it to be the basis of

---

[4] Philippe, *Dix ans au service du Roi Pie IX* (Paris, 1886), ii. 465–6 *bis*.
[5] *Acta Pii IX* (Graz, 1971), I. iii. 220–30.

culture, art, morality, and society. Then the French philosophers, 'inspired from England', started teaching that it was the Church that kept mankind backward and in darkness. The answer to this was easy—one should consider the 'barbarity' of the makers of the medieval cathedrals, of Aquinas or of Dante, of the deeply Christian aspects of parts of the Renaissance. The devastation of Europe by the French Revolution and Napoleon I only stamped home the recognition that the Church was the source of civilization.

But now men see civilization not as art, moral endeavour, education, or the quest for eternal values, but as speed of travel, vast corporations for commerce, the electric telegraph, or (above all) political liberty. This was an odd definition of civilization. It could not be found in the Church's thought. It rested on the theory of an absolute liberty of conscience, an absolute disregard of the future life which thereby made the policeman the only guardian of good behaviour, a quest for wealth which produced also a proletariat. True civilization was not power or expansion. On the contrary, robber-states were cleverer at power than civilized states.

Could the Church ever reconcile itself to such a theory and try to make it humane? It could not be seen how the Church could ever accept such a theory and remain true to its mission.[6]

The idea of an all-embracing condemnation of the errors of the modern world was not in the first instance due to the Pope. Various conservatives round the Curia talked of it during the 1850s. The crisis of 1859, when the kingdom of (North) Italy was created, seemed to the Curia to make the idea more urgent. They asked various churchmen, including French and Belgian, for suggestions on what were the main errors of the modern world which ought to be condemned and what ought to be included in an encyclical which stated the authentic doctrine of the Church in its relation to contemporary society. There was a draft of such an encyclical by 1860.

In discussion beforehand it seemed a rational idea. No one had any notion that it would be twisted into one of the turning-points in the history of the Church.

The draft was much changed and made more pointed by the arrival in Rome of another one written by the bishop of Perpignan, Gerbet. This bishop loved writing mandates and pastoral letters to his diocese, and good judges in France regarded him as one of the best

[6] See esp. the lecture at the Roman Academy of Catholic Religion, the main part printed in *CC* (1863), 7: 257–67; lecture delivered on 2 July 1863 by an anonymous lecturer.

literary stylists of his generation. He issued for his clergy a condemnation of modern errors. No one outside Perpignan took any
notice—until the Pope read it and was struck by it. The Pope, being
the person he was and in the state of mind that he was in, preferred
Gerbet's mandate to the draft existing in Rome. The Curia went to
work on the new one. In April 1862 the majority of cardinals in the
Pope's drafting committee said that this was not the right line to pursue. The Pope took no notice.

The committee argued in a leisurely way: atheism was a modern
error but there was not much of it and everyone knew that the
Church was against it, it seemed a platitude to say so solemnly.
Universal toleration must be condemned because it led to the belief
that the truth does not matter. 'One person one vote' must be condemned because the majority of people had no idea what is just or
right. Revolution ought to be condemned because its object was to
overthrow a legal government. They were not agreed about much
else—but that was a lot.

That summer many bishops came to Rome for the canonization of
the Japanese martyrs. The Pope took the chance to consult them on
the draft. Ninety-six bishops preferred not to give an opinion. About
a third of those 159 bishops who replied were against the plan. They
said the required condemnations had already been published, and
clearly; to add a wholesale condemnation could achieve nothing and
ran risks. The bishop of Pittsburgh was worried about the draft attack
on democracy because the effect was to assail the American constitution.[7]

To consult so many people was to ask for a leak. During 1862 the
North Italian press got wind of it and attacked the backwardness of
the Church. This had the effect of delaying any pronouncement. Just
possibly, if external events had gone differently, the plan would have
stayed only in the archives.

But outside events pushed it ahead. At a Conference in Malines in
Belgium, the French liberal Catholic Montalembert was invited to
speak and saw the chance of reiterating the dream of his life, a reconciliation between Catholic faith and the modern world. He kept
his liberal attitudes after the condemnation of Lamennais and was a
French Lord Acton, an aristocrat for whom religion and freedom
are inseparable. When Louis Napoleon took the dictatorship

[7] G. Martina, *Pio IX (1851–66)* (Rome, 1986), 313.

Montalembert accepted it on the ground of crisis and the need for
order; but within a year he was attacking dictatorship. In 1858 and
1859 he was before the courts on charges of inciting people against
the government and once was sentenced to imprisonment but was
pardoned by the Emperor. He was unpopular now in France; his
constituency refused to elect him and he was out of French politics,
and sad. He revered monks and nuns but was almost heart-broken
when his daughter decided to take the veil. He dedicated his leisure
to writing a romantic but readable *History of the Monks of the West*;[8]
which Lacordaire believed would reconcile the nineteenth century
to monks.

In Belgium the tradition of Lamennais still spoke. Montalembert,
as a famous Catholic liberal in politics, was highly regarded and
cheered at meetings. He could say what he liked. He could and did
say to them that he came to do homage to a country that was both
religious and free.

At Malines, to more than 3,000 listeners, he revived the plea for a
free Church in a free State. He was an intellectual who truly loved
his Church—though he did not love its management. Although he
was a layman his appearance and dress were vaguely ecclesiastical,
with long fair hair and a long frock coat buttoned up to the neck, and
with the face, as was said by more than one observer, of an elderly
child. He had never had charisma, could not sway a constituency, was
gentle but always the aristocrat; and yet he had been capable of great
parliamentary speeches provided they were about ideals and principles, and not about practicable solutions. Enemies in France,
Voltairean or Bonapartist, thought him a pious humbug, a windbag
with too prominent a cross displayed on its top; his friends held him
to be the noblest of their French contemporaries, they admired him
with a little ruefulness as though this selfless crusader was another
Don Quixote.

At Malines he made two speeches, certainly two of the greatest of
his life—for here he could truly talk about ideals. Because he had
been pushed out of French politics there was passion in his sadness.
Too many Catholics, he said, could only think of the Church as a
body of the *ancien régime*. The *ancien régime* had merits but it had one
demerit which it was enough to mention—it was dead. (Sensation
in the hall.) Catholics had to reconcile themselves to civil equality,

[8] *Histoire des moines d'occident* (6 vols.; Paris, 1860–8), two more vols. posthumously in
1870.

religious liberty, and political liberty. He said that he was not a democrat; but 'even less do I believe in absolute rulers'. He prophesied that
democracy, already reigning in half Europe, would soon win the
other half. The whole cast of his speech was against absolutism, and
he urged the Church not to be afraid of democracy because it would
bring it the freedom it must have. He said that democracy may be a
vast turbulent sea but the Church could do nothing but put its boat
out into the waves. It had many dangers—the crowd seen as more
important than the individual, the temptation to use voting mobs for
corrupt ends, democracy easily produced dictators and as easily produced the anarchy that leads to civil war. But democracy was coming anyway and the Church must venture in and try to guide it, and
it had the one compass that could guide it aright. And in accepting
liberty for everyone as the ideal the horrors of past repression had to
be thrown away. 'The faggots set on fire by Catholic authorities to
kill heretics I find as ghastly as the scaffolds on which Protestants
killed Catholic martyrs. When the Spanish Inquisitor said to a
heretic, "Accept the truth or die," I hate it as much as I hated a
French red in the Terror saying to my grandfather, "Accept liberty
and fraternity or die."'

The speeches were interrupted by prolonged cheering and excited
or uneasy rustling and fidgeting. Afterwards Cardinal Sterckx of
Malines was friendly. The nuncio in Brussels, the Pole Ledóchowski,
was glacial, and the information to Rome was not complimentary to
Montalembert. Cardinal Wiseman and some English were present
and were cold. Veuillot's journal said that the speeches were scandalous. But three or four leading French bishops liked them much.

Not long afterwards the professor of church history at Munich,
Döllinger, who by origins was in no way a liberal Catholic, but was
an academic determined to follow an argument wherever it should
lead, made a speech to a scholarly congress at Munich. He spoke for
the free right of scholarship to think as the evidence demanded, irrespective of what the authority of the Church should say. The nub of
his speech was the friction between the duty of Church authorities to
teach doctrines and the duty of Catholic professors, like any other
professors, to follow the evidence which they found. Döllinger was
justly proud of the contemporary advances in German universities
and their rapid raising of the standards of scholarship; but he inferred
that out of these faculties of theology an improved divinity would
come, better than the traditional repetitions of the Roman schools.

The meeting condemned Renan's *Life of Jesus* and agreed to work against errors in Catholic doctrine, and submitted themselves to the infallible authority of the Church which, however, did not remove their scientific freedom. They sent a letter submitting to the pope.

These German critics filled the Pope's mind with suspicion. The Roman schools had distrusted German divinity since the eighteenth century or before. Cardinal Antonelli knew no theology; Pius IX knew it in outline, without subtleties.

A brief, *Tuas libenter*, dated December 1863 but sent in January 1864, went to the archbishop of Munich.[9] It set down that such a meeting ought to be held only with the approval of authority; that school theology is useful in defence of faith, and minds should follow not only defined dogmas but the ordinary teaching of authority for which the see of Rome is responsible.

Bilio was asked to write an opinion on what Montalembert said. His memorandum read thus: (1) Liberty of conscience was bad for both Church and State. There was a traditional opinion that toleration may be allowed by a Catholic State to avert worse evils (such as civil war) and this must be right. But it could not mean that Catholics be allowed to desert the Church without impunity, and if it was conceded it could only be with the consent of the pope. Bilio cited the long line of papal decrees as evidence of this. In the city of Rome apart from the churches only the synagogue was allowed. All other non-Catholic places of worship were outside the city walls. (2) It was wrong to say that States could not use force to encourage religion. Truth had the right to be protected; governments had a duty to care for the welfare of their subjects. Therefore they had a duty to care for the highest in their welfare, the state of their souls. All the practice and thought of the past was in favour of coercion. If the Church was not to be seen to have erred, it must confess that this power to coerce was right. Bilio called for the condemnation of what Montalembert had said. A private letter of rebuke went from Cardinal Antonelli to Montalembert.

Belgium was like the United States in that any Catholic condemnation of democracy would hurt the Church because of the country's constitution and politics; and might hurt it more than in the United States because Belgium had a Catholic people and was the only country in Europe where the government was that of a formally Catholic

[9] Text in *Acta Pii IX*, I. iii. 636–45.

political party. The Prime Minister Dechamps wrote a tough letter to the Pope. Was the Church to condemn liberty? If it did it would condemn itself to decline. The free Belgian constitution had helped Catholicism and there was no sign that the result was to encourage Catholics to become Protestants. An encyclical that condemned liberty of conscience would claim that it was faithful to the past of the Church and would protect the future of the Church—but it would cause the Church to lose the world in which it lived.[10]

In August 1864 the cardinals of the Holy Office again said that the draft condemnations were not well formulated. They asked the Pope to send an encyclical to all the bishops reminding them of what Rome had condemned already and adding any new condemnations that were necessary. The Pope accepted this opinion and told Bilio to draft it.

The September Convention of 1864 used to be regarded as the direct cause of the encyclical. In Rome's eyes two usurpers, the French emperor and the king of Italy, both heads of States where the population was in large majority Catholic, the one owing his power to an illegal coup, the other owing control over most of his lands to robbery, were playing around with the pope's rights and pretending that this was in his interests. All the modern world seemed to be agreed in an attack on the Catholic Church. Thus it was natural to suppose that the Convention provoked the condemnations that followed. That has been shown to be an error. The Convention had only the function of a last small straw. It had no other effect. Bilio already had the draft of an encyclical.

The difficulty was to take a statement out of the context which caused it. Three years before Sardinia-Piedmont was claiming that 'modern civilization' meant the dissolving of monasteries, the institution of civil marriage, and the destruction of the social influence of the Church. To condemn this looked natural. To take it out of its Cavour context and say, 'The Pope condemns modern civilization,' could have no effect but to make him contemptible.

By then the Pope had lost interest in the detailed drafting of this momentous encyclical. Afterwards he was not quite sure himself what one or two of the propositions meant. He approved 82 condemned propositions. But they appeared as 80 because during the night before publication Bilio became afraid of what would happen

---

[10] Martina, *Pio IX (1851–66)*, 332–3; Lecanuet, *Montalembert*, iii. 373 ff.

if two of them were published, so said a prayer and quietly struck out two of them without asking anyone's leave.[11] He would have helped even more if he had struck out the 80th and last proposition.

The two documents—the encyclical *Quanta Cura* and a Syllabus, or list, of errors condemned—reached the bishops just before Christmas 1864. The tone varied. Though Bilio was responsible for the last few propositions which were to alarm Europe and America most, his drafting tone was flat. With the Pope's approval a secretary added a preface to the encyclical and this had the music of desperation, with phrases such as: the criminal intrigues of the irreligious . . . slaves of corruption . . . seeking to ruin the base of civil society and of the Catholic faith, to destroy every virtue and all justice, etc.

Though the principal drafter was Bilio, the Pope did not bother to look at the final version before it was published. Bilio altered language which he thought unwise without asking the Pope; and, extraordinarily, one of the gravest encyclicals ever issued should be composed by a Barnabite with a clear pen for drafting but no theologian, and with no profundity, and the gift only of a compiler; it nevertheless became the Pope's act of defiance to the modern world. He had a sense of the duty to restore Christendom, and an apocalyptic vision of criminals running through the world, ranting of liberty when they were slaves of corruption. He had no capacity for balance. This was a man shocked by what he saw, depressed, pessimistic.

Some statements in this encyclical and syllabus were so offensive to the modern world that it failed to notice that not all parts of the statement were unacceptable and that not all in the modern world was perfect. It condemned some opinions that Christians were united in condemning—for example, that God is the same thing as the universe, or that God does not act upon man or upon the creation, or that God has revealed nothing that helps humanity, or that Jesus never existed. With such propositions most of Europe still disagreed. The only doubt was whether it was necessary for the Pope to say what was hardly in doubt. And a number of other propositions condemned were not likely to meet much disagreement; for example, that all power comes out of the muzzle of a gun; or that the State ought to control the curriculum in colleges for training priests; or that the breaking of oaths, taken in the most solemn form, ought not only

[11] The two were: 'So-called constitutional institutions are always good for society and for religion', and 'What Italy is now doing is nothing to do with religion but is a pure question of politics.' Cf. Martina, *Pio IX (1851–66)*, 345–6.

to be sanctioned, but should receive praise, when it is done for love of one's country.

But other statements were the words of a dying world in conflict with a new world, for instance, that it is always wrong to rebel against lawful governments; it is always wrong to allow divorce; it is wrong to think that if the pope lost the Papal State it would conduce to the freedom and happiness of the Church. It is wrong to believe that nowadays Catholicism should not be the only authorized religion in a State. It is wrong to believe that a Catholic State ought to give the right of public worship to immigrants of a different religion; to think that freedom of the press, and of the expression of opinion, does not lead to decline in public morality.

And finally, the 80th and last, which was to be the only proposition that most of Europe noticed—and at which it laughed: it is wrong to believe that the pope can and ought to reconcile himself with progress, liberalism, and modern civilization.

No sentence ever did more to dig a chasm between the pope and modern European society.

It troubled Catholic consciences. Not all consciences, for some in France, Italy, and Spain thought it a wonderful blow for truth by the Pope. In the Tyrol, an Alpine country that was very Catholic, it was above the heads of the mountain people, and made no impact on their lives or minds. But Catholics in constitutional States wondered whether they could now with a good conscience take an oath of allegiance to maintain those States, because they guaranteed freedom of religion for all. Many people wrote to Rome to ask for clarity and to express their scruples. The Curia explained: it sanctioned the liberty of conscience as practised in the French or Belgian constitutions, though it continued to maintain that, in the absolute, liberty of conscience is an evil. The atmosphere of the explanations was different from that of the Syllabus. They wriggled to slide out of the meaning of the words.

The most helpful of all the explainers was Dupanloup, the bishop of Orleans. He was a hard fighter for every cause in which he engaged. Privately he thought of the Syllabus as mad drafting from which the Church must be protected, but he did not say so publicly. He wished to defend the Church from its managers.

Dupanloup was already famous in France but the Syllabus gave him a European fame. He was of illegitimate birth but an unknown aristocratic father paid for an excellent education. He gained a name in Paris as curate of the Madeleine and pastor to the young, and so became tutor to the young Bourbon princes. But what made him was the death of Talleyrand.

This death-bed was as controversial and almost as important as the dying of Cavour. Talleyrand had changed sides so often. Some said he was the most elegant species of rat. They could never forgive him for being an immoral bishop, and the bishop who helped the French Revolution and resigned his bishopric to do it; for emigrating to America during the Terror and growing rich by skilled manipulation; for being Foreign Secretary under the Directory and then under Napoleon; for being a traitor to Napoleon. The informed were grateful that by his subtlety at the Congress of Vienna he helped to preserve French territory, and later his skill over Belgium fostered its independence; and now he was dying, still a prince, visited on his death-bed by the King. The world watched to see whether it would be scandalous for the Church to absolve such a sinner before he died.

His family—his niece-by-marriage Dorothea who was his last love, and her daughter Pauline who was believed to be his daughter—were devout and longed for him to be reconciled. He summoned the young Dupanloup, the famous confessor from Paris. Dupanloup saw the danger; but after bedside negotiation, and making Talleyrand sign two vague documents of regret, he gave communion and unction just before the death; the first time the ex-bishop had received the sacrament for forty-seven years. The sinner treated his death and his penitence with a princely courtesy and condescension.

Some were glad—the Church is the mother of sinners; others thought it scandalous; Chateaubriand would have preferred Talleyrand to die like a dog and put into his diary several pages about a mass of corruption being dragged unwillingly before its Maker.[12] Thiers called it a *capucinade*, an empty religious show. Rome was not pleased. It made Dupanloup the most famous priest in France—but with a doubt attached to his name, and in a long eminent life the doubt always hung about him. Veuillot and the *Univers* hated him and were perpetually at his throat.

His sermons were rhetoric and theatre. Veuillot had an easy time— 'he's a man of what is outward; with little base in reality; never ceasing to work to raise his own importance to a level above its merit and

---

[12] *Mémoires d'outre-tombe* (1958), vi. 295 ff.

using every means to that end'.[13] But his organizing power was exceptional and he had quality as a negotiator, evident in the making of the Falloux law on religious education. It was Falloux who obtained for him the offer of the see of Orleans, a diocese which he ran efficiently with a rain of pastoral letters while he continued to keep all his work in Paris. He turned out to be exceptional as a pamphleteer. He loved a fight—the nuncio accused him of always being on a war footing. He assailed Cavour in 1859–60 and won the gratitude of Pius IX.

So it seemed that no one could be more qualified than Dupanloup in an effort to extract the poison from the Syllabus of Errors. He made the Syllabus mean what it did not say by distinguishing the stated principles from their application in particular cases; by placing the large, general utterances back into the events out of which they arose, thus reducing their significance. He made a distinction between thesis and hypothesis, the thesis being the general proposition, the hypothesis its application in a special set of circumstances. The pope, for example, did not condemn progress, he only condemned that progress which was decadent—there was not a word against true progress. Political liberty? The Church, he said, rejected no form of government, because it belonged to all times and only asked leave to fulfil its mission. 'There is no need to ask the Pope to reconcile himself with what is good or indifferent in modern civilization . . . It would be like saying to an honest person, you must reconcile yourself with justice': therefore he did not condemn modern civilization sweepingly but only what was bad in it.[14] By the time that Dupanloup had finished with the Syllabus it was almost as though it had never been; at least in its impact upon northern Catholics; and in northern Europe it was left as a sharp weapon only in the hands of anticlericals and Protestants. The tract was an able as well as a brave piece of special pleading.

Dupanloup consoled many Catholics. The pamphlet went through 34 editions in a few weeks and had three Italian translations. As many as 630 bishops wrote to thank him.[15] Minds were relieved. They were even more relieved when moderate men extracted from the Pope a brief to Dupanloup (4 February 1865) which did not say

---

[13] Louis Veuillot to Delor, 4 Dec. 1854, *Correspondance* iv. 251, in *Œuvres*, xviii (1931).

[14] F.-A.-P. Dupanloup, *La Convention du 15 Septembre et l'encyclique du 8 Decembre* (Paris, 1865).

[15] F. Lagrange, *Dupanloup* (Paris, 1894), ii. 255, 263.

that he was right but did congratulate him on having exploded errors in men's opinions about the Syllabus. Liberal Catholicism could continue on its way.

Of course it would have continued on its way in any case. The power of hierarchs in any Church does not extend to stopping the tide as it flows over the beach. But meanwhile, when someone close to the author said that the Syllabus did not mean what it appeared to mean, it was, at that moment, an obstacle removed.

It was also true that less liberal Catholicism could continue on its way more confidently. The editors of *Civiltà Cattolica*[16] were excited by the excellence of the Syllabus as the maintenance of unadulterated truth; and as for the doubt about whether it was the right moment, they trusted that the Pope was guided not only in what he said but in the moment that he chose to say it. The next year Louis Veuillot wrote a powerful book, *L'Illusion libérale*. The Pope said in conversation that it was a good book, and that the ideas that it put forward were his own.[17] The career of a largely liberal mind such as that of the convert Newman in England, who found it necessary to spend much time telling the world that he was not a liberal, shows how disreputable the word 'liberal' now was in the leading minds of the Church.

The relief that flexible interpretation was possible did not mean that the Syllabus left no aftermath. The students of the university of Naples burnt it upon a bonfire. An English Jesuit left his order and the Church, as did a few others. Every liberal newspaper in Europe leapt upon the encyclical with derision. Napoleon was so offended by the Syllabus that he now appointed to the Senate Sainte-Beuve, brilliant as a literary critic but famous also for being an agnostic.

Sainte-Beuve was a journalist from early years, though he also wrote poems which few people read. For a time he was a liberal Christian and disciple of Lamennais. He was attracted to the Jansenists and wrote a big history of their Port-Royal which was fundamental at the time and is still valuable. But he seems to have been thrown by the influence of Renan and the new criticism of the New Testament documents. His journalism moved up a step, becoming the work of an essayist, where he found his vocation, so that his portraits published each Monday were regarded as indispensable reading. He had to leave France at the Revolution of 1848, but Napoleon III allowed him back and he was one of only two eminent French literary men seen to be

[16] *CC* (1865), 1: 273–89.
[17] E. Veuillot, *Louis Veuillot*, iii. 500–3; Martina, *Pio IX (1851–66)*, 354 n.

in favour of the Emperor. He was a very civilized critic and had a gentle nature, and it was a warning to the Church when a mind that understood the stature of the Jansenists and the profundity of their devotion felt the intellectual need to become an agonistic.

Early in 1869 the French government authorized the erection of a statue to Voltaire in a public square. The alliance of Pope and Emperor had fallen apart. This was bad for the Pope, but worse for the Emperor because his right to power had once rested on the support of the Catholic Church, and it was now a question whether he had the warm backing of any category of persons in the State.

The Syllabus left Europe with a poor image of the Pope: as of the extreme right, an obscurantist about the development of thought or politics, an unwise person who could not predict the effect of his words. This impression had a touch of the caricature. But partly it was the right image. There was a sense in which the Pope did choose to live dangerously. But the more resolute he was—and the more dangerously he lived—the more the protective instinct of Catholicism gathered round his person and his throne.

It was an age now when any moderate might be suspected by the Curia of compromising with liberal Catholicism. The Master of the Sacred Palace,[18] whose work was to administer the Vatican Palace on behalf of the pope, was forced out of office on the suspicion that he sympathized with liberal-minded clergy, not least among them Rosmini. Three years later the Vatican archivist Theiner, then a historian of European stature for his contributions to scholarship, was driven from his post on the same suspicion, especially because he helped liberal Catholics who wanted to make historical enquiries, in particular the young English historian Acton who was notorious as a liberal Catholic.

The date when the Italians would occupy Rome now depended only on the date when the French would be forced to withdraw their protection of Rome. In July 1866 Prussia overthrew the Austrians in war and tipped the Catholic–Protestant balance of power in Germany to the Protestant side. The victory made the Prussians powerful enough to be a threat to France. By being on the Prussian side the Italians at last acquired Venice from Austria.

---

[18] A Dominican, Girolamo Giglio. He was one of the first Dominicans in the South Italian revival after the Napoleonic Revolution. In the turbulence of 1849 he was vicar-general for South Italy, acted wisely, and hence became Master of the Sacred Palace. The unification of Italy divided the Italian Dominicans. Cf. *DHGE* xx. 1289–90.

French and Austrian power in Europe was falling as German and Italian power was rising.

THE FIRST VATICAN COUNCIL

A part of living dangerously lay in proving that the world-wide Church had its own independent life apart from modern States and what they decided in politics. The effective way of showing this independence was to assemble large numbers of bishops in Rome; with modern steamships and railways, these assemblies were possible without undue loss to the dioceses, for the first time in papal history. Because the protective instincts of Catholicism reached out towards the confessor-pope, bishops were glad to travel and show their loyalty by answering his invitations. In 1862 and 1867 large assemblies of bishops met in Rome.

The 1862 meeting, where 255 bishops were present, was to bear witness when the Pope canonized twenty-three Franciscans and three Jesuits who had suffered martyrdom in Japan in the late sixteenth century. It was a hitherto unique occasion in that among the bishops present were thirteen Americans and one Canadian, and, a fact unprecedented for so big a meeting of bishops in Rome, hardly any Italian bishops, as they were prevented from coming by their government. By reason of another and different conflict between Church and State no Portuguese bishops came.

The purpose of the meeting began as a pure act of piety, but Rome found that the Turin government suspected it of being a demonstration of international solidarity with the Pope. Foolish and provocative, Turin refused passports to its bishops. Therefore the Pope departed from custom and invited the bishops of all the world, if they could get away without harm to their flocks. The solemnities in Rome warmed the Pope's heart. Twenty thousand people made the way of the cross to the Coliseum, the bishops affirmed the necessity of the Pope's temporal power and its origin in divine providence, and thus a canonization of saints, which started as piety, became politics. To Rome it felt as if Catholicism showed its power and freedom amid its chains. 'It was a slap in the face of the Italian government'—this was stated openly.[19]

---

[19] *CC* (1863), 5: 186; cf. (1862), 1: 749.

The meeting of 1867 was summoned to celebrate the eighteen hundredth anniversary of the death of the apostles Peter and Paul; present were some 490 bishops, the Eastern patriarchs in communion with the see of Rome, and some 14,000 priests; they came not only from Europe as far as Spain, but from China, India, and Africa. It was a vast Church event. Yet it also had a political moment; a symbol that the Church was international and no State may tamper with its life, especially not the Italian State: for the assembled bishops heard the Pope renew the excommunication of the king of Sardinia-Piedmont. They heard more from him: of his faith in the future of the Church, of the vitality and fruitfulness of an institution which the enemies said was moribund, of his gratitude for the backing of the people of Rome, of the canonization of 205 more martyrs from Japan.

At this meeting the Pope announced a third meeting within that decade of the 1860s, the climax of this policy and its culmination: a General Council. There the Pope would be seen to be surrounded by all Catholic Christendom.

He first talked of this plan in December 1864, just before the publication of the Syllabus. The cardinals to whom he talked were cautious but approving, but that was not so with the Curia. The Curia was the normal administration of the Church, and looked upon a possible ecumenical Council as a disturbing new source of authority and an interference with well-tried ways of governing the Church. They were strong against the plan. What is the point of the trouble, expense, and anxiety of holding a General Council to take decisions for the Church when it is the business of Rome to decide more economically and effectively?

The Pope asked about forty bishops to suggest an agenda for a Council. But he went slowly because his administration dragged its feet. Cardinal Antonelli made no secret of his lack of enthusiasm—but then he was not a man of enthusiasms. Various bishops took the same reluctant point of view. 'The only thing the Church needs is the Pope', a French bishop wrote in expressing the opinion that a Council would be useless. Cardinal Pentini wrote laconically, 'I think it is no good summoning a general council.'[20] He was alone among

[20] R. Aubert, *Vatican 1* (Paris, 1964), 70; Pentini had a dramatic start, for the French occupying army of Napoleon found him in Rome as a boy and sent him to be a soldier in France. He deserted, and soon was one of the bodyguard of the king of Sweden. When Pius VII was restored in 1814 he became one of his bodyguards. Then he was taken into the Curia, and rose fast; during the Pope's semi-liberal governments of 1848 he was Home Secretary, stood by the Pope in the troubled days, and held high office on the return from Gaeta. Soon

the cardinals in his outspokenness. But a few other cardinals, though not so negative, had fears—that States would block bishops from coming, the Church would be divided by the resistance of liberal Catholics, debates would be difficult because of pressure from the media, or the arguments between bishops in a Council would display to the world a divided Church.

The leading bishops encouraged the Pope in the plan, and somehow it fitted the mood of setting an international Church visibly before the eyes of divided Europe and nationalistic Italy. Whatever the Curia thought, the plan had its momentum derived from the circumstances of that age.

No one realized it at the time, but the Council was made by modern invention. Early Church councils were possible by the Pax Romana, though even then bishops from Britain could hardly travel to Asia Minor. Medieval ecumenical councils were either Byzantine or purely Western, and the bishops needed to travel only half the distances of those under ancient Rome. In the middle of the sixteenth century the Council of Trent still conformed to this pattern although by then there were a few bishops in India and Latin America. But from 1600 onwards an ecumenical council, if it were to be truly such, became impossible physically, travel over the oceans was too slow. This practical reason explained why the period between Trent and Vatican I was the longest interval of years that ever divided one ecumenical Council from another in the history of the Christian Church. But now again there were routes that were secure on the high seas, and railways over Western Europe. Bishops could leave their dioceses without the fear that they might not see them again for two years.

The bull convoking the Council appeared, after a long delay, in June 1868. It summoned the Council to meet on 8 December 1869.[21]

The archbishop of Tours, Guibert, approved the plan, telling the Pope that a Council in Rome would be 'a new occupation of Rome in the name of Catholicity' and would help to show the moral necessity of papal temporal power.[22] That was an obvious function of the Council, in the eyes of Italian bishops, the most obvious. But a Council cannot meet for the sake of meeting. Even if its importance

afterwards he retired and as a reward for services was made a cardinal. He died a few days after the opening of the Vatican Council.

[21] Bull *Aeterni Patris*, St Peter's Day 1868; text in *Acta Pii IX*, I. iv. 412 ff.

[22] J. Paguelle de Follenay, *La Vie du Cardinal Guibert* (2 vols.; Paris, 1896), ii. 419.

is the meeting—getting to know personally those who have been names at the foot of letters, the comfort brought to lonely outliers in India or Africa, the raising of morale by coming to the centre—it still needs an agenda to discuss. Guibert suggested various items for the agenda—to make the Syllabus of Errors more solemn; arrange for better discipline among priests; and most important in his eyes, discuss the concordats of the States which still allow governments the right to nominate bishops. He mentioned nothing about a definition of the infallibility of the pope.

There happened to be a need for a General Council which had little to do with the reasons for which this Council was summoned, and little to do with the restoration of Catholic Christendom or the defence of the papacy against its assailants. The laws which controlled the pastoral system of the Church were out of date. They rested on the canons of the Council of Trent or the decrees of the popes of the Counter-Reformation. In the middle of the eighteenth century Pope Benedict XIV, who understood the Curia better than any pope, did something to modernize the system. But more than 100 years had elapsed since then.

In addition, modern laws of reforming States affected the Church. Italy instituted civil marriage in 1866, Austria (in breach of its concordat) in 1868. Old habits of mind thought that any marriage not in church was no marriage for Christians, and went on thinking so. But if they suggested that these civil marriages were not marriages in the full sense, what pastoral anxieties might they create about adultery and desertion? It was not a new problem, but the extent to which they faced it was new.

The difficulty to be addressed was not the social situation of Europe. The doctrinal commission of the Council, considering what to put on the agenda, wondered whether to follow the Syllabus in drafting a condemnation of socialism, then decided that the dogmas of socialism and communism dealt with 'absurdities and abominations which it would be unworthy of a Council to spend its time debating'.[23] The compilers of the agenda were not yet ready to treat the nature of society in that sense. That was not their fault, for the argument was not yet hot in the world about them. When they spoke of the problems of society they meant the relations between Church and State.

[23] Aubert, *Vatican 1*, 59.

But the bringing up to date of the pastoral system, though discussed, was not debated by the relevant commission with any originality of ideas. They stood in the old ways, and had no intention of doing anything radical. This was not true of the commission to prepare suggestions about monks and nuns. They received suggestions from the heads of the religious orders and framed a well-documented series of ideas for discussion. On missions, there was an enormous field waiting for debate, owing to the speed of change in Africa, India, China, and Latin America. But the commission on the subject, dominated by the most powerful of the Pope's cardinals, Cardinal Barnabò, the prefect of the Congregation of Propaganda, thought about very little but the Eastern Churches and how to bring them back once more into union with the Western Church. The secretary even asked the meeting if it was not below the dignity of an ecumenical council to discuss missions.[24] The commission decided that it was not and that they needed to draft a memorandum for discussion on the nature of the apostolate. They worked hard, and sat for many meetings. But nothing came out of this committee except two suggestions about the relation between the Western and Eastern sacraments of confirmation. This crucial committee might as well not have met.

Therefore the main agenda before the Council was not to be a pastoral endeavour, or an endeavour towards Christian unity. It was to be doctrinal. And the key point under discussion in the Church, ever since the 1840s with the new influence of the ultramontane movement under Gregory XVI, was the authority of the pope's office. The Church could not err, all were agreed. In what circumstances did the Church speak with the assurance that its voice could not err? The old Gallicans had answered that it could not err when the General Council, properly convoked, made a decision. But Gallicanism was dead, or remote in corners of the Church, among a few unfashionable minds like Bishop Maret in France. For centuries a school of divinity had argued that when the pope spoke as the mouthpiece of the Church he was speaking as Christ's Vicar and was prevented by the Spirit of God from erring. In the word which did not appear in the dictionaries of classical Latin, he was 'infallible'.

It would be an anachronism to say that the fathers of the Council would have done better to concentrate on the pastoral system and not

---

[24] Ibid. 62.

worry about the theory of authority which was not likely to make much difference to the real work of the Church. Many of the political events of that age focused the mind of Europe on the office of the pope and the nature of his authority. Everyone discussed it. As early as 1847 the new English Catholic convert Newman, writing the novel *Loss and Gain*, which purports to describe Oxford student life which he knew well, made one of the undergraduates amuse party-goers by asking their opinion on the pope's infallibility.

If it was so discussed, it was hard for the Council to avoid pronouncing on it. And if they pronounced on it, they would have to do so in such a way as to destroy the Gallican theories, according to which the pope was but the senior bishop among bishops. For if they allowed Gallican theories, they would greatly hurt the authority of the pope just when most Catholics wanted to elevate that authority in the face of his numerous enemies.

In this way the act of summoning the Council made a definition of the infallibility of the pope necessary. To say nothing was impossible in the circumstances which they were in. To say anything would run into ferocious debate sure to be unedifying before the world. Nearly everyone believed that the pope, when he was the organ of the Church, was protected from error. But formidable critics among the bishops would not be willing to accept extreme formulas of authority which were now beloved of ardent ultramontanes and which looked as though they could turn the Catholic Church into a despotism.

And since a declaration about infallibility was on the map once it was certain there would be a Council, the ultramontanes were determined that the Council should not shrink from the subject though it might prove thorny in debate, and that it should be defined in a form that would elevate the office of the pope and destroy the Gallican theories that he was but a chairman with honour among bishops. In Rome on the night before St Peter's Day 1867, when he knew that there was to be a Council, Archbishop Manning of Westminster came together with the bishop of Regensburg, Ignaz von Senestrey, by the tomb of St Peter. They took a vow together 'to do all in our power to obtain the definition of papal infallibility' and daily to recite Latin prayers for that end. The motives of the two bishops were not the same. Senestrey was offended by Döllinger and the Munich professors who said that the academic pursuit of truth could not bow to mere authority; Manning wanted to extend the authority of the pope as far as it was possible to extend it. Manning took the view of the modern world that the Pope took, and wanted to make him as powerful a voice as possible in denouncing its iniquities.[25] General ultramontane opinion was more like Manning's: it wanted the views of the Syllabus made a test of Catholic loyalty. A wide definition of the pope's infallibility would force the Syllabus as a dogma on the Catholic Church and 'liberal illusions' would be crushed.

Early in the preparation they took a decision with far-reaching results: that the titular bishops should be invited, those without proper sees or pastoral responsibility. Afterwards there was an accusation that it gave the Pope a private army in the Council. But the Pope was not comfortable with it. Maret was a titular bishop. Pius IX would have preferred a council without famous Gallicans and at that moment Maret was the most famous of them all.

During 1869 a Congregation drew up rules for the procedure of the Council. This laid down who was to preside—a board of five—and that the debates should be confidential. They stipulated that only the Pope had the right to propose business for debate. The members might put forward requests for a commission of the Council to consider, and membership of the commission that controlled the agenda was to be by papal nomination. This was a different way of running a Council from the way customary in the councils of the fifteenth and sixteenth centuries. It ensured that the Pope—which in so complex a matter meant the Curia—had a tight hold on what could be discussed at the Council. In extenuation it must be remembered that railways and steamships meant that this Council would consist of a far larger number of bishops and hence that some bishops were bound to be eccentric and their proposals for agenda certain to be bizarre.

The proposals for debate were formulated by the preparatory commissions. There was no chance that this Council would debate anything which the Curia did not wish debated. But the subjects were large, and in large subjects almost anything can be made relevant by a skilled debater. This tight control of the agenda affected the freedom of debate surprisingly little.

In drafting the procedure, the Curia took into its counsels Hefele, the Catholic professor of church history at the university of Tübingen (there was, of course, also a Protestant professor of church

[25] E. S. Purcell, *Life of Cardinal Manning* (1896), ii. 420; I. von Senestrey, *Wie es zur Definition der päpstlichen Unfehlbarkeit kam: Tagebuch zum I. Vatikanischen Konzil*, ed. Klaus Schatz (Frankfurt am Main, 1977), 1–3.

history at that historic Protestant university). Hefele had failed to move to any other university because he was suspected by the academic electors or their civil servants of being Roman in his attitudes; a failure which pleased his university and the students, who liked his friendliness and his lectures. His influence lasted long after his death because of his effect upon his students. From 1855 he began to publish a *History of the Councils*. This began a new epoch in that area of historical study: that is, it was useful to both students and canon lawyers for the texts it reprinted. But he had a personal aim, which was only half hidden—to show that the Gallicans were wrong in their doctrines about the superiority of General Councils to popes. Hefele knew about the Council of Trent and its procedures in the sixteenth century and wanted this Council to avoid the inconveniences of debate which the fathers of Trent had suffered. He preferred that the Council should discuss drafts of proposals already formulated, and not be confronted with documents which were pro and con, on the one hand and on the other hand. The commission which he was advising took a subtly different view from his own. The scholar assumed that the bishops would really discuss and alter the drafts; the commission assumed that the bishops were very unlikely to alter the drafts but would mostly approve them without discussion. Hefele soon found that his opinions were so little accepted that he must have been consulted for appearance's sake and not because his advice was required. That June 1869, a few months before the Council opened, Hefele was elected bishop of Rottenburg. The Curia did not like the candidate, but after a delay of a few months they accepted him and he became a bishop shortly after the Council opened. He was strong against definition. He told Acton that if a decree of infallibility were passed Germany would be Protestant within two years.[26]

The Curia knew that it must invite the Orthodox. But the Protestants had appeared, uselessly, at Trent. Must they invite Protestants? They consulted Archbishop Manning of Westminster who approved. An invitation was addressed to all the Protestants 'and other non-Catholics', who 'glory in the name of Christians and own Christ as their redeemer'; and asked them to consider the consequences of their separation from Rome, especially that they could not

[26] See Aubert, *Vatican 1*, 67–8; for Hefele see *TRE* s.v. (by Rudolf Reinhardt) with literature. The *History of the Councils* had a second improved edition of its first 4 volumes 1873–9; others had to revise the next 4 volumes. Hefele's prophecy to Acton is reported by Acton's words to Gregorovius in F. Gregorovius, *Roman Journal* (1911), 343.

be sure of their own salvation. This was not a hostile document but this last phrase meant that it could not be accepted by Protestants of goodwill. The only place where a few non-Catholics (if they were non-Catholics) took the invitation seriously was in England among the heirs of the Oxford Movement. A Scottish Presbyterian minister in London, Dr John Cumming, wrote to the Pope asking whether the invitation meant that he would be able to come and speak and say what he thought; but this letter was more a way of exposing to the world the hollowness of the invitation. For Dr Cumming was a famous controversialist and his nature was not irenical. Even the invitation to the Orthodox did not go well because instead of sending personal invitations to their heads, Rome sent a circular to the Latin representatives in the Orthodox lands, for them to pass on to the Orthodox bishops; this was a sure way to make the invitation unacceptable.

The commission asked itself whether the procedures should be put to the Council for its approval. That had happened at the last General Council to be held in Rome, the fifth Lateran Council of 1512. They decided that such preliminary discussions about procedure would waste the time of the Council and that the Pope should publish the rules, before the Council opened, upon his own authority. This decision caused resentment among the bishops when it was put before them only a few days before the opening of the Council.

In early February 1869 the world suddenly awoke to dangers ahead, real or imagined. The editor of the Jesuit journal *Civiltà Cattolica* asked the Secretary of State Cardinal Antonelli for help in finding out the state of public opinion about the Council. Antonelli asked the nuncios. The nuncio to France sent him two memoranda written by associates of Louis Veuillot, the most extreme of ultramontanes. These texts came to Father Piccirillo the Jesuit editor, who printed extracts. Because people assumed, with reason, that Father Piccirillo was close to the Pope, the effect of this was to make Veuillot's opinions 'official', as though they came from the Pope.

The Protestant world, and the French, Italian, and Spanish anticlericals, believed that the Jesuits were propagators of the opinions of the political right. Protestants took it for granted that Pope Pius IX was under the control of the Jesuits. This was not the truth. During the revolutionary storms of 1847–8 he seemed willing to consider the possibility that the Society should once again be suppressed for the sake of saving the reputation of the Church. So long as Roothaan was the general in command, that is until 1853, the Pope's relations with the Society were not warm. He left the Jesuits free to elect Roothaan's successor and was happy with their choice, by a narrow majority, of the Belgian Beckx, who was a man of sense and moderation.[27]

Pius IX was accustomed to defend the Jesuits against their critics among the bishops. But for many years he was not close to the Society as a whole. His English adviser Monsignor Talbot disapproved of them.

In the preparation for the first Vatican Council during the later 1860s the Pope formed a relationship of trust with the editor of *Civiltà Cattolica*, Pietro Piccirillo. In earlier years the journal had been an intelligent organ of papal theory in politics, society, and the Church. It had able men among its writers, and its conservatism was different from mere legitimism. It had no use for despotism in any form. But as it wrote against any form of liberalism, it could not but help very conservative governments. The choice of Father Piccirillo to be editor of the journal meant that the standard of editing declined. He was not the wisest of editors or of men. But during his time the Pope came closer to *Civiltà*, both as a regular reader and as an adviser. During the first Vatican Council Piccirillo was able to see the Pope almost at will, and took precedence even over archbishops trying to see him. This did not escape the attention of the critics and confirmed their opinion that the Pope was dominated by the Jesuits. As a general proposition, this was not true. What was true was that for a time one Jesuit became one of those private advisers who composed the Pope's kitchen cabinet. And this happened at a crux of papal history.[28]

[27] Pierre Beckx joined the Jesuits at Hildesheim in 1816; he was sent as chaplain to the new convert from Protestantism Duke Ferdinand of Anhalt-Köthen and stayed as chaplain to his widow in Vienna. He was hunted out of Vienna in 1848, but four years later became provincial in Austria and won from the emperor the rescinding of the 1848 ban on Jesuits in the Austro-Hungarian empire. Elected in 1853 and retiring in 1884, he was the longest-serving general in the history of the Jesuits, except for Acquaviva who served thirty-four years and presided over the biggest expansion of the Company ever known. Beckx's generalship was a very bad time for Jesuits in most countries but they steadily rose in numbers and even after being expelled from Rome Beckx seems to have remained relatively imperturbable. Though a Belgian he served only four years of his adult life in Belgium. For Beckx see *DHGE* s.v. and bibliography there.

[28] On C. Piccirillo see Aubert *et al.*, *Chiesa e Stato nell'Ottocento: Miscellanea in onore di P. Pirri* (Padua, 1962), 607 ff. Piccirillo was one of the editorial board of *Civiltà* from 1852 but only from about 1866 controlled policy in the journal. Early in 1865, apropos of the Syllabus of Errors, the British envoy in Rome, Odo Russell, reported to his government the

In the article now published in *Civiltà*, the words were like hammers: True Catholics thought that this Council would be very short. They wished for the doctrines of the Syllabus to be proclaimed. The infallibility of the pope in teaching doctrine would be proclaimed and they would receive this with joy. They hoped that this would be a unanimous bursting forth of the Holy Spirit, uttered through the mouths of the fathers of the Council, and that they would accept it by acclamation.

The key sentences in this effusion disturbed educated Catholics. If a General Council proclaimed the doctrines of the Syllabus it would make the gulf between the Church and society more difficult to bridge. At the moment the Syllabus could be said to be an appendix to a document by a single pope, and no one knew what its authority was. People thought that another and future pope could say something different. To make it the act of a General Council was to give it a status which at the moment it possessed only in the eyes of extremists. Secondly, acceptance by acclamation would deprive bishops of the chance to discuss anything, if the Council was to be so short. The Council seemed in this conception to be a meeting in which bishops from over the world assembled to cheer what the Pope or his close advisers proposed. The article in the *Civiltà Cattolica*, because it was thought to have been given Roman status by the manner and place of its publication, put up the backs of bishops, and roused their resolution. They determined to go to Rome in a mood of refusal to be gagged. If this was a General Council nothing could stop them discussing the agenda. Veuillot mocked the idea of wanting debate, as though the Holy Spirit needed time to form His opinion.

Antonelli was economical with the truth. Asked whether he knew about this publication he said that he was unaware of what was to be published—but it is clear that he was consulted and approved the publication.[29] One of his qualities as a diplomat was skill in leaving

increasing power of the Jesuits, that they were 'masters of the situation', that they had the power to select the next pope, that they exalted obedience above all other virtues and that they had 'long' governed and directed the Roman Church. But the more Russell's reports are studied, the more it will be found that they are more brilliant than accurate. He preferred to write what his correspondents wished to hear. Text in N. Blakiston, *The Roman Question* (1962), 304. Cf. the extraordinary text of Döllinger in Quirinus, *Letters from Rome*, Eng. trans. (1870), 74: 'that great ecclesiastical polypus, with its thousand feelers and arms, the Jesuit Order' working 'under the earth and on the earth'.

[29] Martina, *Pio IX (1867–78)* (Rome, 1990), 156.

questioners with the impression that something was true when it was not and yet he could not be accused of lying.

The article hurt Döllinger of Munich. He was a church historian who believed that history disproved the infallibility of the pope. He was now a liberal Catholic who thought the Syllabus a calamity—and the idea of consecrating it to be a worse calamity. He wrote a series of articles in the *Allgemeine Zeitung*. They were extreme articles, as extreme on the opposite side as Veuillot's on the ultramontane side. They could have been written by a strong and learned Protestant of the seventeenth century, but were written more emotionally than the best Protestant controversialists would have written. He thought papal power was largely based on medieval forgeries. This was his Church, and he was hurt. He then collected the articles in a book, *The Pope and the Council*, by an anonymous author, Janus, by which name the book has ever since been known. The disguise was thin: it was not hard to guess the author.

The disturbance of mind, or fear of what the Council might do, was not during that summer confined to Catholics. Any State with many Catholics among its citizens was nervous about a Council that might elevate the status of the Syllabus. It could affect the attitude of Catholics to constitutional government; to toleration; to divorce; or to education offered by the State. The Austrian and Bavarian governments were nervous, not because they were Catholic but because they were governments. The Prussians were nervous, with their large Catholic minority. The lay Catholic leaders in Prussia were nervous because they wanted to use constitutional freedoms to establish their rights as citizens and make their new Centre Party effective in the Prussian Parliament. The Prime Minister of Great Britain, Gladstone, was nervous because he was trying to do the best he could for Ireland and did not want his relationship to the Irish made more awkward by the Syllabus of Errors. Belgian Catholics were nervous because they were using the freedoms of a constitutional State. The chancelleries of Europe started to send each other messages to ask what could be done to divert the Pope from a course on which he seemed to be set.

No pope ever embarked upon a course of action which so many leaders of European states regretted so ruefully. In the eighteenth century the governments would have given their orders, and the ambassadors in Rome would have spoken courteously to the pope and fiercely to his men, and a pope would have given way. But the world had changed. Cavour and the Piedmontese had done to the pope much worse than the governments of the eighteenth century threatened to do, and had not made Pius IX hesitate in his course.

By the late summer of 1869, three months before the Council was due to open, the situation worried leading bishops in France and Germany. They saw the danger of schism; and that such a schism would have sympathy from both Catholic and Protestant governments. Janus did not suggest that Munich was likely to accept a decree of infallibility. The Austrian bishops could hear talk in Hungary of a separate national Church if the decree went through. Many of the French or German bishops did not think the definition of infallibility so necessary that it was wise to risk the consequences. They felt that the circumstances under which the pope could not err when he spoke as the mouthpiece of the Church needed more careful consideration than so far they had received. And in view of the obvious dangers of definition, a majority of the German bishops reached the private conviction that at that moment any definition was 'inopportune'. They met at Fulda in September, and fourteen out of twenty present signed a letter to the Pope to say so. The most dramatic plea that the definition would be untimely was made by the bishop of Orleans, Dupanloup, in *Observations on the Controversy*, published on 11 November 1869, less than a month before the Council was due to open. The definition of infallibility would be inopportune because it would need more care in thinking it out than it had yet received, and because there was a danger that the Pope would be elevated in such a way as to lessen the proper authority of bishops in the Church.

Others asked their governments to intervene. The Gallicans in France, headed by Archbishop Darboy of Paris, approached the French Emperor. Döllinger approached the Bavarian Prime Minister.

The governments were in a quandary. They wanted to stop the Pope in his tracks. But they did not want to get across their Catholic citizens. If they interfered with the Pope would that help them with their Catholics? The predicament was obvious in the discussions of the British government. If they did nothing and left the Council free, might the Council vote something which would make Irish Catholics more difficult to govern? On the other hand, if they tried to stop the Pope doing what he wanted, that looked certain to make Ireland more difficult to govern. The two chief men of the British cabinet took different views. The Prime Minister, Gladstone, who cared much about the welfare of the Catholic Church if the word 'Catholic' is taken in its widest sense, really wanted political intervention. His Foreign Secretary, Clarendon, who was expert on Ireland, took the opposite view. By interfering with the Pope Gladstone could only make the Irish distrust the English. It was better to leave him to do whatever he wanted. And if, thought Clarendon, the Council declares that the pope is infallible, that will only do good because the world will laugh at him.

A similar view was taken by the British envoy in Rome, Odo Russell. He gave the cardinals the impression that he was on the Pope's side. Certainly he did not want the British government to intervene with the Council. But his reason, not disclosed in Rome, was the same as Clarendon's. He wanted a definition of infallibility so that the public influence of the Roman Catholic Church would be weakened among the nations.

Other governments, which might not take this cynical view, nevertheless believed in restraint. The risk of interference was greater than the risk of doing nothing.

One of the decisions made during preparation for the Council was a novelty. To previous ecumenical councils Catholic heads of State had been invited. The managers asked themselves whether they should follow this precedent. It appeared to be an anachronism. If the heads of State were Catholic their States were multi-religious, even if the majority of the people were Catholic; and Catholic heads of State were doing things that the Pope thought wicked, like allowing civil marriage. But when they consulted Cardinal Antonelli he held that it was not right to cut such a historic link between Church and State. They took the debate to the Pope and with his advice reached a compromise—they should not *invite* the heads of State but should allow them to send a representative if they desired. This meant in practice that their ambassadors in Rome were to be able to make representations to the bishops. The Pope felt that no modern government was a Catholic government in the full sense of the word.

In two States this was resented; in France—but only by a few in Parliament—and in Bavaria by the Chancellor himself, Prince Hohenlohe.[30] The Bavarians wanted the powers to demand that they

---

[30] Hohenlohe married a Radziwill and so became master of great Russian estates. He was a moderate who wanted German unity and became Chancellor of Bavaria after the Prussian defeat of Austria. He had to resign in Feb. 1870, partly because he was too liberal in politics but partly also because he was strong against the infallibility of the pope. When the German Reich was made a unity he was needed as an eminent Bavarian and Catholic who supported it, and became ambassador in Paris, then governor of Alsace-Lorraine, and later, for six years, the German Chancellor under William II.

be given their right of sending an ambassador to the Council. Döllinger drafted for Hohenlohe an appeal to the powers, cast in bizarre language: if the pope were declared infallible there was a danger of the European powers being subjected to the pope and his Curia. The principles of the Syllabus were opposed to the principles of public life in modern States. He suggested common measures by governments and a meeting to enable concerted steps against what they feared from this Council (Hohenlohe's circular of 9 April 1869).

None of the powers thought this a practicable circular, except the Italians. The Swiss did not bother to reply. Bismarck replied that the idea was good but as yet they had no basis for doing anything effective. The Austrian Chancellor Beust (who happened, unusually, to be a Protestant) said that it would be easier to get 200 bishops to agree than three German governments. Württemberg said that the Bavarian fears were excessive.[31]

The French Emperor shared something of the Bavarian viewpoint. But too many influences in France were against him. These were not only those of Veuillot and the ultramontane papalists. Veuillot proclaimed, with an excited satisfaction, that none of the governments was Catholic now. Moderate liberal-minded French Catholics were mostly against intervention. And the French political left, which, though excluded from power had an underlying strength, regarded interference with religion as giving it an importance which it ought not to have. To try to stop the Pope would make it look as though France thought that things he did were important.

These negative responses to Prince Hohenlohe's plan gave the Curia confidence that they could go ahead without fear of interference from the States. To the politicians in the Curia, so far as there were any at that moment, this mattered: for the Council could only meet if the French troops stayed in Rome, otherwise public order in the city would be too insecure to hold it. Theoretically the French Emperor could stop the Council by evacuating his army. In fact this was not an option open to the Emperor. The French attitude to Prince Hohenlohe's plan proved to Rome that this view of the Emperor's predicament was right.

This political consideration, however, was not likely to have entered the Pope's mind. He would do what he believed God

[31] Aubert, *Vatican 1*, 87–8.

wanted him to do and the powers could do whatever they liked, it would make no difference to him.

The fathers of the Council assembled. It was afterwards said by the hostile that the Pope could do what he pleased at the Council because half the members were his pensioners. It was true that the Pope paid the expenses of bishops who travelled far, and he already had many bishops expelled by the Italians from their sees, and then there were the vicars-apostolic who were bishops depending *ex officio* on the Pope, besides various impoverished bishops, including most of the bishops from Greece and the Levant. There were 111 titular bishops, without real dioceses, bishops, as was still said in those days, *in partibus infidelium*, that is, with the names of sees from old Asia Minor of early Christian days, men who were made bishop to give them a rank rather than a pastoral sphere. Rome paid the expenses of something over a third of the members of the Council—to achieve this it put some of them up in primitive accommodation. The French government paid the travelling expenses of a number of more distant missionary bishops. Many of the more remote visitors were hardly aware, before they arrived, of the argument raging through the press of Europe.

North European and American bishops arrived with anxiety, but resolute. They intended to debate. They would not be fobbed off by being asked to greet proposals with acclamation. They had not come to Rome to be rubber stamps to whatever the Curia thought they ought to vote for. And their anxiety increased because none of them knew what they were to debate. Even on the day before the opening of the Council none of them knew the drafts that were to be put forward.

The place of debate did not look suitable for debate: nor was it. The planners thought the acoustics of St Peter's bad for debate and wanted the Council to meet in some other church. The Pope rejected this plan. They tried to make him change his mind with the plea that no one would hear anyone else. The Pope said, with his graphic humour, 'Then they will either shriek a lot or chatter less',[32] and insisted that the fathers met in St Peter's.

The Curia partitioned off the north transept of St Peter's. It was grand in its architecture but so tall and wide that the echoes of voices rose into the roof and it was hard to distinguish a speaker's words. On

---

[32] Tizzani's diary in G. M. Croce, *AHP* 23 (1985), 311.

that day the Church needed a gift different from wisdom or patristic learning. It needed nothing so much as the uninvented microphone. If speakers were to do any good they had to declaim a set speech. No one could argue with anyone else, it would be like conducting an advanced discussion on delicate theological points by shouting across Trafalgar Square. This was a problem never met before at a General Council, and was caused by the expansion of the Church across the world together with the increase of bishops in Europe. The result was so impossible that debates had to be suspended altogether for a month in its course (21 February to 18 March 1870), to the vexation of those who came from afar and wanted to get on with the work. The room for debates was made much smaller by a wooden partition and the seats were arranged much closer. The acoustics were still imperfect but not impossible.

The Council opened solemnly on 8 December 1869, in a rainstorm and before a crowd of pilgrims who had come to pray round the event; the floor of St Peter's was awash from dripping umbrellas and wet clothes, and the steam rose. The empress of Austria, who loved to be always travelling, was stuck in the crowd and had to be helped through by Swiss guards; she was given a special place with five ex-kings or ex-dukes from the old States of Italy. Just before the end of the solemnities, when a Te Deum was sung, the Pope, at times in tears of emotion, gave an address that spoke of the dangers of liberalism, saying how necessary to the Church was the temporal power of the pope and urging all the bishops to loyalty to the Holy See. When the hymn 'Come Holy Ghost' was sung many of the crowd were also in tears.

Out of the nearly 1,000 bishops of the Catholic Church, some 700 were present at most of the early meetings. (The total list had 792 names.) In the later meetings the number was more like 600. It was a kind of General Council new in Christian history. All previous General Councils drew their members from the old Roman empire extended to the Holy Roman empire. They had been Councils of the old world that ran from the Pillars of Hercules to Byzantium and Jerusalem. The Russians would not give any of their sixteen bishops passports to leave the country for the purpose of attending the Council. But this Council had sixty-seven bishops from North America (United States and Canada), twenty-one from Latin America, fifteen from China, fifteen from British India, and eighteen from Australia and the Pacific. About three-quarters of the Catholics of the world lived in Europe. At the Council the Europeans were about two-thirds only of the whole assembly.[33] That is, this was the first General Council under any influence from missionaries outside Europe. It was also the first to have a large number of bishops— fifty—from inside the Ottoman empire. Nearly all the bishops from sees or districts outside Europe were European by origin.

A surprisingly large proportion of the fathers (53 per cent) were Italian or French; Italian because the Curia had many high prelates and because the old diocesan system of Italy was organized in small dioceses; French because many of the missionary bishops were French. More than 35 per cent of the attenders of the Council were Italian; about 17 per cent French; and about 10 per cent German and Austro-Hungarian put together. But the combination of the Irish from Ireland and the Irish bishops from North America produced a strong Irish contingent, some sixty-three bishops, nearly as many as the bishops from Germany and Austro-Hungary combined. Similarly, if the Spanish bishops were added to the bishops from the former Spanish empire in Latin America, that produced a total of eighty-five.

Portugal boycotted the Council: only two bishops came from mainland Portugal, and the leading Portuguese prelates from the empire did not come. Relations between the Portuguese and the Curia were frigid.

The bishops grouped by nations. The Spanish had a tradition of teaching papal infallibility and they stood solidly for it with the learning of their scholastic tradition. The Germans and Austro-Hungarians had the best-educated men, theologically, at the Council and were almost solidly opposed to the definition of the pope's infallibility, though not unanimously against its doctrine. The British and the Americans were divided but they were mostly practical people who wanted to discuss the pastoral system and wished that the Council could get away from matters of theory. The Italians according to their old way followed the Pope and his advisers. The radically divided group were the French; the extreme ultramontanes who liked Veuillot, and wholeheartedly approved of the Syllabus, had no common ground with a Dupanloup who thought a definition inopportune or a Maret who thought the infallibility of the pope proved by history to be untrue, or the liberal minds who were determined that the Council should not condemn the constitutional liberties of modern States.

[33] Figures from Aubert, *Vatican 1*, 98–101.

The majority of bishops at the Council—soon known to the press as the Majority—could see no objection to declaring the infallibility of the pope, which was so widely believed in the Church and had behind it a historic tradition with learned names, such as that of Cardinal Bellarmine. In various regions there were social and political reasons leading the local churches increasingly to look towards Rome. Their people usually believed something vague about authority but would be much more likely to be offended by a denial of the pope's authority than by its reinforcement. If they were bishops who thought about the relations between Church and State, they were determined to condemn all the old expedients by governments to control the Church in a Josephist way; and one of those ways was associated with the Gallican theory that made the pope simply a president. They were the more determined to do this because modern constitutional governments, even of devoutly Catholic countries, had to be less and less openly committed to the Catholic denomination for the sake of equality of rights in religion.

They were given more influence—and after two months of Council, much more influence—by the attitudes of the Pope and the Curia. The Pope believed in the infallibility of his office and wanted the doctrine defined. He found it difficult to think of those who opposed it as loyal to himself. The mass of bishops with not very decided minds on such matters wanted to do all they could for the Pope under the terrible pressure of Italian nationalists and the threats that lay over Rome. The Curia could not bear the idea of a 'defeat' of central Roman authority that would happen if the opponents got their way and, after all this world publicity, forced the Council to say nothing about the pope's teaching office. All the missionary bishops depended upon one Congregation of the Curia, the Congregation of Propaganda, which had a tough government. The Congregation exercised on its dependents a pressure which was unceasing, and which some of them (especially the Easterners) thought at times to be unscrupulous. But in creating the strength of the Majority, the pressure of the Curia was far less important than the devotion, without theological precision, of so many bishops to the person of a confessor-pope.

The opponents of definition—soon known to the press as the Minority—consisted of a surprisingly large number of bishops: at least, the number surprised and vexed the Curia. With vague edges their party had nearly 150 members, a formidable force. They were not so formidable as at first they looked, for they consisted of a few people who thought it untrue that the pope was infallible; and a lot of people who thought that the pope was infallible (in some sense still to be defined), but that in the condition of Europe it was a mistake to try to define it. The people who thought it inopportune could not easily ally with the people who thought it untrue. And to say that it was true but inopportune was a weak plea. If it was true, and if there was a crisis of authority in the modern Church and society, it must be right to say so; and not to say so because Protestants might be offended, or because it would be criticized by doubtfully Catholic German professors, would be an absurd act of weakness. Therefore the Minority was weaker than it looked. And from the point of view of the historical situation, once the Council was summoned the point of infallibility had to be discussed and, if discussed, then defined. For if it was not defined, the Pope would be shatteringly troubled in ecclesiastical influence at just the time when he was shatteringly troubled in politics.

The world's press imagined that the leader of the Minority was Dupanloup the bishop of Orleans, for he was the chief pamphleteer on behalf of the inopportunist doctrine. But inside the Council he commanded less respect than several others of his party. Even among the French the formidable mind was that of the archbishop of Paris, Darboy, who had a subtle, analytical, and cold intelligence that cut through every sort of woolliness or nonsense. The person nearest to a leader of the Minority was the archbishop of Vienna, Cardinal Rauscher. He had rendered extraordinary services at the time of the Austrian Concordat of 1855; no one could doubt his loyalty to the Pope; he had historical learning and a fair, judicious mind. In addition, while Dupanloup and Darboy led only a number of the bishops of their nationality, with many French bishops loud against them, Rauscher stood at the head of an almost solid body of German and Austro-Hungarian bishops.

In the Minority were a few Italian bishops, mostly from North Italy, and with sympathy for a united Italy and therefore not anxious to increase the Pope's authority. There were Americans who, like some of the English, did not want to condemn constitutional government and were afraid of elevating the authority of the Syllabus. And a fairly solid block of Eastern bishops from Greece and the Levant, whose doctrines lay near the traditions of the Eastern Orthodox Churches, did not wish to diminish the historic place of bishops by increasing the authority of a chief bishop.

The inner mental conflict among bishops of the Minority was evident. They also wanted to do all they could for the Pope in his dangerous predicament, and had no desire to be made to feel disloyal when they were loyal. They knew that the priests of their dioceses were ultramontane and that if they went on voting 'against the pope' they would store up trouble for themselves in the pastoral care of their people afterwards.

Each bishop of the Minority might have his particular situation and personal reasons which led him to this stance. This was specially true of the one who became the Minority's ablest speaker and one of its best representatives: Strossmayer, a Croat, the bishop of Djakovo in the Austro-Hungarian empire. Because the languages of that empire were so numerous and so dissimilar, the empire retained Latin as a common means of communication. The debates of the Council were in Latin, which compounded the acoustical problem in making discussion impossible for many of the fathers. The bishops' seminary lectures were in Latin, but not many of them were fluent enough at the language to engage in rapid cross-talk. Moreover, Latin as the English spoke it sounded different from Latin as the French spoke it. To have Latin as the language of debate was not to have so common a language as might be supposed, but in the days before simultaneous interpretation it is not easy to see what else could have been done.

Strossmayer spoke Latin as though it was his native tongue, and brilliantly. Therefore he became the chief orator of the Minority. His motives for resisting the Majority were not the usual. His diocese was full of Slavs in Croatia and Bosnia. He was a Slav nationalist who represented Slav aspirations from his seat in the Vienna Parliament, and was the political leader of the Croats against the not very understanding rule of the Hungarians. He therefore cared about possible union with the Eastern Orthodox Church, from political motives as strongly as from ecclesiastical. He believed that by a return to the Roman obedience the Slavs would gain, not merely religiously but culturally, by being opened up to Western education. Anything that made it more difficult for Slavs to accept reunion with the Western Catholics was a blow to his social and political aspirations, as well as his sense of Christian charity.

In several respects Strossmayer was the most astounding bishop of the century. He set up a record by being bishop of the same see for 55 years; his was a larger-than-life personality who therefore had dedicated disciples and equally dedicated enemies; he carved out an epoch in Croat history and is still looked back upon as a founder of modern Croatia. A man of very able intelligence, noble countenance, and an eminent gift of oratory in Latin, German, or Serbo-Croat, he could be hasty in judgement and too impetuous in decision. His opinions of people he disapproved of were at times expressed in unepiscopal language. His enemies accused him of being vain or even proud and that was natural, but probably untrue; what was true was that he knew that he was right.[34]

At the Council Strossmayer was the most compelling person in the Minority though he could not command a team. The strangest aspect of the Minority was the part played in its creation by a young English Catholic layman, Acton, whom Gladstone had lately made Lord Acton, one of the first two Roman Catholic peers to be created in Britain in modern times. He was a strenuous liberal Catholic. Because the old English universities refused to give degrees to Roman Catholics he went to Munich for his higher education and became the ablest and most learned pupil of Professor Döllinger; earlier he had been a pupil of Bishop Dupanloup. With a command of Italian, German, and French, acquaintance with several important people in each group, a bustling energy, and a determination that a definition of infallibility would justify horrible things like the Inquisition, he rushed about Rome putting bishops of similar opinions but different groups or nationalities in touch with each other. It was an astonishing role for a young layman of only 35 years to play; a role unprecedented in the history of General Councils. In the earlier stages of the Council it certainly had an importance. Acton's weight rested upon the bishops' awareness that he was very close to the British Prime Minister. It was just possible that Acton could persuade Gladstone to influence the French Emperor, who would then stop the Council in its tracks by ordering his soldiers out of Rome and leaving the city a prey to anarchy.

This work of bringing the opposition together was made easier by a political blunder on the part of the extreme members of the Majority. It was evident that the most important of the commissions or committees would be the commission on doctrine, called the

[34] Strossmayer was of Croat family but with one Austrian great-grandfather who married a Croat girl and settled in Croatia. Born 1815; theology at Pest; priest 1838 and parish pastor; DD Vienna 1842; a director of Vienna theological school 1847; hence the prominence at and after the Revolution. The see of Djakovo was a union of the 18th cent. between an earlier diocese and the historic diocese of Sirmium which went back to the days of Constantine the Great.

Deputation on the Faith, for it would take the comments of the fathers about the draft into consideration and present a final version to the Pope. The ultramontanes, headed this time by Archbishop Manning of Westminster, made sure that not a single member of the Minority was put into this commission of twenty-four members—or tried to make sure, because they put in the primate of Hungary, Simor, thinking that he was on the right side, and were surprised later to find that he was one of the Minority. That is, the most important of the commissions was made unrepresentative of opinions in the Council as a whole. This made the Minority angry and pulled them together into a bloc as nothing else could have succeeded in doing. It also gave excuse to the publicists who told the world that the Council was not free. Acton was able to say that this was 'a gagging of the Council'.[35]

One other regulation troubled the Minority, though it should not have done. The regulation of 22 February 1870, confirmed by the Pope, said that the decisions would be reached by majority voting. The old theory of General Councils assumed that the conclusion would be reached unanimously because the bishops were guided by God—'it seemed good to the Holy Spirit and to us . . .' (Acts 15: 28). A Council was not thought to be a counting of votes but a proclaiming of the corporate voice of the Church. Since even in the smaller Councils this ideal of unanimity was not realistic it was interpreted broadly, as substantial agreement; to have a few people voting No was in the nature of humanity; and everyone was agreed that a tiny majority, a decision carried by two or three votes, would not bind the Church. But in resenting the rule of results by majority, the Minority failed to take account of the new numbers of voters; a substantial agreement reached by 200 bishops looked different when the bishops were 600 or more. If the Council were to achieve anything, it must have the rule of result by majority, provided that it was not interpreted to mean bare majority.

The Minority was less critical in its attitude to 'unanimity' than was right for a group led by several church historians. The second ecumenical Council at Constantinople (381) gained unanimity because the minority left before the end. The third ecumenical Council at Ephesus (431) gained unanimity because Cyril of Alexandria refused to wait for his opponents to arrive. The conclusions of

---

[35] Dated 19 Dec. 1869: Quirinus, *Letters from Rome*, 91.

ecumenical Councils had been less unanimous than Strossmayer and Acton asserted, yet had been afterwards accepted as binding on everyone.

In reality the bishops were still free to discuss; even if they needed to shout to discuss. They could say what they liked about the drafts presented; and if they were prepared to risk an air of public disapproval in the city and the meetings they could and did say vehement things against them. Since some of these drafts smelt of the professor who had not kept up his reading into modern times, it was easy to find in them things deserving strong language. The presidents of the Council had the power to carry through the drafts without taking any notice of what was said against them. But they did not. They withdrew them for consideration. And this showed the fathers of the Minority that after all they possessed a freedom of debate. The freedom was seen to be limited by the physical fact inevitable in large assemblies. People made long speeches. The less they had to say the longer they went on saying it. At this rate of progress it would not be possible to get far within a short space of time, nor even in a long space of time. Cardinal Antonelli said wearily as he came out of the first session that at this rate the Council would last ten years.[36] The idea of decision by acclamation was dead.

Nothing ever came out of most of these debates. But the attitudes they showed were a sign of the way the Catholic Church wanted to go. The bishops did not want an excess of centralization in Rome, but they did want the authority of the bishops, under attack from the modern world, to be fortified, not diminished, by Rome. It must not be forgotten that the bishops had a collegial responsibility for the universal Church, not only the care of their own diocese. They did not want the Council to put out statements of obsolete-sounding theology that the world would not understand and which could not profit the Church. They raised the possibility of a reform of the canon law, so that people might have access to it from some codified and up-to-date volume instead of having to fumble among the huge folios of various dates and diversified authority. They wanted the teaching of the young brought up to date by better catechisms but did not want a universal catechism alleged to be suitable for all lands.

On 21 January 1870 the fathers were given a draft for consideration, *On the Church of Christ.* It set out that Christ founded a Church

---

[36] Aubert, *Vatican 1*, 131–2, from the Vienna archive.

with orders of ministry and a visible unity. Therefore to belong to the Church of Rome was necessary for salvation (but this was then interpreted in a far less rigid manner). This Church could not err, for it was guided by the Holy Spirit. In the hierarchy of the Church Christ had invested St Peter and his successors with a primacy which included a universal power of government. The pope was not simply the bishop with the chief honour but had an ordinary jurisdiction over all the pastors and people of the Church. And by providence he had been given a temporal domain to guarantee him freedom and independence of all earthly powers. It was wrong in civil society for Church and State to be separated, but the Church could be united with various forms of civil constitution. Governments were bound to take account of Christian moral teaching. The draft condemned absolutist States which made the State the source of all law. The Church must be allowed to teach the faith to the young. Seminarists ought not to be forced to do military service. Monks and nuns may freely form communities.

This draft was leaked to the European press and caused commotion. The bishops attacked it for lack of balance between pope and bishops: a very short section about bishops, a long section about the pope. It was withdrawn for redrafting and never came back. But meanwhile the Austrian Chancellor Beust warned Cardinal Antonelli that Austria would have to alter its Concordat with Rome. And the French Foreign Secretary Count Daru, the least experienced politician ever to become Foreign Secretary of France, made ominous noises about French intervention. A flurry of anxious letters was again exchanged between the governments.

None of this government activity achieved anything on the face of it, although it might have had an influence behind the scenes. The draft *On the Church* never reappeared in a form that dealt with matters of the Syllabus of Errors. The Council managers quietly put aside, in the later stages of the Council, those matters that directly touched the relations between the Church and the States—which may have been the result of the flurry of letters between governments.

Possibly the European press affected the fathers of the Council; certainly it lowered the reputation of the Council through the world. The international press had only just arrived as an institution. During the 1860s the system of foreign correspondents was organized, and for the first time there were journalists hungry for copy. They had to print something, and if they were not told what was true, they would print what they guessed, a few of them would print what was untrue—but print something they must.

The government of the Papal States, which lived in a world of several decades before the time, had no idea of this new circumstance of society. They accepted the ancient doctrine that as all proceedings were confidential no one ought to be told anything. Cardinal Antonelli kept sedulously away from anyone who wrote casual articles for the press.[37] The Curia did not realize the elementary truth that an assembly of 600 to 700 people could not hide what it did if it was in any way controversial. Bishops talked to their friends, or to their ambassadors. Several bishops felt that the imposed clause of silence, which they had not voted themselves, did not bind them.

Hence documents were leaked. The angriest moments were reported graphically, followed by the issue of denials of what was alleged to be untrue reporting. The solemn secrecy of the Council became a sieve, and the conditions were such that the press was certain to report with a hostile slant. This was particularly true during the first two or three months of the Council, after which the press started to lose interest in what they could no longer make exciting.

Under these conditions a truly informed person, who could find confidential information and was prepared to use it, could control a large public and influence opinion. Acton in Rome was well informed. He knew the British envoy Odo Russell, and the Prussian and Bavarian ambassadors in whose houses he met their national bishops; he knew Dupanloup and French bishops of the Minority, Hefele and several Germans of the Minority, Strossmayer, and English bishops who, unlike their leader Manning, were against a definition of infallibility. All these were a small group in relation to the whole Council, but they were the spearhead of the Minority.

In frequent letters to Döllinger, which Döllinger then edited slightly and published in the *Allgemeine Zeitung*, Acton portrayed the Council from the viewpoint of the most hostile among the Minority and gave Europe a picture of an unscrupulous Majority tyrannizing over minds and consciences. And since he was truly informed, and since no one else was allowed to report with another slant, his

---

[37] L. von Pastor, *Tagebücher, Briefe, Erinnerungen*, ed. W. Wühr (Heidelberg, 1950), 240, evidence of Cardinal Reisach via Cardauns. But Cardauns was the most responsible Catholic journalist of the age, the editor of the Cologne *Volkszeitung* for more than thirty years from 1876 and a lover of the historic Rhineland.

portrait in *Letters from Rome* by Quirinus became the chief source of information on the behaviour of the Council and controlled the picture of it then and for years to come, even among historians.

The ultramontane journalist Louis Veuillot set up house in Rome and tried to do something of the same on the other side. Like Acton he was privileged, because the Pope, who knew that he supported papal infallibility, ordered a monsignor (Mercurelli) to keep him informed of everything that went on in the Council.[38] Veuillot tore into the Minority as heretics, and ridiculed some of their leaders (especially Dupanloup) maliciously. But the effect was very different from that achieved by Acton. He touched French and Italian clergymen and a faithful band of French laymen and laywomen; he caused French priests to question their bishop if he was a member of the Minority and stored up future trouble in the dioceses. That is, Veuillot was read by an ecclesiastical public, Acton affected the view of interested Europe.

The two sides believed something so important to the future of the Church to be at stake, that at times they slid into methods which were hard to justify morally. Clifford, the bishop of Clifton, the diocese of the West Country in England, was one of the best of the English bishops. He was a sweet-natured man from an old aristocratic family of recusants. He was totally against the definition of infallibility. He saw a letter which John Henry Newman, the head of the Oratory in Birmingham, had written to his bishop, Ullathorne of Birmingham. In it Newman, who believed that the pope could not err when speaking on behalf of the whole Church, used violent language against the behaviour of the Majority: 'When has definition of doctrine *de fide* been a luxury of devotion and not a stern painful necessity? Why should an aggressive insolent faction be allowed to make the hearts of the just to mourn? . . . Why can't we be let alone?' Wrongly imagining that publication of this letter could help the opposition, Clifford leaked it to the press, which helped the Minority not at all. It only complicated Newman's life.

Meanwhile, behind the scenes the theologians were busy with the more literate bishops of the Deputation on the Faith in trying to redraft the statement of fundamental theology. They divided the former draft into two parts, and issued the earlier one, *On the Catholic Faith*, to the fathers on 14 March. Most of the fathers of the Minority

---

[38] E. Veuillot, *Louis Veuillot*, iv. 148 ff.

were happy with the new and substantially altered draft, but the discussion of it led to the big scene of the Council (22 March). The preface talked in a hostile way about Protestants. Strossmayer rose to protest, and spoke of the truly Christian nature of many Protestants. There was murmuring, even barracking, and the presidents interrupted a man hard to interrupt; whereupon Strossmayer left the subject to complain that the Council now appeared to be deciding things by a majority when the proper course of a Council was only to decide with a 'moral unanimity'; and meanwhile there were cries of 'Anathema!', 'He's a Lucifer!', or 'This is Luther again, out with him!' The majority of the bishops in the Council had never seen a Protestant in their lives and the word to them was more like the words 'Bolshevist' or 'Fascist' to a later generation.

Nevertheless the text was altered to be less hostile to Protestants: in its better form—as the constitution *Dei Filius* of 24 April 1870— the sentence ran thus: 'Everyone knows that, after they [Protestants] rejected the divine authority of the Church and abandoned themselves to private judgment in religion, the heresies condemned by the Council of Trent divided themselves bit by bit into numerous sects, of which the disagreements and rivalries ended by doing much to ruin faith in Christ.'

The other part of this constitution that caused trouble in debate was an appendix with eighteen anathemas. These looked old-fashioned, and the more liberal bishops thought them unnecessary— 'if anyone denies that there is one true God, Creator and Lord of things visible and invisible, let him be anathema', etc. The old-fashioned air was a little more offensive to some of the northern bishops than the content of the less general anathemas.

Otherwise *Dei Filius* was for the most part a plain statement of fundamental faith and caused problems only of drafting. It was accepted unanimously by the Council, or by all the members present; Strossmayer preferred to absent himself from the vote. A few bishops were vexed that it had taken this Council so many weeks to arrive only at an elementary creed. Yet for the most part the constitution was well drafted. It was beginning to be important in the climate of the world to say aloud rather than take for granted, that God is free, personal, and creative, and revealed Himself to men that they might know him and trust his providence.

From 9 May 1870 the fathers discussed a draft on the infallibility of the pope. The draft called it his 'prerogative' of infallibility; it extended to matters of faith and morals to be held by all the Church; it was exercised when he performed the duty of supreme teacher of all Christians. That is, it was limited. It was not supposed that he had an infallibility on matters other than faith or morals, nor that it applied to everything that he said. It applied only when he made a judgement in his office as Vicar of Christ, and then only when he taught the whole Church and was not dealing with an individual or national question.

Much time and emotion could have been saved if the fathers could have approved this draft at once. But since some of them did not believe it and others thought it a mistake to say it even though it was true, two months of tension ensued while the bishops of the Minority tried to prevent the constitution being agreed; or, if and when they saw that some such constitution was inevitable, tried to introduce drafting changes which would make the pope the mouthpiece of the bishops and the whole Church rather than a sovereign in his own right.

These strenuous endeavours looked at one time as though they might bring a result. But they ended by making the draft decree even more papal, in the sense of separating the pope's infallibility from that of the whole body of the Church. This result was not what the Minority aimed at.

Before the end of April 1870 it was agreed that there should be a separate constitution, *De Romano Pontifice*, concerning the pope's primacy, power, and inability (under conditions) to err. A member of the Majority, Pie of Poitiers, explained that no one wanted to make the pope infallible as a private person, nor to set him up against the whole Church as though the head of the Church could live without its body. These explanations pleased many in the Minority.

In the debates their leaders continued to put forward the difficulties: the historical objections to thinking that decrees of popes could be infallible; the danger to the proper attitude to the power of bishops by an undue exaltation of the pope; the practical difficulties with Protestants, with governments, or with discontented Catholics which might follow from a definition.

The speakers of the Majority denied that infallibility could possibly be called a new doctrine when it was taught by Cardinal Bellarmine of the Counter-Reformation and by St Thomas Aquinas in the high Middle Ages. They had an easy target with the doctrine of unripe time—if the doctrine was true it must be so important that the

Church must declare it. And in Manning they had an ex-Protestant who could tell them how he had found relief in the high doctrine of the authority of the pope from all the disagreements and uncertainties of his Protestant past. So far from the Protestants being offended by such a definition, many of them, he thought, and he alleged publicly, were crying out for such a clear voice to speak the truth with authority.

All May and June of 1870 the debates went on, sometimes dramatic, mostly wearisome, always monologues, occasionally wise, occasionally offensive. And little by little the summer heat of Rome became more oppressive. The most famous scene of these debates, and the most famous quotation of the Council, were produced by the Dominican Cardinal Guidi, who was archbishop of Bologna but not allowed by the Italian government to go to his see. To the surprise of both parties, he said that the Pope must consult the bishops before he defined so that he could inform himself on the content of the Catholic tradition: 'If anyone says that the Pope when he speaks does so by his own will independent of the Church, that is separately and not with the counsel of the bishops who show the tradition of their churches, let him be anathema.' It has been proved that Guidi was speaking not only for himself but on behalf of a group of Dominican theologians.

Observing the Council debates were secretaries whose task was to inform the Pope of everything that went on—and he wanted to know about every detail. At once, therefore, he heard about Guidi's speech. No sooner had Guidi returned to the Dominican house at the Minerva where he lived than a message came that the Pope wished to see him. When he reached the Vatican he could tell from the faces of the staff that a storm was brewing. He said afterwards that he found the Pope 'grave and haughty'. The Pope said that he would never have believed that he could have made such a speech, and that he must have done so only to please the Piedmontese government so that they would grant him a passport to his see of Bologna. Guidi said that he could defend what he said, and that he had said nothing that did not agree with the teachings of St Thomas Aquinas and Bellarmine. The Pope said that this was not true, he had taught error. Guidi denied it. The Pope said: 'Yes, it is an error, because I, I am tradition, I, I am the Church!' He accused Guidi of allowing Strossmayer to kiss his hand and thank him as he came down from the rostrum. Guidi said that he did not know Strossmayer by sight and had no idea who thanked him when he stepped down from the rostrum. The Pope said that he would make Guidi profess true faith to the Council. Guidi said that he would subscribe to the doctrine of infallibility when it was defined. And he asked the Pope to read the actual words of his speech.[39]

When Guidi came back to the Minerva so many carriages arrived, of cardinals and bishops calling to thank him for his speech, that the little piazza at the Minerva was jammed. When they heard about the interview with the Pope they were angry and talked of oppression. 'We have no freedom in this Council. Under this pressure what sort of validity will the decrees of the Council possess? A Pope who doesn't want a debate but defends his own opinion under pain of incurring his anger, is a Pope who destroys the rights of bishops and in consequence the authority of the Council.'

This incident was the lowest point of the effort to influence an individual member of the Council, made all the worse because of its melodrama.

The story represented a truth about the changing attitude of the Pope during the course of the Council. Though Pius IX had always believed in papal infallibility, he had not sought during the first month and a half of the Council to exercise undue influence on the fathers to come to conclusions which he wanted. He had the confidence to leave them relatively free. If the Council in those early weeks was not at liberty, as Acton's letters from Rome alleged, it was not the result of pressure from the Pope upon the Minority but of that of the ultramontane Majority. If at first the Pope exercised influence on members of the Minority it was by charm, not by bullying.

But after February 1870 Pius IX felt that the world was increasingly against the Church, that liberalism was ever more dangerous to

---

[39] Guidi's speech in G. D. Mansi, *Collectio conciliorum recentiorum*, ed. J. B. Martin and L. Petit (Arnhem and Leipzig, 1923–7), lii. 740 ff.; and vast literature on the case. See esp. G. Martina in *DHGE* s.v. Guidi. Various historians denied the probability of the Pope's words but they are now proven by the text of Tizzani, repr. in Martina, *Pio IX (1867–78)*, 555 ff.: excellent modern treatment of evidence in K. Schatz, *Vaticanum I 1869–70* (3 vols.; Paderborn, 1993–), iii. app. 1, 312 ff. For the bizarre rumours about it, U. Horst in *RSCI* 34 (1980), 513 ff. Guidi had never been able to occupy his see of Bologna because the Italians kept him out. After the speech a group of ultramontanes in Bologna asked the Pope to remove him from the see. He resigned it next year, was given two nominal posts in Rome, and was thereafter remote from events till his death in 1879. At the papal election the year before he died someone gave him a vote, but only as a way of throwing it away while he waited to see what would happen.

the truth, that the opponents of the Church were ever more unscrupulous. His training left him with no capacity to understand the difficulty felt by the bishops of the Minority. And since he had never visited a non-Catholic country, he had no capacity for understanding the pastoral problems of the Catholic Church in a Protestant land. He identified the desire for a definition of infallibility with a true understanding of faith.

Therefore the Minority began to appear to him evil. From the spring of 1870 he used the vast influence of his person and office to push members of the Council to define the Pope's infallibility in an ultramontane form. A few of them he treated pastorally, as though they had cause for penitence; to a few of them he was rude. In the last weeks of the Council he fell into conflict even with the presidents whom he had chosen for the Council, and especially the former drafter of the Syllabus Cardinal Bilio, who was more considerate of the wishes of the Minority than the Pope thought right. He sent briefs of thanks to many people who stood for the truth as he saw it— opponents of the Minority bishops of France, priests in dioceses who were active against their bishop if he was of the Minority, ultramontane pamphleteers such as Gaston de Ségur and the Benedictine Prosper Guéranger, an ultramontane journalist in Veuillot.[40]

Much the most important of the successes achieved by the Minority was an addition to the text on the universal power of the pope; that the bishops are true successors of the apostles and true pastors in their dioceses. This was important in meeting in part the fears of those who thought that the elevation of papal power would reduce the apostolic authority of the bishops to nothing.

But what they most wanted to achieve was to make sure that the infallibility of the Pope was placed in the context of the inability of the whole Church to err. They wanted some such formula as 'the Pope is infallible when he speaks as teacher of the Church, with the agreement of the whole Church'. An official speaker from the ultramontane side, Monsignor Gasser, explained to them that the Majority did not wish to claim that the Pope alone was infallible and that it was this that made the Church infallible. But the Minority

[40] The case against Pius IX is admirably summarized by K. Schatz in M. Greschat (ed.), *Gestalten der Kirchengeschichte* (Stuttgart, 1981–6), xii. 198–201. It is overstated by A. B. Hasler, *Pius IX: Papstliche Unfehlbarkeit und I. Vatikanisches Konzil* (Stuttgart, 1977). For the exaggerations of this book see especially the review by G. Martina, *AHP* 16 (1978), 341–69. Balanced discussion in K. Schatz, *Vaticanum I 1869–70* (3 vols., Paderborn, 1993–), iii. 181 ff.

found extreme difficulty whenever they suggested that such explanations ought to be included in the text of the constitution. They would have been happy with the addition of three words only, he is infallible if he speaks *innixus testimonio episcoporum*, 'relying on the witness of the bishops'. But this was impossible. What the Majority would never concede was that the pope was only infallible if first he had the agreement of the Church in what he said.

On 13 July 1870 the fathers voted on the draft. The number of people voting *against* shocked the Majority and disturbed the Pope. Of the bishops, 451 voted for. Some fifty bishops abstained by not coming to the meeting—Antonelli was one of them. Eighty-eight bishops voted against, sixty-two voted 'yes with reservations'—but of these there were some who thought the constitution inadequate because it was not papalist enough. Between a quarter and a third of those present in Rome did not want the constitution as it stood. In that fraction were three cardinals and many of the most celebrated bishops and archbishops of the Catholic church, famous for their defence of the see of Rome under the attacks of the modern world.

They hoped that the size of this negative vote would force a concession at the last minute. It had the contrary effect on the ultramontanes, and a very contrary effect on the Pope. Archbishop Darboy of Paris led a delegation to see the Pope himself, asking for the addition of some phrase such as 'the Pope, resting on the witness of the whole Church'. Any deputation led by Archbishop Darboy was not likely to please Pius IX. The Pope received a contrary plea that such a phrase would leave the door open to Gallican interpretations, and therefore words should rather be added in the opposite sense—for example, that 'definitions made by the Pope cannot be altered and there is no need for the agreement of the bishops'. Under the Pope's stimulus or request or even order the Deputation on the Faith added to the formula the famous clause, *ex sese non autem ex consensu ecclesiae*—'the definitions of the Pope cannot be altered, they have authority from themselves and not by reason of the agreement of the Church'.

The Minority did not know yet that this addition was the Pope's wish, and tried again to get it altered. On 17 July Cardinal Rauscher of Vienna made a last plea to him to abstain from turning an opinion of the schools into a dogma under anathema. It was clear that the constitution was going through in this form. The Minority decided therefore that it was better not to vote against it. They would do better to leave Rome in order not to be present for the vote. Fifty-six bishops wrote to the Pope saying that this was what they were doing and why.

At a solemn session of 18 July, the constitution was approved by 533 votes to 2. Of the two, one was the bishop of a tiny see in South Italy who probably had not heard of the decision of the Minority to abstain. One was the bishop of Little Rock in the United States who possibly—but not probably—meant to cast his vote in favour and made a mistake.

The size of the vote was greeted with prolonged cheering. They sang the Te Deum in the midst of a thunderstorm, which was variously interpreted.

So a majority of the bishops of the Catholic Church formally voted to elevate the pope's authority. Most of them thought that they did nothing new, and that true Catholics had always believed the dogma which they now made formal.

It defined that Christ gave St Peter, and through him the popes, a primacy over the whole Church, and that the pope's authority over the Church was derived from Christ and not from the Church. He was given an episcopal authority over the whole Church, not only concerning faith and morals but on matters of discipline. A decision of the pope could not be altered by any authority but the pope's own, not even by the authority of a General Council. In this power was included the supreme power of teaching the faith. When he taught *ex cathedra*—that is when he officially fulfilled his office as the pastor and teacher of all Christians—that a doctrine or a decision on morals was to be held by the universal Church, he had the help of God promised to St Peter, and therefore his decisions could not be altered and had their authority from themselves and not by reason of any agreement of the Church. The constitution was known from its first words, *Pastor Aeternus*.

6

THE PRISONER OF THE VATICAN

France declared war against Prussia on the day after the infallibility decree. That meant a hurried return to their sees by many bishops. The Council was reduced by departures to something under 150 members. For a time the committees went on drafting. On 6–7 August 1870 the French troops at last left Rome. The September Convention of six years before, whereby Italy promised not to occupy Rome if the French took away their soldiers, was still in force. Napoleon III perhaps imagined that he could rely on it, though it had failed him when he was forced to fight the battle of Mentana. But now the same pressures as those of 1867 made the pope's Rome untenable. Whatever the Italian government promised or wished— and of course it wished for Rome whatever it had promised, though many of its moderates thought it wrong to occupy Rome by a coup and not by treaty—it must march on Rome or it would be over-thrown by Italians. If the king of Italy refused to agree to taking Rome there would not be a king in Italy. They must take Rome or they would be in revolution. The Prime Minister Lanza and the Foreign Secretary Visconti Venosta agreed with the King that they had undertaken by a solemn treaty not to attack Rome and they must not break their word. The radicals in Parliament led by Rattazzi told the Finance Minister Sella, the only cabinet minister to be militant on their side, that if the government did not order its army to occupy Rome, even if it had to fight a papal or French army, they would leave the capital Florence and declare for a republic and for the over-throw of the Savoy line of kings.[1] The threat sharpened the mind of King Victor Emmanuel. He asked the advice of a liberal aristocrat San Martino, who persuaded him that the alternative was a worse fate for the Pope as well as the House of Savoy. The king accepted reluctantly that the only way to keep himself on the throne was to occupy Rome, but he preferred not to use force.

[1] M. L. Rattazzi, *Rattazzi et son temps: Documents inédits* (Paris, 1887), ii. 348 ff.

In the middle of August 1870 the Italian army began to mobilize. Before the end of the month the Italian government told its ambassadors that it would move on Rome. On 2 September the French Emperor surrendered to the Prussians at Sedan. Instantly the pressure on the Italian government multiplied, it was certain now that no French army could resist them. They pleaded, as before Mentana, that they must go to Rome to establish order in place of the French. But no one believed the excuse, there was less reason to do so than before Mentana because the city was orderly. Perhaps the city was orderly in part because possible conspirators believed there was no need to take risks, since the army would come. But the city was calm also because most of the inhabitants liked what they had had for more than 1,000 years and were afraid of what would happen if the Piedmontese arrived. This was not true of the Papal State outside Rome. Sure that a change was coming, the radicals in every other town of the Papal State caused disturbance. Italy had a sufficient excuse to occupy the Papal State except for Rome on grounds of public order. On 8 September San Martino arrived in Rome to tell the Pope that they would occupy the city but would respect his independence. The mission did not help. The interviews were stormy. Cardinal Antonelli told him that he was announcing an act of violence and the Pope told him that the Italian doctrine was, 'right must give way to might'.

The Pope did nothing. He was sure that Rome was a sacred city. No modern army would dare to attack it. God would protect it. If Italy really attacked then the Catholic powers, France and Austria, would see that it was secure. The Pope even thought that Prussia would help to stop the Italians if they were needed. He was happy and serene. Antonelli did nothing. He had not the same illusions as his master. He did nothing because he thought nothing could be done; and was improvident.

But they had a garrison. Someone must tell the garrison what to do. Its commander was Hermann Kanzler, a professional soldier who commanded the papal forces who were with the French when together they beat Garibaldi at Mentana—after which the Pope felt affection for him. First Antonelli and then the Pope told Kanzler that the Italians would not attack, but Kanzler knew better. He brought his troops back into Rome and manned the walls. But he was not satisfied with the order that if the Italians attacked (which, he was told, they would not) he was to let them make a breach and then surrender without firing a shot so that no lives would be lost. He said that his honour and that of his men was in question. This scruple of the soldiers' honour caused a loss of life which the Pope could have avoided by being firm. General Cadorna, as he advanced through Viterbo, sent two messages to Kanzler under a flag of truce asking for leave to occupy the city. Kanzler replied that what Cadorna wanted to do was sacrilege and that he ought to consider his responsibility towards God and history.

On the day before the attack the Pope climbed the Scala Santa on his knees. That 19 September 1870 General Cadorna had 60,000 troops outside Rome and the zouaves and the French volunteers came to about 10,000. The city had walls but they were weak and in disrepair and the wall by the Porta Pia was weakest of all. The fight lasted five hours, from 5 a.m. to 10 a.m., without the Italians penetrating the city. While the artillery exchanged fire at the Porta Pia— and some fifty soldiers from the two sides were killed, one shell destroyed Cardinal Bilio's stable and killed his horses—the Pope addressed the diplomats. Kanzler sent a message that the breach at Porta Pia was made and passable and the Pope ordered a surrender. When the order to surrender came and the white flag must be raised some zouaves talked of disobeying the order but did not. They spent that night camped in St Peter's square; and in the morning were put on trains. Many of them enlisted in the French army to fight against the Prussians; so the last was not heard of zouaves until 1871.

Cadorna was told not to occupy the Leonine City—St Peter's, the Vatican, Castel Sant'Angelo and Trastevere, that is, Rome to the west of the Tiber. This did not work because there were now no proper gendarmes in occupied Rome; for under the honourable truce Kanzler's little army marched out in good order. Wild men started tumults, and there was a physical assault on the Vatican; and Antonelli had to ask Cadorna to complete the occupation and guard even the Piazza of St Peter, except for the Vatican Palace and the cathedral itself, which alone were left under the protection of the Swiss and the papal gendarmes. Cadorna stated that he would withdraw his troops from that side of the Tiber when the Pope asked. This statement had no effect in reconciling the Pope. His words to the diplomats became a motif for himself and for his successor: 'I surrender to violence. From this moment I am the prisoner of King Victor Emmanuel.'

On 2 October the Italian government managed a plebiscite, whereby every male adult was asked whether he said Yes or No to the statement 'I wish to be united with the Kingdom of Italy under the rule of King Victor Emmanuel and his successors'. Only forty-seven Romans voted against. That could only mean that large numbers of Romans took no notice of the plebiscite which therefore carried Yes by a large majority. Antonelli called it 'the iniquitous bit of clumsiness called plebiscite'.

The Quirinal was the Pope's palace. It was now in the area occupied by General Cadorna. Was it a State building, or the Pope's personal property? They took legal opinion which declared it to be the property of the State. Inside it were eighteen armed Swiss guards and 200 old people, poor pensioners and the widows of former officials and such like. The Italians allowed the Swiss to join their compatriots at the Vatican, taking their weapons with them, but in mufti. The poor were far more difficult, where else in Rome could they be put? The chief opponent of a move of the king into the Quirinal was the King. They looked around for other palaces—only the Colonna, the Barberini, and the Rospigliosi had a palace worthy of a king, and with a garden and could they turn out those historic families? The Farnese was full of sad Bourbon memories. The Braschi, which was for sale, was engulfed in noise and traffic. But years before, Cavour had virtually promised that the king would live in the Quirinal.

On 8 November 1870 they took it, room by room, in the space of a fortnight. They were surprised that the Pope kept almost nothing valuable in his palace. The most important things were the archives, especially those of the Revolution of 1848. The king inherited from the Pope, or stole, whichever it was, a few clocks, various desks, pictures (one of the battle of Mentana), table-lights, iron bedsteads, and a billiard table. Antonelli did not fail to tell the European powers that the Italians were burglars.[2]

In 1809 Pius VII had waited until he was taken by force to France. In 1848 Pius IX had fled in disguise to Gaeta. Immediate rumours focused on whether the Pope would now leave Rome. A few responsible Catholics, among them Beckx the general of the Jesuits, argued that if the Pope left Rome on the plea that he was no longer free, this would so shock the powers with Catholic peoples that they would ensure the restoration of Rome, and perhaps of much more than Rome. In Florence the Italian government was nervous that he might go and that their international influence might be weakened.

---

[2] E. Morelli, *AHP* 8 (1970), 239 ff.; the documents between Antonelli and the Italians.

The Pope asked himself the question, 'Is it better to go, and if so, where?' A committee of ten cardinals, which included Bilio and Barnabò, was asked to advise. The Pope had selected his ten cardinals: in Rome at that time were twenty-seven cardinals altogether, but he refused to ask the opinion, for example, of Cardinal Guidi who had said just what he thought during the Vatican Council. The Pope was not likely to be in favour of going because of his experience of the flight in 1848, which led to all the disadvantages of the stay in Gaeta and the restoration to Rome with the aid of a foreign army. Since the ten cardinals could not cross the city safely they could not meet, so gave their opinions by letter.

Six of the ten cardinals, among them Barnabò, were resolute that he should not try to go. Two of them thought it best that he should. Bilio and another refused to give an opinion. The six cardinals argued thus: flight without careful preparation was not possible; he could not know where to go until after negotiation with some State or other. It was hard to decide where the best refuge would be. In present conditions the presence of the Pope might be useful in the city, to avoid worse acts by the invaders and protect church establishments. If the Pope went, very bad things would happen in Rome and probably outside it.

The two who wanted him to go argued that if he stayed he would have to watch helplessly while monasteries were dissolved and the city secularized; that somewhere else he would have freer links with all the Churches of the world, and there was the chance of restoring the honour of the Holy See. When they considered where he could go, they suggested Malta, Belgium, the Tyrol, or the Rhineland. They thought Malta or Belgium the best hope.[3] Malta had a British government but it was a Catholic country and nearest to Rome; and the British, even if they sympathized with the Risorgimento and wanted a united Italy, made plain that they would be neutral in any dispute with the Pope for they had Catholic subjects to consider in Ireland, Quebec, and Australia as well as in Britain. Belgium, though it was a democracy, had a Catholic government. The Belgian bishops formally invited him. Bishop Martin of Paderborn in Germany offered him a sanctuary at Paderborn to which in 799 Pope Leo III escaped from a monastery at Rome (when his enemies had locked him up), and where he first met Charlemagne—an encounter with

[3] G. Martina, *Pio IX (1867–78)* (Rome, 1990), 248–9, the first to examine unpublished archival documents on this cardinals' report.

long consequences for Christendom. The Polish Prussian Archbishop Ledóchowski approached Kaiser William and Bismarck who were engaged in making peace at Versailles; not so much to secure a refuge as to get victorious Prussian power to help restore the Papal State. Bismarck, who was a pious Protestant in a very individualist way, took a cynical view: that if they offered the Pope a refuge (at Cologne perhaps, or Fulda?) it would transfer to Germany the Pope's existing unpopularity and so weaken German Catholicism. But all this was talk: the Prussians had no intention of helping the Pope even by providing sanctuary from the Italians.

Pius IX had no intention of going, as things were; he was an old man, beyond the age of moving. It is clear from the way in which he pre-selected his advisers and from the evidence of those who were close to him at that time. He was not at peace within himself, for observers discerned the sadness and anger of the man though his manner was dignified and his self-control was remarked. His attitude was that God's purposes were dark and mysterious and he could not see the future but he must trust that the right would prevail at last. Antonelli on the other hand was realist enough to know that any theories of quick restoration were (at present) wild. Pius IX accepted that circumstances might change, that if the Italian government failed to protect him he might be unsafe in Rome, that when he died it was certain (he imagined) that the election of a new Pope could not safely be held in Rome and must be held outside Italy. He did not rule out the possibility that he might be forced to move. Antonelli was content that it be known this option was still open because it posed a threat in international politics against the Italian government and constituted a safeguard that they would continue to treat the Pope with respect. But the Pope's personal attitude was that he should stay where he was, protest against usurpation, say his prayers, and trust in what providence held.

THE ACCEPTANCE OF THE COUNCIL

Meanwhile he had a lesser problem. There was still sitting in Rome an ecumenical Council with a heavy agenda of reports from committees in front of it. Most of its members had gone home but the rump was still nominally at work and all the real work of the Council concerning pastoral care, as distinct from broad statements about the nature of the Church, was still untouched. Some of the bishops suggested that they could go with the Pope to Belgium and continue the work of the Council in Malines.

On 20 October the Pope decided that the Council could no longer debate freely and adjourned it to a date to be fixed later. But nothing ever happened: the Council was ended. The drafts about missions, discipline, and pastoral care disappeared into the archives.

The question now was whether the bishops of the Minority, who had refused to vote for the decree of infallibility but had carefully not voted against it, would accept it. For most it was easy to accept. Any who had voted against only on the doctrine of unripe time had now no reason to resist. Some submitted because they realized that they could not be pastors in their diocese if they held out, and some because the occupation of Rome made the Pope a Catholic martyr in Europe and a great wave of Catholic protection rose to do all that was possible for him.

The last handful submitted with a torment of mind, and only because it was better than the alternative, which was encouraging dangerous schism in the Church at just the time when it was under most pressure and needed most support. Not to submit when ninety bishops did not submit was a different act from not submitting when four others refused. Strossmayer and others had argued in the Council that it could decide a fundamental doctrine not by majority but only by a moral unanimity. When so many submitted afterwards, the moral unanimity was in effect attained.

Those in the predicament of having to believe what they did not believe were helped by interpretation. The infallibility decree said that in matters of faith and morals the pope, when speaking formally (*ex cathedra*), is infallible of his own authority and not because of an assent of the Church. Extreme ultramontanes took the view that this meant what it seemed to say, that popes rule the doctrines and moral judgements of the Church without reference to anybody else. But many bishops never supposed that it meant that. For them the Council only declared that the bishops' formal assent in a Council was not necessary to the truth of the pope's formal words. Some continued to hold that the pope must still take regard for the opinions of the bishops before he spoke, even though they never voted on them. The secretary of the Council, the German Fessler, wrote a book, *On True and False Infallibility*, which took a moderate view along these lines, and the Pope made a speech approving Fessler's interpretation.

This book and the Pope's approval relieved many minds that were uncertain. The German bishops met and (defending themselves against Protestants and the Catholic critics) took a very moderate view of the effect of the infallibility decree; and the Pope declared that he approved of what they said. Probably even he was affected by the wave of Protestant contempt and propaganda that followed the decree, by the desire to prevent more Catholics from following the example of Döllinger and the other Catholic professors in Germany who were excommunicated and caused a schism. This moderation of interpretation after the event was weighty in helping the bishops to accept the decree. Once the decree was in place as a constituent of the law of the Church, the mood in the Vatican grew milder. Five years after the Council the Jesuit general Beckx was even able to prise Father Piccirillo from the Pope's side and order him to go to the United States, there to be an obscure teacher.

The agony of Hefele of Rottenburg, a true church historian and an honourable man, was the worst. In a letter to Fessler he even spoke of 'the sacrifice of the intellect'; but when he finally submitted he appealed to Fessler's moderate interpretation. It caused him mental suffering, but did not take him long. He submitted on 10 April 1871, much earlier than a few of the others.

Where a reluctant bishop could be subjected to direct pressure from Rome, that was sometimes applied, perhaps in the form of a refusal to renew the faculties for their pastoral work, or by a call to face the Holy Office. Mérode was summoned by the Holy Office and had to accept a draft submission which they agreed. Maret, most famous Gallican of them all, made less difficulty, he was asked by the Pope to recant his Gallican book and did so, after hesitation, publicly. The Hungarian bishops were particularly slow to send in their adhesions, but, rebuked by Antonelli, one by one sent in the required message.

Strossmayer of Djakovo did nothing for a long time. In December 1872 he published the decrees in his diocesan gazette but did not formally say that he agreed with them. The Pope chose to assume that all was well. Strossmayer had too heavy a weight in Slav affairs for it to be sensible for the Pope to be seen to be against him. Not until eleven years after the Council ended did Strossmayer make a clear statement that he believed its decree on infallibility.

The Pope's sternest critic, Darboy, accepted the decree. He had returned from the Council to the tragedy of Paris. By November

1870 Prussian forces ranged over much of France and besieged Paris and he was cut off from communications with Rome. An armistice was signed at the end of January 1871 between the Prussians and the French government now in Bordeaux. But the Parisian national guardsmen who controlled Paris in its siege were determined to fight on. When the French army tried to disarm them Paris was turned into the Commune. It had no realism. It was as if the barricades had won for a few weeks yet outside there were great French regular armies awaiting only Prussian leave to move on Paris.

Darboy, back inside Paris, believed the French cause to be just, asked prayers for victory, and said mass for Napoleon III the day he left for his fall. His experience of street revolution in 1848 made him hate this mode of bringing about political change. But he refused to leave Paris despite several attempts to persuade him on the plea that his life was not safe. When rioters threatened to attack the archbishop's house he refused to take precautions. He told the clergy that they ought to back the acting government, and he disturbed royalists by asking that the hymn 'Lord, save the republic' be sung. He helped to establish hospital services and handed over seminaries to become field hospitals. He asked his country in its hour of defeat and despair to put its trust in its moral force and its faith. His last pastoral letter in March 1871 asked for requiems for all the French fallen, including those who died in the streets of Paris.

The Commune grew wilder in the siege by the French army. It was put about that the clergy were the accomplices of tyrants, and priests were morally responsible for murdering the masses. It shut churches, destroyed two of them, and said that it found instruments of torture in monastery cellars. Friends kept begging Darboy to go into hiding and organized an escape route to Versailles. He refused. On 4 April 1871 he was arrested as a hostage. They told him that the French army was shooting prisoners and he wrote to Thiers at Versailles asking him to make sure that this did not happen. Friends tried to get him exchanged with the revolutionary Blanqui but Thiers blocked the proposal as a negotiation with criminals. Darboy wore the pectoral cross which Affre his predecessor but two wore when he was killed on the barricade of 1848 and the ring which his predecessor but one Sibour wore when he was murdered. On 21 May the Versailles army forced its way into Paris and the city was delivered to anarchy. The soldiers shot anyone they found whom they suspected of being anything to do with the Commune. By 24

May the guns were close to the gaol and a local *ad hoc* committee ordered the death of the hostages. The prison officers did the best they could, delaying hour after hour. But at last, in the darkening, Darboy and five others, including two Jesuits and a colleague in Paris, were shot in the courtyard by a posse of adolescents aged between 15 and 18. Affre's cross and Sibour's ring were never found. His death spared Darboy the knowledge of how many Parisians were shot by the incoming troops.

The day after the death of Darboy and his five comrades, five Dominicans were killed elsewhere in Paris; two days later, in the Commune's last gasp, fifty-five more hostages were shot, among them several clergy but also thirty-nine gendarmes. On 6 June there was an enormous funeral in Notre Dame. Of the hostages shot five were Jesuits. Twenty-nine clergy who were also hostages in the fateful prison managed to survive in the confusion of the last day when the army besieged the building.

Not long before his arrest Darboy wrote his last letter to the Pope. He told of his pain at what happened at Porta Pia, of this 'sacrilege' committed in Italy, and of the social disorder in France, the sufferings of his diocese, and of his priests' care for the wounded and the poor. Then he said, 'I adhere simply and purely to the decree of 18 July last.'

The Pope replied. Darboy was shot before the letter could arrive so that he never saw the Pope's last reproach. 'It is a sweet consolation that you adhere purely and simply to the dogmatic definition of the ecumenical council of the Vatican. We are sure that you will feel it a duty to tell your people, without any delay, that they must believe what you have said that you yourself believe.' But after this rebuke he assured him of his blessing amid all the great misfortunes of his flock.[4]

Posterity finds it bizarre that a pope, writing to a bishop whose life was at risk, in a city in chaos with gunmen in the streets, more than fifty churches damaged by shells, and seminaries used as field hospitals, should urge him to tell all his people that popes are infallible. It was an extenuation for the Pope that he could not have known quite what was happening in Paris when he wrote the letter, and had no idea what was about to happen.

---

[4] Darboy to Pius IX, 2 Mar. 1871; Pius IX to Darboy, 20 Mar. 1871; both printed in J. A. Foulon, *Histoire de la vie et des œuvres de Mgr Darboy* (Paris, 1889), 502 ff.

ROME AS A LAY CITY

One of the most painful sights for the Pope to watch was what happened to the city of Rome and its institutions. The Quirinal was only a symbol, though to Pius an offensive symbol. But the taking of the University away from the control of the Church and placing it under the Italian ministry of education was grievous to him: he imagined it teaching impiety to the young. He was pleased that the young did not seem to believe in the new state university, the Sapienza—the number of students fell dramatically. He tried to create another and more Christian university, but the state would not let it function. Soon they abolished the theological faculty despite a forcible argument in Parliament that to leave theology to seminaries was a sure way to get narrow-minded priests.

The records of the French Benedictine Cardinal Pitra, who was in Rome as the Vatican librarian, show the new predicament in the city. He spent his days working quietly in the library, and lived in San Callisto (the city 'branch' of the great Benedictine house of St Paul's outside the walls), but he could not cross the city dressed as a cardinal. He secured a passport for Spain in case the Pope decided to move there. He watched, more in sadness than anger, as the Italians took over monastic houses to be government offices. He noticed that the cardinals who used carriages painted out the coats of arms so that they looked like ordinary cabs. When the cardinals were summoned to a meeting at the Vatican they turned up dressed in city suits.[5] It took several months before they could be sure that the mob disorder of a revolution had passed.

It was not only the Pope who regretted the change coming to the city of Rome. The German historian Gregorovius was a stern East Prussian Protestant who believed in progress, despised popes, and wanted the papacy to end. But he loved the city of Rome, had dedicated many years of his life to writing its history, and so knew most of its stones and corners. His was a very readable history, partly because he had rare descriptive talent but partly because it was more than history, it was a private battle with a soul or spirit that he sensed within the city of Rome. He accepted that what had happened was right, but disliked its consequences: Rome, the moral capital of the

[5] A. Battandier, *Le Cardinal J. B. Pitra, évêque de Porto* (Paris, 1893), 560 ff.

world, cosmopolitan, now to be reduced to the capital of just one of the kingdoms of the world. Thinking thus he walked through the city with melancholy, seeing at every turn monuments of popes, such as churches, or fountains, or obelisks, from an age when Rome was not a part of Italy but Italy a piece of Rome. He asked himself how a mere king would look moving into the Quirinal:

The air of Rome is not suited to a young aspiring kingdom . . . The King of Italy will cut a figure here only such as that of one of the Dacian prisoners of war on the triumphal arch of Trajan . . . Rome will forfeit the cosmopolitan, republican atmosphere, which I have breathed here for eighteen years. She will sink into becoming the capital of the Italians, who are too weak for the great position in which our [German] victories have placed them . . . The Middle Ages have been blown away by a tramontana, with all the historic spirit of the past; yes, Rome has completely lost its charm.[6]

THE PRISONER IN THE VATICAN

The new Italian occupiers of Rome were careful to respect the person and the palace of the Pope. The authorities in the Vatican realized that without French troops they had to be policed by Italian soldiers or they would not be secure. The Pope said that he was a prisoner in the Vatican, and the world came to think of him as 'the prisoner in the Vatican'. The Italians said that this was scandalous propaganda, for it caused, for instance, distant Irishmen to imagine the Pope chained to a wall by Italian shackles. An enterprising fraud even sold as relics straw from the palliasse of his cell. The Italians said with truth that the Pope could walk out of the Vatican into the streets of Rome whenever he liked. But although this was true in law, the Pope was correct in saying that he was a prisoner. The mood of anticlericalism among members of the Roman population at that moment was such that if he had walked out into the streets he would have been rabbled. As it was, opprobrious shouts penetrated his rooms in the Vatican palace from the square outside. During 1871 there was shooting in St Peter's Square, with some deaths. Hooligans

[6] F. Gregorovius, *Roman Journal* (1911), 132 (written in Apr. 1861 when he was sure the fall of Rome to Italy must soon happen); and ibid. 389, 30 Oct. 1870. Cf. ibid. 437, 12 Jan. 1873. Gregorovius' Journal is uncheckable, because he destroyed it all and left only a select journal when he died. We have no means of knowing whether whether what he wrote on a date there printed was written then or altered later.

smashed madonnas in the streets and broke down the name of Jesus at the entry to the Collegio Romano, and at a service in the Gesù there were disorders. If these things happened when the Pope was inside the Vatican who could say what would happen if he came out? The carnival of Lent 1871 was turned into an insult to the Pope, and the psychological wall of the Vatican palace grew in height.

The international Church was represented in a few acres behind a high wall, which created in those who grew accustomed to it the mood of a sanctuary, fenced against the world. This was a mood which the old popes of the Quirinal palace and the Papal States never shared. Everyone who grew up in the Curia during this time was stamped by this experience. The last pope to be conditioned by it did not die until 1958. Each pope was restricted to the Vatican palace and St Peter's. Legally, it was voluntary, self-inflicted imprisonment. Actually, it was imposed by the threat of mobs, at least during the earlier decades of the 'imprisonment'. Thirty years later, long after his death, there was no more danger than to any sovereign who walks in public and needs a police guard to protect him or her from cranks; but by then the imprisonment had become a way of life or a habit of mind, with a touch of sacredness about it, that for reasons connected with a Christian legitimacy the Piedmontese government must not be recognized to be the legal government of Italy. For fifty-eight years no pope after his election put a foot down outside the precincts of the Vatican.

The Italians appointed a secret service officer, by name Manfroni, to watch the Pope. He did his duty with discretion, set a line of observers round the walls of the Vatican, and reported the Pope's movements and visitors to his masters. He made friends with several junior monsignors and gained useful information, a practice which would have horrified senior members of the Curia if they knew.

The Italian government was nervous. It was afraid that an unexpected combination of political events would restore the Pope to his State. It ruled a long peninsula where the interests of South and North were different and where people still thought of themselves as Lombards or Neapolitans rather than Italians. It had plenty of other internal tensions; it was afraid that Catholic France might revive; or that the pressures of the Catholic world, Austria, France, Spain, even tolerant Britain, might force it to give Rome back to the Pope. It heard of the debate in the French Parliament where a proposal was made that the Pope be restored by French arms. A French warship, the *Orénoque*, still cruised off Civitavecchia in case it should be needed by the Pope.[7] The Italian army got far more taxpayers' money than it needed or than the State of Italy could afford on the plea that it might be called to defend Italy against foreign invasion on behalf of the Pope. The Italian government was not so strong, nor the Pope's prestige so lacking, that it could afford to have him fleeing to Malta or Fulda, Granada or the Balearic Islands.

Therefore diplomacy found it essential to treat the Pope with the maximum honour. The government realized that it was sane policy to prove to the world—and to half-Catholic Italy—that the Pope, whatever he said about being a prisoner, was still free in the only way that ought to matter to him, free to perform his spiritual duty as head of the Church.

THE LAW OF GUARANTEES

In the conditions for the plebiscite the government announced that there would be a law to ensure the Pope his freedom, including the 'personal prerogatives of a sovereign' and 'territorial freedoms' (*franchigie territoriali*). Whether they liked it or not they were committed to make a law which defined these rights, otherwise they could be too widely interpreted. They therefore passed (March to May 1871) the Law of Guarantees.

The Law recognized the person of the pope as sacred. Insults against him were punishable in the same way as insults against the king of Italy. He was given the right to royal honours, and to maintain a private army of Swiss and noble guards. His palaces, museums, and libraries were exempted from tax. He was given a perpetual right to enjoy the Vatican, the Lateran and the country seat of Castel Gandolfo; no Italian official might intrude into these properties without the pope's permission—that is, the pope's properties were made a no-go area for the State. He was promised total freedom for his spiritual office, and the right to communicate freely with the Churches. Diplomats accredited to the Holy See were given the same rights as

---

[7] The *Orénoque* caused an incident. The French Foreign Minister ordered the officers to follow convention and pay respects to the king of Italy. The French ambassador refused to present them. He was ordered to obey or be dismissed. He left Rome. When it appeared that the commander of the *Orénoque* would do the same Paris did not persist, except to order the officers to pay respects to neither king nor pope.

diplomats accredited to the government of Italy. The government abandoned its right to appoint bishops—but in practice the law allowed a veto, for the *exequatur* must still be applied for; and the government took over the old rights of the Crowns of Savoy, Naples, and Vienna in choosing bishops and kept the appointment to those sees which were numerous—the bishops in Sardinia and Sicily, many of the bishops in the former kingdom of Naples, and five sees in the north including Venice. The law at last abolished, after so many centuries, the Monarchia Sicula, the effective state control, going back to Norman times, of the Church in Sicily. Finally, Italy agreed to pay the pope an annuity of 3,225,000 lire to maintain his palaces, cardinals, and diplomatic service.

This was fought through against a radical opposition which believed that too much was conceded to the pope. Is it really possible, they said, to make a second 'sovereign' inside a State? Is this not a revival of the medieval right of asylum? By allowing a citizen of Italy his own guards, are we not creating a private army—and what will be the effect on public order? In the ablest speech in Parliament against the bill, Mancini said that he could not understand what was meant by creating a sovereign; a sovereign could only be sovereign over territory, and therefore this bill was confessing that to rule a land was necessary to the pope's spiritual freedom, and committing the government's successors, sooner or later, to restore to the pope a State. A State may concede to one of its subjects as elaborate a ritual splendour as it likes, but it cannot concede sovereignty. If this mighty subject is given a private army—'a new corps of Janissaries'—what would happen in the future when the time came for an exchange of fire between papal guards and Italian soldiers? The bill provided that the pope should have protection from abuse similar to that of the king. But was it right that people should be prevented from saying that they thought infallibility nonsense, or that the Syllabus was a great mistake? Crispi said that the bill gave the pope inviolability, which meant that licence was being given to one member of the State to plot against the State without fear of penalty. On the moderate side the best speakers, such as Lanza and Visconti-Venosta, were direct. They held the pope to be an institution that existed and could not be destroyed. The international powers, with so many Catholic citizens, would never consent to the pope being treated as though he had no more rights than any other citizen of Italy. His spiritual authority had to be recognized if Italy were to be stable.

The bill was carried by 185 to 106 in a house of 508—that is, there were as many as 217 abstentions. Garibaldi thought the act wicked; yet it was a measure of the first importance to the well-being of Italy and incidentally of the pope over the next fifty-eight years.

On 15 May 1871 Pope Pius IX issued an encyclical, drafted by Bilio and three other cardinals, *Ubi nos arcano*.[8] It repudiated the Law of Guarantees and called upon the powers to restore him to his just rights and the Papal State. He put the papal treasury into acute difficulty by refusing the annuity from the Italians. The Law of Guarantees was a law which one side observed despite repudiation by the person whom it principally touched. The Pope felt the need to repudiate the Law of Guarantees because not to repudiate it would look like, and perhaps be, recognition of an illegal regime; namely, Italian rule in Rome (or in Bologna). And there was an argument which owed more to common sense than principle: this law depended upon a parliamentary majority; majorities in any Parliament slip and slide. What would happen if the ministers who made the law went out of power? Was the spiritual authority of the pope to be made dependent upon the changes and chances of party politics? The debates on the bill showed how insecure was the majority on which it depended.

Two legal judgments were needed to settle points about the pope's rights. The first concerned Martinucci, one of the two architects who employed 500 workers to construct the rooms inside the Vatican for the Conclave of 1878. He claimed that he was never properly paid for the work, and sued the Secretary of State. Vatican lawyers contended that as the matter was internal the Italian court had no jurisdiction. It was decided that every inhabitant of the Vatican except the pope was liable to the Italian courts.

The second was brought by a trader in maiolica, a white earthenware coloured with metallic glazes. After 1870 valuable pieces of maiolica were brought from Castel Gandolfo and some were sold. Several years later the trader accused the Vatican of robbing national property. The point at issue was whether these pieces were *national* property. It came to a debate in Parliament which settled nothing (15 December 1879). However, the Pope bought them back so that they stayed in the Vatican Museum.

The Pope had justifiable ground for saying that the Law of Guarantees was not well observed by those who made it. The Italian

---

[8] *ASS* 6 (1870–1), 257–63.

government found it impossible to control insults to him on the streets and in the press. On the 1874 anniversary of the coronation of Pius IX St Peter's was crowded for the singing of Te Deum. Afterwards in the square the people cheered, kneeling and shouting 'Long live the Pope!' or 'Long live the Pope-King!' Troops with bayonets moved in to disperse the crowd. Three days later another crowd, only some 300, but angry, advanced on the Vatican to attack it, with cries of 'Death to the Pope!' 'Death to the Jesuits!' There were other times when, if the Law of Guarantees was to be kept, the piazza of St Peter's needed packing with the army. The Pope made extreme attacks on the parliamentarians, but in Parliament the left used language such as no pope had heard: 'Mastai-Ferretti, Italian citizen, profession—vice-God' (laughter from the left). 'The papacy has been judged, gentlemen. It is the negation of the life of the people. The world has rejected it. Italy has suppressed it. Pius IX has paid for his pontificate as Kings Charles I and Louis XVI paid for their monarchy' (cries of 'Bravissimo' from the left).[9] Such language could be heard outside Parliament. A banquet was held in Rome to honour Garibaldi. With the mayor at his side, he made a long speech: 'The papacy has served its time, its priests will disappear like the priests of Jupiter.'[10]

Mazzini died at Pisa and the cities of Italy wanted to demonstrate by remembering him in memorial services. Rome held its service on 17 March 1872. Democratic clubs marched to the Capitol with flags and four white horses drew a car carrying a bust of Mazzini and placards of the names of conspirators whom the papal government had executed; at the Capitol the bust was placed among the designs of Michelangelo. Probably it was contrary to the Law of Guarantees; the government apparently thought so because it refrained from any official part in the celebration. But no government could have prevented it, and none would have wished to.

The government extended to Rome the Piedmontese laws on the dissolution of religious houses and the expulsion of the Jesuits (1873). They had already confiscated eight monasteries needed for buildings to house the administration necessary for Rome to work as the capital.[11]

---

[9] Atti, 3034, in *CC* 6 (1875), 616: the words of Petruccelli Della Gattina, the chief scourge of the pope in the Chamber. But he was a fantastic, whose speeches were not taken too seriously by his colleagues.   [10] *CC* (1875), 5: 613.

[11] e.g. the Ministry of War took over the Twelve Apostles (Conventual Franciscan); the police, San Silvestro in Capite; Santa Croce in Gerusalemme, which was Cistercian, became a barracks; the Carmelite nunnery at Regina Coeli became the city prison. Cf. *CC* (1873), 12: 607.

At that moment there were more than 4,000 monks in the city and a similar number of nuns, but their religious houses together with their gardens owned one-fifth of the residential land of the city of Rome. To this day a high proportion of Italian public buildings are former monasteries.[12]

Jesuit headquarters at the Gesù was taken over and the general, Beckx, moved it to Fiesole by Florence, where Florentines protested vainly against its presence. Such a move sounds easy enough, but there were personal reasons why it was not so. Saverio Patrizi was the son of a marquis whom Napoleon had locked up. He was among the first to become Jesuit, aged 17, after the order was restored when Napoleon fell. At the Roman College he became an eminent Hebraist and had pursued his studies for more than forty years before he was expelled at the age of 77. It helped him not at all that he was a cousin of King Victor Emmanuel and that he did not mind when Rome passed from the rule of the pope.

The Jesuits' library at the Roman College was supplemented by the libraries of various appropriated monasteries and turned into the Italian national library, for many years called the Victor Emmanuel Library but now in a modern building and known as the National Library. It was surprising to discover that the libraries of the monasteries were not in good order. This was the result of a medieval rule still in force that no one could take a book out without being excommunicated. Therefore in more recent times professors put new books not in the library but in their cells where they and their pupils could have access; and so the library itself was neglected and its catalogue not kept up to date. It was discovered that the monks had often sold piles of books by weight; a heap of books from a monastery library was discovered in the warehouse of a butcher at Florence.

A sad fate overtook a few Poor Clare nuns in the province of Naples, at the convent of Polla. Under the dissolution of monasteries at the unification of Italy, their house was suppressed. But as there were seven of them, they were allowed to remain in the house. They did not die off soon: the abbess went on into her 90s. Therefore the

---

[12] The appropriation of the monasteries needed a lawsuit. The government took over two nunneries in Rome, the Camaldolese and the Augustinian. They did not take the churches but closed them. The pope's cardinal-vicar, Monaco, sued the State on the ground that the churches that had not been taken over should still be open to worshippers. The courts held that the only persons with the right to sue were the nunneries and that by the law of 1873 these had ceased to exist. Not all lawyers thought this good law.

local municipality, led by an ardent disciple of Garibaldi and one of his former officers, grew impatient. The municipality started noisy building works next door (in the state-annexed part of the old convent). The nuns maintained their enclosed way of prayer despite the noise. In the years of the 'imprisonment' of the pope the local anticlericals became militant. The State offered the nuns a transfer; they refused to go. They sold what was not on the inventory and passed their more precious possessions to other nunneries. The State insisted, and occupied the building. Of the seven nuns, one went to a surviving house of Benedictine nuns, the others went home, and the local bishop asked Rome for help with these sick old people, and a dispensation to allow them to be cared for at home.[13] Apart from the tears of evicting old women from their home, the sadness lay in the fact that most local people did not mind the end of a community which for generations had educated their girls.

In 1873 the government deconsecrated the Coliseum, which had a chapel, and was sacred as the site of early martyrdoms. They stripped the stones of interesting flowers and weeds.

The religious oath in the lawcourts was abolished (1874) as was religious teaching in elementary schools (there could be voluntary classes); and the law on conscription to military service was applied to the clergy.

The government applied the law on civil marriage to Rome in 1874. The Pope had said that civil marriage without the Church was concubinage. Of denunciations from the Pope this was morally the most doubtful. As early as 1852 he had said that civil marriage without the Church is nothing but adultery, and in so pronouncing he was in line with historic canons. But in that generation it made many difficulties for the bishops, who kept asking Rome for guidance. If the young man married civilly and then tired of his wife he could run away without any suggestion that he offended morals or Church law. Bishops in Protestant or mixed countries could not cope with a ruling that all Protestant marriages were adulteries. There was great difficulty in Hungary which was semi-officially a Catholic country but where a third of the inhabitants were Protestants.

In 1866 with the Italian law of compulsory civil marriage upon them, the Sacred Penitentiary issued an important ruling. It distinguished what happened the other side of the Alps, which was to be

---

[13] V. Bracco, 'L'espulsione delle ultime Clarisse dal monastero di Polla', in *Archivio storico per le province napoletane*, 3rd ser. 95 (1978), 343 ff.

deplored, from what happened this side of the Alps, which was contamination. The ruling stated that there was no marriage valid except that celebrated by the Church, in those countries where the decree of the Council of Trent has been published. In such countries, which included Italy, civil marriage could not bind a couple; and civil law could not separate a couple who had been married in church. The state of marriage by registrar was nothing but concubinage. Nevertheless, to avoid trouble—so as to ensure that the State recognized the children as legitimate, and to avoid the danger of bigamy or polygamy—it was expedient that after marriage in church the faithful obey the law. Therefore parish priests should not marry people whose marriages the State would refuse to recognize. The civil ceremony should not precede the marriage in church. If there were compelling reasons why the civil ceremony should precede the marriage, the couple were to separate after the civil ceremony until the marriage in church. Parish priests then took trouble to persuade people married in church to go through the civil ceremony afterwards. But many of them did not bother.

Later the Chamber brought in a bill to ensure that civil marriage preceded marriage in church and to fine priests who married anyone not previously married by the State. This would face priests with the dilemma either to refuse to marry persons who lived together without civil marriage or to incur a heavy fine and imprisonment. But the Senate threw out the bill, though only by three votes.

The Law of Guarantees created, from the point of view of one side only, very nearly what was done to everybody's satisfaction fifty-eight years later in the making of the Vatican State. For there is little practical difference between a no-go area, which the Law of Guarantees created, and a separate little island State, which is what was created in 1929. Turmoil, trouble, and waste of time and emotion could have been saved if both sides had agreed on the solution in 1871. The law was good in this sense, that it proved to the papacy, in the end, that the temporal power in its old form was not necessary to the spiritual independence of the pope.

But no one can compromise with piracy until it is about fifty years old and has won the right which is brought by time and general acceptance. And on the other side, the Italian government saw all the difference in the world between the no-go area that they created, and a separate State. If their supporters could claim that they had given away a piece of Rome, the capital of Italy, to a foreign ruler (the pope), they would have fallen overnight. The new Italy was not ready to sacrifice an inch of its territory to anyone; especially not from its newly acquired capital. There might be no difference in reality between a separate State and the police keeping out of a particular area, but there was a great difference in political feeling, political expediency, and political possibility.

For the next few decades therefore, the papacy was in a curious situation in Italy. It was hostile to the Italian government, and kept protesting against it. In 1876 the Home Secretary of the new left government, Mancini, introduced the bill of Clerical Abuses, which imposed heavy penalties for political pressure from the pulpit or in the confessional. It was the worst kind of law that radical governments sometimes pass against free speech. If it had succeeded it would have caused an endless series of lawsuits against priests; informers sitting under pulpits; and all the machinery for controlling sermons that the Gestapo was to make systematic. But the bill was passed in the Lower House and only just lost in the Senate (105 to 92).

For this behaviour of the radical government Pius IX shared responsibility. His language was extreme, it affected discontents within the State, and it encouraged his bishops and parish priests to utterances of a like tone. This was not good for the State of Italy. Many Italians were Catholics who needed to be reconciled to their regime, which was having a difficult enough time anyway, trying to make a unified country out of so many different States. The divisions of Italy were deepened because government and Pope could never agree. The Parliament of Italy never won the affections of the Italian people, and this was partly because the Pope wanted Catholics to have nothing to do with electing anyone to that Parliament and so refuse it recognition. This division stored up a legacy for the future of Italy.

From the point of view of the authority of the Church, as an international institution, there was everything to be said for the situation. If Italy took Rome, everyone else would suspect that Italy could control the papacy. The Law of Guarantees was a successful effort to persuade the international world that this would not be so. But the world was more convinced by seeing that the Pope and the Italian government were at loggerheads. To be protesting against the Italian government was a maintenance of spiritual independence, as effective in its way as the possession of a separate tract of territory; perhaps more effective. Pius IX called them wolves, liars, satellites of satan in human flesh, and monsters of hell, a list that is not exhaustive. No one could suppose that the Pope had turned into a private chaplain to the king of Italy.

The Law was also effective in that it cocooned the Pope. Bismarck complained to the Italian government that they had surrounded the Pope with so much cotton wool that no one could bring pressure to bear upon him.

The Law of Guarantees was passed by a moderate Italian government in which the opinions of wise men like Visconti-Venosta or Minghetti were weighty. But in March 1876 the ministry of Minghetti fell to the left and no one knew how the Law of Guarantees would survive under a radical government.

The radical leaders wavered in their attitude to the law. Consider the most famous, effective, and sometimes wild of those leaders, Francesco Crispi. As a young Sicilian lawyer he was fired by Mazzini and had later to flee to France where he prepared Garibaldi's expedition of the Thousand. In the new Italy, though a republican, he helped the left to rally to the monarchy of Savoy as the only way to a united nation. He did not become Prime Minister till 1887. Meanwhile his opinions, though always radical in both Church and State, swung this way and that, his personality so strong that he was never without bitter enemies and reverent disciples.

As an anti-Church person with links to Freemasonry, he had resisted the Law of Guarantees in its making. He was afraid of reaction and clericalism and fancied that the clergy would make conspiracies, though they did not. He did not want 'a free Church in a free State', but believed that Italy needed the old controls of *exequatur*, etc. to be able to restrain the Church. He was not an atheist and refused to patronize atheists, believing religion necessary, but was against popes and priests. 'All our great men', he once told Parliament, 'have been deists. Dante, Michelangelo, Galileo believed in God. Mazzini, Garibaldi believed in God.'[14]

So when he gained responsibility his attitude to the Law of Guarantees wavered. His heart thought it wrong, his head saw that it was necessary to the well-being of the State. Republicans asked him to propose its repeal. He refused, saying that it was an honour to the Italian government that it guards the freedom of the head of the

[14] A. C. Jemolo, *Chiesa e stato in Italia negli ultimi cento anni* (Turin, 1963), 274; F. Crispi, *Discorsi parlamentari*, ed. T. Palamenghi-Crispi, (Rome, 1915), iii. 860, 28 Nov. 1895.

Catholic Church so that other powers cannot say that he is not free. But at other times he would say that the law was good only if the pope was an apostle, but if he was the enemy of Italian unity it was bad law that disarmed the State and made it impossible for it to repress its enemies, 'the clerical sect'. He thought that the most absurd institutions of the Middle Ages were ecclesiastical States: Italy had to have Rome, without it unity could never be secure. With the guarantees the Pope had been given more power than any pope before him. Crispi spoke in the presence of the King and Queen at the erection on the Janiculum hill of a monument to the memory of Garibaldi. He said that there were enemies of Italy who protested that this monument was an offence to the pope. But 'if Christianity could conquer the world by the words of Paul and Chrysostom, without any weapons, we cannot understand why the Vatican still wants a State to fulfil its spiritual work.'[15]

A part of the open breach was a refusal by the Pope to allow Catholics to vote in national elections, or to accept office as members of Parliament. Refusal to vote went back to Margotti and the days when Cavour rigged elections in Piedmont, and gave Margotti ground for saying that democracy is a fraud and it is better to keep away from it. After 1860 the duty to vote or not to vote became a national question. At first the Curia was not sure of its policy; none of its members knew whether, if the Pope told Italians not to vote for candidates, anyone would obey his order. A local Catholic committee which thought that it had a good chance of electing its candidate might appeal to Rome and ask for leave to act. In 1867–8 bishops in the north warmly encouraged their Catholics to vote. But because a member of Parliament must take an oath of allegiance to the Italian State, which the Curia held that no Catholic could recognize, the logic was to prevent people voting if they would obey. This was called the *non expedit*, 'it is not expedient' to vote. The Pope continued to say publicly that it was wrong to use the vote.

In 1876 the Italian political left, headed by such men as Mancini and Nicotera who were known for their hostility to the Church, won power. Was the *non expedit* contributing to the weakness of the liberal party and thereby causing worse trouble for the Church? The word 'socialism' was coming into conversations about politics. Rome had to ask itself again what to do; it was confronted with evidence

[15] Crispi, *Ultimi scritti e discorsi*, 180 ff., 220 ff.; the Janiculum monument was as late as 1897.

that its faithful were going back to the polling booths despite their instructions. The Pope went on being very negative in his speeches. In 1877 the Penitentiary in the Curia, which was the dicastery responsible, changed the words from *non expedit* to *non licet*, that is from 'it is not expedient' to 'it is not permissible'. The change made no difference to what happened. The Curia grew a little more flexible in how it interpreted the *non expedit* because it could sensibly do nothing else.[16]

The situation of the 'monarchs' in Rome produced two courts. The Quirinal had a king who was bad at public functions and a morganatic queen who was worse. The Vatican had a pope-king who was superb with crowds. The Quirinal was cold and formal, the Vatican warm and emotional. The Quirinal refrained from rude remarks about the Vatican, the Vatican made rude remarks about the Quirinal. Most of the old aristocratic families, once the court of the pope-king, stuck with their old allegiance and were known as 'black Rome'—and regarded 'white Rome', the fewer aristocrats who accepted the new king, as not to be invited to parties. Pius IX could say words to them that other sovereigns of that age now blushed to say: 'Jesus Christ loves aristocrats . . . He chose to be born noble. He made known his family tree in the gospel . . . Noble rank is a gift of God . . . Thrones sustained by the ignoble, and by those who are informed by unbelief and hatred towards God and the Church, are ill-founded and worse maintained.'[17]

The division of Italian society was evident not only on the streets of Rome. In the north the rival processions, even in small villages, could turn into demonstrations and lead to blows, and the local authorities were more likely to protect the anticlerical procession than the Catholic procession for a saint's day, Corpus Christi, or the Assumption. At Milan the Church supposed that the relics of the martyrs Gervasius and Protasius, patrons of the city, discovered so dramatically by St Ambrose in the fourth century, were stolen by a German emperor during the Middle Ages. In 1864 the relics were rediscovered, still undisturbed under the high altar of the church of St Ambrose. Ten years later they decided on a solemn procession to put the relics finally to rest. They applied to the prefect who sanctioned a public procession on 11 May and 15 May. The liberals of the

[16] For the *non expedit*: M. F. Mellano, *Cattolici e voto politico in Italia* (Casale, 1982); Martina, *Pio IX (1867–78)*, 273 ff.
[17] *CC* (1873), 9: 232–3.

city said that this was an intrusion into the public domain, an occupation of the streets by Catholics in such a way as to offend consciences. On 11 May they therefore organized a procession in honour of Garibaldi which would start at the cathedral and meet the Catholic procession head-on. They summoned helpers from the countryside and from Genoa and obtained from Genoa the flag with which Garibaldi landed in Sicily. The prefect, who could do nothing else, banned the procession of the relics on the very eve; and the would-be marchers returned home by night under an armed guard.[18]

Partly on the ground of public order the prefects stopped pilgrimages. While in anticlerical France hundreds of thousands went as pilgrims to Lourdes, in Italy the police—but only at first—ringed the Italian sanctuaries: at Assisi there was an infantry battalion, at Loreto a force of *carabinieri*, at other shrines there were infantry and *carabinieri*.

THE NEW BISHOPS

There was a battle over the bishoprics. The Law of Guarantees gave the pope much more say in the choice of bishops but the State retained the *exequatur* as necessary before they could be recognized, occupy their palaces and receive their stipends. Various bishops never got the *exequatur*, though they were harmless men. Cardinal Parocchi was made archbishop of Bologna after his predecessor Guidi had never been able to occupy the see; he waited five years for the *exequatur* and then, like Guidi, resigned. During the vacancies the government took the income but used it for Church purposes, perhaps to restore churches, help poor clergy, or pay for the Ministry of Church Affairs.

Nevertheless the Pope started to appoint bishops to Italian sees after the years of so many vacancies. Though he denounced the Law of Guarantees, it made him able to appoint. Between October 1871 and the following May he chose 102 new Italian bishops; that filled nearly half the dioceses in Italy. They were well-chosen from the point of view of honour, piety, and pastoral experience. Many of them were young and energetic. They were not often very well educated, and without exception they were against Catholic liberalism.

[18] *CC* (1874), 2: 617 ff.

The Law had enabled him to make the bench of bishops more mono-
chrome in its opinions about Church and State.

To obtain their stipends from the endowments these bishops
needed the *exequatur* from the State. But to ask for the *exequatur* was,
in effect, to recognize the State. Because of the Law the State could
not stop the pope appointing bishops to do the work but it could stop
him paying for them except with his own money, prevent them living in their palaces, and refuse to recognize their choices when they
picked a parish priest. It looked odd to be so stiff about not asking for
the *exequatur* when this was cheerfully done in several other Catholic
countries. But in the eyes of the Pope and Antonelli those other governments were legal.

Since their position was weak new bishops asked for permission to
apply to the government. After about four years ways were found of
getting round the difficulty. Friends of a bishop took it upon themselves to send a copy of the bull of appointment and so in effect to
ask on his behalf for the *exequatur*. With reluctance Rome winked at
this manner of proceeding. The Pope stopped it, but then Antonelli
died and six weeks later he allowed bishops to ask for the *exequatur*.
Once the compromise was agreed, the State behaved honourably in
the way it worked the system, and it continued under all the liberal
governments, under Mussolini, and for decades after the Second
World War.[19]

It is instructive to look at three examples of bishops of the time:
first, a bishop of the old Papal States, Carlo Gigli, who might be
called typical, except that he was bishop of Tivoli for forty years
(1840–80), which was the longest reign of any of the mid-Italian
bishops during the nineteenth century. In most respects he was a
bishop after the style of his predecessors of the eighteenth century.
He was of upper-class stock, a good man, who built up his seminary
and schools and revived the Monte di Pietà, the lending bank for the
poor. What was different from the past was not his pastoral method
or experience but the strength of his convictions on new questions.
In the unification of Italy in 1859–60 he ardently defended the temporal power of the pope, not only as an expedient for Church and
State but as an institution founded by God. When the Immaculate
Conception was defined, he warmly welcomed the encyclical and
inculcated the doctrine. When the Vatican Council was summoned,

---

[19] For the bishops and *exequatur*, Martina, *Pio IX (1867–78)*, 261 ff.

he was very pleased, and described it in a Lent letter as 'the end of the shameless atheism which people introduce into all the relations of society'. This description had no truth whatever if we compare it with what happened, but it shows the mental state of a good and honourable Italian bishop during those years.[20]

Bishop Pietro Rota of Mantua preached fiercely against the government. His position was hard because he succeeded Bishop Corti, who ever since the unfrocking and hanging of Professor Tazzoli had been rebellious to Rome, for he sang a Te Deum for the union of Italy and hoped that the Pope would of his own accord resign the temporal power; and refused to answer demands for retractions. Finally he did so, making it clear that this was an act of pure obedience. For three years they could not fill the see. When Bishop Rota arrived his mission was to rule with a heavy hand and clear up the 'laxities' left by Corti and the interregnum. Hence the strength of his language, as a result of which he was put in gaol for six days and fined. Antonelli passed to him that Pius IX had said that it was no wonder they sought excuses to torment bishops and suppress their freedom to preach; and that he was sure that no fear even of death would stop holy pastors from doing the work to which they were called.[21] But Rota's work was impossible, because the government would never give him an *exequatur*. He resigned the see after eight years, with a sense of frustration.

We can see the consequences of the attitude of the prisoner of the Vatican, by way of example, in one northern Italian diocese: that of Verona.[22] Luigi di Canossa, of the old aristocratic family of Verona, was bishop from 1862 to 1900. He first had to cope with the transfer from Austrian rule to Italian rule and early gained a siege mentality. The Piedmontese laws on the Church were extended to his territory. He accepted the Pope's refusal to recognize the Italian Parliamentary system and maintained the ban on anyone voting in national elections. His brother the Marquis refused to sit in Parliament. The bishop believed that liberalism was incompatible with Christian doctrine, and hated the 'immoralities' of the freedom of the press. He saw liberalism as the child of rationalism which in turn was the child of Protestantism. He elevated the papacy and demanded a reverence

[20] Cf. *DHGE* s.v. Gigli, fasc. 119, col. 1287.   [21] Martina, *Pio IX (1867–78)*, 460–1.
[22] There is an excellent study of this diocese and its bishop by Rino Cona, in *La visita pastorale di Luigi di Canossa nella diocesi di Verona (1878–1886)*, Thesaurus ecclesiarum Italiae recentioris aevi, 3 (Rome, 1983), 18.

for the office of pope higher, probably, than any previous bishop of Verona had demanded. One of his first acts was to set up boxes for the collection of Peter's pence to aid the pope. He turned the teachers of the seminary out when he disapproved of their Rosminian attitudes, and put in teachers who would be strict Thomists and would teach divinity analytically and not historically. He founded an extremist journal, called after its first few years *Il Verona fedele*; in its first appearance it compared the crucifixion of the Saviour with the crucifixion of Pius IX. With all this intransigence he organized good social work in the diocese, managed in the end to be on good terms with the local Italian authorities, and finally earned the reputation of a moderate, kindly, and wise man. All his endeavour went into religion and the social efforts that came out of it. He compelled his clergy to wear clerical dress and to come to annual retreats, and found them generally of a high standard. He watched with despondency the decline of old habits as the urban rather than rural parish became dominant; where pubs played the role of antichurches, and where shops opened on Sundays—but he need not have been so depressed for only 8.46 per cent failed to make their confessions (naturally with much variation according to the place). In politics he was sure that God would provide, and therefore that God would restore the papacy to its rights.

The number of clergy fell more because of the dissolution of the monasteries than because fewer young men applied to be ordinands. (In Camerino diocese there was one priest to 174 people in 1854, one priest to 261 people twenty-seven years later.) Many parishes had no parish priest in charge, because of the difficulties with the State, and were served by casual priests; their pay was very poor, and they were often inadequate. But for social reasons ordinands still applied, and usually from uneducated families (the illiteracy rate of the people of some areas was still 80 per cent or more in the middle 1860s). The people preferred the seminaries as places of education to the state schools, therefore many students had no intention of being ordained. Government eyed the seminaries as 'nests' which fostered disloyalty to the State. In 1866 for a few months it shut all the seminaries in the Marches of Central Italy. During the 1860s both the archbishops of the Marches were in gaol as intransigents. The law that refused to exempt ordinands from conscription to the army hurt the seminaries. Because the State taxed them heavily they had to charge fees and hinder the very poor from coming, though bishops created funds for grants to poor ordinands. The education in seminaries was authoritarian, rigid in its rules, with much silence. Churchmen outside the seminaries criticized them for narrowness. But they slowly improved as did the education in state schools. The boys were not taught Greek, nor science, and very little history, but hours of Latin. They were made to commit a lot to memory. Their teachers were selected so far as possible—for example, the teacher in the seminary at Urbino showed how Dante in the *Divine Comedy* defended the temporal power of the Pope. Their knowledge of Scripture was still based upon the books of the eighteenth century.[23]

THE SPEECHES OF PIUS IX

During the last seven years of Pope Pius IX he did nothing to try to get back a papal State—except protest. He once told the French ambassador that it was not all the old Papal State that he minded about, if he were offered it he would refuse it, it was Rome itself that mattered to him. He looked to God, and left it to him, and expected that some time a miracle would occur; and in this state of mind made marvellous speeches to pilgrims that gathered in St Peter's, breathtaking oratory of compelling simplicity. He did not speak wholly unprepared but used headings and then spoke as he was moved; and he was an old man and had always been easily moved.

In the short fight of 20 September 1870 Father Pasquale di Franciscis went along the wall of Rome by the Porta Pia ministering to the dying and wounded of both sides, and afterwards went on with this work in the hospitals. The Pope asked how the wounded were and Father Pasquale led a group of convalescents to see him and took down in shorthand the address which he gave them. This led him to be employed in making typed copies of the Pope's speeches. He suggested that he could print some of them. The Pope hesitated but then agreed and corrected the proofs. When these speeches were printed they looked to the unsympathetic eye like the most disturbing collection of addresses that ever came out of the mouth of a pope. They shocked Protestants and some Italians. Gladstone, free to speak as an

---

[23] G. Brocanelli, 'Seminari e clero nelle Marche nella seconda metà dell'Ottocento', in *RSCI* 31 (1977), 68 ff., 391 ff. As late as 1845 the students in the seminary at Perugia were forbidden to read Dante and hid copies under their mattresses: E. Soderini, *Il pontificato di Leone XIII* (3 vols.; Milan, 1932–3); Eng. trans. (1934–5), i. 71.

ex-Prime Minister, even reviewed the first two volumes in a raging article in the *Quarterly Review* for January 1875. But no one can read them now without a rueful admiration, rueful because of the lack of wisdom, the overstatements, and the harsh words; admiring because of the otherworldly courage of an old pope in his last declining years.[24]

Earlier, as railways made pilgrimages more possible, the audiences grew larger. Pius IX was the first pope to practise what thereafter became characteristic of a pope's relation to his people. He felt, and they felt, that they had a direct and personal meeting, even with a crowd. This warm quality in Pius IX, and the new ability to meet him provided by modern transport, made a curious difference to the Catholic Church's attitude to him. Formerly it revered the institution; the successor of St Peter; the Vicar of Christ; the office; while the person was remote and little known. Now it was more personal; the office was lent a magic by flesh, and speech, and smile, and greeting, and blessing. It was long before the cardinals, in electing a new pope, needed to ask themselves whether their candidate had charisma with the people. But that was what Pius IX already possessed.

The tactic of waiting for miracles did not please those who wanted a policy and did not think that perpetual strife with the government constituted one. Archbishop Manning of Westminster was made a cardinal, very late, in 1875. (Other cardinals had objected to his elevation because he was a widower, a convert, and an extremist, and because he appeared too frequently as a contributor to the secular press.) He visited Rome next year and did not like what he found; old cardinals still in charge, and now hopelessly incompetent. There was the elegant and princely Cardinal Chigi, who all his life backed whatever Cardinal Antonelli wanted and was a humble and tenacious servant of lost causes. Waiting for miracles seemed to Manning to be another name for stagnation: 'No preparation, no provision, no readiness for alternatives.' He thought that some of them did nothing, not because they were looking for a miracle to happen, but because they liked doing nothing.

Are we to shut ourselves in like Noe [Noah in his ark] and wait? or are we to act upon the world, as all the Pontiffs from St Leo the Great? If the world

---

[24] Pasquale di Franciscis, *Discorsi del Summo Pontifice . . . dal principio della sua prigionia fino al presente* (4 vols.; Rome, 1872–8); Gladstone's article was also printed separately; for de Franciscis' career see Martina, *Pio IX (1867–78)*, 292 n. He did the same work for the speeches of Pope Leo XIII.

has fallen off and become corrupt, how is it to be recovered? By leaving it in its corruption till it returns by itself to soundness? . . . Ecclesiastical Quietism . . .

The only hope seemed to be a new pope. Gregorovius met Manning at dinner and summed him up briefly—'a little grey man, looking as if he were tangled in cobwebs'.[25]

CONCILIATION WITH ITALY?

Curci, one of the most famous of Jesuits, made his name by assailing Gioberti's book against the Jesuits; and then, exercising his talents as an organizer, was one of the founders of the Jesuit journal *Civiltà Cattolica*. He was strong for the Pope, dedicated to him, and for a time longed for the French monarchy to be restored so that its army could march into Italy and put Pius IX back upon his throne. Then realism dawned. He ceased to believe that restoration of the Papal State was possible. If this was true, then it became the duty of every Catholic to do what was possible for the new Italy and its moral well-being as well as its economic prosperity. He held that for Catholics not to vote in national elections was blind, for every Catholic ought to join in public life, where that was possible, to help prevent the de-Christianization of Italy. He had been shocked by the murders of archbishop and clergy in the Commune of Paris, and realized that in this so-advanced century serene-looking societies lived with explosive forces under their feet.

In 1874, in an obscure preface to exegetical commentaries on the four gospels, he stated his view. The Jesuit general Beckx demanded that he retract. Curci refused, and three years later was dismissed from being a Jesuit. Then he published at Florence a still more radical book entitled *The Modern Disagreement between the Church and Italy* (*Il moderno dissidio fra la Chiesa e l'Italia*), a book that confirmed the breach between himself and the prevailing mood of papal Rome; he claimed that the great error of Margotti was telling people not to vote when by voting they could help Italy to strength, prosperity, and morality. The book showed a love of his country and the young people growing up there; what could be done for them, he wondered, by a

[25] E. S. Purcell, *The Life of Cardinal Manning* (2 vols.; London, 1892), ii. 375–6; cf. Manning's words to Count Santucci as reported by Soderini, *Il pontificato de Leone XIII*, Eng. trans. ii. 10; Gregorovius, *Roman Journal*, 354.

Church which did not shrink from influence or retreat into its prison of recrimination. He retired to a quiet study away from the world, knowing that his old colleagues and friends were hostile to him, and lived in poverty.

After the accession of the new pope, by whom he was treated more gently, he published a plan of reform, *La nuova Italia e i vecchi zelanti* (*The New Italy and the Old Zealots*) (Florence, 1881), which contained a heavy attack on the Curia as marred by the characteristics of a court, with the faults of a bureaucracy and susceptible to flattery; and a defence of the phrase 'liberal Catholic' as meaning no more than a Catholic trying to do the best for society. Concerning talk of the need for the Pope's independence he said that the Pope was just as dependent on foreign powers before 1870. Curci now accepted that the old Papal State was impossible because it would be an absolute government in a world where that was an anachronism, where the people could rightly take part in influencing governments, and where liberty of conscience was considered right for a State.

This book was put on the Index and Curci was suspended from the right to officiate as a priest. That made him miserable as well as poor, but neither altered his views nor lessened his integrity. It also made him more outspoken—the *scandal* of a Vatican that rules, the essentially Christian nature of liberalism, the massacre of souls wrought by the Syllabus. Ten days before his death in 1891 he was readmitted to the Society of Jesus.

In matters of public opinion it is hard for history to test the relative importance of different events. But in raising the affections of the Catholic Church for the pope, and in further centralizing the Church upon the pope and the Curia, it looks as though the loss of the temporal power by Italian piracy was of more advantage than anything the bishops did at the Vatican Council. For centuries idealists saw that a pope might be benefited in his spiritual office if he were no longer the ruler of a State. The events of the Italian Revolution of 1848 brought the contradiction between spiritual leader and national leader into a unique tension. And once the Italians, or at least the Piedmontese and many of the northern middle classes, were determined to move towards an Italian nation, this tension could do nothing but increase until the moment when the pope surrendered, or was deprived of, his State.

But even before the Italian army took Rome, the Pope was of such a character—it was his single strength as a Pope—that the spiritual office was what mattered to him and his role in international politics meant little. Before his kingdom collapsed, he was already, politically, a helpless old man. The fall of Rome made no difference to his behaviour.

It happened that at the precise moment when Rome must be lost as a papal capital, its ruler was a person who regarded his kingdom as not of this world, however strenuously he might defend his right to Rome as a sacred and historic trust and as necessary to his independence as a spiritual authority. A big part of the rise in the Pope's authority as a churchman was connected with the collapse of his authority as a politician. And this in itself was something to do with the circumstance that the person of the then pope fitted this calamity (if it was a calamity): a confessor, undaunted, Athanasian, one who cared only for the things of the spirit in the face of unscrupulous and worldly men—this was the image that he projected upon the world-wide Church.

But meanwhile, in northern countries, the Syllabus, the Vatican Council, the fall of Rome to the Italians, and the 'imprisonment' of Pius IX, had grave consequences in Church and State. Pius IX died before they affected France so clearly, but during his time there were hard events in Austria, Germany, and Britain.

AUSTRIA

In July 1870 the Austrian government denounced the Concordat which Cardinal Rauscher had made so favourable to Rome and the Church. The Austrian government justified this one-sided breach of a treaty by the plea that the papacy after 19 July 1870 was not the same institution as that with which they negotiated the Concordat.

The liberal members of the Austrian government wanted in any case to do this. After their defeat by Prussia in 1866 they introduced a liberal constitution (valid in Austria to this day) which by its nature must move to a parity of religious denominations in the State and away from a privileged position for the Catholic Church. The Pope complained formally that the non-Catholics in Austria were given more rights than the Catholics. The Austrian Chancellor was for the first time a Protestant, von Beust, who believed that the Concordat had lost Austria respect among the European nations and that, since the Syllabus of Errors it linked Austria with what was backward in

Europe. Some of his radical supporters thought absurdly (or pre-tended to think), that the Concordat was the cause of the defeat by Prussia which ended Austria's primacy of honour in Germany. But the Austrian government was like that of Louis Napoleon in not wishing to offend its Catholic population, and wanted negotiation with Rome. That was not easy because Cardinal Antonelli gave them to understand that Rome believed any attack upon the Concordat to be an attack upon religion.

Cardinal Rauscher was much respected, and staunchly defended the Concordat which he had done most to bring into force. But the constitution and the Concordat could not agree; for example, the rights of citizens under the constitution were not compatible with the clause of the Concordat which insisted that all teachers in schools were to be Catholics. A new law left the authorities of a denomina-tion the right to ensure that the teachers of religion in a school were of their own denomination. In 1868 the State introduced civil mar-riage (by a law which the Pope denounced as 'abominabilis'),[26] not as compulsory but available to citizens who did not want a Church wedding. An apostate from Christian faith was no longer excluded from the law of inheritance. If someone taught what was against the Christian religion it was no longer an offence punishable by the State. But the law continued to ban all work on Sundays and saint's days during the hours of service, especially anywhere near churches where a service was in progress. The Churches were assured of religious education in the State schools.

All this did not happen quite peacefully. Bishop Schaffgotsche of Brünn told his priests to treat civil marriage as concubinage. Bishop Rudigier of Linz issued a pastoral letter against the changes as a breach in an agreed treaty, the Concordat. The police seized the 5,000 copies of the pastoral letter and the Linz court, which he refused to attend on the ground that they had no say in the matter, charged him with provocation against the constitution and sentenced him in his absence to 14 days in gaol. The Emperor Francis Joseph immediately released him but the moment caused a demonstration for the bishop in the streets of Linz and several other bishops issued pastoral letters of the same import. Bishop Rudigier won fame outside Austria.

Bishop Gasser of Brixen in the Tyrol, whom we met speaking at the Vatican Council in an effort to help the Minority by interpreta-

---

[26] *ASS* 4 (1868), 10 ff., all the laws of 1868 and not only the marriage law.

tion, was a tough ultramontane who could rely upon a dedicated flock at his back. He told his clergy to obey the law but to do all in their power to stop civil marriages. If the children of such marriages were christened the priests must leave the entry in the register headed 'legitimate' or 'illegitimate', unfilled, and add a note therein that the parents were married civilly. The State authorities had to ban the clergy from putting the word 'illegitimate' after the names of such babies. This trouble was about nothing, because Gasser, being of the Tyrol, never experienced civil marriages—the people did not use them.

But in another part of his diocese, outside the Tyrol, in the Vorarlberg where Swiss influence was stronger, Gasser ran into real trouble over a divorce case. A husband had run away to America and his wife at first asked for legal separation; but when the divorce law was passed she asked for divorce. The secular court demanded the papers about the case. The bishop refused to give them up. The court then sent a policeman who broke into the diocesan office and ransacked it, but found no papers connected with the case. Bishop Gasser eventually had to pay a punishing fine of 1,000 gulden but never gave up the papers.[27] In tremendous fights between Church and State where principles were at stake it was easy to forget that there remained a wife whose husband had deserted her.

The final denunciation of the Concordat, though it was excused by the Vatican Council, was not caused by it. Beust wanted to restore Austria to the old political power that Prussia had destroyed. To do this he needed alliances with liberal-minded States who were afraid of Prussia; his best hope lay with France and anti-papal Italy. He was given his opportunity by what happened at the Council. Leaders of the Minority were 'his' bishops—Rauscher of Vienna, Schwarzenberg of Prague, the Hungarian primate Simor of Gran, Archbishop Haynald of Kalocsa,[28] and Strossmayer for the South Slavs. The Austro-Hungarian bishops wanted to keep the Concordat but their

---

[27] J. Fontana, *Der Kulturkampf in Tirol (1861–1892)* (Bolzano, 1978), 131.

[28] Kalocsa was a see going back to almost 1000 AD. The occupant was always second in seniority among bishops to the primate who was of Gran. The diocese was long under Turkish occupation and the archbishop in exile but from the 18th cent. it flourished again and in 1870 was the best-endowed see in the Austro-Hungarian empire. Haynald was strong for the Minority at the Council, and even talked of resigning his see if the infallibility decree went through (so he said to Gregorovius), but accepted it, and under Leo XIII became a cardinal. Gregorovius, *Roman Journal*, 369, called him 'a handsome, gentle, eloquent man of sensuous warmth and attraction'.

power in the Minority at the Council contributed to its fall. The Emperor Francis Joseph wrote to his mother on 25 August 1870: 'I have a deep wish to find harmony again with the Church. But that is not possible with the present Pope.'[29]

It was an epoch in Austrian history. This was the successor of the Holy Roman empire. Though Napoleon I forced its ruler to abandon the title Holy Roman Emperor, it retained something of the magic of its tradition in the new world after the Battle of Waterloo. For centuries it stood as the symbol of Christian resistance to the Turks and the figurehead of Christendom. Now this symbol and figurehead disappeared, although the majority of the people were Catholics and many of them were devout. Austria–Hungary became just one of the modern States, no more symbolic of the Catholic inheritance than were France or Spain, which also had a majority of Catholics.

By the end of September 1870 the balance of power in Europe had changed. The pope was a prisoner of the Italians. France was in a new chaos; Spain was in an old chaos; Austria–Hungary was a state moving to neutrality in religion and pushed to the fringe of Germany. The two leading powers in Western and Central Europe were Britain and Prussia, both in mood and temperament Protestant even though Britain ruled many Catholic Irish and Prussia ruled many Catholic Poles. And to the east was the third great power, Russia, dedicated to Orthodoxy and even more hostile than the Protestant powers to the pope because as yet it had no liberalism in its composition. And with all liberal Europe, which was to be the papacy's best hope in the future, the Pope's reputation was as low as it could be because he was thought to have canonized the Syllabus of Errors as the permanent teaching of his Church.

It was a paradox that the old Josephist tradition, of State control of the Church, did not vanish from Austria but revived a little when the Concordat was dropped. All religions were equal before the law but the State still had a say in the religion of the majority. The State could veto appointments to sees or parishes; supervised the endowments and income of the Church; and retained the right to allow the foundation of a monastery. In 1874, in response to a protest by the Pope and Cardinal Rauscher, the State said that it had no desire to control the Church other than for its welfare; on the contrary, it wished to do all it could to foster the Church as the pillar of public morality. The Emperor himself was in part responsible for the moderation with which the new laws of Church and State were carried out in practice. Though there was argument in Parliament about making civil marriage compulsory, the proposal collapsed. Austria was very willing to offer the Pope a refuge if he came to the point of deciding that his place in an anti-papal Italy was untenable. Six times between 1859 and 1888 they offered the Pope asylum. They had in mind Salzburg or Trent. Sometimes, when they made the offer, they accompanied it with the hint that it would be a mistake for the Pope to leave Rome.

An old privilege of the Holy Roman emperor was to appoint to Rome a 'protector of the Austrian nation'. In the age of the Counter-Reformation this office of protector was weighty as an influence of the German emperor on the Curia. But long before the Holy Roman empire was abolished, its real function had been taken by modern types of ambassador and it became an honour and no more. After the Holy Roman empire disappeared the Austrian emperor continued to appoint someone; even Francis Joseph appointed one—the last. The office disappeared in the turmoil over the Austrian Concordat.[30]

THE OLD CATHOLICS

In South Germany, the Rhineland, Switzerland, and Austria the Old Catholic movement formed, led by German Catholic professors in the universities. Thanks to Acton and Döllinger the Vatican Council had a shocking press in Germany. The faithful were not disturbed but Catholic intellectuals were militant against the untruth and unwisdom of the Council's decisions. Anyone who believed that the Council was, not as the minutes show it, but as Acton and Döllinger represented it, could not possibly think it a valid Christian meeting. In the German-speaking lands there was no effort by the Curia to correct the portrait of intrigue and pressure. The German and Austrian bishops, most of whom voted against the infallibility decree, were on a shaky platform if they stood up for what had happened, or defended what only a few months before they attacked.

The excommunication of Döllinger in April 1871—Archbishop Scherr of Munich, who had been his pupil, acted with haste and

[30] Cf. ibid. iv. 71.

rigidity, for the case of such a man as Döllinger needed time—precipitated the forming of a Catholic Church in schism from Rome. Most were university teachers or members of the educated middle class. The group of university professors who joined them in the highest numbers were, naturally, the historians—two-thirds of all Catholics teaching history in German universities became Old Catholics, a disaster for the Roman Catholic study of history. They had hoped for bishops but got none. At one time they had hoped to have many of the Catholics of Germany behind them, but their leaders were not rebellious by nature; they were reluctant protesters because their historical or theological integrity demanded that they refuse to accept the decree, and no one went about like an evangelist to draw a new Church together. They were helped because bishops refused sacraments to people who were well-known for being against the Vatican Council, and if they had no sacraments from a Roman Catholic church they must go somewhere else to receive them; and because if bishops prevented a priest from celebrating mass for the same reason, he would celebrate mass elsewhere.

A Church was in effect founded at a Munich Congress of September 1871; it claimed to be the old, historic Catholic Church before these recent innovations, with its roots in the early Fathers and Catholic tradition, maintaining celibacy of the clergy, private confession, and the liturgy in Latin, and so being less radical than some of the Jansenist reformers of a century before. But it quickly abandoned indulgences, and limited the veneration of saints.

Slowly, within three or four years, it faded to some 60,000 people in Germany, though more in Switzerland. Swiss villages were the one place where it was not a middle-class movement, but had the people with it; at the university of Berne was the only State theological faculty which the Old Catholic movement was able to form. Döllinger never joined it wholeheartedly. His wish was to remain a member of the Catholic Church and he believed that he was that even though, he thought, he was wrongly excommunicated. His reputation made the Old Catholic movement much more important than its numbers. Among the Bavarian educated classes he was a hero. Immediately after the excommunication he was made rector of Munich university, and shortly afterwards the president of the Bavarian Academy of Sciences. Legend reported him as a cold intellectual, and he could give that impression—Gregorovius used to walk with him for three hours on many days, and admired his sincerity but decided that he was cold and 'devoid of enthusiasm for any lofty ideal', and that his character had none of the qualities that make a reformer; but in truth Döllinger was a man of warm feeling and friendships.[31]

To be the Old Catholic Church the movement needed bishops; and in 1873 it elected Reinkens the professor of theology at Breslau and caused him to be consecrated at Rotterdam by one of the Jansenist bishops in the Utrecht church. The position of the new bishops and Old Catholic clergy was made easier because the States were on their side; in Germany several governments recognized that they had the legal right to share in the use of the Catholic parish churches or cemeteries and not to be turned out of their vicarages or their chairs.

A reforming element moved them away from traditional customs of Roman Catholicism. They found that they could not insist on private confession; there was soon a demand for the mass in German; and then a more emotional demand that priests should be allowed to marry; and this was reluctantly conceded though not encouraged.

A congregation of Old Catholics quickly formed in Vienna, for Döllinger was admired by the intellectuals among the Austrian clergy; the municipality gave them a chapel where the first Old Catholic mass was celebrated in October 1871, to be followed at once by an interdict on the chapel launched by Cardinal Rauscher.

The Austrian government recognized the Old Catholic Church by a decree of 1877. The Old Catholics demanded a share in the old endowments of the Catholic Church of which they claimed to be the authentic representatives. In Austria several attempts to that end failed, and they could not elect a bishop till four years later. Unlike their colleagues in Germany and Switzerland they gained no leading personalities. The Austrian State, unlike the governments in Germany and Switzerland, had no desire to complicate its life with Roman Catholics and hindered the development of the Old Catholics where it could lawfully do so. They were very short of money and clergy except in the Sudeten areas of the Czech lands. Some of the priests who looked for pastorates in Austria could not be paid and had to find their work in Germany. They were first given

---

[31] Gregorovius, *Roman Journal*, 406, 434. For Döllinger see the original Life by his pupil Johannes Friedrich, *Ignaz von Döllinger* (3 vols.; Munich, 1899–1901); correspondence with Acton, Victor Conzemius (ed.), *Ignaz von Döllinger Briefwechsel: Lord Acton* (3 vols., Munich, 1963–71), indispensable; modern literature in *TRE* (1981) s.v., by Victor Conzemius; Georg Denzler and E. L. Grasmück (eds.), *Geschichtlichkeit und Glaube: Zum 100. Todestag J. J. Ignaz von Döllingers* (Munich, 1990).

State money towards the end of the First World War. Celibacy and the use of Latin in the mass were early abolished.

During the 1890s the Austrian Old Catholics found their situation changed by the movement called Los-vom-Rom, 'Get rid of Rome'. Some of the resultant 'converts' were more political than religious, but they increased by 20,000 the number of Old Catholics in the Austro-Hungarian empire.

THE *KULTURKAMPF* IN GERMANY

The historic difficulty of the union of Germany as a single State rested partly upon size and particularisms built into the country by geography since the Middle Ages; and partly, since the Reformation, by the division of the country into Catholics and Protestants. The treaty of Westphalia, which ended the wars of religion in 1648, solved the problem by an equal balance of religions but with the Catholics given a slight pre-eminence of honour in that the emperor was always the ruler of Austria and therefore a Catholic. The emperor's Catholic power in Germany rested not only on an alliance with Catholic Bavaria but on the prince-bishoprics of the Rhineland.

Bit by bit this equality was dismantled. Napoleon forced on Germany the secularization of all the independent bishoprics and abbeys; and pieces of Germany, that is the Protestant parts mainly but not solely, were glad to have this chance of strengthening the secular principalities. Then Napoleon forced upon Germany the end of the Holy Roman empire, which was the legal framework for the Catholic primacy of honour. The emperor became the Austrian emperor, but for Germany that was not the same. Then Napoleon was beaten and the peacemakers, needing to strengthen something between France and Russia, strengthened Prussia with the aid of Rhineland provinces. The effect was to produce a new great power in Europe, the first great power apart from Britain, to be Protestant in its feeling, since the Reformation.

In Germany, and in Europe, the balance of power swung towards the Protestants. It could not be said that Protestantism any longer made much of an international link between Protestant States. Even in Germany the pressure towards unity among the Protestant States depended more on economic advantage than on a common religion of the majority.

Most Germans assumed that Austria was part—indeed the leading part—of Germany. But to make a united Germany with Austria was difficult; partly because the dominant Protestants feared a Catholic emperor, and even more because the Austrian empire contained many races that were not Germanic and Germans feared that this would hurt German unity.

The contest for leadership inside Germany was settled in 1866 by the war between Prussia and Austria which Prussia won easily. Everyone including the Pope could see that Protestant Prussia was now dominant in Germany. Pius IX regarded the outcome of this war as a disaster for the Catholic Church. By the treaty Austria agreed to a new organization of Germany excluding Austria; Prussia took the chance to annex Protestant States of the north which had sympathized with Austria—Hanover, the city of Frankfurt, Hesse-Cassel, Nassau. So Prussian power mounted. In 1867 there was a North German confederation with its headship hereditary to the king of Prussia.

The French emperor claimed compensation for France to balance this growth in Prussian power. Bismarck, the Prussian Chancellor, saw that by a successful war against France he could weld the German States, apart from Austria, into a single State under the lead of Prussia. He worked for it, and obtained it under the best conditions. The overthrow of the French emperor at Sedan in 1870 meant the unification of Germany, as well as the Italian occupation of Rome.

The mood of united, Prussian-led Germany was Protestant; the rituals that celebrated union were Protestant; the crowning of the Prussian king as emperor of Germany was a Protestant ceremony. But inside united Germany, even apart from Austria, about a third of the people were Catholics, and these were often opponents of Prussia, Berlin, and Bismarck. They were Bavarians with a strong local tradition and members of a State with a long history and a suspicion of centralization under Berlin; or they were Rhinelanders, influenced by French liberalism and as Catholics suspicious of Berlin; or they were Poles in the east, hostile for reasons of nationality towards the Prussians and expressing their nationality by means of religion. The consciousness of the federal government that the Catholics were against them made the political leaders more anticlerical and more anti-Catholic. The union of Germany prepared a new conflict between the denominations.

On their side the Catholics in Germany were conscious of pressure. They organized in resistance, not by force but by constitutional means. From 1848 onwards they held Congresses (*Katholikentage*) with the object of exercising influence upon State policy, especially in freedom for Catholic education. From the 1859 Congress of Freiburg these meetings became a platform for protests against interference with their rights. They created an influential press, and talked of Catholic universities.

When Germany won the war against France and there was a German Reich, there was an immediate chance to form a Catholic political party to send members to the federal Parliament. The Zentrum, or Centre Party, was founded in October 1870. Its founders wanted a political party which would be general rather than denominational, but for which Catholics would wish to vote. Immediately it became the Catholic party. Its leader, the lawyer Ludwig Windthorst, was a dedicated Catholic, but one who had been opposed to infallibility. Religious questions were not the foundation of his policy. The importance of the party was shown by the first election to the Prussian Diet where the Zentrum put up candidates—and won 58 seats. Windthorst, the ugly little man with a stout heart, became the chief Catholic in Germany, more important to the faithful than any of the archbishops. Behind him sat enough members to cause trouble to the government and to batter away at laws that restricted Catholics, not because they were unjust to them but because they were breaches of the liberty which the State owed its citizens.

Bismarck regarded Catholics as the Germans who were the enemies of the new State. He associated this with the Syllabus of Errors, and the Vatican Council, and the decree of infallibility; but even more he associated it with two pressures of new German politics: (1) the Poles and their representatives in the Reichstag—'disloyal to Germanity'; there were more than two million of them in Prussia; and (2) the formation of the Centre Party. Never since the Thirty Years War was the Catholic Church more unpopular in North Germany than in the two years after the Vatican Council.

Bismarck professed an undogmatic and individualistic piety that valued Luther. He had a strong sense of vocation and obedience, and drew no clear line between politics and religion. He regarded the appearance of the Centre Party as 'monstrous'. Because his personal religion was so individual, he had little regard for Churches, Catholic or Protestant. His superlative sense of the realities of power deserted him when it came to dealing with Churches. He had no idea what power they could exert. After the creation of the German empire and its unity, which everyone confessed to be his work, he regarded anyone who opposed him as wicked as well as stupid. His manner of life made for ill humours: vast meals, gargantuan drinking, sleeplessness, and pains in the head due partly to a refusal to see dentists, the people in the world of whom he was most afraid. If he was opposed he was irritable, and when he was angry his fits of rage frightened even his admirers. He spent months away from Parliament among the woods of his northern estate and took his decisions alone or among a few advisers who would not contradict him. He was well-educated, fascinating in conversation, and a master of prose but had little interest in the areas of culture that were akin to religion in their attitude to humanity, such as art, history, philosophy, or the theatre, though he read poets like Schiller, Shakespeare, and Heine. He loved his wife, who was unpolitical, and loathed the Empress Augusta because she thought his attack upon the Catholic Church wicked. He lay awake at night thinking with hatred, sometimes of Windthorst, sometimes of the Empress.

Much of the best in North German Protestantism or ex-Protestantism stood behind him. Even some Catholics who would not think of joining Döllinger were not against him. The leaders of scientific and historical research regarded the Centre Party and 'Roman influence' in the new united State as a threat which must be countered. They were agreed that the tradition of 'German' culture was Protestant. The freedom of the kind to follow an argument wherever it went, and of the individual against the 'heavy' hand of church authority, were the foundations of German intellectual development. That a mere man could declare himself infallible seemed to them to war against everything they stood for. They identified 'Germany' with the North German Protestant tradition. This was the remarkable consequence of the exclusion of Catholic Austria from Germany.

So began the *Kulturkampf*, the name given to the struggle by the free-thinking scientist Virchow. He used the phrase at a small meeting but it caught on and was taken over by both Catholics and the enemies of Catholics, and then by all the historians. By *Kulturkampf* Virchow meant a battle between the modern cultivated intellect and the obscurantism of a clerical past. That was not what the battle was about, and Bismarck avoided using such a term. The contest was not between two cultures, whether old or new. It was rather a struggle whether the section of German Catholicism that resented the new

Reich would be incorporated into it successfully. It had three political sides: whether the pope would get back his State; whether the Poles would retain their anti-German nationalism; and whether there was room for a Catholic party in a State that was only semi-democratic. Not all the Poles were Catholics, but most of them were, and the right to teach their children in the Polish language, especially the right to teach them religion in Polish, was life or death to them, or was felt to be so; the Poles gave the struggle its worst tensions.

The Centre Party showed the movement towards the political left that characterized so many Catholic parliamentary movements in this age, from Ireland to the United States. Because many Catholics were peasants or members of the urban working class, their political constituency was radical. The Centre Party had a link with the Christian-social movements of Germany, of which the leader was Ketteler, bishop of Mainz. The first Catholic trade union was founded at Essen in 1869 and the next year there was a congress of Catholic trade unions. This radical slant made it easy for the propaganda of the right to represent the Catholics as more radical than they were; with talk of the alliance of the Red and Black internationals.

The battle started slowly. The bishops demanded submission to the infallibility decree of the Vatican Council. Catholic professors at State universities refused to submit. When the bishops tried to remove them they appealed to the State which upheld their rights to their posts and their teaching. The German tradition of 'academic freedom' was firm. The central government of Germany suppressed the Catholic section of its Ministry for Church Affairs and united the two sections under a Lutheran civil servant.

Bismarck did not expect that the Old Catholic movement could win German Catholicism. He saw that it was a movement of intellectuals and that ordinary people were indifferent. The Vatican believed that the aim of Bismarck was to create a National German Catholic Church free from Rome. This was not his idea.

But in the eastern provinces of Posen and Silesia where the Catholics were Poles, the trouble hit schools. A headmaster refused to teach what the bishops ordered; the bishop tried to get rid of him; the State upheld the headmaster. The parents took their children away from school, but the law said they must attend. The Polish population voted with its feet.

The *Kultusminister*, that is, the head of the Ministry for Church Affairs, Mühler, treated Catholics fairly and did not like the hard policy that Bismarck wanted, either in Prussian-ruled Poland or among the Catholics of Alsace-Lorraine where most of the inhabitants resented being taken out of France after the Franco-Prussian war. Müller warned the cabinet against the policy of attacking the Roman Catholic Church. In January 1872 Bismarck replaced him with Adalbert Falk, whose name was always to be associated with this struggle. He was a little-known lawyer, son of a Lutheran pastor, with a true faith and a Prussian patriotism. It has been said that Bismarck fought this battle because he was pugnacious, Falk because he was conscientious. Falk was the best person for the fight because he was the only civil servant whom Bismarck trusted, and because he had a sense of law. History held his name up to reprobation because of the persecuting policy which he was told to pursue, but he made the policy less unjust than his master wanted. Bismarck preferred administrative acts, umbrella laws that allowed magistrates or police to deal capriciously with any priest making trouble. Falk wanted none of that; he was insistent that government must proceed by a legal framework which was clear to everyone. Bismarck disapproved, but he still respected Falk and his judgement. He was the only one of Bismarck's cabinet ministers to be known and popular among the general public.

In March 1872 the first of the *Kulturkampf* laws subjected all schools, public or private, to State inspection. It appeared harmless, if not natural, but the Centre Party fought it passionately in Parliament because it subjected religious education everywhere to a godless State. Evangelical Protestants disliked it as much as did Catholics. It was a good law that was never afterwards altered or withdrawn.

The next crisis was in a Polish school in the diocese of Ermland. Bishop Krementz excommunicated the school chaplain and declared that this had social consequences (those of being ostracized and unemployable). The State persistently demanded that he withdraw. Krementz three times professed his loyalty to the State, but refused to withdraw. In September 1872 the government suspended him from the temporalities of the see, and the first shot in the real war was thus fired. The government put itself in the wrong before most of public opinion, and realized that it did so because it possessed no adequate weapons with which to fight. So began the quest for laws.

That summer of 1872 the pope was entangled in the quarrel. Bismarck nominated as the Prussian ambassador to the Holy See the Bavarian Cardinal Hohenlohe. Years before, Hohenlohe had influence with Pius IX. He was not only a prince, he was nephew of a princely German bishop who was famous for his prayerfulness and gift of healing; and he won the affection of Pius IX when he joined him at Gaeta. In the 1850s he was a papal chamberlain with rooms in the Vatican, and at Castel Gandolfo a lovely view over the lake, and Pius IX was charming to him. When at Rome he lived at the marvellous Villa d'Este at Tivoli (which he leased from the ex-duke of Modena, head and last survivor of the historic Este family). He loved piano music and was himself no mean pianist. At Tivoli he was host for many months to the pianist Liszt, whom all Europe revered as the musical genius of that age. Cardinal Hohenlohe ordained Liszt to minor orders (it was alleged, either to help Liszt not to have to marry the Princess Sayn-Wittgenstein who was determined on wedlock, or at the behest of the princess, to prevent Liszt marrying anyone else; but she denied both legends, and the story is incredible). Hohenlohe was a good patron of artists in Rome.

But he was a pupil of Döllinger, and though he assented to the infallibility of the pope he believed the process of defining it caused untold damage to the Church—'Stupidity and fanaticism are dancing a tarantella together.'[32] His brother was the Bavarian Prime Minister who sat more loosely than he to dogmatic Catholicism and had tried to assemble the powers to stop the Vatican Council, and who was now much in favour of the laws that the Prussians wanted to control the Church. At the Vatican the cardinal was rumoured, though falsely, to have helped Döllinger to secret information about the proceedings within the Council. Historians cannot finally disprove the charge (for which there is no evidence) because the cardinal burnt all his papers about the Vatican Council shortly before his death. Pius IX had now to regard him as an enemy. The cardinal attended the sessions of the Council as little as possible and absented himself in Rome on the day of decision, but told his brother, 'The Council is no longer a council.'[33] He stayed till the Italians occupied the city and then left, with the reluctant leave of the Pope. In Germany he was very popular with Protestants and Old Catholics because he was so moderate or ecumenical in his attitudes.

---

[32] Cardinal Hohenlohe to his brother, 18 Mar. 1870, in F. Curtius (ed.), *Memoirs of Prince Hohenlohe*, Eng. trans. (1906), ii. 3.

[33] Cardinal Hohenlohe to his brother, ibid. ii. 11. The cardinal kept away from Rome till Pius IX died. He took part in the election of Leo XIII but afterwards destroyed his reputation with Leo by going to Munich without the pope's leave and calling on Döllinger and the Italian ambassador to Bavaria.

There were precedents for Catholic States being represented by a cardinal,[34] but there was no precedent for a Protestant State to be so represented. And in the situation the German cardinal, dedicated by his office to loyalty to the pope, could have found himself with the duty of promoting an anti-German policy at Rome. It could be represented as a kindness to the Catholic Church by the German government, thus to choose a cardinal as its representative. Historians have argued that Bismarck knew that Rome would refuse, and made the nomination with the object of causing war. The evidence for that is speculation by contemporaries, and the theory is not probable.

The Pope refused the nomination. Then both sides made things worse by what they said. Bismarck, challenged in the German Parliament, made the single famous remark in this affair—'Have no fear, we are not going to Canossa, either in body or in spirit.' German opinion was ecstatic that their Chancellor should make this utterance. After Bismarck's speech his admirers erected a pillar, with the words upon it, at the Harzburg, the old palace of the Emperor Henry IV who had been forced to do penance before the pope at Canossa in North Italy in 1077.[35] And on 24 June 1872, Pope Pius IX, who in old age said whatever came into his head, made a public attack on Bismarck—'who knows if soon a stone will not crash down from on high to smash the feet of this colossus?' Thus the pope and the German State were at war. At the end of the year the German legation to the Holy See was withdrawn from Rome.

So the legislation began. The foreign Jesuits were expelled from Germany; they mostly went to France, Belgium, Holland, Austria, and the United States. (Austria already had many Jesuits who were refugees from Italy and took precautions that the Germans should not add to their numbers.) Jesuit foundations were illegal in the Reich. The Reichstag, more prejudiced than Falk, strengthened the bill to allow the police to ban individual Jesuits from particular places. Most of the big Liberal Party contradicted their liberalism by voting through this bill.

In 1873 Prussia passed the May Laws. These applied to all Churches. They (1) required a 'scientific' higher education, that is a university degree, for the clergy (and did good to that end), and put

---

[34] Cardinal Fesch, Napoleon's uncle, for France, 1803; Cardinal Häfelin for Bavaria, 1803 onwards; and recently Labastida, bishop of Puebla, for Mexico, 1860.

[35] It has been said (E. Eyck, *Bismarck* (Zurich, 1944), iii. 103), that when Bismarck at last dismantled the *Kulturkampf* the only thing left was the Canossa pillar at the Harzburg.

all seminaries under State supervision; (2) made it compulsory for the Church to notify the State of all appointments, and the State could refuse the choice if there were grounds to believe that it might imperil public order; (3) abolished Roman interference in the disciplinary measures of the Catholic Church; (4) ordered that resignation from the Church was to be regulated by the State courts. In 1874 a law allowed the seizure of the property of all Church posts whose occupants were illegal under these laws. In the same year *compulsory* civil marriage was introduced, and then this was accepted as a law not only for Prussia but for all Germany. (Bismarck was against compulsory civil marriage and was pushed into it by Falk.) In 1874, in the sharpest act of the struggle, a Reich law made possible the exile of illegal clergymen.

Three months later a Catholic cooper's apprentice shot Bismarck in a carriage at the spa at Kissingen, and wounded him in the arm. The would-be assassin said that his motive was anger against the May Laws. The attempt confirmed German opinion that the State was on the right track. In 1875 all monks and nuns, except those caring for the sick, were expelled from Prussia. On 5 February 1875 Pius IX declared the May Laws invalid; that could not make them illegal.

The early biographers of Pope Pius IX represented Bismarck as a new Luther (it was the age when Catholics still saw Luther as nothing but a villain), or even as a new Nero. The laws were contrary to the Prussian tradition of treating denominations fairly—greater than the Prussian tradition, this tolerant attitude was what made the Prussian State. Later historians saw the predicament of the German government in the new situation of Catholics, both politically and in education. Yet the effect of the *Kulturkampf* was bad not just for the Catholic Church in Germany but for the country.

The Prussian government enforced the laws against a resisting Church. It closed seminaries because they did not ask government approval, or the bishops closed them first, and ordinands attended neither universities nor seminaries and could not be ordained. It removed priests appointed to their offices without government approval, so the bishops started leaving parishes vacant. It passed a law which demanded an oath of obedience from bishops or their deputies. If a bishop or priest was fined for disobedience to the laws he would go to prison rather than pay.

These measures united the Catholic Church of Germany under its bishops and the pope—almost united, for Bishop Deinlein of

Bamberg alone disapproved the policy of refusing to obey the State. Many of the cases in the courts ended with trivial fines. The reputation of the priests rose among their congregations as they tried to protect them. The British ambassador, that Vatican expert Odo Russell, reported to his government that 'Bismarck utterly misunderstands and underrates the power of the Church . . . His anticlerical measures have only produced the very state of things the Vatican was working for through the Oecumenical Council—namely, unity and discipline in the clergy under an infallible head—or the Prussian military system applied to the Church.'[36]

The number of monks and nuns had been growing (in 1855 there were 334 monks, rising to 1,032 in 1874; in 1855 there were 579 nuns, rising to 7,763 in 1874).[37] Most of their leaders were not German but from Austria, Holland, Belgium, or France. The law to dissolve them was attacked by the Centre Party as the merest prejudice—most Protestants had never seen a convent and their beliefs about monks and nuns were based on imagination and legend. But the liberal party backed the abolition; convents, they said, are 'obsolete in modern culture'. The law was carried through the upper house of the State Parliament with less than a third of the members appearing. It was not enforced too systematically. Of some 900 houses, 109 were dissolved. These were houses that had no work in nursing or education. Force had to be used to eject three Franciscan communities from their houses. But most left peacefully, and went to the same countries, for the most part, to which the expelled Jesuits went. Some houses which did both teaching and nursing, gave up their school in order to be safe. This created the need for expenditure on secular schools, and the State refused to provide the money.

The turmoil turned opinion, both in Germany and outside it. Britain, with its own tradition of tolerance, at first liked what Bismarck was doing. *The Times* declared the laws wise. English newspapers were on the side of the German government. The French bishops backed the German bishops and accused the German government of being persecutors. The Germans tried to make the French government prosecute the French bishops but got nothing

---

[36] Paul Knaplund (ed.), *Letters from the Berlin Embassy 1871–4, 1880–5*, in Annual Report of the American Historical Association (Washington, 1944), 71.

[37] E. Schmidt-Volkmar, *Der Kulturkampf in Deutschland 1871–90* (Göttingen, 1962), 142, from statistics collected by P. Hinschius in *Preussische Jahrbücher*, 34 (1874), 117–48.

but apologies for their behaviour, a circular warning them to discretion, and the banning of Veuillot's newspaper *Univers* for two months.

What alienated foreign Protestant sympathies from Bismarck was the imprisonment of bishops. The first was the Polish Archbishop Ledochowski. He banned the teaching of religion in the German language to the lower classes of schools for Polish children. The government ordered him to resign his see. He refused. He was put into a fortress and deposed by State action (15 April 1874). He stayed in his cell for over two years and then was banished from Prussia. After he was a prisoner for a year Pius IX made him a cardinal, a promotion not likely to increase peace in Germany. On his release Ledochowski came to Rome and from there tried to govern his diocese.

Only a little time after Ledochowski's arrest, Archbishop Melchers of Cologne was arrested and released after six months but without his stipend. Months later he was told to resign, but preferred to go abroad and was forced to try to govern his diocese from Holland; in his diocese the seminaries were closed, 150 parishes had no pastor, 605 monks had been banished, the ordinands were trained in Holland, Belgium, or France.[38] He never came back to Germany. Archbishop Martin of Paderborn spent a year in prison and then escaped to Holland, but died in exile in Belgium. Two other bishops were in gaol. Those who survived disagreed about the extent to which they could go along with the State—for example, some thought it reasonable to accept state approval of appointments and some could not bear such a compromise.

With the inability to fill sees, only three out of twelve in Prussia had bishops. Four bishops died and five bishops were deprived of their sees by the courts. About 1,400 parishes were vacant. Congregations refused to follow priests who conformed. Secret masses were celebrated in woods. Some priests accepted State approval in order not to lose their State stipends; some monks wanted to stay in Germany and were willing to give up their habits to do so. Such compromises displeased the Catholic authorities.

The worst was in the Polish areas. To many Poles the clergy were maintainers of their nationality; to them, Ledochowski was the leader of their nation. After his release his journey to Rome was a triumph.

---

[38] Melchers to Pius IX, 3 Nov. 1874; Martina, *Pio IX (1867–78)*, 392.

Even the death of Pope Pius IX produced a political demonstration in Polish Prussia. Among the peasants there was growth in cults and devotions, with visions of the blessed Virgin and many pilgrims; and with extraordinary rumours, for example that the government had decided to export all Polish children to England and Turkey. But the people's support of their bishop was not confined to the Polish lands. When the bishop of Münster refused to pay a fine the authorities tried to distrain his goods, but no driver would drive the cart. The authorities hired a Protestant driver, against whom there was a riot; his windows were broken and the army was called in. The bishop emigrated to Holland. When the property was seized and sold at auction, Catholics bought it and gave it back to him.

Prussia could not win this contest. Bismarck had no idea what would ensue when he took on a Church. As early as 1877 he saw that the policy must be reversed; but slowly, so as not to humiliate the State. There could be no change so long as Pius IX lived—it must wait for his successor. When the news of Pius IX's death was brought to him, Bismarck ordered a special bottle of wine to drink a toast. He knew that the policy had failed; but since it was impossible for him to have failed, the fault, he was sure, must lie with Falk.

BRITAIN

Everywhere in the Protestant countries the attack by Protestants on Catholics grew sharper. In every Protestant country except Scandinavia the Catholics were a substantial minority and the Protestants were unhappy with this new growth by immigration, birth rate, or change of frontier. In Britain the Irish immigration into England produced a new militancy among the more controversial Protestants. In the House of Commons Newdegate hammered away obsessively with questions, private bills, and motions for a government inquiry—was it possible that the Pope would take up residence in England? Why was the government trying to do what it could for the preservation of the monastery of Monte Cassino? Why did the British have an envoy in Rome and what was he doing so close to the papal government?[39] Ought we to have a parliamentary paper on

---

[39] The last English ambassador to the Vatican until the later 20th cent., Sir Edward Carne, died in 1561. Queen Henrietta Maria had a personal envoy at Rome and so later did King James II. From the time of the French Revolution common interests caused various

the doctrine of transubstantiation and its social effects? We must at all costs have an inquiry into monasteries and nunneries since what went on in their enclosures was not compatible with the rights of citizens of a free country. The papacy, said Newdegate, has declared its 'direct opposition to modern civilization', and the pope seeks infallibility 'that he might exalt his authority over every monarch, and bind every state to his obedience'.[40] But Newdegate, with his tail of ardent supporters, was regarded by most of the House of Commons as a crank.

But if Newdegate was a fanatic, it was very few years before the ex-Prime Minister of Britain wrote pamphlets against the pope. Gladstone, forced out of office partly by Irish votes, felt himself free to say what he liked; and if he was overheated, no one but Queen Victoria could call him a crank. He revered Döllinger and was shocked by his excommunication; he greatly admired Strossmayer; he regarded Lord Acton as his sage. Half-consciously he may have been influenced by a personal motive, which was the need to clear himself of the widespread suspicion that one who was evidently an Anglo-Catholic in his devotion was a secret friend of the Pope. In 1869–70 he disestablished the Protestant Church in Ireland, and in 1871 abolished the Ecclesiastical Titles Act which penalized Roman Catholic bishops if they took the names of sees in Britain. He was persuaded of a conspiracy to restore the pope to his temporal power, by European war if necessary, and such a war could hardly do other

('unofficial') missions to the Vatican but crown lawyers held that any official embassy was illegal by British law. As Foreign Secretary Lord Palmerston got over the difficulty by making the Tuscan embassy in Florence send an official to take up residence in Rome. In 1848 an act was passed making it legal for the British government to send an official, but nothing happened, and the unofficial system continued. As occupant of the post from 1858 Odo Russell was so brilliant that he had force and influence equal to an ambassador's. When Russell went in 1870 his chargé Clarke Jervoise kept the seat warm for four years, until this was challenged by Newdegate and others in Parliament, and Disraeli ended the mission. The lawyers in 1875 ruled that since there was now no Papal State the act of 1848 legalizing a mission was obsolete. When the war of 1914 broke out, it offended Britain that their German and Austrian enemies were the only powers with weighty ministers at the Vatican, so the modern British representation at the Holy See opened in December 1914.

[40] Hansard, 21 Mar. 1870, 200, col. 341; for the motion for inquiry into monasteries and nunneries, which was carried by the barest majority, Hansard, 1870, 200, cols. 872–908; and Report, PP (1870), vii. 1 ff.; (1871), vii. 181; for the bill on monastic and conventual institutions which kept reappearing but failed, PP (1872), iii. 391; (1873), iii. 331; (1875), iv. 305; (1876), v. 231; (1877), iv. 199. The English were not unique in these attitudes. In Aug. 1869 two Dominicans opened a chapel in Berlin to minister to Catholic workers in a nearby factory. Non-Catholic workers arrived with crowbars, the Dominicans fled over the garden fence, and the chapel was sacked. Cf. K. Bachem, *Vorgeschichte, Geschichte und Politik der deutschen Zentrumspartei* (Cologne, 1927–32), iii. 39.

than draw in Britain. In two violent pamphlets he accused the Vatican Council of making all Catholics disloyal to the State. Acton tried to stop him from publishing, but Gladstone was unstoppable: 'I see this great personage [the Pope], under ill advice, aiming heavily, and so far as he can make them so, deadly blows at the freedom of mankind, and therein not only at the structure of society, but at the very constitution of our nature, and the high designs of Providence for trying and training it . . .'[41] Gladstone took his evidence partly out of the Syllabus of Errors. He maintained that the Pope condemned all who believed in the liberty of the press, of conscience, or worship, or of speech.

The two pamphlets received many Catholic answers of which only one mattered, the *Letter to the Duke of Norfolk* by John Henry Newman. To have an ex-Prime Minister writing pamphlets against him was not in all respects a disadvantage to the Pope. It made him more important to the British.

The serious consequences were longer in their range. Between 1872 and the end of the century the Catholic Church was the victim of prolonged assault, by anticlericals in France and by Protestants in Germany. These attacks were not caused only by the Vatican decrees. There were wider political and social causes in those nations. But they were fostered by the Vatican decrees or by the mood in Europe which the Vatican decrees created. Such assaults may have done good to Catholicism because persecution is said to help Churches if it is inefficient, as these persecutions were inefficient. They helped to make the Catholic Church solid and unified in a way the Vatican decrees would have failed to do. But they had also the consequence, inevitable in all persecutions, of making the Church build its walls still higher against the world.

Or, to put it another way, between 1830 and 1869 the Pope raised his defences against the world because the Italian Revolution was a revolt against him. His chief defence was international; the affection for the apostolic see against the interference of local nationalism. In 1864–70 the Catholic Church converted the resistance to the Italians into a resistance against European society which could produce a phenomenon like Italian nationalism. Thereby the Pope made many more enemies—and simultaneously made his disciples much more dedicated to himself and his office.

[41] *The Vatican Decrees in their bearing on civil allegiance* (1874); *Vaticanism* (1875).

THE DEATHS OF THE POPE AND THE KING OF ITALY

In the first five weeks of 1878 the two men died who were the symbols of the European clash between Church and State: the King of
Italy first, and then Pope Pius IX. Their death-beds, their deaths, and
their funerals were a sign of more than the internal battles of Italian
politics. They were almost like the old Europe and the new: the Pope
who condemned democracy, a free press, and toleration; and the
King, sleazy in his person, but the head of a State that stood for
nationality, encouraged a free press, and insisted on 'toleration'; and
which, if not quite a democracy, was backed by the coming democratic world; on the one side the defence *à outrance* of old ecclesiastical endowments, on the other the opinion that old endowments
should be put to uses which helped the State more—and yet the
ancient clergyman stood for more ideals in his life than the person of
the king who died four weeks before he did. The old had strength
and depth, but grew impossible. The new had vices, but must come
because the needs of society, and the inventions of engineers, and the
new learning, brought it forward, sometimes with humanity and
sometimes with ruthlessness. Because the two funerals were symbols
of so much more than the events themselves, they became as political as they were religious.

Like Te Deums, funerals were a problem. The makers of the
Risorgimento, other than Mazzini, Garibaldi, and a few others, were
Catholics; some bad Catholics, some pious. Were they all excommunicated? Their families, and often they themselves, wanted Christian
burial. Rattazzi died at Alessandria: the bishop was away, the chapter
conducted his funeral in the cathedral. The Pope said that Rattazzi
was Catholic by birth and infidel by conduct, his life was full of anti-
Christian acts, and he had helped Garibaldi to fight at Mentana—and
a humble letter of penitence came from the canons. Two lesser men
were refused Catholic funerals in Sicily because they would not
recant. Lanza, Prime Minister when Rome was seized, accepted the
comforts of religion from his parish priest as he died, and the bishop
made no difficulty about allowing a funeral in church. The Catholic
press then said that he recanted before death—and his widow and
nephew denied it hotly.

So when the King was dying, he faced the Church with a problem
of conscience as sharp as that of the dying Cavour. By Victor

Emmanuel's death-bed, a scene was played out which was like that when Father Giacomo ministered to Cavour's last hours. The Vatican expected this scion of the house of Savoy to be buried in the family crypt at the Superga, just outside Turin. But that was politically impossible. It was necessary to the new Italy that its first king should be buried in its new capital, Rome, to prove that it was indeed his. The funeral must be the final act in making Rome into the capital. It was also necessary that he should be buried with all the rites of the Church. But since the house of Savoy had no family graves in Rome, and since there was no previous king of Italy to be buried in Rome, and since the King could not be buried in either of the cathedrals of Rome—the Lateran and St Peter's—because such a burial would need force and be illegal under the Law of Guarantees, the place of burial was discussed by the family and the cabinet. It had to be in a church which the Vatican did not control because it was not protected by the Law of Guarantees. They decided that it should be the Pantheon, Marcus Agrippa's historic circular temple to the planetary gods, rebuilt by the Emperor Hadrian, turned into a church dedicated to St Mary of the Martyrs, but because of its round structure called thereafter Santa Maria Rotunda. It was a church with majesty and harmony, and it linked modern Italy with imperial Rome. In its rotunda was the tomb of one of the most Christian of all artists, Raphael, who had asked to be buried there. Yet in that place the memory of imperial Rome was even stronger than the memory of Christian Rome. The choice of the Pantheon did not mean that the cabinet or the family wished for a semi-Christian burial. It was necessary to political Italy that the King whom Rome tried to reject should take possession not only of the State but of the religious tradition.

The King's chaplain in the Quirinal was Father Anzino. The Pope thought that the King's heir Humbert had no religion in him but that Victor Emmanuel had. Pius IX had always liked the King, ruefully, even while he excommunicated him, and even though they never met. He gave Anzino leave to hear the King's last confession and if he found him penitent to pronounce the absolution. Anzino, in order to defend himself later, had a motive to report the King's penitence as more articulate than it was, but he must have rightly related the sense of the words. The dying King said to Anzino that he died a Catholic and felt a devotion to the Pope as of a son to a father. He said that he regretted that he had caused the Pope to feel aversion to him but that in all he had done he never meant to hurt religion. He asked pardon for the enmities which he caused. For Anzino as for any normal priest that was enough. He fetched the viaticum and holy oil from a nearby parish church and administered the viaticum before an astounding company, all carrying candles—not only Humbert, who was thought to believe nothing, but cabinet ministers who were suspected of believing as little. Victor Emmanuel died a few hours later (9 January 1878) and a message was sent to the Pope.

And now Anzino's situation was like that of Cavour's Father Giacomo. It was necessary to the Vatican that the King's penitence should repudiate what the Risorgimento had done to the Church; and it must be made public that this coming religious funeral was only possible because the King was penitent for what he had done. It was necessary to the Risorgimento that the King should retract nothing. Anzino found himself between two fires, doubted by some in the Vatican whether he had rightly absolved the King, and threatened by the Home Secretary Crispi if he had implied to the public any word of retraction. Anzino went from Crispi to the new King Humbert and received his authority to tell the Vatican what Victor Emmanuel had said.

The Curia ordered that this funeral should be simple and without pomp—but they had no such power. It is true that kings are usually buried by archbishops and neither bishop nor cardinal appeared at the funeral on 17 January 1878. But nearly everyone else appeared; a procession of four hours, with many detachments of the army, and the imperial crown from Monza on a cushion, escorted by the chapter of Monza cathedral. The trouble came in towns distant from Rome. The Curia ordered no requiems, if they might turn into political demonstrations. But in the circumstances any requiem was a political demonstration. Since many towns were not to be stopped from holding requiems, and could easily find clergy to celebrate them, there were disputes in Italian towns reminiscent of the old war of the Te Deums, with bishops trying to refuse the use of cathedrals. At Bologna and Parma there were riots; the windows of the Bologna seminary were smashed; at Piacenza the bishop's life was at risk; Turin minded that the funeral was not at the Superga. Humbert was proclaimed king. The Pope lodged a solemn protest that this was illegal—no one took any notice.

Three weeks later (7 February 1878) the Pope died. He was 85 years old, only three months short of 86. For a few months chaplains had helped him to stand up. The rites of death were kept perfectly, with Cardinal Bilio intoning. If 100,000 followed the coffin of the King, three times that number turned out for the coffin of the Pope. The Curia was afraid that it could not control such crowds and for the first time invited Italian troops into St Peter's to help maintain order.

His had been the longest reign of any pope in history, he had passed by several years the so-called years of St Peter,[42] and he was the most hated man among some—but only some—of the citizens of Rome. In the international Church he was revered, almost at once as a possible candidate for sainthood.

Three years after his death his last testament was obeyed and he was buried in the church of San Lorenzo in Verano, known as San Lorenzo outside the Walls. It was the church by the old cemetery of Rome. Pius IX had restored the church, which dated to the Emperor Constantine, though it was reconstructed in later centuries. In it was a monument to the papal zouaves who were killed at the battle of Mentana. His wish to be buried there made a claim that the old churches of Rome were still papal; and it linked him with Mentana and the defence of the Papal State against Garibaldi.

This wish presented the Curia with a difficulty. To obey they had to get his body across the city. After all that had happened, if he had crossed the city alive he would have suffered shouts of abuse and probably missiles. The Curia asked themselves whether the same thing would happen to a dead pope, and decided that it would and that they dare not risk a cortège to San Lorenzo in daylight. They ventured to do it only by night and selected the night of 12–13 July 1881. This was a blunder, because by night no police can control demonstrations.

The coffin was almost thrown into the Tiber in the ensuing riot as it crossed the bridge by torchlight in the dark amid stones, and curses,

---

[42] Early among the legends about the origins of the see of Rome came the story that St Peter had ruled the Church in Rome for twenty-five years. During the eleventh century St Peter Damiani, who was trying to preach to his pope, encouraged him to humility by saying that popes always die after a short reign and none of them exceeds at death the twenty-five years of St Peter. He thought this an order of providence to keep popes humble amid their temptations to glories of this world. For a time this was truly thought by some writers to be a divine command. But in modern times life grew longer. The last pope of the eighteenth century lasted twenty-four years. In 1871 Pius IX 'passed the years of St Peter' and inscriptions were put up in St Peter's and the Lateran and St Maria Maggiore to honour him as the first such pope.

and knives, and obscenities. By the railway station troops had to intervene and the hearse had to gallop away. Behind the locked doors of San Lorenzo the interment was reverent despite the milling crowd outside. The Pope's tomb was placed in the crypt under the piece that Constantine built, and later the crypt was richly decorated with mosaics.

This funeral was an international incident. The Catholic powers protested but the Italian government was rude in the way it refused to provide an ordinarily courteous apology. The Prime Minister Depretis regretted the attack in the Chamber, but in language which accused the organizers of wanting a political demonstration. The Foreign Minister Mancini issued a letter to the powers saying that the affair was caused by impudent clerical aggression. Six alleged culprits were put on trial and five of them were convicted, but were given derisory penalties and cheered in court. The Freemasons struck a medal in honour of the accused.

At Turin a new church had been built, with the help of money given by Pius IX. After he died the congregation turned it into a half-memorial, with a large bust of him over the main door. Demonstrators gathered and were not placated till they had brought down the bust.

7

POPE LEO XIII (1878–1903)

THE CONCLAVE OF 1878

Before the Conclave of February 1878 the hard-liners were divided. Was it safe to hold the election in Rome? Would it show the world that they were free from the Italians if they met somewhere else? The cardinals debated whether they could safely hold the election freely in Rome when they were in the power of the Italians, and there was hot debate whether they should ask the British government for leave to hold the Conclave in Malta. It was essential to the Italian government that the papacy should be seen to be workable in Rome. The Austrian Emperor had consulted Cardinal Rauscher about the necessity for ensuring a free election for this pope, not influenced by the new rulers of Rome. There were anxious letters on the matter between the Austrian and Italian governments. The Austrian Chancellor Andrássy tried to curdle blood by threats of the horrors which might happen if the election were not free and in Rome—he imagined the cardinals deciding to leave Rome and electing a pope in some asylum—and then the Italian government might cause another pope to be elected and since he would be the bishop in Rome he would gain the sympathies of many in the Catholic world, and there might be a schism like those of the Middle Ages. It was fanciful, but it had an effect. The Italians publicly gave a guarantee of freedom (which they kept) and privately passed a message that if the cardinals went away they would not come back.[1]

At the first meeting of cardinals, before they were shut into the Conclave, they voted by a large majority (31 : 7) to hold the election outside Italy. But some of them voted that way because the dead Pius IX had wanted it, and when they went away from the meeting many

[1] For the non-Italian anxieties over the election and its place see the Austrians in E. von Wertheimer, *Graf Julius Andrássy, sein Leben und seine Zeit* (Stuttgart, 1913), ii. 216; F. Engel-Janosi, *Österreich und der Vatikan* (Graz, 1960), i. 200–3; the British documents in O. Chadwick, 'The British Ambassador and the Conclave of 1878', in W. Gruber *et al.*, *Wissen Glaube Politik: Festschrift für Paul Asveld* (Graz, 1981), 155 ff.

of them realized that the decision was wrong: they had nowhere to go, had they time to make arrangements with a reluctant foreign government for another place of meeting. Some were old and could not travel easily, and were afraid that it was possible that if they went the Italian government would not let them back. The following day they voted, again by a majority, to stay.

There was evidence that Pius IX had wanted Bilio for his successor, and the wishes of Pius IX mattered to the cardinals, nearly all of whom owed him their hat. Others were afraid that if they chose an ultra such as Cardinal Bilio they would provoke a veto from one of the powers. As he was the author of the Syllabus the choice of Bilio would be seen to continue the policy of Pius IX. Bilio retained support till the very end of the election. But he was so notorious among liberals that he was evidently the one cardinal whom the European powers would hate to have as pope. All the powers were unanimous in wanting a liberal or (for they saw that was not possible) a moderate ('we don't want a zealot Jesuitical Pope', said Vienna[2]), anyway not a pope like Pius IX.

At least three of the powers, France, Austria, and Spain, still claimed the right to veto a papal election. Little Portugal, though now tormented in matters of Church and State, used in old days— not very old days, for Döllinger told them that it was first prominent in 1800—to claim a veto, and talked about claiming that right now. Politicians had a feeling that in the new papacy this historic right might be doubted as obsolete. But Austria entrusted its veto to the cardinals of Vienna and Hungary. Rauscher, to whom the veto was first entrusted, died in 1875 and his successor Kutschker was much less weighty as an archbishop, though he had written five volumes on the Catholic law of marriage. Simor was still primate of Hungary. The Austrian with authority among the cardinals was Prince Schwarzenberg of Prague, a survivor from the reign of Gregory XVI and so without the stigma of being created by Pius IX. Earlier there was Austrian talk of vetoing Cardinal Bilio. Their envoy Paar thought that after so long a pontificate they would ensure a very short

---

[2] Wertheimer, *Andrássy*, ii. 216; Andrássy was a Hungarian who played a wise and moderate part in the predicament of Austrian government between Bismarck, who demanded their full support for his *Kulturkampf*, and the more upper-class Austrian Catholics who wanted him to restore the pope by force if necessary. Andrássy was against the Vatican Council and regretted as an error of policy his predecessor Beust's refusal to join Hohenlohe of Bavaria in trying to stop the Council before it started. He was the only statesman of modern times to achieve the conditions for something like peace in Bosnia.

one, and suggested that they were likely to elect the archbishop of Fermo, De Angelis, more because he was 83 than because he was also a good man. But De Angelis died before the election. The Spanish instructed their cardinals to veto the Sicilian Franciscan Cardinal Panebianco and go for a conciliator[3]—it was an odd decision, for Panebianco was a remote and pious friar, and the Spanish, like many others, wanted someone who knew more of the world. They mentioned the name of Cardinal Franchi as someone whom they liked, for he had made an excellent impression when he was the papal nuncio in Spain. Franchi would have made an able pope and his early death was perhaps a disaster. He was the cardinal of the most liberal opinions then in the Sacred College and so had no chance of being elected; though there were other reasons why he had no chance—as the powerful head of Propaganda he was an excellent talker, loved dinner-parties, and his apartment was furnished lavishly—and other cardinals did not approve.

The Italian government had a problem. They must be seen to ensure the freedom of the election. But more than any other power, they wanted a moderate person elected. Since they dare not say so themselves, nor use their influence with their own cardinals, they privately made their wishes known to the French. They had to have an Italian, if possible a moderate, and someone likely to accept, or if that was impossible, to be seen to tolerate, the new Italy.

The French told the Italians that what they, the French, wanted was a moderate person, and an Italian, who would make up the quarrel with Italy. They had no name they intended to veto, but they said that they were prepared to veto any candidate who was not an Italian.[4] There was a story that they told Cardinal Bonnechose of Rouen to veto Bilio if necessary, but it seems to be without foundation—though it was true that they were against Bilio's election.

The same problem—that they must elect a pope who would be for the first time a subject of the Italians—made some of the cardinals wonder whether they ought not to prove the international status of the papacy by electing a non-Italian, a citizen of another country, to be pope. There was irresponsible talk of electing Cardinal Manning

---

[3] Greppi the Italian chargé in Madrid to the Prime Minister Depretis, 8 Feb. 1878, in *DDI* ser. 2, ix. 407; cf. Greppi to Melegari, 8 Dec. 1877, ibid. 238–9. Panebianco was still given 3 votes at the final scrutiny.

[4] Ressman, Italian chargé at Paris, to the Foreign Secretary Melegari, 25 Dec. 1877, ibid. ix. 273.

of Westminster, who made such a name as an ultramontane in the Vatican Council. Manning would have made an unsatisfactory pope. The Austrians were afraid of Cardinal Ledochowski the Pole, who was stalwart in his fight with Bismarck and was in exile at Rome, and of Franzelin the Jesuit theologian who was a Tyrolese and well-known for his defence of infallibility, and gave their cardinals the order to veto either of these. Ledochowski got one vote in the election, Franzelin none, and the veto was not mentioned. The leaders of the cardinals quickly saw that in their circumstances, where the position of the papacy was central to the problem of Italy, it was unthinkable not to elect an Italian; and that was the preference of the European powers.

As a church historian, Döllinger discouraged this talk of vetos.[5] To exercise a veto successfully, according to him, a power needed to be obviously Catholic and to have so consistent a policy that it had a body of cardinals in the Curia with a common opinion. Spain was said to be a Catholic power but after all the revolutions its influence at Rome was nil; France was by constitution a Catholic power but its government's liberalism was not likely to influence cardinals. Döllinger thought that the Emperor Francis Joseph of Austria was much respected as a Catholic and therefore an Austrian veto was possible; and that Portugal was on such good terms with the Holy See at that moment that its veto might count. This letter of Döllinger to help Portugal was not at all realistic. Events proved that the veto was not obsolete.

The historic law of systems of election ensured that the cardinals, though so largely chosen by Pius IX, must elect someone of a different mettle from Pius IX. But in the circumstances this general rule took a special form. Till his death Cardinal Antonelli had dominated and many cardinals had disliked him. That meant that the person they chose was likely not to be Antonelli's man. The cardinals of the Conclave might or might not want someone different from Pope Pius IX, but above all they wanted someone who was not part of Antonelli's machine. Therefore a prelate disapproved by Antonelli had a chance in the Conclave.

Cardinal Pecci[6] was the archbishop of Perugia. Early in life he had

---

[5] Oldoini at Lisbon to Depretis, 18 Jan. 1878, ibid. ix. 333–4.

[6] Born Vincenzo Gioacchino Pecci at Carpineto in Central Italy in 1810; studied at Rome, doctor of divinity at age 22; joined civil service, was delegate to Benevento in 1838, and tough with brigands; at Perugia, 1841; nuncio in Brussels 1843–6, and proved himself a

(rather painful) experience as nuncio in Belgium, but was abroad only for three years and had little experience of the world of international politics, especially as it changed after the European crisis of 1870. Cardinal Antonelli was opposed to him, and preferred to keep him away from Rome in his 'exile' in Perugia; for after so many years Pecci lamented Perugia as exile.

So Cardinal Pecci was elected, very quickly, at only the third scrutiny, to be Pope Leo XIII: because he was a conservative; because he was a moderate conservative; because he could not be blamed for Cardinal Antonelli; because he was an Italian cardinal who was known to care about Italy and well understood the tense situation of the papacy in Italy; because he was a distinguished person in a group of Italian cardinals who, thanks to the policy of Antonelli in preferring nonentities, lacked figures of distinction; because there were only two other serious candidates one of whom had written the Syllabus of Errors, and the other[7] was such a saint as to be withdrawn from the world, and popes must greet the world, and because Pecci was almost 68 and too long a tenure was not likely. Whether he was also elected because Cardinal Bartolini rushed about canvassing votes and persuaded the Spanish bishops, who had agreed to vote for their former nuncio Franchi, to join for Pecci on the expectation that Pecci would make Franchi his Secretary of State, is possible and was afterwards said. But the ardent canvass was probably not necessary. Once it was clear that there must be an Italian but not of the Curia, Pecci stood out.

He achieved nothing like unanimity. Antonelli's men were against him to the end. They said that at the Perugia 'massacre' of 1859 he had hidden away in his palace and done nothing; that he did nothing to stop bloodshed when the Piedmontese army occupied Perugia a year later; that he compromised by allowing a Te Deum for Cavour; that he was famous for penny-pinching if not avarice . . . and so on. At the third scrutiny which gave him 44 votes out of 61 and so the

statesman, but offended the king and was recalled; bishop of Perugia 1846–80 (for he kept the see two years after he was also bishop of Rome), made cardinal in 1853, cardinal chamberlain in 1877, and so responsible for the arrangements for the Conclave.

[7] Martinelli was an Augustinian. Bilio wanted him. He argued that the Church at this moment of crisis did not need a well-known person but a saint; as he said, 'a gentle man of God'. Bartolini asked him whether he really wanted another Celestine V, who if he had not resigned the papacy would have brought disaster upon it. He would be a weak pope. Martinelli kept two votes to the very end, but not Bilio's.

necessary two-thirds, there were still 17 votes against him, but all divided, 5 votes still for Bilio.

The cardinals obeyed the law of elective constitutions to do something different from the last time, when they had elected so young a pope with consequences for the world which, in the end, not all of them welcomed. They never expected that, like his predecessor, Leo XIII would outlive the years of St Peter and still be pope into his nineties.[8]

THE CHARACTER OF LEO XIII

Leo XIII was always a conservative, and liked the Syllabus of Errors. No one not a conservative could have been elected by the cardinals left by Pius IX. But from the 1860s Pecci wanted a rather more moderate attitude in the government of the Church; not a liberal attitude, but a presentation of the Church as a creative force in modern culture.

He had a good mind and worked hard. He had charm, but his personality was colder than that of Pius IX. Till his last years he was more in control of the Curia, because as there was no Papal State there was no one to fill the role of Cardinal Antonelli. And he was an autocrat: he once did something the like of which no pope before him had done, that is, to insist on the public humiliation of an eminent French cardinal, the Benedictine Pitra, the Vatican librarian, by forcing him to write him a public letter with the words, 'I deplore what you deplore, desire what you desire, condemn what you condemn.'[9]

---

[8] We know much about the Conclave because R. De Cesare's book on it, *Dal Conclave di Leone XIII al'ultimo Concistorio* (Città di Castello, 1899), was based on material from Cardinal Di Pietro and the knowledge of several Conclavists; and Soderini in his *Life of Leo XIII* had a diary of the Conclave kept by the Oratorian Calenzio who was the Conclavist of Cardinal Bartolini. Hence we know of the Bartolini canvassing in detail. Cesare had the actual voting by each cardinal. Cf. also C. Weber, *Quellen und Studien zur Kurie und zur vatikanischen Politik unter Leo XIII* (Tübingen, 1973), 198.

[9] A. Battandier, *Pitra* (Paris, 1893), 723. Jean-Baptiste Pitra, 1812–89, one of Prosper Guéranger's revived Benedictines from the age of 29. He taught history at the Autun seminary and there deciphered an Ichthys inscription of the early Church. His scholarly journeys made him something of an expert on Russia and he soon became adviser to Pius IX on eastern affairs. In 1863 he became a cardinal, and in 1869 Vatican librarian. Pitra rendered important services to history and archaeology. He wrote from Rome a letter to the Dutch editor Brouwers (4 May 1885) singing the praises of Pius IX, and of Solesmes and the religious revival, and the heroism of the zouaves—and 'alas, where are we now?'—Renan and Lamennais, and Loyson, and the pagan monument dominating Aracoeli at the summit of

When he interviewed Pitra (whose offence, if it was an offence, was trivial) he was more like a monarch receiving a rebel than like a father receiving one of his foremost sons. He kept him standing in front of him while he abused him for three-quarters of an hour. No pope ever acted more ruthlessly towards one of the most distinguished of his cardinals. He did not remove him from being a cardinal; but there were threats, and meanwhile he humbled him in the face of Europe. He was an autocrat who preferred to work through the customary channels, summon the cardinals, and listen to what they had to say. Personally he lived a simple life, and hated paying out money unnecessarily, so that some of the Vatican staff disliked him because they received fewer tips. He enjoyed ceremonial. He had a passion for cleanliness: the white cassock of the pope was always spotless. He was shy of giving audiences, and never laughed; but he had a charming smile, and was erect and slim. Despite his cool exterior he was mercurial emotionally, liable to be carried away by exaltation or by anger. He loved the great minds of the Italian Middle Ages, such as Aquinas and Dante. He was much interested in Christian archaeology, and though not himself a scholar liked to encourage scholars, and was keenly conscious of the long history of Italian civilization and the part of the papacy in its continuity.

Unlike his predecessors he was unable to give a blessing to the people in the square of St Peter's because no one knew whether all the crowd would be friendly; he gave it from the balcony inside. The coronation proved awkward. To crown a pope was to make him a king, and new Italians were determined that in Italy there could not be two kings. The words of the coronation rite were traditional—as the cardinal deacon put the tiara on his head he was to say 'You are the father of princes and kings, the head of the world, and the vicar of our Saviour.' Leo decided to be crowned in the hall above the porch where he could be seen by the crowd inside the cathedral, and workmen prepared the benches. The Italian police said that if this happened they could not ensure order in the square or the cathedral; and so the preparations were cancelled at the last moment and he was crowned in the Sistine Chapel where entry could be controlled. This did not fully secure order, for the more faithful inhabitants of Rome illuminated their windows in his honour that evening, and gangs went about with stones smashing the lit windows in the Corso.

Rome. The journals trumpeted a tremendous outcry, accusing him of attacking the new and more liberal pope in comparison with Pius IX—which was false.

Europe expected that the new pope would turn away from the policy of Pius IX and reconcile the papacy with the powers. And the first signs were that he wanted to do that. He chose the liberal-minded Franchi as his Secretary of State. Several of his first actions showed that he was a new broom. He at last abolished the eunuchs or castrati who sang in the Sistine Chapel. He agreed with the cardinals not to reconvene the suspended Vatican Council and at last caused the benches for the meeting in St Peter's to be broken up. He sold the last ship of the papal navy, the *Immaculate Conception*, which, because the pope now had no harbour, was stationed at Toulon. He sold the wretched collection of oil paintings and embroidered slippers that Pius IX had assembled. He ordered that bulls should appear in ordinary writing and not in Gothic lettering.

Such trivial changes were supported by weightier acts. Two or three of his earliest public utterances expressed the desire for reconciliation. In 1879 he marked the change of mood in a dramatic way by making John Henry Newman, who under his predecessor was in disgrace for his independence of mind, into a cardinal. Throughout Leo's reign this desire for reconciliation ran like a motif through some, though only some, of his utterances.

In one respect it was an advantage that he knew more than Pius IX. He had a true sense of the tradition of Italian culture, that the Church was the propagator of the highest civilization of Italy and of Europe. If he refused to accept freedom of the press, he wholeheartedly accepted the doctrine that truth does not need artificial props when in 1883 he formally opened the Vatican archives to researchers of all nations, not necessarily Catholic. When Rome reformed the calendar late in the sixteenth century, the pope founded an observatory at the Vatican. It did not prosper and was abandoned. Leo XIII now recreated it as a work of science, and put in charge a learned astronomer who was a Barnabite, and so pleased the astronomers of Europe.

But because he knew some Italian and papal history, the past could become a burden on the present. He vastly admired Pope Innocent III, under whom the papal monarchy of the Middle Ages attained the zenith of its power. He transferred the remains of Innocent III from Perugia to Rome and asked that he himself be buried near his tomb. He looked back upon the high Middle Ages as the age of faith, and wanted Catholicism to play again the part it played then, and popes to wield the authority of an Innocent among the peoples.

To this end he was a man of encyclicals. No pope before him ever issued so many. Declared by the Church to represent on earth the voice of God, he felt a duty to instruct the world; on morality, the rights of labour, the nature of socialism, the Bible, the nature of philosophy, the culture of Europe, marriage, Freemasons, the unity of the Church, and Anglican orders. But many of the encyclicals were more devotional. He had a particular wish to propagate the use of the rosary; there were no fewer than ten encyclicals with commendations of the rosary. He felt himself to be the international authority on truth, ethics, and religious practice, and was bold to utter what he thought it good for the world to hear.

It was, for the most part, a dream—but he did not think of it as a dream. He did not recognize that the medieval ideal was entangled with social and political conditions which could never return. The dream did not make his practical policies more offensive to the powers; he remained, for the most part, a person who knew that sane policy dealt with facts as they exist. Occasionally he could use such high-flown language out of the past that it became incongruous in the present; as though the office of the pope was God's way of ruling the world. But he did not use such language in situations where it could jeopardize the policy which he pursued.

THE PHILOSOPHY OF ST THOMAS AQUINAS

One result of this mentality came after the first year of his pontificate. It was the encyclical *Aeterni Patris*, of 4 August 1879. This declared not only that the philosophy of St Thomas Aquinas was very commendable for Catholics to study (which was likely to be true) but that it was the truest philosophy for the modern age as well as for the past (which was not so certain). A pope who loved the Middle Ages and wished to revive their impact in the modern world tried to make the supreme exponent of a medieval philosophy the only reliable exponent of modern philosophy.

Nevertheless this encyclical marked a change from the mentality of his untheological predecessor. Leo XIII perceived the errors of Christendom as springing from false axioms on which men and women were now brought up. If society were to be drawn back to the truth it must be turned to authentic first principles. Therefore the language of the encyclical had a confidence not lately heard in

Catholic history, confidence in human reason and its ways of enquiry, and was a poem of conviction that rational and intelligent people come by right reason to apprehend God, His justice, and His knowledge. Though he seemed to close the mind of the Church to so many ways towards truth, and to most of the roads established in the universities of that age, he also opened it. Not totally, however: the encyclical was still a narrow way for theological ideas, in that it assumed that only those who profess the Catholic faith have the balanced minds that move towards a true philosophy of the world. But Leo XIII recommended a large Catholic mind of the past who thought for himself and had a range of apprehension which would allow variety in modern interpretation. The Pope recognized that not everything in the schoolmen was suitable for the present generation and that it was not possible simply to go back to a past world of thought. By that recognition he opened the door to a wider variety of thinking than everyone supposed when they first read press reports of the encyclical.

The document, one of the two encyclicals of Leo XIII with long consequences for the future, had interesting results. First, it shattered the European expectation that this was a liberal pope. The world did not perceive the liberty that was being subtly offered to the theologians, it saw only that the Pope told everyone to believe what was taught seven centuries before. It thought that the Pope was as obscurantist as his predecessor.

Secondly, the encyclical contained not only a commendation but a command. It ordered the young, especially the ordinands, to be trained in the philosophy of Aquinas. Many of them were already so trained, though inefficiently; the next decades saw a sustained endeavour to improve the philosophical training in seminaries with the aid of the study of Thomism. And since Thomism was a good exercise in logic, it constituted an admirable training of the young in logical thinking.

Thirdly, it raised the importance of the Dominican Order, who were the established guardians of the teaching of St Thomas Aquinas. They had been under a cloud after their resistance to the definition of the doctrine of the Immaculate Conception. The cloud was lifted. They began to attract philosophical minds.

The Dominicans were given the task of producing a critical edition of Aquinas. If the schoolmen were so important to the modern mind, it would be helpful to know what they said. The manuscripts were chaotic, the editions poor, the texts hardly available. The encyclical began a scholarly process of study of the thought and of the texts of the schoolmen, not only of Aquinas but of the body of later medieval thought.

The 'establishment' of Thomism had a curious side-effect which showed how even the most pure theology could have political repercussions. Rosmini was nearly made a cardinal at the Roman Revolution; then at Gaeta his liberal ideas appeared as compromise, and two political works were put upon the Index of Prohibited Books. But not long after, Pius IX set up a new committee of inquiry, which reported favourably, and the condemnation was removed. But now under Leo XIII there was difficulty, for Rosmini's philosophy was not compatible with Thomism. After Rosmini died forty passages were extracted from his works and reproved. Cardinal Monaco demanded that the Rosminians accept this decree.

In Rosmini's birthplace at Rovereto in the Trentino, still under Austrian rule, there was a house of Rosminians headed by his heir and executor Francesco Paoli. They cheerfully accepted the Roman decree but said that it was wrong because the passages from Rosmini were taken out of context and he had been wrongly condemned or rather had not been censured. The prince-bishop of Trent demanded that Paoli withdraw his criticism of a Roman decree. Paoli did nothing. And now the politics entered: Italians of South Tyrol, drawn by the magnetism of a united Italy, made Paoli and Rosmini into heroes; nationalist leaders started reading theology which they could not understand; and raged that the Vatican had expelled the Rosminians from the Tyrol (which it had not, quite). When Paoli and his Rosminians left Rovereto voluntarily, a great crowd at the railway station cheered them as martyrs and women hung garlands about them. A pope could not even utter a decree touching theological truth without it making a difference to politics. The controversy made Rosmini suspect to the Church at large for more decades.[10]

LEO XIII AND ITALY

Leo XIII was in a situation where he must keep up the pressure on the Italian government to restore the Papal State. He used less

[10] J. Fontana, *Der Kulturkampf in Tirol (1861–1892)* (Bolzano, 1978), 384 ff.

ferocious language than had his predecessor. He kept the conventions of public diplomacy. He was always master of himself. Unlike his predecessor he did not say the first thing that welled up from his heart. Anyone who talked to Pius IX felt that at that moment he cared about him or her more than about anyone else in the world; those who talked to Leo XIII felt that they were talking to a person who was cool, formal, and courteous. But the claims were the same, and even more frequent in their repetition. And they had no more possibility of fulfilment by anything but a miracle.

But this pope was not like Pius IX with his simple faith that it was right to do nothing and God would provide. He had two more earthly resources that might bring back the Papal States. The first was international; a better relationship with the powers to increase their pressure upon the Italians. Leo wanted once again to make the question of Rome an argument in international politics. The second was internal to Italy. The strength of Italian nationalists was among the middle class, but the strength of Catholics in Italy lay in the old aristocracy and the peasants. The poor of the deep south never liked the union with the north of Italy and fought a terrible civil war against it. In the old Austrian provinces of Lombardy and the Veneto the ordinary people were a churchgoing people and now part of the strength of faith inside the kingdom of Italy.

Leo XIII was in a situation where he must not be seen to jettison the heritage of Pius IX whom Catholics revered; nor had he much wish to do so. He declared again, more than once, how valuable a document was the Syllabus of Errors. He believed in an ordered and hierarchical society. He did not believe in a separation of Church and State. When he was first pope he did not believe in toleration. The message seemed to be the same as the message of Pope Pius IX. It seemed as though only the tone and the manner were different. Slowly the world found that something was new other than the presentation.

Pius IX eschewed the idea of a policy and left the future to God and miracle. Leo XIII had a policy. It was not at first clear what that was, and as it became clear, most of it was a failure. But to have a policy at all, even if it did not work, set the papacy on a subtly new course.

THE RELATIONSHIPS WITH THE POWERS

The Law of Guarantees of 1871 allowed the pope to continue to receive diplomatic representatives from the powers. Should a pope who had no State continue to send diplomatic representatives to the powers? There was still a nuncio in Vienna, what now was his purpose? Pius IX had continued to keep his few representatives in the countries which received them; Leo XIII continued to keep the foreign service and to pay for its upkeep, for the nuncios were in origin not only ambassadors but agents of the pope to the Churches of the countries to which they were accredited. They affected, for example, the choice of bishops, and were the source of information for the Curia. In addition to the nuncios there were the apostolic delegates, of whom one was sent to Greece in 1834 by Pope Gregory XVI, and whom Pius IX and Leo XIII extended to the mission areas; they had only Church duties and were not ambassadors to the State. Both Pius IX and Leo XIII saw reason to keep them in existence.

Not all Catholic prelates thought the same way. The German bishops of the eighteenth century fought against the power of the German nuncio. This was often characteristic of the bishops of a national Church. To them the nuncio was an interference with their work. In the time of Leo XIII there was talk of negotiating a nuncio in London for England and Ireland. Leo XIII once said that he would rather get a nuncio accepted in Britain than in Germany or Russia. The Irish bishops found the idea of a nuncio in London, influenced by the needs of the Protestant British government, intolerable, and Cardinal Manning resisted the idea forcibly. He said that the conception of nuncios was obsolete, that they belonged to a time when Europe was Catholic, and that nowadays the bishops were the Pope's nuncios. This idea was far from the policy of the Curia, for whom the system of nuncios or delegates was a necessary part of the authority of Rome.

The pope therefore, though not the sovereign of a State, had, in a small way, the international relations of a real State. That gave him the illusion of a larger opportunity for influence among the powers than he really had.

THE ENDING OF THE GERMAN *KULTURKAMPF*

Leo XIII was confronted with a German desire to meet his wishes for reconciliation. He courteously told the German emperor of his own election. The German government did not at first believe in the courtesy, they took four weeks to decide whether this was a trick. Then the emperor replied with equal courtesy, and the mood between Germany and the Vatican changed with the pope. Even after his reconciling Secretary of State Franchi dropped dead the policy did not alter.

After what had happened it was difficult to negotiate without loss of face. Negotiations were carried on secretly in Vienna, and Bismarck met the Bavarian nuncio Masella at Bad Kissingen. Bismarck thought that alliance with the Catholic Centre Party could help him against the threat from the Socialists, and wanted peace. The Pope must demand the freedom of seminaries from State control, the reinstatement of priests or bishops driven out of their parishes or dioceses, Catholic teaching in schools, and freedom for monks and nuns. Prussia could only achieve this by more legislation which could not be passed through Parliament.

In August 1879 Adalbert Falk resigned from his office as Prussian Minister of Church Affairs, and that helped the Vatican. The main difficulties were first, how to get enough votes in the Prussian or Reich Parliaments to repeal the May Laws and Reich laws, and secondly, that if the Pope conceded something, not all clergy would obey him, and the Centre Party, whose force was built on resistance to Bismarck, would resent the concession. In February 1880 Leo XIII shocked the rigid, including the Centre Party leader Windthorst (who cried, 'Shot in the back!'), by conceding to Bismarck the duty to inform the State about Church appointments and agreeing that new appointments should have the State's approval. The State passed the first law to restore normal relations with the Church. It was done in the way that Bismarck liked and Falk disapproved—a vague, general law which allowed administrators discretion to make exceptions to the laws. The Centre Party voted against the discretionary bill because they thought there ought to be a law which repealed everything, but such a repeal would not have gone through Parliament. Even the discretionary law was only achieved by a majority of 4.

From 1881, with awkwardness and embarrassment, they began to fill the sees because in the new discretion they could exempt bishops from the need to take the oath. Under it they could give back to the dioceses their endowments, and they had discretion to allow new foundations of convents to nurse or teach children not yet of school age. The Catholic clergy began to co-operate with a moderate exercise of government power. In 1882 the German mission to the Holy See was restored; but there was still the Reich law of exile for clergy to be repealed. Windthorst proposed it and it was carried easily (233 : 115), but the full disability was not repealed till a law of 1890. The *Kulturkampf* was moribund.

Both sides were left with a hangover of discomfort from the past. Prussia refused to accept that Ledóchowski of Posen and Melchers of Cologne could return to their dioceses. Ledóchowski accepted a post in the Curia and eased the situation by allowing a new appointment to the see of Posen. The Pope sacrificed a stalwart warrior for the Church for the sake of peace. Yet still it was awkward in Posen. Bismarck refused a list of thirteen Polish candidates, but at last accepted a German. By January 1886 all dioceses again had bishops.

Both sides were tired of the fight. But it was easier to start than to stop a war. Freedom was given to Catholic schools, and there were fewer restrictions on the monastic orders. State examination before ordination was abolished, as was the appeal from the bishop's court to the State court. The right to found new monasteries was made freer. The Germans considered abolishing the ban on Jesuits but realized that politically they could not get it through, and Rome accepted that that was true. (The Jesuits were not readmitted to Germany for another thirty years, in 1917.) The German liberals accused Bismarck of going, in spite of everything, to Canossa. Windthorst, whose stature and happiness hung upon his fight for liberty and his David-versus-Goliath sling against Bismarck, now found that most of the battle was won, Rome had conceded what he did not want them to; he was an unhappy man, Bismarck purred.

In 1886 Bismarck used the Pope as an international mediator in a quarrel between Germany and Spain over the Caroline Islands in the Pacific. In return the Pope gave Bismarck a medal, the first ever given to a Protestant. It had on one side a portrait of the Pope between Germany and Spain; and on the other the inscription in Latin, 'arbiter of the world'. The inscription did not correspond to the realities of the pope's position in the world, and was a sign how ancient ceremonials still affected what was done in modern political circumstances.

The German State retained State inspection of religious education; compulsory civil marriage; and influence over Church appointments (the right to object, which later the State rarely exercised). But Bismarck failed in his main objective—to crush the Centre Party and make the Roman Catholic Church in Germany what he regarded as 'truly German'. On the contrary, the *Kulturkampf* did for German Catholicism what Napoleon did for French Catholicism—it made them more Roman. Polish resistance to German domination was widened into Catholic resistance to Protestant domination, and for that reason the more Roman. In the Polish provinces the hand of the State was still heavy upon the Church, but now for political rather than religious reasons.

The long-drawn affair proved the quality of Pope Leo XIII as a peace-making diplomat. Without drama and without haste, he used quiet, unostentatious negotiators and, without conceding anything that he regarded as essential, was willing to grant what the Germans on the spot, bishops or leaders of the Centre Party, were not prepared to allow. Pius IX, under whom the quarrel had begun and who helped to start it, could not have achieved peace in this way. But then Leo XIII acted in part under an illusion from which Pius IX could never suffer—that if he achieved peace with Germany, now the mightiest power in Europe, it could help him to get back his Papal States from the Italians.

THE *KULTURKAMPF* IN SWITZERLAND

In several other German States apart from Prussia, similar laws were passed but with less quarrel, and administered with more moderation. The Protestant States had a tradition that the State ought to have a say in Church affairs. Catholic States with a long Josephist tradition, like Bavaria, were familiar with several of the powers that Bismarck took for the Prussian government. Therefore the controversy was never so bitter. And in some States, Württemberg for example, the moderation of both sides maintained peace throughout the age. The Prussian settlement affected Bavaria and Baden, where the fight was settled along Prussian lines. In Hessen there was long delay because, when Bishop Ketteler of Mainz died in 1877, it proved so difficult to find agreement with the State on a successor that the see was vacant for nine years.

In Switzerland it was as bitter as in Prussia. There the Sonderbund War and its aftermath (see p. 44) left a sour heritage between Catholics and Protestants. Then came the Syllabus, the Vatican Council, the excommunication of Döllinger, and the formation of the Old Catholic Church. Switzerland was the one country outside Germany where the Old Catholic Church took stable root. Its bishop was Eduard Herzog, formerly Catholic professor of theology at Lucerne. This was not only a movement of Catholic intellectuals who could not take the Vatican decrees, for in certain cantons whole congregations followed their priests into the Old Catholic Church. The political aspect of the conflict was not the racial difference, as with Polish Prussia, but a constitutional fight. To the Catholics it was vital that Switzerland should be a confederation of separate cantons, with minimal powers to the central government. The Protestants wanted efficiency, control from the Centre, fewer monasteries, and better education everywhere especially in the Catholic cantons. They wanted to make the central government more powerful over the minority cantons.

The conflict was at its worst in French Switzerland. Bishop Lachat of Basle-Solothurn was ejected from his diocese and forced to live elsewhere in Switzerland. Bishop Mermillod was by name bishop of Hebron *in partibus infidelium* but was actually bishop in Geneva. There in 1873 Pius IX provokingly made him apostolic vicar. Mermillod was ejected from Switzerland and tried to run his charge from across the French border. Along the Jura there was a war of congregations. Priests came quietly from across the French frontier to celebrate mass.

All this left a long inheritance in the politics of Switzerland, even into the middle twentieth century. But both sides quickly tired. Protestant canton governments realized that they could not win and remembered that they had a principle of toleration. Leo XIII was prepared to sacrifice a little face for the sake of restoring good feeling in Switzerland. After 1878 the priests in the Jura were no longer troubled, and five years later the Pope consented to withdraw the apostolic vicariate in return for the face-saving appointment of Mermillod as bishop of Lausanne-Geneva though with his see in the Catholic town of Fribourg. The Pope had more difficulty throwing aside Bishop Lachat of Basle-Solothurn for the sake of peace when the cantons of the diocese of Basle-Solothurn refused to have him back.

Eventually he was persuaded to resign and to become apostolic administrator in the diocese of Ticino in Italian-speaking Switzerland. As in Germany, the Pope sacrificed a warrior for the sake of peace.

In both Germany and Switzerland, as later in France, the *Kulturkampf* was the encounter of a more militant Catholicism with a more militant Protestantism. Catholicism was more militant because it felt itself under threat, because in the worst-affected States it was a minority, and because events in Rome produced what never before existed, the mentality of the 'prisoner in the Vatican'. Protestantism was more militant because it was more confident of social and political power, and because the pope seemed still to stand for lost causes and obscurantism. Pope Leo XIII was more moderate in diplomacy than his predecessor, but he still referred to the Syllabus of Errors with approval. And both sides were more militant for two external reasons: first, the movement of populations which mixed Catholics with Protestants as never before, a familiar example being the emigration of so many of the Irish into England (in the long run these emigrations would bring more understanding but in the short run they produced the friction of unfamiliarity); and secondly, because the coming of a widely read press made people aware of what was said, of threats that were uttered or designs that were planned by the other side, as never before.

THE *KULTURKAMPF* IN FRANCE

The twenty years of the Emperor Louis Napoleon constituted something of a honeymoon between government and Church; too affectionate a honeymoon for the comfort of the Church in the future when the emperor fell. It was true that after 1860, when the pope lost most of his possessions, ultramontane Catholics never trusted the emperor again. The State grant of money to the Church (in compensation, of course, for money seized in the French Revolution) rose steadily. Monks and nuns also rose in numbers, as did ordinations. By the fall of Louis Napoleon there were 10,000 more priests in France than when he gained power. Religious education was compulsory in the State secondary schools but meanwhile the number of denominational Catholic schools rose rapidly. The State continued to maintain civil marriage with no divorce.

The anticlericals were not alone in resenting this alliance of emperor and bishops. Liberal Catholics were uneasy at the advertisement of a marriage between the Catholic Church and the bourgeois well-to-do. To them the Church was better based if it rested itself on the right of humanity to liberty, rather than hang upon the favour of a government. But the liberal Catholics, despite the stature of such leaders as Montalembert, were a little group of intellectuals, who hardly touched the mass of the lower clergy. They had to endure constant scorn from Veuillot in the *Univers*. It could not help them to be aware that Pope Pius IX approved of Veuillot and his point of view.

In 1870 the emperor was defeated at the battle of Sedan and his government fell. The communards in Paris and the massacres made new France, by reaction, look as Catholic and conservative as the old empire. What the winners remembered was the shooting of a good and great prelate, Archbishop Darboy. The reaction went far. The national assembly elected in 1871 was two-thirds royalist and Catholic. It expressed, sometimes in strange forms, the penitence of a Catholic nation for the moral weakness, or worse, which they supposed had led to their defeat in war.

The symbol of this penitence was to be the building of a great church on the hill of Montmartre. This was where the communards first broke into rebellion and for centuries an abbey had stood on the hill. After the shocking deaths and massacre, the idea was to 'turn away from their city the effects of divine anger'. The promoters wanted it dedicated to the Sacred Heart. In July 1873, when the mind of France was still shattered by what had happened, they took a bill to Parliament and had the plan approved by a large majority. They selected an architect, had trouble with the foundations, collected money—but by the time the foundation stone was laid in 1875 doubts began to creep in and the mood of France was changing. There began to be violent attacks in the radical press—Paris, the capital of free-thinking in the world, to be dishonoured by so reactionary a building! Two attempts were made in Parliament to repeal the consent given in 1873.

For only a short time, therefore, this Catholic and would-be royalist republic was the hope of Pius IX. France had maintained his temporal power, he believed France should restore it. But restoration by the French would mean war between France and Italy; no French government would be so foolish as to fight a war for that cause alone.

They would give the Holy See what diplomatic protection they could, but if ever there were talk of restoration, they would pretend not to hear. *Univers* called for a crusade. Archbishops and bishops of France appealed for action. No such action was practicable or sensible. And meanwhile royalist, Catholic France lost ground to republican, anticlerical France. The Catholic Church was linked with the political right, and as the right wing in politics failed, so the power of the French Church to help the pope failed.

A symbol of the change was the centenary of Voltaire's death in 1878. Voltaire had done good to the Church but the Church had not liked the abrasive way he did it, and he was most famous for 'Écrasez l'infâme!' a motto understood in legend to mean 'Smash Christianity'.

Bishop Dupanloup was still at Orleans, and still the most celebrated bishop of France. He was considered to succeed the murdered Darboy at the see of Paris; Thiers wanted him, but it would not have done, Rome could hardly approve, the clergy were believed not to want so political a bishop, and Dupanloup himself did not want it. They thought of Lavigerie of Algiers, but were afraid the army would resent him, so finally offered it to Guibert of Tours who was old and gentle; when he declined they made him accept by telling him he would be thought cowardly and would be assumed to have refused because Parisians usually murder their archbishops.[11]

Dupanloup made an eloquent protest against any celebration of Voltaire. He succeeded in preventing the feast from being backed by government and so official (it was the last victory he won before his death). But Voltaire had become for anti-Catholics a symbol like Giordano Bruno for the Italians. Victor Hugo presided at a glorification in the Gaiety Theatre in Paris which was more a demonstration for the moment than gratitude for 100 years earlier. Victor Hugo himself had become an anti-Catholic symbol and when he died his funeral was more eloquent as an anti-religious demonstration than as an act of thanksgiving for his stature.

From 1879 the French presidency, and the majority in both the Chambers, were in the hands of the republicans. Jules Grévy was the first French head of State, since Napoleon smashed the Directory, to be anticlerical, to hate both kings and priests. He was a good husband, but a cold, unimaginative lawyer who helped to make the Third

---

[11] J. Paguelle de Follenay, *La Vie du Cardinal Guibert* (2 vols.; Paris, 1896), ii. 516.

French Republic the most prosaic constitution yet seen. The new cabinet had another anticlerical—indeed a convinced positivist with a faith in human progress—at the key ministry for the Church, that of education: Jules Ferry, free-thinker to his fingertips. He believed that the young of France must be drawn away from the darkening influence of the clergy and brought to light by state schools. That would be no small work since so many of the schools were run by Catholic religious orders. He brought in a bill to make it illegal for any member of a religious order to teach in a school if the order had not government approval. At that moment there were some 500 convents and 20,000 monks and nuns who were teaching French children and had no approval from the State. Ferry said that he would close all the Jesuit houses, because they must prise the soul of French youth from the Jesuits who were essentially alien to France.[12] The press of the French right called Ferry a Nero. His clause failed in the upper house.

But then government could act by decree because the religious houses were not 'authorized' and it could apply outmoded laws, those of the revolution of 1790 and 1792. Many lawyers believed these laws obsolete and the decrees illegal. The monks and nuns decided not to ask for authorization, so in June 1880 the police occupied the Jesuit house in Paris and expelled the fathers; and the same happened in thirty-one other places. The Jesuits locked the doors so that the police broke in, but then they went peacefully. In the Paris house several Parliamentarians of the right went to the house to be expelled with the fathers, and in the street outside there were cries of 'Down with the Republic!'

Pope Leo XIII, committed by his office and by his predicament to the lines of his predecessor, talked of the wickedness of parts of modern civilization. But from time to time he made speeches that sounded a different note. An encyclical, *Immortale Dei*, of 1885 accepted that governments might rightly, to avoid worse evils, tolerate religions that were not Catholic. Dupanloup had said this in his interpretation of the Syllabus, but it was new that a pope should say it formally. It sounded still a grudging concession; for the encyclical condemned as absurd the doctrine that human beings are free to think as they like on any subject, and said that liberty of thought and publishing is the cause of many ills in society. Yet Leo accepted that

---

[12] Cf. M. Reclus, *Jules Ferry* (Paris, 1947), 151 ff., for a remarkable series of speeches on the bill.

sometimes the people may have a share in government, that there are times when they must be given a share. He might have seen it as a duty to say that the Syllabus was a rule that must be obeyed, but in fact he gently said the opposite: 'My eyes are not blind to the spirit of the age. I do not reject the progress of our age where it is certainly useful. Only I want politics and society to move more sanely than they do and to be based upon a strong foundation which does not hurt the people's freedom.'

Three years later an encyclical, *Libertas*, took the line of the Syllabus in blaming toleration as producing evils in modern society, and declared that States had the duty to limit freedom of opinion.[13] But it asked for patience and gentleness with human weakness. It said that it was untrue that the Church looked ill upon modern forms of constitution in politics, and that it repudiated the discoveries of the genius of contemporaries. It accepted that the citizens of a country might work by constitutional means to change the frame of the constitution.

Hence he recognized that the Church could work with all sorts of constitutions, and that more democratic constitutions had advantages of a moral kind. The idea of popular sovereignty was said to be wrong because all power comes from above. But the Pope allowed that in some cases a head of state might be elected—it was necessary to allow this because of the American constitution.

Therefore it became possible for the Pope to think that the French were not to be condemned because they were democrats and republicans. This was far more difficult for the old ultramontanes, the successors of Veuillot, to accept. Catholic France was tied to monarchy. If a French priest said he was a republican he was looked upon as a traitor to his priesthood. Leo XIII would have preferred monarchy in France but he was willing to face facts. France still contained the largest body of Catholics, at least nominal Catholics, in Europe. If the cause of the king were lost in France, then religious people ought not to tie their faith to that cause.

This was difficult for any pope. During the 1880s the French government passed a series of anticlerical laws. In 1880 Ferry became Prime Minister and applied the decree to other non-authorized houses besides the Jesuits. Strange scenes were enacted across France, the closing of houses in the midst of the people's disapproval. Near

---

[13] *Immortale Dei*, ASS 18 (1 Nov. 1885), 161–80; *Libertas*, ASS 20 (20 June 1888), 593–613.

Tarascon it took a battalion of infantry, guns, and cavalry to get rid of thirty-seven Premonstratensian monks. Some 5,000 monks were expelled. The nuns were not affected, they were too valuable as primary school teachers. More than a third of teachers were members of religious orders; in girls' schools nuns were a considerable majority. The illiteracy rate of women was scandalous for the age and nation: a quarter of all new wives signed the marriage register with a cross. To get rid of nuns the State needed to found an entire system of primary education: which it began to do.

Pius IX would have thundered out the unchanging truths of the Catholic religion, and its eternal claims. Leo XIII stayed silent in the face of this French *Kulturkampf*, and as the republican government varied in its anticlericalism, it soon allowed monks other than the Jesuits to return to their houses. It did not pass a law to ban monks or nuns from teaching in the State schools until six years later, and then it was not done too sharply: boys' schools were given five years to remove the religious among the teachers; girls' schools were not to employ any as new members of the staff.

The Bourbon pretender to the French throne, the Count de Chambord, died in 1883. From the following year Leo XIII embarked upon an endeavour, first to free French Catholics from the charge that they were disloyal to the government of France, and then, as time passed, to persuade them to take a positive attitude to the French republic. This policy was sane in theory, but impossible to make successful.

The pope might be infallible and have a plenitude of power over the Church; that did not mean that he was the dictator of the Church as Protestants liked to imagine. The new policy, of trying to reconcile the French Church to the French republic, meant causing offence to the successors of Veuillot, and the public discouragement of the making of a French Catholic political party. A fine French officer, Count Albert de Mun, wanted to form such a party. It would show the Revolution as the enemy of the Church and repeal anticlerical legislation. De Mun's party would have accepted that it was right to work within the constitution of the republic—as Germany already had its Centre Party and Belgium its Catholic party. But in France royalist Catholics were totally opposed to de Mun's party and Pope Leo asked him to desist.

In 1889 a near *coup d'état* against the French republic by General Boulanger, with sympathy from the Catholic right, failed. It revived the forces of anticlericalism and postponed for three years the Pope's desire to reconcile himself and the Church with the French republic.

Meanwhile some French royalists realized that the republic had come to stay, that the people no longer cared about the king, and that it was better to make terms. Being outside France and having other aims than French aims, Pope Leo saw this more clearly than most of the French Catholics. He had a new Secretary of State, Rampolla, a Sicilian of old lineage, and a cultivated man.[14]

Austrian reports gave an unfriendly portrait of Rampolla as a dim mind. But they may not be reliable because they resented his swing of papal policy from friendship with Austria to (attempted) friendship with France. While nuncio in Spain Rampolla faced passionate resistance from extreme Spanish Catholics for his willingness to work with the Spanish regime. His sympathies lay wholly with the policy of making terms with the French republic. It is probable that until Leo XIII's last years and extreme old age, the Pope rather than the Secretary of State was the maker of policy, but no one else in the Curia was so influential under Pope Leo XIII.

The Pope had an imprudent ally in Cardinal Lavigerie, the archbishop of Algiers. French colonial policy and missions were closer than Church and State at home. Lavigerie was accustomed to the backing of the State for his missionary and colonial ventures. He was a great missionary leader with a big reputation not only among Catholics; a man of stature who knew it, and was always in command of himself. He provoked scandal to the monarchists by causing Catholic children of Algiers to greet the French admiral by singing the Marseillaise, which Catholics still thought a revolutionary hymn that in conscience ought not to be sung. All national anthems are militant ('frustrate their knavish tricks') but this was the most militant of all. It was written by a soldier at Strasbourg fighting to defend the French Revolution against invasion from Germany, and its words are full of fierce phrases, the 'bloody standards of tyranny', the soldiers who come to 'strangle our sons and friends' . . . 'vile despots fighting to become the masters of our destinies . . . Tremble you tyrants.' The French Revolution made it the national anthem but since it was

---

[14] After Franchi's sudden death Leo chose Franchi's friend Nina, but they did not get on and he lasted only a few months; then the Pope chose Jacobini (1880–7) who had been nuncio in Vienna. As Secretary of State he maintained the old friendship with Austria and was helpful about the German *Kulturkampf*. When he died there was an interregnum because the Pope could not decide what do to; eventually Rampolla was brought back from Madrid.

directed against armies fighting to restore the king, no royalist liked it, and after the Battle of Waterloo it was no longer the national anthem; the republicans of 1879 restored it to that honour. That an archbishop should have it sung shocked the right.

Lavigerie caused more scandal when at a banquet for military and naval officers in Algiers he received the guests to the sound of the Marseillaise played by the band of his missionary order, the White Fathers. He proposed the health of the navy, and in his toast said that it was time for all Catholics to accept the constitution which most of the French people wanted; and implied that for this proposal he had the backing of the pope. The naval officers sat silent. Pope Leo approved the sentiment of the speech but doubted the Marseillaise. It became the most famous toast in history. For three weeks the press covered this toast and its consequences. Moderate Catholics were pleased with Lavigerie, the ultramontanes regarded him as a blunderer or a traitor ('an unconditional surrender to Freemasonry'), and with them he lost his repute. In the summer he came to Paris and he who once was greeted by Parisian society with veneration was now received coldly.

For the French republic was not only a political constitution, it was a way of life, an outlook upon the world. This outlook regarded clericalism as the enemy and passed laws to hurt the Church; not yet to abolish the Concordat or the Organic Articles, the 'establishment' of the Church or the payment of clergy from State funds; but it diminished the funds, abolished prayers at the beginning of parliamentary sessions, restricted service and hospital chaplaincies, and ended scholarships for ordinands. In 1884 divorce was re-established, which was an essential act for the future of French happiness but which was thought especially shocking. In the following year the Panthéon— once a church, then a Valhalla in the French Revolution, then again a church under Quelen, then a lesser Valhalla after the Revolution of 1830, and then a church again under Louis Napoleon—became once more a non-religious shrine; but the cross that Louis Napoleon restored to the dome was left. Opinions, which in a normal democracy anyone might hold, such as the belief that Church marriages were more likely to promote the good of the family than civil marriages, were treated as though they were incitements to overthrow the republic. How was it possible for a conscientious Catholic to accept such a philosophy enshrined in a constitution? Most of the French bishops were against Pope Leo's policy of reconciliation.

Some were against him on moral principle, some because they did not want to lose wealthy Catholic supporters of their good works, most of whom were monarchists.

In January 1892 the Paris nuncio advised Pope Leo that there now existed a minority of French Catholics who were in favour of reconciliation with the republic. In February that year a papal encyclical addressed to the French, *Aux milieu des sollicitudes*,[15] tried to persuade the French Church to be less uncompromising.

Leo spoke of his love for France. He said how political institutions change with time. This was a platitude for the French who in his lifetime had seen a revolutionary general as a dictator, then a reactionary Bourbon monarch, then a semi-parliamentary system, then a revolutionary assembly, then a dictator made by plebiscite within a democracy, then a royalist sort of democracy, and then a democracy of the left. Leo thought that if all these were studied it might be decided which form of government was best for the country—but ultimately any form of government might in particular circumstances be best, the Church could condemn none. What it should condemn was anarchy. Power always came from God, even if it came by means of a revolution forced upon a society by new conditions. Popes had maintained good relations with all the succeeding governments of France during this century, and this was the wise course for all Catholics. This was not to say that the acts of an anticlerical republic should not be condemned, they took away precious religion from the people. Later in that year, in a letter to a French Cardinal Lecot, he applied the general proposition frankly: the restoration of the monarchy was hardly probable; it hurt the Church to be associated with that cause; it was not right to use religion to create opposition to the powers that be.

This *ralliement* of 1890s marked a stage in papal history. At first sight it was in continuity with the attitude of Gregory XVI sixty years before, when he told the Poles that it was wrong to have a revolution against an oppressive Tsar because the powers that be are ordained by God. Leo was saying, in effect, that the French government was oppressive, but it was wrong to try to overthrow it, therefore Catholics must work within it and try to change what it did. Yet this was a new stage. This French republic was anticlerical and committed to propositions which the Syllabus of Errors condemned. The Pope now said that in certain circumstances Catholics ought to rally

<hr/>

[15] *ASS* 24 (1891–2), 519–29.

to a democracy. Catholics should join with all good men and true to do what they could for the State by constitutional methods, which should not include the forming of a Catholic political party.

What the Pope imagined was a broad conservative party, Catholics on its right moderate republicans on its left, allied to resist anticlerical intolerance by extreme republicans. The Pope had no idea that a time might come when Catholics could be more radical than moderate republicans. If he had guessed he would not have approved any more than his successor, who hated Catholic radicalism. Despite his opening of their minds to democracy and to labour movements, Leo XIII still thought of the Catholic people as the anchor of a conservative Europe. If liberty was good for the Church in the United States, why should it not be good for the Church in France?

This overturning of papal thinking was difficult for French Catholics to accept. They had fought vehemently for everything that Pope Pius IX proclaimed. Some suffered for that cause. They were monarchists, almost all, and their religion was entangled with a politics that could never accept the anticlerical republic. Republicans could not believe in a rallying of Catholics to the republic, they thought that any male who went to church must be in political reaction. Catholics were papalists, almost all, and had a high doctrine of papal authority. But soon they distinguished between the pope's authority in faith and morals, which commanded their obedience, and his authority in politics which commanded their respect but which could be discussed.

French Catholics were not alone in thus repudiating the right of the pope to interfere in the politics of their country, even when those politics touched ecclesiastical questions. Belgian and German Catholics, each in their own political parties, disliked it when Rome told them how to play the politics of their country and saw no necessity to obey.

The French bishops were embarrassed. If they resisted the pope they would damage the Church. If they came out in favour of the pope they might be repudiated in their dioceses. Their money for every sort of church work came from the upper classes, who were monarchists. A few bishops said that the encyclical only meant that Catholics were not to break out in rebellion—which was not Leo's meaning. His effort at reconciliation with a democracy did not succeed because his clergy and laity took their hats off to what he said but were no more reconciled to the republic than before.

The bishops were not helped by the anticlerical radicals. It was necessary to the power and propaganda of the French left to have the clergy as scapegoats. They did all that was possible to make the *ralliement* come to nothing. They liked to have intransigent clergy, whom they could represent as the enemy. From the viewpoint of votes at elections, the principal effect of the Pope's intervention was to divide the party of the right.

In the country which led the world in its ultramontane spirit, the pope's authority did not run so far as everyone pretended or, if they were Protestants, imagined. In a Church where disobedience to the pope was seen as almost equal to disobedience to Christ, clergy and people could still remain deaf to what Rome said and uncooperative in what Rome planned. The Pope had a resounding success when Albert de Mun rallied to his cause. But the best of the French were sad; they stood for old monarchy, legitimism, a Catholic State, the lost union of throne and altar. And now even the pope made them realize that they stood for a past that had vanished, never to return.

In March 1892 a Jesuit at the church of Saint-Merry in Paris said that the French Revolution, drunk with blood, invented socialism and all its errors. He was barracked from the pews. The following week the crowd rushed the pulpit and threw out the speaker. A few days later the two parties, Catholic and radical, rioted against one another, with rival hymns, in the church of Saint-Joseph. These were the social conditions which made the *ralliement* a failure in the France of that moment.

The *ralliement* had a force far beyond France. The Pope offered Catholics everywhere, by implication, the chance of assenting to that form of political arrangement which Western Europe and America were coming to think the most moral of constitutions because it safeguarded individual liberty and human rights. It did not compel Catholics to stop being monarchists, or legitimists, or believers in the old encyclicals which condemned toleration. But, like the Belgian Catholic party and the German Centre Party, it was another step on the road towards the Catholic political parties within the democracies of the twentieth century.

Even in France, the idea was put before the people that it was possible to be a republican and a good Catholic. With time, that became important to the French.

To be in a Catholic political party was already important not only to the Germans but to the Belgians and Dutch. Belgium was a Catholic country, and ultramontane. Every Belgian bishop voted for the decree of infallibility. In the year of Leo XIII's accession a general election returned a radical-liberal government which diminished Church power. The chief dispute lay in education and the provision of schools where no religion was taught. Five years later, in 1884, another general election produced a sweeping Catholic majority which remained in power for the next thirty years. Belgium was the only country in Europe where a Catholic vote along party lines produced Catholic political power at so early a date in a democratic constitution.

CONCILIATION IN ITALY?

In Italy Leo XIII was in a situation where he must disapprove of a Catholic political party. He was not happy about the German Centre Party; it is still a question whether he was right or wrong in discouraging Albert de Mun and a French Catholic party; the Belgian Catholic victory in the polls was due to Belgian Catholics and had nothing to do with Rome—or almost nothing—for the new prestige of the papacy, which was due to the protective instinct towards Pius IX but was encouraged by the outgoing diplomatic attitudes of Leo XIII, had something to do with a rising influence. If reconciliation were possible with Bismarck, and even with France, was it possible with Italy?

The worst moment came in 1887. The *Kulturkampf* in Germany was ended; the *ralliement* with France was soon to begin. A Benedictine monk of Monte Cassino, vice-archivist of the Vatican archives, the learned and godly Tosti, published at this moment a book on reconciliation between the pope and Italy, *La Conciliazione*. Tosti had stature. He went to the school at Monte Cassino when he was a boy and had early links with Rosmini and Gioberti. After the Roman Revolution of 1848 he was accused of being a friend of the revolution and of democracy, and was banished for several years from his monastery. But as a person he was revered by many who met him; a poet, wise and humane, a happy man with a sense of humour and without ambition, soaked in the Benedictine tradition of historical scholarship. Under Leo XIII his learning took him into the Vatican. For a monk of Tosti's weight and place inside the Curia to advocate conciliation suggested that the Pope contemplated an agreement with the Italian State.

The idea collapsed that summer in recriminations between Crispi the Italian minister and the Pope. The Curia objected to the plan. Tosti, who was an ornament to scholarship, to the Vatican, and to the monastic order, was forced to withdraw his book and to resign his post in the Curia. The atmosphere was more irreconcilable than before the half-attempt at reconciliation.

Two years later a North Italian bishop, Bonomelli of Cremona, writing anonymously as a liberal priest, proposed the most part of the solution that was later found. He argued that the time of sterile protest was past; that Italy could not do without Rome as a capital; that the pope could not do without a State of his own; and therefore that Italy and the Pope should agree a miniature State round the Vatican with a corridor to the sea. Bonomelli believed that temporal power was a weakness to the authority of the Church and a discredit to religion, and did not want even a small Papal State. He included the idea only because he saw no practical possibility of commending any solution that did not contain this provision. The proposal was put upon the Index of Prohibited Books and Bishop Bonomelli at once submitted.[16]

The same year of 1889 was the year of the erection of a statue of Giordano Bruno in the Campo dei Fiori in Rome. Bruno was a Dominican priest and philosopher of the Italian Renaissance who fled from inquiries into his heresies which contained, amid eccentricity of language, a Neoplatonic interpretation of Christianity. Invited to Venice he was seized and sent to Rome, refused to recant, and was burnt. In the war between Italy and the pope, Bruno came to be the hero of the radical left. In the municipality of Rome the question whether or not to put up a statue to Bruno became an issue which conditioned the city elections (where Catholics were allowed by the pope to vote). The Catholic-controlled municipality threw out the proposal; whereupon the national government, under Crispi, inter-vened to order a new municipal election and win it for the radicals with the votes of government employees. The statue was unveiled on the day after Whit Sunday 1889 before an audience of 6,000 headed by leading atheists of Europe. It was a surprising apotheosis for Bruno. Its intention was not so much to honour a philosopher of the Renaissance as to dishonour a modern pope by means of the history of his distant predecessors.

[16] Cf. *DBI* s.v. Bonomelli; *Rassegna Nazionale*, Mar. 1889; Index and submission, Apr. 1889: *ASS* 21 (1888–9), 561.

This was one of the three times[17] when Pope Leo XIII talked to ambassadors about the need to leave Rome. That day he expected a mob attack upon the Vatican. The foreign ambassadors stood about him ready to do what they could to repel an invasion of the palace. He felt the erection of the statue of Bruno to be a stab at his breast and was disturbed that 'his' city and 'his' people should countenance such ceremonies.

The *Memoirs* of Crispi show that this time the government were really worried that the pope might go. He wheedled out of the French ambassador to the Vatican that the French government, which was hardly on speaking terms with the Italians that year, had said that it was ready to solve 'the Roman question' if the pope gave them an excuse by fleeing from Rome. If he did so the Italian government would occupy the Vatican and fly the Italian flag from its high point. But suppose that the French meant what was threatened?

Crispi was so perturbed that he chose the most unpromising intermediary he could find, Cardinal Hohenlohe. The most extraordinary moment of this affair is that an Italian Prime Minister, with the resources of a secret service at his disposal, should choose for his agent to influence the pope the very cardinal who was the chief opponent of the pope in the Curia, a person whose advocacy of a cause could only weaken it. Evidently Crispi knew almost nothing about the people round the pope, although he lived only a few hundred yards away.

Cardinal Hohenlohe did not think that Leo would leave Rome—but 'he likes the world to be talking about him, and is subject to fits of nervous excitement . . .'—and promised to try to see him. He was twice refused an audience—'It appears,' he wrote to Crispi, no doubt with his tongue in his cheek, 'that I am mistrusted, I cannot tell why.' He wrote the Pope a letter: 'God has allowed matters to shape themselves so that the Church cannot recover the temporal power. The well-being of many souls demands that we accept the inevitable . . .' The Pope sent Monsignor Sallua to say that he was much upset by this letter and refused an audience and when the cardinal blamed the Pope the monsignor shed tears and excused his master on grounds of old age.[18]

[17] The three times were: 1881, the funeral of Pius IX; Bruno's statue, 1889; the French pilgrimage of 1891.
[18] F. Crispi, *Memoirs*, Eng. trans. by M. Prichard-Agnetti (1912–14), ii. 405–6.

FREEMASONS

Since the eighteenth century the popes condemned Freemasonry and forbade Catholics to join. It is not certain which came first, whether the Continental Freemasons were designed to be anti-Catholic and therefore popes condemned them, or whether they were not of necessity anti-Catholic (as never in England) and only became anti-Catholic because the pope condemned them. Nor is it easy to discover whether Freemasons in France, Italy, and Spain were secret societies designed to destroy the Catholic Church or whether that was a fanciful picture of them which popes adopted by tradition—for the Curia, walled up against society by the Risorgimento, was apt to conjure pictures of modern conspiracy. During the early nineteenth century there were links between the Carbonari and some groups of Freemasons. In the Italian, French, and Spanish governments of the 1880s and 1890s several leading members were Freemasons and others were given political work because they were Freemasons and could be guaranteed to be anti-Catholic. It was even more true of Latin American governments. There were moments when all the members of anticlerical Latin American cabinets were Freemasons. It is also possible that the Church, as with a political party, needed a devil to condemn, a scapegoat, to increase the solidarity of supporters. The importance of this is at present beyond the reach of accurate historical enquiry. But Pope Leo's condemnations of Freemasonry were cast in fierce phrases for one who had abandoned the less courtly language of Pius IX. They were the kingdom of Satan, and he said so in no uncertain terms.[19]

Catholics who became Freemasons were excommunicated. A few unscrupulous French, Italians, or Latin Americans built up legends to appal the public about Freemasons as in a former age they built up legends to appal the public about Jews. A lady was invented named Diana Vaughan who was said to have become an adherent of the cult of Satan and understood all its secrets, and then was converted to Catholicism and had to flee into hiding for otherwise she would be murdered. The hoax was eventually confessed but not till many respectable Catholics, and more ignorant Catholics, had believed it.

[19] Brief *Praeclara*, 20 June 1894, *ASS* 26 (1893–4), 705–17, the epistle on his jubilee as a bishop, paragraphs on the *secta massonica*.

The historical effects of all this were, first, to maintain Catholic belligerency against governments, already developed by the various forms of *Kulturkampf*, and to maintain the separation between Catholics and general society which was so marked a feature of the reign of Pius IX; secondly to encourage a certain sickness within Catholic society of which the affair of Diana Vaughan was a symptom; and thirdly to foster that sense of international community which was to be the strength of the Church of the twentieth century.

Canadian and American Freemasonry was more like the English form, an unpolitical series of brotherly clubs. The Canadian and American Churches were uneasy at the papal language.

Pope Leo's language was more urbane towards Italy and its rulers than the speeches of the old Pius IX. But the matter of the speeches was as uncompromising. As he grew older it became less capable of achieving a sensible end except to prove that the pope was not the private chaplain of Italy. The encyclical to celebrate his eightieth year in October 1890 protested against nearly everything. In 1891 French pilgrims cried 'Viva il Papa Re!', 'Long live the King-Pope!', at the tomb of King Victor Emmanuel in the Pantheon, and French youths scrawled it on the tomb; this provoked the mob, there was violence against pilgrims and a march on the Vatican; pilgrims tried to leave Rome hurriedly and were threatened at the railway station. The Pope called the Catholics of Italy to fight against the Freemasons and the sects, and this speech let loose a storm against him and roused more denunciations of the Law of Guarantees. In 1893 he appealed to the Italian nation and made the Freemasons responsible for the war against religion. In 1894 he contrasted the corruption of Italy and its economic disaster with the happier times when popes ruled. The orators of the left used equal language against the pope.

Some historians regarded the diplomat pope as a diplomatic disaster. Yet no one can think this without qualification of a pope who at whatever cost to honour settled the *Kulturkampf* in Germany and Switzerland. And the Secretary of State during all the later years of Leo XIII, Rampolla, believed in the policy of war with the Italian governments which made so many onslaughts on the old rights of the Church. He thought that the papacy had nothing to lose, and everything to gain, if it was seen by the international community to be at loggerheads with the Italian government.

The bad side of the policy was its effect upon Italy and its parliamentary constitution; it prevented many Italians from accepting the political situation. Yet Catholic Italy slowly reconciled itself to the new Italy. They went to church, heard mass, made their confessions, sought the counsel of their priest, and brought up their sons and daughters as Catholics; but more, they got themselves elected to municipal governments where they co-operated with liberals; they voted unostentatiously in elections and if there were not a candidate whom they could in conscience approve, they chose him whom they thought the least bad; they tried to avoid the fanatics on both sides, refrained from writing pamphlets, and disliked the pamphlets that extremists wrote; they were persuaded that this quarrel of Church and State, from which they suffered, but not to excess, could not go on for ever and that they would work patiently to heal it.

In Italy there were several attempts to found a reformed Catholic Church. These communities were always small; always likely to look to Protestants for help and for money; never lasting long; getting European publicity for a moment and then sliding slowly into nothing much except a link with some historic Protestant Church such as the Waldensians.

The wisest of the Italian rebel-leaders was Count Enrico Campello. He was a priest who organized night schools in the city of Rome and by 1868 was a canon of St Peter's. He was a disciple of Rosmini, looked towards liberal Catholicism, and disliked what happened at the Vatican Council. Like the early Rosmini he had a vision of a democratic hierarchy, bishops, and even pope elected, as in early times, by the clergy and people of their diocese. His work was condemned. But he professed to continue a Catholic of the tradition of Rosmini and Gioberti. In 1881 he announced his separation from the clergy of Rome, worked in Rome towards an Italian national Catholic Church, and started a daily newspaper, *Il Labaro*, 'the Banner' of Catholic reform. He accepted the hierarchy but not papal supremacy, wanted the liturgy in the vernacular, and leave for clergy to marry. Above his chapel in Rome was the national flag of Italy. He appealed to Catholics who believed in the new Italy. He was aided by Archbishop Benson of Canterbury. His excommunication won him notice and sympathy. In 1884 he and his group adhered to the Old Catholic Church. He won support in the country around Spoleto and Terni and soon had a group in San Remo where the newspaper *Labaro* was now published and where Campello was consecrated a bishop. The letters of the last few years of his life show a decaying man, in despair about his work, and praying God that He would close his eyes before he could see the catastrophe coming for the Reform. In December 1902, after a retreat of thirty days in Rome, he abjured, declared his contrition for the harm that he had done to the Catholic Church, and died early in 1903.[20] The movement survived him by only four years.

Later examples of such movements in Poland and Czechoslovakia proved that these attempts at Reformed Catholicism could not find stable ground (except in links with Protestantism) unless they linked with the Old Catholic Church, which itself had wider bonds with the Anglican Communion and outside Europe, but which was Germanic or Dutch in its attitudes and did not attract the Latin minds of French or Italian reformers.

SOCIALISM AND THE WORKERS' MOVEMENT

Most male Catholics in the world earned their living as farmers or the employees of farmers. The Church was, in majority, a peasant Church; with its strength in Italy and Spain, in the French countryside especially in Brittany, the Irish villages, the Tyrol, the Hungarian latifundia, the Polish workers on great estates in Russia, Prussia, and northern Austro-Hungary, and the remote Latin American ranches. But this was changing. A multitudinous Italian immigration to the United States was in progress. The peasant who left a smallholding in southern Italy usually ended in a big American city. A big Irish emigration was still in progress, mainly to Britain, the United States, or Australia; and the son of the Irish peasant was a navvy or industrial worker in London, Liverpool, Birmingham, Sydney, or Boston Massachusetts.

Certain parts of Europe which were quick to foster industry because of favourable natural resources were in Catholic areas. These were not many: the big cities of southern central Europe from Munich and Vienna to North Italy (Turin and Milan); the French cities, especially Lyons and Bordeaux, and all the north of France; a few Spanish cities such as Barcelona and Bilbao; Belgium and the Rhineland near it, from Cologne to Mainz; and in areas of Upper Silesia where, though the State was German, many of the people were Poles.

[20] For Campello see *DBI* s.v.; and A. Robertson, *Count Campello and Catholic Reform in Italy* (London, 1891).

Both Protestant and Catholic Churches discovered that the move from country to city, and life in a big city, meant loss of members. Industrialized Barcelona quickly achieved a reputation for militant anticlericalism. In such a place efforts to develop Catholic trade unions were weak. There appeared to be solid Catholic support within one of the large industrial areas of Europe: Belgium during the nineteenth century remained a deeply Catholic country, with its neighbours in the northern Rhineland round Cologne. The important social thinking of Catholics came from this area or from the North Italian cities.

Not only in so glaring an instance as Barcelona, but in the ring of industrial cities in Belgium, northern France, and northern Rhineland, the worker escaped the Catholic net. He had a feeling that the Church was on the side of conservatives and against his interest in wages and advancement. Money, effort, and self-sacrifice, and original social thinking, was poured into these areas by Church leaders of quality; and still the industrial workers deserted in droves and were indifferent if not hostile.

This caused a predicament for Christian trade unions. They were at their best in the Rhineland. Nowhere in Europe had they more than a minority of the workers in their industry, though in Belgium and Holland it rose to be a large minority. Whether they were a small minority or sizable, they were as much the competitor as the ally of the larger non-denominational trade union. What mattered to the worker was the muscle of a union, not its philosophical principles; the worker did not need to be a Marxist to distrust a Christian trade union which he saw only as dividing the power of his workforce. In Spain Christian trade-unionists were called by their secular counterparts 'the yellows', and were regarded by them as an organization for blacklegs. Nevertheless, the small groups of Christian trade unions delayed the de-Christianization of the worker, and proved that it was possible to be both a worker in a modern industry and a worshipper.

The better practice of medicine meant more people. This led to high morale in all Churches of the nineteenth century. There were more Catholics, more Protestants. Churchmen might feel under attack from anticlericals or scientific critics, but they saw their denomination grow: there were more adherents, more churches built, more schools and more hospitals. The Catholic Church did not see all the old religious orders expand. But small new orders went on flowering, and the number of the professed religious, male and female, grew dramatically.

More people in churches did not mean that the churches housed a larger proportion of the population. It was not at first clear, but during the last decade of the nineteenth century enquirers realized that though the Churches grew, the number of people grew faster. More people escaped from the practice of Christian worship. It came to be realized that the larger the city, the smaller the percentage of people to be found in its churches (of every denomination) on a Sunday. A part of the cause was diagnosed as the separation of the working person from an old milieu. Parents lived in the country, where the middle class and organized charity were present, and where the custom of the village bound behaviour. The son and daughter lived in an area of bad housing where no one but the poor lived and where no customs bound anyone's behaviour, but only the force of the police.

The care of the Churches did not derive only from fear of losing members. Their historic axioms, derived from the Bible, entailed care for the poor. Most Catholics (and Protestants) saw no need to change their attitude towards charity, they would encourage almsgiving, seek out those in need, provide free education and nursing. This historic mode of help to the poor continued all through the nineteenth century and beyond.

But in this world of cities some churchmen accepted the doctrine of some political thinkers, that the structure of society kept the people poor when the resources of society were sufficient for them. If that were true it became a duty to seek to change the structure of society, not by paying out alms but by taxation for the benefit of the poor. In England of 1848, under threat from a Chartist revolution, a tiny handful of Anglican theologians were bold enough to take the label 'Christian socialist'. They were not socialist as the Socialists understood their programme, but it was a symbol to be willing to adopt the name. Such an appellation was impossible for Catholics at that date. Pius IX tried to make it impossible for any Catholic to be a socialist; he associated socialism with the idea of class warfare, the destruction of the rights of property, and the undermining of the rights of the family.

By 1882 an Italian Socialist party, weak but not silent, was in being. Pope Leo XIII saw no reason to withdraw the condemnation of socialism and much reason to maintain it. The French Socialist party, when at last it won seats in the Chamber, was vehemently anticlerical, as was the German Social Democratic party. Protestant pastors who joined the Social Democrats in Germany were excluded by their Churches from the ministry. The only significant Christian Socialist party in Protestant Germany, that of Adolf Stoecker, was wrecked by its anti-Semitism. Just possibly, if Lamennais had not left the Church in 1834–5, he could have created the small beginnings of a Catholic socialism. His departure, and move into non-Christian socialism, was another sign that Church and socialists could not make a treaty. If Lamennais had not been ejected for his liberalism, he would have been ejected for his socialism.

In revolutionary France of April 1849, a banquet was held of 'socialist priests'; thirty-three of them, three in cassocks and the rest dressed as laymen. Six hundred working men joined the festivity, and toasted Jesus of Nazareth, father of socialism. Almost all those priests disappeared into exile or silence under the dictatorship of Louis Napoleon. Nearly all Europe, outside quite a number of Englishmen, a few Austrians, and fewer Germans, was persuaded, during the third quarter of the nineteenth century, that Christianity and Socialism were incompatible.

Catholic bishops cared about the exploitation of the poor by industry. The more we know of their pastoral charges, the more impressive their utterances become. But most of them did not believe that you cure the state of society by laws. They were sure that promises of Utopia round the corner, upon the abolition of property or of capitalism, or the establishment of a minimum wage, were false. They loathed the doctrine of class warfare. They still believed that the troubles of society were due not to structure but to greed; and that only faith could bring moral right into society. They took the view— a relatively new view in Christian history—that it was the duty of the clergy, as pastors of flocks, not to be political partisans; but they usually applied this restriction to those who were politically active for socialists or liberals and applied it more gently, or refrained from applying it, to those who were politically active for monarchists or conservatives.

Yet by 1887 only the blind could not see that the legitimist, paternalist, upper-class world was going or gone; and that in the coming world was a struggle between the bourgeoisie and the muscle of the worker.

Something was due, via the new systems of national education, to articulate laymen and laywomen in the pews. Ecclesiastical power they had none; no one could call the centralized Church a democ-racy. But by the last quarter of the century the idea that the sole province of the Catholic laity, as Monsignor George Talbot once said, was to hunt, to shoot, and to entertain,[21] was still held by the backward but had become absurd because now the laity knew more and cared more about the worship and practices of the Church. They were able to hold international meetings.

Pope Leo XIII was not content with busy Catholic laymen stand-ing on platforms and telling the bishops what the Church ought to do. Without approaching the dictum of Monsignor Talbot, he had a hierarchical idea of the Church, with authority moving from the top downwards, which was common Catholic doctrine.

KETTELER

In Germany the name of one bishop came to be the symbol of new attitudes towards the worker: that of Wilhelm Emmanuel Freiherr von Ketteler. He studied law at the university where he lost the tip of his nose in a duel. He showed no signs of being an ordinand. He became a Westphalian lawyer and civil servant, but resigned from the civil service in protest at the behaviour of the Prussian government in the affair of the archbishop of Cologne and mixed marriages. He was ordained priest and at the constitutional assembly at Frankfurt during the Revolutions of 1848 made an extraordinary name for him-self as a Catholic of the political left; especially by preaching a sermon at the funeral of two men who were murdered in the Revolution; but also by coming out for a people's Germany as opposed to a Germany dominated by a Prussian monarchy. In the following year he became dean of the cathedral at Berlin, and the year after that was elected bishop of Mainz.

The Baden government refused to have him as archbishop of Freiburg. The Prussian government refused to have him as arch-bishop of Cologne. He himself refused the right of succession to the archbishopric of Posen. By the middle of the 1860s he was the lead-ing personality among the German bishops. He disliked the Syllabus of Errors, for he believed the Catholic Church to be the key to free-dom and that the liberty of the Church rested upon constitutional

---

[21] E. S. Purcell, *The Life of Cardinal Manning* (2 vols.; London, 1892), i. 318: 'These mat-ters they understand, but to meddle with ecclesiastical matters they have no right at all.'

liberty. After the Syllabus he tried to restore belief in the rightness of
the doctrines of toleration and a free constitution. Thereby he contributed to forming the Centre Party as the Catholic party in
Germany.

At the Vatican Council he was a strenuous member of the German
opposition to the definition of infallibility, but at once accepted the
decision of the Council and thereafter was loyal to Rome.

Meanwhile he thought, and talked, about the Church and the
working man. He moved from the ancient doctrine that all would be
well if human beings were charitable and loved their neighbours as
themselves, to the newer—though not new—doctrine that the
Church had a responsibility for the shape and structure of society.
Some of his associates were attracted to radical doctrine like that of
Karl Marx. Although Ketteler read Marx's *Das Kapital* on the way to
the Vatican Council, he never went so far. But he accepted that the
only way to solve the problem of the proletariat was to provide that
the worker receive a share of the profits of his labour. He attacked
socialism strenuously because that was his Catholic duty and because
German socialism was anti-religious. But in other countries and con-
texts he would have been known as a Catholic socialist. It was a new
stage of Catholic history when a leading bishop could say from the
pulpit, 'Religion and morality by themselves cannot cure the plight
of the worker.' In a speech of 1869 he demanded the formation of
German trade unions on the lines of the English unions, with the
right to strike.[22]

RERUM NOVARUM, 1891

Ketteler died in 1877 when Pius IX still reigned and before such ideas
affected the leaders of opinion. Leo XIII renewed the condemnation
of socialism shortly after he took office.[23]

But in a united Italy, the Pope's enemies were the bourgeois. His
allies were the peasants of north and south, the peasantry of the north

[22] For Ketteler, *Sämtliche Werke und Briefe*, ed. E. Iserloh (Mainz, 1977–); A. M. Birke,
Bischof Ketteler und der deutsche Liberalismus (Mainz, 1971). For this whole question, Paul
Misner, *Social Catholicism in Europe: From the Onset of Industrialization to the First World War*
(New York, 1991).

[23] *Quod apostolici muneris*, 29 Dec. 1878, 'Epistola encyclica adversus Socialistarum sectas';
Acta Leonis XIII (Graz, 1971), i. 170 ff.

being the more educated. Leo XIII could appeal to the workers of Italy against capitalist masters who dominated the new State.

A popular Catholic party, away from national elections, was built in Italy. Its centre was an organization dating from 1874–5, the Opera dei Congressi, the congress being their annual meeting. They were led by old papal aristocrats, but their appeal was to ordinary people. At first they were conservative in church politics, liked the Syllabus of Errors, disliked toleration, hated liberal Catholicism, and demanded unquestioning discipleship of the pope. They meant to fight the Risorgimento State of Italy, not using violence or conspiracy but using a free press and free association, and to vote in municipal elections. They started small, but even at their third meeting in 1876 they were important enough to be invaded by hooligans and have the meeting banned by the prefect of Bologna on the ground that they were a threat to public order. The same thing happened to their seventh Congress at Lucca. The eighth Congress had to be held in the house of the bishop of Lodi because the prefect threatened to occupy the church with carabinieri.

They carried more political weight because they abstained from the normal political contest. They declared that they were for the real Italy against the legal Italy; that they were for the people against the bourgeois minority that oppressed them. They founded youth clubs, relief work, and working men's societies. They built up peasant banks (like the old Monte di Pietà), and co-operatives, and credit institutions for the rural communities. To begin with they remained in the countryside. At the inaugural meeting a speaker said that the first murderer, Cain, was said to have built the first city, that innocent man was placed in a garden, among flowers and shrubs.

Between the death of Pius IX and the end of the century the social tension in Italy between Catholics and anticlericals was manifest; little towns of the north divided socially, Catholic processions were broken up by roughs, anticlerical ceremonies interrupted by zealous Catholic youths. In parts of the old Legations, Emilia and Romagna, the parties came to an unofficial vendetta. The more ardent the anticlericalism, the more zealous the younger Catholics, the more hostility felt by Catholics to conciliation.

After 1890 the Congress movement made headway in the cities. They organized a public dormitory at Vicenza, a cheap kitchen in Leghorn, service to the unemployed at Piacenza. They were not democratic in theory, but paternalist, like the old squire doing what he could for his tenants. They were influenced by a teacher of political economy at Pisa, a rare Catholic professor at a generally anticlerical university, Giuseppe Toniolo. He had no use for capitalism or socialism, on moral grounds. At that time the new State was stained with scandals of business and banking. Toniolo hated the materialistic State that liberalism created. His ideal was that of the old medieval guilds, adapted for modern life; a corporatist theory of society, where the corporations were constituted without class divisions and brought employer and employed into a common society. The Congress Movement, contrary to the wishes of workers in its branches, was against strikes.

Nor was Italy the only country where such ideas became vocal among Catholics. In France Albert de Mun was shocked by the Commune rising in Paris in 1871, for which he was inclined to blame the bourgeois. He founded a society for Catholic working men and a movement similar to the Italian Opera, called the Catholic Union. Most of the French bishops disliked his social work and the theories it implied.

In Britain the Irish immigrants were the poorest of the poor, and the cardinal of Westminster, Henry Edward Manning, became an advanced advocate of social reform—an unexpected stance, for in person he was stiff and unforthcoming—and helped to settle the London dock strike of 1889, because many Irishmen were among the dockers.

In America a Protestant created a secret order in Philadelphia called the Knights of Labor. It worked for nationalization of railways and road transport, wanted equal pay for both sexes, and built up unions and the right to strike. By 1886 it had three-quarters of a million members and a record of successful strikes. Catholic workers wished to belong, but the Catholic bishops in Canada banned them from membership. Cardinal Gibbons of Baltimore was determined that Catholic membership of the Knights should not be condemned. His influence with Pope Leo XIII prevented a Roman condemnation.

Thus pressure mounted on Rome to say something about the labour question. The perception of Pope Leo XIII was very Italian; he tested everything against the question of what difference it would make to the Catholicism of Italy and perhaps to the recovery of the Papal State.

The encyclical *Rerum novarum* of 1891 maintained the traditional doctrine by condemning socialism and communism because they trampled on the right to property that is a God–given human right; because they hurt the family, which was the basis of sound community; and because they encouraged class warfare, whereas a true doctrine of society would encourage love of one's neighbour. The encyclical was strong on property which it defended against socialism. Therefore, in the history of social thought, it was a very moderate document.

The encyclical accepted the necessity for state intervention to secure justice between the classes and a fair wage for the earners. It recognized the right of the workers to form unions for the defence of their interests, and declared that this was a human right which the State had no business to touch. It talked of the dignity of the workers as men and women, and of their rights under God, and of the moral principle that they were never to be treated as objects or machines. The encyclical was against strikes because they harmed employer and employee alike and because, whatever their peaceable intentions, the consequence was usually violence. The State had the duty of intervening to prevent such strife.

An old–fashioned note was struck by the idea that the primary purpose of the workers' unions must be the encouragement of piety among their members and their families.

This encyclical was obsolete in some phrases, and wrought out of an Italian distress which was not relevant to the rest of the industrial world. But it was the most important encyclical of the nineteenth century. More weighty than what it said was what it allowed or released. It freed the Christian social movement and fostered a range of thinking which was hardly possible under the former regime where the papacy produced nothing but flat condemnations of socialism. The Pope had not himself moved towards socialism, which he still regarded as a mortal enemy, but under the umbrella of his encyclical radical thinkers pursued their arguments almost wherever they wished to go. Remotely the encyclical was one of the foundations of Catholic democratic parties in the politics of the twentieth century.

It was a sign of a new–found self–assurance in the papal office. The decree of infallibility was thought of chiefly as a way of assuring the pope of his right to define Christian doctrine—that Mary was born without sin. A Pope Pius IX who in 1866 declared solemnly that the laws of the Italian State against religion were null and void, and who in the following year declared that the laws of the Russian government against the Catholic religion were null and void, did not lack consciousness of the supreme authority of his office. What now happened was willingness to enter social ethics. Previous popes denied the right of revolution, condemned the separation of Church and State, and toleration. As early as 1859 a Jesuit writer claimed that infallibility in faith and morals must include infallibility in matters of public law. In 1906 another writer of the same school claimed that it was a great error to think that popes could judge faith and morals but were no better than anyone else in judging social action.[24]

Leo XIII entered social theory in a way that caused professors of politics and society to treat his recommendations as one option among others, and even to include his documents in anthologies of texts for the use of students of political theory. 'We approach the subject with confidence', said *Rerum novarum*, 'in the use of a right which we obviously possess.' Leo remembered how the early and medieval Church helped to suppress slavery, and compared that function with what he could do to 'rescue workers', as he said, 'from the suffering into which they are thrust by the way in which society is organized'.[25]

In this way the morality of the strike entered the textbooks of Christian ethics. The most important textbook was *Arbeitsvertrag und Streiksrecht* ('Contract of Work and the Right to Strike'), written by the German Jesuit August Lehmkuhl in 1899. He argued thus: observation proves that capitalists can exploit workers; observation proves that workers can make claims that are excessive. A class war can result.

Pope Leo XIII has laid it down that strikes are to be avoided as far as possible. They hurt everyone, and usually hurt the worker most. All strikes are contrary to law and morality unless society denies justice to the worker. Therefore we cannot condemn all strikes. Some could be justified in the same way as self-defence could be justified. The individual workers were helpless against the employer, and only in union did they have a chance. Workers were therefore justified in claiming that the greater part of the profit should go to them. If the employer said that the industry could not afford the just claim of the worker, then the worker was justified in allowing the industry to collapse.

---

[24] *CC* (1859), 3: 573; (1906), 4: 9; at that moment in 1905–6 the pope (Pius X) was condemning the idea of class struggle.

[25] Brief, 6 Aug. 1893, *ASS* 26 (1893–4), 74–5, expressing pleasure at a meeting of Catholic workers in Switzerland.

These pro-worker definitions were modified by Lehmkuhl in his big handbook of moral theology (*Theologia Moralis* (2 vols.; 1883–4), 12th edn. by 1914). If a strike were not to be unjust, it must fulfil certain conditions. The workers who did not wish to strike should not be forced to do so; the employer had to be given due notice; the strike would not be unjust if the employer had abused the contract with the worker (for example by lowering the wage which he had agreed, refusing due holidays, or forcing the worker to immoral practices). If the strike was only to increase wages, it was generally to be dissuaded—the method was doubtful and carried evils with it, and idle workers could scarcely ever be restrained from excesses like violence or drunkenness.

Such definitions made it clear that Christian trade unions were almost as free to strike as any trade union. But this was not the opinion of every member of a Christian trade union, or of many in secular trade unions.

During the 1870s a Socialist party grew among the workers of Austria as Vienna and other towns developed their industries. Their unions were anticlerical like those of Germany.

The Catholics founded trade unions, the first for Lower Austria in 1892. It was hard to make headway against the earlier Social Democrat trade unions (in 1904 Christian-Social unions had 148,000 members; Social Democrat unions, nearly 723,000[26]). But the Christian-Social Party was very successful among the peasants of the German-speaking lands, especially the Tyrol; and also in Moravia and among the Slovenes. The bishops did not like it that their clergy should belong to a political party if it were called Christian-Social and tried to stop them, but failed. The party talked of the need to divide up the great estates and that alienated the Conservatives who were still a Catholic strength in Austria.

Karl Lueger founded the Christian-Social Party as the first Catholic mass movement that was antiliberal and anti-Semitic. The bishops were against it, the people who voted for it were the lower middle class and artisans. They were much encouraged by *Rerum novarum*.

Whatever the Austrian bishops thought of the Christian-Social Party—not all disapproved, the prince-bishop Kohn of Olmütz disturbed some by approving—Cardinal Rampolla in Rome was in

[26] Peter Leisching in A. Wandruszka and P. Urbanitsch (eds.), *Die Habsburgermonarchie 1848–1918* iv. *Die Confessionen* (Vienna, 1985), 197.

favour of it; and when its programme for anticapitalist reform was put before Pope Leo XIII he approved of it. Vienna elected Lueger its mayor; the Emperor refused to accept the election and ordered another; Lueger was elected again. The party controlled the capital. In the election of 1907 they won the majority of seats in Parliament, achieving it by alliance with the Conservatives. They were moving away from the left.

Galicia with its Poles was a part of the Austro-Hungarian empire where the Church was strong. Stanislaw Stojalowski was a priest of the archdiocese of Lemberg (Lvov). There was a Christian socialist element in him but also a Polish nationalist—that was against the rule of Vienna, and he built up a peasant party. He was fiercely anti-Semitic. He won much support from the country people and from the parish clergy in Galicia. In 1895 he was arrested because of his attacks upon the State, conservatives, capitalists, and Jews, and put in gaol—which made him more famous. The bishops thought him a disgrace to the clergy and threatened him with excommunication. Unable to work in the diocese of Lemberg he disappeared for a time to Montenegro (!) where the archbishop, prompted by Strossmayer (not a socialist, but a prince-bishop if anyone was), defended him from any attempts to extradite him; for Strossmayer had helped the Montenegrin churches to be allowed to retain the old Slavonic liturgy. He submitted, confessed penitence, and was allowed back to this work. Then he was elected a member of Parliament and was not silent in his seat. Rome, though besought by Austria, refused to act against him.[27]

The dilemma is illustrated by the Catholic party in Germany, the Centre. No one but Catholics voted for this party. Yet its leaders were determined that it should be an interdenominational party. Their motive was political: if they could draw in Protestant or agnostic voters who liked their moderate radical programme, they would be stronger in national politics. But they still had a dilemma: since it was the Catholics who voted for them they could not do other than represent Catholic interests, while they tried not to be at the beck and call of the Curia. There was inherent conflict between the duty of the Catholic organs to Catholicism as an institution, and their duty to do what they could for humanity. The world had assumed that to fur-

---

[27] For Stojalowski, Engel-Janosi, *Österreich und der Vatikan*, i. 315–16; E. Winter, *Russland und der slawischen Völker in der Diplomatie des Vatikans, 1878–1903* (Berlin, 1950), 111 ff., documents at 159 ff.; Wandruszka and Urbanitsch (eds.), *Die Habsburgermonarchie*, iv. 229–30.

ther the interests of Catholicism was to do the same for humanity, but now, in the socializing century, these two objectives were not so easy to reconcile. Catholic trade unions were good for the Church, but that could not be their objective, which must be the good of the working people, and they had to be prepared to ally with anyone who had the same goal.

Romolo Murri in Italy was a radical politician and only by consequence a radical about Church authority or policy. He fought to prise the Opera dei Congressi away from its aristocratic heads, and won; he became the leader in Italy of 'Christian democracy' and was near Catholic socialism. Like Lamennais he thought Christianity the foundation of freedom and prophesied a liberation of the poor which would come from the renewal of Catholicism. He said that Christian democrats 'accept from socialism the method, the class struggle, and in part the political realism, apart from the philosophy of historical materialism'. His journal *Cultura Sociale* was the only Christian journal to treat Marxist ideas without blindness.[28] He was willing to justify the resort to violence by the worker because repression was also a form of violence, and 'The Church has justified far more doubtful wars . . . If the workers' struggle is immoral, the proclaimers of crusades were a hundred times more immoral' (*Cultura Sociale*, 1905). The Pope condemned his National Democratic League.

The movement was strong among younger Italian Catholics. In 1908 two young Italian priests formally applied to join the Socialist Party, on condition that they need not renounce their religious faith. The Socialists long discussed whether this was tolerable and their extremists thought it impossible. Though the ordinands were taught in their seminaries that Marxism equals atheism, they did not always believe what they were told.

The arguments were that if a trade union's methods and objectives were moral, a clergyman could join it. But if the union was recognized to have the right to enforce a strike on its members, the clergyman would become part of an organization the purpose of which was an industrial battle, and seeking conflict was wrong; therefore he would be forced into a situation which he regarded as immoral. From the other point of view, every Catholic had to strive for justice in society; and in an industrial society the right to enforce a strike upon the members of a trade union was sometimes the only way in which

[28] L. Bedeschi, *Cattolici e Comunisti* (Milan, 1974), 18.

general justice, as distinct from justice to certain individuals, could be achieved. Catholics therefore had to accept the right to strike, including a corporate or general strike, as a last resort where all else had failed.

Would it then be necessary for Christian trade unions to co-operate with socialist trade unions? The popes taught that co-operation with socialists was wrong. Yet if they did not co-operate, did they not frustrate the purposes of strikes and became a group of organized blacklegs? In Germany this argument grew tense between the Berlin Catholic unions (supported by the Vatican), which denied the right to co-operate with socialism, and the Rhineland Catholic unions (supported by several German bishops), who saw that nothing effective could be done unless they co-operated with socialist trade unions. Cardinal Georg von Kopp, the prince-bishop of Breslau and the bishop most trusted by the then government of Germany, almost succeeded in persuading Pope Pius X to condemn Christian trade unions; but not quite.[29] The Pope decided that membership by Catholics of denominationally mixed unions must be 'tolerated'.

Therefore Catholic trade unions could never be effective; not at least as instruments for the main purposes for which unions were founded. Many bishops thought that they politicized good lay people and turned their minds to material advancement, and infected them with the class warfare that they imagined to be inherent in socialism. They were suspect to the socialist unions which regarded them as too religious to be effective in the class struggle and treated them as enemies instead of allies. In other directions they might be useful, for giving the Catholic working class a place of meeting, social concern, and religious influence. But they could not be more than marginally useful as instruments in a social battle.

DEMOCRACY?

After the encyclical *Rerum novarum* the phrase 'Christian democracy' came into quite widespread use among Catholics. This was surpris-

---

[29] For the argument on Catholic trade unions, K. Bachem, *Vorgeschichte, Geschichte und Politik der deutschen Zentrumspartei* (Cologne, 1927–32), vii. 156 ff.; Schm. iii. 98 ff., 164 ff.; *HJHC* ix. 501 ff.; *LTK* s.v. Gewerkschaften III, with literature; R. Brack, *Deutschen Episkopat und Gewerkschaftstreit 1900–1914* (Cologne, 1976).

ing, for the idea of democracy included ideas of toleration, freedom of the press, liberalism, etc., condemned by both Pius IX and Leo XIII. The phrase was associated with movements of social Catholicism to which the encyclical gave a vague sanction. It became easier to use after the Pope tried to persuade the Catholics of France to rally to the French republic. It became so established that the Pope himself finally used it, in the encyclical of 1901, *Graves de communi*.[30]

From the time of Gregory XVI the popes strenuously condemned the right of revolution even against a tyranny; Gregory himself was in trouble with the Poles in their fight against the Russians, and Pius IX in trouble with the Irish in their fight against the English.

Leo XIII started by accepting the usual doctrine absolutely: the only remedy for tyranny was passive disobedience. Early in his pontificate he not only reiterated the Syllabus of Errors but denounced the doctrine of popular sovereignty and declared a paternalist monarchy to be the most Christian form of government (*Diuturnum illud*, 1881); though even there the wording accepted, grudgingly, the possibility of circumstances where the chief magistrate might best be elected by the people. In the encyclical *Libertas* of 1888 he condemned any resort to violence, but the same encyclical was not as absolute as his first utterances on the theme. He confessed that it was right to want to work to change a regime that was tyrannical, though he did not sanction violence against a tyrant. He condemned the doctrine of human rights as liberals understood it. But the language allowed, without enthusiasm, that if a Catholic preferred a democratic form of government, he or she was not in breach of Catholic duty.[31]

In the United States of America the word 'democracy' became sacred to all Americans including Catholics. And it could not be denied that under that regime the Church flourished. Like the French *ralliement*, this helped the spread of the phrase 'Christian democracy'.

---

[30] 'Grave discussions about economic matters in society'; *ASS* 33 (1900–1), 385 ff. The encyclical pronounced socialism an error. It said that people now used various phrases, e.g. Christian socialists, popular Christian action, social Christians, Christian democracy, Christian democrats; Leo did not condemn such expressions unless used to mean anything other than beneficent Christian action for the poor of society.

[31] *Diuturnum illud* in *ASS* 14 (1881), 3 ff.; *Libertas* in *ASS* 20 (1888), 593 ff. Cf. O. Köhler, in *HJHC* ix. ch. 14, pp. 233 ff., with valuable citations; and Schm. ii. 365 ff.; Misner, *Social Catholicism*.

The encyclical *Graves de communi* of 1901 in which Leo XIII finally used the term 'Christian democracy' was not encouraging (though he had softened the language of his drafters).

At the publication of *Graves de communi* the Pope was nearly 91 years old and left the drafting of messages to members of his staff. He accepted the phrase because it contained the ideas of justice and of the individual's right to property, and because it cared for the interests of the powerless. He said that the phrase should have no political meaning (!), that it recommended no particular constitution (!), and that it did not sanction rebellion against lawful authority.

His Secretary of State, Cardinal Rampolla, said that the phrase 'Christian democracy' was not a novelty because it meant the same as 'Christian charity'. This was directed against the radical leader of the Christian democrats, Romolo Murri; probably it came out of the Curia and was not inspired by the very ancient Pope.

But the use of the phrase 'Christian democracy' by a pope not far from his death encouraged radical Catholics. Qualified though this language was, *Rerum novarum* and its application were prising the Church out of the damning inheritance of the Syllabus of Errors.

THE PRESS

The press was a new force since the 1860s. The power of newspapers made a difference to authority. Good Catholic leaders refused to believe in a free press; such newspapers, they thought, were written by hired people whose object was not truth or wisdom, but selling the newspaper. The paper focused the opinion of parties and caused the parties to vituperate each other because vituperation sells copies. Yet their pronouncements posed as 'public opinion', or 'representative of the country'. Boys who have just left school, said one critic, are astonished to find themselves sitting on a throne and giving out oracles; as they have to utter oracles every day, they have no time to think.[32]

Yet Catholic organs of opinion were needed and were important where they were extreme. The newspapers of those days were less troubled than their successors by a flood of information. Their columns of opinion, and their line in politics, were more weighty

[32] Cf. the critique of the liberal press in 'Gli organi delle opinione' in *CC* (1858), 9: 5–16.

than the news they printed. No one suggested that they ought not to advocate a cause, with all the force at their disposal. In all States they were under the restraint that if they printed slander or false information they were liable to prosecution or suppression. As with later newspapers a few fines or prosecutions could be risked, even coveted, because it was good for circulation.

The papers had not at first many subscribers, but when they were edited trenchantly they were quoted throughout Europe, and influential. The most famous Catholic newspaper of the nineteenth century, Veuillot's *Univers*, had curious origins. It was founded as early as 1833 by the Abbé Migne with the intention of edifying the Catholic public. It ran into financial trouble and was helped out by Montalembert who became a secret co-director until he found that he could not agree with a new editor's policy. That editor was Louis Veuillot.

Veuillot was of poor family, the son of a barrel-maker, and was self-educated, to the extent that he even acquired a passable knowledge of Latin. He obtained work as a journalist on five successive, unimportant papers. Evidently he was already trenchant, for during his time with these newspapers he was forced to fight three duels. In those youthful years he was not pious. In 1838 he went to Rome, as tourist not pilgrim, but he was received by Pope Gregory XVI. This experience had the effect of a conversion. He went on pilgrimage to Loreto, Einsiedeln, and to Mariastein on his way home to France.

He doubted at first whether to be a journalist and a Catholic was compatible. He took work as a civil servant. But his journalistic past soon took hold of him. Someone gave him a copy of the *Acts of the Martyrs*. There he fancied that he found officials in the primitive Church whose job was to carry messages between the bishops and who sometimes had to be pugnacious to get their messages past opponents. He decided that this was what he would do for the modern Church by his journalistic talent.

In 1841 *Univers* was in crisis. Its original inspirer Melchior du Lac wanted to leave and become a Benedictine monk at Solesmes. Veuillot was taken on as joint editor and within two years became editor-in-chief. The tone of the paper changed. Edification vanished, and it became a fighting journal. The managers surrounded him with an editorial committee, but he soon disposed of that.

By 1844 he had already incurred the sentence of a fortnight in prison and a heavy fine, and so his reputation as an editor was made.

In 1840 there were only 1,530 subscribers. The numbers rose rapidly, but bore no relation to the paper's force in public opinion. In 1858 *Univers* sold only 5,000 copies, in 1867 only 4,150.[33] Yet it had a far larger audience than its subscribers. France regarded it as the mouthpiece of French Catholicism. It has even been said that in 1870–2 it exercised a magisterium in the Church of France. Its advocacy then, that defeated France had now the duty of restoring the pope to his States by force, affected for that moment French politics and the international scene. When Bismarck took a hostile interest in the *Univers*, Veuillot was evidently one of the leading men of France.

He was a brilliant writer, one of the literary figures of the nineteenth century. When he attacked Victor Hugo it was not mere abuse, he had an accurate judgement of what could be criticized in a poet or novelist: the onslaught was worth reading. He wrote verse (it was not quite poetry), but it was his prose that mattered. He had verve; he was incapable of being dull; he had vision, albeit misty. His genius lay in satire, and he could mingle eloquence with subtle irony—that is, his gift was destructive. He had an instant perception of the ridiculous, and could hold up opponents to devastating scorn. He revelled in personal attacks, having no respect whatever for dignities anywhere below the pope. He did not believe in the dictum that one should not speak ill of the dead, especially the recent dead, but evidently thought that lamentable bishops should be exposed in their obituaries. And he knew where to get help which would be respected—Guéranger at Solesmes gave him aid, and sometimes he retired to the monastery there to write articles; the learned Pitra was a member of his kitchen cabinet. Sometimes this journalist needed to spend long hours in libraries. For instance, it was used as propaganda against the Catholic Church that the Middle Ages allowed such a scandalous custom as the *droit de seigneur*, the right of a feudal lord to sleep with the new bride of a tenant on her wedding night. Veuillot proved, after hard study, that the alleged custom was a myth.[34]

Archbishop Sibour of Paris ordered his clergy not to read nor contribute to *Univers*. He decreed that it should be read in none of the

---

[33] C. Bellanger (ed.), *Histoire générale de la presse française* (Paris, 1969), ii. 128, 259, 267–8.

[34] L. Veuillot, *Le Droit du seigneur au moyen âge* (Paris, 1854). The myth was probably of the 17th cent. in origin. The Council of Carthage, 398, asked newly married couples to be continent on the night of their wedding, and the custom came to be known as 'the law of the Lord' or *jus primae noctis*.

religious communities of his diocese. He said, 'Demagoguery has invaded the Church by means of a part of the press called Catholic.' Sibour's language was too downright to persuade his colleagues. The Pope and other bishops backed Veuillot and Sibour had to withdraw his ban. Pius IX issued *Inter multiplices*, 21 March 1853,[35] which, amid much else, such as praise of Louis Napoleon for giving peace to the Church and praise of dioceses which used the Roman liturgy, was the first encyclical to mention Catholic journalism in that it recommended moderation of language to journalists. He treated the press as though it mattered to the work of the Church.

Veuillot was committed to the cause as he saw it. He had a satirical glee, a *Schadenfreude*, that society was destroying itself, and that its laicism and anti-religion were its method of suicide. He imagined himself living in an age like that in which the barbarians destroyed the Roman empire; and had a vision that on the ruins of heathen monarchies or republics a body of free peoples, protected in their freedoms by the pope and bound in a unity of faith, would be a baptized and converted democracy which destroyed the idols set up by monarchs. For all his wish for authoritarian government, he was willing to use the phrase 'Christian democracy'. For him, light and truth came from the pope. Veuillot was educated but not an intellectual, for he never had a doubt; his intention was pure, though his expression could be savage. To him everyone who backed the pope was right, everyone who doubted was a compromiser to be scourged. He defended a world of miracles against modern rationalism. Gregorovius called him, charmingly, 'the Voltaire of the dark'.[36] Veuillot maintained that anyone who wanted to keep local Gallican liturgies when they ought in loyalty to be using the Roman form of service, was a compromiser, probably a Gallican or a Jansenist. He claimed that it was he who did most to destroy the historic forms of French liturgy for the sake of Roman uniformity. It was not surprising that liberal Catholics disliked him; especially when he defended, with power and at length, the kidnapping of the baby Mortara from his Jewish parents because he was baptized and must therefore be brought up a Christian. The agnostic About called him a diminutive evangelical Marat.[37]

---

[35] *Acta Pii IX* (Graz, 1971), I. i. 439 ff.

[36] F. Gregorovius, *Roman Journal* (1911), 356.

[37] L. Veuillot, *Mélanges religieux, historiques, politiques et litteraires, 1842–56* (6 vols.; Paris, 1956–7), ii. 217, 264.

When Louis Napoleon seized power Veuillot began by being a clamorous supporter, and when he fought the Crimean war Veuillot sang his praises as the leader of a crusade. The panegyric was distasteful to liberal Catholics who did not like Napoleon's rule:

You have given glory to our arms, and have brought social peace to this country, the greatest good in a nation. Our flags are proud, our altars are elevated. We thank God that He sent you to us and has cared for you. We pray him that he will guard you and inspire you. Sire, walk with pride among your people whose acclamations hail you, *Long live the Emperor!*[38] (*Univers*, 30 Dec. 1855)

But when the war of Italy was fought and the pope lost his lands, this emperor was no longer a hero; and Veuillot said what he thought, despite warning after warning from the censorship. 'My God, this war is bad and what sophisms are put forward to justify it!'[39] From 1860 to 1867 the paper was suppressed for its attacks upon Louis Napoleon for what he had done to the Papal States and Italy. From time to time it was later suspended, for two or three weeks at a time. But, though Veuillot damaged the Church by ferocity and partisanship, he did it service by being stalwart for the liberty of Catholicism. He made the lower clergy of France proud of their faith when it was under attack. He turned the word 'clericalism', which was becoming a dirty word in the French language, into a word of which the clergy were proud. He made it a word of courage, of principle, and of determination. He uttered the fears and hopes of the parish ministers and articulated what they wanted to hear.

He was not much liked among monks (except by Guéranger and Pitra) or nuns. The bishops, mostly, disliked him. Dupanloup, whom he savaged regularly, thought him a calamity. The reason was evident: the question had to be asked, what was Catholic policy in an emerging middle- or working-class world where Catholicism was questioned? Was it to make a fighting cavalry of Catholics which should clash head on with the modern world and the way it was going? Or was it better to be like Montalembert, and try to find what was good in the development of the modern world, and baptize it where possible and criticize it where necessary—but criticize it persuasively rather than damningly?

[38] E. Veuillot, *Veuillot*, iii. 31.
[39] Veuillot to Bishop Parisis, *Correspondance générale*, ed. L. le Guillou (Paris, 1971–), iii. 270; *Œuvres*, ed. E. Veuillot (Paris, 1931), xx. 30.

Veuillot had no doubt which was right. He was much approved in Rome. He kept receiving briefs of thanks and encouragement. One of these briefs reproached him for a 'biting zeal'; a phrase that hurt him; he had to be reassured that the Pope trusted him.

The interesting question about him was whether a successful journalist, in that first generation of the modern press, had to be of the pugnacious school not only because of his private opinions but because of the nature of the new instrument of authority that he wielded. To what extent did inventions in printing, and new possibilities in state education, and a wider circle of readers, make ultramontane views likely, controversial, or necessary?

With the fall of kings in the revolutions, the voice of the laity in the Church was weaker. The hierarchy was more authoritative. The coming of forms of democracy was a precondition of the coming of a defined doctrine of papal infallibility. The *Univers* was the first dazzling sign that the laity recovered some of the power that they were otherwise losing. In many respects it was not a gain when the power in the Church once wielded by a king from Versailles passed to the son of a cooper in an ink-blotted office in a side-street. The new lay voice was more narrowly denominational than the old royal voice. It had less sense of a wide responsibility. But it was still the recovery of a lay voice.

In 1877 Veuillot had a stroke and could do little before his death six years later. The first volume of his biography appeared in 1899, the fourth in 1913. When it was complete, Pope Pius X sent a brief of thanks to the nephew of Louis Veuillot who completed his father Eugène's work. The brief spoke of Veuillot as the stalwart defender of the Church, and as a person on fire with apostolic zeal; with precious gifts as a writer, a thinker of genius who has surpassed the most illustrious masters. 'With what generous frankness he knew how to unmask the liberal theories!' When Emile Amann wrote his hostile notice of Veuillot for the *Dictionnaire de Théologie Catholique*, it was a sign of the many kilometres that the Church had travelled between 1913 and the end of the Second World War.

The status of Catholic newspapers exercised the Church: were they purely denominational or were they to try to capture non-Catholic readers, in which case their editing would be different? Several of the managers of early Catholic papers consciously excluded politics from the subjects they would treat because they did not wish to be 'merely secular' papers. Was it a tenable policy in a world where

Catholicism was embattled? Sometimes they abstained from politics for prudent reasons, so as not to be suppressed; but they needed to defend the pope's temporal power whenever they could, and that was politics.

Some newspapers were little more than trade journals, and very partisan or uncharitable trade journals. These newspapers might compete against each other; ferocity against adherence to some form of liberal Catholicism. They depended upon advertisements and so upon a posse of trade supporters who wanted to prop up their platform.

The press depended upon the right to information. Veuillot might defend censorship, but there was inherent antipathy between censorships and this new instrument of communication.

The Curia was not helpful. It made pronouncements to tell editors to do what the hierarchy wanted, and sent messages to editors to avoid scandalous disagreements. This narrow attitude did not provide what editors needed. They were in a dilemma which could not be solved by obedience to the new hierarchy: it was necessary to their circulation to heighten scandalous divisions. Many of the newspapers had a very small circulation by the standards of national newspapers, hardly more than a few thousand. Margotti's *Armonia* in North Italy only sold 3,000 copies at its maximum circulation, but influenced far more than 3,000 Italians. The brilliance of Margotti's editing, like the brilliance of Veuillot's, ensured that it was quoted far and wide. The article of 8 January 1861, 'Neither elected nor electors', gave a phrase to history and influenced Italian politics for the next fifty years. Unlike Veuillot, Margotti believed in being generous to the dead.[40]

In Milan the *Osservatore Cattolico* was another intransigent paper, founded in 1864. Milan ecclesiastics wished to counter both the Risorgimento and the liberal Lombard compromisers with the new State. Five years later a brilliant journalist joined the board of editors, Davide Albertario, who made himself a Veuillot of North Italy; firm for the Syllabus, fierce against liberal Catholicism and against the Rosminians, devastating against the corruptions of the Italian State, its tax burden, its bureaucracy, its mismanagement of the economy, its absurd ideas of making Italy a great power in Europe. Like Veuillot,

---

[40] Birago, the principal owner of *Armonia*, died in 1863. Margotti left it and moved to a new journal founded with the agreement of Pius IX, *L'Unità Cattolica*. *Armonia* transferred in 1866 to Florence and struggled on until 1878, still on Margotti's line but less brilliant and in decline. Cf. Angelo Majo, *La Stampa cattolica in Italia* (Milan, 1992), 44–5.

Albertario did not eschew personal attacks on bishops. Veuillot had tried to make Dupanloup's life a misery, Albertario did all he could to lower the repute of Calabiana, archbishop of Milan, who disliked this extremism, and Bishop Bonomelli of Cremona who wanted conciliation. After *Rerum novarum*, Albertario moved the journal towards a radical social theory. He, a priest journalist, dominated the opinions of the younger Italian clergy more than any bishop. At the Congress meetings he was greeted with tumults of applause.

The small numbers sold by most of such newspapers resulted because Catholicism was often local in interest. Germany in 1881 had 221 Catholic newspapers. That was healthy, but it meant that few had many readers. In France alone one Catholic newspaper achieved a vast circulation with an extremism in its policy and editing: *La Croix*, which in 1897 had 700,000 readers.[41]

Pope Pius IX had accepted with the top of his head that the press was an instrument for good, but he did not take it seriously. For him it was a way in which a Veuillot could propagate his, the Pope's, opinions. Leo XIII was the first pope to realize that the press, even when it was Catholic, was a fourth estate, and to begin to treat it accordingly.

A newspaper and a journal were founded which established themselves as the principal agents of communication close to the pope, not dictated to by the Curia but trying to interpret the pope's mind. The first number of *Civiltà Cattolica* came out at Naples on 6 April 1850, with the approval of Pope Pius IX and Cardinal Antonelli, who had recently left Gaeta to return to Rome. It was founded by the Jesuits; mainly by Curci, later disreputable in Rome as a conciliator with Italy. It soon moved to Rome; it had a circulation higher than that of most Catholic newspapers—12,000 as early as 1853. Except for the time of the first Vatican Council and the editing of Father Piccirillo, it was edited intelligently and established itself as an organ of the Catholic Church at the centre. It was on the right of politics—that is, it was for the temporal power, against the Risorgimento, against liberalism. But the conservatism was intelligent, it was not a journal that longed for an older world of Bourbons; it thought about the reconstruction of society in an industrializing world.

The *Osservatore Romano* was founded in Rome during 1861 by two lay refugees from the revolution in the northern Papal States and the

---

[41] *HJHC* ix. 216 and n. 96.

Deputy Ministry of the Interior Marcantonio Pacelli. The Ministry, that is the Pope's government, kept the control of policy and aided it with money. In 1870, with the Italian seizure of Rome, the government organ of the Papal States disappeared. The *Osservatore*, in spite of being a private enterprise, took the empty place, though it still kept distance from the Curia. In 1884 the Curia saw that it must control the journal and took hold of it, in the sense that it became the property of the Holy See. But Leo XIII said to the editor in 1890, 'The newspaper ought to depend on no one. It ought not to depend on me nor on my Secretary of State.'[42]

The journal established itself because amid the controversies of that age it retained an absence of acidity. This was a precondition of its work in the time when it became vital not only to the pope but to Italy—the age of Fascism, when all other newspapers were suppressed or tightly controlled, and the *Osservatore* was the only free newspaper in the country.

THE DEATH OF LEO XIII

Leo XIII died in 1903 at the age of 93. He was a unique pope, the first since before Charlemagne not to inherit a State to govern. Not that his successors did not enter international politics, nor that his predecessors were not weak in politics. But Leo was a pope in international politics still, though he had no State as a base from which to act. His successor was chosen because he would be a pope for the Church rather than for the world. It was more than a temporary swing in the system of election. In 1899 he dared—it did not feel to him like daring—to consecrate all humanity to the Heart of Jesus. His predecessors would not have done it, though Pius IX had the large sense of authority that Leo XIII inherited. And in the realm of practical politics, for all his failures, and for all the stern noises he made against the Italian government, he changed the atmosphere between Church and State in Italy and Germany. He looked and sounded like an intransigent, but by the time he died, the possibility was opened of a reconciliation, however distant, between Italy and the Church. He was the first pope to say a yes to democracy; a qualified yes, but a nod of assent at the possibility; a pope who could be called, for all

---

[42] Majo, *Stampa cattolica*, 266.

his hostility to socialism, 'a workers' pope'. Formal, cool if not cold, unsuccessful (except in Germany) in achieving what he designed, out of date with his fancy about what his office could do in the world— he made almost as big a difference to the modern papacy as had his predecessor Pius IX.

8

POPE PIUS X (1903–1914)

The modern age is distinguished from its predecessor by the ease with which popes are elected, if the criterion of ease is the number of days, or scrutinies, which it takes to elect. The first of these quick elections happened in 1846 with Pius IX in only two days. The causes of this speed were the fear of revolution in Italy and of too long a vacuum of power at Rome, and the fear of an Austrian veto if a zealot were elected. But these cannot be the only causes because all subsequent papal elections followed with the same speed.

One difference was a sense of independence among the cardinals. In the eighteenth century they needed the approval of the powers. If the cardinals representing the king of Spain had not arrived they spun out the election till they came, to make sure that the new pope would be acceptable to Spain. In the nineteenth century the cardinals hoped that their chosen person would be acceptable to the governments of France and Austria, but they saw no need to wait until they knew what Vienna wanted. They made papal elections more internal to the hierarchy of the Church, and diminished the outside influence of Catholic governments.

Nevertheless, in all three elections of 1846, 1878, and 1903 governments worked to exclude candidates by old-fashioned methods: that is, either by threatening, or by using, the veto. Those with eyes saw that if the cardinals no longer felt it necessary to wait until they knew what Paris, Vienna, or Madrid wanted, the right of veto by those governments was on its way out.

This process was given an impetus by the union of Italy. To justify its taking of the pope's territory, the Italian government had to prove to the world that nevertheless the pope was a free spiritual leader and not under their control. It was necessary that the election of a pope should be seen to be free. Naturally there were cardinals whom the Italian cabinet would have hated to see as pope. Italian documents of the 1870s show them abstaining from any effort at interference but trying to persuade the French government that it would be disaster to everyone if certain illiberal cardinals were elected. In the election of 1878 the French government hinted at the threat of veto. So did the Austrian; and even the Portuguese talked of using the veto which they claimed but did not possess. An Italian government was not likely to let Frenchmen, Austrians, or Spaniards tell the cardinals which persons they could not elect. The pope refused to recognize the Law of Guarantees, but that law ensured a freedom of election for his successors that popes had not enjoyed for centuries.

Therefore when at the Conclave of 1903 the Austro-Hungarian Cardinal Puzyna of Cracow used the veto on behalf of the Austrian emperor, this was a shock to the cardinals as never before. He used it against Cardinal Rampolla who had been Leo's Secretary of State. Rampolla was committed to the policy of Pope Leo to reconcile the Church with the French republic, and had the reputation of being a 'French' cardinal, and so suspect to Austria; and there were other Habsburg reasons for disliking Rampolla—his pope befriended the Slavs and approved of Bishop Strossmayer and Croat nationalism. Vienna thought that it would be fatal if Rampolla were elected pope; in that event they might even go for a national Church free from Rome. On the evening that Leo XIII died the Austrian government sent a telegram to Rome that Rampolla was to be vetoed at the election.

The Austrians had few cardinals and a majority were nonentities. The prelates at Vienna and Prague seemed to them to be nobodies. Kopp, the prince-bishop of Breslau, was a strong, respected, intelligent man who sat in the Prussian House of Lords and helped to settle the *Kulturkampf*; but his see was mostly German and no one could really call him an Austrian cardinal, though his diocese included a bit of Austria. Puzyna of Cracow at least had a personality, and though he was a Polish nobleman he was also an Austrian cardinal. He had the strong personal opinion that Rampolla would be a disaster, and did not act just out of obedience to his government, but encouraged his government to act.

There were then sixty-four cardinals and all but two were present; Sydney was too far away and Palermo was too ill. The two-thirds needed was 42 votes. The crowds expected Rampolla to be elected because he was the only cardinal most people had heard of; the more well-informed talked of Antonio Gotti the Prefect of Propaganda, who was a theologian, had once helped to stop a little civil war in Brazil, and at Propaganda showed excellent powers of administration. As a cardinal he was very helpful over the reforms which Leo XIII wanted for the monks and nuns; but he was a Carmelite, and it was hard for a monk to be elected. There was talk at first of Capecelatro of Capua who was beloved and very intelligent; but he was an Oratorian, and worse, he had happy links with the king of Italy—and he was 79 years old, which might be an advantage if they failed to agree.

There were two reasons why it was impossible to elect Rampolla. The first was the law of elective constitutions—the right-hand man of the previous head has almost no chance, however good a person, because electors always want somebody with a different approach from the previous person; and second, anyone who is powerful for a long time—and fifteen years was a long time in papal history—makes enemies.

Electoral systems have an alternating bias. Electors look to fulfil a need which has not been met under the previous government. In the Conclave system this worked almost without a pause from 1846 to 1978: pastor—diplomat—pastor—diplomat—scholar but not diplomat—diplomat—pastor—diplomat—pastor. This does not mean that the pastors could not be diplomatic, nor that the diplomats lacked heart, but rather referred to the kind of training that the cardinals looked for. Should their new pope have experience as a nuncio, who had worked among the embassies of courts and understood what politics were about, or who had worked inside the Curia dealing with the commitments which streamed into Rome from abroad? Or should they look this time for one with experience of parishes, and with a reputation as a caring bishop of clergy and people in a diocese, whose strength lay with the ordinary and the uneducated and the parish priest and not with the world of politicians or monsignors?

The diplomats usually served for a time as bishops, the pastors usually served for a short time as nuncios, so most popes had something of both experiences. Only Pius XII had no previous work outside the diplomatic service, except voluntary pastoral service amid the poorer quarters of Rome. Three popes of the twentieth century—Pius X, John Paul I, and John Paul II—never held a diplomatic post.

Part of the alternating system rested upon the attitude to the Curia. Many Italian cardinals were leaders of the Curia. But other cardinals, especially if they were foreign to Italy, suspected the Curia as a civil service which interfered with bishops in their dioceses. At times they had a picture of junior monsignors pretending that they had the pope's authority for a decision taken with small knowledge of the local scene. Centralizing fed these suspicions.

The first Vatican Council declared the Pope to have a universal jurisdiction. This might be interpreted by lesser officials in a preposterous way—as though clergymen in Central Italy would take decisions for clergymen in Western Australia in circumstances which they knew nothing about. Of course popes had always governed distant provinces on information that was partial, slow to arrive, and slow to return—the old missions in China and India were famous examples of this difficulty. The new speed of letters, and the telephone, though they enabled Rome to take decisions on better information, made the hand of the administration still heavier. The combination of a centralized authority with better communications created the twentieth-century problem of the Curia; which had to exist, and had to be powerful, but was resented as legalistic, partisan, clumsy, or slow.

When cardinals came to a Conclave, the attitude to the Curia mattered. Was it better to choose a man from the Curia, who understood its inner workings so well that he could control and reform it? Or was it better to have a pastor who came to the Curia fresh, would not have a curial mentality, and would share the attitudes of many bishops that the Curia needed keeping in order? The danger of the first type would be that he would wish to make the Curia more effective and so strengthen it. The danger of the second type would be that he would be confronted with a powerful machine which he hardly understood and could hardly shift from its traditional ways.

Within the Conclave were parties. Formerly these used to be national—a Spanish party, a French party, an imperial party; against whom would be set the *zelanti* party, the cardinals opposed to any national interference. But with the decline of the States' efforts to interfere, the parties grew 'natural'—liberals and conservatives. No one used the name 'liberal' which was disreputable. But conservative cardinals wanted popes who would have no compromise with Italy, the modern world, liberalism, or socialism. More open-minded cardinals wanted popes who would reach outwards, quietly bury the Syllabus of Errors, and meet the challenge of the times.

The second rule was that prominent persons were less likely to be elected because they had made enemies. To be elected pope, it was better to start, if not obscure, then not too prominent. This rule was

of universal constitutional validity. It had applied in the last two elections, of Pius IX and Leo XIII. It was shatteringly broken for the first
time in 1939, and that could best be accounted for by the imminence
of a Second World War when the electors met. Whatever might
loom within a decade, no such crisis was imminent in 1903.

Another reason for short Conclaves lay in modern means of communication. The cardinals could arrive quickly and have time to talk
together before they entered the Conclave. They could form opinion and parties; they could consult whom they wished; on occasion
they hardly needed to make up their minds after they entered the
Conclave.

An accident made this ease of consultation still easier. American
cardinals became important as the American Church grew. The first,
single, American cardinal appeared at the Conclave of 1903.
Americans had a long way to come for a papal election. The law said
that the cardinals must be shut into the Conclave ten days after the
old pope died. In 1914 Cardinal O'Connell of Boston and Cardinal
Gibbons of Baltimore instantly booked a passage on a liner to Naples.
O'Connell deserted Gibbons at Naples and hired a car. But the car
broke down, so neither cardinal arrived in time for the Conclave. To
say that O'Connell was displeased would understate his mood. To the
next Conclave Cardinal O'Connell again hastened by ship and train,
and arrived half an hour too late. This time he confronted the
Camerlengo with a protest. A *motu proprio* of 1922[1] extended the time
before they must be immured and so gave them still more time when
they could meet, consult, form parties, and get to know candidates.
This extra time was not diminished when airlines made arrival still
easier. For his last Conclave (1939), Cardinal O'Connell arrived in
time.

In this way a part of the election, formerly acted out within the
Conclave perforce, would be done with less hurry before entry into
the Conclave, during a time when no one could stop ambassadors
talking to cardinals.

Pressure from without was reduced because the end of the Papal
State meant that the cardinals elected a spiritual leader and not also a
secular ruler. The distinction was not clear, for the spiritual ruler had
political effect, and the pope was in the position of a secular ruler
who was exiled but had irredentist disciples. Nevertheless, after 1903

---

[1] Gerald Fogarty, *The Vatican and the American Hierarchy 1870–1965*, Päpste und Papsttum,
21 (Stuttgart, 1982), 206, 219–20.

the powers were not so keen to ensure that a pope was elected to suit their needs; their desire to intervene faded. This was not true of the election of 1939 on the eve of another World War, when it mattered much to the powers which pope the cardinals chose. The cardinals did not abandon the claim that they elected a secular ruler: the pope continued to be crowned as the new secular head of a State until John Paul I in 1978. But cardinals no longer needed to ask themselves whether their candidate would make a capable Prime Minister within Italian politics.

They did have to continue to ask themselves questions that were not purely religious. They could not simply ask themselves, 'Is he wise and discerning in the things of the spirit?' For the spiritual head of an international community acted, willy-nilly, in politics. His decisions on moral issues made a difference to what happened in France, Germany, Italy, Spain, or Poland. Cardinals had to ask themselves, not only whether this was a religious man, but whether he understood the world. Gregory XVI was a monk. At his death, criers of 'No foreigners, no monks!' were heard in the streets of Rome. No monk nor friar has since been elected, as yet. The cardinals half-thought about an Augustinian monk, the ascetic and prayerful Martinelli, as possible in 1878. In 1903 the Germans would have liked Gotti the Carmelite to be elected. But this was only a way of saying, 'how pleasant it would be if religion had little to do with the world'.

Cardinal Sarto, the patriarch of Venice, entered the Conclave of 1903 and was asked by his neighbour, in the French language, whether he was an Italian bishop. He said that he could not speak French. They began to converse in Latin. 'It is not possible for you to be Pope,' said the Frenchman, Lecot of Bordeaux, 'a Pope must be able to speak French.' 'Perfectly true, your Eminence,' said Sarto, 'I am not a possible Pope. Thank God.'[2] (It was not true—he could cope in French.) This axiom of the two men that the language of diplomacy was necessary to a pope was a sign that they expected him to be able to converse with envoys in the international language, and to address pilgrims at audiences in a tongue more common among non-Italians than were the Italian or Latin languages. That showed how the function of the pope as an appearer at public occasions grew in weight. As the governing function decreased, the ceremonial duty increased. Yet, eighty years before, Pope Leo XII had a state carriage

---

[2] G. Dal-Gal, *Pius X,* trans. T. F. Murray (Dublin, 1953), 134.

with a cherubic angel, emerging from golden olive branches and half-smiling, flying on each side, together with the keys of St Peter on one side and a golden crown on the other. The pope of 1825 needed such a coach because he was a monarch and on occasion kings must be seen to be splendid. The pope of 1905 had no need of such a relic of worldly magnificence, because he not only did not wish to travel anywhere but could not travel anywhere if he wished. But he needed ceremony even more because the function of meeting the pilgrim was more prominent and he needed to be seen by more people.

The lower pressure upon cardinals hardly changed the kind of man who was chosen. Two modern popes came from social origins lower than those of any pope since the age of the Counter-Reformation. The father of Pius X was a village official, the father of John XXIII was a peasant sharecropper. But this reflected the chances of education for the poor more than any difference in the operation of Conclaves. Nor did the change diminish the average age of the persons elected.

The first scrutiny of 1903 gave Rampolla 24 votes, Gotti 17, and Sarto of Venice, 5. At the second scrutiny, Rampolla had 29, Gotti 16, and Sarto 10. Before the third scrutiny the cardinal of Cracow, worried about what he had to do and a little ashamed of himself, but afraid of Rampolla's votes rising further, pronounced his government's veto.

Rampolla, who was not surprised, for he had been warned that it would happen, stood up and protested against this intrusion of a State into the sovereign rights of the Church. But inside the Conclave there was surprisingly little disturbance; which meant that many of the cardinals knew by then that they would not have ended by electing Rampolla even if there were no veto. The veto was felt an anachronism and they would go on as if nothing untoward had happened. In the scrutiny that followed Sarto had 21 votes and his election began to be possible; at every one of the four following scrutinies his numbers rose and so he was elected, not unanimously, but by receiving 50 votes to Rampolla's 10 and Gotti's 2. Sarto said he was not up to the work and would not serve, but refusal was not possible. So he said that he would be known as Pius X, in remembrance of the popes who had 'fought with courage against the sects and the errors dominant in their time'. This made it clear that the new reign was not to lose its militancy against the contemporary world.

Venice was surprised that its patriarch was elected pope. 'We did not think he had cultural breadth, nor the diplomatic experience, which we had imagined to be necessary in anyone who succeeded Leo XIII.'[3]

One of the first acts of the new pope was to excommunicate everyone who tried to use the veto at future papal elections. No government protested at this throwing overboard of its customary right—but no government was likely to protest because neither the pope nor the Curia dared to publish it to the world. It was odd to decide to excommunicate people for a particular infraction but not tell the people that this was what you intended to do. There may have been another motive for this oddity besides nervousness about the reaction of the powers. Since the Conclave was confidential no one was supposed to know that a veto was lodged, even though the *Giornale d'Italia* published the news two days after it happened. And the closer the news of the excommunication was to the actual pronouncing of the veto the more offensive it would be to the Austro-Hungarian government which had used it. It was also possible that if the pope thus confirmed that there was a veto in the Conclave and pronounced it illegal he could cast a reflected doubt on the validity of his own election. Thus the Curia tried vainly to keep so weighty a document from the public for five years. There was a rumour that such a document existed: enough members of the Curia knew about it to ensure that there were leaks. At last in 1908 a Jesuit writing in *Civiltà Cattolica* confirmed that such a document in fact existed; and in the beginning of 1909 it was formally published. By then no one took much notice.[4]

It still mattered to several governments which cardinal was elected pope. They continued to want their own candidates, or, more often, to hinder the election of some other power's candidate. Through their cardinals or ambassadors they continued to influence elections; but henceforth quietly, discreetly, and as deviously as before.

The veto of 1903 was a sign of the difficulty it would have caused to have the previous pope's Secretary of State as pope, and of the weight of the office; though Cardinal Rampolla carried the more weight because Pope Leo XIII survived till such an age and could

[3] G. Romanato, *Pio X: La vita di papa Sarto* (Milan, 1992), 120, from the depositions for canonization.
[4] M. Scaduto studied the complex situation in *CC* (1944), 2: 140 ff., 236 ff.; text of the encyclical in *Acta Pii X* (Graz, 1971), iii. 289 ff., as an appendix for the year 1906.

bear fewer burdens. Pius X chose as his Secretary of State, Merry del Val, who was a Spaniard with an English mother, and had been born in London when his father was the Spanish ambassador. The choice had sense because he was an experienced diplomat, and the new pope knew nothing about courts and kings but only about parishes and people, monks and churches. None the less, the choice brought disasters with it, especially in France. But, apart from Merry del Val's ability to speak in several languages, he had the merit of not being an Italian and of being able to sit calmly amidst the frictions of the quarrel between the popes and Italy. Much identified with his master's policy, he might have been a possible candidate at the next Conclave in 1914. But he was his master's voice, and an intransigent, and the alternating system ensured that he could not be elected: the cardinals wanted someone more outgoing towards the intellectual world, and gave him hardly a vote. At the election of 1922 he was no longer a retiring Secretary of State, but represented the opposite tack from that of the previous pope, and collected respectable numbers of votes at each scrutiny (17 at the highest)—but nowhere near a lead.

The rule of total secrecy about the proceedings within a Conclave continued to be in force. For centuries it was not kept. Journalists ferreted out rumour and snippets of information, but not a full account of what had happened or of which cardinals voted for which candidate. But from the Conclave of 1903, because the conduct of business had drama, we possess five good sources from five participants. After any Conclave too many people knew—and too many were fascinated by—what happened to make a blanket of discretion possible. A couple of diaries of the Conclave were almost at once sold on the market. Such was the rule of secrecy in the world of modern media.

Pius X was elected partly because he was not identified with the policy of his predecessor; partly because he was a devout man and a good bishop, and not a figure of the Curia, and one of the best-known of the Italian bishops; partly because it was privately clear that he would not be unacceptable to the Italian government. Many cardinals thought it time for the beginnings of reconciliation between the papacy and Italy. As patriarch of Venice Sarto sought a political alliance between Catholics and liberals to keep down socialism; in the Conclave it was not to his disadvantage with the more liberal-minded Cardinals that when at Venice he was suspect to the Curia for liberal tendencies. Nor was it to his disadvantage that he was acceptable to the conservatives as well-known for being as hostile as Pius IX to 'liberal Catholicism', at least in doctrine.

The difference between Rampolla and Sarto the future pope is remarkable evidence for the nature of the system. The cardinals rejected a candidate who had long experience of the running of the machine; who ran it adequately even if key policies failed; who was an intellectual, a higher doctor in four subjects, and the master of five languages. Instead they chose Sarto, who came from a very simple background, knew only Latin apart from Italian and some French, had never left Italy except for a very short sightseeing trip to Vienna, had hardly been out of North Italy except for a short visit to Rome, and who suspected intellectuals. The preference of Sarto over Rampolla is explicable because this time the cardinals wanted a pastor, someone who understood how parishes work, was not rigidly against the Italian government, was a person against whom the Austro-Hungarians would not kick (they remembered at Vienna that he was born an Austrian subject and, unlike some of his colleagues, had never showed sympathy for anti-Austrian conspiracy), and was a friendly, warm-hearted man not given to cold formality. That Leo XIII called himself 'we' was a reason for electing a successor who would never dream of calling himself 'we' except in a formal document.

THE EARLY CAREER OF POPE PIUS X

He was born Giuseppe Melchior Sarto in 1835, in a village of the Veneto, the son of the village secretary. Always top of the class in his seminary he became a parish priest, with St Vincent de Paul as his hero, a curate in his first parish and the incumbent of his second. Though he was one of a large family he was a very reserved personality—that is, though he was easy on social occasions, no one felt close to him, they admired or revered him but did not feel him to be an intimate. He was strong and wiry with a rare capacity to work, beginning at 4 or 5 a.m. and continuing till the late evening, full of vitality and never seeming to tire. His experience was of the parishes (seventeen years), then of running a seminary, and of being part of the Treviso administration where he showed much common sense. He had the reputation of being a tactician, by no means ham-fisted for all his severity; those who disliked him in Mantua or Treviso spoke of him as at times slippery in administration. He had a quick temper. He read with care all the works of the ultramontane Frenchman Cardinal Pie and regarded him as his master. In 1884 he was made bishop of Mantua, and remained so for eleven years, in a diocese notoriously difficult. It was a gloomy town, with its huge fortifications now useless since it passed from Austria to Italy.

One incident fostered the anti-intellectual in him: he found a seminary devastated. Mantua had not forgotten Father Tazzoli who was revered at the seminary, and had been hung outside the gate for conspiracy against the Austrians. The liberal clergy were still strong though the Austrians had gone; and Sarto's two predecessors as bishop (since Tazzoli's bishop Corti resigned) were so far to the right that they only made matters worse, for their clergy and the Mantuan citizenry had made both their lives impossible; and the first of them, Rota, never received the *exequatur* from the Italian government so he could neither draw his pay nor live in the bishop's palace and was once arrested for preaching in the cathedral a sermon which a government spy disliked. One of the executed Father Tazzoli's pupils, Roberto Ardigo, inherited his ideas of a humane, liberal religion and followed him as a professor at the seminary, and was also a canon at Mantua cathedral. At a ceremony he gave a lecture which praised the Protestant Reformers, the French Revolution, and the doctrine of human rights. There was then no bishop because Bishop Corti, who so sympathized with Tazzoli, had resigned the see. Because of this lecture Ardigo was suspended from saying mass. Less than a year later the Vatican Council agreed the decree on infallibility. Canon Ardigo issued a statement to the press that he did not accept the decree and thought it folly. He put off his clerical habit but went on saying his prayers, and launched into an attack upon the government of the Church, its 'despotism' and its 'aversion to culture', calling it a *sillabica* Church, dominated by the Syllabus of Errors. Seven years later it was plain that he had lost his faith; he became a radical democrat and a student of psychology and went on to become the professor of the history of philosophy at Padua university and a very famous intellectual who received many honours including the honorary citizenship of Mantua.[5]

---

[5] He was made a senator in 1913 but was too old to attend. He suffered in the bombing of Padua in 1917 and afterwards twice tried to kill himself, the second attempt caused his death less than three weeks later (1920). His works on education and psychology were in their time influential. For his career see A. Bortone in *DBI* s.v., with literature.

Thus, when Sarto became bishop of Mantua, the most celebrated living Mantuan was now not only one of the handful of leading critics of Christianity in Italy but was famous for apostasy from a devout faith. And this critic's ideas were not theological wool like Mazzini's nor a blunderbuss aimed at the Pope's bosom like Garibaldi's, but the product of a training in divinity and hard reading in philosophy. This was remembered at the seminary. The rector was disliked by the clergy, the professors were not up to their work. After six years Sarto made himself the rector and appointed a good young man of only 24 (!) to run it as vice-rector. He would wander into the seminary unexpectedly, and knew each ordinand personally. Throughout his career he liked young men about him and trusted them. The choice of Merry del Val as Secretary of State though he was under 40 was one example of a habit. He was not the rector of the seminary in name only, but appointed himself to the chair of philosophy to make sure that the ordinands were all taught Thomism. How good the Mantua seminary was when it had a half-absentee head and a half-absentee professor of philosophy we cannot say, but it was very disciplined and its reputation rose; which was not a difficult direction in which to go. It could hardly have sunk further.

The Mantua government decided to celebrate King Humbert's birthday by going in procession to the synagogue after singing the Te Deum in the cathedral—but Sarto ruled that if they intended to do that, there would be no Te Deum, so the procession was cancelled. A book full of untruth was published against him at Mantua, but he would not answer it. Thus Sarto acquired fame at Rome for having brought the most difficult diocese in Italy, if not into order, at least into far less disorder.

Then the patriarch of Venice died. It was a very small diocese, unattractive to any prospective bishop, its only merit apart from the beauty and history of the place being that the old Venetian republic had gained for it the title of patriarch, and the patriarch was almost sure to be a cardinal. Three bishops (at least) refused the see; then the offer came to Sarto of Mantua who also refused it. Evidently Rome did not naturally think of Sarto first because they tried three of his neighbouring bishops before they approached him. When he refused Pope Leo appealed to his conscience, and so he became the patriarch of Venice.

The government refused the *exequatur*. This did not mean that the Italian government specially disliked the repute of Sarto. A constitutional battle was raging. In the Counter-Reformation, Venice, as a reward for its services against the Turks, was given the right to choose its bishop. Then Austria acquired Venice and asked that the privilege be confirmed to them and it was agreed, and written into the grant that the appointment of the bishop was given to the Austrians. When the Italians gained Venice Rome pointed out that the privilege was not conceded to them. The Italian government pressed its claim but Leo XIII said that they had no such right. This quarrel went on so long that there was even talk of saving Rome's face by transferring Sarto to a high post in the Curia; and when he heard this Sarto's comment was characteristic of the attitude of distant bishops to the Curia—'For fifty-nine years I have been a bird in the forest. I don't feel like going to be a bird in a cage.'[6]

With the refusal of the bishops and then the refusal of the *exequatur* the see was vacant for more than three years. Cardinal Rampolla managed to achieve the saving of face by exchanging Sarto's *exequatur* for the concession that in the Italian colonies on the East African coast the missionaries should all be Italian.

Sarto went to Venice with a reputation as a disciplinarian and the clergy were nervous. The mayor (*sindaco*) of Venice closed all his windows so as to show that he took no part in receiving the new prelate. The prefect of Mantua had told the government that Sarto was more respected and feared than loved by the clergy, but that he was intelligent. The clergy had reason to be nervous because it was Venetian custom that no sermons should be preached except on special occasions, and they knew that he would demand sermons in each church every Sunday. As at Mantua he made himself the rector of the seminary and left its running to a young vice-rector. As he grew older, or more used to power, the authoritarian streak in him grew also, he found it harder to bear contradiction. At walkabouts in Venice he was superb. The Venetians gave him a sleek black gondola.

But at Venice two things happened which must have influenced the Conclave that chose the successor to Leo XIII. This non-political person set up an alliance between Catholic voters in the city and the moderates who were not specially Catholic; and this achieved the removal of the *sindaco* who had shut his windows, and put a lasting Catholic government into the city. This was not a breach of the *non licet*—in municipal elections Catholics were allowed to vote. But it showed what might be achieved in wider politics.

[6] Romanato, *Pio X*, 190.

Then King Humbert visited Venice. What was a patriarch to do? Sarto behaved with all the courtesy that was due; and when the King was murdered at Monza, he sent the Queen a warm letter of condolence. The cardinals at the Conclave would know that with such a man as pope, the bitter fight between the papacy and Italy would be likely to be healed or at least oiled.

As pope he was glum on formal occasions. He hated ceremonial. Unlike Leo XIII, he could not bear to be carried round and waved away the carriers on the day of his election. Unlike Leo XIII he could not bear visitors to remain on their knees during a private audience, and always invited them to be seated. Everyone enjoyed an interview with him. He hated his toe being kissed and avoided it when he could. He was a man of compassion with no time for shams. The Curia urged him to make countesses of his sisters, who at Venice used to bring him his sandwiches wrapped in a red handkerchief. He refused. He wore his tiara askew; he did not like to be cheered. Someone gave him a motor-car, but only the Secretary of State used it; since he could not go out he could only have driven in his own garden. When solitary he was prone to suffer from melancholy. He felt imprisonment inside the Vatican a grievous restriction. For 260 years it had been a rigid custom that popes ate all meals alone. He revoked the rule at once, eating with his sisters or secretaries, and the press wrote of it as a most important act. It was the custom to clap the pope when he entered St Peter's. Pius X said that clapping is out of place in church and ordered the custom to stop.

He did not like to have the Noble Guard, which was one of the four groups of Vatican guards—Swiss, Noble, Palatine, and Gendarmerie. Swiss guards went back to the warlike Pope Julius II in 1505, in the days when the Swiss made the best mercenaries in Europe. The French Revolution disbanded the pope's protectors and then the Noble Guard was formed, all of aristocratic rank, all officers, with no ranks below sub-lieutenant, and all wearing high black boots and spurs, but not for riding horses. Leo XIII had liked to have a retinue of Noble guards and chaplains even when he went for a private walk in the garden. Pius X preferred to walk alone or with a secretary. Before the end of his time as pope he opened the Noble Guard to others than Italians, and the newspapers commented that even Irishmen were allowed to enlist. The Palatine Guard had been provided from the people of Rome to protect Pope Pius IX soon after he returned from Gaeta in 1850, and had a uniform of the French type, since the French were occupying the city. The Gendarmes wore a type of Napoleonic uniform and were ex-soldiers of the Italian army. After 1870 the use of guns was a delicate issue in negotiation with the Italian government. Until 1943 it was supposed that such guns were only for ceremonies and need not be modern. In September 1943 the Nazis occupied Rome and suddenly those who carried ceremonial guns realized that they might need to use them.

The Curia was almost as nervous as the clergy of Venice. They had acquired a head who knew nothing whatever about their mode of working. And he did not try to discover, but rather set up his own system of government—with a young Secretary of State and a still younger team of secretaries—and two cardinals whom he specially trusted, the Italian Gaetano de Lai and the Spanish Capuchin Vives y Tutó. Of this team Cardinal de Lai really understood the Curia and used the chance to give directions in several of the dicasteries which were not specially under his own aegis.

MODERNISM

The Protestant Churches struggled with evidence that made it impossible to believe that Genesis was in a literal sense an account of the origin of the world. During the nineteenth century the main Protestant Churches succeeded, without an excess of turmoil, in accepting that persons might be excellent Christians though they thought the Bible unreliable as a historical guide to the movements of Abraham, and even though they rejected, except as parable, the account in Genesis of the creation of the world. And some Protestants, though fewer, accepted that people might still be good Christians if they accepted this also about the New Testament, and believed that, for example, the Virgin Birth was a symbol of St Mary's purity rather than history.

None of this was true of the main stream of Catholic Christianity, in the Roman Catholic and Orthodox Churches. There the acceptance of the Bible in the old way stood firm for the enormous majority of worshippers. No one in the Eastern Churches attempted to deal with intellectual anxieties that made no one in the East anxious. A tiny handful of theologians in the West coped hesitantly with the problem: Cardinal Newman, whose sense of history was perceptive and whose mind was not frightened of new insights, was the most important. They made no impact upon the schools of theology. In Rome a great church historian, the Frenchman Louis Duchesne, accepted the new ways of thinking: but church historians do not influence theological schools directly. And yet, outside Rome, it was impossible for thinking scholars not to read books by Protestant students of the Bible, several of whom appeared to have reached a position a long way from Christianity, but others seemed to be in the authentic Christian tradition even while they wrote upsetting things.

Therefore the clash that came was more agonizing than the clashes in Protestantism. Authority in the Catholic Church was more powerful and more conservative. That authority cared for the expression of truths in dogmatic faith. Pius IX taught the Church to distrust all forms of liberalism. The clash meant a breach with a strong conservative power. And on the other side, those who reached forward to explain faith to a new intellectual world had a sense of liberation in freeing themselves from syllogistic divinity and yet being able still to profess faith.

The controversy started forty years later than in Protestantism. And because the world moved a long way during those forty years, the conservatives looked more obscurantist and the radicals looked more heretical. It was a resounding conflict of ideas and persons; in which the papacy, as the supreme teaching master, could not but be at the centre. Were these new minds teaching truth which the Church must receive if it was to survive as an intellectual force? Or were they heralds of disaster, persons who watered down faith until it was a form of agnosticism?

The battle was bitter for another reason: the newspaper. The first Vatican Council was the first great Church meeting to be covered by the world's press. That had not helped its deliberations. But now a dispute was on the table which concerned high matters of divinity, which a popular press cannot present intelligibly, but which concerned the fate of persons who were reproved, excommunicated, approved, dismissed, or promoted. Journalists dealt more easily with persons than with ideas. And since the leading newspapers of the world were Protestant or agnostic, conservative authority was likely to be blackened in columns of print.

The argument was affected by other issues which were not of the intellect. Many good Catholics did not like the road the Church travelled during the nineteenth century. Though they had not become schismatics, they had not liked the definition of papal infallibility. If they cared about philosophy, they disliked the pressure to make Thomism the basis of their teaching. Others thought that Darwin was obviously right and the Church could not reject the idea of evolution. There were old-fashioned heirs of the Catholic enlightenment of the eighteenth century who wanted the liturgy in the vernacular or the end of compulsory celibacy of the clergy. There was a vague feeling that the ultramontanes shut them into a ghetto and they needed to come out. There were natural radicals who wanted charisma, and freedom, and a Franciscan anarchy rather than a legalistic structure of the Church. Most of them thought the power of Rome to be excessive. Centralization could not occur without critics. In these ways the question about truth was fought out in an environment of less definable discontents.

The Inquisition and Index were powerful, the censors of books were timid. Good men, who wrote books which did not conform to what was accepted in the lower reaches of the Curia, found their work put on the Index and their careers damaged. Some published ideas which were suppressed and never revived because they did not fit the way in which the world was to travel. Others threw out ideas which were suppressed, and since the ideas had truth their authors gained respect anywhere from thirty to sixty years later. During the nineteenth century the defenders of Catholicism dug moats and threw up ravelins: during the second half of the twentieth century the defenders knocked down archaic battlements.

The reputation of persons engaged in the Modernist controversy see-sawed amazingly; miserable in 1910, revered in 1960. This was not true of all the protagonists. Several were on their way out of the Church and did not realize where they were going. But a few men under unjustified suspicion had a miserable time in 1910 and were candidates for canonization fifty years later.

The Church was in conflict with the modern world. Everyone admitted it. Popes made the conflict a matter of faith. Laymen and laywomen who thought themselves modern despised the Church as behind the times. Was this gulf necessary? Was it needful for the Church to despise the world in order to gain its soul? No one ever thought the modern world to be right about everything, in doctrine, philosophy, or morals. If the Church inherited a message from the apostles, it had to say something to each generation which that generation might not like. If churchmen conformed their faith or their morals to the axioms of contemporary fashion, there would soon be not much of a Church. The conservatives argued thus: we may admit that the Church is always in need of reform. But ordinary men and women need not to be disturbed in their faith and way of worship.

The opposite viewpoint argued thus: the new theory of evolution might be understood to deny that God created the world—if so, it was contrary to Christianity. Organs of discipline said that no one could teach evolution, but was it a necessary consequence of a theory of evolution that faith in God the Creator be denied? At least there should be liberty to enquire. This chasm which popes declare to be wide looked unbridgeable, but was it certain that bridges could not be built if faith were retained and minds opened to what truth could be found?

So argued humane minds among the Germans; but they could hardly be heard. If they put forward ideas for change, the old suggestions of the Catholic enlightenment would come out—a liturgy in the vernacular language, an end to the celibacy of the clergy, a change in the Roman mode of censoring books by the Index. And then the Curia would hold up hands in horror, and the humane attitude was lost in pamphleteering. And finally the pope would send a brief approving a pamphlet against reforming theologians; or perhaps not finally—the final act came when a disciple of the reformer was convinced that the cause was hopeless and left the Church to become a Protestant.

Hermann Schell of Würzburg was a reformer who dedicated his considerable mind to showing that Catholicism was not irreconcilable with science and philosophy, and to proving that it is the ally of progress. It was able work, which involved the restatement of the basis of Christian creeds. He was a good pastor with a fine mind. By 1898 his important works were on the Index of Prohibited Books. He gained weighty adherents, but the pressure against him for disloyalty, and the hostile books of criticism by German disciples of Thomas Aquinas, troubled his soul; he died at the age of 56. Pius X sent a brief approving the writing of his most acrimonious opponent, and one of his more able students converted to Protestantism.[7] This was not a wholly untypical scenario for that confused generation.

Like the third quarter of the seventeenth century, this was an age when the Protestant intellectual was powerful. Darwin and the new criticism of biblical texts confronted scholars with a challenge which

---

[7] For Schell, *LTK* s.v.; R. Aubert *et al.*, *The Church in the Industrial Age* (London, 1981), 424 ff., with references.

Catholics were not yet able to meet but which Protestants were free to tackle. And the best of them, a Lightfoot, Schaff, Hort, or Harnack, had an excitement in pursuing truth relentlessly and yet finding that they could profess faith with conviction. This strength, and the excitement, infected open-minded Catholic scholars. They were being more influenced by Protestant minds than at any time for 200 years. The left-wing French Huguenot, Auguste Sabatier, wrote a study of the nature of Christian philosophy on the basis of the ideas of such Germans as Harnack and other Protestants. This work, written by a French Protestant out of the tomes of learned Germans, had an effect upon Catholic students in France and Italy.[8]

The excommunication of Döllinger, the leader of the Catholic historical school, and the departure of so many professors into the Old Catholic Church, damaged Catholic historical writing. Good scholars remained—Kraus in the history of archaeology and art, Hippolyte Delehaye the Belgian Jesuit in the critical study of the lives of the saints, and several others. But they kept away from material touching on the Bible. Louis Duchesne was a Norman who professed church history at the Institut Catholique in Paris. There he was in trouble for lectures on the early history of dogma. In 1895 he became director of the École française in Rome where he remained until his death in 1922. He was a historian of the first rank who dedicated his work to the early history of the Church and the early documents of papal history. He had a sharp wit and a brilliant sarcasm which did not endear him to his foes, and this manner led readers to think him more heretical than he was. He passed through different phases, but for most of the time he disliked the ultramontanes, and his studies in the early papacy gave him no high doctrine of papal authority. He professed not to be a theologian and to wish to keep away from a subject which he did not understand, but his critical history affected men's attitudes to the documents of the first century AD; and his edition of the *Liber pontificalis*, the fundamental document containing the lives of the earlier popes, could not but upset those with traditional minds. He had a cold manner, a brilliant irony, and more fascination with facts than theories, so that he was accused of never probing deep, and of caring nothing for the mystical side of the Christian religion.[9]

---

[8] A. Sabatier, *Esquisse d'une Philosophie de la religion d'après la psychologie et l'histoire* (Paris, 1897).

[9] For Duchesne, see *DHGE* s.v.; *RSI* 92 (1980), 176 ff. (by F. Parente); B. Wache, *Monseigneur Louis Duchesne, 1843–1922* (Rome, 1992).

One of Duchesne's pupils in Paris was Alfred Loisy who dedicated himself to the study of the Old Testament and then the gospels. Nothing that Loisy did was welcome to authorities who had no idea how far the textual criticism of the New Testament had gone—with a measure of certainty in the results—and still less idea how far it would soon go. One example concerns the so-called Johannine Comma; that is, the fourth-century addition of the name of the Trinity to the threefold text of the first epistle of St John (1 John 5: 7). Study of the manuscripts proved that it was not original. Erasmus had known that. But the Holy Office of the Inquisition was still prepared to take on the profession of the historians, and ruled that the Johannine Comma was authentic.[10] This was not typical of Rome during the pontificate of Leo XIII. The old pope showed signs of being disturbed by the news of what scholars were arguing. In November 1893 he issued the encyclical *Providentissimus Deus*,[11] which spoke of the need to defend biblical truth against rationalists and the children of the Reformation, and rejected the theory that the truth of the Bible was guaranteed only in the realm of faith and morals, saying that in authentic Scripture there were no errors. Despite this encyclical he behaved with moderation, and created the Pontifical Biblical Commission with the real intention of fostering biblical study.

Loisy did not mind what he said, nor how much it might disturb, and he was a writer very easy to read, even when he wrote on such technical subjects as textual enquiry.[12] In December 1903 the Holy Office in Rome condemned the works of Loisy.

[10] *ASS* 29 (1897), 637; discussion was permitted again in 1927, cf. *LTK* s.v. Comma.
[11] *ASS* 26 (1893), 269 ff.
[12] In 1902 Adolf von Harnack, famous Protestant church historian of Berlin, published his tract, *The Essence of Christianity*. This was an attractive statement of the nature of Christian faith as love of God and love of neighbour, limiting Christian faith to a very few and simple articles, and accepting the main Protestant conclusions on the documents of the Old and New Testaments.

In November 1902 Loisy answered Harnack with a book *L'Évangile et l'Église* ('The Gospel and the Church'). He had no difficulty in showing that Harnack's simple portrait of the New Testament was conjured out of his own mind and not out of the documents. Harnack seemed to leave out of his Christianity all that part of the New Testament that deals with the last days and the end of the world. According to Loisy the documents showed that Jesus expected the Kingdom of Heaven, and the Church that resulted was not his conscious intention. But the Catholic Church grew out of what happened in Palestine. The essence of Christianity lay not in a stripped-down skeleton, as Harnack imagined, but in fuller growth, or development, or evolution. Therefore doctrine develops in the face of experience and new discoveries, and is never a static, codified object. It is always meeting new

An argument of the first importance was in progress within Catholicism: on the nature of dogma, and with it the nature of decision over dogma; on whether revelation could be said to develop; on the authority of the Bible and of the Church which sanctified the Bible and stood for its truth; on whether the old arguments of apologists had utility in this new world where the historians were working at the texts. It could have been a great debate: at some point of time it was necessary to let the debate happen. But since the radicals worked in an atmosphere of hostility, and since they were thinking out their ideas for the first time, they expressed themselves crudely or provocatively.

In England learned Catholic laymen accepted the research of Protestant scholars about the formation of the Old Testament; the half-German historian Lord Acton was among the first. Another was a half-Austrian scholar, Baron Friedrich von Hügel, who dedicated his intellectual life to maintain the freedom of scholarship and did all he could to protect priests who were in trouble. There was something characteristic of English Catholicism that protection for freedom of thought should be given by two laymen who were both aristocrats and both half-Germanic. The thinking of both was complex, at times tortuous, and their originality was a problem, making difficult reading for the eye that expected to travel along familiar lines. They were very different from each other. Acton was hostile to the papacy and had no element of mysticism in his composition. His certainties about religion were based upon morality. Von Hügel thought that the Curia's methods were discreditable in the extreme but he had loyalty to the papacy, and believed that *The Mystical Element in Religion*, which became the title of his great book of 1908, provided the absolute assurance of the divine which modern disturbances of scholarship or science called into question.

Von Hügel influenced the Irish Jesuit George Tyrrell. As his mind turned rebellious, Tyrrell retired to a house of the Society of Jesus at

responses. The archbishop of Paris, Cardinal Richard, condemned Loisy's book (Jan. 1903). A few months later Loisy published a defence of himself, *Autour d'un petit livre*, in which he became more explicit and more radical. The historians, he said, were not to be hindered by authority: the truth must be sought, and the Church stands for truth. He asserted, for the first time by any Catholic writer, that history could not prove the divinity of Christ, the resurrection, or the virgin birth. The only things that concerned history were the documents, which showed the belief of the disciples in these doctrines. There was a Christ of history and a Christ of faith, and these were not the same. He did not intend to say that therefore the Christ of faith was untrue—but that was what he was accused of saying.

Richmond in Yorkshire, whence he published radical little books, until he was expelled from the Jesuits. He was affected by the reading of liberal Anglican Protestants. He began to suffer from Bright's disease, and whether from the disease or the consciousness of a short future, he became angrier at the restraints put upon him. Expelled from his order he found that the bishops would not accept him for work anywhere and he retired to write at Storrington in Sussex, and finally died excommunicate in 1909.

The problem in Italy lay in a link between liberal religious thought and radical politics. The movement was powerful in Italy because it harmonized with the desire of young Catholics not to be in opposition to the Italy of the Risorgimento, or at any rate to oppose it from the radical left on behalf of true democracy instead of from the traditional right on behalf of conservative legitimacy. Its intellectual head, until he grew too radical to be a representative leader, was Ernesto Buonaiuti, professor of church history at the Roman seminary till he was ejected from the chair, and later professor of the history of Christianity at the university of Rome. Because he was ejected, because he was a good lecturer, and because he was pious and stood for a cause which others wanted to hear, he lectured to rooms crammed with young people. He had been affected by the reading of Newman and then George Tyrrell, and in history by the work of Tosti, the famous abbot of Monte Cassino. He kept half-submitting to demands from the Vatican, but in the end it would not do and for years, with pain, he refrained from saying mass. When he desperately needed work the Swiss university of Lausanne offered him a chair, but he would have to declare himself a Protestant and that was a declaration which in conscience he could not make.

But the storm in Italy raged over a novelist. Antonio Fogazzaro was a devout layman who disobeyed the *non licet* by becoming a senator. Like von Hügel, whom he knew, he sensed the mystical element in religion. He wanted to reconcile faith with Darwin and evolution. He wanted the Church to be less legalist and more a free society of humanity and brotherly love. The novel in which he expressed his ideals was *The Saint*, published in 1905, where in the last pages a saint addresses to the pope a plea for reform. The evils shown up included the denial of modern scholarship, attack upon good folk who stood out for the truth, and the turning of authority into despotism. The novel was translated into several languages.

Faced with this wave of radical thinking Pope Leo XIII was

restrained and sought to keep the door open for scholarship. Even after his death several bishops acted gently towards those who frightened the faithful. The English Cardinal Bourne had no desire to make an example of George Tyrrell.

Pope Pius X was a simple, conservative pastor who could not understand what was happening, and saw only that it was his duty to maintain the apostolic truths. He removed from seminaries well-read professors who accepted the new critical methods in their application to the Bible, and replaced them by ignorant professors who did not. As the ejected professors were usually given no reason for their dismissal, the result was anger, unsettlement, fear, and suspicion of informers. On the Biblical Commission the Pope removed an open-minded secretary and pushed in consultants whose merits lay in orthodoxy rather than scholarship. The Commission declared that Moses wrote all the first five books of the Bible, which no one who studied them could believe, and that the fourth Gospel was certainly written by the apostle St John, which was possible but uncertain. December 1905 first saw the word 'modernism' used as a term by which to describe a dangerous movement, in a pastoral letter of some North Italian bishops.[13] Pius X at first used the term 'religious neo-reformism'.

On 17 July 1907 the Holy Office published its decree, *Lamentabili*.[14] This contained extracts from various modernists, much the largest number (fifty) from the works of Loisy. On the basis of the extracts it condemned theories of authority, inspiration, revelation, and dogma. This decree on doctrine was followed on 8 September by the encyclical *Pascendi*. The Pope did not draft it in detail. Like Leo XIII, he was in the habit of laying down general suggestions and left the drafting to members of the Curia; but there is evidence that he gave the draft a tougher tone than it possessed when it came from the drafters.

This encyclical selected opinions derived from various sources and heaped them together in a lump labelled 'modernism'; so that no one who was a modernist recognized himself or herself in the description. It condemned also agnosticism, 'evolutionism', 'symbolism', and the claims of the academics to be free in the pursuit of truth without any need to pay attention to the authority of the Church. The ominous part of the encyclical contained the measures needed to frustrate the

---

[13] *HJHC* ix. 457.   [14] *ASS* 40 (1907), 470 ff.

evil from spreading. These reinforced the obligation of all ordinands to be taught the scholastic philosophy and the need to watch over the reading material available to them. It set up in each diocese a committee to guard against the corruption of the faith.

The encyclical was not so ill-received as was afterwards thought. It was commonly regarded as a misleading picture of modernism, but the reaction to it was nothing like so contemptuous as the reaction to the Syllabus of Errors nearly half a century earlier. Several of the modernists left the Church on the ground that their position was no longer tenable; and some of these moved, as Lamennais moved, further to the left until they ceased to claim the name of Christian. This happened both to Loisy the biblical scholar and Romolo Murri the radical politician. Tyrrell refused to submit. One French bishop, Lacroix of Tarentaise, resigned his see. Buonaiuti stayed where he was for a time, in a professorship at Rome, and blasted away against obscurantism by means of anonymous pamphlets. A greater number of those associated with the modernist movement submitted to what Rome decreed, though they were not sure what that was.

But now came the bad time—in some ways the worst time for the Church in the modern epoch. Fear led to suspicion, and suspicion led to abuse of power. Centralization intended to give the pope supreme authority in faith and morals, but had not meant to turn the Curia into a tyranny. With conservatives afraid of what was happening to the Bible and doctrine, lesser men could eject honourable scholars from their teaching posts or pastoral work. Pius X was personally afraid, and imagined secret heretics working to undermine the faith. In *Pascendi* he said that such people did not shudder to follow in Luther's footsteps (*Lutheri sequi vestigia non exhorrescentes*), and quoted the bulls that excommunicated Luther and condemned Lamennais.[15] In 1910 he created an oath which all the clergy had to take, known to history as the anti-modernist oath. Part 1 was doctrinal and not difficult to take; part 2 demanded the acceptance of the decree of the Holy Office, *Lamentabili*, and of the encyclical *Pascendi*. Less than fifty clergymen refused to take this oath when it was presented to them, and most of those were German. The oath survived a surprisingly long time, long after the disappearance of the panic which produced it. It was abolished by Pope Paul VI in 1967.

---

[15] *Pascendi*, in *ASS* 49 (1907), 593 ff., certainly one of the longest papal documents of the age, 57 pages of not very large print.

Meanwhile the repressive organs, the Index and the Holy Office, were busy. The Biblical Commission grew still more conservative. Louis Duchesne's brilliant *History of the Early Church* was put on the Index. The good historian Pierre Batiffol was removed from the headship of the Institut Catholique at Toulouse. The Pope came near to suspending the theological faculty at the Swiss university of Fribourg. The Institut Catholique at Paris lay under suspicion. Even Calabiana's successor as archbishop of Milan, Ferrari, who was not an intellectual but a good, conservative pastor, and who gave strong backing to the election of Pius X at the Conclave, fell into grave trouble with Rome because a pair of monsignors attacked his seminary for modernism and he dared to defend it; the Pope said that the archbishop of Milan had caused him the worst grief of his pontificate.

In the Curia a remarkable person gained an ability to hurt. It was an illustration of the rule of constitutions that where government is absolute, or nearly so, a favourite can gain an excess of power because he controls information to the ruler, or because his information is that which the ruler who trusts him is likely to believe. This constitutional law was evident even in a sacred constitution. In an earlier volume[16] we saw how the popes of the seventeenth century tried to protect themselves from this difficulty by means of nepotism, the giving of power to members of their family, such as nephews, whom they knew well; and how when nepotism became disreputable, they built up the Secretary of State so that authority rested not with a favourite but with a constituted official. At times this new authority of the Secretary of State could make the Pope feel that his personal authority was reduced, as in the age after Waterloo Consalvi seemed to draw the authority of the Pope into himself, and in the Second World War Pope Pius XII found his Secretary of State too powerful, and when he died refused to appoint another. But, even under the long career of Cardinal Antonelli, the move from nepotism had been an improvement to the constitution.

Pius X needed a confidant who could tell him how to eradicate the treachery which he believed that he faced. He found Monsignor Umberto Benigni. In the time of Leo XIII Benigni studied in Rome and tried to get work in the Curia but failed. He became one of Romolo Murri's radical disciples and an advocate of Christian democracy. When the new Pope repudiated Murri, Benigni swung

---

[16] O. Chadwick, *The Popes and European Revolution* (Oxford, 1981).

over. Through the vehemence of his onslaught on Murri he was accepted as a member of the Congregation of Extraordinary Affairs. Impressive by appearance, he was organized and hard-working, and rose in the opinion of the Curia till he became an Under-Secretary of State. There he came to know the Pope personally; and Pius X found him an attractive personality and one who shared his fear of a secret onslaught on the Church from inside. Benigni won the confidence not only of the Pope but of the three cardinals who ran the Curia, his superior Merry del Val, Cardinal de Lai whom Pius X regarded as another chief of the Curia, and the Spanish Capuchin Cardinal Vives y Tutó. To them he made himself indispensable. There was a proverb in Rome, *Benigni fa tutto*, 'Benigni does everything'. He was disliked inside the Vatican.

Benigni directed operations against the suspects. He was an oddity. This was proved in the First World War. Germans searching the house of a Belgian lawyer at Ghent unearthed an unexpected archive; the lawyer had been a secret source of information for Benigni. Many of the papers were marked 'Secret', 'Burn', or 'Under the seal of the confessional', but the lawyer had kept them, from 1923 they were published. They showed that Benigni had a secret society for discovering news or rumour through informers and used his own codes to write to his correspondents. He called the Pope 'Mama', and used the pronoun 'she', and intentionally misdated letters or put a wrong place of dispatch. The society was called the League of Pius V, or in secret slang La Sapinière ('the copse of firs').

It was not only modernists who were under suspicion, it was anyone scholarly. He headed what has been called 'a sort of ecclesiastical secret police'. He once uttered this condemnation of a class of scholars who by then were among the best minds in the Church: 'History is nothing but a continual desperate attempt to vomit. For this sort of human being there is only one remedy: the Inquisition.'[17] Ignorant of Germany and history, he had the old-fashioned Italian portrait of the Germans as only half Catholic because they were likely to be tinged with respect for Lutherans. (He was not alone in this opinion, Cardinals Merry del Val and Vives y Tutó thought the same.) He hated the German Centre Party because it was Catholic but

[17] The Belgian letters in K. Bachem, *Vorgeschichte, Geschichte und Politik der deutschen Zentrumspartei* (Cologne, 1927–32), vii. 310 ff.; *CC* (1927), 4: 386–400; (1928), 2: 55–68, 3: 158–61; Erika Weinzierl in M. Greschat (ed.), *Gestalten der Kirchengeschichte: Das Papsttum* (Stuttgart, 1984), xii. 235.

pretended that it was undenominational; Christian trade unions because they had to compromise; anything ecumenical (which he called 'interconfessional'); Archbishop Fischer of Cologne because he was moderate among the German bishops; Archbishop Amette of Paris because he was not so rigid against the French State as he ought to be; all feminists; all democrats because they were ruled by demagogues; the 'Jewish-Masonic sects'; and most of the Jesuits because they were well educated and they argued, and argument was a form of compromise.

In 1911 he was removed from the office of Under-Secretary of State, but he was still potent. The next pope at once got rid of him and all his works and he ended his life as a Fascist.

A system of repression may control what is said, and who is promoted and demoted, but does not control minds except by the lesser motives of patronage, and by making the ignorant regard it as disloyal to have any truck with people who are out of favour. Many suffered in silence, some with agony of mind. Some of the young priests and ordinands were very attracted to the freedom of enquiry which men like Loisy offered them, and were restless at the grinding conservatism of biblical lectures which now were monotoned from rostra. But meanwhile the tradition of scholarship, pushed aside in a key area, found other areas where it flourished: archaeology, church history, canon law, the study of the Hellenistic background to Christianity. The French led the way; the Germans were not far behind; the Jesuit Bollandists in Louvain (not without the suspicions of authority) did wonderful work on the texts of the lives of the saints; an occasional layman in England, like Edmund Bishop, who was privately modernist, became famous for the study of the Catholic liturgy, and the English Benedictine, Cuthbert Butler of Downside, gave new impetus to the study of monastic history. The modernist crisis did not kill Catholic scholarship—except that it strangled work on the New Testament texts, and for a time helped to close the mind of Catholicism against the arguments of contemporaries. For the remaining six years of Pius X's reign, the air of the Vatican was tense.

On the other side, a few able young Protestants, sent into turmoil over their faith in the intellectual struggles of the age, welcomed the Pope's stand, and saw the authority of the Church as the safeguard against the dissolution of Christianity. Ronald Knox, able young Anglican priest and son of an Anglican bishop of the ultra-Protestant school, became a Roman Catholic; and when he was reordained as a

Catholic priest he took the oath against the modernists with pleasure and fervour.

The repression did not depend upon one monsignor. There was a flowing movement of conservatism, appealing to loyalty, in which souls were encouraged not to be content with a watered-down faith but to practise the whole faith of the traditional Church. The notion of wholeness led to the name, taken out of Spain, which at first was a name of honour and later became a name of abuse, that of 'integrist' or 'integralist'. The Pope himself accepted the word. He could speak in Latin of *integre catholici*.

Sometimes the accusation of modernism, which should have been applied only to the realm of thought, smeared other groups of which integralists disapproved, such as advocates of Christian democracy. In France Le Sillon, just such a Catholic society which wanted to show how Catholicism led to justice in the State and to win back the proletariat to the Church, was made disreputable for reasons of 'modernism' which were nothing to do with the case.

THE ENDEAVOUR AT REFORM OF THE CHURCH

The differences which Pius X made to religion caused him to be a pope who affected popular practice more than most of his predecessors; perhaps more than any of his predecessors, for the centralization that he inherited enabled a pope to affect the religion of the people in new ways.

THE REFORM OF CANON LAW

Canon law was found in tomes requiring of lawyers an encyclopedic learning which few of them possessed. The Vatican Council had proposed reform and codification, but this was one of the plans which the forced end of the Council stopped. Since then enterprising scholars had planned and drafted codes of canon law.

As soon as he became pope, Pius X set in motion the codification of the law. The Secretary for the Congregation for Extraordinary Affairs was a former professor of canon law at the Institut Catholique in Paris, Pietro Gasparri, who had produced standard and respected books (in Latin) on the laws of marriage, ordination, and the eucharist. From the first opportunity under Pius X, Gasparri dedicated himself to the plan and became the instrument for carrying it out. Near the end of his life he claimed to have suggested the plan to the pope.

The plan was not popular with everyone. Catholics (and of course Protestants) who disliked the Curia suspected that this was merely another plan to extend its authority. The extreme right, which included many Spanish churchmen, suspected a codification which might align the law of the Church with codes of secular law such as the Code Napoleon. The fears of more centralization were justified. In hindsight the new code became a further instrument in the process. The lawyers who drafted it were very legalistic in their mentality; and in more modern days there have been critics who complained that it is misleading to compare a code of church law with a code of state law, and that it is necessary in the drafting to have not only legal minds, but persons of a historical instinct as well as scholars of the texts of the Bible.

Gasparri went steadily ahead; and by the time that Pius X died the code was almost complete. It was finally published and approved in 1917 and became indispensable. It was clear, easy to use, and complete—with the conscious omission of the relations between Church and State, at that time too thorny to codify. For all its conservatism this was an achievement of law and scholarship: the law at last in an intelligible form which readers could understand. It took canon law out of the mysterious realm of the experts and made it available to administrators of dioceses. It was also the legal sanction for the centralization that took place during the nineteenth century. For example, it declared: 'The Pope nominates bishops freely' (canon 329. 2). For most of the history of the Church the pope did no such thing, and in many countries still did no such thing. But throughout the nineteenth century popes sought to acquire this right. The canon in the codex was aspiration more than reality. But it was now a law of the Church to which popes and Curias afterwards appealed at need, in conflicts over the choice of bishops.[18]

---

[18] The codex of canon law was further revised in a new reformulation of 1983, published under Pope John Paul II.

THE DAILY EUCHARIST

The edition of the Index of Prohibited Books, issued in 1897, silently omitted the ban on translation of the mass into the vernacular. Little had yet changed. The people focused their worship in their private prayers at the mass, or their adoration at the elevation of the Host, not in their infrequent communions or in an intelligent participation in a Latin liturgy which they could not understand. It was still common for communion to be given not from the Hosts consecrated at that mass but from the reserved sacrament. The sacrament was still very priestly: it appeared to be a solitary action by the priest which the people followed—or hardly followed. The people were not so much a congregation as a collection of individuals or families, each with a little treasury of private devotions and a common adoration at the exposition of the sacrament.

In the eighteenth century the Jansenists were no friends of frequent communion. They regarded people who went without due preparation as polluters of the sacrament. Their opponents, though wishing for more frequent communion, also laid much stress on the need for due preparation. Till the end of the nineteenth century most worshippers held to the obligation to hear mass every Sunday but saw no need to communicate more often than two or three times a year. Before each receiving of the sacrament it was needful to cleanse the soul by going to confession; and many laymen and laywomen found frequent confession distasteful or useless. It was also a binding obligation, except in sickness, that the sacrament be received as the first food of the day. Such rules limited lay receiving of the sacrament.

These habits of mind no longer applied in monasteries, or nunneries, or colleges of priests where every week, even every day, was the rule of communion, and where the practice of frequent confession, or of fasting before the liturgy, was no problem. Near the end of his time Leo XIII encouraged more frequent communion. But the belief that to confess before communion was morally desirable was deep in the tradition of confessors and pastors, especially in France and Belgium. Such guides had a fear of cheapening the sacrament by encouraging half-hearted people to go whenever they felt inclined or happened to turn up at church when mass was celebrated.

John Bosco, who ran clubs for boys, sometimes allowed small children to receive the sacrament. Pius X, when he was a priest and then as a bishop, admired John Bosco. The Congregation of the Council (1905) issued a decree 'on the receiving of the sacrament daily'. This said that only two conditions were needed to receive—first that the person should not be in a state of mortal sin, and secondly that he or she should have the intention to do what God wills for them. The laity were asked to receive the sacrament often, even daily. A decree of the following year defined the laity as including children who had received their first communion. The Pope ordered every parish priest to spend an hour each Sunday on the catechism for children. He wanted the people not to watch sacraments passively but to share in them as a congregation. He did not realize the consequences of what he asked.

These acts of Pius X amounted to a revolution in worshipping practices. Historians, in hindsight, if asked which act of which pope did most to affect the Church since 1800, would put their finger on this change of 1905–6, the encouragement of frequent, even daily communion, and the receiving of it by children. An argument went on about the age at which children ought to receive their first communion; for the usual custom was to postpone first communion until the age of 10 or 12 so that the child would understand what was happening. The Congregation of the Sacrament (1910) said that a child needed only to be able to distinguish between sacramental bread and common bread. In many dioceses and parishes the age of first communion was thereupon lowered to 7. In other parishes and dioceses the pastors thought that the new system was bad and that the pope was unwise. But the encouragement to the sacrament fitted what many laity now wanted; and others wanted to take their little children to the altar to kneel or stand at the rails by their side. Societies of devotees were founded, pledged to encourage frequent communion or the communion of children. There came to be a eucharistic 'children's crusade', spreading despite world war. The number of communions made in each year at most churches rose steeply. People accustomed to worship *at* a sacrament rather than *with* a sacrament now expected to be participants in the rites.

Pius X demanded that the people share actively in the prayers of the Church. But if the people were to do so they needed to understand the mass better than they did. Benedictines, with their vocation to think in terms of a shared liturgy, were among the first to perceive what was now to happen. It afterwards came to be called the Liturgical Movement.

The Belgian Lambert Beauduin was a lovable monk. He became a Benedictine in 1907 at the house of Mont-César[19] at Louvain.

Two years later he demanded at a Catholic Congress in Malines that the mass be given to the people, and that a full translation be made available to the ordinary parishioner. The proposal won support in Belgium. Translations into French, for parish use, were made. This making of the mass into a congregational act was taken up with enthusiasm in Germany.

It was easy for a new discovery to run to excess, so that congregations insisted on saying everything, and leaving nothing to the priest, and saying it in too large a voice, and turning the mystery and solemnity of an act of worship into the raucous or the jolly. The movement or its effects met passionate criticism from conservatives in the German-speaking world. Everyone soon recognized that quiet and peace were part of any act of Christian worship. But to combine peace and contemplation with a congregational way was a permanent problem of history, not only within Catholicism.

Conservatives objected to too much vernacular in the mass, which they found a lowering of tone compared with historic and beautiful Latin phrases. They thought it absurd when zealots of the new movement said not only that mass, but that mass with the receiving of communion was of obligation. They were revolted by popular songs used as hymns during the mass. They did not like the way that the law of worship began to affect the law of belief—if the mass was an act of the whole congregation, that revived the idea of the priesthood of the laity, and conservatives suspected an inadequate doctrine of the priest and his holy and set-apart vocation. Rome was brought into the argument, and was wise enough simultaneously to discourage the extremists and to encourage lay participation in the mass.

The colour of Catholic worship changed in the parishes—or in the parishes of some countries—but very slowly. In 1900 the religious experience of the people was individual at the eucharist, infrequent at communion, and fed in its private devotions by the cult of the Sacred Heart and by the affection for St Mary and for some other of the saints. Twenty years later all this was the same, except that communion at the eucharist was much more frequent.

[19] The name did not derive from Caesar but from being a hill with an old castle in which the Emperor Charles V used to reside when he was young. It had no previous monastic history. The monks were temporarily ejected when the German army occupied Belgium in the First World War.

Eucharistic congresses were elaborate processions and public displays while Leo XIII was pope. Under Pius X they became more important as a form of instruction as well as of public demonstration.

MUSIC

In contrast to this warmth over sacramental practice, the Pope's taste in music was austere. Leo XIII could not sing in tune and had small interest in music. Ever since he was a student at the seminary Sarto was careful about its use in worship. In Mantua he met the young man Perosi and found that he responded ably to his ideas. He took him to Venice as director of music at the Capella Marciana and from there recommended him to Rome to be the director of music at the Sistine Chapel; and so rejoined him in Rome when he became pope. He wanted to restore the Gregorian chant, believing it the godly way of singing psalms. He was against orchestras and pianos in churches, only the organ should be used, and he was against 'theatrical' music; church music must be grave, and must be sung in Latin, and solos were allowable but must not dominate. He allowed bands for processions out of doors.

Something of a medieval revival was happening. As Pope Leo XIII made St Thomas Aquinas the key to philosophical theology, so Pius X made the Gregorian chant the perfection of church music. No one ever suggested that popes were infallible in their taste. But centralization made this preference very influential. The Benedictines of the abbey of Solesmes, who had done most to revive the Gregorian music, helped him and guided what he wanted. He made sure that seminarists were taught this way. He particularly praised and caused a revival of interest in Palestrina. He wanted to make the Gregorian chant not just the possession of monks or select choirs but of the people, so that congregations could sing it; and this was hard, because the nature of Gregorian chant does not make it easy in congregational use, it is too contemplative in its spirit. By the end of his pontificate the seminaries took far more interest in good music and its use in worship. As with all committees on liturgies, some of the persons responsible were more interested in scholarship than pastoral care. Some of the work was more antiquarian than helpful to the music of contemporaries. Official editions of the Gregorian melodies were printed.

He also wanted to get rid of women from choirs and have boys—
he demanded that women should not be in choirs because the singers
have a liturgical function and said women are not capable of that—
and to that end wanted more choir schools.[20]

THE DAILY OFFICE

In the age of the Reformation the Protestants complained that the
daily reading of the Bible was interrupted by saints' days and digres-
sions from the regular course which should bring knowledge of the
Scripture. The Counter-Reformation worked at this, for the criticism
was just. Pius V drastically cut the saints' days and restored sufficient
regularity in psalms and readings. But as time went on, more interruptions crept back into the breviary. The Vatican Council had the
idea of reforming the breviary but had no time. Leo XIII was the
worst pope of all for allowing interruptions to the normal course.
When he died the breviary was as much in need of reform as in the
days before Protestant criticism.

In 1911 Pius X reordered the breviary and allowed relief in the
saying of it to priests who were busy in pastoral care. It was still very
long and a burden on priests to say, but only three-quarters as long as
it was before and simpler in its structure. To change liturgies asks for
trouble and critics said that the Pope worked too fast and that hal-
lowed elements of tradition were sacrificed without need. They were
relieved that he died before he had time to reform the liturgy of the
mass.[21]

THE IDEAL OF A PRIEST

Pius X would have liked to make every priest over the world wear
the cassock in the public streets. He would have liked to stop the
ordinands going home in the holidays from their colleges, because
there they might breathe a less clerical air. He refrained from these

---

[20] *Motu proprio*, 22 Nov. 1903; *ASS* 36 (1903–4), 329 ff., an unusually well-written
encyclical.

[21] The breviary was further reformed, or reconstructed, by Pope Paul VI in 1971; much
for the better, if the object is to secure regularity and to see that those who are ordered to
say the office want to say it and are not (often) bored in saying it.

draconian orders but they were what he wanted. He liked to keep the clergy conscious always of their separation from the world, and of the call to follow a standard not expected of laymen. He wanted bishops to refuse to ordain men who were not up to his standard, and would not accept the plea of hard-pressed bishops that their parishes needed pastors and the people needed sacraments. He preferred few and dedicated priests to many and lukewarm. The chief virtue he wanted in ordinands and priests was obedience. He ordered that clergy and ordinands should not go to State universities unless sent there by the bishops who must use great caution about whom they sent. He forbade the ordinands to read newspapers or periodicals unless the bishop selected a few which he thought helpful to their studies. He forbade clergy to edit newspapers or periodicals. He forbade any clergyman to use language which could cause in the poor an aversion for the upper classes for this is contrary to charity.[22]

Since the Council of Trent ruled that every diocese should have its seminary, many dioceses had grossly inadequate colleges. The eighteenth century struggled to improve them, the nineteenth century did what it could, but the men were not there to teach and the money was not there to provide the facilities, and seminaries were hangdog and dilapidated.

Pius X tried to tackle the problem, at least in Italy. He did not achieve much. Visitors pried around the colleges to see that all was well. But there were two defects which this pope could not cure, and they were the chief defects. He could not cure the lack of good teachers because the good teachers were not to be found and those who were found were suspect for original ideas. And he could not cure the remoteness of the institutions from ordinary society and its way of thinking, because that was how he wanted them; he would have distrusted them if they had not been remote.

REFORM OF THE CURIA

Criticism of the Curia was endemic, and the reason was obvious. In any monarchy where the sovereign is revered, the civil service bears the brunt of attack. Part of its function is to draw off criticism from the sovereign. The complaints were those bestowed upon every tribe

---

[22] *Pieni l'animo*, to the archbishops and bishops of Italy, 28 July 1906, *ASS* (1906), 321–30.

of bureaucrats: they would not make decisions; they did not under-stand local issues; they were too remote; were submerged in red tape; played the game with such rigid rules of precedent that they missed chances. They dampened inspiration; feared innovators, and liked to stay within their ruts; pretended that people who assailed them for their inefficiency were disloyal to the sovereign in whose name they acted.

The Curia was unique among bureaucracies in offering an addi-tional ground of complaint: the church was international, the Curia almost wholly Italian.

Complaints were not the only utterances about the dicasteries: at times they were blessed for what they did. They elicited gratitude for pastoral care or discipline; they took the burden of local opposition from a bishop to a realm where the local opposition would be hard put to follow. So widespread a Church could not do without its laws. As with all systems of law, precedent did not fit all new events. Disputes could happen to which old laws gave a ridiculous answer, and then something must be interpreted, and explained away, and supplemented—and who better to do this than an experienced dicastery constantly dealing in the interpretation of laws? The clergy might not like the Curia, but needed what it did.

A disciplinary case might come forward—a rebel priest, or a con-flict of obedience between a monk and his superior: Rome was the highest court. People might doubt whether a book by a theologian was orthodox: only Rome could finally decide. The canons decreed this or that, but could not fit all cases and had to be applied. Documents must be drafted and dispatched; the rights of the Holy See kept secure; its property administered. Since no legislative body existed, and since the one person at the summit could decide only high matters or such small matters as interested him, interpretation by the Curia became a minor legislative power.

It is in the nature of government that when its subjects like it they do not say so. When they dislike it they say so loudly. Good Catholics might be found who said, without disloyalty to the pope, that the Curia was 'past it', stupid, self-centred, and corrupt. Mostly it was not these things, but it gave critics the impression of being some of these things, especially when churchmen found that bright ideas for pas-toral care vanished into complicated machinery and were lost.

If a dicastery in the Curia was determined not to do something, it was hard to shift; the only way to do so was to approach the pope.

And then dicasteries, when they thought an innovation unwise, were known to practise inefficiently the arts of delay and the philosophy of unripe time. Therefore the Curia appeared at its most conservative (or as critics would put it, its most obstructive), when a pope could not, or would not, interfere.

It is a truth about civil services that to control them effectively it is best to have experience of them. If a pope was elected who had served inside the Curia, he was the one who had a chance to alter its ways. The machine was big, and worked by accepted methods. It could hardly be shifted by a new head from outside who could not tell what was valuable and what was hidebound. The popes who made most difference to the Curia had long experience of work inside it.

Since Pope Benedict XIV brought sense into the system of the Counter-Reformation during the middle of the eighteenth century, nothing much had happened to the Curia: except that the crisis of the French Revolution and Napoleon created the Congregation for Extraordinary Affairs, which was meant to deal with crises, and since nearly everything was a crisis it gained power previously administered by routine congregations. But the Curia was designed as a bureaucracy to run a large secular State: inland revenue, courts of law, army, navy, public health. Pope Pius IX refused to recognize the conquest as permanent. He maintained all the dicasteries, and continued to pay their stipends with money which now he hardly possessed. But eight years later Pope Leo XIII could see that the idleness of so many nominal officials was bad and tried to think up work for the unoccupied. He had very small success. Various dicasteries, with no function, survived for decades. It was a hidden problem after 1870—people with nominal but not real responsibility, numerous organs with nothing to do but get in the way. And the reforms of Benedict XIV were so long ago that even without the vast changes of the nineteenth century, the system would still have needed adaptation. Centralization had done for the Curia what it wanted, given it more power. But its system was not well-suited to exercising such power.

The force of gravity, and of vested interest, was strong. Like all historic institutions the Curia could not reform itself. There had to be external force. Only a pope could reform the Curia, and it had to be an authoritarian pope. Pius IX and Leo XIII were both authoritarian, but neither had the least interest in administration, they were interested in finding an effective person who would relieve them of the need to take an interest. Pius IX had Antonelli who was efficient, Leo

XIII had Jacobini who was efficient and Rampolla who was fairly efficient. The Curia served their different needs and they did not ask for more. They did no more than make small changes to suit a particular necessity. And they had a sense of honour in keeping institutions going, even though they were obsolete, because good men must not be made redundant, and the Papal States would be restored and would need their offices again.

But Pius X had not the same sense of duty about keeping offices going when they were not needed. And while he was a bishop he was on the receiving end of the delays, clumsiness, and legalism of an archaic organization. Any open eye allowed to penetrate the habits of the Curia was surprised—the variations in pay and fees seemed to bear little relation to work done; in Rome they smiled at clergy who fell between two stools, when they were absent from choir they were said to be engaged on their work in the office and when they were absent from the office they were said to be doing their duty in choir; since there was no system of selection it worked by friendships, favouritism, or patronage.

It is easy to shuffle offices without making a difference to the result. It is hard to know what effect the shuffling of 1906–8 had.[23] The congregations were reduced to eleven in number but there were also three tribunals and five offices. The Secretary of State was given more power over the Congregation for Extraordinary Affairs. The Congregation of Propaganda lost its authority over countries which were not 'missionary countries', except for all churches called 'Oriental'; that meant it ceased to exercise power in Britain, Holland, America, and Canada. The Consistorial Congregation, with the pope as its president, was given power over the dioceses including the right to nominate bishops except those of Italy (which were personal to the pope) and those in missionary countries under Propaganda. The spheres of authority were tightly drawn in the vain effort to avoid overlaps. Judges in courts were still given the historic ban that they must not listen to oral evidence. The bishops were given no more authority in their dioceses. Propaganda had allowed them more local decision than they were now to get under the Consistorial. The length of time taken to reach decisions was no different; sometimes

---

[23] *Sapienti consilio*, June 1908; *AAS* 1 (1909), 7–19. Pius X abolished ten dicasteries, their business (where it existed) passing to others; created new dicasteries in Discipline of the Sacraments, a Congregation of Religious now separated from its old link with the Congregation of Bishops.

it was slower, for to get a new bishop in America under the old system they needed Propaganda, now they needed the Consistorial which was liable to the old delays. Still, they preferred not to be treated as missionary countries. The entry to the system was made more acceptable; no longer by influence but by examination. Poor plaintiffs were given legal aid in the courts. One could approach the Curia without first passing by an unnecessary official called *spedizionero* who demanded a fee. Numbers of Roman families who had the right to supply these *spedizioneri* thus lost the hereditary right to an income. By a stroke of the pen the Pope abolished colleges of prelates whose only function was to receive a share in a historic endowment. He rid the Curia of an army of civil servants who did nothing. He suffered the fate of all reformers of bureaucracies, in that the changes made him unpopular with members of the Curia.

This made a large formal difference. But it made not much difference to the way the machine worked; the same sort of people went on doing the same sort of things, though with better typewriters and secretaries and more educated officers. One of the old courts, though useless, was too historic yet to be abolished. The Datary, which went back to the fourteenth century, once had a weighty part in taxation and reserving benefices to papal nominees, and later gave out marriage dispensations. After Pius X's reform it had nothing to do but went on doing it and was not finally abolished till 1967.

There was another active Congregation which was useless but which Pius X did not touch: the famous Congregation of the Index of Prohibited Books. The real work of censuring literature or theology was now done by the Holy Office of the Inquisition. The Congregation of the Index had always been an overlapping body. Pope Benedict XV (1917) abolished the Congregation of the Index. The list of prohibited books remained.[24]

The Holy Office of the Inquisition remained in theory the most powerful of the Congregations because truth was what the Church existed to serve. Its prestige remained high. During the eighteenth century its work moved away from doctrine to issues of immorality,

[24] Pius IX (1862) created a Congregation for propagating the faith 'in matters of the Eastern rite'. This title offended the Eastern Orthodox who knew that they had the faith and did not want Rome propagating it in their lands. Benedict XV therefore abolished this Congregation in 1917 and replaced it with the Congregation for the Eastern Church; this only concerned the uniats, Catholics of the Eastern rites, while Catholics of the Latin rites in the east remained under the Congregation of Propaganda. N. Del Re, *La Curia Romana: lineamenti storico-giuridici*, 3rd edn. (Rome, 1970), 107–8.

the canonization of saints, or questions of holy orders. For five years Pius X even made it the examiner of candidates for bishoprics. Among the nations the name Inquisition was a disadvantage, it rang of thumbscrews and the rack, and gave matter to Protestant pamphleteers. But its prestige was too high and its conservatism too fixed to enable it to change without pain. In 1908 Pius X at last changed the name, to be the Congregation of the Holy Office. But it remained very strong, as the guardian of truth, the scourge of heresy, and the maintainer of the faith. The title of Inquisitor-General, which now spoke rather of comic opera than of the rack, was used for the last time in a decree of the Congregation as recently as 1929.[25] Ridicule achieved what pamphleteering could not.

THE CARDINALS

During the pontificate of Pius IX the Papal State still existed and cardinals were still chosen for service in such offices as chief of police or governor of the city or a province. When we compare the cardinals of the middle nineteenth century with the cardinals at the end of the first quarter of the twentieth century, a time when none of them was selected because of secular service in the pope's State, the comparison does not suggest that the later cardinals were marked by striking stature. There were always small men and small jobs. A fraction of the men made into cardinals under any pope consisted of curial officers, who were heard of for the first time when they became cardinals and who then vanished into obscurity, until they rated a few dry lines of obituary in an official journal.

The steady offices which qualified for the cardinal's hat, apart from certain curial positions, were the ex-nuncios of the main States; for the State complained if this did not happen, and two or three States regarded it as a right which they could demand of the pope. It was very desirable that ex-nuncios should become cardinals because they were the members of the Curia with international experience.

Ex-nuncios were few in number; for until 1918 the Holy See kept very few nuncios.[26]

[25] Del Re, *Curia Romana*, 99. Pope Paul VI changed the name again in 1965, and it became the Congregation of the Faith. It continued strong.

[26] In 1916 they were four; by 1923 they were nineteen; by 1961 they were thirty-one and after that they went on rising rapidly. The diplomatic service grew more numerous and more expensive in decades when its functions might have been expected to diminish.

The third group of offices, after the leading curial officials and the ex-nuncios, to qualify as cardinal, were still leading Italian, French and Spanish sees (especially Seville and Toledo), a few German sees (especially Munich and Cologne), and the sees of Catholic capitals: Vienna, Lisbon, and (historic for Belgium) Malines, to which after 1850 the see of Westminster was added, and after 1866, Dublin. The American sees came into the system: James Gibbons of Baltimore in 1886, but it continued to extend; Pius X in 1911 made cardinals of the archbishops of Boston and New York, and in 1914, Quebec. Bologna, Milan, Venice, and Palermo were historic, as in France were Lyons and Rheims—but the system never recovered its assurance after the shock refusal of Pius IX to make Archbishop Darboy of Paris into a cardinal. The Italians at times included Turin, Lucca, Pisa, Florence, or Benevento; the Spanish Burgos, Granada, or Tarragona; the French Marseilles, Lille, Orleans (but not Bishop Dupanloup!), Besançon, Rennes, or Rouen; the Irish, Armagh. The Austro-Hungarians at times included Gran and Prague. The South Americans began to come in. The first Latin American cardinal was of Rio de Janeiro in 1905.

In theory these archbishops were the most important of the cardinals. Usually they were men of stature and wide experience. They were the people who knew what the Church was really like, and what new problems it faced. They were not shut up inside the Vatican but brought into the cardinals' college the knowledge shared by the nuncios but with the added experience of coping with the needs of the clergy. This weight was largely theoretical: most of the time they were busy, and nowhere near Rome. Their influence upon central policy was confined: (1) to the time when they came to Rome, and then their influence counted for little more than other bishops who were not cardinals; (2) to the time of each Conclave, when their weight was not as great as that of the Italian curial cardinals, but was nevertheless strong, and became indispensable for any election to be made with the necessary two-thirds majority; (3) to a little more ability to prise out of the Curia a decision that they wanted. Their stature made them a little closer to the pope and slightly more able to make him intervene with an obstructive Congregation.

To these three groups which made the regular part of the system, popes added their own choice of men; as Pius X chose Merry del Val to be cardinal for his services at the Conclave, and because he could speak several languages and the pope could not, and Bishop Callegari of Padua because he was a friend of his youth. Or a pope might prefer practical men and pastors to diplomats, as did Pius X, or diplomats to practical men.

Among these personal choices was a historic type of cardinal: the scholar. During this age there were very few, unlike previous times; in the past there had been men such as Mai, and in the future those such as Ratti and Tisserant. Pius IX chose a scholar to be cardinal in the French Benedictine Pitra, but more because he was a Benedictine than because he was a scholar. Leo XIII made the historian Hergenröther a cardinal, but the object was curial, to strengthen Leo's liberal policy over the opening of the Vatican archives to reputable comers. Simultaneously with his appointment was that of John Henry Newman, not conservative but a real scholar: the object was not scholarship but to recognize the first Roman Catholic Englishman ever to be admired among the Protestants of England. In 1899 he made the Orientalist Ciasca who had been prefect of the Vatican Archives; but his purpose was to strengthen one who did much for the missions at Propaganda.

Pius X might be expected to disapprove of scholars. But he soon made the learned canonist Gasparri into a cardinal, with important results. During his last year he elevated the English Benedictine Gasquet. The scholarship of Gasquet was more shaky than is usual with academics of his eminence. But his field of study, the monasticism of the English Middle Ages, and his cast of mind, were remote from the modernism which Pope Pius X feared.

Cardinals were not dismissed if they quarrelled with the pope. D'Andrea became a rebel against Pius IX and was humiliated, but remained a cardinal. Pitra was wrongly fancied to be a rebel by Leo XIII and was humiliated but remained a cardinal. Carlo Odescalchi resigned in 1838, after a year's resistance from Gregory XVI, in order to become a Jesuit novice. Neto of Lisbon resigned in 1907 on a plea of ill-health, and he was ill—but a dictator was resolute to be rid of him. Not till the 1920s did a pope presume to turn a cardinal out of the Sacred College.

Not many people minded the predominance of the Italians. Nearly everyone accepted that the Curia carried on business in Italian and that the central staff must be mainly Italian, and that the pope must (except in theory) be an Italian. Everyone took it for granted that since the Curia was mainly Italian, and many of the cardinals came by custom from the Curia, the curial Italians would be strong at the election of a pope. The possibility of a non-Italian pope was remembered at every Conclave. It was less unlikely, though still with long odds against, at moments when the predicament of the papacy amid the contending politics of Europe was specially tense.

The widening of the place from which cardinals came had a curious effect. Seven popes in succession (1773 to 1903) had their origins inside the Papal States. Every Italian pope of the twentieth century except one came from outside the old Papal States. But this did not mean that their origins varied. All but one of these non-Romans were North Italians; Venetian, Lombard, Genoese. This difference might have lessened the intransigence about the old Papal State. All the northerners were readier to be moderate in their attitude towards the kingdom and then the republic of Italy.

According to the Concordats, States could nominate bishops for papal approval or, more commonly in modern times, object ('on political grounds') to bishops who were nominated by the pope. Revolutions jettisoned Concordats and left the pope with more nominal power in the choice of bishops; nominal, because the State kept influence on the choice of bishops in all the countries of Western Europe except Britain, Ireland, and Holland, and all the States of South America except Chile, Brazil, and the former Guianas; even these last did not leave Rome totally free.

Until the reform of 1908 the agent was the Congregation for promoting archbishops and bishops, and then the Consistorial Congregation, a revival of a very historic congregation which at that moment was almost obsolete. Cardinal Gaetano de Lai, most conservative and antimodernist of cardinals, sat at the Consistorial Congregation for the next twenty years and chose many of the bishops.

The visit of all bishops to Rome (*ad limina*) remained the rule. Railway and then aircraft made it easier to obey, distance and disturbances made it harder. Until 1909 the rule said that they must visit Rome every three years. Exceptions were often conceded. Pius X modified the rule, which became every five years for a European bishop, every ten years for a non-European bishop. That faced the facts—as they were before the coming of airlines.

It will shed light on the papal office to compare an early volume of the *Acts of the Holy See* with a volume after the end of this period. The first properly organized volume, called volume 2, ran from June 1866 to June 1867. If we were to take a similar period seventy years later, it would run from June 1936 to June 1937. In the later year more material was printed, the pages were larger in size and more in number. The later period straddled two volumes, no longer called *Acts of the Holy See* but (since 1909) *Acts of the Apostolic See.*

Both were mainly in Latin. The style of curial Latin had not altered, but the later volume gave more Italian translations to important documents. The later pope was guilty of more length, and more repetition, than Pius IX.

The earlier volume was not unlike the minutes of curial congregations a hundred years earlier, during the eighteenth century; it included items on canonizations, indulgences, nullity of marriage, the secularization of a cleric, nominations to sees, the form of the competition for a benefice, the duties of chapters, whether a cathedral may use money from endowment of masses to repair its structure, and whether a relic was authentic. Concerning relics, in the case of the rochet of St Francis de Sales, the Congregation of Rites ruled that it was not certainly authentic and could not be exposed for veneration. What about the four tombs found at Milan, were the bones venerable? Yes. A bit of an arm of St Cecilia, may it be venerated? Yes: 'old traditions of churches that relics are to be venerated are a sign of the authenticity of the relics . . . This is not to be put in doubt because of difficulties arising, unless they arise peremptorily.' The Pope issued a Prayer in the Present Calamities of the Church (for this was 22 October 1866, when he knew that the French would soon withdraw their troops and the Vatican would be helpless before the Italians); and the prayer (indulgences annexed) talked of the nefarious machinations of the Pharisees and begged that the minds of the faithful might be enlightened and not corrupted by the cleverness of those who spread their sophisms everywhere. The Congregation of Rites was asked, 'May chalices be made of aluminium?' No. The Holy Roman and Universal Inquisition, as it styled itself, was not at all ecumenical about suggestions by 198 Anglo-Catholics for corporate reunion.

All this was (so to speak) routine administration and answers to enquiries. But in this volume the pope issued two big allocutions. The first was uttered on 29 October 1866 and was directed against the conduct of the Italian, or rather the 'Subalpine', government, for the pope would not recognize it as Italian. The burden of the allocution was that every day there was worse attack upon the laws of the Church. Every day priests were driven from their parishes or bishops from their dioceses, churches profaned, seminaries closed, schools made unchristian, property stolen. A law of civil marriage encouraged concubinage. The allocution blamed the government for extending its laws instantly to Venice (given to Italy by France that year) and thus abrogating unilaterally the Concordat made with Austria which applied to Venice. The pope declared all these acts of the Piedmontese government to be invalid. 'Destitute of human help,' he said, 'we rely upon God. Miracles will be done. The gates of hell cannot prevail.'

The second allocution was directed against the tsar on behalf of the Poles. It recounted the maltreatment of bishops, priests, and monks by the Russians; and how the Russians strove to make the people Orthodox, which Pope Pius IX called 'a deadly schism', *funestissimum schisma*. He confessed that the revolution by the Poles was very evil and shocking, and totally condemned and reprobated it, and exhorted the Polish clergy and people to abhor the impious principles that lead to rebellion, and to know that as Christians they must loyally obey the higher powers. He declared all the decrees of the Russian government against the Church to be null and void.

Now move forward seventy years and look at the records of 1936–8. The congregations had old problems—the nullity of marriage, nominations to sees; but there were fewer that resembled those of the eighteenth century. And the Curia dealt with new problems, such as that of pilgrimages, which were now so easy that they needed more control, tighter regulations, to distinguish pilgrimages from holidays, to keep them cheap so that the poor could go, and to shift the financial arrangements from clergy to laity. The Curia acted to make the feast of St John Bosco a feast of the whole Church. An act hardly possible in the earlier volume was a speech of the pope saluting the Catholic press and laying down moral guidelines. Another of novelty was sent to the American bishops: *de cinematographicis spectaculis*, 'on the way to restrain the depravity of the cinema'. A custom not known in the earlier minutes was the printing of the pope's letters to cardinals on the jubilee of their priesthood or episcopate.

With regard to States, the enemies of 1866, Italy and Russia, were in 1936–7 Germany and Russia. In the minutes there is no sign of antipathy to Italy, unless it be to condemn a history by the modernist Buonaiuti. There is friendliness to the Portugal of the dictator Salazar (the pope made the Blessed Virgin, St Antony of Padua, and St Francis Borgia joint patrons of Portugal), and an agony at what was happening in Spain at that moment, with a gathering of Spanish refugees at the Vatican to hear the pope speak of the glory of suffering and the heroism of martyrs; that all war is awful but civil war the most awful; and that the 'satanic preparation' came from Russia.[27]

Unlike his predecessor, he did not need to mention Poland; for at this moment the Poles were experiencing their independence of twenty-one years from both Germany and Russia.

PIUS X AND FRANCE

An unpredictable incident changed the course of French history and of Catholicism. A Jewish captain in the French army, Dreyfus, was accused of spying for Germany and convicted.

The eighteenth century in Europe brought various laws of toleration which included those applying to Jews. But this toleration sometimes covered only the right to dwell, work, earn, and worship in existing communities of Jews. The French revolutionary armies demolished the walls of ghettos wherever they went. But when Napoleon fell, several states reinstated their ghettos and a measure of restriction on Jews; as was seen in the Mortara case. Rome had historic synagogues inside the papal city, though no Christian denomination but the Catholic was allowed a chapel inside the city walls until the Italians took it in 1870. The ghetto at Rome still existed till the tragedy of 1943 as the place where Jews lived, but they were no longer compelled to do so. This was the case in other cities. During the nineteenth century Jews no longer need live inside the ghetto, and non-Jews might live there, but in some cities the old ghetto turned from a place of racial or religious to one of social segregation, a very poor part of the city in which many Jews still lived. The Venice ghetto can still be seen as a historic relic, in much the old form in

---

[27] The two condemnations of the behaviour of states both came in March 1937. *Mit brennender Sorge* condemned the misbehaviour of the Nazis to the Catholic Church in Germany and the frequent breaking of the Concordat. *Divini redemptoris* (19 Mar. 1937), 'de communismo atheo', condemned the precepts of communism, especially as propounded by the Bolshevists; its materialism, tyranny over human liberties, destruction of the family. This pope continued to say, as late as 1937, that liberalism prepared the way for it, because the liberal economy caused the religious and moral abandonment of the working man. And finally there was a characteristic touch which showed how Pius XI was still of the mind of Leo XIII: 'we will put all the great action of the Church against atheist Communism throughout the world under the shield of the powerful protector of the Church, St Joseph. He was of the working class and knew the burden of poverty . . .'

which it survived until 1944. Most Jews were still poor traders; their heartland since the expulsions at the end of the Middle Ages was Poland, where in certain towns a good percentage of the people was Jewish. But in certain cities such as Frankfurt, where was the community of Jews with the most continuous history in all Europe, Vienna, Paris, London, and others, there were Jews eminent in business or banking. The Rothschild bank rescued the pope from bankruptcy after the Rome revolution of 1848.[28]

The 1848 Revolutions and their new constitutions everywhere established a legal equality; the Prague ghetto ended in 1852, the Revolutions failed and in the reactions against them came a new anti-Semitism. The arguments were old but they were put in sharper forms because where there was no segregation there was more association and more reaction between different ways of life. In France, Germany, Austria, and Hungary there was a vague feeling among many of the common people that the Jews were not like themselves and were not good for a common life. This rarely broke out in attacks upon Jews because the leaders of States kept public order and the leaders of Churches preached the rights of human beings. The constitutions were late in keeping pace; the French government was paying the stipends of rabbis as of other denominations from 1831; the Austro-Hungarian constitution of 1867, and a Prussian law two years later, introduced equality of civil rights between members of all denominations or religions, or of none.

Many Jews now received the same education as their Christian neighbours, sat loosely to old Jewish customs, were ready or eager to be assimilated into general society, and were welcome among their Christian friends.

Austria had a special difficulty. Since the partitions of Poland between Austria, Russia, and Prussia, Austria contained many more Jews from the Polish areas, especially in Galicia where the Jews were 12 per cent of the people. The Russians treated most Poles with suspicion, and their government was not comfortable for anyone not a Russian, which meant steady Jewish emigration out of Russian Poland westwards, and especially into Austria. Most of the migrants were not educated nor well-to-do, but poor, with the customs and

---

[28] Cf. B. Martin and E. Schulin (eds.), *Die Juden als Minderheit in der Geschichte* (Munich, 1981); J. Bunzl and B. Marin, *Antisemitismus in Österreich* (Innsbruck, 1983); A. Wandruszka and P. Urbanitsch (eds.), *Die Habsburgermonarchie 1848–1918* iv. *Die Confessionen* (Vienna, 1985), 146 ff.

dress of the eastern communities. The lower-middle-class German felt threatened by cheap labour. Anti-Semitic clubs were founded in Austrian towns from 1873 onwards, and though their object was to be against Jews rather than for Christianity, they attracted members by taking a sturdy Catholic stance. Anti-Semitism was much more prominent in the lower classes than the upper. In many parts of Europe the progress of democracy meant more votes for the working men and therefore more appeals to their prejudice. The growth of modern anti-Semitism, which had roots in historic anti-Semitism but in many respects was very different, went hand in hand with the rise of a proletariat. The Jews were partly protected by the still restricted franchise in the chief States. In Germany, where there was enough popular prejudice for some politicians to think they could get votes by appealing to anti-Semitic feeling, the Parliament of 1893 produced its maximum number of anti-Semitic MPs, and they were only sixteen. There was as yet no wave of anti-Semitic nationalism.

Since the taking of power by Hitler and especially since the Holocaust, it is hard for the modern historian to comprehend the mentality that caused rational Catholics or Protestants to be so outspoken in their anti-Semitism. To understand them we have to shut our minds to what was to come, and its direct connection with what they did and thought, and to fail to remember that Hitler was born an Austrian at Braunau in Upper Austria in 1889, into a society then the most anti-Semitic in Europe by reason of the immigration from the east.

As the socialist movements took power among the proletariats they had an anti-religious cast of mind except in Britain. Catholics observed how so many of their intellectual leaders were from the Jewish people, even though they were casting off their Judaism as they cast off, or fancied they cast off, all religion.

In the Catholic Church the leaders were against any such attitudes towards the Jews. In Vienna one cardinal after another, from Rauscher onwards, tried to prevent race-hatred and especially anti-Semitism in the Church. As political anti-Semitism—that is, the attempt to win the votes of the working men and lower middle class by attacking Jews in speeches—grew in Vienna, the bishops issued a joint pastoral letter against anti-Semitism and racialism. The Austrian lawcourts held for Jewish plaintiffs when they sued for libel over scandalous abuse such as the charge of the use of human blood in rituals. The Emperor Francis Joseph walked out of a theatre when anti-Semitic songs were sung. That such songs could be sung at all shows that the social threat was worse than the political, the smallness of which can be registered by noting the largest number of MPs who were of anti-Semitic parties in the Austrian Reichsrat—it was five in 1897. Yet politicians who did not belong to such parties could still draw anti-Semitic votes by the noises they made in speeches. The threat was rather more potent than the tiny number of MPs. In Hungary, nearer to the Jews of Galicia, there were more anti-Semitic MPs and they were more fanatical in what they said.

The bishops in Poland were less able to distance themselves from the views of their people,[29] and all over the Austro-Hungarian empire, priests could be found who shared the opinions of their flocks. Equality in Galicia was far from preventing popular anti-Semitism, it increased it. In 1898 the government had to bring in a state of emergency to stop a pogrom. An amazing trial about ritual murder happened in Bohemia (1897) which was fostered by mass hysteria encouraged by Catholic sermons. And meanwhile refugees from the tsarist regime poured in, different in dress, diet, customs, and worship and almost all nearly destitute and a threat to the poor Hungarian, German, or Slav labourer.

The ablest of the politicians in this area was Karl Lueger the Christian Social leader in Austria and a benefactor of the city of Vienna by his work as mayor over years. He was not a religious person. But he realized that he could attain power by linking the insistence on Catholic rights, which attracted Catholic conservatives, with anti-Semitic prejudice which attracted socialist anticapitalists and proletarian workers. Able Austrian Jews such as Stefan Zweig defended him; historians of the Holocaust saw him as a prototype of the method of attaining power afterwards used by Nazis. Hitler, baptized and confirmed as a Catholic but lapsed, came to Vienna in 1907 at the age of 18 and it was the moment when Lueger ruled the city almost as a local dictator. Later Hitler was accustomed to praise Lueger, in *Mein Kampf* and in speeches. He declared that it was in Vienna that he became anti-Semitic. Lueger was not personally anti-Semitic, that is, he had Jewish friends and treated individual Jews fairly. His anti-Jewishness was for party purposes, not for private life. But he was capable of defending anti-Semite fanatics. There are those who believe that his milder sort of prejudice, though apparently

<hr>

[29] Cf. S. Dubnow, *History of the Jews* (Philadelphia, 1973) (Eng. trans. from the 4th rev. edn.), v. 476 ff.

more pardonable, was more dangerous because it made prejudice socially acceptable.

Cardinal Puzyna, who came from southern Poland and uttered the veto against Cardinal Rampolla, doubted Rampolla partly because he seemed to befriend the party of Karl Lueger in Vienna.

In 1895 the rector of the university of Vienna was a Catholic priest, Laurenz Müllner. He was unusual because though he was the professor of Christian philosophy he had dedicated himself to the study of the consequences of Darwin's theory for Christian thought, and so had been denounced to Rome—but vainly. As rector he delivered a brilliant inaugural lecture on the significance of Galileo for philosophy, which at last caused the archbishop and the university to think that they could not afford to keep him in the theological faculty but must move him into the philosophical school.

In a debate on money for the medical school, an anti-Semite attacked the university as Jew-infested. Müllner took the speaker to pieces.

Read Dante, and what he said about Averroës, a Semite; he was a great spirit. Read Thomas Aquinas, a noble mind and a saint. Even where they do not agree with Jewish scholars they speak in a very different spirit. Every year it is my duty to refute Spinoza. Though I refute him, yet I bow before that great spirit and noble mind.

The anti-Semitic campaign in Vienna and then the Dreyfus case caused an epoch in history. Theodor Herzl was a Jew from Hungary who was sent by a Vienna newspaper to report in Paris and had to study the Dreyfus case. He started by believing that the only hope for full equality for the Jews was by total assimilation, and at moments in his life even thought they must convert to Christianity to achieve this. He once had a dream of leading all the Jews to conversion at St Stephen's cathedral in Vienna. His experience in Budapest, Vienna, and Paris led him to the despairing conviction that however the Jews assimilated to European culture, however patriotic they came to be as citizens of the European States, they would always labour under a prejudice, and so in 1896 he published *Der Judenstaat* ('The Jewish State'), which advocated an independent Jewish homeland; and in the next year he founded, at a meeting in Basle, the Zionist Organization. At first this plan was denounced by many educated Jews. But Zionist headquarters were established in Vienna.

For the belief that Dreyfus was a spy—and disloyal to France as a result, it was said in undertones, of not being properly French, but a Jew—the only evidence was a paper known as the *bordereau*, a list of information for a foreign power, and evidence from an expert in handwriting that this was in his hand. There was also a presumption that if there was a spy among the officers of the army it could not have been a true Frenchman, and the Jewish officer was the obvious suspect. At first the army was inclined to release him for want of evidence—but then extreme newspapers ran an anti-Jewish campaign, one demanded that Dreyfus be shot, and another urged that Jews be expelled from France. Hence he was put on trial before a court-martial, during which a fellow-officer, Henry, who believed in his guilt and wanted to make sure that he did not get away, lied to secure the conviction. The people of France were wholeheartedly against this spy and glad that he was degraded from his rank and sent to Devil's Island.

Nothing yet could be said to affect the Church, unless it was that wise men and women were nauseated by unchristian articles in certain journals.

Six months later an honourable officer, Colonel Picquart, who believed that Dreyfus was guilty, became the head of military intelligence and went through the dossier. He found a little blue note from an unknown in the German embassy in Paris to another French officer, Esterhazy. He followed the trail of Esterhazy and discovered other evidence to suggest that Esterhazy was a German agent. He secured a specimen of Esterhazy's writing and saw that it was the same hand as that which had written the *bordereau*.

He told his superiors. But now reason of state destroyed the moral sense. If Dreyfus was not guilty, not only was another officer a spy, but other officers must have told lies to convict him and, at a time when there was a threat from Germany, the army would be utterly dishonoured if this came out. The credit of the army, which was the security of France, depended upon the verdict of the trial of Dreyfus being right or believed by the public to be right. They told Colonel Picquart to keep his mouth shut, and sent him to a post in Africa. The lying officer Henry, to ensure that doubts did not grow and that his career was not destroyed, forged a letter to prove Dreyfus's guilt. Then all the authority of the army was used to prove that justice was done.

Nothing here, one might think, to throw French Catholicism into a state far worse than disarray. Judges make mistakes, witnesses are corrupt, armies know that on their reputation rests the security of the State and try to cover up what tarnishes their glamour. In such circumstances a Church is not touched. But this turned out not to be true.

In July 1897, when Dreyfus had spent three years in prison and all France, except Picquart and a handful of his superior officers, still believed that he was a spy and was glad, it was suddenly clear that this affair must come back to the public. Picquart disclosed the efforts of the generals to prevent him saying what he had found. The distant Dreyfus was again on trial in the French newspapers. The army command was in this so deeply that it was essential to them to prove that he was guilty.

The first thing all this showed was the extent of a virulent anti-Semitism in the middle class; and incidentally among a number of the lower clergy, monarchist, traditional, conservative, longing for the old France, and fearing liberalism. The next thing was the use of the case for political ends by the anti-Catholic and radical wing. The clericals, they cried, were anti-Semitic and against that equality and liberty which was the gift to Europe of the French Revolution. It seemed to be a battle about human rights—which, in a way, it was. But the Church was identified with the attack upon human rights, for in divided France the officer corps of the army was linked to the Church. Anyone who wanted Dreyfus retried was regarded as an assailant of the honour of France, a trampler upon the flag, a person who wished to weaken France before the coming invasion from the east. The general staff still had this excuse—they did not know that Henry had lied in court, nor that the letter which he produced as evidence was forged. During 1898 monks and religious, especially the Assumptionists who edited *La Croix*, used all their force, sermons, articles, and tracts, to defend the honour of the army against Jews who supported Dreyfus. If an officer in the army or navy was known to be a republican, or a free-thinker, he was not likely to get promotion. There was still loose talk of the possibility of an army coup against the republic.

The Assumptionists, a short name for the Augustinians of the Assumption, were a modern order founded in France. During the 1840s the vicar-general of Nîmes, Emmanuel d'Alzon, set up an association of priests and lay people which was dedicated to teaching in all its forms. They added a fourth vow to the usual three, a vow to struggle mightily for the kingdom of God among Christian and non-Christian souls; and Rome did not quite like the unusual addition of this fourth vow and caused them trouble with their statutes. By 1880 there were 100 fathers, already under threat of expulsion from France.

D'Alzon organized crowded pilgrimages to Lourdes, allowed the first big pilgrimage to La Salette, sent missionaries to Madagascar and Zaire, and founded a scholarly institute of Byzantine studies. He died in 1880 just when his order was under threat of expulsion with the other French orders. Three years later his successor François Picard founded *La Croix*, which by 1900 had the reputation of being the fiercest of the ultramontane journals and its editor the name of being a new Veuillot. The governments hated it.

The monks turned *La Croix* into a daily newspaper, which commanded at its best an enormous circulation for those days, over half a million copies. Its editor Father Bailly had the qualities of a crusading journalist, with cries of resistance to the government even unto death. *La Croix* dedicated itself to the anti-Dreyfus cause. This was the most powerful and extreme journalism ever conducted by an otherworldly religious order during the history of Christendom. And governments of the republican left needed to hold their divided forces together by means of an enemy, and the obvious enemy was the Church.

Esterhazy was put on trial and on 11 January 1898 was acquitted. Two days later Émile Zola published his 'J'Accuse' in the newspaper *L'Aurore*, and so a famous writer exposed the whole cover-up to scorn and fury. Zola made himself fiercely unpopular, for nearly all France still believed that Dreyfus was a spy. Anti-Semites went mad as did Nazis later. Jewish shops were sacked in several towns, synagogues were invaded, windows of Jewish homes and shops were broken, machines in Jewish-owned factories were wrecked, in Algeria 158 Jewish shops were ransacked, and Jewish girls found in the streets were stripped naked and smeared with dung. That moment early in the France of 1898 was comparable with the Crystal Night in the Germany of forty years later.

Amid this surge of nationalism and folly, Colonel Picquart, in bad trouble with his nationalism, stated openly that the letter produced by Colonel Henry was a forgery. He was imprisoned by the Minister of War, Cavaignac. But Picquart's statement, and the fury it produced, caused the minister to order that an officer should once again look at the whole dossier. It took army intelligence one evening to see that Henry's letter was not only a forgery but crude, made out of two different bits of paper. Cavaignac had this checked and then confronted Henry. He confessed the forgery, was sent to prison, and killed himself with a razor, while Esterhazy fled the country. From exile in England he disclosed what he had done. The effect in the French nation was overwhelming. They had believed in Dreyfus's guilt. Now, suddenly, many believed in a corrupt army.

In August 1899 Dreyfus was retried before a court martial at Rennes, amid noisy demonstrations against his supporters round the courtroom. The judges condemned him again, though they allowed extenuating circumstances. President Loubet instantly bestowed a pardon. That he was not acquitted was still a scandal. The conflict of opinion moved out upon the international stage. Protestants everywhere condemned the papacy for the Dreyfus Affair, though the papacy had nothing to do with the matter. So far as he expressed an opinion publicly, Leo XIII was on the side of Dreyfus. In March 1899 he was said to have compared Dreyfus to Jesus on Calvary.[30] The French bishops were prudent and stayed silent, except for Cardinal Mathieu of Toulouse who deplored this attempt to acquit a traitor and attack the French army. But somehow French Catholics, whether or not they stayed silent, really felt themselves on the side of the army and against the defenders of Dreyfus. In Rome the Jesuit journal *Civiltà Cattolica* (January 1898) published an article which forty years later Fascists used to justify their anti-Semitism, and which held the French Revolution wrong to concede French citizenship to the Jews.

Government hoped that now Dreyfus was pardoned the warring parties of France would be reconciled and the case would be forgotten. It was kept going by two campaigns. The smaller was the demand by the family and friends of Dreyfus that he should be rehabilitated; which did not happen until 1906. The more divisive was the government's recognition that the repute of the army needed protection; and therefore the quarrel must be got rid of by a general amnesty for all officers who might have misbehaved during the case. What truculence of speaking this amnesty aroused needs no description. It was carried by large majorities but the debate did nothing to reconcile the French to each other.

The attempt of Leo XIII to make French Catholics reconcile themselves to the republic had failed totally. The articulate republic

---

[30] Leo was talking to the editor of the Paris newspaper *Figaro*. When the editor printed it the Curia did not deny the words.

was now violent against the Church and articulate churchmen were now violent against the republic. The Prime Minister Waldeck-Rousseau started an onslaught upon monks and nuns.

On 24 January 1900 the Assumptionists appeared in court on a charge of using language that was harmful to the State, and were condemned to be dissolved and to pay a fine. Pope Leo XIII did not try to defend them. He asked them not to edit *La Croix*. The government stopped the pay of six French bishops who expressed their sympathy for the order. They then turned the incident into a bill that dissolved all the non-authorized religious congregations unless they obtained authorization within six months (from July 1901). If they won authorization they must be under the bishop and not under a foreign superior.

Most orders or houses asked for authorization because the act left them no alternative if they were to survive. The Benedictines left the country, the Jesuits got permission to go secular, and handed over their schools and colleges to lay teachers.

Waldeck-Rousseau was a cold lawyer who raised anticlericalism to high principle, as an attitude which no State ought to be without. He saw himself as defending the sovereignty of civil society against its ecclesiastical invaders. He needed the Church as an enemy to hold together an uncomfortable alliance of radicals with socialists. He professed a strong liberalism; it was odd to find a strong liberal starting a campaign of intolerance against monks and nuns.

The religious congregations, he argued, were controlled by the old kings of France. Under Napoleonic and republican France monks and nuns grew in number without anyone doing anything, and gained wealth and property. They were bad for the State because they were ultramontane, and educated the young in hostility to modern France, and divided society into democratic and anti-democratic. The State should rid itself of monks that intrigue in politics, and control tightly all other religious. He thought that the Church needed to defend itself against the monks, who usurped the authority, he imagined, of bishops and pastors. They trained most of the clergy, opened chapels which rivalled the parish churches, and carried on conflict with the bishops. Waldeck-Rousseau was under the illusion that bishops and parish priests would welcome his assault upon the monks.

Under the laws of Napoleon and the Restoration, the orders of monks and nuns were only legal if they did certain kinds of pastoral work. The many others were not legal but 'tolerated'. That is, 909 congregations of nuns were legal, and five of monks.[31] A law of 1901 threw all non-legal religious out of teaching posts. To get round the law the monks went through fictitious processes of secularization.

The election of May 1902 was fought largely on religious grounds; anticlerical speeches against ultramontane speeches. The anticlericals increased their majority a little and turned their anger into fury. Waldeck-Rousseau handed over the ministry to Émile Combes, the bitterest anticlerical to attain power in democratic Europe. Combes was a tubby little man with a pious mother, had been an ultramontane young man educated in three seminaries, and had written a thesis on the philosophy of St Thomas Aquinas and another on the battle between Abelard and St Bernard. He prepared for ordination, but was rightly refused. He married and qualified as a doctor, then went into politics as an advanced republican and was determined in demanding revision of the Dreyfus trial; a fanatical anti-Catholic who still thought religion important to the morality of society and had a dream of a national Church where all the *curés* would be like Rousseau, where Rome would have no authority but the State would direct a religiously tinged moral code. This could not be achieved without exploding Catholicism; which he wished to do. France, he thought, must be brought into the modern world of science and progress and get rid of these superstitions. It was said that he was less like a Prime Minister than like the leader of a crusade. It was calculated roughly that no Prime Minister in the history of Prime Ministers in any country had ever been more frequently interrupted in a Parliament. He had an affectionate correspondence with a Carmelite nun who revered him. She was a prioress at Algiers who came to Paris to persuade him not to touch her nunnery; she got her way, and the meeting set up a friendship. In the end she returned to the world.

Combes closed all the schools run by nuns, 2,000 schools and more, whose permit was doubtful or not applied for. In a few villages in Brittany there were peasant barricades, and with an uncharacteristic (for the French) piece of tyranny Combes got his own back by forbidding all priests to use the Breton language under penalty of losing their pay. It took 6,000 troops to ensure order at an unveiling, in the presence of Combes, of a statue of Renan at his Breton birthplace. All through 1903 Combes closed schools or nursing homes run by

---

[31] A. Dansette, *Histoire religieuse de la France contemporaine*, new edn. (1965), 570.

sisters, and refused permits to those which applied. 'The member of
a religious order', said Combes, 'has lost, by the fact of entering a religious order, his rights to the liberties of civil society.'[32]

Two missionary orders, including the White Fathers, and three
other orders, including the Cistercians and the Trappists, were
granted permits. There were demonstrations against closures, the
biggest in Paris at the Place de la Concorde and the garden of the
Tuileries, and in some places physical resistance. The protests were
hottest when the nuns were ejected. In Brittany the peasants gathered
piles of ordure as ammunition to bespatter soldiers and police. 'The
worst incident happened at the Grande Chartreuse. The colonel who
was ordered to close the house and expel the monks resigned.
Thousands of peasants gathered with cudgels, beacons were lit on the
hills, the soldiers had to open the road past blocks of carriages. They
arrested the Carthusians in their chapel one by one at three o'clock
in the morning with a crowd outside singing hymns.'

The monks and nuns went abroad—Belgium, Britain, Italy.
Britain was to benefit permanently from the congregation of French
Benedictines of Solesmes which settled at Quarr Abbey on the Isle of
Wight and Farnborough Abbey near Aldershot.

Some congregations carried out the extreme measure of monks
under persecution and secularized themselves, outwardly, to avoid
the law while continuing privately to follow their calling; that did not
bring them back their public functions. Occasionally they were
helped by locals, who did not want them but wanted the money they
brought. Many nuns teaching in primary schools went on doing so
but discarded their habits; and this compromise saved about 5,000
schools and was a great help to primary education. The local administration in Hautes-Pyrénées was radical but begged Combes to spare
the sanctuary at Lourdes because on it depended the prosperity of the
region.

Demonstrators began to interrupt church services; there were out-
rages in the cathedral at Rheims. In a riot at Lorient workers attacked
a religious procession and in the fight six people were killed and 450
wounded. Combes took the crucifixes out of the lawcourts and
handed over responsibility for all burials to the municipalities. A law
of 1904 banned all monks and nuns from teaching—which was very
serious, for more than 8,000 schools had the proper permit and were

---

[32] A. Dansette, *Histoire religieuse de la France contemporaine*, new edn. (1965), 579.

not yet struck by law or government. President Loubet signed the bill with distaste and his wife, who was pious, said that her husband was dishonoured. It was accepted that an ex-monk or ex-nun could not be stopped from teaching, and there was an argument about whether the right to teach (if qualified) was part of the right of a citizen and whether therefore it could not be right to prohibit a religious from being a teacher—but the argument fell and the monks were banned. The state confiscated the property of the religious communities that it dissolved. As in the dissolution of Henry VIII too much property was sold on the market at once, with a lowering effect on prices.

All this was a curious survival of a vanishing world. A democratic republic in modern educated Europe (in which, it must always be remembered in watching Combes keep his shaky majority, women had no vote) still thought that the State knew enough to distinguish religious truth from error, that it could determine Catholicism to be error, and that its duty as a State doing its best for its people was to get rid of such error by penalties and confiscation. No one must think that the idea of toleration was rapid in its conquest of the world.

Under the French Concordat of 1801 Napoleon took the right to nominate bishops. The pope could give them canonical institution and after a time claimed the right to refuse it, but the French government did the choosing. The system worked well because all governments wanted good bishops. Twice Pope Pius IX refused canonical institution and the see was left vacant. After the fall of Louis Napoleon in 1870 the new republic started the habit of informing the nuncio before it made public its nominations. Combes would have no truck with such courtesies towards Rome. Rome (still with Leo XIII as pope) refused the nominations. Several sees were not filled.

Combes chose clergymen who backed the republic. Leo XIII accepted only one out of five nominations and refused to give reasons for the four refusals. The pope now claimed an absolute right to refuse anyone whom the State named, and this was not compatible with the Concordat. Combes made a speech in Parliament saying that he named irreproachable clergymen to sees and the pope was violating French rights.

Combes wanted the Concordat to hold. He did not wish to lose the right to choose bishops, nor did he want the State to lose the other controls over the Church which the Concordat had given. He liked power and did not want to risk losing his majority in Parliament by a bill for disestablishment which might fail under the combined forces of the Catholic right and antichristian left who would vote to keep controls over the Church. But Combes was driving Parliament into a situation where the establishment of the Church was so ludicrous an anachronism that, to be consistent with himself, he would have to do what he did not wish to do, propose its disestablishment. And on the other side the entire development of the papacy since Gregory XVI had created claims for the pope of such a nature that the old compromises that used to make the Concordat workable were not now possible without Rome knowing that they contradicted moral principles.

The tension was made worse by a tough quarrel over ceremonial acts. As part of a Franco-Italian alliance, the French President Loubet went to Rome to visit the king of Italy. This was important to France because Russia, which it now saw as its chief protector against Germany, was in trouble over the Russo-Japanese war, and it seemed good to the French to try to detach Italy from its German–Austrian alliance. If the head of a non-Catholic country, such as Kaiser William (who actually ruled some 16 million Catholics), visited the king of Italy the pope had nothing to say and the Kaiser could be courteously received by the pope. It was true that when the German sovereign came all did not go as it was planned; for it was made a condition that he should not go straight from the pope to greet King Humbert. But William II did precisely that, and proposed his health as king of Italy. Still, the German emperor drank a toast to the pope at a formal meal, and what was not perfect could be overlooked, for this was a Protestant and could not be expected to know how to behave in a Catholic world.

But France was a country where Catholicism was the established religion. A Catholic head of State was expected to pay a call on the pope and not on the king. Since the pope did not recognize the king of Italy as King of Italy the visit was offensive to the papacy. The French needed the Italian alliance, and did not mind if the result was a break with the pope. Why should modern republican France, which knew that it needed real help against a future German threat, bother with the States of the Church which were a memory of history or a pretence? But ultramontane newspapers said that this was a plot to overthrow the papacy and dechristianize France. Catholics in Parliament were in favour of the visit even though he could not see the pope. Most of them voted for the motion granting the expenses for the expedition.

If Leo were still pope, and Rampolla the Secretary of State, they would have protested gently. But there was a new pope. When the French President arrived in Rome (24 April 1904), the Italians used the visit to make it antipapal—with placards and ceremonies. Cardinal Merry del Val, as Secretary of State, protested to France and all the powers. The message was in very undiplomatic language, describing the king of Italy as 'the person who hangs on (*détient*) to power'. It was not that the French President refused to call upon the pope, it was that the pope refused to receive a call from the French President because he had just visited the king of Italy who in the pope's eyes was not the king of Italy.

Merry del Val's message was supposed to be confidential but since he sent copies to other governments it was sure to leak. The Socialist newspaper in Paris received it from Montecarlo (where the prince disliked the pope) and published it, and Combes used the excuse to break diplomatic relations between Rome and the Holy See. Nuncio and ambassador left. Combes said in Parliament that it was time to finish with this obsolete fiction of the temporal power of the pope. Many Catholics in Parliament must have preferred to end diplomatic relations because they voted on his side, and he carried the motion by 427 to 95.

SEPARATION OF CHURCH AND STATE IN FRANCE

State and Church were in perpetual dispute; bishops were so often deprived of their stipends, priests were so often suspended, monks were driven out of the country. The Dreyfus Affair almost destroyed the reputation of the French army, and with that was entangled the standing of the Church.

Not many Catholic leaders wanted the separation of Church and State. A little handful of bishops thought it good, and believed that disestablishment would restore dignity and pastoral freedom. But Rome had always taught that the separation of Church and State was an evil, and the Syllabus condemned it. Moreover, every Catholic worried about money; how would the clergy be paid, or pastoral work financed, or buildings maintained, if the Church lost the money guaranteed by its establishment under the Concordat?

In January 1905 Combes, whose government in other areas showed huge political incompetence, fell from power. It was discovered to have set up a system of secret informers, mostly Freemasons, over various public offices especially those connected with the army. Nevertheless the bill for disestablishment went forward.

Catholics in the Chamber reminded the members of the terrors that happened after the last French disestablishment. They argued that it was good for a State to profess a faith, that the two institutions of Church and State needed each other for a healthy society; that disestablishment would free bishops and clergy to enter politics and that would be bad for both Church and State; that the French Revolution took the endowments of the Church under an agreement that it would provide a proper budget for the Church. Therefore disestablishment ought in justice to mean the restoration to the Church of its property. They were offended that the government was wreaking revolution in the affairs of the Church without the least consultation with Rome.

The act of disestablishment went through various projects and drafts; some as hostile to the Church as the Bolshevik act in Russia a few years later (with measures to eject Churches from the country, take over all the property including the church buildings, ban religious teaching in any form of school, etc.), others much less hostile but still unfriendly. The final act was less hostile than the first drafts; partly because of international politics and the threat from Germany when France's ally Russia was so weakened by the Russo-Japanese war, partly because the drafter Aristide Briand, though still an extreme socialist, was a humane person, but mainly because government could not succeed with any bill which moderates refused to vote for.

The act as accepted (9 December 1905) gave freedom of worship to everyone provided it was consistent with public order; withdrew all government money from any denomination unless for army chaplaincies, prisons, hospitals, or schools. All Church property that existed before the Concordat of 1801 would return to State ownership.

There were to be inventories of buildings and furniture belonging to churches. Within one year all these properties, including churches, vicarages, bishops' *mensas*, would be transferred to the ownership of 'associations', that is, local associations for worship which alone the State would recognize as corporations with the right to administer Church property. These associations had to act in accordance with the rules of the denomination the worship of which they were to provide for (hence it was later argued successfully that any Catholic association must be under the bishop). If no association was formed in a region within the year given above, all the property of that place would be sequestered and given to public welfare in that region.

Who would belong to these associations to provide for worship? Article 19 said that if the village was less than 1,000 the association should have seven members; if less than 20,000, fifteen members; if more, twenty-five persons, all domiciled in that area. It did not say that the persons would be men, nor that the members of an association to promote Catholic worship must be Catholics. It did not say (though one of the drafts had said) that clergy could not be members of an association.

Any association which had a surplus of money could give it to another association. No political meeting was to be held in a place of worship. Worship was not to be disturbed by intruders. Processions outside church, and the use of bells, would continue (as before) to be subject to local permission.

Children of between 6 and 13 enrolled at state schools could be given religious instruction only outside school hours. For eight years from 1905 ministers were ineligible for public office in the district where they served the church. The money saved from the budget that supported the Churches would be given to the authorities of the local communities. The Concordat of 1801 and its Organic Articles of 1802 were repealed.

All suggestion that Catholicism was the religion of most Frenchmen vanished; the State abandoned its part in choosing bishops. The law brought liberty to the Church, in meetings and synods, nevertheless the Church excommunicated the members of Parliament who voted for the law.

No clumsier scheme for disestablishing a Church could have been devised. It was made slightly less clumsy by Aristide Briand's drafting, but the whole was vitiated by a partisan incompetence. Some of the debaters engaged were rational persons, but the bill had to be got through in spite of disarray among various speakers who supported it, some of whom were determined to smash the Church while others were resolute that shreds of justice and liberality should be preserved. These incompatible wishes gave birth to the contortions of the act, leading to trouble for France and worse trouble for the Church of France.

The first snag was the order to make inventories. The law was passed in December 1905. In the next two months officers visited the churches to list what they owned. In most places this happened peacefully, though with sour looks. But in smaller communities the villagers believed that the officers came to despoil or blaspheme. Throughout France came an unpleasant series of little village battles, when the people resisted the inventory. A very foolish circular from the head of the civil service office told the persons making the lists that they must open and inspect the tabernacles on the altar, which contained the reserved sacrament. Most Church people thought such an intrusion blasphemous; certainly it trampled on sacred feelings. In Brittany peasants afraid of sacrilege put up barricades; knives came out, some fetched their guns. At a village near Tarascon a chandelier dropped on the head of a state officer. In two Paris churches, St Clotilde the worse, there were scenes of violence with well-dressed demonstrators going from church to church singing hymns till dispersed with the hose from a fire engine. In the Basque country they chained Pyrenean bears at the doors of churches. Occasionally mantraps were left lying on the floor of the church. Some villagers stayed up all night, several nights running, to guard the churches. In Haute-Loire all attempts to get inside any of the churches failed. In some areas officials, shut out and not willing to use force, invented lists and sent them in.

The cabinet fell and was replaced with a cabinet in which two sane radicals, Briand and Clemenceau—Briand the saner—had authority. The last straw weighed when in Flanders a demonstrator against an inventory was accidentally shot and killed. Briand instantly stopped the inventories. Clemenceau said in the Senate (20 March 1906), 'Chandeliers are not worth a revolution,' and Briand said, 'I'll not risk human life in order to count up the number of chandeliers.'

In the midst of this turmoil over inventories, Pius X pronounced. The encyclical *Vehementer nos* (11 February 1906: 'We are vehemently troubled and in anguish . . . it is a bad crime . . .'[33]) spoke his grief at what had happened to the eldest daughter of the Church. He said how wrong it was to separate Church and State and to pretend that the State's only function was material prosperity and that it had nothing to do with the eternal happiness of its people. The Concordat of 1801 was a treaty, agreed in solemn terms, by which the French government, who had seized Church endowments in the Revolution, undertook to pay stipends to the clergy and to maintain

---

[33] *ASS* 39 (1906), 3.

worship; in return for which the Pope undertook not to molest the then holders of former Church property. The keeping of treaties was the first condition of peace among the nations. This law of separation had tragically divided the French people. Its associations would give the control of churches and worship into the hands of lay people. Pius X expressed this last in terms which showed how he was a man of the nineteenth century and not of the emerging world: 'By its essential being the Church is an unequal society—with two classes, the pastors and their flocks . . . These two are so distinct that all authority lies with the former; and the people have no other duty than to let themselves be governed by their pastors and to follow obediently.'

The French bishops saw that the Pope hated the associations on high principle. But as the dust cleared some of them saw that they must have associations, by the law within a year, if they were to keep their houses, seminaries, *mensa*, perhaps even their churches. They observed that the encyclical *Vehementer*, despite its vehemence against the law and the associations, did not plainly stop them from forming associations. They had established that the pope allowed not too dissimilar associations to the Germans; and that he accepted the law in so far as he allowed priests to keep the small pensions provided.

Several leading intellectuals, led by the respected writer Brunetière, appealed to the pope and the bishops (26 March 1906) to work the law, which they thought could be made tolerable. The bishops met at the Paris archbishopric (31 May 1906) and by a strong majority (48 to 26) agreed that the associations ought to be made workable to ensure the use of the property and the worship of the churches. That they could meet at all was a curious effect of the law, because under the Concordat they could not meet without the leave of government. But twenty-six bishops were a formidable minority when the pope's opinion was so clear.

The Pope bowed to pressure from the French right and on 10 August 1906 in *Gravissimo officii*[34] ('We are under a very heavy duty of our office') he said that he had taken advice from French bishops and from some cardinals, and that he had said his prayers; and so condemned the parish associations, all of which would violate the sacred rights which were essential to a Church: 'You must find other means of bringing worship to the people. I know that I impose a heavy burden upon you.'

[34] *ASS* 39 (1906), 385–90.

Gravissimo was one of the three disastrous encyclicals of the age with which we deal. It was not approved by the responsible congregation in the Curia, the dicastery for Extraordinary Affairs, nor by the secretary of that congregation, Gasparri. But it was approved by the Secretary of State Merry del Val. It was a shining sign of the growth of power; if Gregory XVI had ordered the French bishops to hand over their money and buildings to the State they would not have obeyed him. Several French bishops of 1906, probably most, thought *Gravissimo* a calamity yet knew they must obey it. They met again at the archbishop's house in Paris in September 1906 and gave an assurance that they would obey. Afterwards they took a pride in their self-sacrifice: 'Holy Father, we have followed you to ruin; if necessary, we shall follow you, with God's help, to death.'[35]

On 11 December 1906, therefore, because there were no associations to take control of the Church and the property, the State ejected the bishops from their palaces, the clergy from their vicarages, and the ordinands from the seminaries, sequestered such property and endowments as they could instantly manage, and expelled the ex-nuncio from France. They distributed the money to the communes and districts for welfare so far as that was practicable. They had a piece of good fortune: in breach of international law, Cardinal Merry del Val told Montagnini the auditor of the nuncio, a dubious character who used a bogus title, to stay in his flat and go on with the work that the nuncio had done. When he was found to be pressing clergy to elect right-wingers in the election of 1906, the police raided the flat and seized his dossier of papers—private and unedifying papers of information to Rome, with comments on bishops, clergy, and not a few politicians ('Clemenceau is a very bad man but he is bribable'). The newspapers of Paris were allowed to print whatever they wanted and the publicity caused Rome to appear sinister.[36]

But the State recognized that somehow the churches must he kept for Catholic worship. Briand passed a supplementary act ensuring that.

Three years later the French Church was poor as never before. They still worshipped in their churches, priests said mass undisturbed, they had no excuse to cry persecution; the bishops had authority, even more authority, the worshippers subscribed generously to make up the moneys which the State cancelled—but that was an impossible task. The legal ownership of new-built churches or new-given

---

[35] H. L. Chapon, *L'Église de France et la loi de 1905: Réponse aux objections* (Paris, 1922), 44.
[36] *Les Fiches de Mgr Montagnini* (Paris, 1908); Clemenceau at p. 127.

moneys was precarious—yet they raised enough money to build many new churches in the suburbs of the big towns. There were fewer retreats because the expense could not be met. By strenuous efforts at raising money the bishops kept the senior seminaries in operation, but they had to put them into buildings that were inconvenient and too small. Many of the French bishops were not displeased to be turned out of their too-large palaces, which were cold and sparsely furnished. What hit them hardest was the sharp decline in the number of ordinands. It was difficult to pay for their training, harder to pay their stipends when they were ordained. The great French bishops of the nineteenth century, such as Darboy or Dupanloup, Lavigerie or Pitra, were to have few successors of that stature in the mid-twentieth century.

But, for the first time in French history, and for the first time in any of the historic Catholic countries except Ireland, the pope could choose bishops without interference from the State. At last the sees were filled. The new bishops were escorted into their cathedrals by cheering crowds. The new freedom had merit because prime ministers sometimes chose bishops for political reasons and it had more merit when the prime ministers were anticlerical. But it was not without loss because the State had brought lay influence into the choice of chief pastors and so prevented apostolic succession from being only a co-optation of clergymen by other clergymen. It also had the loss that sometimes the State had taken wider consultations beforehand than now were taken in Rome. There was soon argument between the French bishops and the Curia over the appointments. Though to free the choice of bishop from the Prime Minister might be expected to rid the search of political bias, the pope also chose for political reasons, though Pius X would not have admitted that his reasons were political.

Pius X had to be admired because his sense of right was such that he cared nothing for the practical. Someone asked him how an archbishop of Paris was to do his job without a house to live in, money to spend, or a church to say his prayers in. He said that then one could appoint as archbishop a Franciscan who by his rule was committed to live off what people gave him.[37]

In the summer of 1906, when the quarrel of the inventories was still at its worst, Pius X performed a political act, though to him it was

---

[37] The story was told by the Italian statesman Orlando; F. Hayward, *Pie X* (Paris, 1951), 106.

purely religious, by beatifying sixteen Carmelite nuns of a Compiègne nunnery, who had been imprisoned in the French Revolution, then accused of hiding arms for conspirators and, though two were 82 and 83, killed; they sang *Veni Creator* as they went to the guillotine. Three years later Pius X pleased the French right, and especially the army, by beatifying Joan of Arc. Forty thousand French pilgrims came to Rome for the ceremony. When Pius X came to the tricolour, symbol of all that monarchist France detested, he kissed it.

Not all France was pleased about Joan of Arc. No member of the French government attended her elevation. The process to get her beatified had continued for thirty-three years—and some said that the act was more political than religious, a sop to the right and a beating of the left, which was the government. Royalists were so ecstatic at the news that they alarmed moderate persons. A German theologian asked what her virtues were and decided that her main merit was patriotism which had never been a cardinal virtue.[38]

Flexibility by the government in not pressing the letter of the law, and by a majority of the bishops who had to comply with the law without seeming to be disloyal to the pope, succeeded together in making the law tolerable. The government was faced with a situation which it had never expected—that most of the historic monuments of France, which were the churches, now belonged to communes, some of which were neither rich enough, nor religious enough, to want to keep them in repair. The churches, if in repair, were still occupied by their priests and congregations, but on insecure tenures. The government quickly got most of the old churches classified as historic monuments and able to receive grants. But churches which were not classified could be valuable artistically, and still more so religiously. As the law of separation stood, the commune was not bound to repair, and the congregation was not bound to repair, yet the French government would be very embarrassed if churches fell down, even though the radical left in Parliament made speeches claiming that nothing could be better for France than all the churches falling down, for then France would be full of rationality and free from superstition.

[38] At the ceremony Bishop Touchet of Orleans made a warm, patriotic speech in thanks. The critics also said that the three miracles all happened to nuns, and they complained about the text, uttering the untruth that the execution was ordered by the ferocious enemies of Rome. *Acta Pii X*, iv. 309 ff.; letters to Bishop Touchet in *AAS* 1 (1909), 230, 250, 489, 502; to Fuzet of Rouen for the setting up of a Joan monument there, AAS 3 (1911), 316, (10 June 1911).

Those not so far to the left said that the plight of the churches was the fault of the pope's intransigence, and it was not Parliament's duty to clear up the mess. The other side kept saying that if religion were removed from the villages, rationalism would not take its place, instead there would be magic, astrology, superstition, and charlatanry. There was no common ground between the two sides except the assent that works of art should be maintained or put in museums.

Across France came strange scenes. Most municipalities, enriched with a share from the former budget of cults, accepted that they must repair the churches. The Caen municipality gave 200,000 francs to put five churches in repair and the county authority added 65,000 more. Others refused to repair but did not stop the congregation collecting money to do so. But some municipalities refused both courses of action, preferring the churches to crack. At Grisny-Suisnes a church was demolished—the commune said it was redundant, and probably it was—but a scene of corpse-shifting was accompanied by gravediggers hunting through the corpses for valuables in the presence of the village schoolchildren, which shocked France. In the Aube someone saw poor and sick women weeping in the porch of a closed village church, too ill to get to the next village. Processions which had formerly passed through the streets were no longer allowed to be public and were held in some large garden near the church. Mayors, now that they owned the churches, used the bells for civil occasions, like summoning the children to school. Near Noyers in the Yonne there was a calvary, sculpted in the early eighteenth century. The commune refused to repair it and refused leave to the congregation to do so on the ground that it was a religious work in a public place and under the law of separation that was not allowed, as it would be propaganda. The Historical Monuments Commission appealed to the government and after twenty months the commune lost and the calvary was put in order.

All France was concerned, in anger, or shame, or laughter, by the latrines of St Martin at Vendôme. The bell-tower of St Martin's was classified as a monument. It belonged to the commune, and the commune needed public lavatories. So the mayor put the latrines into the bell-tower and used tombstones from the graveyard in making them. In the latrine it was possible to read the inscription, 'Here rests the widow Doré, died 1900 aged 85, pray for her soul'. There was to be a ceremonious opening of the latrines on Good Friday. A national storm forced the stones to be returned to the cemetery. A Parisian antique dealer plastered notices on the walls of Lorraine villages that he would give very good prices for old statues, in stone or wood, even if they were damaged.[39]

Slowly, a majority of the bishops made the new situation work. An anticlerical government, where the majority hung on its being anticlerical, could not go into reverse overnight. But it was soon plain that though by majority male France was willing for disestablishment, they had no idea that this would mean that the churches could fall down or be closed, and were not willing for any such consequence. Aristide Briand thought that village churches could be used as rendezvous for peasants, but he was resolute that they should be fairly treated. He was told that he could only achieve the result he wanted if he reopened negotiations with the pope, but this he was not willing to do and to keep his majority he could not afford what would look like weakness. With administrative help the new law began to work and after a time the bishops made it work well.

Many communes behaved very well to the churches of which they were now the legal 'owners'. There was a special decision at Lourdes: on 9 April 1910 a decree confiscated the properties at the shrine and handed them over to the commune. The bishop protested that this was sacrilege and injustice. But he did not need to: the commune voted *unanimously* that they were indeed the legal owners; but that they would hold the shrine in perpetual trusteeship, to leave it at the disposal of the diocesan to hold worship and organize what was needed for all the pilgrims.[40]

The next Pope, Benedict XV, in effect, though not in words, accepted the associations. But this was easier because the government of 1919 was very different in mood from the government of 1910. In 1921, with Briand as Prime Minister, the government restored diplomatic relations with the Vatican. Briand had a continual sense that all was not well with what he had done, though he also knew that things could have been still worse if he had not taken charge of the bill. As early as 1914 he told Bishop Lacroix that, far from pushing the Church out of national life, he wanted it to be 'the great moral teacher of our democracy'.[41] A great war made the fight over anticlericalism irrelevant. In 1924 another pope, Pius XI, openly accepted the associations. The system was fully legal again.

---

[39] M. Barrès, *La Grande Pitié des églises de France* (Paris, 1914), 97–8, 204 ff., 303 ff., 406.
[40] *CC* (1910), 2: 372.　　　　　　[41] F. Siebert, *Aristide Briand* (Zurich, 1973), 79.

Yet the Church never fully recovered from the predicament forced upon it by the single will of Pius X. They had lost about 350 million francs; and that included the bishops' *mensas* and their palaces, many of which became public buildings, schools, or museums—the Paris archbishop's house became the Ministry of Labour;[42] the vicarages, though many communes let the priest continue to use the house at a modest rent (and no commune tried to charge rent for the use of the church); the endowments of chapters and seminaries—the historic seminary of Saint-Sulpice became a museum. It meant that the churches had to be insistent with the collecting bags at services, and raise fees for marriages, funerals, and baptisms, which was the way to make the Church more middle class. The problem of paying the priests even a subsistence wage pressed upon bishops, though richer dioceses did help poorer. The bishops had been helped by donations from the rich but now they were more dependent than before upon those lay people for they needed their money not just for extra charities or new churches but to exist adequately. It was awkward leaving money to a church because the congregation had no legal personality and the money must go to the priest, and risked being passed to his heirs. Slowly bodies of trustees were formed for these purposes. By 1913 some 2,000 churches were under the protection of ancient monuments and so could get repair by State money though the State would only pay half the cost if the other half was raised locally; except in cathedrals, where the State paid all.

It had been a bad act of disestablishment. It needed more acts of Parliament and many acts of the administrations to make it workable at all. Nearly twenty years later it was working. The malady that needed such prolonged cure was caused by: (1) Pope Pius IX saying that the modern world, democracy, and socialism were deplorable; (2) the fatal axiom of the French right wing that Catholicism was its political strength; (3) the fanaticism of some of the left politicians in the French Chamber, a prejudice which meant not only that the measure must be passed, but that it could not be a sensible measure; (4) the decision of Pius X, who was so otherworldly that he did not think money to matter in the work of a Church, to sacrifice the endowments on a principle which was clear to him but was not clear to a majority of the French bishops; and (5) the centralization of authority during the

---

[42] One bishop, Rodez, lived in his old palace and paid a rent to its new owner, the Department.

nineteenth century which made it impossible for the bishops to disregard the Pope's decision.

What happened in France between 1870 and 1914 affected far more than the French Church. Their orders of monks and nuns were among the most flourishing, their contribution to missions in the East and Africa was exceptional, their work in Catholic education indispensable. By 1914 they were turned out of many schools, monks and nuns were in exile, the wealth of French Catholics was more urgently needed to maintain the disestablished Church at home rather than the hospitals and congregations of the Far East or French Africa. That affected what popes were able to do.

THE ROMAN QUESTION AND ITALIAN POLITICS

Soon after the election of Pius X it was clear that the old fight between the pope and the Italian government was obsolete. As late as January 1901 the Duke of Norfolk went on pilgrimage to Rome and in his speech said that the new century would restore to the pope his temporal power. At the Catholic Congress of Taranto in 1901 a fierce bishop of Leghorn raised the historic cry 'Rome or death!'.[43] But with the coming of Pius X such utterances sounded quieter. The struggle against Italy was never to be carried on again with the same fury as under Pius IX and Leo XIII. The protest was maintained, but it turned into ritual, and even the ritual altered. The language seemed to accept that Rome was the capital of Italy, and that the king was not only the king of Savoy but also the king of Italy. Cardinal Svampa, the archbishop of Bologna, was allowed to visit the king and do homage.[44]

It must not be thought that all was peaceable with the Italian left. The Italian troops in St Peter's Square presented arms at the pope's coronation, which was not a little thing because coronation was a ritual claim to temporal power. But if the Italian government was less unfriendly, Italian radicals were hard as ever—every 20 September, the day when Rome fell in 1870, the walls were covered with anticlerical placards, which were often gross; to maintain the memory of the erection of the statue of Giordano Bruno as a way of bashing

[43] G. Spadolini, *Giolitti e i cattolici 1901–14* (Florence, 1960), 75.
[44] But see p. 390 the visit of President Loubet of France. Svampa's visit was not the first. Under Leo XIII Cardinal Ferrari of Milan made a long visit to King Humbert at Monza.

Pope Leo XIII, a Giordano Bruno society acquired an office not far from the pope's windows and hung displays which no pope could enjoy. Nor were the words from the Vatican always of perfect courtesy. King Humbert was murdered by an anarchist at Monza. His son Victor Emmanuel III was the grandson of the king who took Rome and it might be expected that lapse of time would oil civilities between the two crowned heads in Italy.

But the long liberal Parliamentary reign of Italy was in trouble from the left. The dominant politician of the early twentieth century, Giolitti, could not yet say that he needed Catholic votes to defeat socialists, for if he offered Catholics an alliance he would lose liberal supporters. But he did need Catholics, and Catholics saw that he needed them and ceased to obey the order not to vote in national elections. Bishops consulted the Pope about this behaviour and he told them to give the people whatever advice they thought right.

In June 1905 an encyclical (*Il fermo proposito*) at last lifted the papal ban on Catholics taking part in the elections to the Italian Parliament. It seemed to be a half-hearted change, for the Pope allowed only that each bishop decide whether voters in his diocese might take part in political life. He made it clear that voting in elections should be only an exceptional permission. The Jesuit journal *Civiltà Cattolica*[45] compared the permission to eat meat on Fridays, there is a Catholic rule against it but for good reasons it is often allowed. The bishop must think the concession 'wise for the good of souls and the supreme interests of the Church'. But whatever the appearance, this was decisive. To keep out socialists, Catholics already voted in alliance with liberals and the old ban collapsed. The change, in this form, did not allow the possibility of a Catholic political party in Italy, but it was a long step nearer to that event.

Radical deputies might still shout in the Italian Chamber, 'Long live Giordano Bruno!' or 'Down with the clericals!' But the government was more moderate than its predecessors. In Faenza leave was given for a religious procession. The police suppressed a demonstration, aimed in the old form to disrupt the walkers. A question was asked in Parliament (14 June 1904) about this behaviour of the police, and the government affirmed its devotion to religious liberty. This was a change since the government's antipapal remarks after the riot that almost threw the body of Pius IX into the River Tiber.

---

[45] *CC* (1904), 4: 489–90.

In parts of Italy the local struggles went on. Processions on Corpus Christi Day still faced public meetings on the street which the procession had to pass, and then shovings could turn into violence. In 1910 at Milan and Turin agitators cried out for Giordano Bruno, and 'Down with religion!' and trouble started among the crowds.[46] But by now prefects did all they could to avoid turmoil and protect processions.

Before long deputies in Parliament were identifiable as 'Catholic deputies' though there was no Catholic party. In 1911 the prefect of Milan reported that at a festival at Sesto San Giovanni, with a cardinal present, amid feasting and fireworks, the socialists did not dare to run a counter-demonstration. And a 'Catholic deputy' made a speech in favour of universal suffrage, which, he said 'could bring not a few advantages to the Catholic party'.[47] When a deputy talked in this way, the State could not be far from seeing a Catholic political party. Such a thing Pope Pius X could never countenance.

In the general election of 1913 the Pope approved an agreement known as the Gentiloni Pact; whereby Catholics, where they were not strong enough to elect a deputy of their own, agreed to vote for a moderate liberal candidate who would maintain religious liberty in Parliament and support the family and the country.

For the first time Catholics moved into Italian politics wholeheartedly. That was not due to the Pope, it would have happened without his assent, though more slowly. But he could have made it awkward and so his friendliness was important. The stability of the Italian government still required that it was publicly against the Vatican, and it was still important to the Pope not to be seen to be the private chaplain of the king of Italy, and therefore he must be in protest against him. But the protests of both sides moved away into ceremonial; yet slowly, for the Italian government refused the *exequatur* to the see of Genoa as late as 1912 and the Pope inflicted a quarter of an interdict on the city, a weapon that was out of date some centuries before.[48]

It was a time of various irritations. The Pope was very ill in the spring of 1913 and almost died; the Swiss guards at the Vatican

---

[46] *CC* (1910), 2: 748. [47] Spadolini, *Giolitti*, 147.

[48] The ground seemed to be the extreme conservatism of the new Archbishop Andrea Caron; unless Genoa was taking it out of a harmless person because the Curia had driven out its favourite preacher Semeria on grounds of suspect modernism; Caron was still not occupying his see when Pius X died. Cf. the Pope's words of 22 Feb. 1913 on the godless power of the secular authorities in keeping out the new archbishop, *AAS* 5 (1913), 58; the 'interdict' was minimal and pointless, a ban on confirmation and ordination.

mutinied because a commander tried to discipline them; the French government was unkind about its possession of the historic cipher that the Vatican had used for 200 years (though every government must have known how to interpret it), and Pius X had to get rid of four popes from the past—Boniface VI, who in 896 was illegally pushed into the see; Boniface VII, whose party was; John XVI, who was accused in 998 of being a usurper and was paraded round Rome facing backwards on an ass; and Benedict X, who resigned the see legally because the other side told him that he was not validly appointed (1059).

The Pope was ill again Popes John after XVI had the right number. When Archduke Franz Ferdinand and his wife were murdered in the street at Sarajevo, he was reported to be 'depressed' at the news. He had thought it probable that Europe was moving to war and his doctor said afterwards that he communicated with the Austrian emperor on its eve; but it is now certain how far, when he died on 20 August 1914, he understood that this was the start of a world-shattering event which was to mark a new epoch in the history of the popes as of humanity.

9

NATIONALITY AND RELIGION: TYROL AND POLAND

At each end of Europe were deeply Catholic countries where the Churches were in trouble through much of the century; in the East because it was a force of patriotism against a non-Catholic ruler; in the West because of civil wars which bankrupted two countries, made it necessary to take the money of the Church, and caused a long national crisis by stopping the States from accepting any form of constitution happily.

In Europe were other nation-churches, or people's churches, what would later be called *Volkskirchen*, that is, where the people were convinced that the Catholic faith was integral to their being as a community or a State. The Poles, or most of them, thought that way because religion was the means of self-expression against a foreign and non-Catholic ruler. The Spanish, or half of them, thought that way because their national identity was formed in a struggle against Moslems. The southern and western Irish thought that way because religion was their means of self-expression against a non-Catholic ruler from over the sea. These were all peoples of the geographical edges of Catholicism. But at the heart of Central Europe lay a people who also identified membership of their community with their religion: the Tyrolese mountains, and valleys, and hardly passable passes did for them what the frontier did for Poles, Portuguese, or Irish. And this was true even though they, not unlike their western neighbours in Switzerland, had two races and two languages, Italians in the south in the prince-bishopric of Trent, and Germans in the north in the prince-bishopric of Brixen.

TYROL

For centuries the Tyrolese were part of the Holy Roman empire and the Habsburg empire. They thought that they were an 'independent'

State within the empire, like Austria or Saxony. They had no sense of allegiance to Vienna, only to the emperor who lived in Vienna—but to him a deep loyalty.

And here was the problem. They were not in an enclosure because the great road over the Brenner Pass, which joined northern Europe to southern, ran through their midst. But within their mountains they had the mood of the enclosure. Vienna was a key in the State-system of Europe. If northern Europe objected to the Austrian Concordat, Vienna must take notice, but Brixen and Trent need take no notice. If society demanded divorce, or the option of civil marriage, or the freeing of State schools from Church control, Vienna could dismiss none of these demands lightly, but Brixen and Trent thought all such innovations bad. When the Syllabus of Errors was published they hardly noticed, to them it was a succession of platitudes.

Hence a sore difficulty in politics. If Vienna passed a Reich law allowing civil marriage, it must insist that it apply everywhere. The Tyrolese thought this mere interference with their historic liberties. Their Catholic practice was an element in their resistance to modern centralization. They were like another mountain people, the Scots; if the English passed a measure insisting that lay patrons had the right to appoint ministers to parishes, Scotsmen resisted on the ostensible ground that this was unpresbyterian, but the underlying reason was that they could not see why the English should force on them what they did not approve.

So the history of Tyrol during the nineteenth century was a long struggle between Vienna and the mountains—whether they could keep their Catholicism pure, unadultered by Protestants, atheist teachers in schools, or dissenting chapels in the villages. The south Tyrolese, who spoke Italian, had a political threat which the north Tyrolese did not possess. Once Italy came into existence they felt a nationalistic draw away from Vienna. They preferred a Catholic Tyrol to a Milan or a Venice playing fast and loose with the pope. But if Vienna was to force them to be like Milan or Venice, the link of race and language took precedence over the unity in religion.

Since the Reformation there was a community of Protestants in Zillertal. This valley had belonged to the prince-bishops of Salzburg, who winked at their presence. But in the Napoleonic upset the frontier was moved and they came into Tyrol. To be Catholic was part of being Tyrolese. With the coming of more toleration the Zillertalers converted Catholics in the valley. They asked the Emperor Francis for leave to found an open congregation. The Tyrolese felt this to be a stain on their land. The Emperor refused the request and gave the Zillertalers the choice of turning Catholic or moving to another part of Austria where already there were Protestant congregations. The Zillertalers refused either choice and in 1837 436 people were expelled because the Tyrolese could not abide their presence; and Metternich persuaded the Parliament of the German Confederation not to mind the breach of the Vienna Treaty. Separated so long from ordinary Protestant churches, the Zillertalers became unusual in their practices, and Austria claimed that this was not an expulsion of 'Protestants'. The Zillertalers settled in Prussian Silesia until the calamities of that country at the end of the Second World War.

The railways brought fame and travellers to the mountains. Meran grew to be a well-known spa. It was not possible to keep tourists who were non-Catholics from saying their prayers. The first mixed marriage in Meran was in 1853, the first Protestant pastor there four years later (but this was because the king of Prussia came to visit), five years after that they had a Protestant cemetery, but at every non-Catholic funeral there were unseemly protests at the grave. Three years after that the pastor started to marry people; but government still refused the licence to make a legal non-Catholic congregation. By 1866 they seemed to have achieved their struggle, to keep Tyrol purely Catholic.

But then the defeat of Austria by Prussia caused crisis in the State and a new constitution. The Vatican Council gave the excuse for the abolition of the Concordat. There were now big fights in which the Tyrol conservatives were on the losing side, though not till after hard battles—the State oversight of schools, the institution of civil marriage, the attack upon the Jesuit theological faculty at the university of Innsbruck. Yet Tyrol was still a very Catholic country. Pius IX's jubilee in 1869 was celebrated more ecstatically in the Tyrol than anywhere else in the Church, with beacons on the mountains, special pilgrimages, and huge services.

The life of the people and their Church was complicated by politics. That was true also of Southern Ireland. But neither Ireland nor the Tyrol could compare with Poland or the Iberian peninsula where national churches or *Volkskirchen* had to live with States that were almost destroyed or that almost destroyed themselves.

POLAND

The partitions of Poland at the end of the eighteenth century left the Polish people divided between the rule of Russia, Prussia, and Austria. Theirs was the most cultivated society of Eastern Europe. They were still a feudal society of landowners linked to the clergy. In Russian Poland they had a Polish kingdom, called the Kingdom of the Congress because it was set up by the Congress of Vienna, with the Russian tsar as their king but with their own Parliament (Diet), and a measure of local autonomy, and Roman Catholicism as the religion of the State, though with tolerance for the Orthodox and other faiths. But the wars and the partitions left the Church in a bad way, with various forms of corruption and a low standard of priesthood. Beyond the Congress kingdom the Poles reached out, in culture and in landowning, into White Russia, the Ukraine, and Lithuania.

The difference of religion between Pole and Russian was important, but at first the autonomy of the Congress kingdom prevented the difference from being a political conflict. Yet the antagonism between the two races was fed by Napoleon's invasion of Russia, where many Poles fought with the French army, and the Russians did not forget. Nor did the Poles forget how Napoleon worked for them. Their secret anti-Russian societies were often Bonapartist. The clergy were not yet the main bearers of Polish nationalism, the leaders of which were the students or lecturers at the universities, and officers in the army. The clergy later became the sole hope of the nation, when the universities were controlled and the army was suppressed. Before 1831 Polish priests were in the classical tradition of Catholicism, where it was right to obey the law and where conspiracy was wrong.

The French Revolution of 1830 excited the Poles beyond measure, and in November the Polish army carried out a coup in Warsaw. Suddenly a national rebellion was virtue; and the old Dominican prior wandered through the streets of Warsaw, cross in hand, calling the people to arms. Bernardine friars[1] of the countryside arrived with sabres to join the amateur bands of fighters. Yet it was not a national rising. The peasants thought it an upper-class affair and did little.

---

[1] These Bernardines were not to be confused with a form of Cistercians from the age of the Counter-Reformation. They were Observant Franciscans, mostly in Poland, who called themselves after St Bernardino of Siena.

Pope Gregory XVI refused to back the Polish nationalists. Revolution was not an option for Christians. He condemned the revolutionaries as troublemakers: 'Anything that disturbs good order in a State cannot be done by the ministers of the God of peace.' Tsar Nicholas was one of the mainstays of order in Europe, like Metternich in Vienna. All the Polish bishops but one obeyed the Pope.

This condemnation by the Pope was as shocking to Western liberals as it was to the Poles and for thirty years affected the links between the Polish Church and the see of Rome. It caused antipapal fury among Polish refugees in the West. It was a help, not only to Russia but to Prussia, in pacifying their Poles. It was now that the clergy began to be the principal force for Polish nationalism.

With their good professional army the Poles kept the war going for ten months before they were suppressed. This failure of revolution against the tsar destroyed the autonomies of the kingdom in Poland. The Polish Diet was abolished and the tsar was no longer crowned as the king of Poland. A policy of slow Russification was oppressive and was only ended by the Russian Revolution of 1905. The failure of the revolution caused a flight of Poles westward and a body of emigrants, with Paris as their headquarters, determined to do all they could to free Poland from Russian rule.

Russification hit the Catholic Church hard. Polish priests and Polish rites were the public maintainers of the language and way of life. The Russians believed that Catholicism made the Poles disloyal to Russian government. They realized that since some 80 per cent of the inhabitants of Poland were Roman Catholics they must somehow get along with the Catholic Church, but they did what they could to control and discourage it. They suppressed the new archbishopric of Warsaw and the clause in the constitution that gave special protection to Roman Catholicism as the religion of the majority of the people. They shut 197 monasteries—but that still left some 120 communities. This closure of monasteries affected the institutes they ran, the schools and hospices. The worst shock to the Poles was the institution of an Orthodox archbishopric of Warsaw.

Tsar Nicholas I became a believer in Church–State unity as the safeguard and inspirer of his empire. He had faith in a mystical Russia, based on the supreme power of its devout ruler, and a society of which the Orthodox Church was the chief uniting instrument. It was the start of a conflict of allegiances which lasted to the First World War, where high tragedy came upon it, and beyond.

In 1845 the Tsar spent five days incognito in Rome and had a courteous but unsatisfactory interview about Poland with Gregory XIV. Gregory put into his hands a document which said that the Holy See was always teaching the people that they must render unto Caesar what is Caesar's, but this meant that Caesar should never hinder the people from doing their duty to God.[2] Tsar and pope embraced. The next head of a Russian State to meet a pope was Khruschev. The Tsar was astounded that the Romans allowed their dogs to wander about in church, and inferred that Orthodox customs were more reverent than Catholic.

The Russians put up with a Latin liturgy provided that: (1) the relation between the Church and Rome was strictly controlled; (2) Roman Catholics did not try to convert Orthodox to their faith; (3) if there were a mixed marriage it must be celebrated by an Orthodox priest and the children must be brought up as Orthodox.

THE UNIATS

The Russian State could not put up with Uniats, Roman Catholics who kept the Eastern Slav liturgy, had a married clergy, and did not use Latin. Sometimes they were known, not as Uniats, but as 'the Greek-Catholic Church', to distinguish them from the Greek or Russian Orthodox Church. There were many, about a million and a half, with an archbishop and two bishops, most of the members not Poles but Ruthenian or Belorussian.

The special nature of the Uniats—having an Orthodox type of liturgy but with recognition of the pope's authority—did not create a problem because it caused little friction within the Austro-Hungarian empire. But that was because the Austrian emperor was a Catholic, and his government could encourage Uniats. Under an Orthodox government they were sure to be in trouble. For not only was the Russian government Orthodox, but it regarded the profession of Orthodoxy as a great binding force of the Russian empire.

---

[2] In 1862 the Secretary of State's office issued a book of documents on Pius IX's care for the Poles, *Esposizione documentata*. The documents were mostly in French or Italian. Since they were needed by Poles they were turned into Latin and then made ampler; and this was published in Rome in 1870 as *Expositio documentis munita earum curarum quas Summus Pontifex Pius IX assidue gessit in eorum malorum levamen quibus in ditione Russica et Polona Ecclesia Catholica afflictatur*. This is a useful collection. The memorandum which Gregory XVI gave to the Tsar is in *Expositio*, 42 ff.

Uniats were in even worse trouble than Poles, for Poles were Roman Catholics with a Latin way of worship, and their services were unlike those of Orthodox churches. But the Uniats had an Orthodox sort of service—and it could therefore be asked in St Petersburg why they should separate themselves from the great Orthodox Church of the country of which they were citizens.

The acceptance of the pope's authority mattered to the Uniats; not because Pius IX might command them to do things and they would willingly obey, for that could hardly happen; but primarily for national reasons—they were almost all Ruthenians. They must distinguish themselves. The neighbouring Poles said that every authentic Christian should worship God with a Latin liturgy. The neighbouring Russians said that every authentic Christian should worship God with an Orthodox liturgy and reject the Latin innovations of the pope. The Ruthenians knew that they were neither Poles nor Russians. They were used to a Slav form of worship, they had married clergy as had the Orthodox, but they were resolute that the patriarch of Moscow should not be their head.

When it is said that they were resolute against Moscow, that is true of the bishops and leaders, but was much less true of the lay worshipper. If there was a change from being Roman Catholic to being Orthodox the lay worshipper would hardly notice the difference— the name of the pope would disappear from the liturgy of the mass, and in the creed he or she would declare that the Holy Spirit proceeds 'from the Father' and not 'from the Father and the Son', two small omissions which would mean little or nothing to uneducated Slavs saying their prayers. Those were not quite the only differences; for the nearness of Poles and what Poles did in church made acceptable a few Western customs that were not found in Orthodox churches—kneeling in church, ringing bells at the altar, and keeping the feasts of Corpus Christi and of the Immaculate Conception. The Orthodox Church would never allow organs in church but a very few appeared in Uniat churches. A very few Uniats used the Western form of rosary in their private devotions. The illiterate, who were then the majority of Uniats, would only notice the absence of kneeling and bells if they changed to an Orthodox way of worship.

Tsar Nicholas I had something of the spirit of a mystic about his nation and its religion. He could hardly understand how more than a million of his people should worship in the way of his Church and yet say that they were servants of the pope, an intrusive Western authority. Among his few Russian or Uniat advisers there was also an ecumenical dimension—here was Christendom divided in a strange and unusual way, where there was hardly a disagreement on doctrine and almost no difference in the way to say one's prayers, how could that unity for which the New Testament asks be re-established? But on both sides nationalism affected what was done. The Uniats did not wish to be Russian, and had no desire to reunite Christendom. The Tsar wanted to make loyal citizens of Russia, and had small desire to reunite Christendom. The Polish Revolution of 1831, with which the Uniats had almost nothing to do, had taught him the importance of religious unity for national harmony.

In 1832 a government decree abolished the Basilians, the Uniats' monastic order, and took their property—except that five houses were left in the diocese. A decree of the same year ordered that all children of mixed marriages must be brought up as Orthodox. Then a decree ordered that all the Uniat ordinands should be trained in the Orthodox Academy at St Petersburg (then the best of the Orthodox seminaries).

In February 1839 a synod of twenty-three Uniat clergy, including both bishops, meeting at Polotsk, sent a petition with 1,000 signatures to the Tsar, asking for reunion with 'their mother the Orthodox Church'. The Tsar replied by accepting their request and putting the whole community under Orthodox authority. Then it was necessary to persuade or force thousands of Uniats to change their allegiance to the Orthodox Church. For lay people that was easy because the change in the way of worship was so small. There was not much resistance. With the clergy it was different, but still fairly easy. There were something over 2,300 Uniat priests and 1,305 agreed to be Orthodox priests, rather more than a half. If they were tough in resistance they were maltreated; 160 priests were put under house arrest in monasteries and others were forced out of their parishes and had to earn a secular living. It was not a reunion to provoke martyrdoms. Some lay people went on confessing, secretly, to their old pastor even if he was now outed.

Pope Gregory XVI published his sorrow at what happened.[3] The expressions were strong but less militant in their words than his successor was to use. It was a disaster for the popes in eastern Europe, for they not only lost the allegiance of once faithful people, but also a

---

[3] Allocution, *Multa quidem*, 22 Nov. 1839; *Acta Gregorii Papae XVI*, ed. A. M. Bernasconi (Rome, 1901–4), ii. 381 ff.

hope, for they looked upon the Russian Uniats as the means by which they would one day persuade the Russian Orthodox that union with Rome was possible.

The Uniat diocese of Chelm was spared because, under the Treaty of Vienna, Austria still had rights there. In the Russian part they were all Ruthenians. There were more than 200,000 Uniats, a chapter with thirteen members, five monasteries with only twenty monks in all, a nunnery with six nuns, and a seminary where government controlled the syllabus. The Uniat bishop of Chelm was Szumborski to 1851, but he had to flee five years before that. Kalinski, a good man, and the father of thirteen children, could not get himself consecrated bishop. He was accused by government of saying a requiem mass for the dead in the Polish rebellion. For years he went on, unconsecrated, but administering the diocese so far as a bishop was allowed any power, until he was arrested in 1866, sent into exile, and died. Wojcicki was appointed as administrator to succeed him, and was a person who wanted reunion; he encouraged the dropping of the clause 'and the Son' from the creed, getting rid of organs (his advice was to sell the organs and use the money for the benefit of the parish clergy, or break them up if necessary), and discouraging the use of the Western form of rosary. Pius IX excommunicated him.[4] The monks were so few that by state order they were put into a single monastery.

In 1868 the Uniats of Chelm at last won leave for a consecrated bishop, whom Rome accepted: Michael Kuziemski. He had the defect that he was an Austrian citizen and a canon of Lemberg (Lvov) and had somewhere to go if he did not like what he found. He was not only too Uniat for the Russian government, he was too Latin for the Uniats, for he went on celebrating low masses, which were unknown to the Uniats. He soon decided that his situation was impossible, deserted his diocese, and went back to Galicia; his successor Popiel, unconsecrated, cheerfully accepted that the only thing to do with the diocese was to accept union with the Orthodox Church. He abolished the feasts of Corpus Christi and the Immaculate Conception, banned kneeling in church and bells at the altar, removed the pope's name from the liturgy, and ordered the clergy to dress as Orthodox priests, and to put in an iconostasis to divide the nave from the sanctuary. A band of Russian Orthodox

---

[4] Apostolic letter, 17 Oct. 1867, *ASS* 3 (1867), 201: 'a certain presbyter Wajcicki [*sic*] of suspect faith, despising all ecclesiastical penalties, and awaiting the judgment of God upon him, accepts the diocese from the civil power and encourages the most dreadful schism'.

monks was installed in the Uniat house in Warsaw. At Siedlce, where the opposition was worst, government installed an inquisitorial court which summoned and examined Uniat clergymen, gave a large grant to repair Uniat churches provided they accepted Orthodoxy, and put up the stipends of the Uniat clergy who came over.

In Warsaw there happened to be a British consul, Colonel Mansfield. His reports to London on what was happening constitute the best neutral account.[5] The trouble was that although many priests accepted Orthodoxy their people were very attached to the customs they knew from childhood. So in a few parishes there were attacks on vicarages and even on priests, and people stopped going to church. In places the priests appealed to government for protection, and then Cossacks or police came to the village; sometimes the people attacked the Cossacks, and the end was brutality. Sometimes they refused the key of the church to the Orthodox priest, and that brought soldiers who were not gentle. An order came from St Petersburg abolishing organs, pews, and the ringing of bells at mass. There were 266 parishes in the Chelm diocese and disorders in only twenty-six parishes, with violent disorders in only three. But even where there was no disorder parishioners might prefer not to go to church, to bury their dead without prayers and by night, and not to have their children baptized or married—or else to travel up to 70 miles to seek out a priest who had not conformed.

Pius IX wrote a strong encyclical 'to the Ruthenian bishops' (13 May 1874).[6] It only made the troubles worse. The British consul reported that as the troubles died down there was excitement over miracles and visions; a vision of the Virgin; a bleeding crucifix. A priest who explained the bleeding as a natural phenomenon was mal-treated. A quarter of a million people and 240 priests were registered as Orthodox. Sixty-six priests fled to Austria, sixty-four more refused to serve as Orthodox and retired from the pastorate.

Still there were Uniats in Russian Poland, but they were confined to the Ruthenian peasantry remembering how they were nurtured, and they could do nothing in public. Occasionally a secret travelling Jesuit or two (who reminded themselves of the dangerous Jesuit missions to England under Queen Elizabeth I, and about whom Rome, the Jesuit general Beckx, and Pope Pius IX were very uneasy lest they be sending good men to their deaths) came from Galicia to

---

[5] PP (1877), lxxxix. 63 ff.   [6] *ASS* 7 (1872), 593–8.

administer the sacraments in private houses. The first was disguised as a travelling tradesman, with a false passport and a portable chapel. His disguise was penetrated, the passport was exposed, and after imprisonment for nineteen months he was expelled from Russia. But the Ruthenians rumoured that the pope had sent them a priest and that he was now in prison, and the Jesuit's imprisonment did more for the hidden Uniat Church than a surreptitious tour. Large numbers came to visit him in prison and used the chance to make their confessions or even to have their children baptized.[7]

When finally the Russian Revolution of 1905 forced an edict of toleration, the Ruthenian Uniats reappeared in their thousands and processed to their old churches with banners and crucifixes. But they won little. The lawyers told them that they could not qualify under the edict of toleration, and so then the old Uniat rite began to disappear as those who did not want to be Orthodox went over to the Latin rite.

CATHOLICISM AND NATIONALISM IN POLAND

Russian control of the Polish Church after 1831 meant churches in disrepair; too few clergy; long vacancies in bishoprics; tense and sometimes weak bishops; a few churches occupied by Orthodox congregations; some monasteries closed and many banned from receiving novices; Orthodox teachers pushed into office as teachers at Catholic seminaries; sermons that had to be read from printed texts and were liable to a censorship. In 1847 only three out of the eight dioceses had a bishop. This was partly because the government proposed names for bishoprics and Rome refused them; the see of Warsaw had been vacant for nine years.

There were Poles who liked co-operation with the Russians. They were usually upper class or merchants, they wanted the prosperity of Poland, their ideas were influenced by the French Enlightenment and they did not mind that their parish church was closed or weak. There were leading churchmen who could see no reason why

---

[7] A. Boudou, *Le Saint-Siège et la Russie* (Paris, 1925), ii. 442 ff.; the first Jesuit was Henri Jackowski; cf. *LTK* s.v. Chelm; *DHGE* xii. 605 ff.; J. Pelesz, *Geschichte der Union der ruthen. Kirche mit Rom* (2 vols.; Vienna, 1878–80), still indispensable for the Uniats, but written in bitterness of heart; N. Miko in *ZKT* 79 (1957), 467 ff.; E. Winter, *Russland und das Papsttum* (Berlin, 1961), ii. 351.

Orthodox teachers should not lecture in Catholic seminaries nor why Orthodox laymen should not administer Catholic endowments. For most of the population Nicholas I achieved a feeling of identity between Catholicism and Polish nationality and freedom. It was now hard to stop national (nationalist) hymns being sung at Polish funerals. The mourners sang pious words that were legal to the tune of a patriotic song that was illegal. In the long history of Christianity no hymns can ever have been sung so movingly.

During the years after the failed revolution of 1831 a mystic Messianism was observed among the Western refugees, of a nature that for all its otherworldly sound contained faith in the resurrection of Poland: Poland as the suffering servant, Poland as the heart of the future liberation of Europe, Christlike Poland. They drew on the ideas of Lamennais, who was strong in influence on Western Poles. But the mind that was key was that of the poet Adam Mickiewicz. *The Books of the Polish Nation and the Polish Pilgrimage* was written not in verse but in the poetic prose of the Bible; its message was that Poland was the richer and more formative for the future of humanity by its Christlike martyrdom.

Short of parish churches, villages built their own little chapels, often without the consent of the parish priest who preferred to have a large parish under his own control. They were often helped by the squire who then regarded it as 'his' parish. Village chapels became indispensable to the worshipping life of the people. But with the shortage of priests it was hard for a squire to find a chaplain adequate to run his chapel or to know more than just enough to say or sing the liturgy. If monks lived nearby it was easier. It was the expectation in Poland that a priest should not be ordained without an education which could only be provided by a family that was of the upper or middle class; a priest from a peasant family was hardly acceptable even to peasants, and this expectation contributed to the shortage of priests in the countryside. But it helped the respect of the people for education. It was a survival from the past, for until 1822 a person could not be installed as an ecclesiastical dignitary unless he could prove that he came of a noble family.

Pius IX was more friendly than his predecessor to the Polish churches. He wholly disapproved of revolution and would say so in the Syllabus of Errors. Like Gregory XVI he thought the tsar a maintainer of the European order established after the wars of Napoleon; for the Austrians helped to save his Papal State after the Italian

Revolution of 1848–9 and they themselves were saved from revolution partly by the tsar's army in Hungary. But messages from Russia came through to Rome secretly—once slipped into the back of a prayer book. Information came through the nuncio in Vienna. The Pope knew what they suffered; more than one bishop begged him to be allowed to resign; his compassion was roused.

Characteristically one of his early acts was spiritual. He beatified the Jesuit Andreas Bobola, who in the Counter-Reformation worked to recatholicize the country round Vilna and was murdered, and was remembered by Poles and Lithuanians as a hero. It was one of those beatifications which had an aim beyond that of honouring a holy man. When Pius IX made Bobola blessed, he lost into exile two Dominicans of Polotsk (where the body lay) on charges of illegal communication with Rome.[8]

The diocese of Mohilev included Finland and a good part of Siberia, and was the largest diocese in the world. The entire history of this see was troubled until it crashed at the Communist Revolution. In 1848 the Tsar allowed as coadjutor-archbishop with right of succession, Ignacy Holowinski, who was the rector of the Catholic Academy at St Petersburg and one of the founding members of the literary group of Poles who were against democracy and nationalism. He was unusual among the Polish bishops of those days; a person of taste and a cultivated poet, he translated into Polish several of the plays of Shakespeare. He was friendly with the Orthodox bishops and believed that it could be right for a local Catholic Church to choose its bishops without seeking the approval of Rome. He issued a pastoral letter which among much else asked his flock to pray for the emperor—and government made him add 'and for our dear motherland Russia', an addition which he accepted. Hence the government approved of him as a wise Catholic bishop. Tsar Nicholas I was proud to have such a humane and learned Catholic bishop at St Petersburg. Anyone whom the Tsar was proud of was suspected by Poles. Anyone who could talk of motherland Russia was abhorred by nationalist Poles.

Holowinski visited all the seven dioceses and confirmed thousands; he made notes on his visitations and so became an historical source for church life. He also kept Rome informed—though communications were hardly legal—mainly through the nuncio in Vienna. He

[8] In 1938, at another awkward time for Poland in politics, Pius XI made Andreas Bobola a saint.

has been described by a learned authority as the only ruler of the Mohilev diocese throughout the century towards whom we can be drawn in sympathy.[9]

But to work at all was hard. A new diocese was founded in the far south, that of Kherson. An instructed Dominican, Kahn, was found to fill it; the government proposed him and the pope agreed. Holowinski consecrated him bishop at St Petersburg in November 1850. It was not an enchanting prospect: the cathedral was a tiny stone church built by the few Catholic inhabitants, almost all German-speakers; the handful of churches decayed under the harsh winters because they were built of wood; and there were not enough clergy to make a cathedral chapter or give the bishop help. Then government refused to let him have a residence other than St Petersburg because there was no bishop's palace at Kherson. So the diocese of Kherson consisted of a mini-cathedral with no proper clergy and a bishop who lived several hundred miles away. The Dominican seemed to prefer to stay with the culture of St Petersburg than seek the wildness of Kherson. The cathedral of the diocese was soon transferred from Kherson to Tiraspol in Moldavia. Six years later the government transferred the bishop, chapter, and seminary (the last two did not exist) to Saratov and after some trouble Bishop Kahn persuaded Rome to agree. There were German communities down there, and Uniat Armenians. But Kahn soon died and no one replaced him for eight years, and when his successor eventually came he went on living not at Tiraspol but at Saratov, 1,000 kilometres from the title town of his diocese. In 1914 the vast diocese contained 350,000 Roman Catholics, nearly all of whom were Germans, but with 40,000 Uniat Armenians, and altogether some 250 priests. The last bishop was forced to resign by the Soviet authorities in 1929 and the diocese of Tiraspol, which Holowinski did more than anyone to create, vanished.

Holowinski stood up to the Tsar. Government decided, as Catholic governments had decided before, that where monasteries had too few monks they should be closed and the surviving monks transferred so that buildings and land could be better used. They decided to close twenty-one monasteries, each with only a handful of monks. They asked Holowinski to order it. He saw that nothing was more likely to make his diocese think him an agent of government, and refused.

---

[9] Boudou, *Le Saint-Siège*, ii. 9.

Government nevertheless closed the monasteries and left the bishop to sort out the care of the parishes which the monasteries had looked after. International religious orders were not allowed to communicate with their superiors or generals. The master-general of the Dominicans asked leave to visit the Dominican houses in Russia and was refused. So he met a few of them in a bar at the customs-house on the frontier while they treated the customs officers to drinks so that they should get a little time to talk.[10]

In an absolute State, minorities which cannot express dissent politically do so by means of a religious practice which dissents from that of the State. Conversely a government must wish to diminish practice among small denominations and to be ecumenical in a link with large denominations. Because he ruled Poland, much the tsar's most numerous minority denomination was the Catholic. His aim was to persuade them that these two Catholic religions were alike; that it was very wrong to say that if a soul was to be saved it must belong to the Roman Catholic Church, or to try to convert Orthodox persons, on that ground or any other, to the Roman Catholic faith; that it was very wrong of a Catholic priest to tell a couple that mixed marriages were bad, or to tell his people that they ought never to go to a service in the Orthodox church; that there was nothing wrong in open-minded Orthodox teachers lecturing in Catholic seminaries (or vice versa?); there was nothing wrong in a godly ruler, as had often happened in the West, reforming the Church for its own good—for example, closing monasteries that were useless, or making sure that the standard of people chosen to be bishops was high. But he could hardly achieve any such ideal unless he cut all links other than ceremonial between Russian-ruled Catholics and the see of Rome.

But what had a touch of the 'ecumenical ideal'—the phrase was not known—in the Russians, even in the two tsars, was impossible at the parish level. In absolute governments the worst tyrants are petty local officials against whom there can be no appeal to a court. An Orthodox priest might insist on inspecting the baptismal register at the Catholic church to see if any of the Orthodox had changed faith illegally. If an Orthodox was converted to be a Catholic and then came to mass, no priest worth anything could refuse communion—the penalty if it were known would be loss of the parish. Among the

---

[10] H. M. Cormier, *Vie du révérendissime père Alexandre-Vincent Jandel* (Paris, 1890), 311 ff.

poorer people, in places where there were many Catholics, mixed marriages were not uncommon. It was illegal for the marriage to be celebrated by anyone but the Orthodox priest and the children must be brought up as Orthodox—hence a trickle of losses from the Catholic communities. The State said that the Catholics could repair their churches, but if in a mixed country parish they tried they were likely to be stopped by the people or the bureaucrats, so that many country Catholic churches decayed. Holowinski banged away at bureaucrats to do what they ought to have done already: if ardent Catholic priests were likely to say in the pulpit things which reflected on the Orthodox, their sermons would be controlled. In 1852 all sermons were put under censorship (the decree only extended a censorship on anything printed, religious or not) and priests were forbidden to preach sermons, they would have to read from printed books of sermons. This censorship of the pulpit was comically impossible to enforce, and where censors tried they obeyed the historic law of censorships that they were illiterate.

The Orthodox lecturers could be awkward. At Holowinski's seminary in St Petersburg the church history teacher was Orthodox, and he told the students that Thomas Becket was a rebel against the State; which was true if the English king were the State. But Holowinski, as head of the seminary, was offended and scolded the lecturer in the presence of the pupils. History was felt by government to be a dangerous subject and in 1851 it ordered that teachers of history and literature in Catholic seminaries should be members of the Orthodox Church. Under these conditions students from the St Petersburg seminary were likely to graduate as Polish nationalists; in spite of the Orthodox lecturer in Russian literature being a friendly, broadminded man who admired Holowinski, wished to have nothing to do with politics, had no desire to convert Catholics to Orthodoxy, and whose only objective was to enable his students to love Russian literature.

By 1851 Holowinski had become miserable at standing up to State pressures upon him. He started sending secret, woeful letters to Rome: letters that show that his psychological condition rendered him unfit for his work, expressing his feelings that his was a martyrdom that went on and on, that he was quite alone because no one dared to back him knowing that the State officers disapproved of him; he was always afraid, sleepless, and unable to eat proper meals: 'I would rather have a proper martyrdom than be consumed little by little by such small flames'[11]—could he not resign the see? 'Tell me what you want. I will obey.' He wrote that there was no hope for Catholic life there except with the help of the see of St Peter, without it they could have nothing but serfdom and death. If Pius IX and Pope Gregory had not done what they could for them and had left them to their own resources they would have been drowned. If Rome wanted them to fight they would fight to the death. If Holowinski were exiled it would not hurt the Church and the Pope was not to be disturbed. He said there might be attempts to poison him but he took precautions against that. He thought it would help the Church if one of the bishops were martyred.

Pius IX replied with the sort of message that popes send when they can achieve nothing and which nevertheless comfort those who receive them: he said how deeply he felt for him, thanked him for all he could do, encouraged him to stand firm in the faith, trust in God, train good ordinands, teach the young to love truth and abhor schism—he always remembered him in his prayers.[12]

Not surprisingly Holowinski died at the age of 48, of cancer of the stomach. The Orthodox lecturer at his college, Nikitenko, mourned him as a good mind, a true pastor, and a close friend. On his deathbed Holowinski chose the man whom he wanted as his own successor—Zylinski, bishop of Vilna, 'because he is wise and because the government likes him'.[13] The entourage persuaded him to sign a letter to the Tsar, saying that Zylinski combined 'zeal for the welfare of the Church with an ardent devotion to your Majesty'. The government evidently did like him because it sent the name to Rome at once and after six months Rome agreed. It was characteristic of the state of the Catholic Church in Russia that the accusation was later made that this letter was a fake. Zylinski was a pious and hard-working pastor, and a realist. He thought that Rome engaged in a rigid policy and that in a despotic State the only way to get things done for the better was by compromise with the authorities. He was a friend of the Orthodox Lithuanian patriarch, and some Poles thought this a crime. He liked the superior of the Dominicans in St Petersburg, Father Staniewski; and this Dominican was admired for the work he did for Catholics in Russia, and resented by the bigoted because he did not

---

[11] Cf. the mood in Holowinski to Pope Pius IX, 10 May 1851, in *Expositio*, 30 ff.; Pius IX to Holowinski, 1 Dec. 1851, ibid. 47–9.

[12] Pius IX to Holowinski, 1 Dec. 1851, ibid.

[13] Boudou, *Le Saint-Siège*, ii. 68.

mind mixed marriages celebrated by an Orthodox priest and had not supported the stronger line taken by Holowinski. Members of his friary were willing to attend Orthodox weddings or baptisms. The sub-prior often said mass for the tsar and his family. Orthodox Russians went to hear sermons in the Dominican chapel. Archbishop Zylinski got Father Staniewski made his suffragan bishop by a title *in partibus*. He tried to get the next prior, Stacewicz, made a bishop but Pius IX refused his name because he made no protest against the rules of mixed marriages and had conducted them himself. Stacewicz went to Rome taking with him for the Pope a relic of Bobola. The Pope said later that he was a hypocrite, but there is no evidence that he was.[14]

Meanwhile, in the West, the plight of the Poles helped to generate that fury which made Western liberals regard the Tsar as the worst of tyrants. Here from Paris is Veuillot on Tsar Nicholas.

In our day he has renewed the most hateful persecutions of the pagans. He pretends to protect the Eastern Christians. Yet he has killed or buried in Siberian snows or handed over to the mountain people in the Caucasus thousands of martyrs, so that a vile zeal has made whole dioceses into apostates. For thirty years he has insulted the blood of Christ . . .   (E. Veuillot, *Louis Veuillot* (Paris, 1913), ii. 24)

Until the disaster of 1863 there was a flourishing Polish culture; mainly based in Prussia (Silesia and Pomerania) and Austria (Cracow and Galicia) but also among the landowning classes in Russian Poland. They were not always religious; but strong in their thinking was the feeling that in a harsh world the Poles were a fortress of authentic Christianity surrounded by its assailants and corrupters. If the bishops were under such frequent pressure from government, the monks and nuns recovered somewhat from their fate after 1831. No longer allowed to teach, they undertook much of the best work in the parishes. They steadily grew in numbers, the branches of Franciscans, especially Capuchins, in the lead. They were not stopped from parish missions, hearing confessions, making parish brotherhoods, or fostering the devotion of the rosary. The nunneries grew in number, always as nuns in action rather than in contemplation.

In 1855, as the Russians were losing the Crimean war, Tsar Nicholas I was succeeded by his son Alexander II. The loss of the war caused a demand for radical change, and the new tsar shared this

---

[14] Ibid. ii. 80.

feeling. He had ideas of freedom and relaxed the tight Russian control of Poland. The chief measure was the abolition of serfdom in 1861, which affected Polish society as drastically as it affected Russian. The administration was less centralized and more power was handed to local authorities.

The gentleness—a behaviour almost as if this monarch was constitutional—caused more ideas of freedom. Among the Russians themselves revolutionary language began to be heard and this could not but encourage Polish radicals.

In 1861 there was a Polish calamity. Radical Poles began to smash the windows of Poles suspected of being friendly to the Russians. They smashed the carriage of a bishop who had denounced such disorder as wrong.[15] They used churches to make their protests, found clergy who would preach 'patriotic' sermons, used national songs as hymn tunes, celebrated anniversaries that reminded them of the days of Polish freedom, slipped clauses into a litany, such as 'From slavery, good Lord, deliver us', and painted gibbets on the vicarage doors of clergy who told them that this disorder was wrong. They had little use for Pope Pius IX, at first they thought him as much of a dinosaur as his predecessor. The more radical had Gallican ideas and talked of a national Polish Church.

These were protests of the towns, they did not happen in country parishes; in towns the churches were crammed, and the inevitable violence began between crowds outside churches and the police.

In February 1861 troops fired on a crowd of demonstrators who would not obey orders, and five were killed. The funeral of the five was a national feast of mourning. The government eased its attitude, promised a little more autonomy, better schools, and the emancipation of the Jews. In return it demanded that the clergy stop this misuse of their churches. The clergy had no such power, and hardly wished to halt a movement which brought hosts of people surging to their altar.

In April 1861 ten demonstrators were killed and 100 wounded. In October 1861 Archbishop Fijalkowski died. He had started at Warsaw as the administrator of the see when government refused to allow it to be filled in the aftermath of the 1831 Revolution. He was nearly 80 when he became archbishop in 1856. He begged Pius IX

---

[15] H. M. Cormier, *Vie du révérendissime père Alexandre-Vincent Jandel* (Paris, 1890), ii. 123; the bishop was Marszewski of Kalisz, bishop since 1856; one of the only two Polish bishops to be allowed to go to the Japanese canonization in Rome.

not to intervene but to hope only for the reform of the clergy (which government would approve of). Like other bishops he was afraid that if the Pope intervened, it would be like the disaster when Gregory XVI condemned the revolution in Poland. His funeral was turned into another feast of mourning. There were national flags, and ceremonies associated with the old kings of Poland. The dead archbishop was openly hailed as *interrex*, as if he were a regent of Poland between the kings that were abolished and the kings that were to come.

That month of October 1861 the revolutionary committee asked Warsaw cathedral to celebrate the day of the death of Kościuszko who had served as one of George Washington's generals and during the Napoleonic wars led the Polish fight against the Russians. The governor announced a state of siege under martial law and banned processions, divine service on national anniversaries, and prayers not in the liturgy. The result was as bad as could be. The cathedral and the churches overflowed with worshippers, troops surrounded them, the doors were locked, for seventeen hours crowds had no food, nor drink, nor sanitation; and after 4 a.m. the soldiers broke in, found the women praying in rows in front and the men behind, used force on the women and then arrested all the men, not without pollution by drunken privates and the looting of precious objects, but without resistance from the congregations. 'It felt', the new vicar-capitular told the general, 'like the return of Attila the Hun.'

The clergy laid an interdict on the city because the cathedral and five other churches had been soiled by armed drunken men. They closed all the churches in Warsaw; which in the flaming quarrel was equal to putting themselves at the head of the revolutionary party. Their motive was not that, but to avoid collecting assemblies of Poles who might be violent in a demonstration and further provoke the police. The effect was the opposite, to align the clergy with the party ready for force. One of their best members protested—saying that the churches were by this means entering a political rather than a religious fight.[16] The vicar-capitular was arrested, the commander of the military committed suicide. The churches stayed closed for a month; the laity did not seem to mind not going to church. Persons devout

---

[16] Constant Lubienski studied in Paris, Berlin, and Fribourg as well as Warsaw; parish priest from 1849; bishop of Sejny 1863 and nominally till 1869, the diocese when he arrived being in chaos, vacant since 1849. He was a wise, moderate man, unpopular with the Russians because he stood up to them and with the Poles for his moderation; the Russians exiled him so that he was not bishop for long.

or politicized went to kneel outside the shut doors until the police stopped them. At one point 160 priests were in cells in the Warsaw fortress. Rome thought this 'interdict' a gross mistake, for it gave the Russians ground for saying that these movements were not religious but revolutionary.

Everyone agreed that to keep the clergy in order there must be a new archbishop of Warsaw. The Russians easily accepted the name of Felinski, which was surprising because his mother had been a revolutionary and exiled to Siberia. He was an unusual cleric, for he had a degree in mathematics from Moscow and in philosophy from Paris, where he met many of his mother's exiled friends. After ordination he taught philosophy at the seminary in St Petersburg. The Pope agreed to his name and he was consecrated very quickly, in January 1862.[17]

Felinski purified the cathedral and in his sermon told the clergy not to preach political sermons. Neither the radicals nor the clergy liked him, for they thought that one whom the Tsar accepted so rapidly must be a tsar's man and a 'traitor'. Out in the diocese he was a good pastor, but Warsaw was heading for an explosion which nothing could now avert. When the churches reopened congregations still sang patriotic tunes to their hymns, and soldiers still burst in to stop them, and then crowds gathered outside, and there were injuries when the police dispersed the people.

Felinski did his best. On 3 July 1862 there was an attempt at tyrannicide, a man tried to kill the new and humane governor, the Grand Duke Constantine. Felinski preached the stoutest sermon against tyrannicide, and asked the priests to bring to penitence such people who were lost souls and risked bringing the nation into hell. The Russian government had the fatal idea of calling up Poles for military service, especially troublemakers. In the night of 15 January 1863 they started fetching young men out of the houses of Warsaw. Conscripts fled into the woods, and became the soldiers of rebellion—though they had very few guns. Felinski made a last attempt; he summoned the clergy to the cathedral next day and reminded them of the Christian's duty of loyalty to the State. Seven days later revolution broke out.

---

[17] Pius IX to Felinski, 20 Feb. 1862 in *Expositio*, 129 ff.—it is no small consolation to us that you have been chosen but your work will be very difficult; never cease to try to find good priests for the people; keep asking the Tsar for mercy for the Poles in prison for political reasons; we should love to see you in Rome this summer if it is possible; we pray for you and send our blessing (summary).

Unlike the revolt of 1830 this had no chance because the Poles no longer had an army. Sensible people who saw that it had no hope did not support it, it was an untidy guerrilla war against a regular army and was bound to fail. It meant the end of the vestiges of gentle government.

On 15 March 1863 Felinski wrote a letter to the Tsar begging him to consider that the only way forward was to give Poland its independence—'Poland needs a political life'—but to link it with Russia because the Tsar would still be its king: 'this is the only solid base for stopping bloodshed and making peace'. The Poles regarded this courageous act as more treachery. One of the guerrilla leaders was a Capuchin, Father Konarski, who never used arms but ministered as a chaplain. He was condemned to be shot. The governor demanded that Felinski unfrock him first. Felinski said that he had no grounds for unfrocking Konarski; this meant exile from his see for Archbishop Felinski, an exile which lasted for decades.

Pius IX, under pressure from Poles, now wrote to the Tsar a letter of protest (22 April 1863).[18] He was frank and undiplomatic. He accused the Russians of trampling on the rights of the Church and clergy, suppressing monasteries and nunneries, enticing or forcing myriads of Ruthenians from the faith of their fathers, handing over Catholic churches to heretics, forcing children of mixed marriages to be brought up in the Orthodox faith, interfering with the training of clergy, and banning monks from communicating with their superiors; and so it was not surprising that the principles of good order were weak and that clergy had acted in ways not fitting for them. 'We in no way approve it that clergy should mix in political riots or take up arms to overthrow government. We deplore and condemn it as a crime.'

The Tsar replied with a laconic courtesy that the freedom of the Church in Central Italy did not seem to have stopped revolution in the States of the Church.

As a result of this revolution thirty priests were executed, some bishops and about 330 priests were in camps in Siberia, two-thirds of the monasteries closed (some needed closing), there was restriction of public profession of religion, spies sitting in on sermons, and even an attempt at control of the confessional. Monasteries, where they survived, had no oversight, either from effective superiors or from

---

[18] *Expositio*, 155–61, in both Italian and Latin. Treatment of original in G. Martina, *Pio IX (1851–66)* (Rome, 1986), 537.

bishops because the see was unfilled or the bishop powerless. Common life was destroyed because most of the monks had to take over vacant parishes. There was evidence of good religious houses among the Capuchins and Observant Franciscans but they were marked out as exceptions. The monasteries which survived had few monks, the nuns were better off, but they were still few. The system was inflexible as countrymen moved into towns. By the start of the twentieth century there were town parishes with 65,000 or more parishioners—just like London, Paris, or Rome of the same date.

Most bishops were against the revolt but the clergy were almost unanimously in favour. An unknown number of priests went into hiding, but deportation and flight left many parishes without pastors. The bishop of Vilna was exiled for twenty years because he refused to condemn the rebellion. Heavy additional taxes were laid upon the incomes of clergy to pay for the costs of martial law. The government closed all the monasteries but thirty-five (twenty-five for men, each with about fourteen monks, and ten for women, each with about eleven nuns). The other monasteries were banned from receiving novices and the moment the number of monks dropped below eight the remainder must move to another house, to secular life, or to exile with a grant for travel. Monastic endowments were taken by the state to administer. The surplus of the fund was to help parishes, schools, and sick clergy. The Russians did only what Catholic and Protestant rulers had done to monks before them, but the mood in which they did it was more hostile. And the crude driving out of monks from some houses (such as the Benedictines and the Recollects[19] at Pultusk) without warning and in the middle of the night, was handled as badly as in the old days of the Reformation. Meanwhile the Poles in Paris, with both accurate and false information about atrocities committed by Cossacks, were able to fill the newspapers of London and Paris with horror at what was happening in Poland. This lurid information also reached Rome. In France hardly anyone was not on the side of the Poles—Thiers said that they were not yet ripe for independence and Prosper Merimée preferred the Russians to the Poles. But most of Western Europe was vehement against the Tsar. Garibaldi even talked of sending guerrillas to help them. A little group of his men arrived in Poland and was killed or made captive.

---

[19] These were a separate group of Franciscans, numerous till the French Revolution, and amalgamated with the main order by Leo XIII.

Pius IX had a puzzle: the mixture of politics and religion on both sides. Were the Russians using the excuse of revolution, not only to re-establish order, but to do what they could to destroy the Catholic religion in their territories? He was sure that they were. And were the Poles really aiming at the political end of an independent Poland and using the Catholic religion as a good excuse to promote their cause? He had status only to defend the Catholic religion as religion and not as a piece of politics. Therefore he could not make a formal pronouncement in favour of a national Poland. On the other side he was under pressure from the three governments that ruled Poles to condemn Polish revolution. Disobedience to legitimate governments was sin, the Pope should say so, as had his predecessor Gregory XVI.

The tension was not lowered when on 24 April 1864 Pope Pius IX publicly condemned the Tsar. It was in a speech at Propaganda and in speeches he was always carried away and spoke more excitably than his hard-headed advisers wished. There were cardinals of stature present—Patrizi, Reisach, and Bartolini. He spoke of martyrs for their faith, of a ruler who persecuted and killed his Catholic subjects and drove them to an ill-considered revolution, and who expelled a bishop who would still be a bishop even in the catacombs. 'Fool that he is!' (*Stolto!*).[20] He said 'I do not want to be forced to cry one day in the presence of the eternal judge' (and suddenly he moved from Italian to Latin), 'Vae mihi quia tacui!' ('Woe is me, I said nothing!').

Cardinal Antonelli bowdlerized this text, the word *stolto* vanished, but in vain: the published text was less violent than the words that the Pope used in his speech, but was still very strong. Montalembert thought it glorious.

That 30 July 1864 Pius IX issued an encyclical[21] to the bishops of Russia and Poland to protest. It reiterated that Christians must obey their governments; but listed with a flowing bitterness the catalogue of persecution ('the Orthodox Church is a mortal schism') and especially condemned the exile of Archbishop Felinski of Warsaw ('no words are strong enough to express my horror', *verba quidem desunt ad huiusmodi factum reprobandum ac detestandum*), ordering the diocese of Warsaw to continue to obey him in his remote town on the Volga. The government reacted only by sending into exile at Astrakhan the

---

[20] Text in Boudou, *Le Saint-Siège*, ii. 233–4, original. Variations in Martina, *Pio IX (1851–66)*, ii. 542; official text in *CC* 10 (1864), 484 ff.

[21] *Expositio*, 173 ff., and *Acta Pii IX* (Graz, 1971), I. iii. 657–64: *Ubi Urbaniano* ('When I spoke at the Urban College of Propaganda . . .').

suffragan whom Felinski chose as he was leaving, and commanding the chapter to elect a bishop and telling them whom they must elect—Zwolinski, a man believed to be friendly to a Rome-free national church of Poland. The chapter refused to elect, and Zwolinski acted on government authority alone, unconsecrated and unelected. After the exile of two more members of the chapter, Zwolinski could act lawfully, as the delegate of an exiled vicar-general chosen by an exiled archbishop. He established a sort of order in the troubled diocese.

Naturally, relations between St Petersburg and the Vatican ceased, for nearly twenty years. Not a single Polish bishop attended the first Vatican Council, because either the sees were vacant or the bishop was under restraint.

The Poles did not mind this break. They preferred the Pope to have no relations with the Tsar. They remembered several of his strong phrases. At last a pope backed their aspirations; and though he never said a word to approve of force but many words to the contrary, they knew that their aspirations were only to be achieved by rebellion and at least the Pope backed the aspirations.

In Rome was a new college of a religious order, the Resurrectionists. The Paris emigrants after the revolution of 1831 were under the religious influence of the poet Adam Mickiewicz and one of them, Bogdan Jánski, who had been interested in early socialism, came under the influence also of Lacordaire and was converted; he set up a godly community with a few friends. Gregory XVI's Rome heard of them and brought two to the Curia to be informants on Polish affairs. Both had fought in the revolution of 1831 and then escaped to Paris and lost their faith. In 1842 they had a rule and called themselves Brothers of the Resurrection, a name which was certainly about Jesus but also rang of Poland. In 1862 Pius IX showed them a signal proof of trust by giving them the duty of the mission in Bulgaria, though their minds were set upon Poland. They founded the Polish College at Rome (1866) which they directed. They were soon invited by American and Canadian bishops to help with Polish emigrants across the Atlantic. After the death of Pius IX they were at last allowed into a piece of Poland, the Austrian area in Galicia.[22]

All the century the Polish Church, and what little survived of the Uniats, were governed by the state authorities, who made most of the

---

[22] *DIP* vii. 1824 ff. with literature; cf. *DIP* s.v. Jánski, Semenenko, and Kajsiewicz.

appointments, suppressed dioceses (Kamenetz in 1866, Minsk in 1869), and administered the funds at least by remote control; the churches rubbed along somehow, but the friction deepened the loyalty of the laity to them. Early in 1871, of the fourteen surviving dioceses, seven bishops were dead and not replaced, five bishops were in exile, and only two bishops of small dioceses were in office. Fialkowski the bishop of Mohilev, who with all his chapter was in St Petersburg, was 83 in the year 1879; he only went out in summer and then only for a short walk into his garden, but he was allowed no suffragan. This was less disastrous than it sounds because in Poland the squires were still important in running their parishes and their priests as if they were private chapels and chaplains. Occasionally there were suggestions of introducing the Russian language into the Latin liturgy, but they came to nothing, for Poles suspected them of being only a way by which Polish Catholics might be tempted towards Orthodoxy.

Peasants had no idea what the difference was between Rome and the Orthodox and cheerfully sent their Catholic children to Orthodox schools, learnt the Orthodox catechism, sang Orthodox hymns, and went devoutly to the Orthodox parish church with no idea that they were anything but good Roman Catholics. They used the Polish language in supplementary prayers (i.e. not the main liturgy) and had sermons and sometimes readings in Polish (in Lithuanian in Lithuania).

Parish life was traditional—sacrament with hardly any communions, catechism on Sunday, confessions, parish missions, the cult of St Mary, the rosary, pilgrimages to a sanctuary, the feasts of Corpus Christi and the church patron saint, combined with the ignorance of the people about the main Christian creed. Brotherhoods were important in parish life, as were 'circles of penitence'. Ceremonies were elaborate and included old local customs. Because it was a 'national' shrine the old sanctuary of the Black Madonna at Czestochowa now attracted ever more numerous bodies of pilgrims, and from many miles away (only about 45,000 in 1864, but Poland was at a low ebb in the repression of the revolution; then steady growth, half a million forty years later; the revolution had made it a symbol not only of devout religion but of national feeling). The conservative nature of this devotion was partly explained because the Polish religion was the one institution of the people which was theirs during the long subjection between the earlier of the revolutions and the making of modern Poland. The vast numbers of churchgoers did not mean that the Poles were all very moral.

When Leo XIII became pope he took trouble to befriend Slavs in the Balkans and was a strong backer of Bishop Strossmayer with whom his predecessor was so uncomfortable. The Russian government disliked this. They were accustomed to the idea that Russia is the protectress of the Slav peoples of the Balkans and were afraid that these moves of the pope were intended to help a Catholic Austria draw the Balkan Slavs into the orbit of their empire.

Leo tried to establish relations with Russia after the long years of breach since the Polish Revolution. He aimed to achieve more understanding from the Russian government for Poles and Uniats. Many Poles resented that he should have anything to do with a tsar. He had hardly begun when Tsar Alexander II was murdered by a bomb thrown in St Petersburg. Leo used the murder as one example of the terrible direction in which Europe moved as it discarded or attacked faith. He took the occasion to denounce again the doctrine that all power comes from the people—rulers may sometimes be chosen by the people, and a people may opt for the sort of constitution which best suits it provided that the result is justice, but that does not mean that rulers derive their authority from the people, for authority is God-given, and the idea of a social contract is an illusion. Disobedience to a government—unless it commands what is unjust—must be prevented not only by fear of the police but by the moral sense of the citizens; and such a moral sense about obeying the law can only arise if authority is seen to come from God.

But if government acts unjustly or oppressively, then the Church has always and everywhere hated tyranny.

Tsar Alexander III, who did not believe in concessions to liberals or anyone else and thought that the only way to hold Russia together was by absolute government, even by terror, imagined that the papacy might be able to help him control Poles. This opinion and the optimism of Leo XIII achieved a treaty in 1882 and things were a little easier. The Tsar at once released a bishop who had been in exile for twelve years and raised Catholic hopes. The fourteen vacant sees needed bishops and the difficulty was to find men whom St Petersburg would accept and Rome could approve; especially when Leo's key adviser on such names was the Polish Cardinal Ledochowski who had been driven out of Prussia by Bismarck and was now in Rome. But in December 1882 the treaty was signed. By the agreement the pope accepted that three dioceses disappeared. Bishops were given back power over seminaries but the use of the Russian language as a medium of instruction in the seminaries was increased. The worst restrictions on the work of Catholic clergy were lifted. Communications with Rome were reopened. The Tsar allowed Felinski to come out of his remote exile but not again to be bishop of Warsaw. In 1883 Rome was allowed to name twelve bishops for vacant sees in Poland.

But the same exhausting lack of system continued. The bishops were as restricted by bureaucrats as before. Leo XIII, here weak as water for the sake of higher ends, found it necessary to give instructions to his legate to the Tsar's coronation that he was not to mention the Uniats. The partial renewal of diplomatic relations between Russia and the Vatican ended in a quarrel (the Pope mentioned Uniats in a speech) within less than two years. But the Roman Catholic Church was treated with much less crude brutality in these years.

THE POLES IN PRUSSIA

In Prussia the Poles were mostly poor peasants under German Protestant landlords. The Prussians did not respect Polish culture and would have liked to make them both German and Protestant. But Silesia had many Polish speakers and there Polish culture, linked with Catholicism, still flourished. The *Kulturkampf* in Prussia helped to identify Roman Catholicism with Polish patriotism. The Polish peasant in Prussia learnt through the *Kulturkampf* to identify the defence of his Polishness with the defence of the Roman Catholic Church. He also learnt to be more ultramontane in his attitude to Rome. When Pius IX made the imprisoned Archbishop Ledóchowski a cardinal, the Polish people of Prussia felt it to be an honour conferred on their nation. In 1877 600 Polish pilgrims were received by Pius IX, who talked to them of 'the Kingdom of Poland';[23] a phrase which the Polish press of Russia, Germany, and Austria was careful to reproduce.

During the 1890s Prussia engaged in a policy of Germanization, by putting in colonies of German farmers, and struggling against the

[23] G. Castellan, *'Dieu garde la Pologne!': Histoire du catholicisme polonais 1795–1980* (Paris, 1981), 67.

Polish language wherever it was used, especially in schools: after 1901 religious teaching was to be in German. The primatial see of Gnesen-Posen was kept vacant for eight years (1906–14); sermons in Polish were banned in the three western dioceses where the people were partly German.

THE POLES IN GALICIA

In the south, in Galicia, the Poles were under Austrian rule. The Congress of Vienna created a Republic of Cracow under Austrian sovereignty and here Polish life was for a time at its best; until 1846, when a wild movement of peasants in Galicia, massacring nobles and priests, caused occupation and annexation to the Austro-Hungarian empire. As time passed the Austrians treated Poles better, gave them a measure of autonomy, and used them in the Austrian administration. Galicia, with nearly four million Poles, made the stable centre for the Polish people after their own monarchy was destroyed. As Polish nationalism grew expectant, Poles looked upon Galicia as the Italians had looked upon Piedmont, the nucleus of a future united nation. There they had a good university at Lemberg (Lvov), a measure of self-government, and a flourishing Catholic Church which was not under pressure from Orthodox or Protestant regimes. It was the part of Poland to which western refugees looked with hope and where they hatched plans for future independence.

THE CHANGE OF 1905

In 1904–5 Russia fought with Japan over Manchuria and to the astonishment of the world lost the war. The Russian people had little use for the war and before it ended there were signs of revolution, with strikes and terrorism. In October 1905 Tsar Nicholas II summoned a Parliament (Duma) and that December voting rights became almost universal. But the Tsar kept control of the army and foreign policy, and nominated half the upper house which had a veto on laws. Slowly the Duma won the confidence of the people.

The Tsar issued an edict of toleration, incorporated in a bill of the Duma. It cancelled the penalties for changing from the Orthodox faith or for ministering to persons who left the Orthodox faith; it allowed Roman Catholics to travel freely; it recognized the eleven million Old Believers as a true religious denomination. It allowed Poles (or any other persons) to give religious teaching in their own language. The Orthodox Church was still the only Church allowed to evangelize, and still the only Church with a historic endowment. The effect was instantaneous and disturbing. Several eminent Orthodox converted to the Catholic faith.

Naturally there was reaction from the Orthodox leaders and pressure upon government to restrict the freedom given. The law giving religious freedom could not be withdrawn and was confirmed; but the administration issued rules—banning free access to Rome, insisting on the *placet* to publish the decrees of Rome, banning the blessing in church of mixed marriages, refusing free activity to monks and to some bishops.

On 3 December 1905 Pius X sent a letter to the bishops of Russian Poland.[24] What he told them to do was remarkable. They were to keep the faithful in good order; not to attack the Jews; to avoid strikes; to found Catholic schools. But they were allowed to preach in the Russian language and to use the old Slavonic liturgy. Rome accepted that Russian language literature and history should be taught in the Polish seminaries.

What Russia had achieved was a weakening of Catholicism in all the areas which were not Polish. But in the lands where Poles lived the Russian treatment had achieved a true *Volkskirche*, a sense of identity between the Polish nation and its Church. When the new Poland rose as independent in 1918 it was large, because on one side the Allies wanted to punish Germany for the Great War and on the other side Russia was enfeebled by Communist revolution and civil war. Therefore the new Poland had one in five people who were not Poles—Russians, Jews, Ruthenians, Germans. This was all changed in 1945 when the Ruthenians and Russians were now in Russia, the Jews had vanished, and the Germans were expelled westward and there were far fewer Protestants in Poland.

The experience of being ruled as a satellite State after 1945 did nothing to diminish the sense that this was a *Volkskirche*, but the contrary.

[24] *ASS* 38 (1905–6), 321–7.

10

NATIONALITY AND RELIGION:
SPAIN

The Spanish rose as a people against Napoleon's invasion and backed King Ferdinand VII when he returned as an absolute ruler. But he was a bad king, and persecuted anyone with liberal ideas, and was linked—unjustly—to the loss of the American empire. In 1820 an army mutiny overthrew him and left a chaotic Spain under a liberal government until he was restored by a French army three years later.

Then the worst defect of absolute monarchy took its toll on the nation. There was no agreed heir, for there were two different traditions in the Spanish past, whether a woman could rule. Ferdinand died in 1833 leaving a brother Carlos and a daughter Isabella who was a baby. In his will he named the baby as sovereign.

Deep within the folk-memory of Spain lay the part which it had played in Catholic history: Spain the saviour of Europe from the Moors, Spain the saviour of Catholicism from Protestant power, Spain the converter of the New World to Catholic faith. In Poland Catholicism was part of nationalism because it represented Polish identity against Russian or Prussian. In Southern Ireland Catholicism was part of nationalism because it represented Irish identity against the English. Spain had not the same reason, but its memories made Spanish nationalism and Spanish Catholicism feel an entity. If Spanish Catholics met a Spanish Protestant they thought him not merely heretical but not quite Spanish.

During the nineteenth century this Spanish Catholicism met a new enemy, which at first was called the principles of the French Revolution, but later came to be called liberalism. Liberalism meant the struggle between rival parties, instead of the unity of the Spanish people. Liberalism meant freedom of the press, or of religious practice and propaganda, and therefore the encouragement of influences working against the unity of Spain. Many Spanish believed that the greatness of Spain rested on its religious past, and that its modern weakness sprang from the divisions which liberalism fostered.

Protestant missionaries who came in during the years of liberal governments had tiny success. There came to be a few Baptist or independent chapels scattered across the country. Their members were thought bizarre or unpatriotic by the remainder of their community.

Therefore the division of the country during the nineteenth century ran between traditional Catholics, still with many illiterate peasants among them, and the Spanish liberals, who might or might not be Catholics in a practising sense, but were almost always hostile to Church power. A few had attitudes descending from the deism of the Enlightenment. More derived their liberalism from the French, for France was the strong source of Spanish ideas in the nineteenth century.

There were two other groups who had nothing liberal about them but who could only justify their attacks upon the Church by supporting liberal politicians.

When it is said that the mass of the peasantry was strong for the Church, that meant the northern two-thirds of Spain. In the Basque country and the north-east the practice of church attendance was astonishingly high, in many places over 90 per cent of the people. This was not true of Andalusia in the south. There, in some areas, the people refused to go near the church and hated the clergy. Attendance at mass might be as high as 13 per cent or even more but it might be as low as 2 or 3 per cent, in places less than 1 per cent. The people were very poor and classed the clergy among their oppressors. The theory has been put forward that these were the old citizens of Moorish Spain and had never been reconciled to the Church after the conquest. Poverty and bad landlords over centuries make a more probable theory. They had the superstitions, the occasional processions, and the statues. But they did not associate these dramas of the streets with churchgoing.

Andalusia was not the only area of Spain where the devotion of the peasant was weak or non-existent. If a 'liberal' government was seen to attack the Church, it usually happened that a few churches were burnt, or a few monasteries sacked, or a few priests beaten or murdered. When Spanish Catholics talked so gratefully of the Catholic unity of the Spanish, they overlooked facts.

The Church passed through the Counter-Reformation, and through the benevolent despotism of the eighteenth century, with its lands and privileges. In a bad time of harvest or of poverty, which was much of the nineteenth century, any government cast its eye on these lands in a desperate effort to avoid bankruptcy. If it was necessary, for the sake of the country or the government, that a general should steal the money of the Church, that was welcome to members of the middle classes who were affected by French ideas and who would be likely to profit—and who did profit—from the taking of the lands. Illiberal generals, who rose to power by a coup, found allies among liberals.

Since the death of Ferdinand VII there was no agreed constitution. All governments had uncertain mandates. In southern and western parts of the country were peasants who hated priests. Men of the upper and middle class wanted reform in the State. The Church was tired, archaic, and compromised with absolutism. This combination produced a devastating series of attacks upon the Church which stamped into its leaders a hatred of liberalism.

THE CARLIST WAR

Immediately there was a civil war over the succession, daughter versus brother; no one sure whether a woman was entitled to succeed. The queen was backed by the moderates, the brother (Don Carlos) by ultraconservatives, with whom stood Basque separatists and the men of Navarre.

To survive in power Queen Isabella's mother Maria Cristina, as regent, had to allow parliamentary forms of government. In the conditions of civil war, with the extreme ecclesiastical right wing on the side of Don Carlos, and a need for church money to fight a war, there were the classic conditions for anticlerical legislation.

Maria Cristina issued a proclamation, that

religion and monarchy are the bases of the life of Spain and will be respected, protected, and maintained in all their strength and purity. The Spanish people has an inborn zeal for the faith and worship of its ancestors and has a complete assurance that no one can rule it without respecting the sacred things of its creed and worship. I am happy to help preside over a nation so eminently Catholic, and give the assurance that the religion which we profess, its doctrines and churches and ministers will be the most grateful care of my government.

The words were too strong for the moment. They were uttered because many conservatives did not believe that the baby daughter could be queen, were afraid of a liberal government taking hold of the regency, and so were out to back Don Carlos as the true and lawful sovereign of Spain. It was a civil war of seven years, 1833 to 1840. The liberals could not have won the war but for the help which France gave them across the Pyrenees.

Not many clergy backed the Carlist rising. With few exceptions Church leaders held that at all costs civil war should be averted and that the baby Isabella was the best hope of Spain. The bishop of León, Abarca, was an exception among bishops in telling them all to back Carlos. Later he became Carlos's Prime Minister. Canon Echevarría joined the Carlists and was shot when he was captured. The priest Merino, who had fought as a famous guerrilla, recognized Carlos as King Carlos V and raided south to the Escorial. The shooting of priests found in the rebel bands was shocking to their bishops, turning them against Isabella's government, and causing some priests in the north to think it a moral duty to lay aside their cassocks and join the fight for Don Carlos. In the Pyrenean areas friars, monks, and canons in plenty joined the Carlists. But churchmen were almost as uncomfortable in Carlist as in liberal Spain because the Carlists were as desperate as the liberals for money.

The government assailed the clergy as disloyal and started to treat them badly. It tried to control what was said in pulpits. People on the streets abused the clergy as they passed. The government was so bankrupt it could not borrow money.

A quarter of the bishops were monks. They had been loyal to King Ferdinand and were likely to be loyal to the daughter whom he chose as his successor. They were well chosen as religious pastors but were inflexible and disliked the notion of 'reform' whether it was in the constitution of the State or in the Church, which they saw no need to reform.

The first trouble came from the diplomatic action of the Holy See. The pope had a nuncio in Spain. It was the prudent custom of Rome not to recognize a new government until it was clear who would win a civil war. The pope did not recognize Queen Isabella—and gave mortal offence to her government because it implied that the pope might be a Carlist. After a Carlist protest in Rome, the pope delayed any appointment of new bishops in Spain because the government would have to approve them—and which government? Gregory XVI relied too much on a Spanish Capuchin, Fermín Sánchez Artesero,[1] who was dedicated to Don Carlos, and put every act of

---

[1] For whom see V. Cárcel Ortí, *Historia de la Iglesia en España* (Madrid, 1979), v. 188–9.

Carlos in the most favourable light and every act of the Madrid government in the most unfavourable. Carlos did all he could to appear as the defender of the Catholic faith against heretics and revolutionaries. His army fought under the banner of the Virgin of Sufferings.

The next trouble was the behaviour of the head of the Spanish Church, Cardinal Inguanzo, the archbishop of Toledo. He was a dry, intelligent lawyer. He pleaded ill-health and advanced age as an excuse not to attend the service recognizing the young Queen and not to swear an oath of allegiance to her. They were about to confiscate his goods and exile him, but then accepted the argument of health and the cardinal recognized Isabella as queen of Spain.

Because some monks and friars joined the Carlists, there was feeling against monks. There were formed societies called Isabelinos, with the purpose of violence against the other side. There was cholera in Madrid and it was put about that the monks poisoned the water. These rumours led to murder. The heat of summer, the story that monks poisoned the wells and caused the plague, the false rumour that Carlos advanced on the city, and the high price of bread caused mob emotion in Madrid.

On 17 July 1834 a gang climbed into the monastery of the Colegio Imperial of the Jesuits and murdered several fathers and destroyed the relics of the saints. The assassins went from monastery to monastery—St Thomas, as the monks said their office; St Francis the Great, as they were ending supper; the Mercedarians when they were in bed; and behind the murderers came looters. The dead numbered between seventy-eight and eighty-one, fifty of them at St Francis the Great where some were thrown off the roof whither they had fled for refuge, and some thirty wounded. In the streets women put on vestments that had been flung out, and danced. The casualties of the police were one soldier hanged for looting a chalice. The Carmelite house was saved by a police guard. The day of 17 July 1834 changed the history of the Church in Spain and was remembered with horror for decades.

The example of Madrid was catching—but not till April next year. At Saragossa the archbishop cancelled the licences of clergy who were outspoken liberals and there were cries in the streets of 'Death to the archbishop!' and 'Death to the cathedral chapter!' The loss of life was small compared with Madrid, but it was a canon, six monks, and a lay brother, as well as a few wounded. At Murcia the bishop fled and a mob sacked his palace. There were murders of eighteen monks in Barcelona, and then of the entire Franciscan and Discalced Carmelite communities; total deaths about 200, and some twenty-five monasteries destroyed. Rumours followed: the Franciscans at Bilbao were believed to have manufactured two million cartridges for the Carlist army. In Tarragona, where the archbishop fled to a ship in harbour, the crowd took his baggage from the quay and paraded through the town in mitres, copes, and rochets.

In 1835 came the dissolution of almost all the monasteries and a taking of their endowments for national needs: this, in the most Catholic country in Europe, or so everyone had supposed. A law abolished the Jesuits, though with pensions for the expelled. Another law suppressed all monasteries with fewer than twelve monks, except for those engaged in teaching, missions abroad, or in hospitals. A third law suppressed all houses of nuns and canons regular. There were exempted the houses at the great shrines at Montserrat (Benedictine), Guadalupe and the Escorial (both Hieronymian), and five other houses: the Cistercians at Poblet, the Carthusians at El Paular, the Basilians in Seville and two at Valladolid. But the exemptions did not stop them suffering.

Poblet was a daughter-house of Clairvaux, founded by the Count of Barcelona in 1150. It was rich and the burial-place for the kings of Aragon, a service to which it owed its exemption. Then it was the headquarters of the Catalan resistance to Napoleon. But exemption could not prevent its fate. The monks left, the house was sacked, part of it was burnt down, the mob polluted the tombs of the kings, the rich endowments went to the national treasury. Poblet remained a ruin till 1930 and ten years later Cistercian life began again.

Montserrat, one of the great sanctuaries of St Mary in Spain, suffered catastrophe in the war against Napoleon when it was destroyed. It had been repeopled when peace came but was struggling; and the exemption of 1835 did not stop it being closed. Only nine years later a handful of monks started to keep it going, with much difficulty, and in the later nineteenth century it flowered as it had not for 300 years. Even so, twenty-one monks were murdered in the Spanish civil war of 1936. After that war it regained its prosperity.

The two Hieronymian houses which were exempt were also closed; and this meant the practical end of the Hieronymian order (which at that time had about 1,000 members and forty-three houses), because it did not extend much outside the peninsula and to end it in Spain was to end it altogether.

When all the houses were closed some 30,000 male religious were thrown onto the streets—though many with pensions. The bishops were able to use some as parish priests, and government allowed those in colleges to go on teaching. About a quarter of them found church work of some sort.[2]

Not all nunneries were closed. The nuns were allowed to continue if their work was with the sick or in primary teaching—and if the convent housed more than twenty. These exceptions ended in 1837. But quietly many nunneries were allowed to go on if they did not flaunt themselves, because the towns could not do without their nursing or teaching.

Under the radical regime pastoral care was not easy. In 1839 five bishops were exiled within Spain, five in France, one in Piedmont, and two were in prison; seven bishops, though still in their dioceses, were prevented by the local authorities from doing anything. Where they were in office and able to act, they had lost their monks, nuns, tithes, and a lot of their money. Twice governments ordered them not to ordain anyone. The northern bishops sent young men over the Pyrenees to be ordained by French bishops, but it hardly felt a loyal act. From time to time the press was free enough to print pornography as well as atheism and they were not used to it, nor were they used to someone like George Borrow from England touring round to sell Protestant Bibles. Six bishops of 1839 were clearly for the liberal cause and liable to the charge of being quislings, and did not find it easy to care for an intransigent clergy. By 1847 there were forty dioceses without a bishop.[3] For a time people refused to receive the sacrament from bishops sent to occupy the sees of colleagues in exile.

The clergy were still very numerous, almost as in the Middle Ages in Europe, some 100,000. The people were pious though they suffered continually from the civil war, violent men taking over their cottages and destroying images, or the loss of their favourite pastor if he was too outspoken. That made them more pious.

The minister, Mendizabal, one of the few liberal statesmen of Spain, exhausted the money of the monasteries and had to turn to other forms of church property. He needed a law to abolish mortmain. He saw, like the advisers of Henry VIII, that the sharing out of Church property would create people who had an interest in revo-

---

[2] Excellent statistics in Cárcel Ortí, *Historia*, 139–43.

[3] Cárcel Ortí, *Historia*, 178–81; and *Politica eclesiál de los gobiernos liberales españoles 1830–40* (Pamplona, 1975), 455 ff.

lution. This sale of church endowments was done corruptly because the state was not capable of supervising it properly. The upper and middle classes, not the poor, won the benefit.

The new liberal constitution of 1837 included toleration of religions. But this provision troubled Spain for the whole of the nineteenth century and after. How could Catholic Spain think a law right which allowed error to be taught, even if only by few people? To persuade Spanish Catholics that toleration was good proved to be as difficult as persuading Pius IX. This difficulty was worse than with Pius IX because sooner or later there had to be a compromise between liberal ideas and the Catholic Church of Spain; and such a compromise continued to be impossible to achieve because most churchmen would not accept that legislation for toleration was right and most liberals would not accept a constitution without it.

In 1843 the regime of anticlericals, then headed by General Espartero, who had won fame fighting the Carlists, and who as dictator toyed with the idea of a national Spanish Church similar to the Church of England, was overthrown in a coup and the fiercer anticlericalism of ten years of Spanish government ended. It was difficult to make Pope Gregory XVI think any good of Spanish liberals, but Pius IX was readier to talk. It was time for him to be brought in since forty-seven sees were unfilled; the primatial see of Toledo had been vacant for thirteen years. A Spanish force helped the pope at Gaeta.

Spain remained officially 'a Catholic State' throughout. A governor of Toledo still imposed fines and prison on persons who failed to fulfil their obligations at Easter. Processions on feast-days continued, with members of government and detachments of the national guard walking as of old, and municipalities still paying handsomely for expenses. The number fulfilling their Easter duties, so far as can be known from various tests, did not fall much during these worst years. Some lamented that Sunday observance was failing in Madrid, but that was a comment applicable to European large cities rather than connected with revolution. Police curbed hooligan attacks upon church services when they could. Though the religious orders were mostly driven out of education, religious teaching was preserved in the schools—it had been taught badly and was now taught worse. The government took all the property of the parish clergy, and promised to pay them adequate stipends by a mixture of fees for church services and a church tax to be assessed and levied by the local authorities. But the local authorities often refused to co-operate, and therefore the State was unable to honour its promise to replace the parish endowments with a stipend. The clergy depended on local charity, and some were desperate.

THE SPANISH CONCORDAT

From 1844 Spain was more stable, bishops and clergy returned, the sale of ecclesiastical property was stopped. These better relations culminated in a Concordat with Rome in 1851, whereby the Catholic religion was declared to be the religion of Spain (article 1) and the Catholic religion had to be taught in schools (article 2). No other religion was allowed to be practised publicly, all teaching in schools and universities must conform to Catholic teaching, and the bishops were given the power to see that it did so conform. The State kept its right to appoint to bishoprics and benefices, and undertook to maintain the parish clergy and church buildings, and allowed a limited revival of the male religious orders. The undertaking of government, in the Concordat of 1851, to maintain priests and buildings was never implemented. The State budgeted for a church grant not much more than half the minimum that the Church thought itself to need. Still, the parish priest need starve no longer. The number of parish clergy again began to rise. There were 8,000 more seminarists in 1862 than in 1853. Only a limited number of these were eligible for government stipends; the others managed with fees or travelling services as mass priests, and revived the clerical proletariat of the *ancien régime*. The salaries of bishops were rationalized, the number of canonries reduced. The power of bishops was increased by the dissolution of monasteries, long exempt from their control, and the Concordat also gave them oversight of seminaries. Government closed the theological faculties of the universities, so that every priest had to be given higher education in a seminary; the bishops were enthusiasts for this change.

The Jesuits reappeared in 1852 and had twenty-five houses only eleven years later; the Benedictines were allowed back to the sanctuary at Montserrat. With limitations it was possible again to be a monk or a nun. They were many fewer: before the death of Ferdinand VII there had been more than 60,000 monks and nuns in Spain. The nuns were still numerous, more than 13,000, but the monks were few. The most important part for the Church was the restoration of the right to acquire endowments; and to achieve this the pope rescinded the condemnation of those who had bought Church property in the great sale.

A constitution of this sort, in the Europe of 1851, could only mean that the party of the right was in harness; all the clergy were ordered to wear cassock and clerical collar. This alliance would cause trouble when the right fell from power, and they were sure to fall at some time because the new factory labourers began to organize and strikes happened. But with a break, and with Queen Isabella's help, a moderate right-wing government and a Church which supported it lasted for nearly fifteen years; and, with a break after that, was important in Spain until 1931. For two years, 1854–6, there was another radical government, and sales of Church property began again; but it had no force and the moderate right came back to power. It was a decade of economic prosperity for Spain and that helped stability. Even while a radical government was in power it hardly affected the devotion of the ordinary Spaniard. Spain thought it a high moment of faith when Pope Pius IX defined the Immaculate Conception.

Queen Isabella, whose marriage was a misery and sex life dramatic, has been called the last sovereign in the history of Europe who pursued a steady Catholic policy. Despite her promiscuity there was a side to her character which was very caring. With her unloved husband she washed the feet of the aged poor, she in her jewels and he in the uniform of a Field Marshal. The people saw her kneeling for hours on cold stones, and it was plain to them that she experienced mystic emotion; she fasted in Holy Week, and no one doubted that all this was sincere. She had an impulsiveness which led to sudden gestures of munificence to a charity or a person. She had a 'Rasputin', a Franciscan nun upon whom she depended and whom she thought holy, Sor Patrocinio (her real name was Quiroga), known as 'the nun with the stigmata', for she claimed to bear the stigmata of the crucifixion on her body and to see visions of truth, which included saying which side was about to win the Spanish civil war. Successive governments kept putting her under house arrest in nunneries or exiling her, but she kept returning to influence because the Queen believed in her.[4]

---

[4] For Patrocinio see *AHP* 4 (1966), 295; 21 (1983), 153 ff.; G. Martina, *Pio IX (1851–66)* (Rome, 1986), 570 ff.

FATHER CLARET

The Queen also came under the influence of a much more reputable and godly man, Father Claret, but though he tried not to be wrongly political he did not easily see a frontier between his deep piety and the politics of the right wing. The Queen believed in him as one who worked miracles. She asked his advice on bishoprics, and the advice was good.

Claret had a very unusual career which illustrated the great strength and a certain weakness in Spanish Catholicism. He was a Catalan, one of eleven children of a pious family, who was trained to be a textile worker. While at work in Barcelona he decided to be a Carthusian, but he interpreted a storm on his way to the monastery as a sign to him that the plan was wrong. So he went to the seminary at Vich to train for orders, but his training coincided with the riots of 1835 and the murder of monks in Barcelona; the troubles shut the seminary and it was now illegal to become a monk. So instead he was ordained and became a curate. He decided to go to Rome and become a missionary to distant worlds but the Congregation of Propaganda told him to go back to Spain. By 1841 he was famous as a preacher and the diocese relieved him of his curacy and told him to go round the parishes preaching. He walked from village to village in all weathers, wearing his cassock, an itinerant evangelist. The civil wars caused a dearth of doctors in the villages, so he studied the uses of herbs and healed bodies as well as souls, knowing how important faith can be in bodily cures. He was so good at the work, and so popular in the villages, that government suspected him of fomenting the guerrillas in the mountains.

He tried to get over the ban on monks and nuns. There were still religious women with nowhere to go and still a desperate need for nurses, carers, and primary educators. He organized women in a 'community'; it could not be a nunnery, so they had to live at home and keep a rule. The authorities frowned on this venture but could not call it illegal. Then he did the same for men—because missionaries were legal, it was called the Congregation of Missionaries, Sons of the Immaculate Conception of Mary; but they could not take vows because that was illegal.

Then in 1850 he was selected, astonishingly, to be archbishop of Santiago in Cuba, about the most difficult post under Spanish rule because it was a corrupt and half-ruined relic of the Spanish

American empire, and was liable to raids from adventurers backed by the United States. He achieved 12,000 marriages of unmarried couples, reconciled 80,000 adults who had been put out of the Church, legitimized 40,000 illegitimate babies, and won massive unpopularity among the whites for his hostile attitude to slavery. Most priests could not read Latin and so could not take the service properly, and most openly had 'wives' and children and almost no pay. Many villages had no church and others had a ruin which used to be their church. A resenter stabbed him in the face as he came down from a pulpit. He was six years in Cuba while white conservatives besieged Madrid with requests to take him away.

This was achieved when Queen Isabella summoned him to be her confessor in 1857. He accepted on the conditions that he need not live in the Palace and could preach in the parishes. Since he was directing the soul of a woman who was hardly on speaking terms with her husband but was on speaking terms with too many young men, and was so indiscreet that the public knew what was happening, this was another work of extreme difficulty. Unlike other courtiers he told her the truth. She became, in three-quarters of her private life, the most devout queen of the nineteenth century. She charged him with restoring the Escorial to religious life.

As her chief confidant he was fiercely attacked as a secret interferer in politics and shared all her growing unpopularity. He aimed to be wholly non-political and believed that he was. He was accused of making cabinets, which was an absurd charge. But to think the Syllabus of Errors good, to advise the choice of a certain kind of bishop, to back the pope to the utmost, and even to despise political parties—as he did, because to despise parties was to be against Parliaments—had, in that moment of history, political consequence. The left-wing world asked why he did not dissuade the Queen from acts that were either illiberal or immoral. They spread scandal about him—even of a liaison with Sor Patrocinio.

The Syllabus did more damage in Spain than in any other country. It condemned democracy and toleration and made it far harder for Spanish churchmen to find compromise with the liberals' ideas—which was its intention; but on such a compromise hung the happiness of Spain. Nearly all the bishops published it, though they had no legal right to do so without government approval. The government finally allowed it to be published with the proviso 'saving the rights of the crown and the rights and prerogatives of the nation'; which showed how the old tradition of Bourbon regalism lived on in moderate-conservative Spain. The bishops were pleased that a document was accepted that denounced State interference with the work of the Church; the moderates were pleased that the bishops accepted a regalist proviso which ensured State control of the Church.

It was obvious to the left and to many moderates that Spain must recognize the new kingdom of Italy, which had already existed for five years. Spain was a Catholic country and the pope thought it impossible for any true Catholic to recognize the usurping Piedmontese kingdom which called itself Italy. Queen Isabella had a conscientious reluctance to allow recognition. The near-Carlist right held that the pope was spiritual king of Italy and it must be Spanish duty to defend his independence to the end, and refuse to recognize bandits who claimed the Pope's State. Liberals and moderates held that every wise Spaniard ought to support the arrival of a new liberal nation and wish it prosperity.

The government forced the Queen to recognize Italy in August 1865. Father Claret left his place at her side and went to Rome in protest against this weakness of her conscience. The Spanish bishops protested. Pius IX was more sympathetic to the predicament in which the Queen found herself. He sent Claret back to the Queen.

The new bishops were more likely to be ultramontane than their predecessors. They looked to Rome as the outside support against the State. Though they were much poorer than their predecessors, they raised large sums of money to help the pope in his poverty after the Piedmontese took North Italy away from him—it was the first time in history that huge collections of voluntary aid passed from Spain to help the pope. They also raised money for missions in Africa and for the desperate clergy in Poland after the failed revolution of 1863. They even sent a contribution to help build the Catholic cathedral in London.

Queen Isabella was at last turned off her throne by an army coup of 1868, and Spain became a republic. On the train, as she crossed the border into exile, was Father Claret, who was never allowed to return to Spain. The local juntas seized power and rescinded all the liberties: freedom of the press, freedom of religion, and the rest, and were violent until the central government forced them back into order. In this chaos Andalusia was the worst place for the Church; the junta in Seville destroyed forty-nine churches.[5] This country where the people

[5] Cárcel Ortí, *Historia*, 231.

were most Catholic seemed to long to destroy churches, church schools, and cathedrals, and hunt out clergymen. It was very possible to be superstitious in religion and simultaneously so antichurch as to want to deliver murderous blows to churches and their officers.

THE QUEST FOR ORDER IN THE STATE

To establish order the central government had to be seen to satisfy the crowds. In October 1868 it dissolved all monasteries and nunneries founded since the dissolving decree of 1837 and took their properties, including libraries, archives, pictures, and other works of art. Some orders devoted to charity or teaching, but not all, managed to survive. But government gave orders that these decrees should be executed with a measure of gentleness. Even the Jesuits could go on teaching if they did not wear cassocks.

These months of near-chaos did not represent what most of Spain wanted, which was order. When the Constituent Cortes met to plan the new constitution, two bishops sat among its members. They soon went home, because their interventions were fruitless. When all was settled and the new Cortes was to be opened, the bishops were invited to bless it with inaugural prayers. They refused to come. The State then tried to exact from bishops and clergy the same oath of allegiance that it demanded of civil servants. This caused one of the worst tensions of the century between Church and State. The Curia at Rome ruled that the clergy might only swear if they were compelled by force and if they swore with the reservation 'saving the Law of God'; but then Pope Pius IX ruled more gently that they could rightly swear with the due reservation. The Spanish bishops were not willing to follow the Pope's gentler line. They refused to compromise about the oath and forbade their clergy to swear. They were not quite unanimous. The primate of Toledo, Alameda,[6] swore the oath,

---

[6] Alameda, study by A. Arce, *Hispania Sacra*, 24 (1971), ii. 1–89; and see *DHEE* s.v. He was a Franciscan from the age of 16 and one of the last of the old world, for he did splendid political work for Spain in the revolt of the Argentines and his rise was meteoric; he became a bishop under Ferdinand VII and in 1833 accepted Don Carlos as king. He was in danger of being murdered and escaped to France, then Italy, and did not come back till 1848. Nevertheless he was accepted as archbishop of Burgos. After he moved to Toledo in 1857 (becoming cardinal, 1858) he was 76 and so old and decrepit that he did nothing, and was a passenger among the bishops. But both his person and his career have mystery in them. During his service to the most right-wing of kings and then his standing for Don Carlos, he was a secret Freemason.

as did the bishop of Almería, with the question, 'Why not, if this is what the Pope approves?' It showed the difference between the Spanish Catholics and others that the French were cheerfully able to take such an oath without a qualm of conscience.

Parish priests continued in their parishes and if their pay was cut they were usually helped by their people. Their life was made much more difficult in 1869–70 because the Carlist war broke out again; Isabella being an exile, there was a chance for the grandson of Don Carlos to claim the throne and the loyalties of the old Carlist party. It was a much smaller war, and the Carlists hardly had a chance. A few priests again took up arms on the Carlist side and gave an excuse to the government to oppress more clergy than those few, and to hooligans once more to abuse clergy in the streets.

In 1869–70 the government conceded toleration to Protestants and other religions and instituted civil marriage. The first public Protestant service was held in Madrid on 24 January 1869. There were still many Spaniards who thought it shameful to treat a non-Catholic as a Spanish citizen, and some of them said this in Parliament. To the unity of a society, it was said, worshipping together is more important than political arrangements. They held up to scorn the example of Italy—politically united by the Risorgimento, but because of the new quarrels of religion and irreligion, a country worse divided than in the time before political union.

The law ruled that only civil marriages had legal effect (and therefore the child of a couple married only in church was illegitimate). This was so contrary to the tradition of the people that it did more damage to the republican cause than any other act. Most Spaniards went on being married in church and took no notice of civil marriage; only a few used civil marriage alone without also going to church. Government was alarmed to find that the ruling caused polygamous males to marry one wife in church and another in the registry office without committing bigamy.

Four years later government again recognized the legality of marriage in church, and later still recognized the children of those who married only in church after 1870 as legitimate. In 1873 the Cortes actively planned the separation between Church and State and quoted Cavour's phrase, 'a free Church in a free State'. Not all Spanish Catholics were against such a separation, but most followed the lead of Rome in being resolute against it.

There succeeded five years of constitutional quest and disturbance.

They could not do without a king. Looking round for kings was not the easiest of tasks when there was no one with a conceivable claim to the throne. The crown of Spain was a comedy, hawked round Europe and refused in Britain, Portugal, and Italy. A German princeling accepted it, then withdrew after helping to cause the Prussian-French war. At last they persuaded Amadeus of Savoy, the son of King Victor Emmanuel of Italy; a choice which had few merits because the need for a king was to reconcile divided Spain and much of Spain did not want the son of the person held responsible for robbing the pope.

Amadeus did not have an easy time. Spain was again nearly bankrupt (by the new Carlist war), and the worst anarchy was in Andalusia: the price of bread made the poor desperate. The bishops went to the Vatican Council and made excellent speeches on the side of Pope Pius IX. Processions for Corpus Christi became impossible in any big town, they would be attacked. There was little that Amadeus could bear in his kingly office, he was treated with studied contempt, and he resigned in January 1873, and sent a letter of penitence to the pope which made him unpopular in the anticlerical part of Spain. Again there was a republic, and renewed talk of a separation of Church and State.

A bill presented by Castelar to effect the separation gave the Church complete freedom and the right to acquire property, abolished the State's control over bulls and the right to nominate bishops, and allowed the nuns or ex-nuns their guaranteed pensions. The bill never came to the vote because the Cortes was suppressed by General Pavia early in 1874. By the end of that year Queen Isabella's son was accepted as King Alfonso XII.

It took him two years to establish control of all Spain against Carlists and Basques. Educated in Switzerland and at Sandhurst, he was the first capable king for more than a century. Though he was conservative and backed by conservatives it was sufficient of a parliamentary government to last, eventually with alternation of parties, which could only mean that there was basic agreement on the principles of government. It constituted, in comparison with all the coups of the last forty years, a fairly stable government in Spain from 1875 to 1931.

The freedom of universities was curtailed, and some professors were dismissed. Civil marriage was emended in the sense that religious marriage was also made legal. Toleration was maintained, but in the modified sense that other religions and cults than the Catholic must not be seen in public. The religious orders again attracted novices—some of them many novices.

CLERICALISM AND ANTICLERICALISM

All this pain left a country where religion was still a dividing force. Anticlericalism in Barcelona or Valencia was more bitter than the bitterest of the French. It was a city symptom; in the countryside, in Castile, in Navarre, among the Basques, old devout Spain lived on. The one could not get on with the other, and neither side had any understanding of the other. Every government was in trouble over harmony in the nation. It had an effect on Church practice. The statistics show a fall for Easter obligations in certain towns. But whether anticlericalism had anything to do with this, or whether it was due to the European problem of what happened in the bigger cities and the changing fashions of social conduct, is not certain. Figures for a parish at Longroño show people not fulfilling their Easter duties in 1828 to be about 1 per cent; then in 1836, during the religious and constitutional revolution, 6 per cent—still very small; in 1841, 4.5 per cent—still smaller; then in 1887, 58.3 per cent:[7] yet much more damage was done to the Church in the earlier time than the later.

In Barcelona in 1909 came the Tragic Week, the worst sign of division and a pointer to what might be. It occurred over a call-up by government for a Moroccan war, which Catholics supported. A workers' anarchist organization called a strike; the tram-drivers refused to join in, so it developed into a street fight between strikers and blacklegs. The police lost control, and then anticlericalism rose to the surface: forty-two churches were burnt or partly destroyed, there was some loss of clerical life, nuns were maltreated, workmen danced in the streets with mummies of nuns they had dug up.[8]

A mysterious social force was at work, most of the time under the surface, but liable suddenly to erupt into the open.

[7] W. J. Callahan, *Church, Politics and Society in Spain*, 181.

[8] As always in that age of Spain, violence bred worse violence. The forces of order, when they gained control again, shot 175 workmen in the streets and afterwards excluded radicals though they had nothing to do with the riot. Cf. Gerald Brenan, *The Spanish Labyrinth* (Cambridge, 1990), 45.

Anticlerical mobs were strangely unpredictable. It is not certain what can be inferred from their acts about opinion among the people. An angry mob needed to do something wild before it was sated. In the revolution of 1854, for example, the crowd rioted for four days in Madrid and ended by burning and sacking a royal palace and the houses of several government ministers. Not a church nor clergyman was touched. In the 1868 and 1873 revolutions the anticlerical acts were more moderate—guns fired at statues, shouting or smoking in church services, a republican flag draped on an altar, red dye dropped into holy water stoups, Garibaldi's march played outside a church at the time of a service, the monstrance of Cadiz Cathedral put up for auction, the throwing of a bishop out of his palace—very different from the massacres of 1834–5 and 1936.

In 1904 was the fiftieth anniversary of the declaration of the Immaculate Conception. The church in Valencia, where anticlericals were as strong as anywhere except Barcelona, decided to celebrate it with a procession. They accompanied the statue of the Virgin with bands and 9,000 people singing hymns. Gangs tried to shout down the hymns with obscenities; and when the people reached the cathedral they were called 'the army of Mary'—and 9,000 people had been made to feel confessors for their faith.

One other example shows how religion divided Spain despite all that a humane government could do: 1882 was the second centenary of Murillo, who died after falling from the scaffolding while he painted at the Capuchin church in Cadiz. He had worked in Seville all his life and was especially employed by the Franciscans. Here was a great Spanish religious artist, it was natural to commemorate his centenary. A local canon organized it, but then a young brotherhood of students with Carlist opinions used it as a demonstration. The intention had been to show gratitude to Murillo, and to glorify Christian art and the Immaculate Conception of the Blessed Virgin, which was the subject of two of his celebrated paintings. But that time also saw the crisis in Rome over the body of Pope Pius IX; and so Pius IX became a symbol for the festival because he had defined the doctrine of the Immaculate Conception. The liberals in Seville would have nothing to do with it, the anticlericals determined to disrupt it, the Carlist students resolved to demonstrate at it, and no tribute to a great painter was ever sunk in a worse bucket of mud.

But this was the antichristian south. The junta at Cadiz was specially anticlerical. Here, unusually, they changed the names of the streets, and their heroes are interesting—Voltaire, Fourier the founder of French socialism, Garibaldi, Mazzini, Juárez the Mexican dictator who drove out the French, and Abraham Lincoln.[9]

INTEGRISM VERSUS LIBERALISM

The division of the nation was not the only one. The civil wars and persecutions left the Church divided in itself. Here was a country with an established Church, with a population the majority of which went to church, and in which an even larger majority cared for the Church; but within it was rancour—which is a common experience in churches after a persecution. The bishops were chosen with Rome's approval and were more of a single type; but the priests and the monks were numerous and had many rebels. Out of persecution the Spanish Church had not achieved peace and harmony.

The first cause was the toleration of other faiths now written into the constitution. It meant that the half-Carlist Catholics renewed their attacks on Catholics who supported the constitution and the kingship of the son of Queen Isabella. They now began to be known as 'integrists', those who stood for 'Catholicism in its wholeness'. Like Veuillot's *Univers* in France, their integrist periodical *El Siglo Futuro* (*The Next Century*) was read by many of the clergy and was amazingly long-lived, from 1875 till the outbreak of the civil war in 1936.

Ramón Nocedal was the founder of the periodical and demanded that Catholics should resist a moderate government totally, stating that they could not ally themselves with moderate liberals to keep out radicals because liberalism was wicked. He put the programme to 'King' Carlos who refused to approve its extremism. Then he attacked the pretender as a compromiser and was excluded from the Carlist party. Therefore he founded the integrists as a new Catholic party further right than the Carlists.

His journalism was the nearest in Europe to that of Veuillot in France: the periodical called for the old Spain which linked nationality to the Catholic faith, which allowed the State no say at all in the doctrine of the Church, that was not disgraced by liberalism. His stance was, 'we are to defend liberty but never open our doors to

---

[9] Callahan, 'Spanish Parish Clergy', 265.

heretics, and must abhor governments that accept freedom of worship, and allow books of pornography, error, and rapine to be published; we are against Parliaments because they do not represent the people, they only represent the interests of party organizations.'

For some twenty years this integrist programme gained surprising support. Integrist pulpits denied absolution to Catholics of other parties. They received support from a majority though not all of the Jesuits. Their best moment and widest support came in 1901 when a moderate government threatened the monasteries and for a moment integrists were the core of resistance. Two years later Pius X was Pope and Merry del Val Secretary of State, and for eleven years there was strife between the Vatican and Spanish governments about the choice of bishops—and no bishops at all were appointed between April 1909 and July 1913. For a time that helped the integrists. But before the death of Pius X their force in Spanish politics had faded.

In 1884 a priest, Félix Sarda y Salvany published a tract called *Liberalism is Sin* after two bishops refused to let it appear. He was a Catalan whose health prevented him from pastoral cures and he started to write pamphlets, and soon became the most popular Christian apologist of that generation. The success of this tract was prodigious; twenty editions by 1960, and translations into seven other languages. It was an exposition of the teachings of Popes Pius IX and Leo XIII in an integrist sense, with pointed applications to Spanish politics, and became the handbook of integrists. It was delated to the Congregation of the Index in Rome, which said that it was meritorious. Spanish bishops appealed against the verdict. The prefect of the Index replied tactfully that the praise applied only to the general principle and not to the detailed applications. Sarda y Salvany received a message of pleasure from Pope Leo XIII. Right into the 1920s some textbooks and catechisms taught the children that liberalism is sin, and that to vote for a liberal party is sin.

The law on liberty meant freedom to meet and talk, and therefore freedom for Catholics. Not unlike the Italian congresses in a similar political situation, Spaniards at last organized themselves *qua* Catholics. They called themselves the Catholic Union. As in Italy they were led at first by aristocrats. The founding leader, the marquis of Pidal, was the son of the minister who sent Spanish forces to help Pius IX at Gaeta; and as in Italy the vocal element grew less aristocratic and more willing to think radical ideas. As in Italy they constituted a movement of lay people to which the bishops assented and

456 *Nationality and Religion: Spain*

which was not initiated by the clergy. The difficulty was that a Catholic party must be 'broad-minded' to collect a lot of votes, as the Centre Party found in Germany, and the later Christian Democratic party in Italy. Therefore this Catholic Union was regarded with hostility by the integrists as a compromise, weak on principle for the sake of power. Anticlericals in the Cortes kept attacking it as an unconstitutional party which the government had no right to protect.

Because the Church was so clerical, the most important man in the Union was the primate of Toledo, Moreno, one of the bishops of stature of the century.[10] But his prestige did not stop a campaign being unleashed against him and everyone else who supported the Union, and a habit of contempt for bishops springing up among ordinary clergy and monks. Moreno became suspect to the monsignors in the Curia.

On 8 December 1882 Pope Leo XIII issued the encyclical *Cum multa* to tell the Spanish Catholics to be at harmony. It made no difference.[11]

THE SEMINARIES

Standards were low. No one could decide the place of the theological faculties. Were they harmful because they could not be controlled by the bishops: so was it best not to have such faculties and to keep all education of priests in seminaries? Or had a university-trained clergy a better chance of serving in parishes where the people were

[10] Moreno y Maisonave (1817–84); born in Guatemala his parents took him, as a baby, on a British ship to escape the revolution when Guatemala went independent of Spain; he studied law and was not ordained till he was 32 and was immediately made archdeacon of Burgos by Alameda (!). Only seven years later he became bishop of Oviedo (consecrated by Alameda and Claret!), and five years after that went to Rome (1862) and instantly won the affection of Pius IX. Next year he was archbishop of Valladolid and was the first to publish the Syllabus in his diocese without State leave; he was made cardinal in 1868. At the Vatican Council he led the Spanish bishops in favour of infallibility from the Palazzo Caborelli (his speech for it in Mansi, *Collectio conciliorum recentiorum*, ed. I. B. Martin and L. Petit (Arnhem and Leipzig, 1923–7), xvi, 19 May 1870). In 1875 he became primate; see *DHEE* s.v.; Cárcel Ortí, *Leon XIII y Los Catolicos Españoles* (Pamplona, 1988), 27 ff.

[11] *ASS* 15 (1882), 241 ff. To the makers of the Concordat of 1851 it had seemed absurd that the capital Madrid should not have its own archbishop but be in the diocese of Toledo. They agreed that a see of Madrid should be founded. Nothing happened. Years passed. At last the see was founded and in 1885 they consecrated its first archbishop, an able prelate, the bishop of Salamanca, Martínez Izquierdo. He was murdered by a discontented curate who shot him down on the steps of his own cathedral, after just over a year in office.

educated? The State wavered between extreme anticlericals who wanted the clergy to be as ignorant as possible and thought it wrong use of State money to help train pastors of any denomination, and moderates who needed moderate clergymen to support a moderate State and thought that they were more likely to be moderate if they were educated at universities rather than seminaries.

The State thought it impossible to concede to bishops liberty to control their seminaries. The Concordat of 1851 gave to the State the control of the academic courses and to the bishops control of the way of life and the devotion. To compensate for the end of theological faculties in universities, the State created central seminaries with the right to give higher degrees including Doctor of Divinity and Doctor of Canon Law; there were four, at Toledo, Granada, Salamanca, and Valencia. Later they added two more, Compostela and the Canaries. There was serious abuse of the higher degrees which could be achieved with payment and a nominal residence. It was necessary to show one of these degrees if one was to be a canon or gain one of the higher posts, and bishops often dispensed candidates from the necessity of attending the courses.

The result was that the six central seminaries were no more central than any other; their standards no higher, their libraries as poor, their teachers no better equipped. The Church lost its theological faculties, of its own wish, without gaining. Rome suggested a single central seminary, in the Escorial. The bishops would have none of it. A Rome report of 1891 listed the Spanish seminaries in three classes, good, adequate, and bad. Among the bad were two of the central seminaries, including the largest, Valencia, though three were among the good.

By the standard of other countries these central seminaries were large. Valencia was always the largest; in 1890–1 it had seventeen professors, three assistants, and 1,208 students, of whom 451 were in theology.[12]

Seminaries were cut off from the world; students wore clerical dress and had no novels, newspapers, cinema, theatre, and only limited communication with the family. Thomist philosophy was learnt by rote; the syllabuses were narrow; Latin was the medium of instruction; and they were segregated from the world and ordinary humanity—priests were much better prepared intellectually in the old

[12] Cárcel Ortí, *Leon XIII*, 139.

university. But now they were trained to be more ecclesiastical, and this was seen as the need of the time. It was the priest's work to be with God, and he should keep away from the normal world and lead his people to the sacred which he was supposed to inhabit.

THE PARISHES

The pastors thought little of the duty of preaching. They did not teach much but gave devotional addresses, sometimes mixed with politics. They liked rhetoric and enjoyed being dramatic; the congregations were not used to the necessity of silence at sermons and were accustomed to laughing or clapping. The exception to these standards, as through all previous history since the coming of the friars, was the parish mission, taken by a member of a religious order who was practised and could be effective. Mass on Sunday could be a popular feast, happy even to excess; at times it also carried superstitions left uneradicated from the Middle Ages. The parishioners did not mind if the priest's housekeeper was also his mistress; he hardly lost credit in their eyes, sometimes the contrary, because it made him seem more like one of themselves; but they agreed with the bishop in not tolerating a married priest.

The number of priests who were not monks slowly fell while the number of people rose. Half the priests and more came from country smallholders, so that recruitment was affected by the slow movement of the people from country to town. Naturally priests were more likely to come from the more religious parts of the country, such as Navarre and Old Castile, and far fewer from Andalusia or Estremadura.

The weight of pastoral work in Spain had always rested on the religious orders. Their fate meant that the secular parish priest became more indispensable. He was seldom of the same standard as the priest trained by a religious order. There is a memory of a parish in the Asturias, then a religious part of Spain, from the 1880s: for nearly all the Sundays in the year no one received the sacrament, and there were only two sermons preached in the year, on the name day of the church and at Corpus Christi.[13]

---

[13] W. J. Callahan, *Church, Politics and Society in Spain, 1750–1874* (Cambridge, Mass., 1984), 234.

The church revival showed the persistence of religious faith and practice among the Spanish people. The urban poor, and the peasants of Andalusia, were still not to be touched by it; and the intelligentsia, all the century under French or German influence but more French than German, were not to be weaned from their principles by a very traditional Catholicism, even after the best of the Jesuits and Dominicans tried to modernize Thomism into a Christian philosophy that would be intellectually acceptable.

Of the cult practices, the rosary was very common and was not dependent on priests. Its affection, and its individual nature, was shown at many masses where most of the congregation could be seen telling their beads during the prayers. The 'attendance' at mass—a people's devotion—rosaries, novenas, visits to shrines, pictures, or statues—was not liturgical though it took place at the time of liturgy. The priest went on saying the mass while the people said their private prayers around him. He had his back to the people and said the prayers in Latin which few in the congregation understood; though they were trained in catechism to understand the outline of what happened at the climax of the mass.

Pilgrimage to shrines was common and was encouraged by the clergy, though the encouragement was unnecessary, for it was a popular movement. The brotherhoods continued strong, often linked with trades, or, as in the Holy Week processions, with the right to carry a float with an image. These processions were very religious in a way, but need not be in the least churchy. They were acts of the whole people rather than of the people organized in a liturgical way to say prayers to God. At times they could be demonstrations. The radicals got up a centenary of the rights of man in 1889. Huge Catholic processions made it clear that they were in opposition, to celebrate the reign of God. Such demonstrative processions led to violence in the streets, but that was rare.

The Daughters of Mary were Italian in origin, but their big expansion was in Spain; they were associated with the crowning of statues of the Virgin, the first at Montserrat, and these events were very popular.

The clergy encouraged the cult of the Sacred Heart of Jesus, a warm, emotional, pictured form of devotion. The Jesuits were its especial propagators. Since they were banned so often they could only do so from late in the century. They founded a monthly journal, *The Messenger of the Sacred Heart (Mensajero del Corazón de Jesús y del Apostolado de Oración*) copied in part from the French. The cult was associated by its opponents with the right wing in politics. It tried to get the picture of the Sacred Heart not only into homes but into schools, universities, banks, and shops. It was enormously successful, so much so that in 1919 King Alfonso XIII with the government consecrated the nation to the Sacred Heart.[14]

Something in it was still political as well as religious. The uniform of Carlist soldiers had a Sacred Heart badge on the left breast. Ernest Hemingway had a true instinct in *For Whom the Bell Tolls* when he described how in the civil war after 1936 a republican shot to kill a Navarrese soldier but aimed so as not to hit his Sacred Heart badge.

As literacy rose—it rose slowly—there was a huge new production of devotional books, pamphlets, and catechisms. The Sunday school first found in northern Protestantism passed into Spain.

THE REVIVAL OF RELIGIOUS ORDERS

After the coming of King Alfonso XII, freedom was conceded to the monks. The government, faced with radicals and anarchists, had the idea that it would help stability if it allowed the opening of monasteries in the radical areas; so that the first of these houses was opened in Andalusia. In the four following years thirty-two monasteries were opened. In the last of the four years, 1880, the French started expelling their monks and though some of them went to England, America, or Italy, many went to Spain and there were plenty of monks to fill the newly-opened monasteries. A historic Benedictine monastery, Santo Domingo de Silos, with wonderful romanesque architecture and once a house for copying splendid manuscripts, had been dissolved in 1837 and its manuscripts sold at auction. Now in 1881 Benedictines returned and reopened it and it has stayed open till now.

The dissolution of 1837 treated nunneries gently in the sense of allowing many to continue while they still had nuns; and so in 1850 there were still open some 700 to 800 nunneries, though each of them had a much smaller number of nuns because they had not been able to accept novices. The Concordat of 1851 allowed nuns provided they combined their contemplation with service in teaching or

---

[14] F. Lannon, *Privilege, Persecution and Prophecy* (Oxford, 1987), 29–30.

to the sick. The nunneries were again able to admit novices. The demand that contemplative nuns should also be active in schools or hospitals had the effect that nunneries were hard-pressed to practise contemplation.

Under existing social conditions a nunnery offered a woman not only a disciplined life but liberty, a chance to become a teacher or headmistress, a nurse, hospital matron, or administrator, which she could hardly achieve in any other way. There were more than three times as many nuns as monks (counting novices, etc.); and more than twice as many nunneries as monasteries. This had always been so in Spain since society became safer. In 1892 the grand total of religious was 47,511, but this included refugee French monks and nuns. The largest number of active nuns were the Sisters of St Vincent de Paul, nearly 4,000; of enclosed nuns the most numerous were not, as we should now expect, the Carmelites, but the Poor Clares, over 2,000. The largest numbers of monks were, as we should expect, in the houses of Franciscans and Jesuits; but the Escolapians (ministering in primary schools) were nearly as numerous, and so, surprisingly, were the Dominicans.

These large numbers should be seen in comparison with the census of 1797 which listed nearly 50,000 monks in Spain; more than four times the number of monks in the revival of 1892. It should also be seen in comparison with the numbers of 1930: 60,000 and more nuns, and 20,000 and more monks. The number of monks and nuns in the Spain of 1904 was still extraordinary—about 11,000 men and more than 40,000 women.[15] It meant that most schools in Spain were run by religious, and that nuns were indispensable to the care of the sick.

The State had not the money to create a welfare system. In 1909, the year of the destruction of religious houses in the Tragic Week, Barcelona's hospices were mostly owned and run by nuns. Sixteen hospices were not of their foundation or in their ownership, but they were staffed by nuns and monks. This ought to have made for popularity, but did not. In the civil war of 1936–9, 283 nuns and 2,365 monks were murdered. That compares with more than 4,000 parish priests murdered over the same period.

---

[15] Lannon, *Privilege, Persecution, Prophecy*, 61, from the government's report of that year. In 1965, in Franco's State, they had risen to about 34,000 men and about 85,000 women. Ibid. 62.

THE JESUITS

The Spanish Jesuits were abolished before Pope Clement XIV abolished all Jesuits. The fall of Napoleon meant the restoration of what was supposed to be 'the old order' in Europe and Pope Pius VII restored the Jesuits. The illiberal King Ferdinand VII thought that they were an instrument of order against revolution and fatally associated them from that moment with the extreme right in politics. He gave them back some of their old houses. But this restoration was not easy, for those recalled numbered only 122; the youngest was 65 and some of them were bedridden.

They were given their old charge of education and to do their work they enlisted large numbers of novices and professed fathers too quickly and with lower standards than before. Only six years later they were already 436 fathers. Then in 1820 a revolution overthrew Ferdinand VII and abolished the Spanish Jesuits (second dissolution); and three years after that a French army restored Ferdinand, and so they reappeared.

So came the civil or first Carlist war. Seventeen Jesuits were murdered in their house at Madrid in the riot of July 1834. In the following year they were again abolished (third dissolution), but not in the parts of Spain controlled by Don Carlos, for the house at Loyola was an armoury for Carlist soldiers. Some went to work in the Argentine, others started up Jesuit communities in Belgium and France, others disappeared into Spain; some of these last held secret and illegal meetings as a community.

The Concordat of 1851 did not expect a revival of Spanish Jesuits. But under the loose wording, of help to foreign missions or to bishops, they again opened communities. Though they could not found communities legally and did not occupy their old buildings, they did not hide their light, and were soon prominent—too prominent for safety. The radicals of 1854 threw out all their students into the Balearics or France, though they came back two years afterwards.

In the 1860s they got leave to found houses, almost always for the purpose of missions; they attracted young men to join them and grew fast. In 1867 they achieved the biggest victory yet by getting leave from government to found higher colleges which could give degrees. These colleges were really seminaries but by the time of the next revolution there were six. In 1864 the Spanish Jesuits numbered 964.

Because of the legal situation which allowed them a measure of freedom they were more directed towards training missionaries than ever before. Something like a third of them were destined for the missions, usually in Latin America or the Antilles, but also in the Philippines and in Fernando Po. The average age was low. At the beginning of 1868 the society was prospering exceedingly.

When the revolution of 1868 came one of its first acts was to abolish the Jesuits (fourth dissolution). But this was unlike the dissolutions of 1767, 1820, and 1835 (and 1932). All the others were done by law, by government decree. This was done by a rolling series of local attacks. Some Jesuits fled with the consent of their superiors. Others were ordered by the superiors to disappear.

Take the two houses at Puerto de Santa Maria, near Cadiz. There was a college of seventy, La Victoria, mostly young novices; and a secondary school with a high reputation, San Luis. The coup started when Admiral Topete (father of two of their boys) sent his rebel fleet into Cadiz harbour. Then order broke down, mobs were in the streets, others came from Cadiz, the windows were broken. The admiral offered marines to escort the fathers to a ship; the move was planned for 2 a.m., and all were to be dressed in lay clothes. At the embarkation they were just in time before the boat was seen and attacked. They were put on a merchant ship where they were treated harshly but eventually they arrived at Gibraltar, where at first the British refused to receive them—though by then they were starving—because they had no passports. After a time all was well.

From La Victoria they had to sneak out through the vegetable garden at the back as the mob attacked the front, and were hidden in a shed for the night by a workman. Admiral Topete's marines rescued thirteen fathers from the mob and put them on the same merchant ship. Many of the novices were taken in and hidden in middle-class houses. But these hide-outs were soon known in the town and to save more violence the junta ordered them all to leave town within 48 hours. Cloth intended to make cassocks ended as jackets and trousers for the lower classes of Puerto. Most of the articles in the houses were guarded from looting but were not recovered by the Jesuits till seven years later.

It was typical: hatred by the mob who were sure that they were friends of a tyrannical government, and were told they were like the Inquisition and tortured people in their cellars. There was no loss of life, though many were in danger, or loss of property; much kindness from charitable folk, even at risk to their own safety; and expulsion by the junta, partly motivated by the twin desires to protect them from violence and to avoid riots in the town.

The Jesuits from Seville also found a refuge in Gibraltar; the Seville junta sold their church at auction. Their good library was preserved for the future and twelve years later reappeared in the college at Málaga.

At Valencia the Jesuit church, a magnificent historic building, was destroyed by a junta order which was as vandalistic as it was emotional. At Santander, in former Carlist country, the house was destroyed when during the street fighting a rebel posse used it as a fort and one of their own bombs exploded inside.

At Durango, east of Bilbao and also in ex-Carlist country, the community was much liked; they had one father whom the town revered as a saint, and the society was so small that officialdom hardly took any notice of it, and it just went on as before. At Salamanca a famous college was shut but without any violence, and then carried on as before with non-Jesuits as the professors.

When all this dissolution was over there were some 336 Jesuits scattered in private houses over Spain. The French houses welcomed large numbers of students and novices, with Toulouse as their centre.

Loyola was the oldest of the colleges and dedicated to foreign missions, and was expected therefore to survive. It was in Basque country and the Basques were devoted to St Ignatius. So confidently was this believed that it became a refuge for Jesuits fleeing from other parts of Spain. Three hundred Jesuits collected there in too small a house and they began to move out into France. At Loyola was the great, over-ornate church built after the plans of Carlo Fontana, and the chapels made out of the rooms of the old castle where Ignatius was born and where he recovered from his wounds. As well as the sanctuary there was a large college for training novices. Like other houses, the college and the novitiate were suppressed in the dissolution of autumn 1868. Some 6,000 volumes of the library were taken to San Sebastian. The shrine itself did not belong to the Jesuits but to the province of Guipuzcoa. Therefore two Jesuits stayed as chaplains to the shrine but were not allowed to sleep at Loyola. After a few months these two quietly began to sleep in the house and no one noticed. Then other Jesuits joined them, not as such, but as chaplains to the shrine. In the winter of 1869–70 there were thirteen of them looking after the sanctuary.

But in the spring of 1870 Navarre rose in the second Carlist war. That August the Carlist army neared Loyola and republican troops shut the sanctuary and put the superior in prison. On 5 September 500 men ransacked church and college for secret arms, even hunting through the roof and cutting up the oranges. It is clear that the superior and every Jesuit in Loyola at that moment was a convinced supporter of King Carlos. They were all ejected from the Basque provinces.

In 1877 they came back again, but not as Jesuits, only as chaplains to the shrine, and only two at first. The Basques took no notice of this distinction. Loyola had become their logo, the Jesuits had become their heroes. On St Ignatius' Day vast numbers of Basques appeared at the shrine. Beaten in battle, they affirmed their solidarity in a religious act; with a colourful procession, the highest of masses, the largest of orchestras, dazzling illuminations above the altar and from the chandeliers, queues for confession and communion. This centre of pilgrimage attracted far more people than ever before. But for the rest of the year it was not happy: it was a vast shrine, empty; a grand library with no books on the shelves; magnificent ornate Fontana buildings, with nothing but the cold inside.

Government at last realized that the formal illegality could be represented as persecution and that it aided the Jesuits, Loyola, and the ex-Carlists. They yielded in 1880, giving leave at first for only twelve Jesuits. Then in May 1880 the French Ferry government ordered the expulsion of Jesuits from France. The Spanish government could gain credit for a wider tolerance. It removed all restrictions on the Jesuits at Loyola and the novices started to come back across the border.

THE HOLY FAMILY AT BARCELONA

The devout yet curious side of Spanish religion was given rare expression in the building of the church dedicated to the Holy Family at Barcelona, the Templo de la Sagrada Familia. The ground had been set aside for a race-course. A pious bookseller was moved by going on pilgrimage to the Holy House at Loreto in North Italy, and wished for a monument in Spain to the Holy Family, as a symbol of the ideal of family life. He bought the ground and collected money. The plan started in 1882; but a year later it was handed over to a very pious architect, son of a coppersmith, Gaudí. His scheme was a monument far too big for the money likely to be available or for the needs of Barcelona. There were to be thirteen very tall and elaborate spires, and complicated vaulting, and ornate carving in the arches, like no architectural style before or since, though he was interested in the old Moslem buildings of Spain and Morocco, and was affected by them, using a terracotta of varied colourings. The expense was colossal, the money short: sometimes Gaudí begged in the streets for funds. He was a Catalan patriot who always spoke Catalan even to the king, and went to mass every day, and looked like a very poor man, and when he was at last run over in the street by a trolley-bus in 1926 no one knew who he was—he was put into a paupers' hospital to die. His workshop and most of his papers were burnt by the mob at the outbreak of the civil war ten years later, and for eighteen years work was abandoned. There his monument stands to this day, still incomplete, still in progress, demanding money that no one can yet find, the wonder of Barcelona, which some think a monstrosity and others, though fewer, think a work of genius.

The Church of the Holy Family illustrates the exceptional quality of the Spanish religious mind of the nineteenth century. The age of looming divorce demanded an outward witness to family life at its best. The inspiration was an Italian legend which had won the affections of Catholic Christendom. The maker was of a humble home, who had learnt to be a lover of sacramental worship, and who saw a vision which in the past could only be brought into effect by a great king who controlled the taxes, like the Emperor Justinian with St Sophia or the popes of Rome with St Peter's. Here in Barcelona was the only Christian building of stature where the architect, easily mistaken for a tramp by his appearance, begged in the streets for money to enable him to go on with his plan; and if the structure was odd, that was in part because of the unique Spanish past with its injection of Muslim culture over centuries.

THE SPANISH PROTESTANTS

During the radical years English evangelical missionaries opened chapels in Spain. Far the most famous, because he wrote a book about it which is a treasure of literature, was the eccentric itinerant giant— both literary and in stature—George Borrow. He was paid by the British and Foreign Bible Society in London to go round Spain distributing Spanish Bibles. He made three long stays there until the Bible Society found him unsuitable and got rid of him. *The Bible in Spain* came out as three volumes in London in 1842. In this epic book readers are never sure whether they read fact or fiction, but the truth predominates and it throws a light on social Spain of that anticlerical age. He printed 5,000 Bibles in Madrid and distributed them to bookshops in various towns. He was unimportant so far as religion went because no one could think his quaint character that of an evangelist; but he looms in the reports of bishops, because it was so disturbing to them to have had a now famous person distributing non-approved Bibles.

In 1849 the English set up a Spanish journal, *The Real Catholicism* (*El Catolicismo Neto*), but the number of readers was tiny. One of the professors at Valladolid, Usoz y Río, republished the best of the Spanish Protestant writings of the sixteenth century, which perforce were nearly all written in exile from Spain. More notorious than Borrow was the Methodist Dr Rule of Aldershot, who in 1831 was made Wesleyan minister in Gibraltar and there made Spanish translations of biblical books and hymns, which were more used in Latin America than in Spain. Under the radical government of 1835 he held missions in Andalusia and opened a chapel in Cadiz and when he came into difficulties retired to Gibraltar. In London Parker published another journal, *El Alba* (*The Dawn*) which was widely read in Andalusia. Francisco Ruet was a Catalan who had been a silversmith and a singer in the theatre. He came over to the Protestant faith while in Turin and gathered a community in Barcelona. When the conservative moderates returned to power in 1856 he was exiled; but he left a disciple, Matamoros, who made converts in Andalusia, especially in Granada but also in Seville, Jaen, and Málaga. In October 1860 he was seized in Barcelona and sent to Granada to stand trial for opening a chapel in Granada; the trial and the sentence of eight years imprisonment had international repercussions. He became a hero, international relations were affected, and Queen Isabella stepped in to diminish the penalty.

Then the radicals came in again in 1868 and the evangelical missionaries returned and opened their chapels. There was formed a Reformed Church of Spain, with its headquarters in Andalusia, at Seville. The first time its synod met was in July 1869. Four years later they founded a seminary to train pastors. This freedom was never altogether lost. The chapels and the primary schools continued—

except in Madrid, four in Barcelona, three in Seville; and several of the big towns of Andalusia had a chapel. The numbers were very small, some 8,000 in all Spain; but such was the Catholic mood that these 8,000 seemed momentous.

The Catholic leaders were steadily against such toleration. In 1869 Cardinal García Cuesta published a *Catechism about Protestantism* which had a large sale, 300,000 copies and more. When the liberal government of 1869 proposed total toleration, a huge petition, with nearly 3,000,000 signatures, was presented to no avail against the article, which was carried 164 to 40; some bishops asked churches to hold services to make atonement for the proposed sacrilege.[16]

The constitution of 1876 reaffirmed Catholicism as the religion of the State and insisted that all education must be Catholic. It allowed toleration of other cults provided that there was no public sign of chapels. At last, in 1910, Protestant chapels were allowed to put up notices outside in the street.

[16] Cárcel Ortí, *Historia*, 246, 447; Callahan, *Church, Politics and Society*, 257.

I I

NATIONALITY AND RELIGION: PORTUGAL

The Church in Portugal, like the Portuguese people, had always been careful to turn their backs on Spain. They looked outwards, to their overseas colonies, especially Brazil, or to the English and their sea allies. Yet astonishing similarities of society and of history appear. The Spanish south was far less Catholic than the Spanish north. The Portuguese south was far less Catholic than the Portuguese north— 90 per cent doing Easter duties in the north, 10 per cent in the south. The south did not throw up such violent anticlericalism as the Spanish south but it was equally capable of despising the clergy or viewing them with indifference. The upper class looked back upon the Enlightenment of the eighteenth century. The name of Pombal, with all that he achieved to modernize the country in the face of Church resistance, was still potent. His writings were much republished during the nineteenth century. The university of Coimbra, in the age of the Counter-Reformation a place of learning that counted, ceased to matter among European universities after 1640, but it still conditioned the higher education of Portuguese clergy. Since the reforms of the Enlightenment it was consistently anticlerical in its feeling. The close association with the English made for an indirect doubt about Catholicism which was not felt to be Protestant but none the less had the result that the educated sat more closely to Catholicism than did the educated Spanish. In the north, and in parts of the centre of the country, was a pious and church-going common people. But, more than in Spain, the upper and upper-middle classes behaved at times as though religion was useful rather for peasants than for the educated. Freemasonry was strong in government, and was of anti-Catholic brand. The lot of the clergy could be hard. Despite the coming of so many people to their ministrations, they felt the pressure, in different ways, of upper-class ridicule, and in the south of peasant indifference. Hundreds of churches were profaned and some destroyed during the eighty years between 1832 and 1912. The special clerical courts for trying criminal clergy were finally abolished in 1833, long before Piedmont.

There were strange similarities in the political development of the two countries of the peninsula; a constitution and a monarchy contested, and so a civil war; a liberal party versus a conservative and/or absolutist party—though in Portugal the churchmen were more divided between the two parties than was normally the case in Spain. (Six priests in Lisbon celebrated a requiem mass for the soul of Cavour, in the presence of the municipal officers of the city.) The politics about securing a legitimate government were as difficult as those in Spain, with *pronunciamentos* by generals and a weak crown. The timing of political change was curiously parallel. Two brothers were at war, Pedro IV with liberal backing, Miguel, the younger, who believed that parliamentary government was a bad system. When Miguel got power many liberals were executed in a reign of terror. When in 1832–4 a liberal government came to power, it associated the Church with Miguel's ultra-dictatorial regime, because Miguel had depended in part on the support of some leading clergy. So when he was overthrown the Church had a bad time for ten or fifteen years. As the liberal forces advanced through Portugal, bishop after bishop fled from his see in fear of his life, until only the patriarch of Lisbon, Patricio da Silva, survived in his diocese; a strange survival, because he had authorized clergy, whether monks or secular priests, to take up weapons on Miguel's side. Miguelite clergy were forced to make humiliating professions of penitence and a number were hidden in the mountains for many months. Cardinal da Silva played the political game with such finesse (or weakness) and such reticence—though he wrote a pastoral letter to his clergy 86 pages long—that he was regarded as a nonentity whose presence and title happened to be useful to a revolutionary government.

This roughness started schisms in several dioceses; Pedro's government installed vicar-generals for the missing bishops, or forced canons to elect vicar-capitulars; and naturally there were clergy who refused to recognize these but thought them intruders and their installations invalid. Canons who were the electors played absentee games, hardly any of the intruders were elected by a majority of canons. Leiria was a Counter-Reformation see which the nineteenth century at last abolished but which was revived in the twentieth century, and then grew important because it contained the modern shrine of Fatima. In the trouble of 1833–4 government wanted it to have a bishop, but could not find a single canon to make the election respectable and forced the complaisant patriarch of Lisbon to nominate a bishop on his own authority. The new vicar-capitular at Lamego drove out of office, on political grounds, twenty-four canons, several parish priests, and even a verger at the cathedral. Life was complicated; at Porto (Oporto) the ancient bishop, aged 80, disappeared, and Pedro ordered the canons to elect another, but there was only one canon who had not disappeared. He was ordered to summon all the clergy in the town to elect the right man; they chose the general of the Austin Friars, who had suffered under Miguel. In this condition Pedro's man could not expect a willing obedience, either from the clergy or from the lay people. But the intruder did well by his diocese so far as he could. Several of the intruders spoiled their see and maltreated the clergy, but several others became conscientious diocesans. Clergy were soon disposed to give recognition to an intruder because only the person in authority had the power to bestow parishes or canonries upon them. The worst schism occurred when a 'legitimate' bishop in exile declared that all ordinations by an intruded ordainer were invalid and the new priests were not priests.

Evora was a see from the fourth century which vanished under the Moors and was restored in the reconquest, and then the Counter-Reformation turned it into an archbishopric. The archbishop, Fortunato, was a Cistercian, and a scholar who had professed history at Coimbra. He owed his see to Miguel, and therefore disappeared. He was one of the two bishops who fled to Rome, and so became the chief adviser to Gregory XVI on Portuguese affairs, and caused Pope Gregory to look with less than kindness on the new regime in Portugal. But the Pope made moderate decisions to limit the harshness of the schism in Portugal. Fortunato had a miserable time in his Rome exile, surrounded by untrue scandal about his way of life. He complicated the running of his diocese by refusing to resign and by living until 1844. The bishop of Guarda was the second who went to Italy, first to Rome and then to Loreto. He complicated his diocese still longer by refusing to resign and by living till 1857, twenty-four years after he fled.

Bishop Lobo of Viseu, who was a Benedictine with a conscience, escaped on an English ship and went via Falmouth to Paris where he lived modestly in the house of foreign missions. When the bishops were being restored in 1841–4 the government refused to let him back to the see but he came to Lisbon all the same and lived quietly

in a monastery. Partly through his stiffness Viseu was the worst diocese for schism. There was a shocking murder—the abbot of
Guardão was strong for Miguel and sternly resolute that no one must
obey intruder-bishops. When they sent to arrest him, he took a gun
and locked himself in his house. They broke the door with an axe but
he shot through the hole and wounded the axeman. After retiring to
think what to do they brought wood and set fire to the house. The
abbot leapt from a window, but they shot him, and he fell back into
the house and was burnt to death.

If a bishop had been driven out in 1833 and lived in exile, he might
disdain the idea that he should either come back or resign, and it might
be decided not to appoint another to fill the see. This happened notoriously with the see of Beja, a very ancient see that vanished under
Moorish occupation, was revived in the eighteenth century, but
remained a little diocese. Government thought with reason that
Portugal had too many bishops and chose not to fill five of the sees;
after forty years it won an assent from Rome that this was sensible.

In the new occupied dioceses the officers forced cathedrals to sing
Te Deums and history wonders how the music sounded.

The government demolished churches freely. Bigger towns had
too many churches if utility were to be the guide. Lisbon lost two
churches to make schools, another to make space for a theatre, two
as barracks, one a warehouse and another a factory, and one for a lawcourt and legal archive.[1] The patriarch was hardly consulted.

In 1839–41 there were long frustrating negotiations with Rome
over the state of the Church in Portugal and in 1841 the process of
making bishops valid in the eyes of everyone began. In the next year
Gregory XVI, famous in the world for sternness, even sent a Golden
Rose to honour Queen Maria II of Portugal, the ugly, fat daughter of
Pedro; and Maria was legally the sovereign responsible for much that
had happened, though she was only 15 when she became queen and
was as weak against her ministers as Isabella of Spain, or even weaker.
(She was married to Ferdinand of Saxe-Coburg who was king-
consort from 1837, but a nonentity.) The letter by which Gregory
sent Maria the Golden Rose was full of affection for his dearest lady
and showed how outside Italy this was a more flexible pope than
people thought from his reputation.[2]

[1] F. de Almeida, *História da Igreja en Portugal* (Porto-Lisbon, 1970), iii. 325.
[2] Gregory XVI to Queen Maria, *Acta*, iii. 204. The Golden Rose was a rose made of gold
and scented with musk and balsam; it was known as an object in 1049 but clearly of an

Government filled the see of Lisbon, soon after da Silva died, with a learned Benedictine who had suffered as a prisoner under Miguel, but at the same time had made good use of the library, and had then become Speaker of the upper house in the revolutionary government. Because of this record Rome at first refused to confirm him or make him a cardinal, but after three years gave way.

The new valid bishops did not have an easy time because they succeeded to years of vacancy and the relics of schism. Bishop da Nazare of Coimbra was a Miguelite. He had been imprisoned in Lisbon Castle. After five months they released him, but he went on living quietly in Lisbon and sending rulings to the diocese of Coimbra. The government would not have this and ordered him to resign the see. He refused, and under threat of assassination vanished into hiding and stayed in a refuge given him by friends for another fifteen years. It was no easy task inherited by the incoming bishop of Coimbra.

In 1848 a Concordat was achieved. From that year a constitutional monarchy reigned which was not at first friendly to the Church. There was tension because government, used to controlling ordinations while there were no effective bishops, went on doing so, though the bishops were valid and claimed the right as their God-given duty. The State even tightened its hold on ordinations through a law of 1862 by which ordinands must pass a State examination. During the 1860s, at the time of the Syllabus of Errors, the liberals were able to represent that the pope condemned parliamentary government. But gradually the government began to treat the Church with equity.

THE MONKS

In 1833–4 Pedro's government suppressed the male orders, expelled novices from nunneries, prevented the nuns from accepting further novices and closed smaller houses, moving the nuns elsewhere. The Jesuits, only sixteen in number, were escorted from Coimbra by a band of volunteers and put on a ship. No one protested: the Portuguese people did not mind any of this, for the monasteries of

earlier custom then; first known as a gift from a pope, by Urban II during the preaching of the First Crusade; then used as a mark of respect especially to sovereigns but to anyone eminent; after the end of the eighteenth century restricted to queens; for example the Empress Eugénie of France, and Queen Isabella of Spain in the year of her flight from the country. Pius X never gave it. The gift was revived by Pius XI, first with another queen of Spain.

Portugal were much of the old regime. In 1800 there were 577 monasteries and nunneries but many hardly counted; after the invasion by Napoleon's marshals many ceased to exist and those that survived counted still less. Several were in a parlous condition. Some works of art, and a lot of library books, were lost while the convents stood empty. The country was poorer than Spain and the properties of the Church even more useful to bankrupt governments. The monks were given pensions, but these were usually in arrears.

From 1848 the country was politically calmer and the Concordat that year ruled that Rome and Portugal should agree on numbers of religious and that government would not hinder recruitment. Most of this was a dead letter for they went on limiting monasteries and nunneries as they thought best. But the orders came back quietly: the Jesuits first, from 1858—and by 1910 there were 161 priests of whom 147 were Portuguese, with seventeen houses, including two colleges, one of which was said to be the best school in the country, and a seminary. The Franciscans came in 1861, and flourished. Benedictines restarted in 1875 but remained few. The Holy Spirit Fathers[3] did a lot in the Portuguese colonies, and their school of tropical agriculture at Cintra was respected throughout Europe. The nuns were indispensable to the education of girls. None of these orders were accepted in general society. They had the feeling of being on sufferance from the government even when they prospered. It was toleration rather than welcome. Yet they still filled needs not otherwise met, especially in schools, nursing, asylums, orphanages, and old people's homes. French Vincentian Sisters of Charity were driven out of the country after a savage campaign of slander. A community of British nuns left because they hoped for more liberty in England. When 'incidents' happened, such as stones thrown at nuns, or arson at night, it was awkward to ask the help of the authorities because the legal situation was insecure.

A curious incident of 1901 precipitated a renewed campaign against the orders. Rosa Calmon was the daughter of the Brazilian

---

[3] In the 12th cent. Guido founded at Montpellier a 'hospital of the Holy Spirit'. He also founded one in Rome which became famous. Being much needed, the order's hospitals quickly spread, especially in France and then in Italy. The expansion in Spain and Portugal came during the age of the Counter-Reformation, but was too fast: the generous gave them so much money for the poor and the sick that corruption crept in. The order disappeared in France at the Revolution, and the male side was abolished in Spain in 1835 and in Portugal the year before. That reduced the once great order to a handful of monks in Rome, and Pius IX abolished them in 1847. The nuns, hard hit by the abolition of their male counterparts, continued in a small way in Spain.

consul at Oporto. She wanted to be a nun, but her parents forbade her. Since she was 32, she decided to do what they forbade. She went with them to church on Sunday and escaped in a waiting carriage. The parents raised the alarm and brought her back by force. This resulted in priests being insulted in the streets, and the windows of colleges or clergy-houses being smashed with stones: the police watched. Government tried to satisfy the wave of hostility by shutting seventeen convents, and by decreeing that no religious house could work without a government licence, and that these would be given only to communities engaged in education, charity, or missions.

Portugal offered Pius IX sanctuary after his flight to Gaeta, and even sent a ship. They allowed the cardinal-patriarch to collect money to help the pope. When the news came that Pius IX was back in Rome, the Portuguese government ordered the bishops to organize masses of thanksgiving. The professors of the university of Coimbra, where throughout the century the textbooks were far from being ultramontane, and several of them came into the Index of Prohibited Books, joined in sending the pope a protest when the Italians deprived him of his dominions in 1860. The seizure of Rome in 1870 sent a wave of pro-papal feeling coursing through Portugal. But the faculty of theology at Coimbra, asked to send a message of congratulation to Leo XIII on his jubilee, refused. Fifteen years later they did it for Pius X.

The people could riot against heretics as vehemently as against monks. A Protestant missionary from Scotland, Robert Kelley, set up a church in Madeira, but after five years was hunted off the island by the mob.

CHURCH AND STATE

The country was officially a Catholic country. Catholicism was recognized to be the religion of the State. In 1864, against strong opposition from the Church, the State allowed a universal toleration, but the official recognition of a State religion remained until 1911. Bishops sat in the upper house of Parliament, and spoke there effectively, though with small practical result: ministers would assent that what they said was right and something should be done, but something was not done. Clergy could be elected deputies in the lower house. The Church suffered because the parish priests lost their income by the abolition of tithe. They lived on a combination of parish fees and a miserable government grant, at first paid through a local tax, which anticlerical localities refused to levy, later paid from central funds in a less invidious way but still wretched in amount. Their pay was substantially lower than that of the teachers in primary schools. During the 1860s the State took over all the parochial endowments; a 'desamortization' quite like the Spanish, and at much the same period.[4]

The Church was affected not only by the loss of its endowments, but by a division between the clergy. The bishops were State nominees; and though good men got through the appointments system, governments were corrupt in their use of patronage. Ministers who were Freemasons were capable of appointing a bishop for motives of party or of friendship. On occasion Rome was known to refuse to accept a nomination, but disliked doing this because the Portuguese government told the bishop to get on with his work and take no notice of Rome's refusal. In 1869 when Rome was being difficult, Portugal threatened not to appoint anyone to ten sees. The government liked a long interregnum even in a see which it intended to fill because then the stipend was available.

The bishops were trained at the university of Coimbra which, apart from Munich, was the only Catholic theological faculty in Europe still to be Gallican in its attitude to papal authority—a sign of how Portugal lived in an older world. For its Gallicanism was not militant like that of the ex-ultramontane who knew a lot of history, such as Döllinger, it was like the old Gallicanism of the eighteenth century which serenely assumed that it was right. Neither Rome nor bishops could do anything except keep the professors of the faculty out of bishoprics. Yet several of the bishops during the century had taught theology, canon law, or history at Coimbra.

The government retained in force the old *placet*, the rule that no papal decree would be published in Portugal without its licence. Portugal refused a *placet* to the encyclical of Leo XIII, *Humanum genus* (1884), which condemned Freemasonry. When the government appointed a bishop they allowed him vast ritual prestige, with reception by State procession and illuminations on houses, under a canopy of honour held by State officers—but little actual power. The

---

[4] Tithe abolished 1832. Mortmain laws 1861, 1866, 1869.

Church was run by the Minister of Justice, without whom nothing could be done. In a moment of independence the bishops made a supplication to the king (2 January 1862) to the effect that they were not so much bishops as ghosts of bishops. They compared their lot adversely with that of their colleagues in any other Catholic country, complaining that they needed a royal licence even to ordain a priest, and were allowed little say in the control of seminaries which trained their ordinands. In the following year government deprived the bishops of any right to be consulted over candidates for benefices. The bishop of Oporto, João de Franca, and the patriarch of Lisbon, Rodrigues, protested against this measure in Parliament. Their successors accepted it meekly. Patriarch Rodrigues was so mortified by his difficulties with the State that he asked leave from Rome to resign his see, but was made to soldier on.

The bishops were under an illusion in thinking themselves ghosts. When one of them was missing from his diocese it had grave consequences. For example, Joao de Aguiar was 'elected' bishop of Braganza, a small diocese founded in the Counter-Reformation. He suspended an abbot for misconduct. A local magnate met him and threatened him with a dagger. The next day he left for Evora and never came back; he lived comfortably there on the stipend of the see. Meanwhile the seminary was in disarray, the ecclesiastical court did not function, priests left their parishes, conferences of clergy were not held. For fifteen years this state of affairs went on. The government tried to settle the matter by nominating Aguiar to the see of Beja. Pope Pius IX refused to sanction the appointment after what had happened, so government refused to nominate anyone else for the see of Beja which in this way was also in trouble, with a vacancy of twenty years. Aguiar finally resigned Braganza in 1871, he had never returned to his see. At last Beja got a new bishop in 1883, de Sousa Monteiro, who opened a seminary, and was a good painter and musician, but also lived outside his diocese, in Coimbra, and visited the diocese for about two months a year. The seminary at Beja became a refuge for ordinands expelled from other seminaries. The bishop's absences did nothing to remedy the state of the diocese of Beja, and he did not die till 1906. Thus the see had a bishop in proper residence for only two years between 1862 and 1919. It was cared for, after a fashion, by vicar-generals or the metropolitan.

These events showed that the bishops' opinion that they were merely shadows because of government interference was far from true. If they were absent, their dioceses went downhill rapidly. Perhaps there were a few ghost-bishops. Archbishop Azevedo e Moura of Braga (archbishop for twenty years, 1856–76) is not recorded as ever doing anything, except once when he recommended that his people vote for government candidates at the election. The bishop of Coimbra, Correia de Bastos Pina (1872–1913) liked to please the secular power, and there was a Catholic campaign in the press against his nomination, on the grounds, among other things, that he was neither serious nor serene; and alleging that he was a Freemason and against monks and nuns. But de Bastos Pina turned out to be no ghost of a bishop, for with the help of Queen Amelia he did wonderful things for the seminary and for learning generally, protected asylums, hospitals, and hospices, erected a sanctuary to Our Lady of Lourdes, and created a museum of sacred art in his cathedral. When government kept a diocese vacant, which was very often, the results in the diocese and in the seminary were bad.

The keeping of parish registers became the law in most churches, Protestant or Catholic, during the sixteenth century. In Portugal the rule was ill-kept even in the earlier nineteenth century and only began to be fully observed after government decrees of 1859–62.

The chapters of cathedrals and collegiate churches, where the canons usually made a link between bishops and lower clergy, were also under pressure from the State, which suppressed numbers of them and restricted the canonries in the others.

In such conditions it was natural that clergy and bishops should look to Rome for help against the State. The constitutional kings of the later nineteenth century needed to recognize this in their formal relations with Rome.

Portuguese presence at the Vatican Council was modest. The patriarch had just died and a dispute had begun over who would be the right successor. Six bishops pleaded ill-health and were dispensed from coming. Four bishops travelled to Rome but two of them came from remote colonial sees and the two who came from Portugal itself were from minor dioceses. In February 1870 the people of Portugal were offended at the news that their bishops had joined in the petition of the Minority that a definition of the infallibility of the pope was inopportune; and the protests were such that the bishops had to tell Bishop Dupanloup that the Church of Portugal believed in the infallibility of the pope, and withdraw their signatures.

One ancient dispute between Rome and Portugal was settled during the century: the Padroado. The Portuguese Crown had the right to appoint all bishops in its overseas dominions. As the dominions shrank they still insisted on the right, even when the diocese covered areas ruled by the British or Dutch. The areas were too vast for proper supervision. From the time when Rome created the Congregation of Propaganda there was friction as it pushed its missionaries into Portuguese areas which it regarded as unsupervised. In 1843–8 at Goa, the Portuguese capital in the East, there came to be lasting schism between Catholics who followed the Portuguese archbishop and Portuguese who followed the Italian vicar-apostolic from Rome; a schism which lasted well into the twentieth century.

In 1886 Pope Leo XIII at last reached agreement with the Portuguese government. He allowed Goa and two other dioceses for the Padroado; and some other parishes in other dioceses were to remain under the jurisdiction of the Portuguese bishops. The archbishop of Goa was given the title of patriarch of the Indies, to show his ritual seniority over everyone else. But the pope, with the agreement of Portugal, went ahead with creating a Roman-based system of dioceses in the East.

THE PIETY OF THE PEOPLE

Many of the common people were still very pious. The rosary was much used. Queen Maria II was devoted to the cult of Our Lady Immaculate and all Portugal seemed to rejoice when the pope defined the doctrine. The cult of the Sacred Heart, already strong among a few in the eighteenth century, was thin during the revolutionary years but afterwards was fostered, especially in the later part of the century. In 1873 the bishop of Guarda dedicated his diocese to the Sacred Heart and one by one other bishops slowly followed his example. Public celebrations could go wrong, as in Spain at the same epoch. Church leaders decided to celebrate the centenary of St Antony of Padua, who despite the link to Padua was a Portuguese by origin and a kind of patron saint for the country. Though the feast was splendid it was wrecked by an anticlerical riot. The forms of service retained their local varieties longer than in France; till almost the end of the century many priests in the diocese of Braga still used the old Braga rite and not the Roman, and it was not until the time of Pius X that more conformity to Rome came. During the later

nineteenth century parishes revived those church dramas of the
Passion or other scenes, performed outside churches, which the
Catholic Enlightenment of the eighteenth century tried to restrict as
unedifying. This revival did not please all educated Portuguese.

In that later part of the century, with more friendly relations
between Church and State, diocesan reconstruction and improvement of seminaries was carried out. The bishops raised money for the
seminaries, and found them less poky buildings. They won more
control over them, and over appointments, with the complaisance of
the State. But no one could say that the seminaries were ideal.
Portugal was too small a country to make the system of the Council
of Trent, a bishop's seminary in each diocese, workable. During
those years the choice of bishops was on the whole good.

In the last decade of the century, plagued by republicans, government leaned on the aid of the Church. That carried its dangers, but
for two decades it was at last a prosperous time for the Portuguese
Church. In 1888 King Luis sent to Pope Leo XIII a richly jewelled
chalice to greet his jubilee.

The reliance on the Church brought the son of Luis, weak King
Carlos, into trouble. The King decided to make visits to friendly
States, especially Paris, Berlin, and Rome. It was natural to go to Rome
as a political act but also because his mother was the sister of King
Humbert of Italy. He had already started on his voyage towards Paris
when the nuncio in Lisbon said that if he came to Rome to see King
Humbert the pope would end diplomatic relations with Portugal,
withdraw the nuncio, and refuse to receive King Carlos in the Vatican.
Carlos asked King Humbert to receive him not in Rome but at his
home in Monza in North Italy. Humbert refused, on the ground that
this was an official visit. The Italian Prime Minister, Crispi, wrote to
Humbert's aide—'We in Italy do not need this insignificant King of
Portugal, who counts not at all in the European concert of powers.'

So in Paris Carlos decided not to go to Rome. It was too public a
change of mind, but it was more important to his stability to keep in
with the wishes of the Catholic Church than with Italy. The incompetence with which Carlos's ministers managed the affair was a big
blow to the king's reputation. Crispi thought it one more case where
the Vatican, in pursuing its own interests, made life troublesome for
an already troubled State and risked the welfare of the Church in that
State.[5]

5 F. Crispi, *Memoirs*, Eng. trans. by M. Prichard-Agnetti (1912–14), iii. 236.

THE PORTUGUESE REVOLUTION OF 1910

Carlos was an intelligent and artistic king who wanted to encourage culture and science, but also a moderate and pleasant person who could not cope with the troubles that hit the State. Economic and political crisis meant that the parliamentary system was no longer workable and could face neither the deadlocks in Parliament nor riots and unsettlement in the country. Carlos agreed to suspend the constitution and appointed Franco to rule by decree, and so drew the howling unpopularity of government upon himself. The next year he was murdered in the street with his crown prince as they travelled in an open carriage. He was succeeded by his second son Manuel, but soon the republican revolution overthrew the monarchy and with it the Church.

The republic was very anticlerical in its origins. Several convents were burnt down, several priests were murdered by mobs, there was vandalism in churches.

The bill of disestablishment decreed the separation of Church and State, more or less along the lines of the French separation five years earlier. It continued the stipends of clergy in office and ensured that the existing Roman Catholic churches could only be used for Catholic worship. The churches were handed over to local lay associations for cult, on which clergy were not allowed to sit and the members of which could be chosen by the local authority. In the anticlerical climate these associations were more dangerous than the French associations which the pope had condemned. The bishops wrote pastoral letters against them and were ejected from their dioceses for two years, in Guarda soldiers had to be used to keep the bishop away from a sympathetic people. Religion was removed from the schools. The religious orders were again suppressed. The regime banned the wearing of religious dress in the streets, and expelled the nuncio, closed the theological faculty at Coimbra and shut all the seminaries but five, abolished all religious holidays except Sunday, abolished army chaplains, legalized divorce, and made marriage civil. For two or three years the Church had a bad time. Pius X condemned the law of separation in the most agonized encyclical of his reign.[6]

---

[6] *Iamdudum in Lusitania*, 24 May 1911, *AAS* 3 (1911), 217–24.

The fate of the bishops varied in these bad years. Cardinal Neto of Lisbon was a good man whose career was sad. His father had fought in the Peninsular war, and he was unusual in that he had little academic background; he had been a monk and then a colonial bishop in Angola and the Congo. He was a man of humble and penitent piety, and of extreme diffidence except when he stood in a pulpit. He became a friend of King Luis and ministered at his death-bed and conducted his funeral. He married the crown prince Carlos to his French Bourbon princess Amelia and baptized their son. But by then (1886–7) the conflict between the monarchy and the republicans took to violence. Twice he refused a requiem mass for cabinet ministers because they were prominent Freemasons, and that caused scandal. When King Luis died Neto offended everyone by his panegyric at the funeral (where a phrase suggested that the king was not quite perfect yet) and newspapers published vulgarities about him. He began to work towards resignation—until he realized who might be chosen in his place. Then he tried to withdraw his plea of resignation, but the government was determined to get rid of him and forced the process of retirement to go ahead. Finally the retirement was accepted by Pius X. When his resignation was made public there was almost a riot because the people believed that he was forced out. Government announced that the patriarch's resignation was at his own wish, but no one believed them.

At the revolution Neto sought refuge in a house at Estoril, meaning to catch a train into Spain. On the way to the station he was caught by revolutionary guards; he had a bad time at police headquarters, but then was allowed to board a train. He never came back, but lived out his years as a simple friar in a house of refugee Portuguese Franciscans at Vilarinho, a few miles south of Vigo and so not far from the Spanish frontier. In his last years in Spain he was the object of deep veneration among the Spanish people as well as the Portuguese exiles, for his own sake and as a confessor of the faith.[7]

Sousa Barrosa[8] was a beloved bishop of Oporto, whose doors were open to everyone; he had been bishop of Mylapore-Madras in India, and so was another of those who came back from the empire. He became bishop of Oporto when the State was so friendly that a column of troops escorted him to his installation. He was a valued preached who followed the teaching of Pius X about modernism and

[7] Neto died in 1920. In 1928 his remains were brought back to Lisbon.
[8] Cf. Almeida, *História*, iii. 586 ff.

daily communion, and did very well for the Oporto seminary. The people's affection could not protect him when the revolution came. Government expelled him from the see, seized his seminary buildings, converted his palace into a political prison, and summoned him to Lisbon where he was attacked by a crowd while being taken by car to stand before the Minister of Justice. He was banned from entering his diocese and after a short house arrest he went into 'exile' in a village. But he returned to his diocese illegally to act as a godfather at a baptism, was prosecuted but acquitted in court. After three years exile, he was allowed to return to his diocese. In August 1917 he was accused of sanctioning a nunnery and again left Oporto to live in the annexe of a hotel at Coimbra. But that December the extremist government was overthrown and he finally returned, though soon to die.

After Neto they chose another Coimbra academic for the see of Lisbon, Mendes Belo, who had served Neto as his vicar-general. He was soon confronted by the murder of the king, the flight to Gibraltar and Britain of the new king, and the bill to disestablish the Church. Portugal had an agreement with Rome that the patriarch of Lisbon should always be a cardinal. Pius X dared not be seen to make Mendes Belo a cardinal lest it provoke republicans, but made him one secretly, *in petto*. The patriarch was exiled from the Lisbon district for two years—all the bishops but Coimbra, who was senile, were in exile at this time—but they were able to hold a Te Deum at his return and the Pope found it not imprudent to make public the bestowal of the cardinal's hat.

The worst of it was that the attack upon the Church was not unpopular with many of the urban working and middle class. Among the middle class there was a belief that Catholicism was the reason for the backwardness of Portugal compared with the rest of Europe. The attack upon the Church in Portugal of 1910–12 was only equalled in modern Europe by that in Russia after 1917 and that in Spain after 1936. In 1913 militants threw bombs into a religious procession for St Antony of Padua and killed several children. An enraged crowd attacked, significantly, the trade union headquarters.

An anticlerical society and a pious common people brought about the right conditions for visions. As mystical appearances happened at Lourdes in anticlerical France, at Marpingen in the Prussia of the *Kulturkampf*, and at Medjugorje in Communist Bosnia, the visions at Fatima in Portugal happened in 1917 and, not immediately but in the end, stirred a new stream of piety and pilgrimage.

THE RELIGIOUS

It might have been expected that the romantic age, with its affection for the Middle Ages and for old ruins, would have loved the idea of monks and nuns, not so much because they did good by prayer or service, as because the dress, architecture, and plainsong fitted a romantic portrait of what Europe was like when it had a heart. That romance conditioned outward forms which the revival of the nineteenth century fostered. But its chief importance was not in the making of vocations to the religious life. It scented the public atmosphere with an aroma of respect for the retired way of life which the Enlightenment pooh-poohed. In Bavaria King Ludwig I was a too-passionate romantic. After a time, and mostly for that reason, he allowed the Benedictines to reopen and restore historic houses of Bavaria, starting with the great abbey of Metten, founded from Reichenau on Lake Constance in 776, celebrated for its scriptorium, so prosperous in the baroque age that it offended puritans by the ornateness on its walls, secularized under Napoleon, revived by King Ludwig in 1830, and thereafter closed only under Nazi rule. From his private purse King Ludwig created or recreated a grandiose abbey, St Boniface at Munich. But royal founders were rare enough. Most monasteries were founded by monks, perhaps as colonies of other monasteries; a few were founded by secular priests, individuals or groups; nunneries were founded by monks, or nuns, or holy women who wished to be nuns. In a very few cases they had rich founders and no problem with money, but most of the houses created during the nineteenth century had to beg. If the house was just a little group of friends who joined for a special task, it could be reach-me-down in its chapel, appurtenances, and way of life. But if it was to see itself, and to be regarded by the world, as a proper abbey, it needed a great chapel, a good library, and many rooms. Maredsous in Belgium was founded by rich benefactors who owned the land. In 1873 they brought in nine men from another monastery, Beuron, and started to build. The superior warned the owner that this project was far more expensive than he expected—a church big enough to accommodate many altars and for liturgical grandeur, an abbey with a chapter-house, cloisters, library, workshops, and guesthouse—and an endowment demanded by the canons to sustain the monks.[1] Though or because they were well-endowed they won an undesirable local reputation for riches and had to go round begging to get money for the building of the abbey church.

There was a quest to repeople historic houses closed by revolution. Since the sites were now owned by government or private estates this was exceedingly difficult and mostly it failed, yet there were some astonishing successes.

With much reluctance from Guéranger, the Benedictines were persuaded to occupy buildings given to them for nothing on the property of John Cassian's old St Victor in Marseilles, one of the two oldest monastic sites in France. It did not work. In return for occupying a historic site the monks lived in cramped quarters and endured unbearable heat in summer and noisy traffic all the year. Expelled by the French government, they took refuge at Chiari in Italy, where Montini, who was to be the future Pope Paul VI, learnt to revere the Benedictine way of life. In 1922 they moved back to France but did not return to the site of St Victor for all its history. They went to the beautiful setting of Hautecombe by the Lac du Bourget in Savoy.

Hautecombe was the place where forty-three early members of the House of Savoy were buried, until the line became the kings of Sardinia, whereafter they were buried at the chapel of the Superga near Turin; when later they became the rulers of Italy, they were buried at the Pantheon in Rome. The Revolution dissolved Hautecombe. But after the Battle of Waterloo there were again kings of the family of Savoy, and Hautecombe was rebuilt. When Cavour traded Savoy to France in return for the making of a kingdom of North Italy, a treaty ensured that Hautecombe should survive and be under the protection of the House of Savoy. Hence it struggled along in the general dissolution, but not easily, and Solesmes was needed to re-establish Benedictine life.

Cluny, the most famous French house of the Middle Ages, was offered for sale for 200,000 francs in 1835. It remained a ruin; except for little shops in the cloister, until a school was established but did not last. Archbishop Guibert of Tours tried to resurrect the house of

[1] Hildebrand de Hemptinne to Victor Mousty, 5 Apr. 1872, in *RB* 83 (1973), 230.

his predecessor St Martin, Marmoutier, which in the Revolution was a vast military hospital for the civil war in the Vendée. He failed to find monks. At last the house, such as was left amid ruins, was taken by some Ladies of the Sacred Heart. Famous abbeys like Clairvaux never recovered monks.

Le Thoronet in Provence was a great-granddaughter of Cîteaux, with lovely romanesque buildings, and one of its early abbots even appeared in Dante's *Paradiso*. It had a bad time in the wars of religion and when the revolution suppressed it there were only seven monks. It was used as a warehouse and partly as a farm. But already under Louis Philippe, Prosper Merimée, who was chosen as Minister for Historic Buildings, said that at all costs the State must preserve this gem of medieval architecture. The State bought the abbey and later the estate and began the hesitant process of keeping it in order and making it a tourist attraction. Hence it never revived as a monastery, except that in the 1980s some monks who settled a few miles away were allowed to celebrate mass on Sundays in the historic church and made it reverent again. Properly speaking such an abbey survived only as a building without a life.

The flowering of monks and nuns in the nineteenth century, however, was less in the historic orders than in little groups. A few like-minded people gathered under a charismatic leader to meet a need, for prayer, or care of the young or the dying, a new plan in education or missionary evangelism, the care of the insane, the promotion of devotion to the Blessed Virgin or to the sacrament of the Eucharist, or (as with the Sisters of St Joseph of Cluny) work among the African missions. This was an age of vast expansion in popular education, until it merged into national systems of education; and an age when at last women's education spread more widely among working people. In France, Italy, Spain, and Portugal, more than in Germany and Austria, there was a crying need for teaching sisters: it was still the acceptable way in which a young, unmarried girl could engage in employment. Bishops and parish priests needed help from monks and nuns and looked to the old religious orders, but could not get enough because those orders suffered so severely in the storms of the nineteenth century.

Because these bodies were almost always small, they depended more upon local church authorities, the bishop, or the parish priest. The old rule of exemption for religious orders needed adapting to a different, smaller, and freer type of religious order. Most of these little orders did not spread far, or have many members. They met the need of their diocese or their neighbourhood, and then perhaps spread to one other diocese or one other neighbourhood, and occasionally, more by chance than design, into another country. They were often encouraged by their bishop, for bishops had struggled in vain with the historic, independent, international orders of religious, and were more likely to exert influence on these smaller groups of monks and nuns.

Each plan needed an authorization from Rome if it were to be canonical. This sudden flowering of religious groups or orders was another area in which the power of Rome was needed. In the old world the pope dealt with the heads of powerful religious orders; now his Curia dealt with a mass of smaller applications from weaker bodies which could not protect themselves from interference by hierarchs without the umbrella of Roman authority.

The number of monks and nuns grew all the century. This did not mean that all the historic orders grew. Some, like the Praemonstratensians, never recovered from the fate that struck them in the French Revolution and its aftermath. But new orders, little parish or diocesan orders, meant that the number of male and female religious increased until about the time of the Second World War, though with much variety according to the country and the level of its anticlericalism, and the dissolutions ordered by anti-monastic governments.

The expansion of the religious communities was the most remarkable feature of Catholicism during that age: the more remarkable because so many governments suppressed or limited religious orders. Take, by way of example, the Prussian numbers, not forgetting that the population of Germany was rising fast: in 1871 there were 9,048 monks and nuns, which was not many in a Catholic population when compared with France, Spain, or Italy; in 1886, during the *Kulturkampf*, there were 7,248 monks and nuns. When the *Kulturkampf* was ended, there was steady expansion—in 1896 there were 17,398, and in 1906, 29,796. Nuns were far more numerous than monks, some 4,000 males compared with 26,000 females. Most of these were engaged in hospitals or schools.[2] Many were of Polish origin rather than German, for as Catholicism in Britain was changed by Irish immigration, so Catholicism in north Germany was lifted by the coming of Poles as workers.

[2] Statistics in K. Bachem, *Vorgeschichte, Geschichte und Politik der deutschen Zentrumspartei* (Cologne, 1927–32), vii. 361.

As canon law became accessible it had a more detailed impact upon the life of the religious. Its tendency was towards uniformity; until the time came when some orders differed more in their name, their history, and their public costume than in the way in which they worked in the twentieth century. This trend remedied certain well-established abuses, but it caused the demand for far greater freedoms in the monastic way of life that was evident after the Second World War.

Industrial society presented monks and nuns with a new problem. In origin they were in retreat from secular society, so that they could be undisturbed in prayer and free from the corruptions of the world. As the centuries passed they took up other work in education, nursing, or scholarship which modified this principle; and the friars and then the Jesuits and Counter-Reformation orders were dedicated to the mission in the town. The Oratorians had to site their oratory in a big town. Industrial society provoked a new form of the flight to the countryside—not to the desert like the first monks, nor to the forests like the first Cistercians, but to fresh air, and quiet, and peace; so that again the monastery was a city of God set amid the corruptions of the world; and yet it was not the same as the old idea—it resembled the city-dweller retiring at weekends to his country cottage to escape the fumes. In the eighteenth century monks preferred the town house of their order and regarded residence in their country house as a penance. Now it could be the other way round. The Carthusian house in Rome was built by Michelangelo in the baths of Diocletian. By the 1880s, even before the coming of the car, it was one of the busiest places for traffic in Rome, and perforce they abandoned it. The quest for peace was given a push in the twentieth century: the Carthusians in the woods near Düsseldorf found themselves under the flight path of the airport and work or sleep became impossible.

This change did not lack critics. To find peace in a peaceful place, it was said, was of less value than finding peace in an unpeaceful place. But such a criticism did not move the leaders of the orders.

In the country they met another hazard. If they occupied a historic house, in a remote and lovely place, they began to be much disturbed by tourists. It was admitted that pilgrims had never been easy to distinguish from tourists and that crowds of pilgrims/tourists eased their treasury. A monastery was committed by its past ideals to accept every traveller as though he or she might be an angel of God. But if they welcomed train-loads, and later charabancs, their peace, quiet, and sense of prayerfulness could be destroyed. The most dramatic disturbance of this sort happened far away on Mount Sinai, but it affected both France and Italy. The Carthusians left their houses in Pavia, Florence, and Pisa not only because of the laws against monks but because they were driven away by too many visitors.

The old orders had a sense of history. Their historic houses had been taken from them by Henry VIII, or by 'enlightened' Catholic sovereigns, and then sweepingly by the revolution, and then by a revolutionary government of the nineteenth century. The orders were joyful if they could buy again some house of their past which had been confiscated and decades later came onto the market for private purchase; or, if they could not buy one of their own old houses, then the ruins that once were inhabited by another order.

Such purchases enabled famous shrines to be peopled again by monks: Montserrat, the Grande Chartreuse, Cîteaux, Silos, and others. A church or pious landowner acquired the site of a historic abbey at an auction and then looked around for an order to reoccupy the place or even founded a new community with that object. These were cases where the community did not precede the building but the building preceded the community.

This was largely true of the Benedictine revival at Solesmes in the diocese of Le Mans in north-west France. Prosper Guéranger was a lad there during the age of Napoleon and was told by his pious parents of the old life of the vanished monks and formed a portrait of the past touched by a romantic spirit. He loved the place, the scenery, and the memories conjured up by the imposing half-ruined and empty buildings. When the buildings came onto the market from a set of property investors, Guéranger, who then was a priest and a bishop's secretary, determined that it must be reacquired for the Church and that the only way to do this was to gather a community of monks to reoccupy it even if they had no money and lived on credit and in poverty. The only well-to-do member of Lamennais's group, the Count de Montalembert, provided enough help to prevent them soon closing their doors, and to enable them to establish themselves as a pride of the French Church.

Yet such restorations had problems. One was that if the object was to save an old monastery, it was more important to have monks quickly than to have good monks. Guéranger started with seven men but only one beside himself persevered. Another was size. An old

house was designed for large numbers of monks. Probably it was decorated to excess by baroque artists and architects. It was an important
piece of cultural history which needed to be maintained. Usually the
State insisted that it should be maintained as a historic monument.
Such houses were much too large for the modern population of a
monastery; were too draughty, needed too much repair, required
much time from the monks as restorers, guides, and cleaners, and
demanded sums of money which were not easy to find. Several of the
early Benedictines of Solesmes, the future Cardinal Pitra among
them, who had come to the quietness of the country to say their
prayers, found that for the sake of their house and its dependencies
they needed to travel all round Europe begging for money and were
far from St Benedict's picture of a monk stable in his cell.

To live in a cold, ill-furnished palace of echoing corridors was the
new form of asceticism for modern monks in old monasteries. And
there were occasions when this quest to preserve the old went
wrong: a former house would be acquired. There would not be
enough monks to make a real community. A handful, perhaps two,
or three, or four, would hang on in too big a palace because their
order hoped that novices would join them, and then novices did not
join them. The Augustinian Eremites reopened an old house of
Rodulfo in Central Italy: its last solitary occupant died in 1908 at the
age of 72.

But this was not always true. Sometimes the novices came.
Miraflores in northern Spain was an old Carthusian house founded
by one of the last kings of Castile before it was united with Aragon
to make Spain, and it housed the tomb of its royal founder under a
noble monument. It was shut in the Spanish dissolution, though a
couple were allowed to live there as caretakers. In 1880 contemplative orders such as the Carthusians were still (strictly speaking) illegal
in Spain. But revivals were little troubled, and the archbishop of
Burgos asked the Grande Chartreuse to repeople their historic house.
They did so, and the novices came—though of course they were
helped by the French dissolution which drove so many out of France
to Spain.

The most surprising part of the experience of monks and nuns was
their prosperity, most of the time, in a world which so disliked them.
Modern governments were not invariably unkind to monks. At one
time Kaiser William II, not the most pious of Protestants, was kind
to the Benedictines of Beuron because he needed Catholic help

against the socialists, and because his government thought that missionaries would help them with the education of the German colonies in Africa. He even gave the high altar to the new priory of Maria Laach. The German Franciscans had a bad time during the *Kulturkampf* but ten years later they found in the Rhineland, to their surprise, that they were encouraged by the Prussians as a help to government against socialism.[3] When sovereigns of either denomination wanted to say good words about monks in public, they talked about their services to scholarship and art. They did not mention prayer. Even Catholic politicians in Germany, like the leader of the Centre Party, Windthorst, were capable of pleading with the government that they should admit the Jesuits back into Germany as a safeguard against socialism. When the law against Jesuits was finally abolished, it was as a consequence of the revolution in Russia.

But this sort of behaviour was not common. At various times the governments of Spain, Portugal, France, Italy, Germany, Switzerland, Hungary, and Russia abolished them or expelled them. Yet there they were, still ready to return when allowed, still demanded by the people, still providing for very diverse vocations.

They had to be prepared to move, sometimes with suffering, sometimes without. Fortunately for them the laws against them did not apply all at the same time in all countries. Expelled from Spain they could go to France; expelled from France they could go to Spain; expelled from Germany in the *Kulturkampf* they could go to Holland or Belgium. They were vastly helped by the Protestant countries, which (except for the bigger Swiss cantons) now believed in toleration—the Netherlands, Great Britain, Denmark, and Sweden, and by Catholic Belgium and Ireland. The mobility was not all loss. The plight of the religious orders in their old lands built up the Catholic Church in the Protestant lands. Without that plight the strong Catholic presence in the United States and Australia would have come about far less quickly. The Spanish Benedictines who were driven out of the shrine of Compostella founded a house in Australia. And when countries like France and Germany made difficulties for monks and nuns they were less hard on the missionary orders, which, they believed, helped their colonial governments in their civilizing mission. In the forced relocation there was an element of the providential.

[3] G. Fleckenstein, *Die Franziskaner im Rheinland 1875–1918*, Franziskanische Forschungen, 38 (Werl, 1992).

But no one must imagine that this was all without agony: no one wishes to be turned forcibly out of a familiar home. And the quest for a new home could be misjudged. The French Trappists made three misjudgements. They fled from the revolution into Switzerland, to Valsainte. Then the French army occupied Switzerland, and they fled into Bavaria. But Bavaria was soon against monks and they went further east into Russia. Not long afterwards Russian policy changed and they were hunted out—and their suffering was intense until they reached the Protestant city of Danzig (Gdansk) which gave them shelter in an old convent of the Brigittines. This was the community which after the fall of Napoleon was able to buy back La Trappe and start the expansion of the nineteenth century.

The fate of a famous Capuchin was not typical but shows how the mobility of monks was not simple. It was a sign how the martyrdoms of the religious orders produced confessors who, because they were confessors received a confidence that could be misplaced.

Vives y Tutó was a very nervous boy from a simple Spanish home. When he was 14 the Capuchins, who were expelled from Spain, came round offering education in Guatemala. With a group of boys he sailed for Guatemala and was educated there, not without nervous turmoil. Three years later the Capuchins were violently expelled from Guatemala. After roundabout journeyings Vives ended at a refugee Capuchin college at Toulouse, for this was before the French expelled monks and when Spaniards took shelter across the Pyrenees; there he had a nervous breakdown. At that moment there was a very pious Catholic dictator in Ecuador, García Moreno, and Vives was sent to the Capuchin house in Ecuador. Soon after he arrived the dictator was murdered, the Capuchins were in physical danger, and the revolution threw them out of the country. Vives, suffering badly in body and in nerves, took refuge in a Capuchin house at Perpignan in south-west France. Here, after a dispensation because of his illness, he was ordained priest; the ordination brought an almost magical cure of his nervous problem. Three years later France dissolved the religious orders, the police turned Vives out of his college, and he crossed into Spain where monks were now again legal.

In 1884 the Capuchin order held in Rome its first general chapter for many decades. It was the low point of the order, they had lost 218 of their friaries in only thirty-four years and something had to be done—they elected as their general the Swiss Bernard Christen of Andermatt, who was to be the remaker of the Capuchins in the modern world. To this general chapter Vives was sent. He impressed Pope Leo XIII who kept him in the Curia and had him near him on his death-bed. He remained in Rome for the rest of his life, entrusted with manifold important business, including the commission about Anglican Orders. In Rome he ran a very successful Latin American Conference and became a cardinal. Perhaps because they both came from humble backgrounds, he felt that he and Pius X were 'twin souls'. In his last years the nervous problem returned and he died at the age of only 59.[4]

Violently ejected from Guatemala, kept out of his homeland for years, forcibly expelled from Ecuador, then turned out of France—such a career of melodrama was likely to make him respected, especially as he had an organized mind and wrote large textbooks. Nothing in his career gave him any chance of understanding French, English, or Italian modernism, yet he was one of the drafters of *Pascendi*; nor had he any chance of understanding German Catholicism.

THE BENEDICTINES

The reason for the existence of the Benedictines was to worship God through the formal liturgy and psalmody, whatever other works of scholarship, education, or agriculture they might undertake.

French Benedictines realized that they had a vocation to teach the Church and the world something about worship. Prosper Guéranger was a warm disciple of Lamennais, almost to the point of adulation, and contributed articles to *L'Avenir*, but withdrew from the master when Rome condemned him. He thought that what was wrong with France was the antipapal Jansenist Gallican spirit. He was an ultramontane, not in the least political, but devotional. Solesmes, in the diocese of Le Mans, dated as a monastery from 1010 and was shut at the French Revolution. In 1832 Guéranger bought the property and next year opened a small Benedictine house, the first such revival in France of the nineteenth century. For a time it suffered from debt. Before the revolution Solesmes had about sixty monks, but Guéranger began with very few. He had no previous Benedictine experience except from books, and his customs were odd. The

---

[4] For Vives y Tutó, see the fine article in *DHEE* s.v. He died at Monte Porzio in 1913, seeking a cure; Capuchin statistics in *DIP* s.v. Cappuccini, 235.

monks wore brown. There were four hours of worship in the day, seven or eight hours on feast-days, and it was soon splendid both musically and liturgically; at other times the house was filled with silence. The rise in vocations meant that within three decades he was building more accommodation—building, without enough money, very uncomfortable cells. The abbey flourished only with the coming of Louis Napoleon and the encouragement to the Church which that meant for France.

Guéranger was aware that each French diocese had its own liturgy, usually marked by what he took to be Gallican or Jansenist formulas. There were still more than twenty forms of service in France, a few historic in the old Gallican tradition, more of them due to the Jansenist reforms of the last century. Guéranger wrote the history of the liturgy, learnedly but not critically. The work of an abbot did not prevent him from issuing volume after volume on the history and practice of worship.[5] It was a protest against 'undisciplined' variety in the manner of services, and he argued that it was moral and loyal as well as sensible that everyone should follow the Roman texts of services. Many dioceses valued their old customs and resented the idea that they were not loyal. But the drive towards uniformity was relentless. Pope Gregory XVI was openly on its side. He admitted that to go back on such diversity could not be the work of a moment, but declared that bishops who tried to bring their services to the Roman pattern were to be strongly encouraged.[6]

Thus Guéranger and his abbey became the focus of the Romanizing movement in liturgy in France, by which the dioceses surrendered their varieties. The house became a centre of the revival of the Gregorian chant in church music, and acquired a European fame.

In France, Benedictines now existed again, though they were illegal unless they won a licence from the State for a particular work. They went ahead, taking no notice of the State. The Benedictines of the 1840s and 1850s were proud to wear their habits in the streets of Paris without asking leave from the State. They did not always have a high opinion of Rome's understanding of their problems.

[5] Important are *Les Institutions liturgiques* (3 vols.; Paris, 1840–51), and *L'Année liturgique* (9 vols.; Le Mans, 1841–66).

[6] Gregory XVI to Archbishop Gousset of Rheims, 6 Aug. 1842; in A. M. Bernasconi (ed.), *Acta Gregorii Papae XVI*, iii. 224–5; Gousset had asked about the variety of liturgies. Under Pius IX he became a cardinal and did all he could for the Roman liturgy and the fight against Jansenism and Gallicanism.

Guéranger owed his ability to found Solesmes to the personal decision of Gregory XVI, who resisted prudent pressures from the Curia that this would be illegal under French law. Yet Guéranger accused Gregory XVI of excessive timidity in the face of modern governments—this because he was determined that the house should be exempt from the bishop, and under the pressure of the French State the pope agreed that it should come under the bishop's authority. When Pius IX succeeded as pope, Guéranger was grateful to him for conceding the exemption that he demanded. Yet his experience made him sure that neither pope nor Curia understood the monastic ideal and its needs. Certainly it was odd that at Guéranger's death Pius IX should issue a brief (19 March 1875)[7] which praised his learning and fervour, and thanked him for the part he played over the doctrines of the Immaculate Conception and papal infallibility, and mentioned what he did to persuade French dioceses to accept the Roman liturgy—but only hinted at his true claim to stature, the revival of the Benedictine way of life, both in France and beyond.[8]

The monks of Solesmes were exiled in 1880 and 1882 but were not finally expelled from France until 1901. They settled first at Appuldurcombe House near Wroxall in the Isle of Wight. Then they acquired the estate of Quarr, the site of a medieval Cistercian abbey near Ryde on the island. They recolonized Solesmes after the First World War, but Quarr remained as a Benedictine house.

The abbey at Farnborough near Aldershot, which owed an impetus to the exiled Empress Eugénie, was already planned by 1896 when the Solesmes Benedictine scholar Fernand Cabrol was elected prior. In 1903 he became the first abbot, received more refugee French monks, and with Henri Leclercq turned the abbey into a centre of historical scholarship. The group that collected at Farnborough could rival the old eighteenth-century school of Saint-Maur: Wilmart, Férotin, Quentin, Gougaud, and others. They made a superb monastic library which lay about the corridors in heaps—a disorder that was only apparent.

At Rome the historic Benedictine house was St Paul's outside the Walls, where St Paul was said to be buried. They were brought to nothing in Napoleonic Italy although one of their monks was elected as Pope Pius VII. After 1814 their Benedictine pope instantly set to

[7] *ASS* 8 (1875), 375–7.
[8] Cf. L. Soltner, *Solesmes et Dom Guéranger (1805–1875)* (Saint-Pierre de Solesmes, 1974), 69, 72, 176.

work to restore them, which was needed as the abbey was falling down. An expensive work of reconstruction was ended when carelessness by restorers caused the fire of July 1823 which destroyed almost the whole church. They did not tell the dying pope of the fate of his money and care. They started again. Gregory XVI dedicated the high altar. They were still not complete when the Roman republic of 1849 drove from St Paul's all the monks but two retained as caretakers, and Mazzini with his triumvirs took their city house of St Callisto in Trastevere as a gaol. During the siege of the city wild men tried to blow up St Paul's but the French army arrived in time. The monks expressed pleasure with Garibaldi because he retreated, and refused to fight through the city, and therefore saved its monuments and churches from the devastations of a street battle. Pius IX, who loved the abbey and came often, was at last able to rededicate its church in December 1854.

After the fight at Porta Pia one of their monks was stabbed in the street in daylight. Since the Pope could no longer visit the abbey, the monks regularly took gifts to him. The 1873 application of the Piedmontese law dissolved the monastery legally, but the State took it over as a historic building, made sure that it was in repair, and allowed the abbot and one monk at least to be its caretakers—and slowly the community gathered again. Cardinal Pitra of Solesmes lived all his later life in the town house of St Paul's. The monks engaged not only in the care of a great house and of the tourists and pilgrims who came, but had a parish out towards Ostia and others up the Tiber valley, and therefore several monks were parish priests. The life of the monks was varied in that seminarists lived there, as did a few secular priests to help with the parishes and the services. That made for an odd situation, and after the 1850s the monks preferred their novices not to be at St Paul's but to try their vocation at the monastery of San Pietro in Perugia.

The numbers at St Paul's in 1786 were: 27 priests, 8 novices, 8 *conversi*, and 20 secular clergy. In 1853 (under Abbot Pappalettere): 15 priests (including 2 Benedictines from Solesmes), 5 postulants, 5 *conversi*, and more than 40 other people including secular clergy and 10 lay servants not *conversi*. In 1858 there were 20 priests, and a total community of 71 (including 1 Irish, 1 French, 1 English, 5 Prussians, and 1 Pole).

There was a big difference between a community such as St Paul's, where the continuity from old times was only broken briefly twice, and a community such as Solesmes, where its founder had not an hour's Benedictine experience. Guéranger first came to St Paul's four years after he founded Solesmes, to find out what a Benedictine community was like. A house with historic continuity was likely to be more leisured, to the outer eye less zealous, than the newcomer. The monks of St Paul's did not even have a common purse for their moneys till Abbot Pappalettere instituted one in 1855. The old house was more likely to be open-minded in politics than the new. Guéranger was an ultramontane, but at St Paul's they were not all conservatives. Abbot Pappalettere was turned out of Monte Cassino, where he went after his time at St Paul's, for being friendly to King Victor Emmanuel. Pappalettere's successor at St Paul's, Pescetelli, was for a time the professor of canon law at Modena but during the revolution of 1848 he had to flee from the Duke of Modena's wrath.[9]

Bishop Pie of Poitiers had the chance of buying St Martin's historic house at Ligugé. He applied to Guéranger at Solesmes, who said that he could spare neither money nor men. Bishop Pie went ahead nevertheless, and the first four monks were brought to Ligugé by Guéranger in 1853. They prospered moderately until the expulsion of French monks at the end of the century. They returned to Ligugé in 1923 and made themselves a centre of art, music, and ecumenical study.[10]

To their surprise, the monks of Solesmes discovered German disciples at Beuron. This was an early house in the Upper Danube valley founded as Augustinian. It was famous for a *pietà* of the fifteenth century which drew many pilgrims. In the prosperous decades it acquired fine baroque and rococo buildings. The house was secularized under Napoleon and the lands passed to the Hohenzollern prince. A Hohenzollern widow met the brothers Wolter, both Benedictines, at St Paul's outside the Walls, and went with them on pilgrimage to Palestine. In 1863 she bought the estate of Beuron and gave it to the brothers, who, like Guéranger, cared about liturgy— Maurus Wolter went immediately to study at Solesmes. The revived house prospered and made other foundations and so became the mother of the Beuron congregation. Its own famous foundation was Maredsous in the province of Namur in Belgium (1872) to which

---

[9] See Giuseppe Turbessi's use of the abbey's internal chronicle in 'Vita monastica dell'abbazia di San Paolo nel secolo XIX', in *RB* 83 (1973), 49 ff.

[10] Ligugé, during its years of exile, started the *Revue Mabillon*, an important contributor to monastic studies.

one of the Wolter brothers, Placidus, went as first abbot. The third abbot of Maredsous was an Irishman, Columba Marmion, whose spiritual writings dominated much monastic thinking in the second quarter of the twentieth century.

The German *Kulturkampf* turned them out of Beuron (1875–87), first to the Tyrol and then to Bohemia. They happened to attract Anselm Schott, who during the *Kulturkampf* had fled to Maredsous and whose *Messbuch der heiligen Kirche* had an enormous circulation and helped to create the modern liturgical movement in German-speaking lands. In the twentieth century Beuron became a centre for study of the Gregorian chant, of the oldest Latin translation of the Bible, of palimpsests, and of ecclesiastical art.

A daughter-house of Beuron was Maria Laach near Coblenz; it was of early medieval origin and had at first followed the uses of Cluny. Protected during the Reformation by the Rhineland arch-bishoprics, it continued to flourish. When the French armies of the Revolution occupied the Rhineland it was suppressed and the prop-erties sold. In 1863 the Jesuits bought it, built a library, and turned it into a centre for scholarship which published a learned periodical, *Stimmen aus Maria Laach* and a collection of Councils which became indispensable to the church historians, especially for the history of the first Vatican Council: *Collectio Lacensis*. But three years after the end of the Vatican Council the *Kulturkampf* expelled the Jesuits from Germany and the house was not freed till 1892 when the Beuron congregation was able to take it over as Benedictine. Thus it was not till the twentieth century that Maria Laach became the centre of the Benedictine influence on the liturgical movement. The most cele-brated of their students of worship, Odo Casel, entered Maria Laach at the age of 19 and in his maturity gave an exceptional impulse to the study of the history of church services and the manner in which that study could affect modern ways of prayer.

The revival based upon Solesmes aimed partly at loyalty to Rome and partly at a more worthy monastic rite; that is, there was little sign at first from these endeavours that the Benedictines were about to start a transformation of the people's way of worship.

The ideal was that each abbey should be independent. The indi-viduality went back thirteen centuries to the Rule of St Benedict and stamped Benedictine spirituality and customs. Built into the philoso-phy of the religious life was the special nature of each religious fam-ily and the possibility of differences, which was freedom of choice, in vocation and way of contemplation. Some of them ran schools, some revived the old tradition of scholarship. As the Curia took more control it administered the canon law touching monks and nuns in a more uniform way. They thought that it would be better if they were federated. They were still few by 1900, far fewer than in the eighteenth century, only about 2,000 monks altogether in some 120 monasteries, which meant some very small communities. There arose the odd-sounding new rank of archabbot, to signify the head of a group of abbeys.

With weaker branches of orders—formerly strong but weakened by the modern dissolutions—amalgamation was needed to ensure continuity. The congregation of Montevergine, with its venerated picture of the Madonna, had at its height nineteen abbeys and sixteen priories, mostly in southern Italy and Sicily. In the Napoleonic revolution all vanished. Revived after the Battle of Waterloo, it was suppressed by the Italians in the 1860s. Its few surviving members had to amalgamate with an existing Benedictine congregation, so they united to that of the historic house at Subiaco.[11] The history of this amalgamation shows the turmoil into which an order was put by the actions of the State.

However historic their mother-house, the congregation of Subiaco was then only seven years old. Pietro Casaretto became a Benedictine in his teens, and at the age of 26 was the prior of a little community of ten monks near Genoa. He was young and earnest and had the idea of reviving the authentic Benedictine way of life—the exact observance of the Rule of St Benedict: rising in the middle of the night for the mattins office, stiff asceticism, and absolute community of property. Pius IX admired him. The revolution in Piedmont drove him and his monks out of their house and gave him Subiaco not far from Rome, where five monks hung sadly on. There his northerners joined him and in 1851, after being allowed a separate Subiaco province distinct from the rest not by its area but by its way of life, the pope pushed the general chapter of Monte Cassino to elect him president of the Cassinese congregation (i.e. the group headed by Monte Cassino, always regarded as the chief of all Benedictine houses).

Casaretto had the idea of reforming all the Benedictine world on his austere lines, but that ran counter to the ideals of other men

[11] They managed to open a new abbey church at Montevergine in 1961.

reviving Benedictine life in Germany or France (Guéranger had no use for him) and even more to the ideals of the other Cassinese. They thought in terms of liturgical revival, and how monasteries could teach the Church as a whole to worship better; or they thought in terms of education and scholarship, and how the monasteries could help the mind of the Church in the modern world. Without rejecting the need for austerity, they had other plans for the future development of their communities. Casaretto could see only the need for personal self-sacrifice.

Other Benedictine houses then joined the rule and the group. Nominally they were still within the federation based upon Monte Cassino. He won over historic houses: Praglia near Trieste, Montserrat near Barcelona. In France he fostered an austere abbey, La Pierre-qui-vire. Therefore he needed to effect the separation of his own group of houses from the Cassinese congregation. In 1867 Pius IX approved the group as 'the Cassinese monks of the primitive observance' and five years later Casaretto rose to the summit as abbot-general. The Benedictines were in a state of rumbling disturbance; and when the new Piedmontese laws of dissolution were applied to his houses the plight of the Congregation was beyond him. In 1875 he was forced to resign. Pius IX did not accept the resignation, but for everyone's sake he needed to be out; he slipped away into a little home near Nice, where he died.

In such a way a federation could affect even the spirituality of a single house; by bringing it up against customs, or ideals, or even antipathies, which the old independent abbey would not have met in the same intimate way.[12]

Pope Leo XIII was eager about the federation of Benedictine houses. During the later seventeenth century Sant'Anselmo was opened at Rome as a teaching college for Benedictines of the congregation of Monte Cassino. Young monks were sent there for three years to study theology and canon law. The place was closed by Napoleon and afterwards there were too few Benedictines to revive it. Pius IX tried to reopen it but was immediately stopped by the Italian laws. In 1888 Pope Leo XIII caused it to be opened in Rome, no longer as a house only for Cassinese, but as a central or even head house for the entire Benedictine order. A monk from the new abbey of Maredsous, Hildebrand de Hemptinne, who started adult life as a

[12] For Casaretto, see *DIP*, ii. col. 630 ff.; *DBI* s.v. with literature; full bibliography in *RB* 83 (1973), 26.

papal zouave, was brought in to organize it on the Aventine Hill and there all the abbots were told to meet to make a Benedictine order. Leo XIII pushed the abbots into electing a chief abbot, or abbot-primate, who should live in Sant'Anselmo, hold office for twelve years, and preside over the confederation.[13] All this was contrary to the old characteristics of Benedictinism which gloried in the independence of the abbey. Even so it was a compromise between the pope's desire for good order and the abbeys' desire to keep their freedoms.[14] For example, in a federation it was sensible to bring the novices together in a special house for their training. Guéranger was passionate against such a plan; each house should be a family with its own novices.

There was dispute over the tenure of abbots. St Benedict and his successors expected a tenure for life after election. The nineteenth century was used to the pensioning of the old in all walks of life. Several modern statutes for the monasteries expected an abbot to be elected for a limited tenure. Leo XIII evidently thought that a wise piece of modernity. Guéranger regarded it with extreme hostility: life tenure was for him a constituent of the Benedictine way. He believed, and was not alone in believing, that limited tenures made the abbots more like governors and their monks more like subjects, the life tenure kept the ideal of the father of a family with his sons.

The French house at La Pierre-qui-vire was founded on old Cistercian land near a granite rock that moved, hence the name. Father Muard its founder had been a village boy who wanted to be a missionary, and grew to become the head of a group of mission priests at the diocese of Sens. He was troubled in soul and mind by the anticlericalism of France and decided that there was a need for a penitential community living in solitude. He passed the winter of 1848–9—while the revolution raged in Rome—in a hermitage hard by Subiaco, and a few months later began to build at La Pierre-qui-vire. He was a man of strange, mystical experiences. He soon died, and his draft statutes for his 'order' were rejected by Rome as too rigorous. The house followed the austere ideals of contemporary Subiaco under Abbot Casaretto and had no interest in liturgical ideals

[13] *Summum semper*, 12 July 1893, *ASS* 26 (1893), 371, *DIP* viii. 760 ff. The house was closed during the First World War and became an army hospital but was soon reopened at the peace.

[14] Among its professors were found able students of the history of monks: Jean Leclercq, Jean Gribomont, etc. The periodical *Studia Anselmiana* dates from 1933.

or learning. From 1880 to about 1920 Benedictine life was hardly possible in France; a group came to Buckfast in Devonshire where was the site of a historic abbey; but then La Pierre-qui-vire was revived, with wider perspectives but still with the ideals of austere simplicity and faithfulness to the Rule of St Benedict.[15]

The most historic of them all was St Benedict's house at Monte Cassino. The monks had been driven out by the Saracens, and by the kings of Naples, and by an earthquake of 1349. During the eighteenth century it was steadily peopled by about seventy monks, which was not quite enough for the buildings. The Napoleonic Revolution abolished the monastery but let the monks stay in the house as priests; and at the restoration they instantly became monks again. In 1867 the Italian government suppressed the house, but again let the monks remain, this time as 'custodians of the national monument'. They were not only custodians and guides, because Abbot Tosti was an eminent historian, and another monk, Postiglione, an eminent surgeon in the medical faculty of the university of Naples. The monument was caught in the middle of the Italian war of 1943–5, and was destroyed by Allied bombs on 15 February 1944. It was reconstructed as it was before, though the old buildings were hardly well-adapted to modern needs (there were twenty-eight monks in 1979). The small number of monks had to maintain the worship, keep up the buildings, guide visitors, administer the diocese, see that their parishes were looked after, run a diocesan seminary for clergy and a school, and continue the tradition of scholarly publication. No one need think that modern monks were persons with uninterrupted leisure.

Before the Revolution the house at Cava near Salerno was one of the richest houses in Europe. Its works of art were splendid and its headship therefore went into *commendam* to provide incomes for cardinals. In the Counter-Reformation the abbey was revived as a monastic house though mostly for the younger sons of the nobility. This glorious architectural and artistic past preserved the monastery through the modern troubles. The Napoleonic Revolution left twenty-five monks in lay dress to be custodians of the treasure. Afterwards it was restored but then the Italian dissolution left only a few monks for the same purpose. Their life, lived amid magnificence,

---

[15] Cf. *DIP* v. col. 455, and vi. col. 186–7. In 1933 the congregation was joined by the English community of Prinknash, formerly a community of Anglican monks from the island of Caldey off the coast of Wales. Not until 1959 did the federation take the name of the Benedictine Congregation of Subiaco.

was for a time wretched. But thereby Cava was saved, a community rare in remembering a continuous history.

Einsiedeln in Switzerland, another historic Benedictine house, was fortunate. Like all houses which lasted over centuries it had its vicissitudes—in the third quarter of the fifteenth century it was reduced to three monks. During the early eighteenth century the abbot created the wonderful buildings which have survived. In the Revolution French troops sacked and suppressed the abbey. Most of the monks took refuge in the Tyrol and the miraculous statue of the Virgin was taken for safe keeping to Trieste. But soon they, and the statue, were allowed back and they revived the school and made it more famous. The monks of Einsiedeln were under threat twice during the 1830s and had difficulty in surviving during the 1840s, when monastery after monastery suffered forcible closure, and then came the time of the Sonderbund war (see p. 44). But the revival of pilgrimage by modern transport helped their income and their reputation. The pilgrims came mostly from Austria, southern Germany, and Alsace. It was the most continuously untroubled of the historic Benedictine houses. This was due not so much to the wisdom of its abbots as to its siting in that country of Europe which suffered the least political trouble of the modern age.[16]

Praglia was a Benedictine abbey not far from Padua. It had a history of many centuries before Napoleon suppressed it. Twenty years after his fall the monks were brought back by the Austrian emperor. Thirty-two years after that their land was changed from an Austrian possession to an Italian and the Italians promptly suppressed them again; the monks took refuge at a house given to them by a count in the Istria peninsula, which was still Austrian territory. In 1904 they came back to Praglia and bought part of the buildings from the family which now owned them, and became caretakers of the remainder, which by then had been declared a national monument. They managed to survive as a community. In almost all cases it proved difficult for monks to prosper when their main function was to look after a historic monument. But the monks of Praglia had the honour during the Second World War of sheltering refugees, and of taking care of the magnificent horses from Constantinople which adorned the façade of St Mark's at Venice, and the winged lion of St Mark

---

[16] The pilgrims continued to come: after the Second World War, when pilgrimage was even more mixed with tourism than before, some 150,000 a year came. The monks were able to colonize four houses in North America and one in the Argentine.

from the Piazzetta. The remains of the archives, which were ill-treated during the Napoleonic suppression, went to the city archives at Padua. The monks' library and the archives suffered from the two suppressions of the nineteenth century, but Padua university library preserved parts of the library and some of the manuscripts. The monks of Praglia looked after both a parish and a little hill sanctuary to the Madonna and did not omit to collect a large modern library to replace what they lost.

CAMALDOLI

The historic house at Camaldoli, home of the Camaldolese order of Benedictine hermits, was suppressed by the Italian government in 1866 and lost all the endowments. But, with caution, they kept the place on its mountain. They were divided into three main communities—Camaldoli which practised the hermit life, Murano in the Venice lagoon which practised the community life, and the loosely knit hermitage of Monte Corona near Perugia which had a special attraction for the Poles. Monte Corona had to be abandoned in the Italian dissolution and the headquarters moved near Frascati to be close to Rome.[17]

THE OLIVETANS

Monte Oliveto was an important abbey not far from Siena in Tuscany, once revered by St Catherine of Siena and later visited as a pilgrim by the Emperor Charles V. It had a fine library. Under it was a chain of priories with at their peak some 1,200 monks. The Napoleonic Revolution suppressed the house. The library was lost. At the fall of Napoleon a few monks came back and found everything in ruin. The Italian Revolution took away the old endowments and left a single monk as the custodian. Gradually other monks collected at Monte Oliveto and in 1928 they again had an abbot.

[17] Pope Pius XI decided that the three branches ought to be united as a single Camaldolese order. To marry a monastic way of life to a hermit way of life was not easy. The project took ten years to carry through, in uniting Murano to Camaldoli, two out of the three branches. The hermits of Monte Corona had in 1975 nine communities of hermits, of which four were in Italy and two in Poland. In that year there were seventy-five hermits in all in the Monte Corona group.

Bec was the greatest of the Norman houses while the English ruled Normandy. But afterwards it was a house with a chequered history; sacked by the Huguenots in the wars of religion, and then children of 9 or 10, and once a married man, made the abbot; it was part of the learned congregation of Saint-Maur and its monks were in trouble with Rome for Jansenism. It was suppressed by the French Revolution and taken over as a barracks for the cavalry. No revival was possible all the century because the French army kept it and did not release it until after the Second World War.[18]

Then a group of Olivetans took over Bec. Because the medieval monastery had housed monks beloved in English history, such as Anselm and Lanfranc, the new Olivetan house became important to the modern English, including—or especially—the Anglicans. The new or old abbey thus became a channel by which the Anglicans nourished their affection for the English medieval past and its devotion.

THE FRANCISCANS

The push to centralize was not well received. The Franciscans were militant against the plans. Some proposals were revolutionary; for example a suggestion by a Turin Observant that the four orders of Observants, Reformed, Discalced, and Recollects should be united into a single body and called simply Franciscans. Though they already had a council on which sat representatives of all four bodies, their discussions about internal reform were chaotic and unpromising. They were so militant that Leo XIII took a high line and appointed a Dominican to preside over the general Franciscan chapter in the church of St Mary of the Angels at Assisi in 1895. In appointing the Dominican he made it clear to the Franciscans that his aim was to unite the four branches.

Nearly all the Observants wanted union. The Recollects were happy if holy poverty were safeguarded in the united order. Few Discalced or Reformed were present. After complex voting the general chapter agreed by a big majority to accept what the pope wished. The union took effect in 1897. The single order was to be called Friars Minor. They were all to wear the same colour of habit.

[18] *DIP* s.v. Monte Oliveto Maggiore, and Congregazione Benedettina Olivetana; *DHGE* s.v. Bec.

At times it was like a schism; various Franciscans refused the union and had to be allotted special houses to continue their old way. Even Franciscans who did not refuse the union resisted, successfully, when visitors tried to make them change the customs of their houses. Pius X was forced to half the process of unification.[19]

The Franciscans never again became very numerous in the way in which they dominated so much of religious life before their sufferings in the French Revolution and then in the bans by anticlerical states. In 1762 there were nearly 77,000 Franciscans. In 1897, when the union came into force, they had 14,798, plus nearly 1,500 Conventuals, which was few compared with the past, plus about 7,500 Capuchins, who had been nearly four times as many a century before. For historical reasons the Conventuals inherited the largest and richest churches and houses, and therefore lost most (materially) to cities which needed barracks, warehouses, prisons, schools, or guildhalls.

From the union they began to grow again and faster, especially in the Americas. In 1889, 51 per cent of Franciscans were in Italy, 91 per cent in Europe. In Italy the number went on declining until 1924.[20]

They were affected because the reputation of St Francis of Assisi rose in Europe. It was never low among Franciscans nor among most Catholics. To them Francis was a beloved saint. But St Francis began to capture the esteem of Protestants, who had despised his simplicity and thought the begging ideal of life bad for society. The scholarly life of St Francis by the French Protestant Paul Sabatier, first published in 1894 and revised in later editions, was the mark of a new attitude within Protestantism. By 1922 there was an Anglican Society of Franciscans who wore brown habits in the streets. The reputation of the little man of Assisi rose in the world at large. That carried good news for the prestige of the Friars Minor in the modern world.

[19] Pius XII, three times from 1940 onwards, pushed again at the unifying of customs, *DIP* iv. col. 865; and this effort at last achieved success, though not popularity. It was not certain what was gained from all this effort between 1862 and 1949. The numbers in the four branches in 1897 were unequal. Incomplete statistics showed Observants 6,228; Reformed 5,733; Recollects 1,621; Discalced 858. So *DIP* vii. col. 1739.

[20] By 1924 between a quarter and a fifth of the order was American, south or north; by 1963 the Americans were not far short of half the order. They prospered; and their third order, for the laity, with simple rules of devotion which they made much simpler for this purpose, saw a vast expansion and was their biggest contribution to the life of the Church.

THE CISTERCIANS

Cîteaux in France, the original house and head of the Cistercian order, had trouble in the wars of the sixteenth and seventeenth centuries, for it lay too near the routes where armies passed. The French Revolution closed it, sold the property, and destroyed the church and almost all the buildings except the library and a great hall. Cistercians and Trappists had a particularly bad time in the various revolutions, Napoleonic, Spanish, Portuguese, and Italian. When they revived, their endowments were lost and they had difficulty in surviving. But their endowments earlier were liable to abuse through commendatory abbots of the *ancien régime* who drew off the main part of their income, so that problems about money were not new. The old way of life, in which agriculture was still important, gave way in part to teaching and pastoral care.

Their reconstruction as an Order during the nineteenth century was the more difficult because the destruction of Cîteaux left them without a proper central authority. Napoleon made their most famous abbey, Clairvaux, into a prison and demolished the historic church, and in better times the prison service refused to do without it. Sénanque, one of the grandchildren of Cîteaux, in its remote and lovely Provençal valley, with a very austere Romanesque church and less austere cloister, had a better fate. It was sacked by the Vaudois during the wars of religion and when the revolution came to suppress it there were no monks to suppress. But in 1854 a Provençal priest, Barnouin, occupied it, in a dormitory open to the rain and the church full of wood, with a gentler Cistercian rule, and made it formally Cistercian three years later. But the official Cistercians disliked the gentler modifications made by Barnouin and there was a long battle in which Sénanque tried to keep its new way of life. That way, and the valley of such glorious solitude, were attractive, and enabled Sénanque to colonize other houses: Fontfroide (Narbonne), Hautecombe near Chambéry in Savoy, a nunnery at Mane not far away, and Garde-Dieu near Montauban from which they were driven out almost at once because they settled without any leave from the government of Napoleon III.

Some communities survived in another country; as with Quarr Abbey in the Isle of Wight, peopled by French monks. The house at Fontfroide near Narbonne, which was a medieval Cistercian priory, was colonized again from Sénanque. It was a weak community. Fontfroide gave shelter to Father Claret, an exile from Spain because he stayed with his queen when she lost her throne; he was still a bishop by rank and so was at the Vatican Council where he even made a speech—a very short one in comparison with the *longueurs* of most bishops, but hot words, the most passionate speech ever delivered at that Council, recalling how he had been stabbed when he came down from a Spanish pulpit, and how he was willing to die for the cause of the Pope's infallibility—'let us not be prudent, prudence is the enemy of God'.[21] He could not go home to Spain, nor to his queen in Paris because of the French war, he found shelter at Fontfroide, where the Cistercians cared for him during ten weeks till he died and put up an inscription to his memory, the famous words of Gregory VII—'I have loved righteousness and hated iniquity, therefore I die in exile.'

When Fontfroide was abolished in the general French dissolution, the surviving monks went to Spain and kept their community in being. When France was more friendly after the First World War they came to the historic place on the Pyrenees, Cuxa, where one of the abbots was the first priest ever to serve in America, in the time of Christopher Columbus. Cuxa had eight monks at the revolution, of whom three stayed to watch its sack; later the roof fell in, the tower collapsed, and the place was a ruin.[22]

The group of islands of Lérins off the French Riviera was the original home of monasticism in France. It became Benedictine after a time (and, in two phases, Cluniac) but when it grew rich its site made it an easy prey to pirates. The Spanish army used it as a base in the Thirty Years War. It was closed just before the French Revolution, during which the property was sold.

When it came onto the market in 1859 the bishop of Fréjus bought it. He offered to make the island of Lérins a gift to the Benedictines of Solesmes. Guéranger refused it because his monks there would be 'too isolated' (!). The Benedictines had a mission which was more than the daily office and the life of prayer: they wanted to teach the ethos of worship, and so had to be accessible. The bishop of Fréjus

---

[21] Speech in G. D. Mansi, *Collectio conciliorum recentiorum*, ed. I. B. Martin and L. Petit (Arnhem and Leipzig, 1923–7), xvi. 363–4, 31 May 1870.

[22] In 1965 Cuxa, reduced to a handful of monks, offered the house to Montserrat, which sent a community there who were rather free in their adaptation of the traditional life of monks. Cf. *DIP* s.v. Cuxa; *DHGE* xiii. 1121 ff.

had to wait eleven years before he persuaded Cistercians to occupy the island. It was Barnouin's men from Sénanque who satisfied his longing that this earliest of French monastic sites should be repeopled; to occupy Lérins was an acceptance of suffering for the sake of a saintly past, since the chapel was then in ruins, the refectory was a stable, and the cloister a store for barrels of wine. To achieve the move they needed to abandon Sénanque; which in any case was shut in the French dissolution and had become a farm; the Cistercians did not succeed in opening it again for more than a very short time. In 1988 six monks from Lérins returned to Sénanque.

The Trappist branch of the Cistercians had worse trouble. From 1847 there were two different branches of the Trappists in France, each with its own vicar-general. Attempts were made to unite the whole order with its parent-order the Cistercians. The union could not be achieved. But in 1892, meeting at Rome by papal command, the Trappists were constituted a unified order separate from the Cistercians with their own abbot-general. Six years later they managed to buy the property of Cîteaux. Their head became its abbot. They were now to be called officially, the Order of Reformed Cistercians, or, ten years later, the Cistercian Order of the Strict Observance.[23]

The affection for the contemplative spirit, and for silence, remained. A French army officer, Charles de Foucauld, turned to be a Trappist in France and Syria. Then he became a hermit at Nazareth, and finally a hermit in the Sahara desert, where he was murdered by Tuaregs. It was not the ideal of a pure contemplation, because he hoped, by a hermit way of worship, to bring faith to the wilder tribes of the desert. And yet his way was not by mission in the old sense, nor by evangelism in the old sense, nor even by saying anything, but just by being solitary and conscious of God among a hostile people.

He meant to found an order of people who would do as he did, but did not succeed before his death.[24]

---

[23] However, the archabbot of Cîteaux, as he was called after 1963, needed to live not at Cîteaux but in Rome. In 1965 they had 4,104 monks. *LTK* s.v. Trappisten.

[24] He was killed in 1916. In 1933 a group of Frenchmen founded, on the edge of the Sahara, a body to do the sort of work that he wanted. They called themselves the Little Brothers of Jesus. Six years later they were followed by a group of nuns, also near the edge of the Sahara. Other groups followed, all inspired by the model of de Foucauld, to live simply and in poverty, and in an ordinary way but prayerfully, with a little group of brothers or sisters in the midst of a hostile or indifferent world. That is, it became the ideal of an approach not to a real desert and wild tribesmen, but to the desert of slums, inner cities, and industrialized indifference. For de Foucauld, see esp. R. Aubert in *DHGE* s.v.

One modern Trappist became famous throughout the Christian world. Thomas Merton

The separation between Cistercians left a small Cistercian order not Trappist—twenty-four houses in 1894, about 1,000 members altogether four years later. They never advanced more than a few hundred above this number.

THE CARTHUSIANS

The Carthusians lost almost all in the age of revolutions; sixty-seven houses in France alone. The Grande Chartreuse was burnt during the wars of religion, when the fire destroyed valuable manuscripts though the treasures were saved by flight the night before. It was reoccupied twelve years later but the society found it hard to recover from the losses. It was again ruined by fire, twice by accident. In 1792 the thirty-eight monks were expelled by the French revolutionary government and six lost their lives by execution. After the Battle of Waterloo the Grande Chartreuse was reoccupied and from this source the Order spread again. It bought back several of the old houses.

It was not easy, the restoration. There was the awkwardness between the survivors of the old who remembered great days, and the young novices who saw the new world with open eyes and knew little of the tradition. They were fortunate to choose out of the new-comers an excellent general, Jean-Baptiste Motaize, who ruled from 1831 to 1863.

(1915–58) dabbled in literature and in communism, and was then moved by the silence and penitence when he visited the Trappist house at Gethsemane in Kentucky. He was accepted there as a novice on 10 December 1941 and remained there, nominally, the rest of his life. He began to write about the life of the spirit. He first published a book in 1948, *The Seven Storey Mountain*, as an account of his own spiritual life. He proved to have a gift for writing attractively. If the Benedictine of Maredsous in Belgium, Columba Marmion, was the author of the earlier twentieth century who best instructed the monastic élite and the secular clergy, Merton was the writer on spirituality who could write for the laity, even for popular consumption. He represented the monastic vocation as a humane life amid an industrializing and technological society. His notion of the life of spirit was contemplative. But during the 1950s he grew conscious that society also had its needs and he wrote about social justice and world peace. Part of his fame was that at first he was the only Catholic to be an acrid critic of American policy in Vietnam. He turned the monastery at Kentucky into a meeting-place for pacifist leaders. He had critics who doubted whether publicity, and a social gospel, were suited to his Trappist vocation. In 1964 he began to exercise the hermit life at his monastery and grew interested in Buddhist contemplation, especially Zen. He was accidentally electrocuted at Bangkok when he attended a meeting of different religions on the theme of contemplation.

The original recipe for the Chartreuse liqueur was invented in the sixteenth century and given to the Paris Carthusians. The Grande Chartreuse had it by the middle of the eighteenth century and sold it to the neighbourhood as medicine. The papers were lost for a time in the sack of the monastery in the Revolution but they were back at the Grande Chartreuse by 1835. Then a talented lay brother in the distillery experimented further, intending now not to make a medicine but an enjoyable liqueur. The monastery started to make a fortune, in 1888 they sold three million bottles and had legally protected their copyright on the recipe.

The Grande Chartreuse itself (and ten other French houses) were again closed in the French suppression; the Chamber refused them the authorization for which they applied, using the excuse that because of their wealth they were really a trading organization. They were not moved out by force until April 1903, with local demonstrations in their favour, and the need for a break-in with axes and locksmiths; a soldier climbed over the screen into the choir where the survivors were saying their office. The monks were led out amid crowds cheering them and jeering the troops. They sought refuge at Farneta near Lucca, an old Carthusian house suppressed under Napoleon and bought back on the market in this very year. It was much too small for them. But under the Vichy government in 1940 the Grande Chartreuse reopened.

THE DOMINICANS

Lacordaire, disciple of Lamennais, who broke with him even before Lamennais broke with the Pope, was a famous preacher. In his vision of the religious life he was drawn to the Order of Friar Preachers. He became a Dominican at Rome in 1839 and refounded the Dominican order in France, beginning with a community at Nancy. He had an open mind that wished to adapt religious life to meet the needs of the modern age. And this desire met the inward tension inevitable in these revivals of the old religious orders.

The purpose of these revivals, to a clear mind, was not the romantic remaking of a past world in reconstructed ruins. Catholicism would not be itself without persons dedicating themselves to the way of chastity, poverty, and obedience. But the world cried for less generalized needs. It could not be denied that the vocation designed by

St Dominic so many centuries ago, of an order which would teach and preach, was a crying need of the nineteenth century. When Lacordaire entered the Dominicans in Italy, they did very little preaching or teaching, they were like pleasant clubs of unmarried gentlemen. It was difficult to recover momentum after the losses of the Napoleonic age. When the convert Newman looked around for a religious order to enter, his informants vehemently discouraged him from the Dominicans: 'We found that the said Dominicans were manufacturers of scented water etc., and had very choice wines in their cellar.' This was a Florence house evidently trading for enough money to survive. As for Lacordaire, Newman was told—he had heard of him but did not know how to spell him—that he 'was quite a new beginning, a sort of knight errant and not a monk'.[25]

To recreate a true teaching and preaching order was tough. It meant reform of the Dominican way of life as it then existed, and finding the people with the intellectual qualities to teach and preach. It also meant a realistic facing of the modern world by the new friars. They would not do good in the industrial world unless they under-stood it; and to understand is to penetrate and to feel a measure of sympathy, an awareness of the benefits of modernity. The preacher would do no good if he spoke in a manner fit only for the past. To talk to republicans as though they should become Bourbons, or to the literate as though they were illiterate, or to the slum-dwellers as though they ought to babble of green fields, might sound pious but was not likely to make a profitable sermon.

Therefore it would be natural for a revived Dominican order, with its special vocation, to try to understand democracy, or liberalism, or life in industry, or what happened as the towns grew bigger—in short, to comprehend the middle nineteenth century. And Lacordaire himself, one-time disciple of Lamennais, was fitted to learn. Apart from his brilliance of language and imaginative insight, it was the ability to speak to his own age which made him the cele-brated preacher of France. As a preacher he was midway between the glorious rhetoric of the old Massillon tradition and the modern social preacher, so that now he is hard to read because the age of that rhetoric is gone; yet his hearers at Notre Dame in 1835 were moved by the language and crowded the cathedral. He was not literary for he hardly ever used notes in the pulpit: words came easily to him.

[25] *Letters and Diaries of Newman*, ed. C. S. Dessain (1961–), xi. 263.

He was no systematic theologian and the austere combed through the texts and sent lists of heresies to Rome, and charged his mind with being an anarchy, and anyone who was known to have been an intimate of Lamennais had to live with distrust. Archbishop Quelen of Paris was afraid that if he was allowed to set up a Dominican house it would be a refuge for radical disciples of Lamennais. The Curia made difficulties about the establishment of French Dominicans.

The Curia wanted religious orders which behaved in the same way as they had before the French Revolution threw them into the dustbin. It could not be denied that some of those former traditions were good and still needed. But an attitude hung about the Curia—the more traditional the better, the more innovating the more suspect. They were nervous of Lacordaire. They fancied that he was sure to baptize democracy, or think little of the need for the pope to rule his Papal States. And it was true that this friend of Lamennais, though a monarchist who thought that France would be best served not by a republic but by kings who were constitutional, was fully willing to accept a democratic republic if the people of France decided that this was what they wanted. He believed that the pope ought to be independent but saw no reason why that independence must mean that he was secular governor of a sizeable State. After the revolution of 1848 he even appeared on the platform at two rowdy election meetings and allowed himself to be elected a member for Marseilles of the constituent assembly, sitting uncomfortably in his Dominican habit on the extreme left near Lamennais; a minister challenged whether it was legal to attend a parliamentary assembly in a monk's habit, but no one else bothered, though there was doubt in both Church and State whether a parliament was the proper place for a friar. This lasted only for eleven days of May 1848, during which he spoke twice, only for a few minutes, once to deny that it could be wrong to come in a religious habit. On 15 May the mob occupied the Assembly while they were sitting and for three hours the legal government of France was helpless. He sat silent in his place, thinking all the time, 'The Republic is lost!' Wild men threatened this member conspicuous by his 'reactionary' costume. He resigned the seat next day. Before he resigned he was one of the most popular men in France. When he resigned he lost his reputation, accused of cowardice.

Archbishop Affre, who had helped him, was murdered on the barricade that June and was succeeded by Sibour who regarded Lacordaire as a kindred spirit; he handed over to the Dominicans the

Carmelite church and part of the Carmelite house, which had a lugubrious sanctity because it was where the September Massacre happened during the French Revolution.

Chalais was a medieval Benedictine abbey in the massif not far from Grenoble. The Benedictines there were overshadowed by the Carthusians in the Grande-Chartreuse not far away, and after some difficulty they were taken over by the Grande-Chartreuse. The French Revolution ruined Chalais. Lacordaire bought the buildings and site, and turned it into a house of study for his revived Dominican order.

Then in 1850 Pius IX summoned Lacordaire's chief disciple, Jandel, to Rome, and made him the head of the Dominicans. That was a stern act. Lacordaire had only to open his mouth and young Frenchmen collected round him to try their vocations as Dominicans. Jandel was known to them because he had run their house of study. The difficulty was less between the founder and the Curia than between the founder and his disciples. The young men who joined the Dominican order might enlist either because they were moved by Lacordaire or because it was Dominican—that is, what they valued and expected to find were the old rules of St Dominic: but it was questionable whether the rules of the thirteenth century were suitable for the modern world.

A preacher and teacher needs time to think and prepare. He cannot weaken himself with an excess of fasting, or by refusing to take a proper night's sleep. There were novices who wanted the old rules literally observed—Jandel was their leader, an older man than most of them; when the pope, nervous about Lacordaire, made Jandel head of the order, he had support for his choice.

The conflict within the revived order apparently centred on how far the old rules had to be observed and in what way. Everyone agreed that the 'essentials' of the old rule must be maintained, but they disagreed on what was essential. 'I had not', wrote Lacordaire, '. . . absolute respect for the primitive text. I did not believe in the idea of my being a lifeless founder, and considered myself free, in the midst of the distress of my soul, to take a step which would settle what I deemed to be the measure for us of what was possible and right.' He argued that the rules were drafted for a time when there were many friars and the burden of maintaining the work of the house, as well as of preaching and teaching, was less; and for a time when the outside world had all the priests it needed, whereas now the demands upon the Dominicans from outside reached them every day; and 'we are certainly weaker bodily than our forefathers'. Insistence on a literal keeping of the old rules made the monastic life dominant and diminished the apostolate—but the purpose of the revival was an apostolate to the modern world. To Father Jandel the object of revival was observance. To do otherwise than observe the old rules would introduce the Protestant principle of private judgement into a community based upon obedience, and would in the end, whatever the situation now, lead to laxity and to the decline of the order back into clubs of comfortable unmarried gentlemen. At the time of his profession Jandel took a private vow that he would never co-operate in any weakening of the ruler of the Order.[26]

During the 1850s the controversy—faithfulness to old rules versus adaptation to the needs of the age—was incessant and disturbing for the young French province. It was even more trouble for the Italian province because unlike the French they had continuity with the amenities of the eighteenth century and they did not take kindly to Jandel. Entangled with the controversy was the ultramontane fear of liberalism and the knowledge that Lacordaire was tinged with the liberal spirit. The argument led to a double standard of observance in different houses, and to an appeal by both sides to the pope. The battle focused curiously on what looked like a trivial question but was not—the hour at which the friars should rise in the night to pray their office. The division led to the founding of a house of Lyons which was under stricter rules than the other French houses and designed to be a model to show that the old rules were not impossible. This creation of a house with different rules led to a crisis in the French province, and in 1858 to a separation of France into two provinces, one with Lacordaire, the other based at Lyons. Rome was steadily on the side of Jandel. Pope Leo XIII in 1870 told a large audience that Father Jandel was a holy man who well understood the spirit of the Order of Preachers: 'its basis is observance'.[27] After Lacordaire's death things were easier but Dominicans of the south-west still demanded a separate province from that of the rest of France.

The men of Jandel thought that the object was to make holy priests. The men of Lacordaire thought that the object was to make teachers and preachers. There was a large overlap between the two

---

[26] Dominic only gave his order the outline Rule of St Augustine, and the actual rules were resolutions built up by chapters till the 17th cent.

[27] R. Devas, *Ex Umbris* (Rugeley, 1921), 54, 153–4, 165, 172.

ideals, but someone whose first aim is to be a holy priest will take less notice of the world around him than the person whose first object is to learn how to be persuasive. The division was made worse by the inability of Lacordaire and Jandel to understand each other. It was not that Jandel was ascetic and Lacordaire lax, for Lacordaire was over-hard on his novices, and even harder on himself. If the essence of being the head of a religious order is to be inspiring and creative he was superb. If it is to be a governor he had the gravest defects, for he was a masochist the focus of whose mysticism was the suffering Christ. He made his novices whip him daily, and then kissed the feet of the scourgers. When he came back from preaching to thousands, and knew himself to be a 'success' and to be touched with pride, he would not go to bed without being humiliated by being beaten. He once had himself tied to a pillar in the crypt of the Carmelite house, and beaten by two novices. He wore a hairshirt, and once he spent Good Friday roped to a cross for three hours. He made confession frequently and to anyone, not necessarily to priests. The need for humiliation had exceptions, he accepted election to the French Academy in Tocqueville's seat.

The Dominicans could not do without Lacordaire because he was the charisma of their venture. But it was not surprising that hard-headed men doubted and infected the Pope with their doubt, nor is it surprising that another, stabler, more prosaic, and more conserva-tive, Father Jandel, became the real head of the Dominican revival. Before he died Lacordaire destroyed all the letters between Jandel and himself. Jandel wrote about the conflict in a private memorandum which first saw the light in 1989.[28]

In the eighteenth century the Dominicans had 25,000 members in the whole Order. The Napoleonic Revolution left them with almost none. For a time they remained under a cloud at Rome because of their opposition, which was traditional, to the doctrine of the Immaculate Conception of the Virgin. In 1876 they were still only 3,341. But when that doctrine was defined, and even more when Pope Leo XIII turned to St Thomas Aquinas as the philosopher of the Church and entrusted the Dominicans with the duty of caring

---

[28] B. Bonvin, *Lacordaire–Jandel* (Paris, 1989). The oddities of Lacordaire's behaviour were first disclosed reverently by his disciple B. Chocarne in a book on his inner life, *Le R. P. H. D. Lacordaire; Sa vie intime et religieuse*, 7th edn. (2 vols.; Paris, 1886), Eng. trans. (Dublin, 1867). The evidence was then confirmed by the official biographer J. T. Foisset, *Vie du R. P. Lacordaire* (2 vols.; Paris, 1870).

for his texts and propagating his doctrines, they began again to expand.

Latent in every revival was the tension between freedom and discipline. A founder like Lacordaire knew that he needed to be free and was so self-tormenting that he could be free without risk to the standards of the order. But such a man, with his affection for the human race, expected everyone else to be as free as himself, without risk. The monastic legislators, beginning with St Benedict, knew that *naïveté* imagines all monks to be Lacordaires who will be safe if they are free. They were conscious, from experience, that the success of the community, and its permanence, needs a rule which is kept.

Lacordaire's life threw light upon another side of religion, that amid the charismata of Catholicism women could be as powerful as men. His director of soul was a Russian woman, Madame Swetchine (in Russian, Swjetschin). She married a Russian general and was one of the tsar's court but converted to Catholicism when de Maistre, famous theorist of the pope's supreme authority, came to St Petersburg to be the Savoy ambassador. From 1825 she and her much older husband stayed in Paris, and she presided over a salon with de Maistre's portrait in the place of honour. She had an extraordinary effect as a religious sage for the 'liberal Catholic' group, almost a prophetess, dominating Lacordaire, powerfully influencing the young politician Falloux who was to be her biographer, and a close friend of Montalembert. Such an influence can only be explained by the mysterious force of personality, but the Russian Orthodox dedication of her earlier years affected the way in which she understood Catholicism and gave fresh insights to those who came into touch with her. It was easy then to be malicious about women who were directors of souls and Sainte-Beuve wrote an essay which was witty at her expense. But both Lacordaire and Falloux came to her death-bed and Lacordaire was heart-broken when she died.[29]

---

[29] C. de Falloux published her life in 1860, as *Madame Swetchine: Sa vie et ses œuvres*, 19th edn. (2 vols.; Paris, 1916), her letters, *Madame Swetchine: Lettres*, 4th edn. (3 vols.; Paris, 1873), and meditations, *Madame Swetchine: Choix de méditations et de pensées chrétiennes* (Tours, 1867); see also the remarkable correspondence with Lacordaire, *Correspondance du R. P. Lacordaire et de Madame Swetchine* (Paris, 1864), which went through several editions. Shorter life in English, M. V. Woodgate, *Madame Swetchine, 1782–1857* (Dublin, 1948).

THE JESUITS

There was paradox in the history of the Jesuits. They carried out of
the Counter-Reformation such a burden of ill-repute that no religious order was more likely to be suppressed by governments that
aimed to be popular. Britain banned them in 1829, and did not lift
the ban for nearly a century, though it made no attempt to enforce it.
During the century after 1833 they were allowed officially into
Portugal for a period of only twenty-eight years. United Italy banned
them from living in community. The constitution of Norway banned
them from the country and this was not lifted till 1956. The German
Kulturkampf ejected them and the law was not repealed till 1917. The
Sonderbund war ejected them from Switzerland where the ban on
them was not lifted till a referendum of 1973; and the most astonishing proof of the perpetuity of legend was shown by the statistics of
this referendum, where in one of the most liberal-minded countries
in Europe only 55 per cent of the people voted in favour of the lift-
ing of the ban, though freedom of religion was one of the fundamental liberal axioms and though the country had a big Catholic
minority in the population. Catholic Spain banished them at various
long periods during the nineteenth century and again in 1932 (which
saved their lives in the civil war four years later).

Yet the number of Jesuits steadily increased. There were two
epochs of big expansion. In the revolution of 1848 they were at a low
ebb. The next twenty-five years, when Beckx was general, was a
time of growth (in 1850 there were 4,600 Jesuits; in 1875, 9,385; in
1900, 15,073; in 1910, 16,293; in 1950, 30,579).[30]

A Spaniard, Luis Martín, was elected general of the Jesuits in 1892.
It was the only election of a Jesuit general ever held outside Rome. It
was not surprising that he was Spanish, no Italian general was elected
during this period—Roothaan was Dutch, Beckx Belgian, Anderledy
Swiss, and after Martín a German, and then a Pole. Martín kept a
secret autobiography, only published in 1988. It is an astonishing document. It was too frank, and he wondered whether it was a disor-
dered affection, but it was a refreshment to his ego, and he never
destroyed it, though he thought of doing so. He was an intelligent,
disciplined personality who wrote Ciceronian Latin and was fluent in

---

[30] Statistics in *DIP* ii. col. 1280; smaller growth, but still growth, after 1950; decline of
numbers after 1965.

English, French, and Italian. He rendered service to scholarship by organizing the writing of Jesuit history and by aiding the publication of the original Jesuit documents of the sixteenth century. He moved the Jesuit archives from Rome to Holland to protect them from the threat that the Italian government would take them over as State property. And at last, in 1895, he was able to move Jesuit headquarters back to Rome from Fiesole whither it fled after Rome fell in 1870.

The move of the archives was a sign of his defensive mood against the world which was natural to a Spanish religious. He saw everything in black or white, the world was good or evil and not mixed up. He was a man for minutiae, and believed in a rigid interpretation when rules were in question: faithfulness to the founders did not allow the flexibility of thought that they lived in a different age and their rules could hardly have an exact application to a new age. For some fathers the minutiae became oppressive. Privately he was a Carlist, but he thought it very wrong for any Jesuit to show a political allegiance and he supported Pope Leo XIII's doctrine that Catholics could work with a liberal State for the sake of the Church; that is, he was an integrist who yet was determined that the Jesuits should not be publicly committed to integrism, and he therefore allowed other points of view in the Jesuits of other countries. But his rigidity could not succeed in keeping the Jesuits from quarrelling among themselves on whether it was possible or not to co-operate with liberals. The division passed from teachers in seminaries to their students.

The assault which the Jesuits found saddest was that by one of their own, Miguel Mir. For Mir was a respected person, a fine scholar, a friendly and cultivated personality, more than three decades a Jesuit, a specialist in the history of the Jesuits, and one of the editors of the letters of St Ignatius. In other ages of that society he would have been one of its ornaments. But in the age of Spanish integrism, and of the fussing generalship of Luis Martín, he found his community impossible to live in; he liked liberals, and associated with not very religious scholars, and joined the Spanish Academy though his general said he was not to. Mir finally left the society at the beginning of 1892. Nearly four years later he published a book of resentment: on the cold obedience that made for the absence of a family spirit, small-mindedness among the superiors, the ostentation of buildings, the evangelism too evidently aimed at the upper class and pious women, the extremism of integrists. He mixed this with anecdotes about individuals, some of which, as usual in similar circumstances, were untrue. Other Jesuits did not treat it with rueful sympathy for a person who did not fit: the provincial of Castile called it the 'vomit of Judas' and by request it was put on the Index of Prohibited Books. Mir died in 1912 and the next year were published his personal memories, which were still more bitter.

Another Jesuit scholar found the community life of Martín's time, and the age of integrism, not to be endured. Julio Cejador was an orphan whom the Jesuits brought up, educated, and turned into a brilliant professor of Greek at their private university of Deusto. He was gentle and sensitive, and after a time realized that he was unhappy because he had to live in community. He asked to be released on the plea that his character did not fit, but it is clear that he found the superiors narrow and their politics rigid. He left the Jesuits with permission in 1899, and went on to be professor at three universities and to produce a history of Castilian literature in 14 volumes. But meanwhile he produced a novel, *Mirando a Loyola*, the monotony and boredom of being a novice at Loyola: how dry and uncultivated were the teachers; how repugnant that the base of the system is moral espionage; how wearing to the freedom of the soul the Spiritual Exercises of St Ignatius; how contrary it all was to the simplicity of Jesus. After he died his memories were published and showed a friendlier and more understanding attitude to his experiences.

Compared with Mir and Cejador, their own scholars, all other attacks were something the Jesuits now expected. They had no need to read such pamphlets, and were ordered not to.

During the first years of the twentieth century they were polemical and ultra-conservative on the antimodernist side. This did not cohere with that quest for effective upper education which was their mark and their duty. The growth, after times when nearly every government conspired to do what it could to discourage them, and when their reputation, even among Catholics, retained the shadow that once they were abolished by a pope on charges of evil conduct, could only be due to the meeting of a need, higher and better education. They had other tasks, like the conducting of missions and retreats. But higher education was what mattered. The nineteenth century turned vast illiterate Catholic populations into half-literate Catholic populations, the first half of the twentieth century turned half-literate Catholic populations into an almost entirely literate people;

and this could only be achieved by secondary schools and universities. This was a realm where the Jesuits were the specialists. Eventually they were responsible for 710 places of education, including fifty-three universities and forty-five university colleges.

That meant research. The new standards of academic work complicated the life of the society: such as that, for example, of the Bollandists, who since the seventeenth century had been responsible for the publication of the lives of the saints, each saint under his day in the calendar. By the time the society was suppressed in 1773 they had reached the third quarter of October. Yet the rest of the year limped, and to this day the work is nowhere near completion. This was due first to the interval of suppression, then to the difficulty of restoration. From 1882, when they founded the periodical *Analecta Bollandiana* with the aim of revising the texts of the past and preparing for the texts of the future, and then with the coming of Hippolyte Delehaye who developed the modern scientific study of saints' lives, the Bollandists passed through a dazzling period. The academic advance was fast: new standards, new texts. But in terms of the calendar, if the object was to reach 31 December, the work went slower and slower as the standards of scholarship rose.[31]

THE ORATORIANS

The Oratory was not regarded by monks as an order of monks because they took no vows. Each Oratory was an independent society of priests (although laymen could join) to encourage each other in the priestly life and do pastoral work. Before the revolution there had been many houses in Italy and some fifteen in France and twenty-two in Spain; which were all destroyed. The restoration of the Papal States made it easy to restore a few in Italy.

In France, the first attempt was almost a failure. Alphonse Gratry was the son of an officer in Napoleon's Grand Army. After a short army career he decided on ordination and then had a bitty career in teaching. In 1852 he founded an oratory, called the Oratory of the Immaculate Conception. It did not work well, and this was mainly the fault of Gratry who spent his time away on a serious endeavour

[31] P. Peeters (who after Delehaye dedicated himself to the oriental texts), 'Après un siècle, l'œuvre des Bollandistes de 1837–1937', in *Analecta Bollandiana*, 55 (1937), v–xliv; David Knowles, *Great Historical Enterprises* (1963).

to reconcile religion with science, and achieved enough to become professor of theology at the university of Paris. He had much influence on the conversion of General Lamoricière and wrote a devotional book which was often reprinted and valued by two generations of French Catholic intellectuals.[32] Though he was still an Oratorian in name he did not live in community. When Renan's Life of Jesus appeared, he published an answer, *The Sophists and Criticism*, which was so acceptable that it won him a seat in the French Academy.

Then came the Vatican Council. Dupanloup knew that Gratry had Gallican views about the pope and persuaded him to publish the main arguments against papal infallibility, which he did, while the Council was in progress, in a book entitled *The Bishop of Orleans and the Archbishop of Malines*, a contrast between what Dupanloup wanted and what Dechamps of Malines wanted. Nothing could do the Oratory more harm in its repute than to publish such a book at such a moment. His struggling little community forced him to resign. He published his submission to the Vatican decree but died a very sad man soon afterwards. Later three other small communities were set up but they all perished in the French dissolution of monasteries and did not afterwards reappear.

In England the ideal had success because of a single priest, John Henry Newman. After being an Anglican leader he became a Roman Catholic and threw himself with loyalty into the Catholic system which he found in his training at Rome. But he did not like the negative attitude to the modern world that he met there. He found, he wrote to his sister about the Jesuits, 'a deep suspicion of *change*, with a perfect incapacity to create anything *positive* for the wants of the times'.[33] He had an ardent desire to do something positive for the Catholic Church in the modern world.

He wondered whether to be a Dominican (a natural idea, for he had been the best of Anglican preachers), but found nothing to attract him. He wondered about becoming a Jesuit, but decided that the Jesuits whom he met, and respected, were too conservative for him. He wondered whether to be an Oratorian but was told that he would have to keep all the old rules. When he discovered what the old rules

---

[32] *Sources, conseils pour la conduite de l'esprit* (1861). The correspondence with Hyacinthe Loyson was published by the modernist Houtin in 1927. Gratry left unpublished his own memories when he died in 1872. They were printed two years later, *Souvenirs de ma jeunesse* (Paris, 1874) and *Méditations inédites* (Paris, 1874).

[33] *Letters and Diaries of Newman*, ed. Dessain, xii. 104.

were he realized that they were impossible for him. And yet the ideal of the Oratory suited him. They had to be sited in large cities, where they had a mission to the people; they were teachers and confessors; and despite the old rules they were flexible in their ways, for their constitution was freer and more democratic than the constitution of some of the orders proper. He discovered that they had few rules and much freedom. He would have the leisure and the library, he supposed, to write books which would help the English to see the nature of Catholicism. In 1847 Pope Pius IX approved that he should found the Oratory in England, and he did so in Birmingham.

In the following year Frederick Faber, another ex-Anglican with an existing small community round him, took himself and his men into Newman's Oratory. In the year after that Faber set up another branch of the Oratory in London, first in the Strand and later in Brompton, and became the superior.

The subsequent conflict between Newman and Faber, or between the Birmingham Oratory and the London Oratory, had parallels with the conflict among the French Dominicans. There was a personal difficulty in both cases; they were different types of religious leader. In Birmingham was a man of stature with a wide reputation, and with one of the most original minds of his age, who wished to create a new kind of work for the Church in England and did not shrink from experiments of practice and language. Newman revered the pope, but was incapable of surrendering his critical faculty, which he could apply unmercifully to the Curia. He was therefore suspect to curial officials. Faber was an ultramontane with the emotionalism of the convert. His men soon decided that Newman was not loyal to his Church.

The climax of the battle came in 1855 when Newman thought that the Londoners had created a false impression in Rome of the Oratorian rule at Birmingham. He asked London to correct the misunderstanding; the Londoners refused. As with the arguments of the Dominicans in France, the argument between the Oratorians centred upon what now appear as trivialities. It was one of the afflictions of community life that perspective about minor matters was not easy to achieve. Throughout the argument the sympathies of Rome lay with Faber.

Both Oratories were established and continue to this day. Newman's hope to put an Oratory into every big town was not achieved.

THE MERCEDARIANS

The Mercedarians were founded in Spain during the Middle Ages with the mission to ransom Christian slaves from the Moors. In the age of the Reformation and afterwards they were important in Latin America, with much more varied work. In 1700 there were 5,200 members. The destruction of the Spanish and Portuguese empires during the age of Napoleon and afterwards devastated their welfare as an order. For forty-six years after 1834 they were not even able to meet in chapter to elect a general. By 1885 the total membership had fallen to 243, and many of those were dispersed. The order seemed on the way to extinction.

In 1880 Leo XIII imposed a general upon them, Valenzuela from Valparaiso, who took up residence in Rome. He elicited new statutes from the pope to allow the order to dedicate itself to teaching and the young. The number of members started to climb again—but very slowly.[34]

THE SALESIANS

John Bosco was a Piedmontese of a worker's family who was a voracious reader as a boy. After his seminary he was encouraged to go to work among the poor adolescents. In 1841 he founded an oratory at Valdocco in a poor quarter of Turin, and at once became concerned with helping delinquents when they came out of prison. He was an enthusiast, warm-natured, and an optimist about adolescents.

Bosco's oratory tried to give its members an elementary education, so that one of Bosco's first little books was a simple explanation of the metric system. Soon he opened a lodging house or hospice, which slowly turned into a technical school. He wrote popular biography, the history of the Church (presented as a sequence of struggles and victories by the Roman Church), lives of saints, devotional meditations, works of devotion to the Virgin, a history of Italy. When the conflict between Church and State in Piedmont began, he published apologies for the Catholic Church, especially against Protestant claims. He was always a man of marvels, and decisions taken after dreams, and of visions.

[34] There were 440 in 1900, 996 in 1965, 773 in 1978, *DIP* v. 1223.

He started with a devotion to St Francis de Sales, and in 1859 founded an order to be a community with boys' work as its vocation. Being in the world, it had no special habit. In the conflicts with Piedmont it was difficult to train priests, so the work extended to cover that. His plans met a need in the growing cities, and the society founded colonies. Bosco went round encouraging and begging for money. He was already revered as a saint by the people in his work. He died at Turin in 1888.[35] The oratory at Valdocco is to this day the centre of the order.

The chief work always remained the helping of the adolescent boy; but after Bosco's death it expanded to parish work, provision of retreats, and running of parish missions. At Bosco's death there were 774 members, and by 1963, 21,847 members.[36] This later growth made them almost as numerous as were the Jesuits in the heyday of the middle eighteenth century; and for the same reason; except that their educational vocation, unlike the vocation of the Jesuits, was forged by the industrial city.

A work parallel but curiously different was created by another priest of Turin, thirteen years younger than Bosco: Leonardo Murialdo, who was of more middle-class origins. Soon after he became a priest Bosco began to use him. He went to Paris to broaden his ideas, and then returned to be head of a big technical college; he directed Bosco's Turin reformatory for delinquents, with a modern agricultural training. In 1873 he created an order to carry out his educational ideals. It was called the Congregation of St Joseph (because St Joseph was the patron saint of workers). But he also founded the Union of Catholic Operatives, which grew into the first Catholic trade union in Italy. Its original object was not the protection of the labour force, but evening religious instruction, a circulating library, insurance to pay for funerals, a labour exchange to help the unemployed find work, funds to help the widows or orphans of workers, or sick workers, or those forced to go on strike. He founded for them a labour journal, *Voice of the Worker* (*La voce dell'operaio*). He was one of the founders of the Congress movement in Italy (see pp. 313–14) and studied the social theorists. He worked to raise the standards of the press and tried to make Catholic journalists more conscious of their mission. It was he who dared to publish the journal under the name *Christian Democracy* (*La democrazia cristiana*). To run a journal

---

[35] John Bosco was made a saint by Pope Pius XI in 1934.
[36] Statistics in *LTK* s.v. Salesianer.

with such a title in the age of Romolo Murri (see pp. 320–1) did not make him respectable in the eyes of the hierarchy. It was seventy years after his death before he was declared a saint by Pope Paul VI in 1970. His order never compared in number with the Salesians.[37]

THE NUNS

Nunneries, accustomed to being the homes of the less marriageable daughters of upper- or middle-class families, had required a certain standard of manners and education not to mention a dowry. The monastic world before the revolution was middle class or higher. It was still that, in part. But the doors were now open to a wider background because the need was there, and education was widening, and a house could train a simple peasant girl and turn her into an excellent nurse or schoolmistress. They had always done that, but in the nineteenth century they did it far more often.

Nuns were indispensable to work with the dying, the very old, or the very young. Hostile governments allowed loopholes in the law by which they could continue this work. Spain abolished nuns in theory but since the State could not care for the old, the orphans, or the sick without nuns, it quietly allowed them to continue. In Protestant countries they were effective and persuaded Protestants, for the first time since the Reformation, of the value of nuns.

Most of the recruits, until well into the twentieth century, went into the active orders, into education, hospitals, orphanages, missions, or retreats. This preference for the active over the contemplative lasted till the Second World War. Only after that convulsion did the trend change and then it was the contemplative orders which attracted novices more easily. The period after 1920 saw a rise in the number of novices which, judged in historical terms, was astonishing. Naturally the rise was accompanied by a large rise in the number of novices who did not persist to make a full profession. Various theories have been put forward to account for this rapid rise. Was there a time-lag between the greater number of educated women which schools now produced and the possibilities for female employment outside the nunnery? Or was it simply a religious fact, one aspect (like the otherwise inexplicable fame of St Thérèse of Lisieux)

[37] In 1974 there were 773 members. *DIP* s.v. S. Leonardo Murialdo and s.v. Congregazione di San Giuseppe.

of the felt contrast between the otherworldliness of the good life and the social circumstances of life in the 1920s and 1930s.

For the first time (except where there had been 'double monasteries', that is, male and female religious in adjacent buildings with the same chapel, and double monasteries were formally disapproved) the nuns experienced retirement in deep country. Most nuns of the nineteenth century were in geriatric wards, orphanages, or little schools, which were usually in or near towns. Before the nineteenth century they were almost always in towns because they were not safe in the countryside and because they could not get enough supplies. But in the nineteenth century the countryside was safe, and in the twentieth century it was safer than the towns. Therefore nunneries also were to be found retiring from towns to the quietness of a rural retreat.

The austere side of ultramontane spirituality, which could produce rigidity about practices in monasteries, had something of the same effect in traditional orders of nuns. Where they tried to follow a historic rule, they became more literal in its interpretation and harder in their refusal to concede to human weakness. Their rules of enclosure were enforced without the humane flexibilities of the eighteenth century. And while this could help an enclosed contemplative community, or a group seeking perpetual adoration, it could also make them very enclosed in mind, with little escape from narrowness. The austere regime over years exercised a pressure on nuns which generated psychological problems or personal difficulties in the community. The majority of nuns were less liable to these perils, partly because so many governments forced them to educate or nurse if they were to survive, partly because many of them wished to educate or nurse, whether forced or not, and treated the rules of enclosure flexibly, and partly because the growth in vocations to nunneries was often in new pastoral groups, who were not under a historic rule and had no need to conform to any rules except what their founders invented and their bishop or Rome approved. They were free to make their own understanding of austerity, except so far as they were affected by canon law.

There was a rub between the practices of nunneries in nursing and educating, and the rules laid down by the Council of Trent and the Counter-Reformation. This difficulty was not settled until after the Second World War.[38]

---

[38] Pius XII constitutions, 21 Dec. 1950 and 21 Mar. 1952; Paul VI, 6 Aug. 1966. Pius XII set up two grades of enclosure, greater and lesser, one suitable for contemplatives, the other for nuns engaged in a work in the world. Paul VI allowed freedom. Cf. *DIP* i. col. 1240.

Like the monks, nuns realized that the historic constitution of an abbot or abbess elected for life, which ancient rules usually expected, might not be the best constitution for a modern world. They replaced the old system with the election of an abbess or prioress who held office for a limited period, most often for three years at a time.

The troubles of the Church could bring agony even to very good nuns. Here is one example. The superior of the community of St Vincent de Paul in Bonn was a revered nun, Sister Augustine. She was a Lasaulx, of an eminent Rhineland family of Catholics. Her brother was a well-known professor of classics at Munich university and next to Döllinger was the important force in Lord Acton's higher education. She had been trained by the sisters as a dispenser and as a Mother Superior ran a hospital for the poor; and when Prussia fell into wars—in Schleswig-Holstein on the Danish border, against Austria on the Bohemian border—she went to the seat of the fighting and made field-stations for the wounded, for the enemy as well as the Prussian casualties; when the war against France came she was too old to serve at the front but worked in fifteen hospitals set up in Bonn; and the work was tough, treating the wounds of war and dying men.

Her piety was strong and dedicated but plain and austere; she loved the openness of St Francis de Sales and was not attracted to the new emotionalism of contemporary devotion. She loved Protestant hymns as vehicles of prayer and knew some of them by heart, and disliked the extravagant expressions sometimes used by writers like Faber. A Jesuit reproached her that there was no picture of the Sacred Heart hanging in her hospital. Her brother's connection with the university of Munich led her to admire Döllinger. When the Syllabus was published she thought that it condemned her in several clauses, though that hardly mattered. But when the Vatican Council voted for infallibility she knew that she could not accept the decree because she did not believe it, and the person whom she revered was Bishop Strossmayer ('Long live the Croats!'). For some months she was left alone. When excommunicated Old Catholics were dying and asked for the sacrament, she quietly arranged for it to be administered to them from the hospital chapel. She had no desire for schism, nor for the founding of a separate Church. She respected Protestant friends but thought their structure of faith too vague. She knew that she was a Catholic.

But in October 1871 the superior of the mother-house asked for her views on infallibility; and then tragedy ensued—on 7 November two superiors arrived at her bedside to say that she was deposed from her headship. They ordered her to leave the hospital—'we cannot keep a heretic in the order'. On reflection they allowed her to leave for a small neighbouring hospital at Vallendar; but the press discovered what was happening. As she lay dying the priest was banned from any ministry to her. A priest who was a student at Bonn secretly administered the last sacraments to her, and various visitors to her death-bed tried to persuade her to accept the faith of the Church. An excommunicated priest offered to bury her but the family refused, and the superior of Vallendar took the nun's robes from her body. They altered the time of the funeral to avoid a demonstration and there was no service at the grave except that the handful of mourners said the Lord's Prayer.[39]

THE MARIAVITES

The strangest of the failures occurred in Poland. The disaster happened because of the illegality of so many monasteries. After the Polish rebellion of 1863 the Russians suppressed most monks and nuns in Poland. A Capuchin named Honorat Kozminski founded secret religious communities of both sexes. But he could not persuade bishops to approve, for they risked being sent to Siberia if it was discovered.

One of his religious, Feliksa Kozlowska, he sent to minister to the sick in Warsaw. She was 8 months old when her father was killed as a guerrilla in the revolution of 1863. She wanted to be a Poor Clare and Kozminski gave her leave to start a community at Plock, 'the Sisters of the Poor Clares of the Perpetual Adoration and Reparation'. For a year she was alone. Then a few girls joined her to live a life of prayer and penitence. To Russian police they were a group of girls earning a living by sewing. The need for secrecy affected the future of the community. Five years later, in 1893, she had a vision in the chapel of the seminary at Plock. She was commanded by the vision to found a community which would take the Blessed Virgin as its model of life. Hence the sisters came to be called Mariaviti.

---

[39] Her life in Anon., *Sister Augustine*, Eng. trans. (1880), the English is fuller than the German original.

Because there were few other communities to meet the need for a place where men and women could fulfil such vocations, priests sent her recruits. There came to be a secret order across Poland, with Mother Felicia (as she came to be known) in a reputation for sanctity. The priests who came to visit her at Plock could say that they sought vestments from the workshop. The key figure was Kowalski, who, after three years as a priest was unsettled, and was advised to go to Mother Felicia; when he arrived he found a profound religious rapport and came to depend upon her. The group was very emotional; perhaps that also was due to the risk they ran.

With the numbers, secrecy was soon broken. They were ascetic, fasted much, wore slightly different clothes, were self-sacrificial in pastoral work, knelt in adoration night and day, and encouraged the laity to frequent communion. A parish priest in Plock attacked Mother Felicia from the pulpit, and this was how she first became known.

It seemed necessary to get the approval of Rome. In 1903 Mother Felicia and fifteen priests went to Rome. While they waited for the election of the new pope, they chose Father Kowalski of Warsaw as their superior. Pius X received them kindly. They elicited all Rome's feelings of protection for confessors in persecuted Poland. He blessed them, and passed their petition to a commission.

Back in Poland the new order said that it had the blessing of the pope. But then the bishop of Plock ordered Mother Felicia to give an account of her visions, and banned her from directing the souls of priests. When he was told about the visions he thought them illusions. In the following year Rome dissolved the order, and banned its members from having anything to do with Mother Felicia, and said that her visions were hallucinations, and subjected all her order to the bishops. Some priests left the order, but others took little notice of these decrees, and the people revered Mother Felicia and her community. She and some of the Mariaviti refused to obey the bishops. A new religious order moved into a schism.

The Roman Inquisition excommunicated Mother Felicia and twelve of her priests and gave twenty others twenty days to submit, which they did not. In many parishes the people backed the Mariavites. There were bloody fights in villages for the possession of the church—at Leszno near Warsaw six were killed, and twenty-seven wounded. When the local authorities ruled that the Mariavites had no rights to the churches, they built their own. In Russian-occupied Poland, they had about 120,000 followers. In 1906 the Russian government made the schism a legal sect. They built churches, had a chief monastic community at Plock, founded schools and hospitals, and created sixty-three parishes. Their drawing power increased greatly when they adopted Polish instead of Latin as the language of worship.

In 1909 Father Kowalski the superior attended the conference of Old Catholics at Vienna and asked to be consecrated bishop. He became an archbishop and head of 'the Old Catholic Church of the Mariavites in Poland'. He accepted clerical marriage. In 1914 he was able to open a great new church ('temple') in Plock.

In 1921 Mother Felicia died and the leadership passed to Archbishop Kowalski, with disastrous results. He encouraged mystical (non-sexual) marriages between monks and nuns. The babies born from these marriages were taken away from their parents to be brought up strictly as the seed of a new and godly community. The Polish people could not endure the marriage of the clergy. Whole parishes returned to the Roman Church.

In 1929 Kowalski ordained nuns to be priests and one nun to be a bishop. Normally they concelebrated the eucharist with male priests so that the faithful should have no doubt of the validity of the sacrament. This meant that the Old Catholic Church was no longer willing to accept the Mariavites as a true part of itself. Short of priests, Kowalski allowed laity to celebrate a simplified liturgy of the sacrament in private houses. He rescinded the duty to go to private confession at least once a year. Then the Mariavites forced Kowalski to resign. They abolished women priests and women bishops and mystical marriages, but not clerical marriage. Nevertheless they continued to prefer priests to be celibate.[40]

The Mariavites were the biggest single disaster generated by the conflict between the age with its State repression of monks and the revival of the monastic ideal among a people growing educated and aware. The disaster was helped by Russian repression in Poland and the inability of Rome to exercise discipline over a new order; by the growing awareness among the Poles of their nationality, and of

[40] In 1978 they had about 23,000 members and some eighty nuns. A small group of some 3,000 remained faithful to Kowalski's ideas and went on ordaining women as priests and revering Mother Felicia. Kowalski retired to a Mariavite convent not far from Plock and was joined there by women priests and bishops. When Hitler seized Poland the Nazis put Kowalski into the concentration camp at Dachau where he died.

the place of religion in that nationality; and eventually by the rise in the number of educated women who were no longer content with their historic roles within the Church.[41]

[41] Excellent article on the Mariavites in *DIP* v. cols. 987 ff.; with literature: J. Peterkiewicz, *The Third Adam* (London, 1975); *ASS* 39 (1906), 129; 40 (1907), 69. The Mariavites should not be confused with the Mariavite Sisters founded at Vilna in 1737 with the principal aim of converting the Jews. Later, to avoid suppression by the Russians, they turned to nursing. Nevertheless they failed to survive successive Russian onslaughts on Polish religious communities during the 19th century.

13

CATHOLIC UNIVERSITIES

In the pre-revolutionary world the religious orders had much influence in the universities. One of them, usually the Jesuits, provided the professors for the theological faculty, sometimes for other faculties, most commonly philosophy. In the world after the revolutions the State took over the universities and showed much reluctance to allow private universities, which in any case were difficult to found because of shortage of the former endowments. It could only be done under liberal social conditions or through loopholes in antiliberal conditions. Cardinal Manning tried to found a Catholic university college at Kensington in London, but it soon collapsed. Newman was brought over to Ireland in 1852 to be the first head of a Catholic university of Dublin, but only during the twentieth century can it be said to have flourished.

The most successful of the Catholic universities was historic Louvain in Belgium. It was founded in the age of Burgundian prosperity in the fifteenth century, with a college system and close association with Oxford and Cambridge, and made its academic name as a scholarly opponent of the Reformation. During the eighteenth century it was as miserable as most universities, but helped the Gallican tradition, and then the French revolutionaries abolished it. After the Battle of Waterloo the king of Holland refounded it as a State university, towards which the Catholics of Belgium felt suspicion or worse. When Belgium rebelled and became independent of Holland, the State university was closed and Louvain was refounded in 1835 as a Catholic private (non-State) university. The founders argued with each other on whether the approval of the pope must be asked. There had never yet been a Catholic university founded without papal sanction; but if they asked the approval of Gregory XVI, the act would cause Belgian liberals antipathy to the new foundation. They asked, and were promptly given what they wanted.

What the Belgian bishops did was welcome to the pope. They were worried that the first head of the university had no doctorate and did not hesitate to get him a doctor's title from Rome. The university was to be under the control of the bishops, who appointed professors on the nomination of the rector. To achieve what they wanted, they needed to concede the abolition of theology from the State universities. Louvain started small in numbers but grew steadily, and by 1900 was the largest and most important university in Belgium.

The condemnation of Lamennais, who was so influential upon the new Belgian constitution, produced a crisis in Belgium and not least at Louvain. Would it be possible to find worthy professors who were not disciples of Lamennais? They had the idea of calling it the Free Catholic University, which was what it was, but the bull *Singulari nos* against Lamennais made them drop the word 'Free' from the title, it was better at that moment not to talk loudly about freedom. During part of the nineteenth century the university was suspect to educational authorities in Rome; until Pope Leo XIII, who knew it well because he had served as nuncio in Belgium, gave it encouragement. Louvain provided the best higher education in Belgium. The pope pushed the bishops to found a chair of Thomist philosophy, and this apparently retrograde plan was turned into an important intellectual movement by the first professor, Mercier, afterwards to be the most famous of Belgians in the twentieth century.

The university blessed the church historians by founding in 1900 the *Revue d'histoire ecclésiastique*. One of its founders was Ladeuze, the scholar who as rector did most to recover the university after the German occupation of the First World War, which saw the accidental military destruction of the great library by fire, with the loss of 300,000 books and many irreplaceable manuscripts. His effort to recreate a great library ended when it was burnt down anew in the fight of 1940—its tower was wrongly suspected of being used by snipers. The remainder of the old university was destroyed by British bombs, which mistook their target, in 1944. Ladeuze was the first to order that some lectures be delivered in Flemish and not in French. The racial or linguistic conflict within Belgium during the 1960s forced the division of the historic university into two universities according to the medium of instruction; a dismal decision, not only for Belgium.[1]

[1] For the history of Louvain, from its foundation under Gregory XVI, R. Mathes, *Löwen und Rom* (Essen, 1975); for its later history, R Aubert, *et al.*, *The University of Louvain, 1425–1975* (Louvain, 1976).

Germany did not need a Catholic university because (with Austria-Hungary) it was the country in Europe where Catholic faculties of theology were still in State universities. The French Revolution abolished the old universities of Trier, Cologne, Mainz, and Strasbourg; and the abolition of the Jesuits had meant the fall of the Bavarian university of Ingolstadt. In 1815 there was not a single Catholic faculty of theology in Western Germany. Since the university of Basle went Protestant in the Reformation, there was not one Catholic faculty of theology in Switzerland.

It was Protestant Prussia which came to the rescue. It had a model to follow. When Frederick the Great conquered Silesia, he found a Jesuit university at Breslau. He reorganized it, gave it better endowments from dissolved Silesian monasteries, and from the same source a fine library, and two faculties of theology, one Protestant and the other Catholic.

Therefore when Prussia by the treaty of Vienna acquired the Rhineland they could follow the Breslau model. They founded the university of Bonn, with two theological faculties. The strife between the faculties was not comfortable, nor was the strife between ultramontanes and others in the Catholic faculty. But both faculties attracted eminent scholars. It was more important than Breslau because that remained rather local and educated mostly Silesians, whereas Bonn drew students from all Germany and beyond.

The same pattern was followed by the Protestant kingdom of Württemberg which had acquired many Catholics among the Suabian mountains. The government created for its historic Protestant university at Tübingen a Catholic theological faculty which within a few years became the leader of Catholic thought in Germany by its courageous restatements of historical theology and the willingness to face up to the radical enquiries of contemporary Protestant theologians.

Bavaria was in the opposite situation in that it was a Catholic State which had acquired many Protestants. Its old Jesuit university at Ingolstadt had been wrecked by the abolition of the Jesuits. The government took the remains and reopened it at Munich, where Döllinger began to teach in 1826.

The bishopric of Würzburg had a Jesuit university from the Counter-Reformation and despite or because of the disappearance of the Jesuits it was the best Catholic university of Germany during the later eighteenth century. After the revolution it was part of Bavaria, had two faculties of theology, and prospered.

Hessen-Darmstadt tried to follow the Prussian example by opening, in 1831, a Catholic theological faculty in its university of Giessen; but it was a feeble affair, and lasted only twenty-one years because its new bishop, Ketteler of Mainz, preferred his ordinands to be trained in a seminary.

Erasmus had taught at Freiburg im Breisgau and later its theology was Jesuit. It almost disappeared in the revolution but the Protestant ruler of Baden wanted to retain it and helped with money. It was not much of a place until after the Vatican Council, when Franz Xaver Kraus was given a chair and changed the face of Christian archaeology.[2]

The other Fribourg (Freiburg) in Switzerland was more modern. Swiss Catholics were not university-minded. The shock came when the Old Catholics were given a State theological faculty at the university of Berne; for it was certainly disturbing that the Old Catholics should possess a State faculty while Roman Catholics did not. In 1889 the canton of Fribourg used State money to open a university with a theological faculty. But it was a dim business until after the First World War, for it could not compete with the German universities which were its natural world.

The university of Vienna had most drawing-power of all the Catholic universities in German-speaking lands and this continued despite the abolition of the Jesuits, who had been given the theological faculty during the Counter-Reformation. Until as late as 1873 the rector and the dean had to be Catholics. Austrian Protestants kept trying to found a Protestant faculty of theology in the university but without success until after the First World War and the coming of republican Austria.

The university of Innsbruck was founded when the Tyrol was specially important in the age after the Thirty Years War. Short of State money, it needed the religious orders with their resources, and from the first the Jesuits taught philosophy, theology, and several other subjects. Then in the eighteenth century Vienna regarded it as a backwater, and thought everything was too theological, and wanted the university to beget civil servants. The pope pushed this process further by abolishing the Jesuits; and the Emperor Joseph II pushed it still further by abolishing it as a university and turning it into a school for training civil servants. The university was not fully restored till

---

[2] For a long debate on how to create a 'free university' in Catholic Germany, see H. J. Brandt, *Einer Katholische Universität in Deutschland?*, Bonner Beiträge zur Kirchengeschichte, 12 (Cologne, 1981).

1826, but it was a miserable place of learning. In the age of the Concordat and Cardinal Rauscher the restored Jesuits were put back to run the theological faculty. In the reactions against the Concordat and the Vatican Council liberals tried to abolish theology, but they achieved only that the professors need not be Jesuits—but some professors went on being Jesuits; and in the 1880s the now conservative State went on pressing it to be more Catholic. The symbol of this was the pushing into Innsbruck's chair of 'universal history' in 1882 Ludwig Pastor, who was writing an enormous (and still valuable) history of the popes wherein he made no secret of his papalist convictions. He had the merit that he was one of those who persuaded Leo XIII to open the Vatican Archives to research. But it became as difficult as ever for this university, which was evidently within the German network, to win repute as an equal of other German universities.

The Austro-Hungarian empire had other universities in its non-German lands. Prague was historic and its theological faculty had been Franciscan; Cracow in Galicia was historic, and Lemberg/Lvov had an old Jesuit university from the age of the Counter-Reformation. All these had difficulties; Cracow was miserable in the eighteenth century, even before the partitions of Poland, and not until Austrian action in its favour in 1870 was it recreated. Prague was disturbed by the conflict between the two races which was settled only in 1882 when it became two universities and afterwards acquired two theological faculties; the two Polish universities because despite their fame they were very important to the maintenance of the Polish nation and because they taught in Polish it meant that they did not attract students from elsewhere.

In Hungary there was a Jesuit college at Buda which, when the Jesuits were abolished, was turned into a university. After the ending of the Concordat the government founded a university for the Romanians at Cluj and another, with the aid of Bishop Strossmayer, for the Croats at Zagreb. But most who wished to study theology headed for Vienna.

Thus Germany and the Austrian empire were the lands, still, of State Catholic faculties of theology; and in the *Kulturkampf* Falk made a university degree necessary for a future priest. But most priests all over Europe were trained in seminaries. The standard of seminaries was so uneven and could be so deplorable that good Catholic bishops, especially in France, still tried for universities. Such universities were founded in France during the 1870s, at Paris, Lyons, Toulouse, Lille, and Angers; their aim being to supply teachers in Catholic schools. A degree-giving university that was not the State's was impossible in France. These colleges were forced by government to stop using the description 'university'. An anticlerical law of 1880 forbad any private institution to call itself a university and this compelled them to change the name to Institut Catholique. The Institut Catholique in Paris nevertheless became a famous place of research, serving such as Duchesne the historian, Loisy the critic of the New Testament texts, Gasparri the canonist, and Maritain the philosopher. None of these famous names of the Institut Catholique in Paris was a monk or a friar.

In the United States private universities were easily founded but at first were little places. The foundation of the Catholic university of Washington in the United States in 1887 caused others to try to copy it, but they did not succeed until after the First World War.[3]

In Italy were historic universities of Europe, headed by Bologna, Padua the daughter of Bologna, and Naples; and then by the Jesuit Roman College. The new Italian State made sure that after 1870 they could not properly be called Catholic universities. It seemed necessary to the popes to have a university in Rome. Their place of higher learning had been the Collegio Romano founded by Ignatius Loyola. The Italian government took its buildings in 1874 and what was left of it moved to the old German College in the Palazzo Borromeo. As the Gregorian university it was a form of private college unless the Law of Guarantees were regarded as empowering the pope to organize a university. But it took some thirty years before the Gregorian adapted to the new conditions of being a university. The name 'uni-

---

[3] e.g. Milan for Italy in 1921 and Nijmegen for Holland in 1923. The university of Milan was helped by gaining state recognition in 1924 (once the Fascists came to power) but its first rector, and rector for life, was the most unusual head of a Catholic university, the Franciscan Edoardo Gemelli. He was the child of middle-class anticlericals and son of a Freemason. He started life as a Socialist propagandist in North Italy, and all his life retained Marxist ideas about social justice. He was converted, in some unknown way, while he did military service. He was a leading member of Luigi Sturzo's Italian People's Party and was not an obvious choice to be rector of a new Catholic university. He ruled the university like a dictator, a mode of government which did not attract professors. But during the Fascist regime he helped the university by being close enough to the Vatican to be able to resist Fascist demands from time to time. See *DHGE* s.v. Gemelli. The most interesting of all the Catholic universities of Europe after Louvain was Lublin, founded in newly independent Poland in 1918. Lublin was strange because it was a semi-private Catholic university in a country where there existed State universities which were Catholic.

versity' was special because nothing was taught there but theology and its kindred subjects.

The work of the Catholic faculties was hampered in the early years, not only by shortage of money, but by the antimodernist reaction, which made it hard to find teachers adequate to a university.[4]

All this was very unlike the Middle Ages when universities dominated the religious thought of the Middle Ages. Excellent work was done in some of the newer faculties; but unlike the rest of human knowledge the best of Christian scholarship might still be found in monasteries. There were now two broad theological traditions in Catholicism—the pope's men in Rome, inheriting the old Thomist tradition of thought, and the German theological faculties who faced Protestant critics in the same university and sometimes the same library. In the nineteenth century this difference produced conflict; in the twentieth century it might still generate war but could also be fruitful in the development of Christian thinking.

Jacques Paul Migne was a priest who fell into trouble with his bishop over liberal attitudes during the French Revolution of 1830. He turned to ecclesiastical journalism and was even one of the founders of the *Univers*, but no newspaper prospered while he was in its management. In 1836 he started publishing a library for clergymen. He invented his own publishing firm and used cheap scholarly labour such as priests in trouble with their bishop and not able to find employment. The *Patrologia latina*—the name was inaccurate because he printed texts not only of all the Fathers but every text he could find into the High Middle Ages—in 221 volumes, then the *Patrologia graeca* in 161 volumes, took him twenty-four years to produce. No great scholar himself, he used a real scholar, the Benedictine Pitra, to make sure of his standards, and he took endless trouble to see that the texts which he printed from earlier editions were correct. Thus this was not an edition based on new manuscripts but an attempt to put together the best editions then existing. It had an influence momentous in itself and all the more so because designed and created by a clergyman who was slightly disreputable in the eyes of the Church and was not himself a person of deep learning or even of wide education, and who began with no capital at his command. Everyone ran

---

[4] In Germany this difficulty was much increased by the division caused by the Vatican Council. For Bonn, the most hit, see A. Franzen, *Die Katholisch-Theologische Facultät Bonn im Streit um das Erste Vatikanische Konzil*, Bonner Beiträge zur Kirchengeschichte, 6 (Cologne, 1974).

him down personally, everyone used his work and profited by it. The history of medieval Europe and of the early Church became far more accessible at just the time when the universities produced early Christian and medieval scholars who needed such easy access. To this day the series is much used. In 1868 a fire destroyed all his printing works and the stock. His methods to restart the venture caused worse trouble with the archbishop. This not holy man did more academic good than any other French priest of the century.

THE IDEA OF REUNION

The mood of the nineteenth century ensured that this is a short chapter.

Leo XIII's idea of reunion between the Churches was still based on the axiom that the only way was for other Churches to submit to the authority of the see of Rome. His language might be diplomatic or courteous but his thought remained set in the old ways. The glaring example of the conflict between manner and matter came in 1896 in the bull *Apostolicae curae*, which condemned the validity of Anglican orders.[1] This was a strange affair because though it began with the unpractical idealism of the Anglo-Catholic Lord Halifax and his French liberal-Catholic friend Abbé Portal, it was encouraged by a vague intention on the part of the Pope to achieve better relations with the Anglicans; and by Cardinal Rampolla who had the same charitable idea and seems to have been persuaded before the event that the evidence pointed to the validity of Anglican orders. On the Anglican side Lord Halifax cared much about reunion with Rome and believed that a recognition of Anglican orders would help, and knew that modern historical study pointed to the validity of the orders in Roman terms. The best historical mind in Rome, Louis Duchesne, was of this opinion. But some English Roman Catholics were not, their Cardinal Vaughan was not, the Roman tradition of thought was not, and the Roman theologians did not easily welcome new evidence; so the Pope who set out to be friendly with the Anglicans achieved a condemnation which hurt relations between Rome and Canterbury more than any act of the pope since Dr Wiseman's letter about the new hierarchy. The bull was a supreme instance of a self-contradictory policy in Rome. It was a sign that the Pope himself was ageing. In 1896 he was 86 years old.

With the Lutherans Pius X had a disaster equal to that of Leo XIII with the Anglicans, and equally unintentional in its origins. Charles Borromeo, the archbishop of Milan, was looked upon as a saint by

[1] *ASS* 29 (1896), 193–203: 1 Sept. 1896.

the Counter-Reformation and set a standard in pastoral care by bishops. In 1610, only twenty-six years after his death, he was declared to be a saint. Therefore the third century of his canonization came in the time of Pius X. On 29 May 1910 the Pope issued an encyclical which held Borromeo up as a model of pastoral zeal. He meant to speak to the Italians and issued it in Italian as well as Latin. But he took the opportunity not only to praise Borromeo but to denounce modernism. The chief drafter was the Spanish cardinal Vives y Tutó. But Monsignor Benigni, hammer of the modernists, took a hand and pushed into the wording of the bull about Charles Borromeo quotations on Luther and the Reformers. He called them enemies of Christ's cross, and said that their belly was their god, and they were men of carnal mind and seducers of the people. The texts were of obsolete controversy of 200 years before. Since the encyclical, being about an archbishop of Milan, was intended for Italy, no one in Rome thought of the effect in Germany.

These phrases soured relations with the Lutherans as Leo XIII's efforts damaged amity with the Anglicans; and worse, for this time there were discussions in the Parliaments of Prussia, Hessen, Bavaria, and Saxony, talk of 'the smearing of the German nation by a foreign priest', protests in pulpits and press articles, and official representations in Rome from the governments of Prussia and Saxony.

Neither Pius X nor his Secretary of State were pleased at the wording which the drafters had put into the pope's mouth. Merry del Val said he first heard of the encyclical when it appeared in the *Osservatore Romano*. The Pope told the German bishops not to publish it. Merry del Val gave the Prussian ambassador a note—that the pope is sorry that he has been misunderstood and that he has much sympathy for all the German nation. This ended the controversy; though some Protestant journalists were glad because, so they claimed, this was the first time that a pope publicly recanted one of his formal acts.

For the difficulty that the first Vatican Council wrought was illustrated here. The decree of the Council that popes, in formal utterance, can never be mistaken, seemed like a great promulgation of authority. But in truth Pius IX trammelled the freedom of his successors. In the past, for the good of the Church in changed circumstances, popes had always needed from time to time to do what one of their predecessors condemned in a different time, with different crises, and with different ethical axioms. A freedom to amend the past was a necessary part of papal authority and was inherent in the relation of the pope's office both to Church and world. The popes of the twentieth century must be as able to amend the past as the popes of the eighteenth. A whole area of ethical questions in family life, from contraception to divorce, was about to come up which could not be settled by saying that it was settled long ago. Pius IX had made such necessary amendment more awkward for his successors.

In the year of the Borromeo encyclical was held the conference at Edinburgh which historians take to mark the start of the ecumenical movement. The encyclical of that year was an old-fashioned piece of anti-ecumenical literature.[2]

For centuries popes wanted happier relations with the Orthodox Churches of the East and never gave up the hope that one day the schism between East and West might be ended; since both Churches still shared so much of a common Catholicism. Pius IX, looking forward to his Vatican Council, addressed to the Orthodox bishops of the East a letter pleading with them to return to unity with and under the see of Rome. Both the language, and the way policy in the East was formulated, were not calculated to persuade Eastern bishops and patriarchs.

Leo XIII, as so often, was more open and diplomatic but hardly more persuasive. His public utterances kept coming back to the possibility of union with the East. The Ottoman empire was breaking up and what would happen to the Christian bodies which were its subject populations in the Balkans and the Middle East? This pope felt an urgency which his predecessors never felt.

He made a concession, only in ritual but still important. When the pope appointed titular bishops, he chose the titles of ancient vanished sees from the ancient world, which was the modern Greek and Turkish world. These bishops were therefore known as sees *in partibus infidelium*—the bishops of 'sees now in the hands of the infidels', and so able to be seconded for work as suffragans or administrators in Western Europe. The Orthodox bishops regarded it as an insult to their Church that their territories should be regarded as infidel. Several of the Greek former sees were now under a Greek government which was not Muslim. The Greek government asked that these words, *in partibus infidelium* be not used. Leo XIII agreed in 1882, and the former bishops *in partibus* became 'titular bishops'. It

---

[2] *Editae saepe*, *AAS* 2 (1910), 357–80; account of the controversy in K. Bachem, *Vorgeschichte, Geschichte und Politik der deutschen Zentrumspartei* (Cologne, 1927–32), vii. 329 ff.

did not help the Greek bishops much because they resented Latin sees in the country as a schismatic act.

Another act of courtesy, still more important, was to stop calling the Easterner heretics or schismatics and start calling them 'those who dissent' or still better, 'brothers who are separate'.

Leo XIII tried to use the Uniat Churches of the East, with their married clergy and their Slavonic or Byzantine rites but their union with Rome, as a model for the Eastern Orthodox Church. He abandoned the centralizing policy of Latinizing the Uniat Churches and now wanted their historic liturgies preserved. He caused the Byzantine rite[3] to be used at the Greek abbey of Grottaferrata near Rome. He gave large sums of money to Uniat seminaries and schools all over the Middle East. Some of these schools failed to work well because they met hostility from the local people. This did very little for union with the Eastern Orthodox but a lot for Uniat Christians who no longer felt that Rome regarded them as second-class Catholics.

It was a case of the Pope wanting something and the Curia being unwilling to carry it out. The staff in Rome suspected his friendly words towards the Eastern Churches. Religious orders which were engaged in trying to Latinize Uniat Churches went on with their endeavours whatever the Pope said. Nor was Leo XIII naïve enough to expect reunion in his lifetime. Nevertheless the atmosphere between the Churches was less grim when he died than when he was elected.

The Balkan peoples, subject to the Ottomans but evidently soon breaking loose from the control of Islam, were Slavs and mostly Orthodox. There in Croatia and with duties in Serbia was a great Catholic bishop, Strossmayer. The Vatican Council prevented Pius IX from having any but a low opinion of Strossmayer. But Leo XIII could see that he was a key in the Balkan predicament, a Catholic

---

[3] The Uniats used rites as follows: (1) the Byzantine rite, otherwise called the Greek rite, in several different editions; Uniats in Russia, Ruthenia, Hungary, Serbia, and Bulgaria; then in Greece and in Syria, and among a few of the Armenian Catholics in Georgia, until it was banned by the tsarist Russian government; and at Grottaferrata; (2) the Hungarian rite, in effect a version of the Byzantine rite in Hungarian, used by some but only some of the Hungarian Uniats and not quite liked by Rome; (3) the Alexandrian rite, used by the few thousand Uniats in Egypt, and by the fewer thousands in Ethiopia; (4) the Antiochene rite, used by the Maronites in Lebanon; (5) the Chaldean rite, used by Uniat Nestorians in Mesopotamia and by their kindred congregations in South India; (6) the Armenian rite, used by a majority of the Uniat Armenians, but there were few because, like the rest of the Armenian peoples so many of them were murdered.

Slav who was respected by Uniats and by some of the Orthodox. Only three years after Leo XIII became pope, Strossmayer led to Rome a very numerous pilgrimage of Slavs, to whom Leo XIII spoke of the destiny of the Slav races to power and of what they could give to faith. Strossmayer believed that a much wider concession of the Glagolitic forms of service, at least to all Croatia and possibly to Slav peoples under Ottoman rule, would much help the Slavs towards reunion. He had the vision of a Yugoslav Church accepting the supremacy of the see of Rome. The vision was too remote for the Curia. It refused to allow Glagolitic except in a small area round Split and Zara where they were used to it.

In 1886 a devout Russian Orthodox, Soloviev, who cared about reunion from the Orthodox viewpoint, travelled to Croatia to learn from Strossmayer. He was unusual for a Russian: he had come through atheism, had read Renan, Schopenhauer, and Hegel, had studied mysticism, and had lectured on the incarnation in St Petersburg to an audience which included Dostoevsky, who was a friend, and Tolstoy. Then he was forced out of teaching because he publicly asked the government to grant mercy to the assassins of Tsar Alexander II. Slowly he became convinced that the Orthodox Church, while remaining what it was, should rightly accept the primacy of the pope. This was when, still only 35, he went to stay with Strossmayer. Afterwards he visited Paris and then published his belief that it would be right for the Russian Church to be fully a member of the universal Church by accepting the primacy of Rome. 'It is a lovely idea' said Leo XIII, 'but it needs a miracle to bring about.'[4] His book made him very unpopular in Moscow. In 1896 he formally became a Roman Catholic but died near Moscow at the age of only 47, receiving the sacrament from a Russian Orthodox priest and evidently believing that Orthodoxy and Catholicism, whatever the hierarchs said, were in communion.

In 1889 Russia celebrated the ninth century of the baptism of St Vladimir and the conversion of Russia to Christianity. Strossmayer shocked the Austrian government, and the Emperor Francis Joseph, who never forgave him, by sending a telegram of congratulation to the celebrations. The Vatican was not pleased.

This work with the Orthodox East produced some first-class scholarship. In 1897 the French Assumptionist Father Louis Petit

---

[4] J. Hajjar, *Le Vatican, la France et le catholicisme oriental (1878–1914)* (Paris, 1979), 99.

started at Istanbul a review of Byzantine history and the Orthodox Churches; at first called *Échos d'Orient*. He was the first modern to journey to Greece to make a serious catalogue of the Christian inscriptions on Mount Athos and the charters of Greek monasteries. He finished his active work by becoming Latin archbishop of Athens (not a popular office in Athens) but that did not stop him continuing with a range of scholarly work.[5]

Pius X did not go back on the policy of support for the Uniats of the East. He also wanted to revive their life, encourage their Eastern liturgies, foster their national traditions, and abandon the Latinizing endeavour.

The attitude was still that of Leo XIII: to respect the Catholicity within Eastern Orthodoxy; to use the Uniat Churches as the way of showing how it was possible for those of an Eastern rite to be Roman Catholic; therefore to try to create in Western Catholicism less suspicion of the Uniats; to give a better grounding for clergy sent out to work among Uniat areas; and to encourage the study of the history, doctrine, and liturgy of the Eastern tradition; to do what could be done to help and recognize its leaders, especially (after Strossmayer's death in 1905) Archbishop Szepticky of Lvov;[6] and all this against opposition from Latinizing clergy in the Balkans and the Levant, who thought the Uniat rites a compromise and the marriage of clergy to be deplored.

In Italy a monastery which survived the dissolutions because it was a national monument had something to contribute. Grottaferrata was not far from Rome, built upon a wealthy ancient Roman villa, perhaps Cicero's Tusculum. It was a monastery for Greek monks from about 1000 AD or earlier. It became the centre for the numerous Basilian monks of South Italy, with a Greek rite. The Western

[5] His journal later became the *Revue des études byzantines*; it moved to Bucharest in 1937 and to Paris in 1946. Partly as a result of his work Benedict XV created higher organs in Rome for the purpose of reunion with the Eastern Orthodox Church; in the Curia a Congregation for the Oriental Church, which had the Uniat Churches as its main responsibility; and the Pontifical Institute of Oriental Studies which was to dedicate itself to a fundamental study of the Eastern Churches and to train men who would work in the field of Christian unification. An encyclical of 1920 made the early Syrian Father St Ephraem of Edessa, whom the Syriac tradition of Christianity held to be its teacher, into a Doctor of the Church.

[6] Szepticky (various Western spellings of the name), the most famous Uniat of the 20th cent., was already a Basilian monk in 1888 and became the Uniat archbishop of Lemberg (Lvov) under Pope Leo XIII and thereafter spent his stalwart life in defending Uniats from oppression, first by Russians, then by Poles, and finally by Nazis.

Middle Ages called all Greek monks Basilians because they thought that their rule was derived from St Basil of Caesarea. In South Italy there had been many Greek speakers from Roman times; and then in the seventeenth century Greeks or Albanians fleeing from the Ottoman rule in the Balkans came to South Italy or Sicily. Hence the name Basilian came to mean a monk who is a Roman Catholic but uses an Eastern rather than the Latin liturgy. An abbot was called by the Greek word *hegumen*.

The abbey of Grottaferrata, nearest to Rome, became rich, and so a monastery *in commendam* which paid the stipend of a cardinal. In the Counter-Reformation Pope Gregory XIII united all the Greek monks of Italy and Sicily in a congregation of Basilian monks of Italy, with an abbot-general who lived in Rome. The community grew more Latin and less Greek, and from time to time popes resisted demands that the Greek liturgy be allowed to vanish. The Napoleonic Revolution destroyed the community at Grottaferrata. But some monks were back soon after the restoration. From 1834 onwards it was ruled by a prior dependent directly upon Rome. It had dependencies in Spain but these disappeared in the Spanish dissolutions.

The Italian dissolution of the 1870s preserved it as a national monument and allowed its few monks to be the custodians. Here it became the nucleus of a revived community of Basilians. An able young abbot consciously went out to attract the Albanians of South Italy and Sicily to the house.[7]

Into this unpromising and yet attractive world of relations between Rome and Eastern Orthodoxy, came a very unusual Western priest. Max of Saxony was the son of the Catholic king of Saxony. All Saxony had followed Luther and the people were still Lutheran. But in 1697 King Augustus the Strong was a convert to the Catholic Church and the royal family remained Catholic. The Napoleonic wars gave equality to the two denominations but the Catholics were still a small minority; until the growth of industry drew in workers from Bavarian families.

---

[7] Pius XI with his interest in the Greeks gave it a more independent status, with its *hegumen* now called archimandrite. It again had communities in Sicily and southern Italy, and two missions in Albania, which were destroyed by the Communist regime at the end of the Second World War. Such a community in ecumenical times regarded as its principal work the return of unity between the Church of Rome and the Eastern Orthodox Church. At first it was very ineffective. But that was because neither the Catholic nor the Orthodox world was yet ecumenical. For Pius XI, *AAS* 30 (1938), 183 ff.; *DIP* i. col. 1081; iv. cols. 1444–8.

Since Max was the son of a king, the press was full of it when they heard that he was preparing for Catholic ordination, and when he became a priest in 1896. He was soon a professor of liturgical studies at the new university of Fribourg in Switzerland. He was fascinated by Eastern Orthodoxy and its way of worship. Every year he went to Palestine, Syria, Constantinople, Russia, or Mount Athos, and became a friend of many of the leaders of Orthodoxy. For four years he taught in his vacations at the Uniat seminary of Lemberg (Lvov) and was a friend of Archbishop Szepticky.

In November 1910 he published an article in a new periodical edited at the abbey of Grottaferrata, *Roma e l'Oriente*. It was very powerful, with its burden that the Catholic Church ought to unite with the East and should recognize the Orthodox as equals. The two could agree on the ecumenical Councils of the first thousand years of Christian history, and the Roman primary should not be pressed upon the Orthodox. They should be allowed to go their own way over purgatory, the consecration rite in the eucharist, and the manner and time of the sacrament of confirmation. How this could help the Churches and the world!

The Curia was disturbed. Amid much publicity the Pope condemned the article. He said that it had many errors in theology and in history: the article said that all the ecumenical Councils from the eighth to the Vatican Council could be dropped. It said that the *filioque* in the creed did not come from Scripture. It doubted whether purgatory or the Immaculate Conception were taught by the early Christians. It thought that during the first four centuries the Church was not a monarchy. It thought that confirmation by a priest can be valid, and that it is possible to allow that the consecration at the mass comes by the invocation of the Holy Spirit rather than by the words of institution at the Last Supper. It attacked the popes of the eleventh century, when the schism of East and West was commonly thought to happen, for arrogance and ambition. It said that the crusades, which were holy wars, were burglary.

Prince Max did not persist. He accepted what the pope declared, withdrew for the time from his teaching at Fribourg and kept his own opinion.[8] After teaching at Cologne he became an army chaplain in the First World War. But outspoken remarks about the army command caused him to be shut up in a castle and he only got out in

---

[8] Condemnation, *AAS* 3 (1911), 118; See *NDB* s.v. and literature.

1918. Then, refusing to be a personal chaplain to the Pope, he went back to Fribourg—though to the philosophical faculty because they dared not have him back in theology—and stayed there for the rest of his long life, till he died in 1951; chaplain to prisoners, revered for his love to humanity, and affected by the Eastern devotional ideal of 'the fool for Christ's sake'.

I 5

SAINTS IN THE MODERN WORLD

The religious ideal appeared in many forms. If any one articulate teacher is studied, nothing typical can be found. But confessors and directors of souls move in a world of what is expected, and use language which minds find creative or inspiring. To look at one such teacher should disclose more than knowledge of an individual. No one ever suggested that Bishop Dupanloup ought to be declared a saint. No bishop used fiercer language in his pamphlets. But to look at his devotion will show one type of expectation common in that generation.

He was famous as a director of souls. He never tired of the work. He was eager in his reading of classics of spirituality, and possessed an excellent memory that could easily quote from them, in Latin or French. His favourite readings were classics of the French tradition—especially Fénelon and Bossuet, from both of whom he could quote many passages, Francis de Sales, Chantal, and Vincent de Paul. Another favourite group was from the Counter-Reformation, very different in tone from the French, above all Theresa of Avila but also Charles Borromeo, and in this realm the anti-Jansenist moralist Alfonso Ligouri. Still a third group comprised the French contemporaries round Lacordaire—Madame Swetchine, and his friend Montalembert's romantic *Monks of the West*, and Lacordaire's letters. He read none of the Jesuits, nor the Easterners, nor the Latin Fathers, nor the schoolmen, nor any of the Protestants, nor John of the Cross. He knew the Bible well, best through passages in the breviary and the liturgy. He made two retreats each year, and visited the reserved sacrament several times a day if he could. He celebrated mass every day and those who were present felt the devotion of the celebrant. He loved the rosary. Meanwhile he poured out into his private prayers, into his sermons, or into notes on his meditations, many words, too many words, fervent with too burning an ardour, the loftiest language, on glory, beauty, sacrifice, love, transformation, the hidden sweetness of the cross, or strength in desolation.

Such a waterfall of idealism hints at a lonely heart. The office of a famous bishop who worked too hard brought its own solitude. But he had a special friend to whom he often went on holiday and in whose house he died, du Boys the squire of a château at Lacombe in Savoy.

Between ardent devotion like Dupanloup's and sanctity lies a wide gap, the edges of which are impossible to draw upon any map.

The making of saints remained traditional in its manner of working. The Congregation of Rites controlled the investigation of a proposed title of 'Blessed' or a candidate to be a saint. The process was expensive, in that long research needed to be done and officials needed stipends. A saint could not be made without the assent of a pope. But some popes took a livelier interest and shared more actively in this sort of work, which was a mixture of historical enquiry, examination of witnesses as in a court, and propagation of types of devotional ideal. The medieval schoolman Albertus Magnus would not have attained the status of saint if that former scholar and librarian Pius XI had not taken keen interest in his cause. And sometimes a pope intervened to cut short a long enquiry and be content with the widespread evidence of a people's cult.

The old rules continued to apply. To become a saint, it was not indispensable, but best to be: (1) the founder or at least a member of a religious order, for a religious order did not die, had a strong interest in pushing its originator into the highest recognition, and could prosecute the cause over decades; everyone could see what good was now done in the world by the saint's children, grandchildren, or great-grandchildren—it was the only place where the achievement of sanctity was in a curious way measurable; (2) a woman (why? Was it that the system of canonization was worked by men, and men are more likely to revere the virtues of women than the virtues of men? Was it that nuns, with a ministry to the dying, the senile, or the orphan, touched the heart of the world as few male orders could do? Or was it statistical, that ever since the world became safer for female communities, there were more nuns than male religious?); (3) a member of the Latin races rather than the Germanic, that is, it was better to be French, Spanish, or Italian; and that may be only a reflection of the statistics of Catholic schools; but it might be affected because the Congregation of Rites consisted almost entirely of Italians and a majority of the cardinals in those days was always Italian, as were popes, and the kind of sanctity most easily preferred was likely to have a 'romance' feel about its expressions of fervour or about the achievements that were possible; or, it cannot be excluded that the generosity or warmth of the Latin races threw up more examples of that sort of personality; (4) unless one of a group of martyrs it was almost essential to be unmarried.

Popes could cut short the process. But where they did not, it was long and labour-consuming. Take a single example: Claret died in a French exile in October 1870. He was the founder of more than one order. His disciple and friend Clotet was sure that he was a saint, and started collecting material: his life, austerities, charity, and miracles. This produced, after ten years, a very large book. But to proceed needed money which the Congregation did not have, and there was a six-year delay. Then a man who believed himself healed by Claret's intercession revived the process and twenty years after Claret's death two vast volumes were presented to the Congregation of Rites and the formal process was opened at the Curia, backed by appeals to Pope Leo XIII from Spaniards of the political right and Queen Isabella who was still an exile in Paris. Then two years were needed to translate the Spanish material into Italian, and seventeen months to ensure the translation was correct, and twenty-nine years after the death he was declared Venerable and a committee was chosen to consider whether he should be beatified. It took another twenty-seven years before Claret was pronounced by the pope to be of heroic virtue and eight years after that he was declared blessed and the pope sanctioned a service for his day, but only to be used in the diocese of Vich where he was born, Carcassone where he died, Santiago de Cuba where he was archbishop, and in the houses of the two orders which he founded; and allowed that his picture might be shown in church with rays round his head. Then 269 of his professed Claretines were murdered in the Spanish civil war, so that he had bred more martyrs in that calamity than the founder of any other order. Eleven years after the war, when the world was more peaceful and the Spanish right was in power, he was made a saint; and then John XXIII made his feast day universal; so it took ninety years from his death; even though he was a very good man, was of a Latin race, and had founded two religious orders.

Part of the lapse of time was mere delay, but not all. The decision had to be right. Claret wrote large numbers of pamphlets on religious matters, an official eye must read them all, critically. Scandal said that he had an affair with Sor Patrocinio, that must be nailed. Wild scandal said that he had an affair with the queen, that must be nailed. More gravely, the left said that he misused his power with Queen Isabella for wrongful political ends, was there any truth? And another motive entered with Rome—if a man or woman who was regarded by a political party in any country as an enemy were made a saint, would that be an undesirable political act on the part of the pope? If Claret was to be made a saint, that aspect also needed thought.

Until 1846 popes were restrained about making saints. Pius IX started the modern habit of being freer in recognition. He accepted the older ways, for example canonizing Paul of the Cross, who was the founder of the order of Passionists, and beatified another founder.[1] But he wanted to recognize a world-wide field of godliness, such as the twenty-six martyrs of Japan in 1862 and 205 more Japanese later, and Latin Americans—he canonized Peter Claver, the apostle of the Africans in South America.

Pius IX was not an intellectual and was suspicious of intellectual clergymen. Usually his saints were not so much parish priests as modern martyrs, or famous mission-preachers, or holy monks or nuns. Pius X had a childlike veneration for the Curé d'Ars, the very simple parish priest who only learnt to read when he was 17, could hardly learn Latin, could not pass examinations, and was a refugee from the call-up, hidden in the hills at the time of Napoleon I, once under a pile of hay; but when at last he was allowed through to take orders (because the wars made a dire shortage of priests) he had to get to his ordination at Grenoble Cathedral through a countryside infested with Austrian troops advancing towards Napoleon who had just been beaten at Waterloo. He was sent to the least responsible of posts, a very small village of Ars, where French revolutionaries destroyed the steeple during the Terror, and there he converted the village; he prepared long sermons, often borrowing those of other people, but could not remember them, so he preached emotional sermonettes with little sharp phrases and staccato repetition. Converting the village included stopping dancing, preventing the carting of manure on

---

[1] One was John of God, of the Fatebenefratelli, a Spanish order of the 16th cent., an order of nursing brothers—its hospital at Paris became a famous school of medicine, La Charité; the Spanish Revolution destroyed much of it, and ninety-nine were murdered in the Spanish civil war, but it still progressed. The order was charged with the medical services in the Vatican. He beatified John Leonardi, founder of the Regular Clerks of the Mother of God, an Italian order of the 16th cent. designed to help parish life, with special devotion to St Mary. The Passionists were founded in 1720 in Italy for missions to the people—the founder, Paul, was himself a well-known preacher.

Sunday, shutting the four pubs, founding a girls' school and a home for abandoned girls, and putting up with scandalous graffiti on his door, anonymous letters to the bishop, and stories that he was plagued at night by demons. He was much helped by someone afterwards forgotten, the lady of the manor. His life was old-fashioned piety, with daily self-flagellation and very little sleep. More than once he asked the bishop's leave to become a Trappist or Carthusian, and once he was accepted for a nearby Trappist monastery but a crowd of villagers stopped him leaving. The village became famous, and he was in demand as a confessor to pilgrims, and he sat for hour after hour after hour in the confessional, a terrible monotony, and the village prospered at the thousands who came. Long before his death people collected his relics, and he was ruthless about them, cheerfully selling cassock, handkerchiefs, or books to make money for the parish work. He became a symbol of the otherworldly peasant without gifts of this world who yet was the best of pastors. Pope Pius X kept his portrait on his desk. It was he who beatified the Curé d'Ars in 1904.[2] Parish priests were not common in the system of making saints, especially parish priests of tiny parishes, or those who could not pass their examinations before they were ordained. It was a rural ideal; still, as with the Anglican veneration for John Keble, a commemoration of the roots of the old Church in the countryside, with the little corresponding danger of the inability to see that where the Church now stood for much of the time was in cities.

Some of the canonizations had a particular significance and aimed at an object beyond that of honouring the person, recognizing a beloved cult among a people, or praising the religious order to which the person belonged. It is possible to tell something about a pope and his ideals, even his personality, by looking at the history of the people whom he made saints.

Pius IX canonized Pedro d'Arbues. This was an extraordinary act. D'Arbues was of Saragossa and was sent to graduate at Bologna, where he won his doctorate, and came back to be a cathedral canon. In 1484 he was appointed the first inquisitor for Aragon. He worked

---

[2] Pope Pius made him a saint in 1925. Life by F. Trochu, *The Curé d'Ars: St Jean-Marie-Baptiste Vianney, 1786–1859* (Paris, 1928), Eng. trans. E. Graf (1927); R. Fourrey, *The Curé d'Ars: A Pictorial Biography* (Paris, 1971), Eng. trans. R. M. Bethell (1959); weighty article by B. Nodet in *DS* (1976), viii. 840. Letters (Paris, 1958); sermons (Paris, 1956), but care is needed over sermons because enterprising publishers made money by faking sermons under his name.

to convert thousands of Jews after Ferdinand and Isabella ordered the expulsion of all Jews. In Jewish eyes the work of 'conversion' was brutal. Afterwards the rumour went about that he was responsible for the deaths of some 6,000 Jews. He was known to be at risk and friends tried to get him to resign for his own safety, but he refused to take precautions. A little group of Jews led by a merchant whose sister had lately been condemned to death attacked him in the cathedral choir while he was in the middle of a psalm at the evening office and stabbed him in the neck. He died next day.

Miracles happened at the tomb. The Emperor Charles V pressed his case; two other Spanish kings tried with two other popes. In 1661 Pope Alexander VII allowed him the honour of being a martyr and gave him the title 'Blessed'. To make him saint could only be accounted for by a wish in Pius IX to declare that, whatever Protestants and liberals said, the Inquisition was good. Attacks ensued. Döllinger of Munich, then still a respected Roman Catholic and revered by many as the best of church historians then working, used his history to hold up d'Arbues to reprobation. A Jesuit defended the canonization on the illogical ground that the other inquisitors in Spain of his time were worse. Acton was shocked by the canonization and it made him more radical in his attitudes to the popes and the Curia.[3] The Pope wanted to say as loudly as he could: the axioms of the modern world are wrong; it is right to stop error from being spread; it is right to use force to prevent error. The Syllabus carried more weight in the canonization of d'Arbues than research into the history of what he did and how he suffered.

Where the making of a saint was meant to fly in the face of modern axioms, the drafting could pain contemporaries and those who came after. The Jews were accused of murdering d'Arbues. Some in the Curia suspected that modern liberal Jewry was responsible for the quarrel that developed over this canonization. The text said, 'The divine wisdom has arranged that in these sad days, when Jews help the enemies of the Church with their books and money, this decree of sanctity has been brought to fulfilment.' There was no need to say this. It could not but offend—and must have been intended to do so. Its presence in the text is a sign that the making of d'Arbues into a

---

[3] Döllinger in J. Friedrich, *Ignaz von Döllinger* (Munich, 1899–1901), iii. 444 ff.; Father Brunengo in *CC* (1867), 11, 273–88, 385 ff.; for Brunengo see *DBI* s.v.; and for the whole, G. Martina, *Pio IX (1851–66)* (Rome, 1986), 703 ff. Cf. *DHEE*; and *Acta Sanctorum*, 17 Sept., v. 728 ff.

saint had other motives besides commemorating a specially devout man (if that was what he was). And what was then done showed how the events of an age brought to the fore a particular person. In the history of the papacy there were only seventeen years when Pedro d'Arbues could have been made a saint—the years beginning with the unification of Italy and ending with the last illness of Pius IX, the years when people of that generation believed the Syllabus of Errors to be what the world needed.

Miracles were both important and surprisingly unimportant. They were treated with respect, for the most part not with credulity, by the researchers. It was accepted that saints are so close to God that his power passes through them to work miracles. If no miracle were recorded that was a bad mark. But if a soul was evidently so near God that people who knew him or her used words such as 'saint', strange things happened; like the healing of a body thought till then to be incurable. Of the modern popes the two with a simple faith were Pius IX and Pius X. Neither of them was drawn to admire visionaries and thaumaturges. Pius IX kept a certain distance from the visions of Lourdes and La Salette, though he felt no contempt. A nun fleeing from persecution in Russia reached Posen in Prussia, and said she was Mother Makryna and was the abbess of the Basilian nunnery at Minsk; she was brought to the Polish refugees in Paris and told a story of savage, inhuman torment of herself and her nuns, because they refused to obey the order to become Orthodox. She was treated by many French as a saint-martyr and sent on to Rome. Meanwhile the Russians and various Poles accused her of being a fraud and an adventuress and even denied that any Basilian convent at Minsk ever existed. She was probably an exaggerator rather than a fraud. Pius IX made no advertisement of her, he let her stay quietly in a nunnery until her death.[4]

Queen Isabella of Spain in her affection for Sister Patrocinio commended her to Pius IX as a holy woman and even secured from him a leave for her to found a few nunneries. But the Pope was no enthusiast for Patrocinio. He suspected contemporary nuns when they had visions. The Holy Office, in close touch with him, was hard-boiled about women who went into ecstasies, though they accepted that stigmata were sometimes real rather than imaginary. One woman who said that she was inspired had her papers examined personally by

---

[4] Best studied by her defender, H. de Riancey, who printed documents, *Les Religieuses basiliennes de Pologne et la diplomatie russe* (Paris, 1846).

the Pope, and was sent to twelve years of penitence in a nunnery. A Foligno girl had continual ecstasies and revelations and had to be stopped. Three years before the Pope died the Holy Office issued a decree condemning a woman who was promoting devotion to the blood of Mary and warning people against starting new cults 'under the appearance of piety'.[5]

But Pius IX gave one visionary the title 'Blessed', to help a doctrine. In the later seventeenth century Margaret Mary Alacoque saw visions. Her visions were weighty in the direction of prayers towards the Sacred Heart of Jesus; a devotion which had the merit of being warm enough to draw the superstitious peasant away from the historic cults which were barely Christian. Hence making her a *beata* was an encouragement for that devotion. As Arbues had a social or moral aim in the present, Alacoque had a devotional aim in the present.

Pius X beatified a lot of people but made few of them into saints.[6] In 1909 he gave Joan of Arc the appellation Blessed. It was controversial: she had visions; she was a woman soldier; the Church had delivered her to the secular arm to be burnt as a heretic (though under the pressure of armed Englishmen). A German Catholic critic remarked that patriotism was never one of the cardinal virtues and that courage in war is a human rather than a Christian virtue. French anticlericals doubted even her heroism. But apart from the attractiveness of Joan as a human person, and her death in a judicial murder, her character had two sides which fitted the mood of the Church at that moment. The first was that, four years after the separation of Church and State in France and the unjust anticlerical laws, her name stood for the tradition of French royalism, the connection of the French monarchy with religion, and the honour of the French army, so recently smeared by the Dreyfus case. And she fitted another part of the Catholic mood of the moment: the simple and direct experience of God amid the complexities of a brutal war. She had something of the same appeal as that of the Curé d'Ars, that of simplicity.

---

[5] *ASS* 8 (1874), 269–70.

[6] Pius XI probably made more saints than any other pope in the history of the papal office. In his seven first years only, he either beatified or made into saints 343 people (Schm. iv. 54). This was partly because the system now commemorated groups more than ever before—e.g. whole bands of martyrs murdered in the mission field, in Africa or Vietnam; and in that way was part of the new impact upon the Church of the Catholic expansion out of Europe during the 19th cent. But also it was a real reflection of the personality of a pope with an interest in history.

She embodied the ideals of the village maiden, purity, voices from heaven. When in 1920 Benedict XV turned the beatified girl into a saint, there was less complaint. During four of the previous five years the French army recovered all its honour; and the ferocity of the conflict between clerical and anticlerical in France was diminished by the sufferings of war. France was still anticlerical in constitutional and political formality, not so anticlerical in its guts.

Don Bosco was a boy and a man who often had dreams. Late in his life he became convinced that these were not dreams of the imagination but real visions. In the process for his canonization a disciple assured the court that the dreams were true visions. When Bosco went to see Pope Pius IX about the founding of the Salesian order, the Pope asked him whether he had had any experience that he took to be supernatural. Bosco told the Pope about his dream, when he was a boy of 10, of a lady who told him how it must be his vocation in life to make rough boys gentle; and how he was persuaded that she was Mary and remembered her as he set out on his work for boys. Pius IX gave him a down-to-earth reply. He should write down an account of the dream and leave it as an encouragement to members of his order.[7]

Visionary experiences are diverse in their origins, effects, and aftermath. The commonest form was found in children, and, in spite of John Bosco, usually girls. They were almost always to persons, like Joan of Arc, who came from poor homes in the countryside. In the society in which they occurred Catholicism was under pressure— Germany of the *Kulturkampf* (Marpingen, etc.), Ireland in its torment (Knock), the half-anticlerical France, revolutionary antichristian Portugal (Fatima), the several Spanish shrines, statutes that moved hands or eyes in or near Rome as the Piedmontese army besieged it, the children at Portmain near Mayenne which was by the front line between the French and German armies, the children at Neuholz in Alsace just after the province was annexed to Germany—but since Catholicism was under pressure in all countries, the nearby crises may not be a cause of what happened. Invariably the visions were met with disbelief and scorn, especially by the local priest or bishop who had to put up with the consequences and who was educated enough to be hostile to superstition. They only became important if they were followed by miracles, usually of healing, sometimes by the

---

[7] John Bosco, *Memoirs of the Oratory of Saint Francis de Sales*, Eng. trans. (New York, 1989), 20–1.

quick running of a spring of fresh water; and in a less dramatic form the sudden conversion of a bystander who came to jeer and was over-powered by such faith as was witnessed in so many people. The eventual approval of the cult by the bishop and later by Rome meant only that a lot of people went to say their prayers at that spot and were helped; it did not mean that bishop or pope certified that the original vision was not a dream or that the events which drew the people were historically accurate. Some events, or utterances of a vision, might be absurd or bizarre. No educated person could be attracted to what happened in the origins of the shrine at La Salette; and many felt discomfort about the origins at Fatima. If the pope canonized the visionary as in the end he made Bernadette of Lourdes a saint, that certified the belief of the Church that this girl saw what she said she saw. It did not certify that everything she saw was accurately described. But sometimes the quality of the child or the childlike adult who saw perfectly fitted the cult which grew around what they saw. In the cases which were not soon proved to be pretence, the evidence was of sincerity among those who experienced the happening. It was impossible for such an event to rise to be a cult unless honourable people believed that what they experienced was real.

Once the cult existed—that is, as soon as numerous persons came to say their prayers at the spot—a lowly motive came in. The pilgrims needed food and drink, and roofs above their heads, and trinkets to take away. At this point there was a risk in the early development of a cult. The persons who provided these necessities in a remote spot had no interest in the vision, only in the money which they could earn by supplying those who were concerned about the vision. It became the interest of the marketeers that the vision should be as famous as possible and that persons should be prevented from saying that all this was rubbish or superstition. This made a dangerous stage between the cult which was new and the cult which was so popular that such hucksters were irrelevant.

If the trinket, or, putting it higher, the cult-object, was to be taken away by the pilgrim, it became part of the extension of the cult. Catherine Labouré came from a modest farming home to be a nun at the Daughters of Charity at their house in the Rue de Bac in Paris. She was always a person for the farm, the cows, the milk, and the sheep, a practical person—though she kept losing money on the cows—and she also ministered in their hospital. She was not the sort to see visions. But early as a nun, in 1830, the year when Paris was soon in revolution, she saw them. The climax of these was a sight of the woman clothed by the sun (Revelation 12 : 1), with rays coming out of her hands. Believing that she did what she was ordered she asked her confessor that this be made into a picture on a medal. He had no desire to do what she asked, but when he found that Archbishop Quelen approved it as a beautiful image, he asked a jeweller to strike a medal. A priest started to give the medal as a consolation to patients in the Paris cholera, and the sufferers associated it with healing. This medal spread. The still Anglican Newman took it as devotional (22 August 1845). By 1842 there were a hundred million medals, though only three of four people then knew for certain that Catherine Labouré was the nun of the vision, and she spent the rest of a long life answering gruffly if anyone asked her about it. By the year of her death there were a million million medals. But no pope of the nineteenth century made her into a saint.[8] The effect was a revival of her order, the Daughters of Charity, and of their male counterpart, the Vincentians. Yet what mattered was the object, not the person behind the object.

These experiences were almost always impervious to people who said that they were untrue. The critic, the academic, the scoffer, came along and might study the events carefully and reach the conclusion that a cult was founded on little or nothing. What sceptics said made no difference whatever to those who came to say their prayers at a shrine.

In a few cases outside pressure choked the cult. The children at Marpingen in the diocese of Trier were as genuine as possible in saying what they saw. The bishop was in prison because of the *Kulturkampf* and unable to control events. The children and their helpers eventually persuaded a sceptical parish priest and one of the leading theologians of Catholic Germany[9] to believe in them. The Prussian State was ready to do everything in its power to suppress this enthusiasm and many German churchmen preferred that in the tensions of the *Kulturkampf* their parishes should give no excuse to the press for the charge of superstition. The children were treated with mental cruelty and put in prison, there was a military occupation of the village with requisitioning. The troubles at Marpingen lowered

---

[8] She was canonized by Pius XII in 1947.

[9] Matthias Scheeben, for whose work see a long article in *LTK*. A pupil of Passaglia and Franzelin he had a vast range of learning in the Greek Fathers and the schoolmen, and wrote one of the best books of that age on Catholic dogmatics. He was professor at Cologne.

still further the reputation for injustice of the Prussian government but there, unusually, State intervention successfully ended the cult except for the occasional person who remembered, and an attempt at revival in the 1930s.

Another sign of the devotion to simplicity of heart was the canonization of Thérèse of Lisieux. She fitted the specifications: a religious, for she was a Carmelite; a woman; and a member of a Latin race, for she was of Normandy. She sounds a conventional nun-saint but was not. Her mother died when she was 4 and she was brought up by the two eldest of her four sisters, all of whom wished to be nuns. She longed to join them and even held fast to the Pope's knees after kissing his slipper when she went to Rome to beg him to order that she be admitted, and had to be lifted away physically by the guards, an episode which the elder sister, coming next in the queue, thought a shameful humiliation. She longed to be a priest, or a crusader, or a papal zouave, or a doctor of the Church, and she resented the way men had an easier time than women. She was allowed to be a nun from the age of 15, an entry organized by her sister who was already a Carmelite, at an age contrary to the normal discipline in those days. The result was psychological torment which left her a prey to guessers and speculators after her death. She had a masochist streak, for she yearned to experience all the worst pains of the martyrs. She compensated by a shining simplicity, not in personality but in faith, and an astounding ability to express it despite or because of her absence of a sophisticated education. She had no desire for nor need of ecstasies or mystical visions. She thought she had found a new way to go to God, by the way of childhood. She knew well the *Imitation of Christ*, and revered strong women, Joan of Arc and Theresa of Avila. She knew nothing about the world outside. She died of tuberculosis at the age of only 24 in 1897.

To experience a rare Catholic devotion of that age, it is necessary only to read her autobiography, *The History of a Soul*, which she wrote two years before she died at the order of one of her sisters who was the Mother-Superior—the aim not being to gain a public but to quiet the young girl's scruples. It was heavily edited by the Carmelites—she had told Mother Agnes that she could alter whatever she liked—and Mother Agnes altered so drastically that it is now impossible to determine what some passages in the original said. It was published in 1898. Not all Carmelite convents liked it; some readers had their teeth set on edge, for they found it not childlike but childish. Thérèse scattered as many notes of exclamation as Queen Victoria used underlinings. But soon it became one of the classics of modern devotional writing. The pilgrims came in their thousands, and associated her with roses which played a part in her devotional sense of beauty. Some of the most sophisticated of the French and English were enchanted by her. Mother Theresa of Calcutta chose her name to be her own.

After 1956 critical editions showed how the Carmelites transformed what she wrote to make it more edifying in the convention of that day. Between the publication of the book and her canonization as a saint in 1925 more than 30 million pictures of her were sold. A cheap edition of the book sold two and a half million copies.[10]

Her life proved something about the popes and the French bishops. Her bishop was Hugonin, an intellectual, who had been the Gallican Maret's assistant, professor of theology at Paris, and a friend of Archbishop Darboy. The censors of divinity in Rome disliked his teaching of theology and he had publicly criticized the acts of Rome in the Mortara case where the Jewish boy was taken away to be a Christian. He was a frank doubter whether the Church possessed any coercive power. When Hugonin was proposed by the French government of Louis Napoleon, the Pope demurred. But he could not resist long if the government were determined and the candidate was educated and not immoral. Hugonin was made by Rome to sign a statement that he did not now approve the doctrine of *ontologism* which he taught as a professor (!). At last he was allowed to be consecrated by Dupanloup in the church of St Genevieve, which for the moment was a Christian church but was soon to be turned back into the Panthéon, and became the bishop of Bayeux. Rome was sure that this was a bad choice. Hugonin not only became an excellent pastor in his diocese, but it was he who allowed Thérèse to enter her Carmelite nunnery at Lisieux so young, and it was he who later sanctioned the publication of her book (over which most bishops would have hesitated). When Pius IX objected to the choice of a bishop (as not seldom in Latin America) he was often right. But the case of

[10] She was canonized by Pius XI in 1925, as St Theresa of the Infant Jesus and the Holy Face; see the modern Life by Pierre Descouvement, ed. Gaucher (Paris, 1982); Ronald Knox translated the *Histoire d'une Âme* into English but he did not then know the most modern text. Important article in *DS* (1991), xv. 576 ff.; 266 letters in *Correspondance générale*, ed. L. le Guillou (Paris, 1971– (2 vols., 1972–4)); fifty-four poems, mostly prayers, *Thérèse* (2 vols., 1979).

Hugonin proved also that prejudice could seek to stop a good pastor from being elevated.[11]

As illiterate Catholics grew literate with the development of elementary schools, they affected the wishes of congregations on what should be said, sung, or done in church. They had little use now for the fear of excess left by the Catholic Enlightenment. The restrained devotion inherited from the eighteenth century pleased them as little as the restraint of the Jansenist tradition. Catholicism experienced a wave of warm, popular, uninhibited devotion; which liked the outspoken language of earthly love, crude pictures, dramatic ceremonial.

The invention of the railway and the creation of the modern newspaper revived pilgrimage. It was easier to be a pilgrim to one of the distant sanctuaries and much more difficult to distinguish a pilgrim from a tourist. The old resorts still held their magnetism and received many more pilgrims—Loreto, Assisi, Compostela, Mariazell, for example. But several of the frequented pilgrimage sites of modern pilgrims were new. Goals of pilgrimage, once established, were made famous by newspapers. In the eighteenth century a nun would have a vision, or a peasant be healed at a spring, and the cult stayed local. That could still happen, but now, with modern media, the local shrine could turn into a national or even an international shrine.

During the first year of Pius IX the Virgin appeared on the mountain of La Salette in the diocese of Grenoble, to a shepherd's two children aged 11 and 15 while they were herding the cows; and there a spring flowed, and people were cured; a normality of popular devotion, but now (just) within the time when the press could seize upon the unusual event. Pilgrims and sightseers gathered, and the place and the cult became national; a blessing to everyone in the village except the two little children. After five years the Church authorities officially recognized the cult as valid.

Sometimes an earlier vision which had remained obscure was rediscovered. Anna Katharina Emmerich died in 1824, bearing the stigmata of the crucifixion on her body, which a commission inspected and certified. During her life she had visions of the home of the Blessed Virgin when she lived her later years with St John at Ephesus. For decades nothing further occurred, but then a pious man searched among the hills near Ephesus and found what Anna

---

[11] Hugonin's case in Martina, *Pio IX (1851–66)*, 677 ff.; J. Maurain, *La Politique ecclésiastique* (Paris, 1930), 788 ff.; *DBF* s.v. Hugonin.

Katharina had seen, and built a shrine by the stream, and the quiet little sanctuary stands to this day.

That the Virgin should be the centre of a very devout cult in two new sanctuaries, Lourdes and La Salette, within twelve years of each other, was a sign of the people's devotion being prominent in the leading of the Church. While Church authority was more centralized in Rome and hierarchical, the worshipper fostered practices or expressions in Church life in a way which was a democracy in devotion.

In February 1858 at Lourdes in south-west France a lady appeared in a vision, eighteen times, to a maiden of very poor family, Bernadette Soubirous, 14 years old. The girl was told by the lady to drink and wash herself from a spot in the cave, and when she did so a spring of water came flowing out. She was beaten by her mother and by her schoolmistress for pretending. By 1 March there was a crowd of 1,000 in the cave. Already in the summer of 1858 there was a commission of inquiry by the bishop into the healings that occurred, and the cult which was practised, and an argument whether these were authentic visions of the St Mary. Surprisingly quickly, less than four years later, Bishop Laurence of Tarbes accepted the truth of the visions but referred them to Rome for a final verdict. The Pope said nothing. Within ten or fifteen years the shrine of Lourdes became a centre of the Catholic revival in the France of Napoleon III and the years afterwards. It represented the simplest, purest, form of the French revival of religion in these years.

To become the centre of a cult in one's teens is not an easy moral fate for a mortal. In Joan of Arc's experience it took her to the stake. Thérèse was protected because the cult was posthumous, Catherine Labouré was protected because she and her confessor prevented the world from knowing her part. Bernadette was known. Her later life fitted the reverence which was felt but was a strain to her. She was persuaded to be a nun at Nevers. The community did not think her a particularly holy nun, she could be difficult; they tried to refuse access to a Jesuit charged to write her life. Yet the pilgrims came and the healings happened, and Lourdes grew and grew as a centre of devotion.[12]

---

[12] She died in 1879 but was not called 'Blessed' until 1925 (a sign of caution), and was made a saint in 1933. During the 20th cent. Lourdes has attracted about 2 million growing to 4 million pilgrims a year. Up to 1959 some 5,000 healings were reported, and of these fifty-eight were accepted by church authority, after investigation by a commission of medical men, as authentic miracles.

During the French conflicts over religion and clericalism the pilgrimage to Lourdes became a Catholic political demonstration. But it retained its simplicity, and the atmosphere of a place of healing, and pilgrims came from, among other places, Italy, Ireland, and across the Atlantic. It was 1891 before Pope Leo XIII sanctioned a church liturgy for the day of the appearance (11 February) and then only for local use in that province. But the international attraction was marked when in 1907—the year after the separation of Church and State in France, and influenced in its timing by those events—Pope Pius X extended the day of the Lourdes appearance to be a feast of the whole Church. It helped to transform modern pilgrimage. In the long run it was more influential in the history of Catholicism than the first Vatican Council.

The making of saints might be controversial; but the writing or reprinting of former saints' lives could also be controversial. With the ease of printing, good Catholics (or Anglicans) published lives of saints in series and in translation; and this was one of the places where the intellectual gulf was most apparent—between the growing sense of historical reality and awareness of historical doubt about sources on one side, and the growing fervour of devotion on the other. There was a controversy over St Joseph of Cupertino near Brindisi, who was notorious for being the clumsiest person ever to try to be a monk, and was said to have smashed more plates in the refectory than any other washer-up, and was famous for ecstasies in which he was lifted up into the air and at times flew in church, and even carried other people in his flight. In the France of the 1850s, with Renan and Sainte-Beuve at the height of their powers, a Life of St Joseph caused mockery. It was a French translation of 1856 of a 1722 biography by Bernino, who particularly relished flights in ecstasy. Veuillot was capable of defending the absurdity of devout simplicity with conviction and yet humour. Two years later he was in action over sophisticated mockery of the visions of Bernadette at Lourdes. He did not claim that reported miracles were true, what he asserted was that the witnesses were sincere in saying what they saw and that disdain of them was arrogance.

Leo XIII, the sophisticated, dared to make blessed, and Pius X the anti-intellectual dared to make a saint, of a lay brother who was famous for flying; and famous for another form of miracle which made intellectuals smile, that of being in two places at once (bilocation); though for many other miracles also: Gerard Majella (beatified in 1893, canonized in 1904). His claim was that he was one of the most popular saints in South Italy and was more famous for miracles than any other person of that region. A widespread cult existed among the people of the south before it was recognized by Rome. Majella was a gardener, sacristan, tailor, and infirmarian at a Redemptorist house, and died when he was only 29, probably of begging during the heat of a south Italian summer. A religious order was there to promote his process, he was a disciple under Alfonso Ligouri. But his claim, to modern popes, was that he was not some famous bishop nor church leader but the lowliest, a lay brother who did the chores. He was not typical of lay brothers for uniquely (perhaps) among them he was director of souls to more than one nunnery. The canonization was part of the growing desire to tell the world that holiness is within the reach of the worker.

Another sign of the devotion to simplicity was the cult of St Philomena. In 1802 was found in an ancient tomb in the catacombs of St Priscilla a skeleton in a wall-cavity closed with three tiles. Nearby was a small phial with brown matter within and on the three tiles were drawings of a winged arrow, an anchor, and a palm. Anatomists said that the body was that of a girl aged 13 to 15. In the then state of knowledge a phial of blood and a palm were believed to be a sign of a martyr. The finders handed over the skeleton to the custodian of relics. The three tiles had letters—LUMENA, PAXTE, and CUM FI. The theory was put forward that the three tiles were out of order, and that originally they read PAX TECUM FILOMENA, 'Peace be with you, Philomena'. Three years later a parish priest of a village near Naples came to Rome to ask for relics for his altar and was given these remains. On his way home healings happened. He put the bones in his village shrine of Mugnano and wrote a 'Life' of Philomena based on the healings, for there was nothing else on which to base it except visions of a nun in Naples. One devotion was the wearing of a cord of Philomena. Jean Vianney, the Curé d'Ars, had a special devotion to St Philomena, his 'dear little saint', his 'agent in heaven'; Pope Gregory XVI met a French religious who was cured at the shrine, and accepted the cult; Pius IX created a mass for her day; and Pius X made her day a feast of the whole Church.

Nothing was known about her, her name was uncertain for the word Philomena meant 'beloved', the belief in her depended upon a people's fervour and the sanction of the Curia. In Spain her cult was associated with the right, for Spanish liberals called her the Carlist saint. It was a special sign of devotion to think of an unknown little girl whom Romans killed for being a Christian and who was holy because such good things happened after her body was discovered.

But then, early in the twentieth century, the archaeologists doubted whether any of this could be true. They proved that the tiles were of an earlier date than the body, and that a phial and palm need not be a sign of a martyr; they doubted whether there was any such person called Philomena, and believed that the girl in the cavity was a Christian but buried later than the age of persecution. Rome did not strike her out of the list of saints to be commemorated until 1961, when it did so because the historical evidence about her was too doubtful.[13]

Old ideas remained strong; at Manresa a hermit not only showed travellers the cave of St Ignatius, but sold them its dust as a medicine for their bodily infirmities. The smoke of the lamps in the shrine of Santa Engracia at Saragossa was believed to cure scrofula. In Valencia, a man was cured of cholera by drinking from a well at the house of St Vincent Ferrer.[14] One unusual mystic was Gemma Galgani; rare because health prevented her from becoming a nun, and because of the nature of her experiences. She was the child of poor parents who lived near Lucca. Although she could not become a nun she determined to be a sort of private nun. She took the vows for herself and kept the nun's way of life. She found herself to have the marks of the crucifixion on her hands and feet, the stigmata. Her mystical experiences were recorded and are among the most extraordinary of modern times, though they conformed to tradition, even to mystical marriage with the Saviour. She felt physically the crown of thorns, the flagellation, the thirst and the agony of Calvary. She was rare in that her depressions of spirit from time to time caused a belief that she was demon-possessed. Attention was called to her experiences in 1907 when her confessor, the Passionist Germano di S. Stanislao, published her Life.[15]

---

[13] A. Butler, *Lives of the Saints*, ed., rev., and supp. H. Thurston and D. Attwater (1956), s.v. August 11; *NCE* and *LTK* s.v. Philomena; *Clergy Review* 41 (1956), 462–71.

[14] Richard Ford, *A Handbook for Travellers in Spain* (2 vols.; London, 1845), ii. 158–9; W. J. Callahan, *Church, Politics and Society in Spain 1750–1874* (Cambridge, Mass., 1984), 232–3.

[15] Pius XII canonized her in 1940. Passionists edited the letters, diary, and autobiography in 1941–3. Life by the Passionist Father Amedeo, *Blessed Gemma Galgani 1878–1903*, Eng. trans. O. Thorpe (1935).

These happenings cry for explanation: (1) The deep devotion of a simple people, especially to the Blessed Virgin; (2) the fact that, where such a faith took root, healings took place and made the cult powerful and independent of its childlike origins; (3) the willingness of local church authorities, and later central church authorities, once they were satisfied that the makers of this cult were sincere and not charlatans, to sanction a cult which fostered local faith; (4) the anti-clerical atmosphere of the society (as with Lourdes), which made the site of the new pilgrimage a rallying point for religious manifestations which were political as well as religious; and (5) the growth of a restored Catholicism which needed a devotional focus for the people, amid the storms of a sometimes hostile world.

DOCTORS OF THE CHURCH

The idea of a recognized teacher of the Church went back to the age of the Fathers where the writings of men like Jerome, Augustine, or Gregory the Great were given a particular respect as the teaching of 'the Fathers'. In the age of Charlemagne the Western Fathers were numbered as four, those three with St Ambrose; but without system for most of the Middle Ages. From about the same time the Eastern Church recognized as three great doctors Basil, Gregory Nazianzene, and John Chrysostom. In the West Pope Boniface VIII in 1295 fixed the number of Fathers as four in the liturgy.

The new knowledge of the Renaissance widened these attitudes. In 1567 the Dominican Thomas Aquinas was declared by a Dominican pope to be a doctor of the Church, and the year afterwards the Western Church accepted the three Greek fathers plus Athanasius as also doctors of the Church. The only addition of the age of the Counter-Reformation happened when a Franciscan pope added the Franciscan Bonaventura. The additions of Aquinas and Bonaventura showed how the rivalry of religious orders affected the list.

But in the eighteenth century the list grew—such medieval divines as Anselm of Canterbury, Isidore of Seville, Bernard of Clairvaux, and Peter Damian; Fathers such as Peter Chrysologus and Pope Leo the Great (the first pope after Gregory the Great).[16]

---

[16] In the 1920s Pius XI went back to the Counter-Reformation, making doctors Canisius, John of the Cross, and Bellarmine; but also the schoolman Albertus Magnus. Pius XII chose Antony of Padua; John XXIII chose the most obscure in the list, the Capuchin Laurence of

Popes had used the power to make doctors of the Church in order to encourage a strand of theology within the breadth of Catholicism. They had used this authority sparingly. In his many years Pius IX made only three doctors: Hilary of Poitiers the ancient Church Father, a safe conventional elevation which aimed to please the province of Bordeaux; Alfonso Liguori, the man of the eighteenth century most identified with the cult of the Virgin and with resistance to the stricter Jansenist moral theology, both of which fitted the mood of 1871; and in 1877 Francis de Sales who was identified with the mysticism of the Counter-Reformation and represented the attractive side of the less strict moral theology.

Liguori was controversial. He was made a saint by Gregory XVI but that did not stop attacks on him for laxity in his moral teaching and he became a moral *bête noire* of Protestants. He was the founder of the Redemptorist order which at that moment the Pope was successfully reuniting after a schism. The Redemptorists wanted him recognized because it would make their order better known and because it would end the blame about his ethical teaching. They appealed to the Pope and brought pressure to bear upon him by request from various bishops. At first Pius IX saw that this would be an undiplomatic act and hesitated. But after a time he ceased to mind about diplomacy. A vast dossier was compiled; it was referred to two advisers, one of whom said that he should certainly be a doctor of the Church and the other said that he was not fitted to be so. The cardinals considered the evidence and recommended Alfonso to the Pope; and so he was made a doctor of the Church, not without nasty comment in the press. But the moods of Alfonso—papalist, gentle in moral teaching and the confessional, warm in piety, hostile to the austerities of Jansenists and puritans though puritan in his personal life—fitted the devotion which Pius IX wished to encourage.

Francis de Sales had written books of devotion widely read by the laity, such as the *Introduction to the Devout Life*. He had called everyone to the perfect life and they must not think that it was necessary to be a monk or nun to go the way of contemplative prayer. His writing was simple and easy to read. He had early ideas about the cult of the Sacred Heart; and he defended the rights of the pope. His form of prayerfulness fitted the personal devotion felt by the Pope in his own life.

Brindisi; in 1970 Paul VI chose, evidently with a motive not solely concerned with their doctrines, the first two women as doctors; Teresa of Avila and Catherine of Siena. John Paul II added Thérèse of Lisieux. List of doctors in *LTK* s.v. Kirchenlehrer.

But again there was a political reason. Francis de Sales had been bishop of Geneva, though he was never able to go to Protestant Geneva, and lived in Annecy in Savoy, and his bones still rested in the church at Annecy. In 1872 there was a big quarrel in progress between Pius IX and the Swiss government, partly caused by the Old Catholic movement against the infallibility decree. The Swiss government accused the Vatican of behaving illegally. Pius IX reacted by making Mermillod vicar-apostolic of Geneva. The idea of a Catholic bishop of Calvin's Geneva shocked many Swiss. They expelled Mermillod from Geneva. He retreated to Voltaire's Ferney on the border and tried to continue to administer his Geneva flock. It was characteristic of Pope Pius IX that he replied to these battles of Church and State with a spiritual act. He made Francis de Sales, the most famous Bishop of Geneva, a doctor of the Church.

Leo XIII followed with more from the Fathers—the two Cyrils (of Jerusalem and Alexandria, not everyone was sure about him of Alexandria) and John Damascene, for he fitted Leo XIII desire for humane understanding with the Eastern Orthodox Church; then, to the pleasure of more than the English, a historian, the Venerable Bede. It had not been the expectation of historians that they would be treated as if their work was seen to have something to do with understanding the faith of the Churches.

SELECT BIBLIOGRAPHY

Four writers are basic to a bibliography of the subject:

1. Josef Schmidlin was an Alsatian born in 1876; after studying history at the university of Freiburg im Breisgau he was invited by Ludwig Pastor to help him with the enormous History of the Popes. He was present among the crowd in St Peter's Square when Pius X was elected pope in 1903. From 1906 he held lectureships in Germany and then became the first professor of the history of missions at the newly revived university of Münster. Here he laid the foundation of much of Catholic missionary history, at that time a new subject. He went on a voyage of enquiry and mission in the Far East and had a very uncomfortable time coming back through Siberia in the spring of 1914, seeing the predicaments of both Catholic and Orthodox Churches in Russia of that day. Reluctantly and under pressure he wrote a short autobiography which tells the reader little of what they would like to know (in *Religionswissenschaft der Gegenwart in Selbstdarstellungen* (Leipzig, 1927), iii, but says enough to show a vaguely explosive personality who won the reputation of being difficult.

Pastor ended his History of the Popes from the age of the Renaissance at 1800. Schmidlin then took on the duty of bringing the history up to date. He completed three volumes, taking it up to 1922. Then the Nazis came to power and his work suffered constant interruption, for he was an idealist. In 1934 the Nazis forced him to retire from his chair, and he was repeatedly arrested and imprisoned; and at last was interned in an asylum before being murdered in a concentration camp. Before the worst happened he succeeded in bringing out the first part of his fourth volume in 1939 which was the pontificate of Pius XI (1922–39). It necessarily left much unsaid.

Schmidlin had great range and extraordinary unremitting endeavour. The reader feels that he has presented the materials for history rather than history itself; but those materials are valuable, and sometimes indispensable as a guide. In those days he had little access to the papal archives (for a time Cardinal de Lai tried to stop him getting into the archives) but his knowledge of the printed materials was unique.

2. Hubert Jedin, who died in the summer of 1980, also wrote his own autobiography: *Lebensbericht* (Mainz, 1984), which his colleague and friend Konrad Repgen published posthumously (Veröffentlichungen der

Kommission für Zeitgeschichte, ser. A: Sources, vol. 35). Jedin was the son of a Breslau schoolmaster and was just old enough to serve in the First World War; he was threatened with death by Communist marines in 1919. He studied at three German universities and then for four years (1926–30) in Rome as a preparation for teaching at his own university of Breslau. He took no notice of the Nazis, or indeed of politics, until the Nazis came to power. (He never in all his life possessed a radio.) At first he hoped, as did many German Catholics, that as the Church had reached a *modus vivendi* with Fascist Italy, it would do the same with Fascist Germany. He was undeceived by the onslaughts on the Jews that spring, for his mother was a Jewish convert to the Catholic faith. After 1 May 1933 he was told that he could teach no more in the university. He wrote to the Berlin nuncio Orsenigo to say that this dismissal was in flagrant contradiction with the Prussian Concordat of 1929. The letter received no answer, as was sometimes the case with embarrassing letters to Monsignor Orsenigo. He was bitter that, however kind were his colleagues, they dared to say nothing in protest, and that the Church made it clear that it would not support such as himself by agreeing the Concordat with Hitler of July 1933—it made, he felt, its 'arrangement' with Fascism. It bothered him that in those heady months even the Benedictines of Maria Laach showed their sympathy for the new regime (*Lebensbericht*, 78). At the end of October 1933 he left for Rome. He expected help there from Monsignor Kaas, the leader of the Centre Party who had also disappeared to Rome and was high in the confidence of the pope's Secretary of State Cardinal Pacelli, and Jedin was bitter that he did not get that help. He lived for the second time at the Campo Santo Teutonico by St Peter's. Bishop Berning of Osnabrück, who was among the weaker German bishops towards the Nazis, came to stay, and was cool to him.

The enforced leisure turned him into the historian of the Council of Trent, though not immediately; at first he studied its tractates. In 1936 he was able to return to Breslau as diocesan archivist. The post was not without its dangers because part of it was genealogical enquiry which in race-conscious Germany could mean a charge that the evidence of descent was faked. He was even allowed to teach a little church history to the ordinands. It was still more remarkable when he was asked to teach on Luther to ordinands in Berlin, a course attended by some Protestants; for Jedin had reached the same conviction that Lortz then was also reaching, that Luther was not to be understood, as Denifle understood him, as a runaway monk, nor as the psychopath portrayed by Hartmann Grisar, but as a deeply religious man, a true theologian, and a man with a passionate pastoral concern (*Lebensbericht*, 90).

In November 1939, soon after the Crystal Night, he just escaped with his life through the intervention of a friendly police officer. It was clear that he must get out. After the possibility of going to Ushaw College in England failed, he finally got a visa to go to Rome in November 1939. Now his object was fixed, to write the history of the Council of Trent. All through the Italian war, even in the worst crises, and despite bad food, bad health, and hardly any pay, he was able to work away at his history. When the Germans seized Rome in September 1943, the Vatican Library was closed lest its readers be spies passing information and it was not reopened to him until a fortnight after the British and American armies entered Rome.

After the war, though he fiercely resented the loss of his home to the Poles, a German academic career opened to him at last. He was professor of church history at Bonn from 1949 to 1965. The volumes of the history of the Council of Trent made him famous. In 1956 he decided that a general new handbook of church history was an absolute necessity; it must be short enough for students but must be up to date in scholarship. He collected a team and had the usual difficulties with tardy authors. But it appeared in seven volumes between 1963 and 1979 and was translated into English, rendering important services to scholarship. Jedin's health began to fail in 1973 and he died on 16 July 1980.

3. Giacomo Martina was born in Libya and was a Jesuit from the age of 15; he taught history at the Gregorian university from 1964. His work, chiefly but not only via the Vatican archives, soon became indispensable to any student of papal history during the nineteenth century; especially the three volumes listed below on the life of Pius IX (see Chapters 2–6, Pius IX), and in these and other work he made available a mass of hitherto unknown or little-known materials which he was able to set in a coherent form, so that he was never a mere collector of information as Schmidlin could sometimes be accused of being.

4. Roger Aubert, a Belgian, who inherited the mantle of modern church history from weighty predecessors. The chief of these was Alfred Baudrillart; a Parisian and an Oratorian, who became professor of history at the Institut Catholique in the age when Catholics were not allowed theological faculties at French universities. From 1907 he ruled the Institut Catholique as rector in the most difficult times, the aftermath of the French disestablishment and the modernist troubles (which were worst in Paris), and ruled it wisely. In 1909 he founded the *Dictionnaire d'histoire ecclésiastique*, which in time was to transform the work of the church historians. He won respect and honour—a member of the French Academy, a chevalier of the Legion of Honour, a Roman count, and (1935) a cardinal. He lost this great reputation at the age of 80, when, from a fear of Communism, he backed the Vichy regime and wanted acceptance of Nazi rule: the Prime Minister Laval attended his funeral. The progress of the *Dictionnaire* which he founded, hampered by world wars and their results, limped; it did not recover until Aubert took over the main direction. He had started as a

philosopher in theology and from 1952 became a professor at Louvain, and then one of the directors of the Louvain-based *Revue d'histoire ecclésiastique*. Thenceforward he became the wisest guide to the history of the popes of the nineteenth century, one whose work, like that of Schmidlin and Martina, was indispensable to the progress of knowledge; and the *Dictionnaire* which Baudrillart had founded soon had the name of Aubert upon its binding.

The following titles are grouped under the topics for which they are a source, and/or by chapter. Place of publication is London unless otherwise stated.

Papal Documents

Acta Sanctae Sedis (Rome, 1865–1908); became *Acta Apostolicae Sedis* (Rome, 1909–).

Denziger, H., *Enchiridion Symbolorum*, 33rd edn. (Barcelona, 1965).

La Documentation catholique (Paris, 1919–), a record invaluable for the twentieth century, unfortunately begun only in 1919; its first four volumes often throw a retrospective light on the recent past.

Schöppe, L. (ed.), *Konkordate seit 1800* (Frankfurt, 1964), contains the original texts and German translations of the then valid Concordats.

For documents of Councils:

Collectio Lacensis (7 vols.; Freiburg im Breisgau, 1870–90).

Maclear, J. F. (ed.), *Church and State in the Modern Age* (Oxford, 1995), for selected documents on Church and State.

For Vatican 1 see under Chapter 5 below.

General Studies and Political Background

Adriányi, Gabriel, *et al.*, *The Church in the Modern Age*, History of the Church, 10, Eng. trans. (1981).

Aubert, R., *et al.*, *The Church between Revolution and Restoration*, History of the Church, Eng. trans. (1981).

—— *The Church in the Age of Liberalism*, History of the Church, 8, Eng. trans. (1981).

—— *The Church in the Industrial Age*, History of the Church, 9, Eng. trans. (1981).

—— *The Church in a Secularized Society*, The Christian Centuries, 5, Eng. trans. (1978).

The above five volumes have bibliographies.

Gerbod, P., *L'Europe culturelle et religieuse de 1818 a nos jours* (Paris, 1977), general introduction, materials, and methods.

Greschat, M. (ed.), *Gestalten der Kirchengeschichte*, xii. *Das Papsttum*, 2 (Stuttgart, 1984), biographical sketches of popes from Pius IX onwards, with original material.

Latourette, K. S., *Christianity in a Revolutionary Age*, i. *The Nineteenth Century in Europe* (1958).

Maron, G., *Die romisch-katholische Kirche von 1870 bis 1970*, Die Kirche in ihrer Geschichte, 4/2 (Göttingen, 1972).

Nielsen, F., *The History of the Papacy in the Nineteenth Century*, Eng. trans. (2 vols.; 1906).

On the Roman Question as a whole:

Bastgen, Hubert, *Die Römische Frage* (3 vols.; Freiburg im Breisgau, 1917–19), documents.

Gregory XVI, Chapter 1

Bernasconi, A. M. (ed.), *Acta Gregorii Papae XVI* (4 vols.; Rome, 1901–4).

Miscellanea Commemorativa (Rome, 1948).

Wiseman, N., *Recollections of the Last Four Popes* (1958). There were those who thought this too friendly and it had a reply the same year from Alessandro Gavazzi, but it is still useful as a portrait.

Le Guillou, Louis, *Le Condamnation de Lamennais* (Paris, 1982).

Vidler, A. R., *Lamennais* (1954).

Schnabel, F., *Deutsche Geschichte im 19. Jahrhundert*, rev. edn. (Freiburg im Breisgau, 1948–55), iv.

The above are all concerned with the time before the 1848 Revolution: the Görres circle, the Cologne marriage troubles, social Catholicism in that generation.

Remak, Joachim, *A Very Civil War: The Swiss Sonderbund War of 1847* (Boulder, Colo., 1993).

Schwegler, Th., *Geschichte der Katholischen Kirche in der Schweiz*, 2nd edn. (Stans, 1943).

Pius IX, Chapters 2–6

Acta (9 vols.; Graz, 1971), copy of 1857 edn.

Aubert, R., *Le Pontificat de Pie IX (1846–78)*, 2nd edn. (Paris, 1963). The Italian edn. had additional notes by G. Martina, and is therefore to be preferred: *Il pontificato di Pio IX* (2 vols.; Turin, 1969).

Hales, E. E. Y., *Pio Nono* (1954).

Hayward, F., *Pie IX et son temps* (Paris, 1948).

Martina, G., *Pio IX (1846–1850)* (Rome, 1974); *Pio IX (1851–1866)* (Rome,

1986); *Pio IX (1867–78)* (Rome, 1990), Miscellanea Historiae Pontificiae, 38, 51, 58.

The Liberal Time of Pius IX, Chapter 2

Documents:

Guizot, F. *Mémoires pour servir à l'histoire de mon temps* (Paris, 1865).

Liedekerke-Beaufort, F. C. A., *Rapporti delle cose di Roma (1848–9)*, ed. A. M. Ghisalberti (Rome, 1949), the reports of the Dutch envoy.

Metternich, R., *Aus Metternichs Nachgelassenen Papieren* (Vienna, 1883).

Stock, L. R., *United States Ministers to the Papal States, 1848–68* (Washington, 1933), the reports of the American envoy in Rome (the USA had a minister there from 1848 until he was withdrawn by a resolution of 1867).

Biographies of Pellegrino Rossi:

Giovagnoli, R., *Pellegrino Rossi e la rivoluzione romana su documenti nuovi* (3 vols.; Rome, 1908–11), Rossi dies at the end of vol. i, vol. ii is the police hunt for the assassin.

Ledermann, L., *Pellegrino Rossi, l'homme et l'économiste, 1787–1848: Une grande carrière internationale au xixe siècle, avec de nombreux documents inédits* (Paris, 1929).

Catholic Power and Italian Unification, Chapters 3–4

Documents:

Blakiston, N., *The Roman Question* (1962): reports of the British envoy Odo Russell. During the years 1858–70 the British had this unofficial envoy in Rome (unofficial because any official envoy was illegal by British law). He had been well trained when he served Stratford Canning in Istanbul, and wrote brilliantly.

Cavour, C., *Epistolario* (Commissione Nazionale per la Publicazione dei Corteggi del Conte Cavour, Florence, 1992–).

—— *Carteggio Cavour–Nigra* (Bologna, 1926–9).

—— *Carteggio Cavour: La Questione Romana* (Bologna, 1929).

Gregorovius, *The Roman Journals, 1852–72*, ed. F. Althaus, Eng. trans. (1911).

Pirri, P. (ed.), *Pio IX e Vittorio Emanuele II da loro carteggio privato*, MHP (Rome, 1944–), the letters of Pius IX and King Victor Emmanuel.

Alberigo, G., in *TRE* s.v. Italien; with literature.

Spellanzon, Cesare, and di Nolfo, *Storio del Risorgimento e dell'unità Italia* (Milan, 1933–).

Martina, G., see above, *passim*.

Trevelyan, G. M., *Garibaldi's Defence of the Roman Republic*, 2nd edn. (1907).

—— *Garibaldi and the Thousand* (1909).

—— *Garibaldi and the Making of Italy* (1911).

Biographies:

Falconi, Carlo, *Il cardinale Antonelli: Vita e carriere del Richelieu italiano nella chiesa di Pio IX* (Milan, 1983).

Flornoy, E., *La Moricière*, 4th edn. (Paris, 1912).

Mack Smith, Denis, *Cavour* (1985), with literature.

—— *Mazzini* (1994).

Romeo, R., *Cavour e il suo tempo* (4 vols.; Bari, 1977–84).

Thayer, W. R., *The Life and Times of Cavour* (Boston, 1911).

The Vatican Council, Chapter 5

Mansi, G. D., *Collectio conciliorum recentiorum*, ed. J. B. Martin and L. Petit (Arnhem and Leipzig, 1923–7, unaltered at Graz, 1960–1), for Council minutes. Martin was professor at Louvain, Petit an Augustinian.

Aubert, R., *Vatican I*, Histoire des conciles oecumeniques, 12 (Paris, 1964), still the best single volume.

Friedrich, J., *Geschichte des Vatikanischen Konzils* (3 vols.; Bonn, 1877–87), from the school of Döllinger.

Granderath, Theodor, *Geschichte des Vatikanischen Konzils* (3 vols.; Freiburg im Breisgau, 1903–6). A kind of official history.

Hasler, A. B., *Pius IX: Päpstliche Unfehlbarkeit und I. Vatikanisches Konzil: Dogmatisierung und Durchsetzung einer Ideologie* (2 vols.; Stuttgart, 1977), to be used with caution.

Schatz, Klaus, *Vaticanum I, 1869–70* (3 vols.; Paderborn, 1993–). This is now the indispensable account of the Council.

Britain:

Butler, C., *The Vatican Council* (1962), the outlook of Ullathorne, Bishop of Birmingham.

Cwiekowski, F. J., *The English Bishops and the First Vatican Council* (Louvain, 1971).

Italy:

Bellone, B., *I Vescovi dello Stato Pontificio al Concilio Vaticano 1* (Rome, 1966).

DDI, ser. 1, vol. xii, has interesting government papers.

Tizzani, Vincenzo, *Il Concilio Vaticano 1: Diario*, ed. L. Pázstor (2 vols.; Stuttgart, 1991–2).

France:

Ollivier, E., *L'Église et l'état au concile du Vatican* (Paris, 1879).

Germany:

Acton's letters from Rome, partly in Quirinus, *Letters from Rome*, 1870.

Conzemius, V., *Döllingers Briefwechsel* (Munich, 1963–), i–ii, for originals of Acton's letters from Rome.

Schatz, K., *Kirchenbild und päpstliche Unfehlbarkeit bei den deutschsprachigen Minoritätsbischöfen auf dem 1. Vatikanum* (Rome, 1975).

Hungary:

Adriányi, G., *Ungarn und das 1. Vaticanum* (Cologne, 1975).

Liberal Catholics:

Conzemius, V., *Katholizismus ohne Rom* (Zurich, 1969).

Les Catholiques libéraux au 19e siècle, Actes du Colloque internationale d'histoire religieuse de Grenoble (Grenoble, 1974), minutes of a Colloquy.

Old Catholics:

Conzemius, V., *TRE* s.v. Döllinger, with literature.

Denzler, G., and Grasmück, E. L. (eds.), *Geschichtlichkeit und Glaube: Gedenkschrift zum 100. Todestag Ignaz von Döllingers* (Munich, 1990), with the literature.

Friedrich, J., *Ignaz von Döllinger* (3 vols.; Munich, 1899–1901).

Küry, E., *Die Altkatholische Kirche* (Stuttgart, 1966).

Moss, C. B., *The Old Catholic Movement* (1964).

Schulte, J. F. von, *Der Altkatholizismus* (Giessen, 1887; repr. Hildesheim, 1961).

Sieben, H. J. (ed.), *Joseph Hubert Reinkens: Briefe an seinen Bruder Wilhelm (1840–1873)*, Bonner Beiträge zur Kirchengeschichte, 10 (3 vols.; Cologne, 1979).

Biographies:

Baunard, J., *Histoire de Cardinal Pie*, 2nd edn. (2 vols.; Poitiers, 1886); see also A. Gough, 'Bishop Pie's Campaign against the Nineteenth Century', in T. Zeldin (ed.), *Conflicts in French Society* (1970).

Foulon, J. A., *Histoire de la vie et des œuvres de Mgr Darboy* (Paris, 1889).

Lagrange, C., *Vie de Mgr Dupanloup éveque d'Orléans*, 7th edn. (3 vols.; Paris, 1894); Lady Herbert made an Eng. trans. of an earlier edn. (2 vols.; 1885); M. U. Maynard, *Mgr Dupanloup et M. Lagrange son historien*, 2nd edn. (Paris, 1884), is an attack on Lagrange. Cf. J. Cabanis, below, under Monasteries etc., Chapter 12.

Lecanuet, R. P., *Montalembert* (3 vols.; Paris, 1895–1902); R. Aubert published the correspondence of Montalembert with Dechamps, *Correspondance entre Charles de Montalembert et Adolphe Dechamps, 1838–1870* (Brussels, 1993).

Limouzin-Lamothe, R., *Monseigneur de Quelen, archevêque de Paris: Son rôle dans l'Église de France 1815 à 1839, d'après ses archives privées* (2 vols.; Paris, 1955–7).

Veuillot, Eugène, *Louis Veuillot* (4 vols.; Paris, 1899–1913); cf. M. L. Brown, *Louis Veuillot* (Durham, NC, 1977).

See also Guéranger and Lacordaire, below, under Religious.

The Prisoner of the Vatican, Chapter 6

Gambasin, A., *Gerarchia e Laicato in Italia nel Secondo Ottocento* (Padua, 1969).

—— *Religione et società dalla riforme napoleoniche all'età liberale* (Padua, 1974).

Halperin, S. W., *Italy and the Vatican at War* (Chicago, 1939).

Jemolo, A. C., *Chiesa e stato in Italia negli ultimi cento anni*, new rev. edn. (Turin, 1963); Eng. trans. of 1st edn. (1960).

Mussolini, B. (ed.), *Italia, Roma e Papato nelle discussione parliamentari dal 1860 al 1871* (Rome, 1975).

Seton-Watson, C., *Italy from Liberalism to Fascism 1870–1925* (1967).

Spadolini, G., *Le due Rome: Chiesa e stato fra '800 e '900*, 3rd edn. (Florence, 1975).

Traniello, F., and Campanini, G. (eds.), *Dizionario storico del Movimento Cattolico in Italia 1860–1980* (3 vols.; Turin-Casale, 1981–4).

Kulturkampf:

Bachem, K., *Vorgeschichte, Geschichte und Politik der deutschen Zentrumspartei* (9 vols.; Cologne, 1927–32).

Buchheim, Karl, *Ultramontanismus und Demokratie: Der Weg der deutschen Katholiken im 19. Jahrhundert* (Munich, 1963).

Franz, Georg, *Kulturkampf: Staat und katholische Kirche in Mitteleuropa von der Säkularisation bis zum Abschluss des preussischen Kulturkampfes* (Munich, 1954).

Kissling, J. B., *Geschichte des Kulturkampfes* (3 vols.; Freiburg im Breisgau, 1911–16).

Schmidt-Volkmar, E., *Der Kulturkampf in Deutschland, 1871–90* (Göttingen, 1963).

These were written before the opening of the Vatican archives. See now:

Besier, Gerhard, *TRE* s.v. Kulturkampf (1990), with literature.

Fontana, Josef, *Der Kulturkampf in Tirol (1861–1892)* (Bolzano, 1978), of wider interest than the Tyrol.

Lill, R. (ed.), *Vatikanische Akten zur Geschichte des deutschen Kulturkampfes* (Tübingen, 1970), i.

Ross, Ronald, 'The Kulturkampf and the Limitations of Power in Bismarck's Germany', *JEH* 46/4 (1995), 669 ff.

Ross, K. J., *The Beleaguered Tower: The Dilemma of Political Catholicism in Wilhelmine Germany* (Notre Dame, Ind., 1976).

Stadler, P., *Der Kulturkampf in der Schweiz* (Frauenfeld and Stuttgart, 1984).

Biographies:

Anderson, M. L., *Windthorst: A Political Biography* (Oxford, 1981).

Eyck, Erich, *Bismarck* (3 vols.; Zurich, 1941–4).

Foerster, Erich, *Adalbert Falk: Sein Leben und Wirken als Preussischer*

Kultusminister, dargestellt auf Grund des Nachlasses unter Beihilfe des Generals A. von Falk (Gotha, 1927).

Iserloh, E., *TRE* s.v. Ketteler; see also Iserloh *et al.* (eds.), *Wilhelm Emmanuel Freiherr von Ketteler: Sämtliche Werke und Briefe* (Mainz, 1977–).

Pflanze, Otto, *Bismarck and the Development of Germany*, Eng. trans., 2nd edn. (Princeton, 1990).

Reinhardt, R., *TRE* s.v. Hefele, with literature.

Leo XIII, Chapter 7

Acta Leonis XIII, 23 vols. in 8, repr. (Graz, 1971).

Crispolti, C., and Aureli, G., *La politica di Leone XIII da Luigi Galimberti a Mariano Rampolla* (Rome, 1912), there are many documents in an appendix.

Soderini, E., *Il Pontificato di Leone XIII* (3 vols.; Milan, 1932–3); Eng. trans. B. B. Carter, vols. i, ii (1934–5).

Spadolini, G., *L'opposizione cattolica da Porta Pia al '98*, new edn. (Florence, 1972).

——*I radicali dell'Ottocento, da Garibaldi a Cavallotti*, 3rd edn. (Florence, 1972).

T'Serklaes, C. M., *Le Papa Léon XIII* (3 vols.; Lille, 1894–1906).

Venturi, G., *Episcopato, Cattolici e Comune a Bologna 1870–1904* (Bologna, 1976).

For the social theory see Social Catholicism below.

The Curia:

Del Re, N., *La Curia Romana*, 2nd edn. (Rome, 1952).

de Marchi, G., *Le nunziature apostoliche dal 1800 al 1956* (Rome, 1957).

Kent, P. C., and Pollard, J. F. (eds.), *Papal Diplomacy in the Modern Age* (Westport, Conn., 1994), mostly about the twentieth century, but the first three essays matter to our period.

Torquebiau, P., *DDC* s.v. Curie romaine (1939).

Weber, C., *Kardinäle und Pralaten in den letzten Jahrzehnten des Kirchenstaates* (2 vols.; Stuttgart, 1978).

——*Quellen und Studien zur Kurie und zur vatikanischen Politik unter Leo XIII* (Tübingen, 1973); cf. id., 'Papsttum und Adel im 19. Jahrhundert', in *Colloquy of Rome 1985*, Collection de l'École française de Rome, 107 (Rome, 1988).

Belgium:

Biographie nationale de Belgique (Brussels, 1866–1914).

Brouette, E., *TRE* s.v. Belgien, with literature.

DHGE s.v. Belgique.

Moreau, E. de, *L'Église en Belgique des origines au début du XXe siècle* (Paris, 1944).

Simon, A., *L'Église catholique et les débuts de la Belgique independante* (Wetteren, 1949).

——*Réunions des évêques de Belgique 1830–67* (Louvain, 1960).

Vatican archives and their opening:

Chadwick, Owen, *Catholicism and History* (Cambridge, 1978).

Pastor, Ludwig von, *Tagebücher, Briefe, Erinnerungen*, ed. Wühr (Heidelberg, 1959); use with caution.

Pius X, Chapter 8

Acta Pii X (Graz, 1971), copy of Vatican edn. (1905–14).

Bazin, R., *Pius X*, 2nd edn., Eng. trans. (1928).

Hayward, F., *Pie X* (Paris, 1951).

Romanati, G., *Pio X: La vita di papa Sarto* (Milan, 1992).

Schmidlin, J., *Papstgeschichte der neuesten Zeit* (4 vols.; Munich, 1933–9).

Frei, P., *Die Papstwahl des Jahres 1903* (Berne, 1977).

Pernot, Maurice, *La Politique de Pie X (1906–10)* (Paris, 1910).

Spadolini, G., *Giolitti e i cattolici 1901–14*, 6th edn. (1990); cf. Jemolo, above, Prisoner of the Vatican, Chapter 6.

Merry del Val:

Buehrle, M. C., *Rafael, Cardinal Merry del Val* (1957).

Cenci, Pio, *Il cardinal R. Merry del Val* (Rome, 1933); Eng. trans. (abridged), V. Dalpiaz (1937).

Modernism:

Barmann, Lawrence, *Baron Friedrich von Hügel and the Modernist Crisis in England* (Cambridge, 1972).

Bedeschi, Lorenzo, *La Curia Romana durante la crisi modernista: Episodi e metodi di governo* (Parma, 1975).

Poulat, E., *Histoire, dogme et critique dans la crise moderniste*, 2nd edn. (Paris, 1979).

——*Intégrisme et Catholicisme intégral, un reseau secret international antimoderniste: La Sapinière (1909–21)* (Paris, 1969).

Rivière, J., *Le Modernisme dans l'église* (Paris, 1929).

Sagovsky, N., *'On God's Side': A Life of George Tyrrell* (Oxford, 1990).

Scoppola, P., *Crisi Modernista e rinnovamento cattolico in Italia* (Bologna, 1961).

Vidler, A. R., *The Modernist Movement in the Roman Church* (Cambridge, 1934).

——*A Variety of Catholic Modernists* (Cambridge, 1970).

Wache, Brigitte, *Monsieur Louis Duchesne, 1843–1922*, École française de Rome, 167 (Rome, 1992).

France, and the separation of Church and State:

Brugerette, J., *Le Prêtre français et la société contemporaine* (3 vols.; Paris, 1933–8).

Burnichon, J., *La Compagnie de Jésus en France: Histoire d'un siècle* (4 vols.; Paris, 1914–22).

Charle, C., *Histoire Sociale de la France au XIXe siècle* (Paris, 1991).

Chastenet, Jacques, *Histoire de la Troisième République* (Paris, 1954), iii, iv.

Combes, Émile, *Une Campagne Laique (1902–3)* (Paris, 1903), with preface by Anatole France.

Dansette, A., *Histoire religieuse de la France contemporaine* (2 vols.; Paris, 1948–51).

Debidour, A., *Histoire des rapports de l'Église et l'État en France de 1789 à 1870* (2 vols.; Paris, 1891).

——*L'Église catholique et l'état sous la Troisième République, 1870–1906* (2 vols.; Paris, 1906–9).

Ferrata, Domenico, *Mémoires* (3 vols.; 1920–1).

Gibson, Ralph, *A Social History of French Catholicism* (1989).

Hilaire, Yves-Marie, *Une Chrétienté au XIXe siècle? [sic]: La Vie religieuse des populations du diocese d'Arras (1840–1914)* (2 vols.; Lille, 1977).

Larkin, Maurice, *Church and State after the Dreyfus Affair* (1974).

Latreille, A., *et al.*, *Histoire du Catholicisme en France* (Paris, 1962), iii.

Lebrun, F. (ed.), *Histoire des Catholiques en France du XVe siècle a nos jours* (Toulouse, 1980).

Lecanuet, R. P., *L'Église de France sous la troisième République*, new edn. (5 vols.; Paris, 1931).

Maurain, Jean, *La Politique ecclésiastique du Second Empire de 1852 à 1869* (Paris, 1930).

Mun, Albert de, *Contre la Séparation* (Paris, 1905).

Partin, M. O., *Waldeck-Rousseau, Combes and the Church: The Politics of Anticlericalism 1899–1905* (Durham, NC, 1969).

Paul, H. W., *The Second Ralliement: The Rapprochement between the Church and the State in Twentieth Century France* (Washington, DC, 1967).

Schurer, Wilhelm, *Aristide Briand und die Trennung von Kirche und Staat in Frankreich* (Leipzig, 1939).

Sorlin, P., *'La Croix' et le juifs* (Paris, 1967).

Thouvenel, L., *Le Secret de l'empereur* (Paris, 1889); Thouvenel was close to Napoleon III in the crisis of the Roman question.

Popular religion in Germany:

Blackbourn, D., *Class, Religion and Local Politics in Wilhelmine Germany* (New Haven, Conn., 1980).

Götz von Olenhusen, I., *Klerus und abweichendes Verhalten: Zur sozialgeschichte katholischer Priester im 19. Jahrhundert* (Göttingen, 1994) (but see for this a review by Helmut Walser Smith in *Bulletin of the German Historical Institute*, 18/1 (1996), 21 ff.).

Hagen, A., *Gestalten aus dem Schwäbischen Katholizismus* (3 vols.; Stuttgart, 1948–54).

—— *Staat und katholische Kirche in Württemberg in den Jahren 1848–62* (2 vols.; Stuttgart, 1928).

Sperber, J., *Popular Catholicism in Nineteenth-Century Germany* (Princeton, 1984).

Austria:

Bernath, M., and Schroeder, F. von, *Biographisches Lexikon zur Geschichte Südosteuropas* (4 vols.; Munich, 1974–81).

Österreichisches Biographisches Lexikon (Graz, 1954–).

Bunzl, J., and Marin, B., *Antisemitismus in Österreich* (Innsbruck, 1983).

Dubnov, S., *History of the Jews*, Eng. trans., 4th edn. (1973), v.

TRE s.v. Antisemitismus, with literature.

Adriányi, G., and Gottschalk, J., *Festschrift für Bernhard Stasiewski: Beiträge zur ostdeutschen und osteuropäischen Kirchengeschichte* (Cologne and Vienna, 1975).

Engel-Janosi, F., *Österreich und der Vatikan* (2 vols.; Graz, 1960).

Mai, P., 'Die tschechische Nation und die Los-von-Rom-Bewegung', *LTK* s.v. Los-von-Rom-Bewegung.

Wandruszka, Adam, and Urbanitsch, Peter (eds.), *Die Habsburgermonarchie 1848–1918*, iv. *Die Confessionen* (Vienna, 1985).

For the Christian Social Movement, see J. W. Bowyer, see below, under Social Catholicism, Chapter 12.

Hungary:

Adriányi, Gabriel, *Fünfzig Jahre ungarische Kirchengeschichte 1895–1945* (Munich, 1974); Studia Hungarica, 6, many documents.

Bödy, Paul, *Eötvös and the Modernization of Hungary* (Philadelphia, 1972).

See A. Wandruszka and P. Urbanitsch, above.

Seton-Watson, R. W., *Racial Problems in Hungary* (1908).

Eastern Europe:

Ammann, A. M., *Abriss der ostslawischen Kirchengeschichte* (Vienna, 1950).

Hajjar, J., *Le Vatican, la France et le catholicisme oriental (1878–1914)* (Paris, 1979).

Neue Österreichische Biographie (Vienna, 1956), ix, s.v. Strossmayer (J. Matl).

Wendel, Hermann, *Der Kampf der Südslawen um Freiheit und Einheit* (Frankfurt, 1925).

Poland, Chapter 9

Documents:

Expositio documentis munita earum curarum quas Summus Pontifex Pius IX assidue gessit in eorum malorum levamen quibus in ditione Russica et Polona Ecclesia Catholica afflictatur (Rome, 1870).

Boudou, A., *Le Saint-Siège et la Russie: Leurs relations diplomatiques au XIX siècle* (2 vols.; Paris, 1922–5).

Castellan, G., *'Dieu Garde La Pologne!': Histoire du catholicisme polonais 1795–1980* (Paris, 1981).

The Cambridge History of Poland, ed. W. F. Reddaway, *et al.* (Cambridge, 1941), ii.

Kloczowski, Jerzy (ed.), *Histoire religieuse de la Pologne*, French trans. (Paris, 1987).

Lescœur, L., *L'Église catholique et le governement russe* (Paris, 1903).

Peterkiewicz, J., *The Third Adam* (1975), (the Mariavites).

Stehle, H., *Eastern Politics of the Vatican, 1917–1979*, Eng. trans. (Athens, Ohio, 1979).

Winter, E., *Russland und das Papsttum* (Berlin, 1961), ii.

—— *Russland und die Slawischen Völker in der Diplomatie des Vatikans, 1878–1903* (Berlin, 1950); not just of Russian interest.

Spain, Chapter 10

Aldea Vaquero, Q., *et al.* (eds.), *Diccionario de Historia Eclesiástica de España* (4 vols.; Madrid, 1972–5; supp. vol. 1987).

Alvarez Lázaro, P. F., *Masoneria y librepensiamento en la España de la Restauración* (Madrid, 1985).

Callahan, W. H., *Church, Politics and Society in Spain, 1750–1874* (Cambridge, Mass., 1984).

—— 'The Spanish Parish Clergy 1874–1930', *CHR* 125 (1989), 405–22.

Cárcel Ortí, Vicente, *et al.*, *Historia de la Iglesia en España*, v. *La Iglesia en la España contemporanea* (Madrid, 1979).

—— *Iglesia y revolución en España, 1868–1874* (Pamplona, 1979).

—— *Leon XIII y las Católicos Españoles* (Pamplona, 1988); reports from the nuncios on the state of the Church.

Christian, W. A., *Person and God in a Spanish Valley* (1972).

Fuente, V. de la, *Historia eclesiástica de España*, 2nd edn. (Madrid, 1873–4), vi.

Lannon, F., *Privilege, Persecution and Prophecy: The Catholic Church in Spain, 1875–1975* (Oxford, 1987).

Religious orders in Spain:

Cuenca Toribio, J. M., *Estudios sobre la Iglesia española del XIX* (Madrid, 1973); includes a survey of Church and State, and an important essay on the effect of *Rerum Novarum* in Spain.

—— *Sociedad y clero en la España del XIX* (Córdoba, 1980).

—— *Sociología de una elité de poder . . . La jerarquía eclésiastica 1789–1965* (Córdoba, 1976); the bishops, their origins, mode of selection, education, etc.

Eguillor, J. R., *et al.* (eds.), *Memorias del P. Luis Martín, General de la Compañia de Jesús* (2 vols.; Rome, 1988).

Mir y Noguera, Miguel, *Historia interna documentada de la Compañia de Jesús* (2 vols.; Madrid, 1913; French trans., 1922).

Peers, E. Allison, *Spain, the Church and the Orders* (1945).

Peset, M., and Peset, J. L., *La universidad española: despotismo illustrado y revolución liberal* (Madrid, 1974).

—— *La exclaustración, 1833–40* (Madrid, 1976).

Revuelta González, M., *La Compañia de Jesús en la España Contemporánea: Supresión y reinstalación (1868–1883)* (Madrid, 1984; ii. 1991).

Simón Segura, F., *La desamortización española* (Madrid, 1973).

Ullman, J. Connelly, *The Tragic Week: A Study of Anticlericalism in Spain 1875–1912* (Cambridge, Mass., 1968).

Zabala, P., *Claret* (Barcelona, 1936).

For Portugal, Chapter 11

Almeida, F. de, *História da Igreja em Portugal*, new edn. by D. Peres (Porto–Lisbon, 1970), iii.

Dicionário de História de Portugal (4 vols.; Lisbon, 1971).

Dicionário de História da Igreja em Portugal, ed. A. Banha de Andrade (Lisbon, 1980–).

NCE s.v. Portugal, with bibliography.

Robinson, R. A. H., 'The Religious Question and the Catholic Revival in Portugal, 1900–1930', *JCH* 12 (1977), 345–62.

Wheeler, D. L., *Republican Portugal* (Madison, Wis., 1978).

Britain:

Atholtz, J., *The Liberal Catholic Movement in England* (Montreal, 1962).

Newman, J. H., *The Letters and Diaries of J. H. Newman*, ed. C. S. Dessain, *et al.* (1961–).

Norman, Edward, *The English Catholic Church in the 19th Century* (Oxford, 1984), with bibliography.

Paz, D. G., *Popular Anti-Catholicism in Victorian England* (Stanford, Calif., 1992).

Biography:

Chapman, R., *Father Faber* (1961).

Gilley, Sheridan, *Newman and his Age* (1990).

Ker, I. T., *John Henry Newman: A Biography* (Oxford, 1990).

McClelland, V. A., *Cardinal Manning, his Public Life and Influence, 1865–92* (1962).

Newsome, David, *The Convert Cardinals: John Henry Newman and Henry Edward Manning* (1993).

Purcell, E. S., *Life of Cardinal Manning, Archbishop of Westminster*, 2nd edn. (1896).

Snead-Cox, J. G., *The Life of Cardinal Vaughan*, 2 vols. (1910).

United States of America:

Ellis, J. Tracy, *American Catholicism* (Chicago, 1956).

——*Cardinal Gibbons* (2 vols.; Milwaukee, 1952).

——(ed.), *Documents of American Catholic History*, 2nd edn. (Milwaukee, 1962).

Fogarty, Gerald, *The Vatican and the American Hierarchy from 1870 to 1965* (Stuttgart, 1982).

Handy, R. T., *A History of the Churches in the United States and Canada* (Oxford, 1976), with literature.

Social Catholicism:

Calvez, J. Y., and Perrin, J., *The Church and Social Justice: The Social Teaching of the Popes from Leo XIII to Pius XII (1878–1958)*, Eng. trans. (1961).

Iserloh, E., *et al.* (eds.), see above, under The Prisoner of the Vatican, Ch. 6, Biographies.

Murri, Romolo, *Carteggio*, ed. L. Bedeschi (Rome, 1970–).

Agoes, S., 'Christian Democracy and Social Modernism in Italy during the Papacy of Pius X', in *Church History* (March 1973, 73–88).

Antonazzi, G., and de Rosa, G. (eds.), *L'enciclica Rerum novarum e il suo tempo* (Rome, 1991).

Bedeschi, L., *Cattolici e Comunisti, del socialismo cristiano ai cristiani marxisti* (Milan, 1974).

Birke, A. M., *Bischof Ketteler und der deutsche Liberalismus* (Mainz, 1971).

Boyer, J. W., *Political Radicalism in Late Imperial Vienna: Origins of the Christian Social Movement 1848–1897* (Chicago, 1981).

Chadwick, O., 'The Crisis of the Nineteenth Century: Christianity and Industrial Society', in G. Barraclough (ed.), *The Christian World* (London, 1981).

Duroselle, J. B., *Les Débuts du catholicisme social en France 1822–70* (Paris, 1951).

Fogarty, M. P., *Christian Democracy in Western Europe, 1820–1953* (1957).

Geehr, R. S., *Karl Lueger* (Detroit, 1990).

Koehler, O., in Aubert *et al.*, *The Church in the Industrial Age* (see above under General Studies and Political Background), ch. 12, 'The development of Catholicism in Modern Society', with bibliography.

Lenhart, L., in *LTK* s.v. Ketteler, with literature.

Misner, P., *Social Catholicism in Europe: From the Onset of Industrialism to the First World War* (New York, 1991).

Piou, J., *Albert de Mun* (Paris, 1925).

Schmidt, M., and Schwaiger, G. (eds.), *Kirchen und Liberalismus im 19. Jahrhundert* (Göttingen, 1976).

Wallace, L. P., *Leo XIII and the Rise of Socialism* (Durham, NC, 1966).

Monasteries etc., Chapter 12

Heimbucher, M. J., *Die Orden und Kongregationen der katholischen Kirche* (2 vols.; orig. Paderborn, 1896–7), 3rd edn. (Paderborn, 1933), repr. (Paderborn, 1965).

Pelliccia, G., and Rocca, G. (eds.), *Dizionario degli Istituti di Perfezione* (Rome, 1974–).

Battandier, A., *Le Cardinal Jean-Baptiste Pitra* (Paris, 1893).

Quitslund, S. A., *Beauduin* (New York, 1973).

RB 83 (1973), 1; the proceedings of a colloquy on the Benedictine restoration of the nineteenth century.

Schmitz, Ph., *Histoire de l'Ordre de S. Benoît* (7 vols.; Maredsous, 1942–56).

Soltner, L., *Solesmes et Dom Guéranger (1805–1875)* (St Pierre de Solesmes, 1974).

Capuchins:

Bibliography in *DIP* s.v. Cappuccini, and *LTK* s.v. Kapuziner.

Carmelites:

DIP s.v. Carmelitani, Carmelitani Scalzi, Carmelitane, and Carmelitane Scalze, and literature.

McCaffrey, P., *The White Friars* (Dublin, 1926); outline.

Dominicans:

Lacordaire, H.-D., *Œuvres* (6 vols.; Paris, 1860–1911); letters to various correspondents in various books but see especially the letters to Madame Swetchine, *Correspondance du R. P. Lacordaire et de Madame Swetchine*, ed. Comte de Falloux (Paris, 1864).

Biography:

Cabanis, J., *Lacordaire et quelques autres* (Paris, 1982).

Chocarne, B., *Le R. P. H.-D. Lacordaire: Sa vie intime et religieuse*, 7th edn. (2 vols.; Paris, 1866); inner life.

Foisset, T., *Vie du R. P. Lacordaire* (2 vols.; Paris, 1870).

Cormier, H. M., *Vie de Jandel* (Paris, 1890).

Franciscans:

For bibliography, see:

Clasen, S., *LTK* s.v. Franziskaner.

Péano, F., *DIP* s.v. Frati Minori simpliciter dicti.

Jesuits:

In France, see J. Burnichon, above under Pius X, Chapter 8: *France and the separation of Church and State*.

In Spain, see Revuelta Gonzáles, see above, under Spain, Chapter 10: *Religious orders*.

Rosminians:
DIP s.v. Rosmini-Serbati; a guide.
DIP s.v. Istituto dell Carità.
Leetham, C., *Rosmini* (1957).
Mellano, M. F., *Anni decisivi nella vita di A. Rosmini 1848–54* (Rome, 1988).
Radice, G., *Pio IX e Antonio Rosmini* (Vatican City, 1974).
Bloch, R. Howard, *God's Plagiarist* (Chicago, 1994); on Migne.

Ecumenical Movement, Chapter 14

Bell, G. K. A., *Documents on Christian Unity* (4 vols., 1924–58).
Baum, Gregory, *That They May Be One: A Study of Papal Doctrine, Leo XIII–Pius XII* (1958).
Fouilloux, E., *Les Catholiques et l'unité chrétienne du 19e au 20e siècle* (Paris, 1982).
Franklin, William (ed.), *Anglican Orders* (1996).
Hughes, J. J., *Absolutely Null and Utterly Void* (1968); on *Apostolicae curae* and the Anglicans.
Perchenet, A., *The Revival of the Religious Life and Christian Unity*, Eng. trans. (1969).
Rouse, R., and Neill, S. C. (eds.), *A History of the Ecumenical Movement 1517–1948*, 2nd edn. (1966).
Tavard, G. H., *Two Centuries of Ecumenism*, Eng. trans. (1960).

The press:
Bellanger, C., *Histoire générale de la presse française* (Paris, 1969–76). And see Eugène Veuillot, under Vatican Council: Biographies.
Löffler, K., *Geschichte der katholischen Presse Deutschlands* (Münchengladbach, 1924).
Majo, Angelo, *La Stampa cattolica in Italia* (Milan, 1992).

Visions, etc., and Chapter 15

Beinert, W., and Petri, H., *Handbuch der Marienkunde* (Regensburg, 1984).
Blackbourn, D., *Marpingen* (Oxford, 1993), with literature.
Devlin, J., *The Superstitious Mind: French Peasants and the Supernatural in the Nineteenth Century* (New Haven, Conn., 1987).
Kselman, T. A., *Miracles and Prophecies in Nineteenth-Century France* (New Brunswick, 1983).
Lannon, F., see above, under Spain and Chapter 10.
Laurentin, R., *Life of Catherine Labouré*, Eng. trans. (1983).
Lourdes:
Laurentin, R., *Lourdes: Dossier des documents authentiques* (7 vols.; Paris, 1958–66).

Neame, A., *The Happening at Lourdes* (1968); cf. T. Taylor, ' "So many extraordinary things to tell": Letters from Lourdes 1858', in *JEH* 46/3 (1995), 457 ff.

Nolan, M. L., and S., *Christian Pilgrimage in Modern Western Europe* (Chapel Hill, NC, 1989).

Thurston, H., *Beauraing and other Apparitions* (1934).

INDEX